Praise for *Hiding in Plain Sight*

"*Hiding in Plain Sight* is a wonderfully comprehensive and clearly worded work that everyone should read. If you want to understand the war criminals of modern times and the dogged pursuit of justice for them, this is the only book you need to read, and you must read it."
—Peter Maass, author of *Love Thy Neighbor: The Story of War*

"*Hiding in Plain Sight* deals a much-needed blow to impunity by revealing how governments and international institutions have sometimes succeeded—but more often failed—to live up to their legal obligations to bring war criminals to justice. This thoroughly researched book is both extremely timely and long overdue."
—Navi Pillay, former United Nations High Commissioner for Human Rights and
    former President of the International Criminal Tribunal for Rwanda

"The cycle of impunity for atrocity crimes is closing slowly but surely. Telling a complex story in a highly readable way, the authors make their own significant contribution to accountability and justice for human rights crimes. The torturer still runs, but he can no longer hide."
—Juan Mendez, UN Special Rapporteur on Torture

"A riveting modern history, on the trail of international justice in the face of politics and self-interest, *Hiding in Plain Sight* is a must-read for anyone who wants to know from whence we have come and the obstacles that will fill the road that lies ahead."
—Philippe Sands, author of *Torture Team: Uncovering War Crimes in the Land of the Free*

Hiding in Plain Sight

Hiding in Plain Sight

The Pursuit of War Criminals from
Nuremberg to the War on Terror

Eric Stover
Victor Peskin
Alexa Koenig

UNIVERSITY OF CALIFORNIA PRESS

University of California Press, one of the most
distinguished university presses in the United States,
enriches lives around the world by advancing scholarship
in the humanities, social sciences, and natural sciences. Its
activities are supported by the UC Press Foundation and
by philanthropic contributions from individuals and
institutions. For more information, visit www.ucpress.edu.

University of California Press
Oakland, California

First paperback printing 2017

Library of Congress Cataloging-in-Publication Data

Stover, Eric, author.
    Hiding in plain sight : the pursuit of war criminals
from Nuremberg to the War on Terror / Eric Stover,
Victor Peskin, Alexa Koenig. — First edition.
        pages   cm
    Includes bibliographical references and index.
    ISBN 978-0-520-27805-9 (cloth : alk. paper) — ISBN
978-0-520-29604-6 (pbk. : alk. paper) — ISBN 978-0-520-
96276-7 (ebook) — ISBN 0-520-96276-1 (ebook)
    1. War crime trials. 2. War crimes investigation.
3. International criminal courts. I. Peskin, Victor,
1967- author. II. Koenig, Alexa, 1972-
author. III. Title.
    KZ1168.5.S76   2016
    341.6′9—dc23   2015028398

Manufactured in the United States of America

25 24 23 22 21 20 19 18 17
10 9 8 7 6 5 4 3 2 1

In keeping with a commitment to support
environmentally responsible and sustainable printing
practices, UC Press has printed this book on Natures
Natural, a fiber that contains 30% post-consumer waste
and meets the minimum requirements of ANSI/NISO
Z39.48-1992 (R 1997) (Permanence of Paper).

In memory of Clyde Snow

Contents

Acknowledgments

Foremost among those who helped us bring this project to fruition is Jonathan Cobb, our friend and editor (though that may be an oxymoron), who shepherded our prose with acumen and compassion and kept it from wandering into unchartered territory. Five years ago, Darian Swig and David Keller helped us begin our research by providing a generous start-up grant. Jonathan Silvers of Saybrook Productions kindly shared transcripts from his PBS documentaries *Elusive Justice: The Search for Nazi War Criminals* and *Dead Reckoning: Postwar Justice from World War II to the War on Terror*. UC Berkeley students Peggy O'Donnell and Aynur Jafar helped with research and fact-checking. Andrea Lampros, the communications manager for the Human Rights Center at UC Berkeley, provided invaluable assistance in securing funding, photographs, and artwork.

Victor Peskin wishes to thank the Melikian Center and the School of Politics and Global Studies at Arizona State University for funding portions of his research for this book. He is particularly grateful to Professor Yuval Shany and his research project, Assessing the Conditions for Effective International Adjudication, at the Hebrew University Faculty of Law in Jerusalem for a sabbatical fellowship year that provided time for writing and intellectual engagement.

Eric Stover wishes to thank the National Endowment for the Humanities and the Institute on Global Conflict and Cooperation of UC San Diego for their generous support of his research for this book.

Alexa Koenig wishes to thank the American Association of University Women for its financial support while she was researching this project and her dissertation.

In addition to Andrea Lampros, our colleagues at the Human Rights Center—Alexey Berlind, Camille Crittenden, Julie Freccero, Keith Hiatt, Julie Lagarde, Kat Madrigal, Cristián Orrego, Stephen Smith Cody, and Kim Thuy Seelinger—were always available to give us sage advice and encouragement. A special thanks to Kevin Reyes for proofreading parts of the manuscript. We are indebted to Naomi Schneider at University of California Press and our copyeditor, Roy Sablosky, for guiding this project to port.

We applied a wide range of research methods in our study of the pursuit of war criminals since the end of World War II. Using a semistructured questionnaire, we conducted in-depth interviews with more than a hundred historians, judges, prosecutors, investigators, journalists, human rights activists, legal scholars, government officials, UN administrators, victims of war crimes, and family members of suspects. We also read widely, relying as much as possible on primary documents and first-person narratives. Several books were particularly helpful to us and deserve special mention: Guy Walters, *Hunting Evil: The Nazi War Criminals Who Escaped Justice & The Quest to Bring Them to Justice*; Richard Breitman, Norman J. W. Goda, Timothy Naftali, and Robert Wolfe (eds.), *US Intelligence and the Nazis*; Richard P. Bix, *Hirohito and the Making of Modern Japan*; David Scheffer, *All the Missing Souls: A Personal History of the War Crimes Tribunals*; David Rohde, *Endgame: The Betrayal and Fall of Srebrenica—Europe's Worst Massacre Since World War II*; Roméo Dallaire, *Shake Hands with the Devil: The Failure of Humanity in Rwanda*; Thierry Cruvellier, *Court of Remorse: Inside the International Criminal Tribunal for Rwanda*; Carla Del Ponte and Chuck Sudetic, *Madame Prosecutor: Confrontations with Humanity's Worst Criminals and the Culture of Impunity*; Benjamin N. Schiff, *Building the International Criminal Court*; Luc Reydams, Jan Wouters, and Cedric Ryngaert (eds.), *International Prosecutors*; Christophe Paulussen, *Male Captus, Bene Detenus: Surrendering Suspects to the International Criminal Court*; Jane Mayer, *The Dark Side: The Inside Story of How the War on Terror Turned Into a War on American Ideals;* and Jess Bravin, *Terror Courts: Rough Justice at Guantánamo Bay*. We highly recommend these books to anyone wishing to pursue a deeper analysis of this topic.

Finally, we wish to thank our families for their unwavering patience and support during our many years of research and writing.

CHAPTER I

Introduction

The Promise of International Justice

The year 2011 was a perilous one for some of the world's most wanted fugitives. The first to feel the squeeze was Osama bin Laden, the al-Qaeda leader who had evaded justice since the September 11, 2001 attacks on the World Trade Center and the Pentagon that claimed 2,996 lives and prompted the Bush Administration to launch its "war on terror." On a pitch-black night in early May 2011—fifty years after Israeli agents snatched former Nazi SS officer Adolf Eichmann off a Buenos Aires street and smuggled him to Israel to face trial for the extermination of millions of Jews—U.S. Black Hawk helicopters carrying Navy SEALs landed on a dirt road next to a high-walled compound just outside of Abbottabad, Pakistan. Within minutes, bursts of gunfire echoed through the corridors of the compound and bin Laden lay dead. Hours later, aboard the USS *Carl Vinson* idling in the North Arabian Sea, the body was washed in an Islamic ritual of ablution, wrapped in a white sheet, placed in a weighted bag, and dropped into the sea.[1]

Next was Ratko Mladic, the sixty-eight-year-old Bosnian Serb general wanted by the International Criminal Tribunal for the former Yugoslavia for his alleged role in the massacre of more than 8,000 Muslim men and boys following the siege of the Bosnian town of Srebrenica in July 1995. The murders constituted the single worst atrocity on European soil since World War II. For sixteen years, Mladic had been a fugitive—sometimes living openly in the Serbian capital of Belgrade, sometimes hiding in a shabby military barracks on the city's outskirts. That all ended at dawn on May 26, 2011, when masked Serbian police officers raided the home of Mladic's elderly cousin, in the village of Lazarevo, north of Belgrade. The arresting officers found Mladic sitting in the front room, wearing a faded track suit, his face drawn and pale. "Good work," he said, handing over a pair of pistols. "You've found the one you're looking for."

Five months later, on October 20, 2011, Colonel Muammar Gaddafi was traveling in a heavily armed convoy across the Sahara Desert trying to avoid roadblocks set up by anti-government rebels. Earlier in the year, the International Criminal Court had issued an arrest warrant for the Libyan leader for his role in the torture and murder of hundreds of protesters who had taken to the streets to demand an end to his forty-two-year dictatorship. As Gaddafi's convoy sped through the desert, an American drone, launched from a NATO base in Sicily and controlled from a U.S. base outside Las Vegas, sped through the sky above the snaking line of black SUVs. The drone pilot, seated in a leather arm-chair in a trailer in the Mojave Desert, drew a bead on the convoy's lead vehicle and let go a fusillade of Hellfire missiles. As the convoy ground to a halt, a NATO warplane struck it with airburst bombs, incinerating dozens of Gaddafi's fighters. Still unharmed, Gaddafi and several members of his inner circle fled to a large storm drain, but were quickly set upon by rebels. One man plunged a bayonet into Gaddafi's back while others pummeled him. Later that afternoon, Gaddafi's lifeless body was put on display in a meat-packing plant in the northwestern city of Mirasta before being buried in an unmarked desert grave.

Bin Laden's assassination, Mladic's arrest, and Gaddafi's demise[2]—as well as Eichmann's kidnapping fifty years earlier—are among the episodes we examine in this book. Our principal aim is to explore the political, legal, and operational dimensions of the pursuit of war crimes suspects in the seven decades since Word War II. In doing so, we look critically at the range of diplomatic and military strategies—both successful and unsuccessful—that states and international criminal courts have adopted to promote and carry out international arrests.

The fact that governments and international criminal courts are now, decades after the Nuremberg and Tokyo war crimes trials, pursuing once-untouchable military and political figures like Mladic and Gaddafi is in itself a remarkable development—and one that threatens to pierce state impunity, alter traditional notions of sovereignty, and transform international affairs. Still, the pursuit of international justice faces enormous challenges. States that are implicated in mass atrocities often resist handing over suspects for trial in international courts. At the same time, the international community is often ambivalent about pursuing indicted heads of state and warlords out of fear that such endeavors will upset quests for peace and regional stability.

So how have these challenges been confronted and, at times, overcome? We endeavor to answer that question by tracking the variation over time in efforts to pursue and prosecute suspects indicted by international tribunals. We begin by analyzing the challenges Allied powers faced in their pursuit of German and Japanese war criminals in the aftermath of World War II. We then focus on subsequent international tribunals, including the International Criminal Court, and their efforts to enlist states, regional organizations, and individuals to capture suspects. We close with an examination of the post-9/11 landscape and the United States' increasing reliance on military force (as opposed to diplomatic means) to capture—or more often to simply kill—terrorist suspects, with little or no judicial scrutiny.

In the mid-1990s, when the United Nations created the International Criminal Tribunal for the former Yugoslavia, the first international war crimes tribunal of the modern era, many observers predicted that it had little chance of persuading states to hand over suspects for trial. Yet, as we explain in chapters 5 and 6, changing global and domestic political dynamics eventually helped the Yugoslavia tribunal gain custody of all its remaining indictees by summer 2011 and enabled its sister court, the International Criminal Tribunal for Rwanda, to obtain custody of most of its indictees. That said, such progress is by no means inevitable for today's international tribunals. As we note in chapter 7, hybrid or mixed international courts—usually located in the countries where the crimes occurred and designed to apply a mixture of international and national law—have had mixed success in gaining custody of their indictees. The International Criminal Court, meanwhile, has faced an uphill battle in garnering cooperation in arresting and handing over suspects—even from many states that have joined the court and pledged their assistance—as we describe in chapter 8.

In sharp contrast to the International Criminal Court and other modern-day tribunals, the Nuremberg and Tokyo tribunals, the subject of chapter 2, had scores of high-level suspects in custody very soon after their establishment, thanks to the fact that the Allies had vanquished the German and Japanese armies and were now occupiers of their lands. Territorial control as military occupiers was key, but it wasn't the only factor. As we document in chapters 3 and 4, the Allies' initially strong commitment to pursuing criminal accountability in the wake of World War II soon waned, despite relatively favorable conditions, as Cold War political interests began to take priority. The U.S. government, intent on recruiting Germans as intelligence assets and as scientists to help the West outpace the Soviets, helped many Nazis evade justice. As we'll see time and again, the ebb and flow of political will on the part of states and the international community as a whole has been the common denominator in the pursuit of international justice since World War II.

In our work on this book, we drew on extensive historical research, including media and war crimes reports, as well as more than a hundred in-depth interviews conducted in Africa, Europe, Asia, and North America with a range of individuals who have been heavily involved in the pursuit of war crimes suspects over the past seventy years. Among those we interviewed were international and domestic investigators, judges, diplomats, government officials, military personnel, politicians, historians, and human rights activists, who helped us understand the diverse strategies that governments, international criminal courts, international law enforcement, and nongovernmental organizations have used to pursue and capture war criminals.

LAW OUT OF THE RUBBLE

The first known international trial for war crimes took place in Breisach, Germany, in 1474, when twenty-seven judges of the Holy Roman Empire ruled that Peter van Hagenback—a mercenary hired by the Duke of Burgundy to wrest taxes from the people—had violated the "laws of God and man" by allowing his troops to rape, murder, and pillage. Hagenback's conviction underscored one of the defining—if unrealized—ideas of civilized society since antiquity: even in war, unnecessary suffering inflicted on civilians is forbidden. Yet it was not until the nineteenth century that states accepted and ratified formal international agreements embodying this principle.

In the mid-1860s, a handful of European states met to plot a new international humanitarian legal order that would govern the interactions between combatant forces and between those forces and noncombatants during times of armed conflict. This effort was sparked by two recent wars and the mayhem and massive loss of life that ensued. The first was the Crimean War of 1854, in which some eighty thousand members of the Franco-British expeditionary force perished in horrendous and chaotic conditions. Five years later, in June 1859, tens of thousands of Austrian, French, and Italian soldiers were killed in the Battle of Solferino in northern Italy (or later died of untreated wounds). The day after the battle, a young Swiss businessman named Jean-Henri Dunant visited the site and was so shocked by the carnage he worked with the Swiss government to establish the International Committee of the Red Cross in 1863 to provide better medical care to all sides in military conflicts. A year later, twelve European governments met in Geneva to sign the Convention for the Amelioration of the Condition of the Wounded in Armies in the Field, the first international agreement on the laws of war. Referred to as the First Geneva Convention, the agreement provides specific protections for civilians, as well as medical and religious personnel, in battle zones, and for soldiers who are *hors de combat* (outside the fight and therefore noncombatants).

Meanwhile, in the United States, president Abraham Lincoln in 1863 authorized the War Department to promulgate guidelines, known as the Lieber Code, to govern the conduct of the Union Army during the Civil War. Consisting of 159 articles, the code mandated the humane treatment of civilian populations in occupied areas, forbade the use of torture to extract confessions, and set out the rights and protections of prisoners of war. Thirty-six years later, in 1899, the Convention with Respect to the Laws and Customs of War on Land was adopted in The Hague, codifying generally accepted principles of customary international law, including the protection of civilian institutions, such as hospitals and churches. Taken together, these conventions represented the first steps toward establishing the boundaries of what was legally permissible and not permissible in international, and eventually in non-international, armed conflicts.[3]

Following World War I, the Allied Powers tried to prosecute nearly a thousand German suspects of war crimes ranging from mistreating prisoners of war to attacks on nonmilitary targets such as hospital ships, but that effort quickly fizzled when the German government refused to hand over the defendants. It wasn't until the end of World War II that the first sustained effort to hold war criminals accountable finally took root. During the 1940s and early 1950s, thousands of trials of German and Japanese military and civilian officials accused of wartime crimes were held throughout Europe and Asia. These proceedings—most notably the Nuremberg trial of major Nazi civilian and military leaders— established many of the core legal principles of international criminal law that are still in force today.

According to legal scholars Ronald Slye and Beth Van Schaack, the most salient of the Nuremberg Principles, as they became known, are

(1) that individuals—and not societies—should be held accountable for crimes committed in war; (2) that international law has primacy over domestic law; (3) that those who commit "crimes against humanity" are—like the pirate and slave trader before them—*hostis humani generis,* enemies of all mankind, and thus may be arrested and tried by any state; (4) that international courts, freed from the legal and political restraints often placed on their domestic counterparts, are often better positioned to prosecute war crimes suspects; (5) that high-ranking officials are no longer shielded by head-of-state and sovereign-immunity claims and, like common soldiers, should be held criminally responsible for international crimes committed in war; and (6) that private actors—financiers and industrialists, for example—as well as state officials can be convicted for war crimes.[4]

Nuremberg's greatest legacy was the introduction of a new international crime: crimes against humanity. Defined in the charter of the Nuremberg tribunal, crimes against humanity include a constellation of criminal acts—murder, extermination, enslavement, deportation, persecution, and other inhumane acts—committed as part of a widespread or systematic attack against a civilian population. Though not included in the Nuremberg charter, a second international crime, "genocide"— often called "the crime of crimes"—became the subject of a multilateral treaty when the UN General Assembly adopted the Convention on the Prevention and Punishment of the Crime of Genocide in 1948. Genocide was defined as "acts committed with the intent to destroy, in whole or in part, a national, ethnical, racial or religious group."[5] Such acts include killings, causing serious bodily or mental harm, deliberately inflicting on a group conditions of life to bring about its physical destruction in whole or in part, imposing measures intended to prevent births within the group, and forcibly transferring children of the group to another group. Genocide and crimes against humanity are considered crimes against *all* humanity, not just the individual victims or their immediate communities, and states are legally obliged to prevent them and prosecute offenders or extradite them elsewhere for prosecution.[6] In this book we use *war crimes suspect* as an umbrella term to include any individual accused of committing a serious international crime—such as genocide, crimes against humanity, war crimes, or terrorism—in the context of an armed conflict.

The years immediately after World War II also witnessed the establishment of the United Nations itself, the intergovernmental agency dedicated to maintaining international peace and security, fostering human rights and social and economic development, and providing humanitarian aid in cases of famine, natural disaster, and armed conflict. In 1948, the UN General Assembly adopted the Universal Declaration of Human Rights, which one of its principal drafters, Eleanor Roosevelt, called "the international Magna Carta for all men everywhere."[7] The agreement set out universally accepted norms of human dignity and freedom and encouraged states to incorporate them into their constitutions. Subsequent human rights treaties sought to uphold political and civil rights, prohibit torture, and protect and guarantee equal treatment for racial and ethnic groups, women, children, indigenous people, and the disabled.

In 1949, states came together independently of the United Nations to further bolster the laws regulating armed conflicts. In a relatively short time, they adopted four new Geneva Conventions codifying the war crimes recognized at Nuremberg and Tokyo and officially deeming them "grave breaches" of international humanitarian law when committed against the wounded and sick on land or sea, prisoners of war, or civilians. The list of grave breaches included willful killing; torture or inhuman treatment (including medical experiments); extensive destruction and appropriation of property not justified by military necessity and carried out unlawfully and wantonly; willfully depriving a prisoner of war or civilian of the rights of a fair and regular trial; and the taking of hostages.[8] Like genocide and crimes against humanity, such grave breaches invoked the principle of *aut dedere aut judicare* (Latin for "extradite or prosecute"), requiring states to either prosecute offenders in their own courts or send them elsewhere for prosecution.

Diplomats and human rights advocates hoped this proliferation of multilateral treaties would usher in a new era of human rights observance and enforcement, but such expectations were soon dashed by the advent of the Cold War. As much of the world quickly divided into Communist and non-Communist camps, the Soviet and U.S. governments began ignoring their treaty obligations and instead often promoted and maintained brutal authoritarian regimes to protect and extend their own economic and security interests.[9]

By the late 1940s, Allied interest in pursuing German and Japanese war crimes suspects had plummeted, only to be taken up by a new breed of unconventional sleuths.

These independent nonstate actors—sometimes in collaboration with sympathetic state prosecutors, parliamentarians, and spymasters— worked out of makeshift offices, compiling dossiers on some of the most notorious Nazi war criminals—men like Adolf Eichmann, Josef Mengele, and Klaus Barbie—who had apparently slipped out of Europe to parts unknown. Often one step ahead of their pursuers, many Nazi fugitives lived out their lives in South American backwaters, while others held prominent civil service posts in Germany itself; some were eventually captured and sent to France, Germany, or Israel to stand trial. Their pursuers—like concentration camp survivor Simon Wiesenthal and Israel's spy agency, Mossad—rarely played by the rules, prompting some governments to denounce their plots to kidnap Nazi fugitives as counterproductive to the fundamental legal principles established in Nuremberg and Tokyo.

It was only with the end of the Cold War in the early 1990s that the precedents established in Nuremberg and Tokyo could finally take root and flourish on the international stage. Within a span of eighteen months beginning in May 1993, two tribunals—the ad hoc International Criminal Tribunals for the former Yugoslavia and Rwanda— were established by the United Nations to prosecute suspects accused of war crimes, crimes against humanity, and genocide in the Balkans and Rwanda. As "ad hoc" institutions, the tribunals were limited to prosecuting crimes that had taken place in a given territory and over a specified period of time. Their creation was a watershed event that has dramatically altered the landscape of post-conflict interventions and served as a model for future international tribunals. As former chief prosecutor Louise Arbour said in a press conference in 1999, "We have moved international criminal justice . . . to a point of no return."[10]

The Yugoslavia and Rwanda tribunals were quickly followed by a new set of judicial institutions, established under the auspices of the United Nations and known as *hybrid* or *mixed* courts, to enforce the principles embodied in the Geneva Conventions and UN treaties.[11] So far, hybrid courts have been established for Kosovo, East Timor, Sierra Leone, Cambodia, and Bosnia-Herzegovina. In 2009, the UN also established a hybrid tribunal for Lebanon to prosecute those persons responsible for the February 2005 terrorist attack that resulted in the deaths of former prime minister Rafiq Hariri and twenty-two others.

When the UN was first created, following World War II, its founders hoped that a permanent criminal court could be established to carry on the legacy of Nuremberg. Such a court, it was thought, would be the first advance in the fight against impunity for those who perpetrate atrocious crimes. A victim of Cold War politics, this plan languished for more than four decades in the backwater of obscure UN committees.

Then on November 25, 1992, the General Assembly adopted a resolution calling on the International Law Commission to draft a statute for a permanent international criminal court.

Six years later, in 1998, more than a hundred states met in Rome, under the watchful eyes of nongovernmental organizations, to hammer out a multinational treaty to establish the International Criminal Court (ICC). Unlike the ad hoc and hybrid tribunals, the ICC would have universal jurisdiction, at least in theory if not in practice, enabling it to prosecute serious international crimes anywhere in the world. The treaty came into force on July 1, 2002, after ratification by sixty states, and the court, based in The Hague, began operations soon thereafter. At the time of writing, more than 120 countries are member states, but numerous others, including the United States, Russia, China, India, Pakistan, Turkey, Israel, and Indonesia, have so far decided not to join. By August 2015, the ICC had opened investigations in eight African countries—the Democratic Republic of the Congo, Uganda, the Central African Republic, Sudan, Kenya, Libya, Côte d'Ivoire, and Mali—and was considering opening investigations in other regions of the world.

PURSUIT AND CAPTURE

Since the statutes of the various contemporary tribunals (with the exception of the Special Tribunal for Lebanon) prohibit trials *in absentia,* these courts must gain custody of their accused in order to hold trials. Writes Gavin Ruxton, a former prosecutor with the Yugoslavia tribunal: "The arrest process lies at the very heart of the criminal justice process: unless the accused are taken into custody, we will have no trials; no development of the law by courts; and ultimately, no international justice."[12]

Today's international tribunals, in sharp contrast to the situation at the Allied-run Nuremberg and Tokyo military tribunals, lack any enforcement powers of their own to ensure that indicted suspects will be taken into custody. Chief prosecutors must rely on the cooperation of states, including international peacekeepers, to enforce arrest warrants. Because the Yugoslavia and Rwanda tribunals were created under Chapter VII of the UN Charter, granting them primacy over domestic courts, states are legally obliged to transfer suspects into their custody.[13] Theoretically, any state that refuses to cooperate with these tribunals is subject to sanction by the UN Security Council, although the council has been reluctant to act. Still, at various times the United States and

European states in particular have pressed noncompliant states for action on behalf of these two UN tribunals.[14] Lacking Chapter VII powers, the hybrid tribunals have had a less robust legal basis from which to seek the cooperation of states to turn over suspects who have taken refuge in their territories. And, as we'll see in chapter 8, the ICC has also faced a difficult challenge in its quest for state cooperation because its recourse to the Security Council is limited and its legal foundation for insisting that those indicted be handed over is generally weaker when compared to the legal authority of the Yugoslavia and Rwanda tribunals.

The statutes of these courts set out specific steps that prosecutors and their staff must follow to ensure that suspects are afforded due-process protections before and during trial. That said, defense attorneys at today's international tribunals have challenged, though generally unsuccessfully, the manner in which some of their clients have been apprehended and transferred to the tribunals' jurisdiction. In quashing these challenges, many judges have relied on the legal doctrine *male captus, bene detentus* (Latin for "wrongly captured, properly detained"), which states that an improper capture can nonetheless result in a valid detention and does not necessarily prejudice a defendant's trial.[15] Sometimes called the tough-luck rule, this doctrine has been upheld by numerous domestic and international courts since the 1970s. Still, judges at international criminal courts have not given prosecutors carte blanche to find creative ways to apprehend suspects. The Yugoslavia tribunal, for example, has acknowledged that if a defendant was seriously mistreated before being surrendered to the tribunal there could be legal impediments to the court's jurisdiction over the case.[16]

While our book focuses primarily on the pursuit of suspects in the context of international tribunals, we also pay attention to the increasingly salient role of domestic war crimes trials. As the UN ad hoc and hybrid tribunals complete years of work, domestic courts are now emerging as the venue of choice for war crimes prosecutions. The legal principle known as universal jurisdiction provides another route for states to prosecute individuals who are believed to have committed international crimes that are considered especially heinous—including piracy, slavery, war crimes, crimes against peace, crimes against humanity, genocide, and torture—even if the prosecuting state has no special link to those crimes other than the bonds of common humanity.[17] The most provocative case of universal jurisdiction to emerge in recent years was one filed in 1998 by a Spanish magistrate named Baltasar Garzón. Judge Garzón invoked the principle of universal jurisdiction to seek the arrest and transfer to Spain of Chilean dictator Augusto Pinochet, who was in London recovering from back surgery, to stand trial for numerous counts of torture of Spanish citizens previously held in the custody of the Chilean police. British police detained Pinochet and placed him under house arrest, where he remained for sixteen months. After a hard-fought legal battle, and appeals by former prime minister Margaret Thatcher and former U.S. president George H. W. Bush for Pinochet's release, Home Secretary Jack Straw—citing Pinochet's poor health—ruled in February 2000 that the Chilean leader should not be extradited to Spain, triggering widespread protests by international human rights organizations. In early March, Pinochet returned to Chile. After his plane landed, he triumphantly rose from his wheelchair and waved vigorously to his supporters. Six years later, at the age of ninety-one, Pinochet succumbed to a fatal heart attack. He died with a total wealth of $28 million and without having been convicted of a single crime committed during his dictatorship.[18]

Despite the Pinochet setback, universal jurisdiction cases increased significantly in the wake of that high-profile case, but national courts have become increasingly wary of them, especially when they target government officials of powerful states.

Outside the context of seeking to prosecute suspects in national and international courts, states have long resorted to killing war crimes and terrorist suspects within and beyond their territories—often with few, if any, legal repercussions. Indeed, illegal abductions, torture of detainees, and assassinations were common features of the Cold War era. In this regard, the actions of the United States in the post-9/11 era have marked a return to the Cold War past. Our discussion of the United States' "war on terror" highlights the ways in which states have acted outside the rule-of-law paradigm that lies at the core of national and international trials. A number of American policymakers and other commentators believe that among nations, the United States is somehow "exceptional" and should not be bound by international laws applicable to others. These commentators argue that the United States should only support international treaties and agreements as long as U.S. citizens are exempt, and that the United States should criticize other states for not heeding the findings of international human rights bodies, but ignore what these bodies say about U.S. behavior.[19] The irony is, as U.S. historian Alfred W. McCoy notes, that the United States, "more than any other power, created the modern international community of laws and treaties, yet it now reserves the right to defy those same laws with impunity."[20]

In this vein, following the September 11 attacks, the George W. Bush administration pursued an aggressive hunt for terrorist suspects that featured the use of what it called "extraordinary rendition," a process whereby terrorist suspects were captured and held in "black sites," or clandestine prisons, outside of the United States, and subjected to interrogation and torture. The United States has explicitly denied "war on terror" detainees the protection of the Third Geneva Convention, also known as the Geneva Convention relative to the Treatment of Prisoners of War, which since 1950 has established the rules governing the capture and detention of enemy fighters. Numerous international human rights bodies, including the UN Committee Against Torture and the Human Rights Committee, have concluded that such renditions violate the Convention Against Torture[21] and the International Covenant on Civil and Political Rights,[22] respectively.

The post-9/11 dragnet led to the rendition of many suspects from Afghanistan, Iraq, and other countries, who appear to have had little or no connection to war crimes or acts of terrorism.[23] These renditions were in addition to the detention of hundreds of "enemy combatants" in Afghanistan and Pakistan, some of whom were falsely identified or sold into captivity, and incarcerated in U.S. detention facilities at the Kandahar and Bagram air bases in Afghanistan before being transferred to the U.S. naval base at Guantánamo Bay, Cuba. Several European states have brought suits *in absentia* against CIA operatives who abducted suspects on European soil. But, so far, only one case—concerning the abduction of a Muslim cleric, Osama Mustapha Hassan Nasr, who was snatched from a street in Milan, Italy, in 2003 by a team of CIA operatives and flown to Egypt, where he was held for more than three years without charges and tortured—has resulted in the conviction (*in absentia*) of CIA operatives, all of whom remain free.[24] As of early 2015 no mid- or high-level U.S. government official has been held accountable for serious violations of international humanitarian law committed since 9/11, although, as we shall see, survivors and human rights activists have turned to foreign courts in an attempt to break this circle of impunity.

STATE COOPERATION AND POLITICAL WILL

Over a decade ago, South African jurist Richard Goldstone, first chief prosecutor at the Yugoslav and Rwanda tribunals, wrote, "The most serious threat to the credibility . . . of the Tribunals has come from the politically inspired delays in the arrest of indicted war criminals."[25] Justice Goldstone's admonition remains true today. While the legal foundation needed to apprehend and deliver indicted war criminals to justice is largely in place, the political will on the part of states to consistently to do so remains elusive.

State cooperation is the *sine qua non* of international justice. Nonstate actors—like Nazi-hunter Simon Wiesenthal and NGOs like Amnesty International and Human Rights Watch—can find and expose war crimes suspects, but it takes states to actually bring them into custody and hand them over to international courts. Antonio Cassese, an Italian jurist and the Yugoslav tribunal's first president, wrote that the Yugoslavia tribunal "is very much like a giant without arms and legs—it needs artificial limbs to walk and work. And these artificial limbs are state authorities. If the cooperation is not forthcoming, they cannot fulfill their functions."[26] Such functions include executing arrest warrants, assisting and protecting investigators in the field, locating witnesses, and bringing them to the tribunal to testify.

The ability of states to defy international tribunals does not mean that the contemporary international tribunals are without recourse. As we document in the book's chapters on contemporary justice, international prosecutors have developed a range of diplomatic, legal, and operational strategies designed to prod the international community and recalcitrant states to cooperate in the pursuit of war crimes suspects. Some of these prosecutorial strategies, though, especially when they involve concessions to states, have compromised the integrity and legitimacy of the international justice project.

Calls for the arrest and prosecution of war criminals arise during war or in its immediate aftermath, or reemerge decades later, but seldom disappear. Victims and their domestic and international backers have launched powerful movements for legal redress, as they did after both the 1994 Rwandan genocide and the 1995 massacre of thousands of Muslim men and boys outside of the Bosnian town of Srebrenica in the former Yugoslavia. Likewise, individuals have acted on their own initiative to collect evidence and protect witnesses in anticipation of future trials. An example is that of Lt. General Roméo Dallaire, the head of the UN peacekeeping force during the Rwandan genocide. Shortly after the slaughter began, he vowed to do everything in his power "to protect the last surviving Tutsi" and to "save every goddamn piece of paper so that some day [a prosecutor could] incriminate" the killers in a modern-day reprise of the Nuremberg trials.[27]

Still, the moral resonance of justice is often met by political obstruction or manipulation, especially if government officials fear that arrests and trials will undermine state interests. In the war against Nazi Germany, for example, President Franklin Roosevelt at first hesitated with respect to Allied plans to put Hitler and other top Nazi leaders on a public list of war criminals for fear that this might jeopardize the safety of Allied POWs who fell into German hands. But once the Allies adopted their policy of pursuing unconditional surrender, Roosevelt and his counterparts began advancing plans for a postwar military tribunal to prosecute the most senior Nazi leaders. More recently, at the start of the NATO-led attack on Libya in spring 2011, the United States and its European partners championed the ICC's indictment of Libyan leader Muammar Gaddafi as a means to isolate him internationally. But when the war effort foundered a few months later, Western diplomats worried that the ICC indictment would be an impediment to NATO's objective to end the war quickly. This led some key Western states to signal for a time that they would offer Gaddafi free passage to exile if he laid down his arms.

These examples and many others discussed in the pages that follow underscore that the pursuit of postwar accountability rarely beats a straight path toward the endgame of capture and prosecution. Time and again, pursuits are marked by the gains and setbacks that are the hallmark of the highly contested world of domestic and international politics. And while popular pressure for courtroom justice can exert a strong pull on governments to track down and arrest suspected perpetrators, the temptation to let bygones be bygones and to allow suspects to remain fugitives—or even tacitly let them off the hook—is a powerful force in its own right.

Despite its importance, political will is not always sufficient to bring suspects to trial. Even when states devote substantial political and operational resources to the task, the resourcefulness of fugitives and their support networks can be formidable. Some fugitives adopt new names and reinvent themselves, as was the case for countless German Nazis and their European collaborators and for former Bosnian Serb President Radovan Karadzic, who took on the identity of a New Age healer and vitamin salesman living in Belgrade. Other suspects deploy their sizable fortunes to buy protection from corrupt police and politicians, as the Rwandan Hutu businessman and prime genocide suspect Félicien Kabuga has for much of the past two decades in Kenya.

This book describes the efforts by states and nonstate networks, including national, ethnic, and religious groups, to hide and shield suspects from capture. In some cases, protection is as inadvertent as it is literal: in the aftermath of the Rwandan genocide, for example, tens of thousands of Hutus implicated in the mass murder of the Tutsi minority lived openly in the sprawling UN refugee camps in neighboring Zaire and Tanzania; half a world away and a few decades earlier, Cambodia's Khmer Rouge forces took advantage of refugee camps in neighboring Thailand to evade capture after they were driven from their homes by Vietnamese forces.

International criminal courts often stir up a hornet's nest when they issue arrest warrants. A host of actors—states, international and local NGOs, and activists—often disagree on when—or even *if*—an international criminal court should issue arrest warrants, especially if peace negotiations are underway. Because the arrest of high-level suspects can trigger controversy, states often back away from a previous commitment to international justice in favor of short-tem diplomatic or political needs. Even when the pursuit of trials is uncontroversial, a state may limit the number of its own war crimes prosecutions in order to concentrate on what it considers more pressing matters. Israel's approach to prosecuting German Nazi suspects is a case in point. After its famous prosecution of Adolf Eichmann in the early 1960s, Israel showed little interest in capturing and prosecuting the scores of other Nazi fugitives worldwide. Then and now, Israel has been far more focused on the security and foreign policy challenges of the present.

International and domestic courts gain legitimacy when they are perceived as operating above politics. But the fact is that international justice is at its core a political endeavor: international tribunals remain highly dependent on individual states and the international community for funding, logistical support, and the apprehension of war crimes suspects. This hard reality, as we shall see, poses an enduring challenge not just to international prosecutors who must turn to states to make arrests, but to the global justice movement as a whole. Despite these limitations, politics need not prevent the purveyors of justice—be they judges, prosecutors, or administrators—from acting in a just and forthright manner. Nor does politics need to prevent states from working collectively to end impunity or from carrying out arrests of those suspected of mass atrocities. Justice matters, and it matters most when it gives voice to those silenced by the gravest crimes.

PART ONE

CHAPTER 2

To Nuremberg and Beyond

"It fills me with horror to think of our Reich hacked to pieces by the victors, our peoples exposed to the savage excesses of the Bolsheviks and the American gangsters," Adolf Hitler wrote in his diary on April 2, 1945.[1] Far from becoming Europe's masters for a thousand years, as the Führer had once promised, Germany now faced the prospect of being overrun by occupying armies. U.S.-led Allied troops had already opened a road to Berlin and were encircling Hitler's huge military-industrial complex in the Ruhr Valley, while British and Canadian troops were sweeping across northern Germany. To the east, on the banks of the Oder River, Joseph Stalin had amassed more than a million soldiers and 22,000 pieces of artillery, all poised to descend on Berlin, a mere fifty-six kilometers away. Nazi Germany was by mid-April on the verge of collapse, its transport, gas, water, currency, communications, and health care systems in ruins, causing food shortages and spreading disease. Months of incessant Allied bombing had claimed the lives of nearly half a million people and left millions more homeless and destitute.

Yet Hitler remained defiant. Hidden deep inside his thirty-room bunker on the grounds of the Reich Chancellery in Berlin, he rose each morning and dispatched orders to his soldiers to fight to the end. On the eve of the Soviet assault on Berlin, he issued what was to be his last Order of the Day. "Whoever gives you orders to retreat," he said, "is to be arrested immediately and, if necessary, to be eliminated straight away—no matter what rank he holds."[2]

On Sunday, April 29, as American and British bombers wracked Berlin with high-explosive and incendiary bombs, news arrived at the bunker that partisans had captured and summarily executed the Italian dictator Benito Mussolini and his mistress, Clara Petacci, dumping their bodies in Milan's Piazzale Loreto, where an angry mob kicked and spat on the corpses before hanging them upside down on meat hooks from the roof of an Esso gas station.

Hitler was horrified. Just nine days earlier, on the occasion of his fifty-sixth birthday, he had received a congratulatory telegram from Mussolini. Now fearing he might meet the same fate, Hitler ordered his favorite German shepherd, Blondi, poisoned and her five puppies shot, then married his thirty-three-year-old mistress, Eva Braun, and, after saying goodbye to his staff, retreated to his study with his bride.[3] A single shot rang out. Martin Bormann, Hitler's private secretary, ran to the door and opened it. Hitler was slumped with his head on the table. Eva Braun lay on the sofa, her head towards him, knees drawn tightly up to her chest, an ampoule of cyanide crushed in her mouth.[4] Bormann barked an order, and guards carried the corpses out of the bunker and laid them in a freshly dug pit in the Chancellery garden. As the Führer's top aides watched, the guards doused petrol over the bodies and set them alight.[5]

With Hitler dead and Soviet troops scrambling over the smoldering embers of the Reichstag building, the remainder of the *Führerbunker* community faced stark choices. They could flee; wait to be captured; or follow their Führer's example and die by their own hand.

Joseph Goebbels, Hitler's minister of propaganda, was the first to choose. Widely known for having planned the *Kristallnacht* attacks that over the course of two November nights in 1938 had left nearly 2,000 Jewish synagogues in Germany and Austria ransacked or destroyed, he told a close associate there was only one way left: "the one Hitler chose."[6] He arranged for his six young children to be killed by Hitler's personal physician, and then he and his wife, Magda, ascended to the Chancellery garden and killed themselves.[7]

It was Bormann who then took nominal command of Hitler's remaining bunker staff[8]—men like Werner Naumann, the newly appointed head of what was left of the propaganda ministry; Hitler Youth leader Artur Axmann; Hitler's pilot, Hans Baur; and Ludwig Stumpfegger, the Führer's personal physician, who had just poisoned Goebbels's children.

The men formed small groups in the Chancellery garden and agreed to meet outside the Friedrichstrasse Station. From there, they would head north to the town of Plon, where the last vestiges of the Third

Reich were gathering.[9] Bormann, Stumpfegger, and Axmann set out together, but at some point the two older Germans became separated from Axmann.[10] Years later, Axmann would tell a West German de-Nazification court that he had lost sight of his companions but a few hours later found them lying face up in the moonlight behind a railway bridge.[11] He quickly examined the two bodies: they were dead, he was sure of it, but he wasn't sure how they had died. Then, as the sound of Russian artillery drew closer, he fled.[12]

For the next five decades, the "Bormann is alive" myth would live on in the press, novels, and cinema. As historian Guy Walters writes, sightings of Martin Bormann became "as ubiquitous as those of Elvis Presley decades later, and in some instances, no less comedic. Bormann was a monk in Rome . . . Bormann had landed in Argentina by submarine . . . Bormann was a hunter called 'Carlo' in the Tyrol . . . Bormann frequented the Ali Baba nightclub in Asunción, Paraguay, with Josef Mengele."[13] The lack of a corpse and the West German government's posting of a $25,000 reward for Bormann's capture made such chimerical sightings inevitable.

Bormann's demise was finally settled in the early 1970s after workmen in Berlin unearthed two sets of human remains near Lehrter Station. Scientists at the West Berlin Institute for Forensic Medicine identified the skeletons as those of Bormann and Stumpfegger. Lodged in their jawbones were microscopic fragments of glass, suggesting that they had committed suicide by biting cyanide capsules.[14]

As Allied troops took control of Germany and the Occupied Territories, tens of thousands of Nazis and Axis collaborators were on the run.

Some, like the Auschwitz doctor Josef Mengele, known as *der Totenengel* (the Angel of Death) because of his hideous experiments on inmates and his power to decide who would live and die, had already taken flight.[15] On the night of January 17, 1945, with the sound of the Red Army's artillery echoing ever closer, Mengele made one last visit to his office, where he hurriedly stuffed records from his experiments on twins, cripples, and dwarfs into a small suitcase and left Auschwitz. As the Red Army closed in, he found anonymity in the growing exodus of German soldiers heading west. For two months Mengele stayed with a Wehrmacht unit and later joined the ranks of a motorized German field hospital unit, Kriegslazarett 2/591.[16]

On May 8, 1945, the date Field Marshal Keitel signed the instrument of unconditional surrender, Mengele's adopted unit crossed into Saxony from Czechoslovakia and settled into a narrow strip of forested land that served as a buffer between American and Soviet troops. For the next five weeks, this no man's land became a collecting center for thousands of German soldiers. When American troops descended on the forest, Mengele and his unit slipped through the American checkpoints and travelled to Bavaria, where they were finally captured.[17]

By the time of Mengele's arrest, Germany had become a seething mass of humanity, its roads clogged with hundreds of thousands of refugees, liberated foreign workers, and released concentration camp survivors either returning to their home or seeking a new one.[18] Mingled within this horde were tens of thousands of Nazi war criminals and their Axis collaborators—former Eastern European government officials, concentration camp guards, and paramilitary leaders who had carried out some of the worst atrocities of the Holocaust and were now hoping to slip away. Allied troops worked through this chaos, erecting roadblocks and conducting sweeps through the countryside, in search of German soldiers. Those who were captured were dispatched to one of a vast constellation of hastily built prison camps, where they were screened in an attempt to discover whether they were members of the SS (Schutzstaffel), Hitler's elite paramilitary organization, or other units suspected of committing war crimes. Never before had a group of victorious powers sought to secure a defeated country and create a judicial process to prosecute thousands of war crimes suspects while detaining and interrogating enemy soldiers on such a massive scale. The closest precedent had been a frustrating, far less ambitious attempt by the Allies and Associated Powers following the First World War.[19]

In January 1919, largely in response to persistent clamor in the French, Belgian, and British press, the Allied Powers appointed a Commission on the Responsibility of the Authors of the War and on Enforcement of Penalties to inquire into the causes of and responsibility for the war. The commission concluded that the Central Powers (Germany, Austria-Hungary, the Ottoman Empire, and Bulgaria) had used "barbarous or illegitimate methods" in their conduct of the war and recommended that a tribunal be established to try those responsible for war crimes and violations of the "laws of humanity."[20] The commission's findings caused considerable debate among the Allies, with the Americans and Japanese vigorously challenging a number of its recommendations. The U.S. representatives were particularly opposed to any attempt to assign criminal responsibility for such a vague notion as the "laws of humanity." They also flatly rejected the establishment of an international court, "for which there is no precedent, precept, practice, or procedure," and instead proposed that each of the aggrieved countries create military commissions or tribunals to try the accused.[21]

When later drawing up the Treaty of Versailles, which would formally end World War I, the Allies took into account the commission's conclusions, but only in part. The final text of the treaty did not include provisions for an international tribunal to try those suspected of crimes against the laws of humanity, which the commission had recommended, but it did include a provision for the prosecution of Kaiser Wilhelm II of Germany, which the commission had rejected.[22]

The Allies presented the Germans with a list of 895 suspects (a sharp contrast from the twenty thousand originally named by the commission) to be tried separately by six countries, not including the United States, which was an Associated rather than an Allied Power. The list included the Kaiser, who was accused of offences against "international morality and the sanctity of treaties," as well as lower-ranking military officers allegedly responsible for mass killings of Belgian civilians and French prisoners of war and for torpedoing British hospital ships. The German government bluntly refused to hand over the defendants, and the Allies, lacking an occupying army, could do little else but consent to what they considered a humiliating compromise: Germany would try the suspects, but the Allies would be allowed to send observers to the trials. If the observers were dissatisfied by the verdicts, the Allies could retry the accused.[23] The Kaiser was not included in this arrangement: in November 1918 he had sought and been granted asylum in the Netherlands, which refused to hand him over for trial.

The trials opened before the German Supreme Court (Reichsgericht) in Leipzig on May 23, 1921. The first case involved two German U-boat commanders who had torpedoed the hospital ships *Dover Castle* and *Llandovery Castle* and later shelled the ships' crowded lifeboats. The court sentenced the two defendants to four years' imprisonment. Another case involved a German general who had allegedly ordered his troops to shoot surrendering French soldiers. When the judges acquitted the officer, the spectators applauded and shouted insults at the French observers.[24] A group of men placed a garland around the general's neck and carried him into the streets like a hero.

By January 1922, with acquittals stacking up like so many pieces of firewood, the Allies withdrew their observers in protest and demanded that the remaining defendants be surrendered to Allied courts. The Germans responded by holding closed trials. Of the 901 German defendants, only 13 were convicted and remanded to prison. And, within months, all of them had "escaped."[25]

Recollection of what had happened in Leipzig and Versailles would weigh heavily on the minds of a new generation of British and American policymakers twenty years later as they began to confront German atrocities of a magnitude never before seen. Fortunately, this time around the victors were in a stronger position. Because Allied forces occupied Germany and her former territories, they were better able to band together and develop a war crimes tribunal that—at least, in theory—transcended many specific national interests.

THE LONG, TWISTING ROAD TO NUREMBERG

During the first two years of the Second World War, Britain and its allies struggled against a relentless, often victorious German onslaught, with little attention to spare for developing a war crimes policy in the event their fortunes changed. By September 1941, U.S. intelligence had begun receiving weekly totals, corroborated by Polish underground and British intelligence, of thousands of Jews being murdered. Aerial photographs were even available of the early extermination sites, including the Babi Yar ravine outside Kiev, where Nazi soldiers massacred 34,000 Russian Jews. As evidence mounted of massive German crimes, President Franklin D. Roosevelt of the United States—then a neutral nation—stated on October 25, 1941, that "the Nazi treatment of civilian populations revolts the world," while British Prime Minister Winston Churchill declared that "retribution for these crimes must henceforward take its place among the major purposes of the war."[26]

Of all the Allied leaders, Franklin Roosevelt was by far the most cautious, often playing down controversial issues that he felt might complicate the war effort, as well as avoiding any commitments to postwar planning. If the Allies publicly threatened specific postwar punishment of German malefactors, he feared, Hitler might retaliate with a wholesale slaughter of Anglo-American prisoners of war. This reticence even extended to closed-door planning: even in late 1944, when prospects for ultimate victory were far brighter than they had been two years earlier, no U.S. task force was yet at work on the practical tasks of gathering evidence of war crimes, interrogating witnesses and suspects, tracking down wanted men, and establishing courts.

In Britain, Winston Churchill was far more outspoken about Nazi crimes, often lacing his radio broadcasts with threats that Britain would seek both ultimate victory and revenge against the Reich and their collaborators. "Any man or State who marches with Hitler is our foe," he thundered in a June 22, 1941 broadcast, adding that Britain was fully committed to delivering "the tools and agents of the Nazi regime . . . like the Nazi leaders to justice."[27] But Churchill's rhetoric on Nazi accountability didn't always sit well with officials in the Foreign Office, who worried that the prime minister was boxing Britain into postwar commitments it couldn't keep. When members of Parliament called on the Foreign Office to expound on Churchill's June 22 remarks, Sir Roger Makin, a Foreign Office legal officer, denied that his ministry was compiling lists of suspected war criminals and warned that the government should "studiously refrain from saying what we propose to do with [Nazi criminals] in the unlikely event [of] our catching any after the war."[28]

Not everyone in London and Washington was so reticent on the matter of postwar justice, however. Ever since they had learned of the Babi Yar massacre, the American Jewish Conference and other Jewish organizations in the United States had been campaigning incessantly in the press and in Congress for punitive action. In addition, the eight governments in exile (Belgium, Czechoslovakia, Greece, Luxembourg, the Netherlands, Norway, Poland, and Yugoslavia)—together with the French National Committee—were beseeching the Allies to announce a tougher policy of war crimes prosecutions.

On January 13, 1942, moved by a need for concerted action, the governments in exile met at St. James's Palace, organized themselves as the Inter-Allied Commission on the Punishment of War Crimes, and issued what became known as the Declaration of St. James's. The declaration repudiated retribution "by acts of vengeance on the part of the general public" and required that the signatory powers place among their principal war aims the punishment, through the channel of organized justice, of those guilty of or responsible for these crimes, whether they had ordered them, perpetrated them, or participated in them.[29]

The Declaration of St. James's notwithstanding, Churchill let it be known that he had no patience for formal judicial trials of what he called the "Hitler gang." He believed that the Nazi leaders should be deemed "world outlaws" and brought before a court simply to verify their identities. That accomplished, they were to be "shot to death . . . without reference to higher authority." Such a policy, which remained Britain's position until early 1945, would avoid, in Churchill's words, the "tangles of legal procedure."[30] Roosevelt and Stalin, however, rejected the idea of a quick execution in favor of a full trial. Of the two, it was, interestingly, Stalin who played the greater part in ultimately persuading both of his partners that a judicial process was the best way forward. He saw German defeat as a great opportunity for what his critics dismissed as a "show trial," much as he had used such trials against "deviationists" and "counter-revolutionary filth" during Soviet purges in the 1930s.[31]

In October 1943, the United States, Great Britain, and the Soviet Union—the Big Three—signed the Moscow Declaration, pledging to pursue war criminals "to the uttermost ends of the earth and [to] deliver them to the accusers in order that justice may be done."[32] Fine rhetoric indeed, but the declaration, when read in its entirety, seemed more intent on justifying a call to arms on the part of the Allies than actually pursuing justice. Nowhere in the text was there any mention of whether those suspected of war crimes would be prosecuted, or simply executed on the spot.[33]

In the meantime, the British Lord Chancellor, Viscount Simon, had introduced a proposal in the House of Lords to establish an international commission—later named the United Nations War Crimes Commission (UNWCC)—to investigate and name those Nazis responsible for war crimes. The commission's name did not refer to the United Nations itself, as that institution would not come into existence until late 1945, but instead to the "Declaration of the United Nations," a term coined by President Roosevelt in January 1942, in which twenty-six nations pledged their unity to stop the expansion of the Axis powers.[34] The thirteen-member UNWCC, comprising the governments in exile plus the United Kingdom, United States, China, Australia, and India, held its first meeting in London in October 1943.

From the start, the UNWCC was plagued with operational problems. The Soviet Union, although a victim of massive German atrocities and initially invited to be a member of the commission, refused to participate, claiming it had established its own machinery for collecting evidence of Nazi crimes. Even worse, the commission's mandate, despite intense lobbying by the Jewish World Congress, was never amended to include Holocaust-related crimes. Further, though the commission was mandated to investigate and collect evidence of war crimes, it lacked staff trained in investigatory procedures. And so it went: the commission met, subcommittees proliferated, and meetings bogged down in legalistic haggling over definitional matters and protocol.[35]

The UNWCC soon became viewed on both sides of the Atlantic as ineffective.[36] Undoubtedly the commission's most embarrassing moment took place during a press conference on August 30, 1944, convened by its chairman, Sir Cecil Hurst. When a reporter asked whether Adolf Hitler was on the commission's list of war crimes suspects, Hurst tried to evade the question, but finally admitted that, in fact, Hitler had been singled out for separate treatment, but stopped short of providing more details. In the end, Hurst's blundering further tarnished the UNWCC's blemished image.[37]

It would take a series of sparks and added kindling to reignite the World War II Allies' now-smoldering attempt to create a war crimes program. Fortunately, a thoughtful and bookish American lawyer named Murray C. Bernays was already at work in Washington, DC, drawing up a blueprint for a radical new approach to prosecuting Nazi war criminals. Bernays had served in the U.S. Army in France during World War I and, at the age of fifty, had been promoted to Lieutenant Colonel and appointed head of the Special Projects Branch at the U.S. War Department. He was well versed in the ways of war, having tackled a wide range of problems, including the treatment of POWs in German hands and the development of procedures to help protect them.[38]

In September 1944, Bernays presented a six-page memorandum on the "Trial of European War Criminals" to his superior, Assistant Secretary of War John J. McCloy. Bernays proposed that Nazi Germany be purged through a judicial process that would move swiftly through the ranks of the Third Reich from top to bottom. Leaders and members of six organizations—the Schutzstaffel (SS) and Sturmabteilung (SA), the two major Nazi paramilitary organizations; the Sicherheitspolizei (SiPo), the security police made up of the combined forces of the Gestapo (secret state police) and the Kripo (criminal police); the High Command of the Armed Forces, and the major leaders of the Nazi Party—would be tried before an international tribunal. In what would become known as the Nuremberg Trial Plan, the defendants would be charged with "conspiracy . . . to commit murder, terrorism, and destruction of peaceful populations in violation of the laws of war."[39] Built on a traditionally Anglo-American legal doctrine, that of criminal conspiracy, Bernays's approach would criminalize "everything done in the furtherance of the conspiracy . . . including domestic atrocities induced or procured by the German Government to be committed by other Axis nations against their respective nationals."[40]

McCloy sent the memorandum to Secretary of War Henry Stimson, who was greatly impressed by the proposal, and especially enthusiastic about the conspiracy concept. At seventy-seven, Stimson was one of the oldest and most venerable officials in the Roosevelt administration. A former Wall Street lawyer and military officer who had served in World War I, he was highly regarded by both military and civil officials. At about the time Bernays's criminal/conspiracy proposal landed on Stimson's desk, the secretary of war was trying to quash another plan for postwar Germany, one that had been put forward to the president by Secretary of the Treasury Henry Morgenthau. The so-called Morgenthau Plan aimed to prevent Germany's rearmament by closing down the Ruhr and Saar industries, effectively turning the country into an agricultural and pastoral backwater. The plan also included provisions for "group detention, the creation of labor battalions, and the summary execution, without hearing or trial, of Nazi leaders."[41]

On September 9, Stimson wrote to Roosevelt condemning every aspect of the Morgenthau Plan and recommending the establishment of an international tribunal to try Nazi war criminals. Stimson argued that only "through apprehension, investigation, and trial of all the Nazi leaders and instruments of the Nazi system of terrorism such as the Gestapo" would the Third Reich be eviscerated.[42]

Two months later, Stimson and his War Department colleagues received further fodder for their tribunal idea from A. N. Trainin, head of the Soviet Extraordinary State Commission for the Investigation of German War Crimes. Trainin sent a précis of the Soviet plan for a tribunal at which the major war criminals would be tried for conspiring to wage aggressive war (crimes against peace) and for waging that war with premeditated brutality (crimes against the laws of war).[43] Stimson and his aides saw the Soviet plan as a tool for outmaneuvering both Morgenthau and those who favored execution. On November 9, the War Department hosted a meeting on war crimes at the Pentagon, where the idea of a full-dress war guilt–conspiracy trial, as originally proposed by Bernays, was approved.

In mid-December 1944 news reached Washington that SS troops had machine-gunned seventy American prisoners at Malmédy, Belgium. Almost immediately newspaper editorial boards across the United States began calling for retribution. "Malmédy fever," as it was called, helped galvanize War Department proponents of an international tribunal. In January 1945, the secretary of war, supported by the secretary of state and the U.S. attorney general, presented Roosevelt with a proposal for an international tribunal to try the leading German war criminals. Even Morgenthau grudgingly accepted the plan.[44]

A month would pass before Roosevelt gave an indication that he fully supported war crimes trials of Nazi perpetrators. On February 24 he issued a directive ordering U.S. army groups stationed in Europe to establish special units to investigate "alleged war crimes against members of the armed forces of the United States."[45] A month later, the president issued a statement declaring that Nazi leaders would be tried and that the defendants would include those who had "participated in planning or carrying out Nazi enterprises involving or resulting in atrocities or war crimes."[46]

Still, the British stood firm, categorically rejecting the idea of a judicial tribunal as "neither good nor practicable."[47] What the British feared most was a lengthy trial in which Hitler and his cronies could dismantle a loosely worded conspiracy theory. The end goal for the British was a firing squad, so why take the risk of holding a trial that could potentially turn into a farce?[48]

In the end, it was Harry S. Truman who would make the final break with the British on the issue of summary execution. On May 2, 1945, just three weeks after Roosevelt's death, President Truman issued a statement from the White House announcing America's commitment to the judicial path: "It is our objective to establish as soon as possible an international military tribunal; and to provide a trial procedure which will be expeditious in nature and which will permit no evasion or delay—but one which is in keeping with our tradition of fairness toward those accused of crime."[49] The following day, in a stunning concession that surprised the Americans, the British war cabinet, possibly in response to Truman's emphatic announcement, reversed its policy on summary executions. News of the British turnabout spread quickly among delegates in San Francisco attending the founding conference of the United Nations. On May 6, American, British, Soviet, and French delegates emerged from a meeting to announce they had reached a tentative agreement to establish an international military tribunal based on judicial principles, with one judge and one chief attorney from each of the four states. Nothing was formally signed, but it was a Rubicon moment: Senior Nazi leaders who fell into Allied hands would be investigated and tried.[50] Only time would tell whether this endeavor would be an anomaly in world affairs, or the beginning of something new and ultimately enduring: the development of a sense of international justice among nation states and a means of adjudicating it.

While the Allies were still arguing over a process for holding Nazis accountable for their crimes, the Supreme Headquarters Allied Expeditionary Force in Paris had established a Central Registry of War Criminals and Security Suspects (CROWCASS). Building on the experience of both Scotland Yard and the FBI, it was to be the largest database of war criminals ever assembled and would serve as the hub for gathering information on war crimes suspects throughout Europe—or so it was hoped. At its helm was British Lieutenant Colonel William Palfrey, who hired four hundred French women to set up a huge card index, into which they would punch the names of the eight-million-strong German army. This index was to be matched against two datasets: lists of war crimes suspects compiled by the UNWCC, and the names that came up on standard detention forms, on which arresting officers were to place a photograph of the detainee, his fingerprints, and a breakdown of his main physical characteristics. From this mass of information, the women of the central registry were to produce lists of war crimes suspects and distribute them to field commanders and POW camp administrators.

CROWCASS faced a daunting and unprecedented task and suffered as a result. Both its first list of war crimes suspects, published in May 1945, and its second list, released five months later, were deeply flawed. Much of the information was simply incorrect: names were misspelled, ranks and military affiliations mismatched, and the like. By May 1946, CROWCASS had moved from Paris to Berlin, where it was placed under the wing of the Allied Control Council, the governing occupation body, jointly directed by the Soviet Union, the United States, and the United Kingdom. By then, Lieutenant Colonel R. F. Luck had replaced the unfortunate Palfrey as the agency's director. Even so, now with only eight employees, the registry soon became overwhelmed, prompting Luck to send a desperate message to his superior in London, begging for more staff and resources. When the beleaguered agency tried to publish a new list of suspected war criminals, it was unable to do so because of a shortage of typewriter ribbons.[51]

By the time CROWCASS suspended operations in 1948, though, it had processed over a hundred thousand detention requests to investigative teams from a dozen countries and published a total of forty book-length registries of persons being sought for war crimes—the most extensive database on such suspects ever created.[52]

But CROWCASS, like so many postwar intelligence projects, also had a second, more surreptitious function. The crosschecking capacity that helped ferret out the names and backgrounds of possible war crimes suspects could also be used to create a pool of possible candidates from within the Nazi ranks for Allied police and intelligence work. There was nothing overtly nefarious about using such information to develop a network of local informants: the intelligence agencies wanted to keep tabs on a restive population, hoping to prevent the resurgence of a Nazi threat in Allied-occupied Germany, and this seemed to them an ideal way to do it. As Gene Bramel, a young U.S. army intelligence officer who supervised a number of Nazi informants, put it:

> They say, "Why did you use Nazis?" That is a stupid question. It would have been impossible for us to operate in southern Germany without using Nazis. We were Americans. I spoke pretty good German, but by the time I got through ordering dinner they would have suspected I was an American. And who knew Germany better than anyone else? Who were the most organized? Who were the most anti-Communist? Former Nazis. Not to use them would mean complete emasculation. And we used them, the British used them, the French used them, and the Russians used them.[53]

But it was a Faustian pact bound in all the trappings of a utilitarian rationalization. Leon G. Turrou, an American intelligence officer and CROWCASS's operations chief, oversaw the task of culling lists to find former Nazi officials who could serve as informants. He also became the inside contact for his American intelligence colleagues who wanted incriminating information purged about Nazis who had gone to work for them. Turrou did this by deleting the names of informants that appeared on CROWCASS lists of either wanted suspects or German POWs or by simply sanitizing an informant's file of any incriminating information. Such selective whitewashing of Nazi personal histories became *de rigueur* as American and British intelligence agents swept through the occupied zones in search of potential German spies to infiltrate Nazi resistance groups. But the process did not end there; these same informants would also be used to penetrate nascent Communist organizations in Eastern Europe, and to track down German and Austrian scientists to send to Britain and the United States to bolster their science and technology efforts.[54]

Allied war crimes investigators faced daunting psychological challenges and operational difficulties as they took control of Germany and Austria in the spring of 1945. Not only did they have to deal with immense human suffering, especially among survivors of the extermination and concentration camps, they also had to make legal sense of the sheer volume of criminality they were uncovering. For the British and Canadians, the horror especially hit home when a combined infantry unit entered Bergen-Belsen, in northern Germany, on the afternoon of April 15, 1945. The camp was packed with nearly 40,000 inmates in the grips of a typhus epidemic, its grounds pocked with half-filled burial pits and strewn with mounds of corpses in various stages of decomposition. Inside the huts were more bodies, some even in the same bunks as the living.[55]

The Allied soldiers arrested the camp's commander, Josef Kramer, and called in a British war crimes team, which soon became overwhelmed by the task of interviewing dozens of uncooperative camp staff and hundreds of emaciated and highly traumatized survivors. "The evidence flowed in like a deluge and we were submerged in it," an investigator recalled. "Our efforts then and later were like a man standing at the edge of the sea dropping lumps of sugar into it, and saying: 'Behold it is sweet.' We were failing because the wave of criminality was so great and our resources were so inadequate." And as it would turn out, many of the depositions taken from witnesses and victims at Bergen-Belsen and other concentration camps would be worthless as trial evidence: the interrogators, few of whom were trained in law, often asked questions that failed to gather sufficient or appropriate evidence.[56]

Corporal Ben Ferencz, a Jewish-American war crimes investigator, who was born in the mountains of Transylvania and grew up in New York's Hell's Kitchen neighborhood before going on to receive a Harvard law degree, was assigned to investigate concentration camps at Buchenwald, Mauthausen, and Dachau. (He would later be appointed, at the age of twenty-seven, a chief prosecutor of one of twelve U.S.-led trials of Nazi suspects following the famous Nuremberg Tribunal.) He recalled adopting a sort of stoic professionalism to cope with the tremendous anger he felt when he first entered the camps:

> Entering a concentration camp very soon after it is liberated is entering hell. Total chaos. The troops are coming in, trucks are coming in, SS are running out into the woods. The inmates—those of them who can still move—many of them are just lying there, dead or dying. And I've got to go in and find out where's the office, where are the records for all of this. . . . Seize all the records. Take testimony wherever [I] can. Go back to headquarters, sit down, type up the report, which subsequently became the basis for war crimes trials.[57]

Now in his mid-nineties, Ferencz goes on to recall how he coped with the emotional stress of witnessing such horrors:

I somehow, automatically I guess by way of self-preservation, created a mental block. This was not real, these were not humans, this is a case. I need the evidence of what is happening here, I need to record it in a manner which is indisputable, I need to determine who could be responsible for these crimes, and I have to move on to the next camp. And I did that, in almost a mechanical fashion. I sometimes thought I was like a doctor on the battlefield having to do triage. Now the effect on me was a permanent trauma, from which I suffer to this day, and that couldn't be concealed, and that couldn't be overcome, but it was put in a side drawer because there was a job to do and that had to be done and it was important and I had no time to waste with emotion or sentiment. I had to get it down and move on to the next camp.[58]

Robert E. Matteson, a former political-science teacher from Wisconsin who was a war crimes investigator with the U.S. 80th Infantry Division, recalled what he and his interpreter, Sydney Bruskin, encountered as they entered the gates of the Ebensee concentration camp early in the morning of May 5, 1945:

Bodies that one would never have believed existed were walking around, covered with sores and lice. The filth was indescribable. Adjacent to the crematorium were rooms piled high with shrunken nude bodies, lye thrown over them to combat the stench and vermin. . . . Worse still was the hospital, where the dying and sick had been herded for experimentation before being carted off to the crematorium. There were no beds in the [hospital]; the inmates lay on shelves covered with dirty rags, groups of two or three huddled together like mice to keep warm. As we entered they put their hands out and begged for food.[59]

After leaving Ebensee, Matteson and Bruskin traveled with an army detachment to the Austrian Alpine resort of Altausee in search of Ernst Kaltenbrunner, the head of the Reichssicherheitshauptamt (Reich Security Main Office), the branch within the SS that ran the domestic and foreign intelligence services, the Gestapo, and the criminal police. In 1943, Kaltenbrunner had ordered the creation of a complex of Austrian camps, including Ebensee, to provide slave labor for the construction of enormous underground tunnels in which German armaments were housed.

In April 1945, the American Office of Strategic Services, the forerunner of the Central Intelligence Agency, had learned that Kaltenbrunner and some other high-ranking Nazis had fled to the mountains above Altausee to establish a redoubt from which they could descend to prey on the Allied occupation forces. Among those who had gathered there were Wilhelm Höttl of the Sicherheitsdienst, the SS intelligence service; Adolf Eichmann, the operational manager of the Final Solution;

General Erich Alt of the Luftwaffe; Walter Riedel, the construction chief of the V-2 rocket program at Peenemünde; and William Knothe, general counsel of the Foreign Office.

Shortly after their arrival in Altausee, Matteson and Bruskin oversaw the capture and initial interrogation of Höttl, Alt, Riedel, and Knothe. Days later, Matteson captured Kaltenbrunner and three SS guards in a small, snow-bound hunting lodge in the mountains above Altausee. Eichmann, however, managed to evade capture.[60]

Allied war crimes teams faced, albeit to varying degrees, three significant challenges in the postwar years: a shortage of personnel and resources, administrative indecision, and, after initial enthusiasm, flagging political support from their governments.[61] Ian Neilson, the head of the British war crimes effort, spoke ruefully to Guy Walters about his constant battle to acquire equipment and personnel:

> If the [British War Crimes Unit] had started in the early spring of 1945, I think we would have caught a lot more chaps—and witnesses' memories would have been a lot better than they were. Generally speaking, the whole thing was on a shoestring . . .[62]

Without proper manpower, many British investigators were absurdly overworked. In August 1946, one desperate team leader beseeched London to send more pathologists to deal with the mass graves his men were uncovering, but to no avail. Another team leader grew incensed when he learned that his team was to be cut by sixty investigators. "It does not seem to be appreciated in certain branches of this Headquarters that the War Investigation Unit is engaged in priority work or that it is a highly specialized unit," he wrote to his superiors.[63] Still, the cuts held, and as his caseload grew, so did the backlog of unresolved investigations.

What neither of these investigators knew was that senior British officials were quickly losing their appetite for Nazi hunting. In November 1946, the Cabinet decided in principle to begin winding down British war crimes trials. In August 1948, Britain effectively ended its war crimes investigations altogether. "I was really upset," one investigator later told Guy Walters. "We still had ten thousand people on the books. These were criminals, murderers, concentration camp guards—and they disbanded it because they wanted to concentrate on the Russians. It was just filthy politics."[64]

Why was Britain abandoning its war crimes effort? Sir Hartley Shawcross, the chief British prosecutor at Nuremberg, later recalled that the decision was made because Churchill was worried that future Axis trials might bring attention to the crimes committed by the investigators themselves.[65] Allied war crimes teams, true enough, did face allegations of torture and ill-treatment, especially in the early years. The French became the subject of criticism by their Anglo-American counterparts for using beatings and dog attacks, among other methods, in their attempts to extract information from German prisoners. In one instance, a French interrogator unleashed an Alsatian and a Boxer on a prisoner, who finally acquiesced and signed a confession written in French.[66]

But the French weren't the only ones who had taken up abusive interrogation methods. Ben Ferencz, who decades later became an influential advocate of enshrining due-process principles through the establishment of the International Criminal Court, described to Guy Walters how he handled cases in which he suspected U.S. airmen had been murdered after they were shot down:

> I'd drive to where it happened and detain the Burgermeister or the most senior guy, and get some witnesses together. I'd line them up against a wall and threaten to shoot them unless they wrote down exactly what happened. I wasn't going to shoot, but they didn't know that, because I damn well made them know that I was going to blow their heads off. Anyway, they'd soon started scribbling![67]

British investigators also faced allegations of torture and abuse in their handling of Nazi prisoners. In June 1945, British intelligence opened an interrogation center in Bad Nenndorf, near Hanover, Germany, where ex-Nazis and suspected communist agents were subjected to systematic beatings, whippings, prolonged solitary confinement, exposure to extreme cold, and starvation, according to Inspector Thomas Hayward of Scotland Yard, who later investigated abuse at the facility. Hayward revealed that guards at Bad Nenndorf had been "instructed to carry out physical assaults on certain prisoners with the object of reducing them to a state of physical collapse and of making them more amenable to interrogations."[68] He also found that some detainees were tortured with thumbscrews and other instruments recovered from a Gestapo prison in Hamburg. Hayward's findings dismayed British officials. "I doubt if I can put too strongly the parliamentary consequences of publicity," one foreign officer wrote in a memorandum to then Foreign Secretary Ernest Bevin. "Whenever we have any allegations to make about the political police methods in Eastern European states it will be enough to call out in the House 'Bad Nenndorf,' and no reply is left to us."[69]

Equally serious charges were directed at British interrogators working in the Combined Services Detailed Interrogation Centre, known col-
loquially as the London Cage, which operated out of three houses in the
posh neighborhood of Kensington Palace Gardens. In total, 3,573 German prisoners, military and civilian alike, passed through the Cage
between July 1940 and September 1948 without the knowledge of the
International Committee of the Red Cross, and more than 1,000 were
persuaded to give statements about war crimes. According to two official inquiries, London Cage interrogators used beatings, sleep deprivation, and forced standing, while threatening the use of electric devices
and summary execution, to coerce inmates to talk.[70]

Most of the U.S. investigations of Nazi crimes were conducted by a little-
known army organization called the Counter Intelligence Corps (CIC).
Established in August 1917 as the Corps of Intelligence Police, the unit
ran counterintelligence operations in northern France toward the end of
the First World War. After the Japanese attack on Pearl Harbor the corps
was renamed the CIC and its numbers swelled to nearly 5,000 commis-
sioned and noncommissioned officers. The men selected for the CIC were
often multilingual, high-status professionals—bankers, professors,
county sheriffs, lawyers, and journalists—with little or no investigative
experience. A few agents would become notable figures, such as novelist
J. D. Salinger, author of *The Catcher in the Rye*; composer Leroy Anderson; and Aaron Bank, father of the Vietnam special operations commandos, the Green Berets. Once in the "Corps," agents were expected to
remain discreet, wearing plain clothes or uniforms bearing no unit identification or designation of rank.[71]

As U.S. army divisions occupied Germany and Austria, they were
accompanied by CIC detachments that provided security for military
installations and staging areas, located enemy agents, and acted to
counter Nazi stay-behind networks. They also provided training to
combat units in security, censorship, the seizure of documents, and the
dangers of booby traps. Once in Germany, CIC personnel were
regrouped into a single detachment headquartered in Berlin. The CIC's
operational mandate, at least in its early postwar years, was drawn
largely from a 120-page counterintelligence directive issued by the
Twelfth Army Group in April 1945. The directive was as blunt as it was
all-embracing. Germany was to be sealed off from the rest of the world,
with martial law imposed on all its inhabitants. Curfews would be
enforced, meaning no German could move without an ID pass, and

never more than six kilometers from his or her home. Army check-points, backed up by surveillance aircraft, were to be posted along Germany's borders and a "blackout" imposed to stop all communication between Germans and their relatives, friends, and associates outside the country.[72]

The directive also instructed the CIC to carry out a range of special tasks, among them tracking down German scientists and industrial technologists (lest they fall into Soviet hands), detaining anyone who represented a threat to the Allied forces, securing Nazi Party buildings to safeguard documents, and arresting and interrogating suspected war criminals. Some CIC agents were dispatched to POW camps to weed out SS and Nazi Party members from the rank and file. One of the least desirable jobs was being attached to a "CI Annex," a warren of communal and solitary confinement cells and soundproof interrogation rooms, usually located next to a POW camp, where CIC agents would spend hours eavesdropping on interrogations and conversations among internees in the hope of gleaning some actionable intelligence.[73]

The CIC's Berlin office maintained two subsections: the Central Registry, which cataloged all counterintelligence information, and Case Direction, which evaluated all counterintelligence information coming from its field offices, checked it against information already on file, and passed it on to other interested agencies. Case Direction was further divided into two subsections known as the internal and external desks.

The internal desk concerned itself with pursuing war criminals, maintaining security, and implementing an ambitious denazification program. During the first ten months of the occupation the CIC apprehended some 120,000 Germans listed for automatic arrest. This group included top Nazi leaders, SS and Gestapo members, high-ranking military officers, and suspected war criminals.[74] The CIC was also pulled, along with other U.S. intelligence agencies, into a secret project authorized by the Joint Chiefs of Staff in July 1945. The clandestine program, known as Project Overcast, was to "exploit . . . chosen, rare minds whose continuing intellectual productivity we wish to use." The chiefs directed that up to 350 identified specialists in chemical warfare, submarine design, and missile research, mainly from Germany and Austria, should be immediately brought to the United States to work in the then continuing war with Japan and the emerging conflict with the Soviet Union.[75]

By early 1946, the Pentagon's Joint Intelligence Objectives Agency (JIOA) had begun pushing for a revised and larger program, given the clandestine name Operation Paperclip, to recruit German and Austrian scientists and technicians. In September, President Truman approved Operation Paperclip, contingent on the effort's remaining secret from the public and recruitment restricted to "nominal" Nazis (and not "active supporters" of Nazism). In the recruitment process the Office of Military Government United States (OMGUS) in Germany would prepare a dossier on each scientist and technician based on CIC investigations. These dossiers would then be sent in batches to the JIOA and on to a panel of representatives from the Departments of Justice and State, who would rule on the admissibility of each individual and report back to the JIOA.[76]

But there was a problem. In early 1947, the review panel actually rejected the first batch of dossiers, largely because the OMGUS reports pointed out that at least half of the recruits were Nazi Party members or SS veterans and some were without question still "ardent Nazis." According to Christopher Simson, CIC investigations revealed that some candidates "were accused of participating in murderous medical experiments on human subjects at concentration camps, for example, or brutalizing slave laborers. Another was reported to have established an institute for biological warfare experimentation on humans in Poland."[77]

In response, the JIOA director, Bosquet Wev, wired the director of intelligence at the U.S. European Command: "There is very little possibility that the State and Justice Departments will agree to immigrate any specialist who has been classified as an actual or potential security threat to the United States. This may result in the return [to] Germany of specialists whose skill and knowledge should be denied to other nations in the interest of national security. . . . It is requested . . . that new security reports be submitted where such action is appropriate."[78]

In other words, the files were to be cleansed of any incriminating information. Weeks later, OMGUS sent back new dossiers with all offending language expunged, and subsequent dossiers were careful to point out that the Nazi and SS past of each recruit "did not constitute a security threat to the U.S."[79] This action prompted two members of the screening board to resign. From then on, the Pentagon's recruitment of German scientists ran without a hitch.

Congressional inquiries in the 1980s and 1990s into Operation Paperclip revealed that between 1945 and 1955 alone, 765 scientists, engineers, and technicians were brought to the United States. At least half, and perhaps as many as 80 percent, of these specialists were former Nazi Party members, including some who were responsible for war crimes.[80]

If the CIC's internal desk in Berlin was focused on seeking out war criminals, its external desk was mainly responsible for monitoring the activities of the Soviet Union and its satellites. When General Dwight Eisenhower, commander of U.S. Forces in Europe, was directed by the Joint Chiefs of Staff in May 1945 to arrest and hold war criminals, he was advised: "In your discretion, you may make such exceptions as you deem advisable for intelligence and other military reasons."[81] By the late 1940s, the CIC had established a wide network of informants and agents, some of whom had tainted wartime backgrounds, within the Allied occupation zones and extending into Eastern Europe. Decades later it would be revealed that in Austria alone the CIC had employed as intelligence informants at least fourteen suspected Nazi war criminals, a number of whom were likely involved in the murder of Jews in occupied Europe.[82]

As the war in Europe came to a close, in May 1945, the CIC began to lose some of its best agents, who were seizing their first opportunity to return to the States and civilian life. To make up for these losses, the CIC scoured American troops throughout Europe to find suitable replacements. The process produced disappointing results, as most of the young soldiers had had no training in intelligence or police work and many were simply attracted to the trappings of authority and benefits that came with a cloak-and-dagger lifestyle. One such recruit was twenty-two-year-old Henry Kissinger, a U.S. Army officer born in the Bavaria region of Germany to an Orthodox Jewish family. As anti-Semitism intensified in Nazi Germany, the Kissinger family had departed for New York in August 1938. Now, several years later, the future secretary of state was posted to southwestern Germany, where, according to CIC historians Ian Sayer and Douglas Botting, Sergeant Kissinger spent his days ferreting out Gestapo and SS officers who were hiding in the town and surrounding countryside, but after hours "lived like a lord in a luxurious villa": "After a visit to the Kissinger ménage an old friend from Washington wrote in his diary for 21 October 1945: 'What a setup! Like a castle. Had dinner with [Kissinger]. What an intelligent girlfriend.' The girlfriend was German. So were the cook, the maid, the housekeeper and the secretary—and the white 1938 Mercedes-Benz he had confiscated from a Nazi baby powder manufacturer."[83]

Such excesses earned the scorn of hard-boiled British agents like Anthony Terry, a British commando who also worked as an interrogator in the London Cage and later as a journalist. Terry found many of the CIC agents he encountered after the war to be posturing, skirt-chasing "nabobs" who were haphazard in their jobs and couldn't keep their files secure. "They may have been effective in the combat situation during the war," he said, "but they were running to seed a bit by the time I met them afterwards. They ran around with a lot of fancy ideas and wrote vast memos full of sound and fury and not signifying very much."[84]

For a week in February 1945, as Allied forces advanced toward Berlin, the soon-to-be victors—Winston Churchill, Franklin D. Roosevelt, and Joseph Stalin—met at the Black Sea resort of Yalta to discuss Europe's postwar reorganization. They agreed that Nazi Germany had to surrender unconditionally and that both Germany and Berlin would be split into four occupied zones. France would occupy one of the zones, but it would have to be formed out of the American and British zones. The Big Three also agreed to "remove all Nazi and militarist influences from public office and from the cultural and economic life of the German people."[85] In effect, the occupying powers, in addition to seeking and trying those suspected of major war crimes, would implement an ambitious denazification program to rid German and Austrian society of any remnants of the Third Reich.

Each of the occupiers took a somewhat different approach to denazification. The Americans viewed their mission as a moral crusade and were by far the most zealous of the occupying powers. They required every German over the age of eighteen to answer a questionnaire or *Fragebogen,* which contained 131 questions in six pages about his or her association with the Nazi Party. After the *Fragebogen* had been filled in, a denazification court would classify the respondent in one of five categories: major offender, offender, lesser offender, follower, or exonerated person. Each of the first four categories carried a penalty, ranging from imprisonment to fines, and those considered some of the worst offenders could potentially be tried for war crimes. In the Soviet zone, the denazification process—at least, in the initial phase—was used to remove capitalists, large landowners, and anyone who seemed hostile to the communist experiment. The British, faced with the responsibility for the zone with the largest concentration of industry and the greatest degree of damage due to the bombing, tended to be more willing to allow people to remain at their jobs for the sake of economic recovery. The French were less interested in purging people on the basis of their Nazi Party membership than in decentralizing and weakening Germany.[86] In all, the Allies penalized nearly a million German nationals for their Nazi Party affiliations.[87]

Denazification tended to be rough justice. This was especially true in the American zone, where the CIC had unlimited powers of search and arrest, prompting many Germans to refer to them as the "American

Gestapo." CIC agents, frequently armed with more prejudice than knowledge, arrested individuals based on tips provided by shady informers who were seeking revenge or hoping to gain personal advantage. Nor did the American occupiers appreciate that joining the Nazi Party might in some cases have been more a matter of necessity than conviction. Indeed, many teachers and public officials had become party members simply to protect their employment or to improve their career prospects. According to one assessment, approximately 65 percent of all primary-school teachers in the American zone were removed from their posts.[88]

In late 1945 the Allies, mindful of the rising fear and anger among Germans regarding the denazification program, began to relax their occupation regime. German advisory committees worked alongside American and British authorities to help usher in German-run administrations at the regional and district levels.[89] Of all the occupiers, the French were the most lenient toward their German subjects and the first to turn the vetting process over to trusted German officials. Meanwhile, in the Soviet zone, nominal members of the Nazi Party were offered the opportunity to join rehabilitation programs if they broke with their political past and agreed to devote themselves to the task of reconstruction.

DAYS OF JUDGMENT

By late 1949, when the victors handed power back to a new German government, the Allies and authorities in Greece, Netherlands, Norway, Poland, and Yugoslavia had conducted 969 war crimes trials, in which 3,470 German defendants were tried. Death sentences were passed for 952; 1,905 were sentenced to varying prison terms; and 613 were acquitted.[90] Of all the postwar trials, the Trial of the Major War Criminals that opened in Nuremberg, in the American Occupation Zone, on November 20, 1945, would be, in the words of British historian Richard Bressel, "the most important expression of the Allied campaign to impose morality through legal proceedings, and simultaneously to establish a record of what the Nazi regime had done."[91]

Allied representatives had met in London in June 1945 to create the charter for what would become known as the Nuremberg tribunal. They agreed that the court would have jurisdiction over only Nazi crimes committed in connection with Germany's waging of aggressive war. Each of the representatives had reasons of their own for holding only the German side responsible for war crimes committed during the conflict. The Americans and British, for example, knew that their forces had killed civilians and wanted to avoid a *tu quoque* argument from the defense that they were equally responsible for war crimes.[92] Of particular concern to the Anglo-American representatives were the bombing raids over Dresden between February 13 and 15, 1945, in which British and American warplanes dropped more than 3,900 tons of high-explosive bombs and incendiary devices on the city, destroying much of the city center and killing more than 23,000 people.[93] Similarly, the Soviets did not want to be charged with the massacre of more than 20,000 Polish officers and civilians at Katyn in April and May 1940, though they included this massacre as a charge in the indictment against the Germans.[94]

On August 8, 1945, after a summer of debate, the four major powers—the Soviet Union, France, Great Britain, and the United States—met again in London to sign the charter establishing the International Military Tribunal in Nuremberg. The charter laid the scaffolding for the Nuremberg trial of the surviving leaders of the Third Reich by determining the structure of the trial, the roles of the countries involved (and their prosecutors), and the rules intended to ensure a fair and public trial for the defendants. Paragraph 6 of the charter defined the crimes that would be prosecuted:

- *Crimes against Peace*: namely, planning, preparation, initiation or waging of a war of aggression, or a war in violation of international treaties, agreements or assurances, or participation in a common plan or conspiracy for the accomplishment of any of the foregoing.

- *War Crimes*: namely, violations of the laws or customs of war. Such violations shall include, but not be limited to, murder, ill-treatment or deportation to slave labor or for any other purpose of civilian population of or in occupied territory, murder or ill-treatment of prisoners of war or persons on the seas, killing of hostages, plunder of public or private property, wanton destruction of cities, towns or villages, or devastation not justified by military necessity.

- *Crimes against Humanity*: namely, murder, extermination, enslavement, deportation, and other inhumane acts committed against any civilian population, before or during the war; or persecutions on political, racial or religious grounds in execution of or in connection with any crime within the jurisdiction of the Tribunal, whether or not in violation of domestic law of the country where perpetrated.[95]

Three weeks later, the chief prosecutors released a list of twenty-four Nazi leaders to be tried before the tribunal.[96] Between their arrests and their transfer to Nuremberg prison, most of the suspects were held in an American internment camp, known by the derogatory code-name Ashcan, in Mondorf-les-Bains, a small spa town in Luxembourg. A small number were held by the British at Kransberg Castle, outside Frankfurt am Main, under the code-name Dustbin. The American facility was by far the less accommodating. The prisoners slept in rooms featuring only a bunk and straw mattress (which was removed as a punishment for rule violations), a small table, and a straight-backed chair. The food was limited to 1,550 calories per day, the amount allowed for ordinary German civilians. Once in prison and out of the hands of their army captors, the detainees were rarely physically abused, although there were reports of psychological pressure, including threats to turn them over to the Soviets if they failed to tell interrogators what they wanted to know.[97]

The twenty defendants who had already been transferred to the Nuremberg jail were served copies of the indictment and given a list of German lawyers who might be available to represent them in case they had no choice of their own. Two of the accused, Erich Raeder, the supreme commander of the navy, and Hans Fritzsche, head of the Radio Division of the Propaganda Ministry, were still in Soviet hands. Martin Bormann, who was still believed to be alive, was to be tried *in absentia*. The twenty-fourth suspect, German industrialist Gustav Krupp, was considered too frail to stand trial and remained confined at his hunting lodge in Austria.[98]

On October 18, 1945, the Nuremberg Trial began, and a month later, on November 20, 1945, the indictments were read. The chief American prosecutor, Justice Robert Jackson, opened the proceedings by delivering one of the most memorable and often-quoted prosecutorial statements in modern history. Jackson began:

> The wrongs which we seek to condemn and punish have been so calculated, so malignant, and so devastating, that civilization cannot tolerate their being ignored, because it cannot survive their being repeated. That four great nations, flushed with victory and stung with injury, stay the hand of vengeance and voluntarily submit their captive enemies to the judgment of the law is one of the most significant tributes that Power has ever paid to reason. . . . We must never forget that the record on which we judge these defendants is the record on which history will judge us tomorrow. To pass these defendants a poisoned chalice is to put it to our lips as well. We must summon such detachment and intellectual integrity to our task that this Trial

will commend itself to posterity as fulfilling humanity's aspirations to do justice.[99]

Jackson insisted on a strategy of *symbolic* justice that would prove German crimes not from the mouths of witnesses (whom some might consider unreliable) but from the defendant's own documents, drawn from a pool of more than 100,000 captured German documents, of which 4,000 were entered as trial exhibits, along with 1,800 still photographs.[100]

Much of the testimony offered by the witnesses at the Nuremberg trial was of questionable legal relevance: meandering commentaries on German history or sententious endorsements of the character of the defendants which, as Rebecca West, who reported on the trial for the *New Yorker,* recalled, left many spectators "puffy with boredom."[101] Yet at times there were moments of high drama. George Krevit, who, at the age of nineteen, served as a court page in the Nuremberg court, recalled how he was struck by the testimony of survivors of Nazi medical experiments:

> Witnesses started to come forward, and it was probably the most horrible time in my life. Men and women came into court, showed the results of operations, torture. I don't even want to mention some things—they were too horrible. . . . I mean, opening up a man's leg and putting seaweed into his veins to see how he reacted to foreign bodies. Castrating people of low moral character, or just to get them off the face of the earth. Experimenting on twins who had the same color eyes. And [the defendants] just sat in the dark and showed no emotion whatsoever.[102]

On the morning of October 1, 1946, the tribunal read the judgments: twelve of the defendants were sentenced to death, three to life imprisonment; four were given prison sentences ranging from ten to twenty years, and three were acquitted. (One of the original defendants, Robert Ley, the leader of the German Labor Front, had hanged himself before the trial began.) Of those given prison sentences, Albert Speer, Hitler's chief architect and minister of armaments and war production, was jailed for twenty years for his use of forced labor. The man who supplied the slave labor, Fritz Sauckel, was hanged. Hermann Göring, also sentenced to hang, killed himself with cyanide the night before his scheduled execution.

Following this landmark trial, the United States held twelve more trials in Nuremberg, involving 144 relatively high-level defendants from the German High Command, the medical profession, big business, the

judiciary, government ministries, SS economic officials, and, most notably, the *Einsatzgruppen,* special SS and Gestapo execution squads that
murdered approximately a million Jews in the conquered German territories in Eastern Europe and the Soviet Union, and scores of trials of
German camp personnel and others.

What satisfactory justice is, of course, can be interpreted in a variety
of ways. According to historian Rebecca Wittmann, many Germans
believed the Allied judges at the Nuremberg trials had violated Germany's constitution, which contained a strict ban on retroactivity, by
imposing ex post facto adjudication on crimes that were not defined as
such at the time the acts were supposedly committed. Similarly, there
was considerable resentment, particularly among Germans who had
been victims of British and American bombing attacks, that no Allied
leaders had been held to account for their crimes.[103] "It was a time when
Germany couldn't care less about war crimes trials," American investigator Ben Ferencz recalled. "The German public was interested in finding a place to sleep and getting a loaf of bread to eat. They had been
beaten to a pulp. And their primary concern was their own self-preservation, the war crimes trials were viewed as victor's justice, as an inevitable price which some people had to pay for the war."[104]

But, for all its flaws and shortcomings, the Nuremberg tribunal
established the precedent that individual leaders and administrators,
not only states, could be held accountable by the international community for actions that violated widely accepted standards of conduct. It
also served as a model, with some variations, for what came to be col-
loquially known as the Tokyo war crimes trials. Most importantly, the
Nuremberg Tribunal established a number of enduring legal principles
and procedures that would serve as models for future international and
national war crimes tribunals. The world had turned a corner: the vast
unregulated gray area of what was permissible in war was now at least
a little less gray.

THE TOKYO TRIALS: SELECTIVE JUSTICE, STOLEN SECRETS

On August 15, 1945, as Allied prosecutors in Nuremberg were preparing for the trial of the Third Reich's most important political and military leaders, forty-four-year-old Japanese Emperor Hirohito, over 5,000
miles away in the smoldering ruins of Tokyo, made a rare radio address
to his subjects. Speaking in such formal Japanese that interpreters were

needed to translate his message, Hirohito announced that his country, which had pledged to fight to the last man, had surrendered the day before to the Allied Powers.[105] Hirohito's announcement came nine days after an American B-29 bomber dropped an atomic bomb dubbed Little Boy over the city of Hiroshima, and six days after a second nuclear bomb, Fat Man, destroyed the city of Nagasaki. Together, these two atomic bombs killed over 200,000 people, the vast majority civilians.

"The enemy has for the first time used cruel bombs to kill and maim extremely large numbers of the innocent and the heavy casualties are beyond measure," Hirohito told his listeners. "To continue the war further could lead in the end not only to the extermination of our race, but also to the destruction of all human civilization."[106] Japan, Hirohito said, was selflessly conceding the war, to save humanity.

Hirohito's picture of Japanese magnanimity and his inferred role as a pacifist was of course not widely shared beyond Japan itself. A month earlier, on July 26, 1945, the United States, Britain, and China adopted the Potsdam Declaration, pledging to punish Japanese leaders for their wartime atrocities:

> There must be eliminated for all time the authority and influence of those who have deceived and misled the people of Japan into embarking on world conquest, for we insist that a new order of peace, security, and justice will be impossible until irresponsible militarism is driven from the world. . . . We do not intend that the Japanese shall be enslaved as a race or destroyed as a nation, but stern justice shall be meted out to all war criminals, including those who have visited cruelties upon our prisoners.[107]

By mid-October 1945, a finished plan for the establishment of the International Military Tribunal for the Far East, more commonly remembered as the Tokyo trial, was presented to the Allied Powers (Australia, Canada, China, France, India, Netherlands, New Zealand, Philippines, Soviet Union, United Kingdom, and United States).[108] In January 1946, the Allied Powers established the Tokyo tribunal and soon charged twenty-eight wartime Japanese political and military leaders with a range of crimes. The principal charge against them was the planning and execution of aggressive war in the Asia-Pacific region, dating to the invasion of Manchuria in September 1931. They were also charged with atrocities committed by the Japanese armed forces against millions of civilians and prisoners of war in various theaters of war. The Allied Powers also created some fifty separate special war crimes courts throughout Asia, including in Australia, Burma, China, Hong Kong, Indonesia, Malaysia, the Philippines, Singapore, and on other Pacific islands. These courts would go on to hold more than 2,200 trials of 5,600 war crimes suspects.[109]

War crimes investigations had begun in earnest shortly after General Douglas MacArthur, commander of U.S. armed forces in the Far East, arrived in Tokyo on August 30. Months earlier, while stationed in the Philippines, MacArthur and a top aide, General Bonner Fellers, had hatched a plan for occupying Japan and rounding up war criminals. Once in Tokyo, MacArthur quickly compiled a list of the forty most wanted Japanese suspects, all of whom would be charged with crimes by the Tokyo tribunal. As with the Nuremberg tribunal, justice at the Allied-run Tokyo trials would also be one-sided: it avoided any targeting of Allied military actions—such as the firebombing of Tokyo and the destruction of Hiroshima and Nagasaki—that might well have been considered crimes against humanity. In the meantime, Fellers, an expert in psychological warfare, sought to separate the emperor, in the words of the American historian Herbert Bix, "from the militarists, retaining him as a constitutional monarch but only as a figurehead, and using him to bring about a great spiritual transformation of the Japanese people. Because retaining the emperor was crucial to ensuring control over the population, the occupying forces aimed to immunize him from war responsibility, never debase him or demean his authority, and at the same time make maximum use of his existing Japanese government organizations."[110]

On September 11, 1945, the United States issued arrest orders for the men on MacArthur's list.[111] Among the most wanted were Hideki Tojo, Japan's prime minister and war minister, who had ordered the attacks on Pearl Harbor; and Matsuhiro Watanabe, a notoriously sadistic guard at the Omori and Naoetsu prisoner-of-war camps. By December, the Allies' public list of prominent accused had grown to 218.[112]

Solis Horwitz, an American war crimes investigator, has written that the Allies selected the defendants from a representative group of Japanese suspects. The group was designed to represent both the major organs of wartime Japan's government and the major phases of the war.[113] The accused were divided into categories, based on the types of crimes they had allegedly committed. Crimes against humanity were identified as class B war crimes; class C crimes included the planning, ordering, authorization of, or failure to prevent war crimes.[114] Those charged with class A crimes, crimes against peace, included some of Japan's top military, political, and diplomatic leaders named in General MacArthur's original list. Of these, twenty-eight were tried before the Tokyo tribunal.[115] Like the trial of the major war criminals that opened the Nuremberg trials, the trials of class A suspects would attempt to showcase both the Allied commitment to fair and impartial justice and the extent of Japanese war crimes. Class B and C war crimes trials were held in many different places in Asia and around the Pacific and dealt with the vast majority of those accused: a total of 5,700 individuals were indicted for class B and C crimes. Of these, 1,018 were acquitted, 475 were given life sentences, and 984 were condemned to death.[116]

In the auditorium of the former War Ministry in Tokyo on May 3, 1946, the International Military Tribunal for the Far East opened the trial against the twenty-eight wartime Japanese political and military leaders. The recently refurbished courtroom—with its soaring ceilings, walnut-toned paneling, imposing daises, klieg lights, and well-positioned balconies for cameramen—seemed like the perfect venue for giving the Japanese public a history lesson. But few journalists covering the opening ceremonies saw it that way. In its first article about the trial, entitled "Road Show," *Time* magazine openly lampooned the setting: "Nuremberg's impresarios had used simpler furnishings [and] relied on the majesty of the concept to set the tone." By contrast, the Tokyo courtroom, *Time* wrote, "looked . . . like a third-string road company of the Nuremberg show."[117]

The trials consumed two and a half years, compared to a single year at Nuremberg. From the beginning, they were plagued by a rapid waning of political will, most notably on the part of the Americans, who were intent on shifting their attention away from righting past wrongs and increasingly toward building their own national security state dedicated to the global containment of communism. One of the tribunal's most bitter critics was the State Department's George Kennan, who visited Japan in March 1948 and filed a top-secret report to the department's Policy Planning Staff. In it he castigated the Tokyo trials and subsequent proceedings as "profoundly misconceived from the start." Punishment of enemy leaders, he wrote, had been "surrounded by the hocus-pocus of a judicial procedure which belies its real nature." Endless delays and "humiliating ordeals" plagued the proceedings. He dismissed the very effort as "political trials . . . not law."[118]

Yuma Totani, a Japanese historian who has written extensively about the Tokyo tribunal, points to President Truman's glaringly different choices of chief prosecutors and judges for the Nuremberg and Tokyo tribunals. To Nuremberg Truman sent Robert Jackson, an associate judge of the U.S. Supreme Court; Francis Biddle, attorney general in Roosevelt's administration; and John J. Parker, presiding judge of the Federal Appeals Court for the Fourth Circuit. For Tokyo, in contrast, Truman picked Joseph B. Keenan, the director of the criminal division in the Justice Department (with a noted drinking problem), and John P. Higgins, the chief justice of the state court of Massachusetts. "The decision to send someone who on paper ranked far below Jackson suggests Truman's general indifference to the success of the Tokyo trial," Totani comments. "Had Tokyo been as important as Nuremberg, he would have taken great care in his selection of personnel, making sure that someone who matched Jackson—at least in qualifications—would be sent to Tokyo."[119]

Paucity of appropriate documentation also dogged the tribunal. Perhaps second only to shock and grief, the reaction of the Japanese to Hirohito's surrender announcement was the start of a campaign to destroy as much of the documentation of Japan's wartime activities as possible. Writes historian John Dower: "Although the emperor's broadcast put an end to the American air raids, it was said, with a fine touch of hyperbole, that the skies over Tokyo remained black with smoke for days to come. Bonfires of documents replaced napalm's hell fires as wartime elites followed the lead of their sovereign and devoted themselves to obscuring their wartime deeds."[120] By the time the first advance contingent of Americans arrived, on August 28, Japanese elites had spent nearly two weeks destroying documents. Although large numbers of Japanese were placed in prison camps at the start of the occupation, the Tribunal's prosecution was in many cases ill prepared to bring charges against individual defendants because adequate documentation was missing.[121]

There was also the challenge of tracking down and arresting the accused. George H. Johnston, a journalist from the Melbourne daily newspaper, the *Argus*, complained bitterly on September 11 that, twelve days into the Allied occupation of Japan, no accused war criminals had been arrested. On September 25, Johnston noted that, though thirty-four of the thirty-nine accused war criminals whose names were posted on the first list of suspects had been arrested, four of the five that remained were "little men," such as noncommissioned guards stationed at prison camps. "It will be recalled," Johnston wrote, "that some days before General MacArthur issued his first black list, I pleaded for immediate action against the war guilty, particularly against 'little men' . . . because it was obvious that escape and disappearance would be easier for these men than for leading public and military figures."[122]

One of those five "little men" still at large was the prison guard Mutsuhiro Watanabe, known as the Bird. Watanabe's cruelty was infamous among Allied POWs who had contact with him. He regularly forced prisoners to stand for hours or beat them mercilessly. One of his favorite amusements was ordering enlisted men to punch their officers in the head. If they refused or punched too lightly, Watanabe would hit them repeatedly in the head with a stick.[123]

Watanabe fled Naoetsu Camp 4-B, where he had been stationed, soon after hearing a radio broadcast that included his name on the list of class A war criminals and disappeared into the mountains around Nagano, a city northwest of Tokyo that would host the 1998 Winter Olympics.[124] Thousands of Japanese police officers were deployed to find him. The Ministry of Home Affairs sent photographs and descriptions of the Bird to every police chief in Japan and ordered them to report regularly on their progress.[125]

On his arrival in the Nagano-area resort town of Manza Spa, Watanabe took on the alias of Saburo Ohta. He grew a mustache and told people that—like many others—he was a refugee from Tokyo whose family had perished during the war. Keeping his real identity hidden, he arranged with a local farmer to work as a laborer in exchange for room and board.[126] That winter, a police officer knocked at the farmer's door and was invited in for tea with the farmer, his wife, and their hired hand—Watanabe. As Watanabe made the tea, the officer produced a photograph of the Bird, dressed in a sergeant's uniform, and asked whether they recognized the war criminal in the photo. The couple honestly replied that they did not.[127]

One day Watanabe paid his family in Tokyo—many of whom believed he was dead—a surprise visit. Despite his family's protest that he must leave quickly because detectives visited their home every afternoon, Watanabe assured them that nothing would happen. Yet, on cue, detectives arrived. Hearing them outside, Watanabe's family hid his clothes while he raced to hide in the tearoom. While detectives questioned his mother and sister just feet away, the former prison guard quietly pried open a closet, squeezing himself inside. He dared not close the door in case it squeaked. Just before leaving, a detective glanced into the room, but did not look toward the closet—if he had, Watanabe would have been in full view, his hand tightly over his own mouth to muffle his breathing.[128]

Later, back in the Nagano area, Watanabe worked as a waiter in a coffee shop the farmer's son had opened, and then as a cowherd. Meanwhile, the police, having located the bodies of a man and a woman in the mountains, took the Bird's family to view them. Yes, they confirmed, the man was Watanabe, and soon after, Japanese newspapers ran a story that the Bird was dead.[129]

Watanabe, still very much alive, continued to hide out in the hills of Nagano for seven years, until the war crimes prosecutions ended, along with the Allied Occupation of Japan, and a general amnesty was granted to any remaining Japanese war criminals. All charges against the Bird were officially dropped in 1952.[130] Watanabe emerged from hiding, married, sold life insurance, and became wealthy.[131]

Hideki Tojo, Japan's prime minister for much of the war and the man directly responsible for the 1941 attack on Pearl Harbor, was easier to find than Watanabe. Within hours of General MacArthur's September announcement of the forty most wanted criminals, American reporters had surrounded Tojo's simple terra cotta house on the outskirts of Tokyo.[132] One of the officers sent to arrest Tojo, First Lieutenant John J. Wilpers of the 308th Counter Intelligence Corps, later recalled, "The best way of finding Tojo was to find our own U.S. newspaper people, because they were there well ahead of us."[133]

Arresting Tojo, however, would prove somewhat more dramatic. According to Wilpers, as the U.S. soldiers surrounded the cottage, Tojo opened a sliding window and announced to the gathered crowd, "I am Tojo." He then closed the window, and a shot rang out.[134] When the soldiers broke down the front door, they found Tojo still standing, "wavering on his feet with smoke curling from his .32 Colt automatic."[135] Tojo had shot himself through the chest, which a doctor had marked with an "X" to show him the spot to plant the muzzle. However, the bullet only nicked his heart, traveling upward and out of his back about six inches below the top of his shoulder.[136]

Suicide was, Japan's military men had been taught, the only acceptable option; surrender was not, and capture was humiliating.[137] Civilians, too, had been indoctrinated to fight to the end and to die, in the historian John Dower's descriptive phrase, "like shattered jewels."[138] One might thus have expected a wave of suicides in the wake of Japan's surrender, and certainly after MacArthur's announcement of wanted war criminals. After the emperor's surrender announcement, several hundred individuals did commit suicide, but roughly the same number of Nazis took their own lives after the surrender of Germany, where there was no culture of suicide.[139]

Yet Tojo did try. For twenty minutes his breathing was labored, while the Americans stood watch. Through interpreters, Tojo told the Americans, "I am sorry for the peoples of Greater East Asia. I will shoulder the whole responsibility. The war of Greater East Asia was a just war. When all our strength was gone, we finally fell. I did not want to stand before the victors to be tried as a vanquished. I wanted to kill myself at one stroke."[140] He added, "I am very sorry it is taking so much time to die."[141]

Lieutenant Wilpers recalled: "We managed, at gunpoint practically, to get a next-door neighbor to get a doctor."[142] When the doctor arrived, however, it quickly became obvious that he would prefer to let the former prime minister die. Wilpers, holding his gun to the doctor's head, provided sufficient motivation, and the doctor kept Tojo alive until American doctors and medical staff arrived.[143]

By the time Tojo was placed in U.S. medical care, he was showing signs of a change of heart. Forty-eight hours after his suicide attempt, the former prime minister ate a good breakfast, acknowledged the quality of care he was receiving, and was on his way to recovery.[144] While awaiting trial in Sugano Prison, Tojo was examined by a Navy dentist named Jack Mallory. Mallory immediately realized the former prime minister's mouth was a mess: all of the upper teeth had been extracted, and only seven of his lower teeth were still intact. Mallory recommended full dentures, but Tojo declined, explaining that he probably would not need his teeth at all in six months. So Mallory agreed to only make an upper denture.[145]

When Mallory's colleagues caught wind of his task, they encouraged him to play a prank. Military procedure dictated that all dental appliances were to be engraved with the recipient's name, rank, and serial number. Mallory's colleagues urged him to etch the phrase "Remember Pearl Harbor" into Tojo's dentures.[146] Mallory decided to inscribe the message into Tojo's dentures using the dots and dashes of Morse code to make the phrase less obvious. But word of the prank leaked out, and was soon circulating in newspapers worldwide. "That's funny as hell," Mallory's superior officer, Major William Hill, commented when he ordered that the engraving be removed, "but we could get our asses kicked for doing it."[147] In the middle of the night on Valentine's Day, 1947, Mallory woke up Tojo, extracted his dentures, and ground away any trace of his artistry.

Tojo was later found guilty of war crimes, and sentenced to death, on November 12, 1948. Forty-one days later, he was executed by hanging.

Though Tojo was clearly a symbol—and a practitioner—of Japanese military aggression, several prominent historians of Japan, including Herbert Bix, Lucien Pye, and John Dower, believe that the former prime minister's prosecution and subsequent conviction helped General MacArthur cover up Emperor Hirohito's role in World War II. Writes Pye: "The emperor was not a passive figurehead manipulated by war-minded militarists but an active strategic plotter of Japanese wars of aggression—and a certifiable war criminal."[148] In the early years of the Japanese invasion of China, Hirohito tried unsuccessfully to slow down the escalation of the war. But, according to Bix, from late 1937 forward, the emperor accepted the mantle of "a real war leader, influencing the planning, strategy and conduct of operations in China. Slowly but surely, he became caught up in the fervor of territorial expansion and war."[149]

Bix argues that MacArthur's aide Bonner Fellers played a critical role in shielding Hirohito from ever standing trial. Fellers apparently told Japan's former naval minister, Admiral Mitsumasa Yonai, soon after his arrival in Tokyo: "It would be most convenient if the Japanese side could prove to us that the emperor is completely blameless. . . . Tojo, in particular, should be made to bear all responsibility at his trial."[150] Fellers also conducted private interviews, mainly in Sugamo Prison, with about forty Japanese leaders, including many who would later be charged as class A war criminals. He reportedly conveyed to them the U.S. desire not to prosecute the emperor and encouraged them to coordinate their stories accordingly. When the Allied prosecutors later interviewed the accused war leaders, they found they all had the same story: "the emperor had acted heroically and single-handedly to end the war."[151]

Both sides had motivation to shield Hirohito from prosecution. Japanese leaders, loyal to the end, willingly adjusted their stories to shift blame away from their emperor and onto themselves. While Tojo was recovering from his suicide attempt, his former staffers sent word that he must live in order to take on himself responsibility for the war and, in doing so, protect the emperor.[152] When pressured by U.S. prosecutors not to implicate the emperor in his testimony, Tojo complied.[153]

Although the United States left open the possibility of trying Hirohito,[154] it had a clear rationale for absolving the emperor of responsibility for the crimes of his country: postwar political stability. During the war, the Allies followed a policy of not attacking Hirohito in their propaganda. The stated reason, Dower explains, was that the Japanese viewed their emperor as an almost divine figure, and attacking him would only make the Japanese more determined to fight to the end. Even during the war, the Office of Strategic Services issued an internal report that observed, "the desirability of eliminating the present Emperor is questionable; it is probable that he inclines personally toward the more moderate faction and might prove a useful influence later."[155]

Throughout the occupation the Allies governed Japan indirectly, that is, through existing organs of government.[156] Allowing the emperor to remain in place—and to do so untainted by criminal indictment—would help solidify the legitimacy and stability of the U.S. occupation. Dower notes: "The Western propagandists, in a word, were ready to take a hand in reimagining an emperor divorced from the policies imperial Japan had pursued in his name, under his authority, and with his active cooperation for almost two decades."[157]

By not trying the emperor, and by creating a myth of a peace-loving man who was taken advantage of by his subordinates, the American occupiers cleansed Hirohito of any involvement in Japan's war crimes. Even today, neither country is eager for a full review of Hirohito's involvement in Japan's war; the U.S. government still has not opened to the public all of the records it holds on Hirohito, such as his conversations with General MacArthur and a folder in the U.S. National Archives that bears his name.[158]

Another Japanese war criminal who got away scot-free as a result of Cold War politics was Shiro Ishii, Japan's answer to Josef Mengele. In the late 1920s, as a young army doctor, Ishii studied medicine in Europe, where he became fascinated with the bacteriological weapons used during World War I.[159] On his return to Japan in 1932, Ishii was appointed professor of immunology at the Tokyo Army Medical School and given the rank of major. He eventually travelled to the Chinese region of Manchuria—which had been occupied by the Japanese military since 1931—where he began lobbying army leaders to allow him to begin biological warfare research. Three years later, he was given free rein—virtually unlimited resources and unquestioned authority—to pursue the development of biological and bacteriological weapons for war at a huge research complex spread over six square kilometers in the town of Pingfan, Manchuria.[160] The fifty-plus buildings there included laboratories, warehouses, and housing for animals and between 80 and 120 prisoners.[161] By 1939, more than 3,000 technicians, soldiers, and scientists would be stationed at Pingfan under Ishii. Yet this was only the largest of seven facilities in Manchuria under Ishii's direction as head of Unit 731.[162]

Ishii and his researchers at Pingfan used human subjects in their experiments with tuberculosis, tetanus, gas gangrene, influenza, anthrax, and bubonic plague. They were particularly interested in creating a bomb that could carry and spread an infection; based on laboratory experiments with human subjects, they found that only anthrax and plague were suitable.[163] On twelve occasions, the weapon was used against Chinese military and civilian populations. Typically, a Japanese battalion would first advance toward Chinese lines, pushing the Chinese back temporarily. They would spray or spread a biological agent, and then retreat, allowing the Chinese troops and civilians to re-enter the infected area. Within days, many of those who had entered the area showed symptoms of plague or cholera.[164] With the goal of preventing outbreaks of syphilis among Japanese soldiers, Ishii deliberately infected Chinese women with syphilis so that research could be done on how to prevent the disease's transmission.[165] In all, some 400,000 Chinese reportedly died as a result of experiments committed in Ishii's name.[166]

Many sources claim that by May 1944 American intelligence officers were well aware of Ishii's experiments.[167] At the start of the occupation, Allied forces swept Japan for suspected war criminals, and for two years investigators followed leads that suggested Shiro Ishii might have been responsible for war crimes. Over the course of eight days in January 1946, U.S. investigators even interrogated Ishii about his role at Unit 731. He managed to convince them that information he could provide made him incredibly useful.

The U.S. military completed a lengthy report on Ishii in April 1947. In it more than a dozen informants claimed that Ishii had also conducted experiments on Allied POWs.[168] Yet U.S. officials dismissed these charges as propaganda; Ishii was simply too valuable to prosecute. A top-secret cable from occupied Tokyo to Washington, DC, on May 6, 1947, stated, "Experiments on humans were . . . described by three Japanese and confirmed tacitly by Ishii; . . . Ishii states that if guaranteed immunity from 'war crimes' in documentary form for himself, superiors and subordinates, he can describe the program in detail. Ishii claims to have extensive theoretical high-level knowledge including strategic and tactical use of BW [biological warfare] on defense and offense."[169]

Seven months later, Dr. Edwin Hill, chief of basic sciences at Camp Detrick in Maryland, wrote a report arguing in favor of granting Ishii and his colleagues immunity. First, Hill said, the material was a financial bargain for the United States. "Evidence gathered . . . has greatly supplemented and amplified previous aspects of this field. It represents data which have been obtained by Japanese scientists at the expenditure of many millions of dollars and years of work." He continued, "Such information could not be obtained in our own laboratories because of the scruples attached to human experimentation."[170]

Dr. Ishii, his subordinates, and his superiors were all shielded from prosecution as war criminals thanks to the American desire, fueled by the Cold War, to acquire information about biological warfare. The

American investigators and Ishii reached an agreement: Ishii would be granted immunity from prosecution for himself and every one of his subordinates in exchange for the notes and photographs of their experiments at Unit 731 and records of the effective systems for delivering chemical and biological weapons. There were also financial transactions, although not much money was necessary to convince Ishii and his men that freedom would be better than trial.[171] The initial offerings from Ishii and his subordinates included a sixty-page report on experiments on humans and 8,000 slides of tissues from autopsies of humans and animals that had undergone biological warfare experimentation.[172]

Ishii disappeared from public life in 1948, although it is rumored that he was brought to the United States to give lectures on biological warfare at Fort Detrick, in Maryland.[173] The United States was accused of using Ishii's research in attacks with biological agents during the Korean War, although it denies those allegations.[174] Shiro Ishii died in Japan of lung cancer in 1958, at the age of sixty-six, still very much a free man.[175]

On November 4, 1948, the International Military Tribunal for the Far East delivered its judgment: twenty-five of the accused were guilty. Eight days later, the tribunal announced their sentences: seven defendants, including Tojo, were to be hanged; sixteen were to spend their lives in prison; and two others were to be imprisoned, for seven and twenty years, respectively. One defendant had been deemed unfit for trial, and two others had died during the proceedings.[176]

For nearly seventy years, historians have debated the legal and historical significance of the Tokyo trial and the scores of local Allied trials convened in countries formerly under Japanese occupation. By and large, the latter trials had little, if any, lasting impact on the Japanese people. While Japanese newspapers, at the insistence of the occupiers, ran articles about these trials, readers at the time soon lost interest as they, like their German counterparts, had a country to rebuild and their own dead to mourn. Writes historian John Dower:

> After a long war that saw the death of several million Japanese servicemen and civilians, the fate of [a] few thousand accused war criminals in faraway places did not initially attract attention within Japan. Although the revelation of widespread Japanese atrocities did make an impact on the general populace, many appear to have regarded these distant exercises in Allied justice as little more than another example of how, in war and in peace, individuals lower in the hierarchy of authority had to pay for the misdeeds of

men with real power. When all was said and done, it was obvious that only a small number of high army and navy officers, few high bureaucrats, no captains of the war economy, and virtually none of the civilian ideologues in politics, academe, and the media who helped prime the pump of racial arrogance and financial militarism paid for the terrible crimes that men on the front committed.[177]

As for the Tokyo trial itself, many of the early commentators believed that it had successfully disclosed the facts about the war and the role played by Japan's political and military leaders, while others dismissed it as a pseudolegal event driven less by the law and more by "victor's justice."[178] In the 1980s, a new crop of historians emerged armed with a trove of trial-related records that had been recently declassified around the world. Kentarō Awaya, a historian at Rikkyo University, studied the records of the Allied occupation authorities, as well as the pretrial records pertaining to investigations of potential war crimes suspects contained in the National Archives in College Park, Maryland. In his view, the "trial was neither a revenge trial nor a just trial, but one that fell somewhere in between."[179] While he agreed with earlier historians that the trial was an important vehicle for disclosing the major facts about the war, he was troubled by what he saw as significant acts of American obstructionism that allowed several high-ranking Japanese civilian and military officials to escape justice and thus denied the Japanese people the truth of the extent and nature of the wartime behavior of their leaders.

Kentarō identified several incidences during the pretrial phase when American officials intervened to withhold evidence for political or military reasons. First, evidence American prosecutors had collected from Shiro Ishii and other commanders on the biological experiments at Unit 731 failed to appear in the charge sheet because of its scientific and military value. Second, evidence that Japan had used poisonous gas in China was omitted from the indictment, in Kentarō's view, because the defense, similar to the *tu quoque* argument over Allied air raids at Nuremberg, "would confute it by citing the American use of atomic bombs."[180] Finally, the failure to indict Emperor Hirohito was a *fait accompli* because General MacArthur needed to use him to entrench American politico-military domination over postwar Japan.

Such political machinations, in the view of Kentarō Awaya and others, turned the Tokyo trial into a decidedly selective process.[181] As we shall see, however, prosecutorial selectivity in the pursuit of suspected war criminals—whether for political, legal, or simply practical reasons—would not end in Tokyo or Nuremberg.

CHAPTER 3

The Hunters and the Hunted

One day in June 1945, as agents with the Counter Intelligence Corps (CIC) were vetting Germans for denazification courts, the American army was busy transferring Dr. Ishii's German counterpart, Josef Mengele, to the Schauenstein displaced-persons camp, some seventy-five miles north of Nuremberg. Although camp authorities made Mengele fill in a form about his military service, they failed to identify him as an SS officer. For that, the German doctor had his own vanity to thank. Contrary to SS regulations, Mengele had decided not to have his blood group tattooed on his chest or arm because he didn't want to mar the smoothness of his skin.[1] Such a tattoo would have been a dead giveaway to the Americans that they had an SS member on their hands.

The SS doctor had no idea of how lucky he was. A month before his capture, the Allied Command in Paris had added his name to the Central Registry of War Criminals and Security Suspects, but the voluminous directory was still at the printer, in England.[2] Mengele was number 240 on a list compiled by the United Nations War Crimes Commission, but that, too, hadn't reached the Bavarian camps where he was being held.[3] Mengele's name also appeared on a blacklist of police and SS officers compiled by M14, the intelligence section of the British War Office that dealt with German and German-occupied territory. He was also fortunate that the Americans, overwhelmed by the sheer number of German soldiers they had captured, were freeing hundreds of thousands of prisoners to avoid their starvation. This in turn led to a policy of processing prisoners as rapidly as possible, among them Josef Mengele.[4]

Freed by the U.S. Army, Mengele found shelter among Nazi sympathizers until he reached Munich. From there he traveled south to Rosenheim, near the Austrian border, where friends arranged for him to work as a farm laborer. He stayed at the farm until August 1948, when he settled near his hometown of Günzberg. By the following spring, however, Mengele realized that his luck might be running out and decided to slip into a "ratline" run by a Catholic priest based in Rome.[5] Ratlines were a system of escape routes for Nazis and other fascists fleeing Europe. There were two primary routes. The first went from Germany to Spain, then to Argentina; the second, from Germany to Rome to Genoa, then Argentina and other ports in South America. Other destinations included the United States, Great Britain, Canada, and the Middle East.

Mengele fled to South Tyrol, in the Italian Alps, which had become a bolthole for the Italian route. From there he traveled to Genoa, where he obtained an International Red Cross passport under the name of Helmut Gregor. Finally, in mid-July, clutching a small suitcase, he boarded the *North King*, a passenger ship bound for Argentina, and slipped out of sight.[6]

As Mengele stood on deck and watched the Italian coastline recede, another Nazi fugitive, living under the assumed name of Otto Henninger, was tending his chicken coops on a rough patch of earth eight hundred miles to the north, in a town near Hamburg, Germany. Henninger's real name was Adolf Eichmann. He was one of an estimated 30,000 Nazis hiding from Allied forces.

Born in 1906 to a Lutheran family in Solingen, Germany, Adolf Eichmann got off to an inauspicious start. After dropping out of high school, he worked as a mechanic before clerking at his father's mining company. He later took employment as a district agent for the Vacuum Oil Company, a subsidiary of Standard Oil, where he managed shipping and transportation. In 1932, he joined the Nazi Party. A year later, when the Nazis came to power, Eichmann became an active-duty SS officer and some years later, in 1938, was assigned to Vienna to run the Central Office for Jewish Emigration. His first major task was to resettle 500,000 Poles and other so-called undesirables—Jews and Gypsies—expelled from the incorporated territories in central Poland to make room for ethnic Germans, or *Volksdeutsche*.[7]

On January 20, 1942, Eichmann joined fifteen leading Reich officials at a lakeside villa in the Berlin suburb of Wannsee. The agenda was to create systematic plans for a "Final Solution to the Jewish Question" and to centralize their execution under the SS. Eichmann prepared background papers for the meeting on anti-Jewish measures and a country-by-country breakdown of the 11 million European Jews targeted for extermination. Following the meeting, he was put in charge of coordinating all matters related to the Final Solution. He excelled at his task, delivering millions of Jews throughout Europe to their deaths. In 1944, Heinrich Himmler sent Eichmann to Budapest, where, over a period of three months, he deported over 400,000 Hungarian Jews to be gassed at Birkenau.[8]

On Christmas Eve of 1944, as Soviet and Romanian troops were closing in on Budapest, Eichmann fled to Berlin, where he set up an office in the cavernous building of oversized rooms and marble stairways that served as headquarters for the Gestapo. One day he came across officers crowded around a table where a department official was taking notes so that he could create a new identity for each officer, complete with forged employment certificates, company correspondence, and other papers. Eichmann looked on, disgusted by the scene of his fellow SS officers looking to become "insurance agents and the like to avoid arrest by the Allies."[9]

By late April 1945, Eichmann was on the move again. First he went to Prague, where he learned that the Soviets were within days of seizing Berlin. Uncertain what to do next, he telephoned an old family friend, Ernst Kaltenbrunner, who, as previously noted, encouraged Eichmann to come to Altaussee.[10] When Eichmann arrived there on May 2, Kaltenbrunner told him to take some combat troops to Blaa-Alm, an inn-cum-hunting lodge hidden in a secluded valley three miles north of Altaussee, and to establish a resistance.[11]

Dressed in his SS uniform, Eichmann led his company of soldiers up to Blaa-Alm. They waited there until May 7, when an orderly arrived with a directive from Himmler that all German troops were now prohibited from firing on Englishmen and Americans. The following day, Eichmann informed his men they were free to go. The war was over; Germany had surrendered. There would be no resistance.[12]

Eichmann left the Austrian Alps with his adjunct, Rudolf Jänish, and headed north to Salzburg and then into Germany, sleeping in the open or in barns. Eichmann was not at all prepared to be a man on the run. He had no money, and the possibility of capture was everywhere. At some point, the two men disposed of their SS uniforms and took on new identities as Luftwaffe corporals. Eichmann tried to obscure his SS blood-group brand by burning it with cigarettes, but the painful process failed. Years later, Eichmann would recall how he and Jänish had marveled at the abundance of wildlife they spotted along the trail. There were foxes and deer and wild hares. "Anyhow, I was the quarry now," he lamented in his memoir. "The hunted animal. Unprotected by 'out of season' rules."[13]

An American patrol picked up Eichmann and Jänish shortly after they entered Germany and took them to a displaced-persons camp, sixty miles east of Nuremberg, where they were interned until late August 1945. Eichmann was then sent to a larger camp at Oberdachstetten, thirty miles west of Nuremberg, while Jänish was sent to a different camp. By then, Eichmann had taken on the identity of Lieutenant Otto Eckmann of the 22nd Waffen-SS Cavalry Division. His new identity served him well and, though there was no chance of denying his SS membership, he survived several interrogations by American military investigators who had no idea with whom they were talking.

Eichmann worried constantly that he might be spotted by someone among the groups of Jewish concentration camp survivors and resistance fighters who regularly came to the camp to identify war criminals.[14] Proudly calling themselves *nokmim* (Hebrew for "avengers"), some groups captured and summarily killed Gestapo and other SS men who, they were convinced, had committed crimes against the Jews.[15] "The Haganah, the underground Jewish defense force based in Palestine, directed some of these squads," writes Neal Bascomb. "Others operated on their own. Often masquerading as British military police, the squads seized their victims at night, drove them to a secluded spot in the woods or by a lake, and then shot or drowned them."[16] One group of conspirators from Palestine even attempted—unsuccessfully—to poison the water supply in several German cities. They next infiltrated an American POW camp holding 15,000 inmates near Nuremberg and sprinkled white arsenic powder on the prisoners' bread.[17] More than 2,000 inmates fell ill, though none died.[18]

On two occasions Eichmann was shuffled into lineups of captured SS officers and scrutinized by concentration camp survivors, who failed to recognize him. His reserved nature, in his past professional and private life, was paying off. Apart from his time in Vienna and Hungary, Eichmann had never spoken directly with Jewish representatives from the Ghettos, leaving such meetings to his underlings. He had also avoided having his photograph taken under any circumstances. For his identity cards, he had used an official Gestapo photograph and destroyed the negatives.[19]

Eichmann's criminal past would be exposed not by one of his victims but by a former associate testifying in a courtroom literally down the road from the POW camp where he was being held. On January 3, 1946, Dieter Wisliceny, an SS officer who had worked for eleven years as Eichmann's deputy in Greece, Slovakia, and Hungary, took the stand at the International Military Tribunal in Nuremberg. His testimony would lay bare the key role Eichmann had played in the Holocaust. Under questioning by an American prosecutor, Wisliceny recalled an extraordinary meeting he had had in Eichmann's office in Berlin in the summer of 1942. Eichmann had shown him a secret document, signed by Himmler, stating that Hitler wanted "the final solution of the Jewish problem."[20] When the prosecutor asked the witness what was meant by the term "final solution," Wisliceny replied: "[Eichmann] said that the planned biological annihilation of the Jewish race in the Eastern Territories was disguised by the concept and wording 'final solution.'" Wisliceny observed that the order "gave Eichmann authority to kill millions of people."[21]

When Eichmann learned of Wisliceny's testimony through the POW grapevine, he began planning his escape from the camp. He paid a fellow prisoner to forge a new identity card in the name of Otto Henninger, a Bavarian woodsman from the town of Prein. Then, late one February night, he snipped his way through the barbed-wire fence and slipped into the forest.[22]

For the next two years, Eichmann eked out a living as a forester in a town near Hamburg. Unlike Mengele, who despised manual labor, Eichmann found some enjoyment in his "simple communion with nature." He liked the way his body had grown hard and how his hands had taken on the "calloused look of the bark of the very trees [he] was hewing."[23] When his employer went bust, Eichmann took up chicken farming. His business, transacted mainly on the black market, went well; he even sold eggs to British soldiers stationed near the town. "At first I was nervous to meet them," he later wrote in his memoir, "but no one was suspicious of the quiet little egg farmer."[24]

Still, Eichmann was growing restless with a life in the shadows and was troubled by the notoriety he was receiving in the media. "I heard of the existence of some organizations which had helped others leave Germany," he later wrote. "In early 1950 I established contact with one of these organizations."[25] Within a month, Eichmann's name was being passed through a network whose connections reached into the Vatican and the highest levels of the Argentine government.[26] One day a man appeared at his door and handed him a landing permit for Buenos Aires and an Italian ID issued under the name of Ricardo Klement. It was time to move.

Since Germany's defeat, Argentina's president, Juan Perón, had worked hard to secure the immigration of Nazi scientists and technocrats to benefit his country's military research and to promote industrialization. A nationalist and a fervent Catholic who had little taste for democratic principles, Perón considered the Nuremberg trials an "outrage that history will never forgive"[27] and welcomed Germans and others from the Axis states. Over 66,000 Germans migrated to Argentina between 1946 and 1955. Of these, some 300 to 800 were senior SS officials or Reich collaborators, including at least 50 war criminals,[28] in spite of Peron's promise in 1945 not to "grant refuge to those guilty and responsible of war crimes."[29]

Most Nazi fugitives made their way to the Southern Cone via a ratline set up by the head of the Argentine secret service, Rodolfo Freude. Scattered throughout Europe, Freude's agents would dispense bribes to local officials, arrange safe houses, hustle the necessary paperwork through the Argentine consulates to produce the requisite landing permits and visas, and liaise with Vatican representatives.[30] Near the top of Freude's organization was Bishop Alois "Luigi" Hudal, rector of Santa Maria dell'Anima, an Austro-German church and seminary located two blocks east of Rome's Piazza Navona. During the war, Hudal was reputed to drive around Rome with a Greater Germany flag on his car and had earned a reputation as an ardent admirer of Hitler. After the war, Hudal headed the Pope's Pontifical Commission of Assistance, a position that allowed him to tour internment camps to tend to Catholic internees and to set the groundwork for the Argentine escape network. "I thank God that He [allowed me] to visit and comfort many in their prisons and concentration camps," Hudal would later write, "and [to help] them escape with false identity papers."[31]

Hudal's link to SS fugitives wishing to flee Germany was Reinhard Kopps, a former Abwehr (military intelligence) captain who had escaped to Italy in 1947 after being incarcerated by the British in Hamburg. Kopps also served as Hudal's link to the Delegation for Argentine

Immigration in Europe in Genoa, where his primary contact was Franz Ruffinengo, a former Italian officer who reported directly to the Argentine spy chief, Rodolfo Freude. And so the circle was complete. All an enterprising SS officer like Eichmann had to do was find an entrée and the cash to pay his way into the circle. From there on, writes Gerald Steinacher, the system took over:

> The Catholic Church provided accommodation and shelter, the Red Cross supplied the documentation, and the Argentine general consulate in Genoa distributed the visas in agreement with the immigration authorities in Buenos Aires and in many cases sorted out the sea crossing. If passengers— mostly Italians—had not appeared before a ship was due to leave . . . the passenger list [would be] filled with German fugitives and emigrants. Officially, the new passengers were identified as Italians from South Tyrol, which was supposed to explain the fact that they spoke German.[32]

Eichmann slipped smoothly into this system. Arriving in Genoa by train, he went to the Church of San Antonio, on a narrow cobbled street a stone's throw from the harbor. He knocked on the door and was greeted by Father Edoardo Dömöter. The old Franciscan priest clasped the German's hand and led him down a corridor to his room. One of Bishop Hudal's most trusted "associates," Dömöter had provided lodging to a number of Nazi fugitives as he helped them with their final travel preparations.

The following day, Eichmann went to the city headquarters of the International Committee of the Red Cross (ICRC), where he presented a letter from Father Dömöter and a copy of the landing permit issued to him under Argentine Immigration file 231489/48. The official reviewed the documents and issued him a Red Cross passport, stamped June 1, 1950, under the name of Ricardo Klement. In the years following World War II, the ICRC regularly issued passports to displaced persons who had lost their identity papers. In theory the ICRC would perform background checks on applicants, but in practice the word of a priest or particularly a bishop was good enough. The passports could then be used to apply for visas.

Two weeks later, Eichmann appeared at the Argentine consulate in Rome, where his Red Cross passport was stamped with a "permanent" visa and he was issued the mandatory "identification certificate" he would need to obtain a valid ID from the Buenos Aires police. Next he appeared at the Argentine immigration office, where his papers were checked and he was subjected to a routine medical examination.[33] Everything went without a hitch, leaving one to wonder whether Eichmann, the consummate bureaucrat, wasn't impressed by the system's efficiency and alacrity.

On the morning of June 17, 1950, Eichmann bid farewell to Dömöter, walked down to the harbor, suitcase in hand, and boarded the passenger ship *Giovanna C* bound for Buenos Aires. With him on the trip were two other former Nazis whom Peron's network had assisted: SS Captain Herbert Kuhlmann, a former commander of the Hitler Youth Panzer Division, and SS Brigadier Wilhelm Mohnke, the former commander of Hitler's bunker in Berlin, who had been with Bormann and the others up to the moment of the Fuhrer's suicide.

Prior to Eichmann's departure a number of other Nazi fugitives had used the Genoa ratline. In addition to Mengele, they included Eduard Roschmann, the second-in-command of the Riga Ghetto, where he had earned the sobriquet "the Butcher of Riga" by overseeing the murder of some 35,000 Jews; Erich Priebke, the SS *Hauptsturmführer* in Rome, who was responsible for the revenge killings of 335 captured partisans in the Ardeatine Caves on March 24, 1944; Gerhard Bohne, the so-called "mercy killer" who had provided the legal and organizational framework for Hitler's euthanasia program; Josef Schwammberger, the dreaded SS commandant at the Przemysl work camp, where he reportedly killed 250 people with his own hands and ordered several thousands more to extermination camps; and Franz Stangl, the former commandant of the Treblinka camp, where hundreds of thousands died.

Bishop Hudal was not the only Catholic cleric using his position to help war criminals flee justice. As Nazi Germany began to collapse in late 1944 and early 1945, many senior church officials in Rome helped organize camps and safe shelters for refugees fleeing from Eastern Europe. The vast majority had left their homelands for reasons unrelated to war crimes; they had simply fled when German or Soviet armies stormed through their villages and cities. However, several church officials who were sympathetic to the Nazis' extreme anti-Communist stand used these refugee routes to facilitate the escape of tens of thousand of Nazis and collaborators from Germany, Austria, the Ukraine, Croatia, Slovakia, and other Eastern European countries. At the head of one of the largest such operations was a forty-four-year-old Croatian priest named Krunoslav Draganovic.

Draganovic had originally come to Rome in August 1943, ostensibly as a delegate of the Croatian Red Cross to attend to Yugoslavs fleeing the war back home, but his real mission was to help Croatian fascists escape punishment for their crimes. Draganovic was an arresting figure: rigid in posture, always dressed in a long, flowing black cloak and a wide-brimmed hat. When Croatia became a Nazi puppet state in April 1941, Draganovic became a leading figure in the Bureau of Colonization, where he tried to force Orthodox Serbs to convert to Catholicism. A rabid anti-communist, he was an ardent supporter of the Ustasha, the fascist movement that ruled Croatia during the war. Fiercely nationalistic, the Ustasha had set out to cleanse Croatia of Serbs, Jews, and Roma. Just in Croatia's Jasenovac concentration camp, where Draganovic had served as a chaplain, the Ustasha had tormented and killed over 80,000 people in unspeakable ways.

At the end of the war, hundreds of Ustasha, sought by Tito's partisans for war crimes, had taken refuge in Italy and Austria. One American intelligence report estimated that 475 Ustasha war criminals were living in Italy in 1946. Of these, more than thirty, including the Ustasha leader Anton Pavelic, were hiding at Draganovic's San Girolamo monastery on Via Tomacelli, or other Church properties in Rome.[34] Many years later, a British intelligence officer would claim that Draganovic had the backing of Pope Pius XII, a speculation that still generates heat among historians.[35] Either way, American and British intelligence reports at the time clearly reveal that elements within the Vatican directly supported Draganovic, or at the very least turned a blind eye to his venal activities.

In early 1946, the CIC and its British counterpart began monitoring Draganovic's human smuggling operation. Under the codename Operation Circle, the CIC placed an agent inside the monastery to find out the names of the Croatian fugitives, collect details about the Vatican's role in their concealment, and develop a plan to capture Pavelic and send him to Yugoslavia to stand trial.[36] But the infiltrator had to suspend his work abruptly when it became too dangerous.[37] Despite the setback, the CIC continued to watch Draganovic until some point in 1947, when, in the words decades later of William Gowen, the CIC agent in charge of the operation, "We received an order from above [CIC headquarters] to stop the investigation . . . but we believed the network headed by Draganovic was actually functioning as the Ratline network that served the Germans—whether it's Eichmann, Mengele, or Barbie and all the rest of them. They escaped and then they went to Argentina. That ended the whole Operation Circle investigation, which was not complete. And as far I know, no one ever investigated the Ratline after that."[38]

Ironically, Operation Circle's demise would soon bring Draganovic new clients, this time from the CIC itself.

One day in December 1950, CIC special agent John Hobbins arrived in Salzburg, Austria, with a problem that he hoped his CIC colleagues there could fix. For the past year, Hobbins and other agents had been hiding a CIC informant named Klaus Barbie, and his family, in a safe house near their offices in Augsburg, Germany.

During most of the war, Barbie had been head of the Gestapo in Lyon, where he was directly responsible for the deaths of up to 14,000 people, including several French resistance leaders. In late 1945, Barbie assumed the name Becker and moved to Marburg, Germany, where he joined a resistance movement called the Organisation für den Deutschen Sozialismus (ODS, Organization for German Socialism), led by a former Luftwaffe lieutenant colonel. Barbie rose quickly in the ranks of the ODS, the aim of which was to be accepted by the Allies as the real power in Germany in the event of a war with the Soviet Union. Over time, the ODS had build up a formidable network of contacts throughout Germany and eastern Europe, some of whom were communist agitators of interest to the CIC. Barbie in the meantime had become a con man, both to finance the resistance movement and to line his own pockets. He forged ration cards and identification documents and traded hard-to-find goods, such as radio equipment and printing presses, on the black market. Unbeknownst to his ODS colleagues, Barbie also worked as an informer for the CIC, which was gradually being taken over by the newly formed Central Intelligence Agency.[39]

Hobbins and his CIC colleagues knew of Barbie's infamous past, but his experience infiltrating communist networks in Eastern Europe had been invaluable. As one of his CIC handlers wrote at the time, Barbie's "value as an informant infinitely outweighs any use he may have in prison."[40] Still, the informant had become somewhat of an embarrassment, and it was time to get rid of him.[41]

The CIC's difficulties with Klaus Barbie had been brewing for some time but had only come to a head in November 1949. For some time now, French intelligence had been aware or at least suspected that Barbie was working for the Americans. The French embassy in Washington, DC, delivered a formal request to the State Department insisting that Barbie was a war criminal and that he should be arrested and placed before French justice. What happened next amounted to a charade of denials and obfuscations. The State Department informed the French that their request would have to be handled by the U.S. High Commissioner in Germany, or HICOG. The French then sent an extradition request to James McGraw, chief of HICOG's Public Safety Branch. He in turn claimed that the High Commission had never heard of Barbie, and that the inference of the several communications from the French authorities that Barbie was being granted refuge in the U.S. zone was "unjustified and unwarranted."[42]

Matters grew worse. In April 1950, a French court opened proceedings against a former resistance fighter, René Hardy, for having betrayed Jean Moulin, the famous underground leader, to the Gestapo during the war. Barbie's name came up repeatedly. In court, Harding's lawyer impugned the Americans for protecting Barbie and asked how anyone, especially an ally, could protect someone who, as the Gestapo chief in Lyon, had tortured resistance fighters with his bare hands and overseen the deportation of hundreds of Jews to Auschwitz.

When Barbie's CIC supervisor, Eugene Kolb, asked Barbie about the charges, the former Gestapo chief admitted that he had used "duress during interrogations" but claimed that he had never tortured anybody. Kolb seemed satisfied, but told his informant to stay out of sight. "I did that," Kolb recalled later, "on my own initiative."[43] Deeply distrustful of the French, Kolb believed that France was riddled with communists and was only pressing for Barbie's extradition so they could interrogate him about the extent of American penetration of the German Communist Party. "If the French had got Barbie," explained Kolb, "I have no doubt that he would have been in Moscow within a few days."[44]

Back in the CIC office in Salzburg, Hobbins was pleased with what he was hearing from his colleagues: Barbie and his family could easily slip into Monsignor Draganovic's ratline to Italy. The process was fairly straightforward: once the "body" arrived in Salzburg it would be placed in a safe house, known as the "rat house," while arrangements were made to secure the proper travel documents and visas for safe passage to Italy. Once the paperwork was completed, a three-man team would accompany the "body" by jeep to the Italian border and then by train to Genoa, where Draganovic would meet them. The total cost to the American taxpayer was around $1,400.[45]

American intelligence files released in 1983 reveal that the CIC approved Barbie's entrance into the ratline on January 25, 1951.[46] Five weeks later, the former SS officer, traveling under the alias Klaus Altmann, arrived with his family at the Genoa railway station, where they were met by a tall and austere-looking priest in black flowing robes. The priest took the group to a safe house, whose occupants, Barbie would discover later, were all Nazi fugitives.[47]

On March 22, Barbie and his wife and two children boarded the *Corrientes*, a converted liberty ship headed for Buenos Aires. For years, the details of the Butcher of Lyon's escape would remain one of the CIC's best-kept secrets.[48]

A NEW BREED OF SLEUTHS

By the late 1940s, the political will of the Allies to pursue Nazi war crimes suspects had plummeted. Many Allied leaders believed that the Nuremberg convictions and the subsequent trials of *Einsatzgruppen* commanders and high-level Nazi industrialists, jurists, and doctors had meted out enough justice for German atrocities. There was also a growing belief among the Allies that Germany and the countries it had occupied should begin shouldering the burden of investigations and trials. Some Allied leaders, like Winston Churchill, feared that the longer the spotlight was kept on Axis war crimes the more likely it was that the Allied abuses, from some of its interrogation practices to the use of war criminals for intelligence purposes, might be exposed and tarnish a hard-won victory.

But most importantly, Western leaders among the Allies were worried that war crimes trials were drawing attention away from their new enemy: the Soviet Union. Explains David Marwell, an American historian and former investigator with the U.S. Department of Justice's Office of Special Investigations:

> The Cold War created a situation where it became nearly impossible to have any meaningful achievement of justice. The focus of the U.S. and Western Allies shifted from prosecuting Nazi war criminals to combating the Soviets. . . . You see it beginning with the refusal to extradite war criminals to the East bloc. You see it in our own recruitment of former German scientists and specialists to work for us against the Soviets. The new enemy, and the perception that that enemy was potent, powerful, and extremely dangerous, destroyed the effort to prosecute Nazi war criminals in any effective way.[49]

Had realpolitik gained the upper hand over the values of justice? In one sense it had: the United States and its wartime Allies were ready to wipe the slate clean and move on. But in another sense, the prime pursuit of Nazi war crimes suspects had simply shifted from the desks of the victors to the file-strewn offices of a new breed of sleuths, Holocaust survivors like Tuviah Friedman and Simon Wiesenthal, as well as the husband-and-wife team of Serge and Beate Klarsfeld, who, as private citizens, wielded neither political nor police power but had already begun collecting information about the crimes and whereabouts of hundreds of Nazi fugitives. In an age before international human rights organizations such as Amnesty International and Human Rights Watch began to appear on the scene, these private citizens-cum-Nazi-hunters largely constituted the citizens' movement seeking accountability for crimes against humanity. And though they became superlative investigators, flushing war crimes suspects from their hiding places, and publicity stuntmen, putting pressure on states to arrest fugitives, it still required the power of states and the authority of their courts to bring war criminals to justice.

Tuviah Friedman was one of the first concentration camp survivors to adopt the mantle of Nazi-hunter. Born to a Jewish couple in the small Polish industrial city of Radom, where his father owned a printing shop, Friedman lost his entire family, save a sister, during the German occupation. Like other able-bodied men in the vicinity, he had been forced to work in the Szkona Street camp, a German munitions and weapons factory near Radom. In July 1944, he and a friend escaped through the camp's sewer system and fled into a nearby forest, where they survived on raw potatoes they stole from a farmer's fields. When the Soviets liberated Radom, the twenty-two-year-old Friedman emerged from the woods and joined a local Polish militia. Spurred on by grief and anger, he set out to avenge the deaths of his parents and siblings, rounding up and, by his own account, brutalizing scores of Nazis and their Polish collaborators.[50]

In March 1945, Friedman joined the Soviet army and was sent to Danzig, where he received interrogation training and took command of a special team charged with capturing and interrogating Germans, Poles, and Ukrainians suspected of war crimes. One day, Friedman took on an assignment that would haunt him for the rest of his life. A Polish soldier had entered a large house on the outskirts of Danzig previously occupied by German officers and found hundreds of dead bodies. The soldier ran to the headquarters of Friedman's unit and a group returned to investigate. "Even today I cannot describe the scene," Friedman recalled in his memoir. "We felt that we were visiting hell. One room was filled with naked corpses. Another room was filled with boards on which were stretched human skins. We found records and medical and surgical instruments in another part of the building. . . . Nearby was a smaller building, with a heavy padlock. We broke in and found an oven in which the Germans had experimented in the manufacture of soap, using human fat as raw material. Several bars of this "soap" were lying nearby."[51]

Such encounters hardened Friedman, who—again, by his own account—often beat his captives with a whip to obtain confessions, earning him the nickname of the Merciless One. Some days he beat up to twenty prisoners in an effort to weed out SS officers. "It gave me satisfaction," he recalled. "I wanted to see if they would cry or beg for mercy."[52] He acted that way, he later said, "because I felt that precious time was being lost as we worked, sometimes around the clock so as not to allow a single Nazi war criminal to escape arrest and punishment."[53]

By late 1945, Friedman had grown tired of his war crimes work in Danzig, his days spent mostly in the office shuffling through a seemingly endless onslaught of paperwork. The previous autumn he had befriended a group of young Jews who had organized themselves into a *kibbutz* near Danzig and were planning to emigrate to Palestine.[54] With the aid of Briha—an underground organization that helped Holocaust survivors emigrate to Palestine (*briha* is Hebrew for "flight" or "escape")[55]— Friedman and his new-found group traveled to Lodz and from there were smuggled out of the country, finally arriving in Vienna, where they were to await arrangements for travel on to Salzburg and then Italy.

With no job, Friedman spent his days strolling through the City of Dreams, the sobriquet given Vienna in honor of psychoanalyst Sigmund Freud. One morning on the Ringstrasse he met an old childhood friend named Heinrich Rakocz. After they embraced, Rakocz told him that he had chanced by a butcher shop weeks earlier and seen Konrad Buchmayer inside serving customers. This was the same Buchmayer who had taken special delight in randomly shooting Jews as he roamed through the streets of Friedman's hometown of Radom. Friedman insisted that Rakocz take him to the shop. But it was too late: the Austrian police had recently arrested Buchmayer and sent him to an American prison camp near Salzburg.

Undeterred, Friedman and Rakocz related their story at Vienna's police headquarters to a high-ranking official who had himself been interned in a concentration camp during the war. Five days later, Friedman took a train to Salzburg and then a bus to the POW camp. He introduced himself to the camp commander, an American major, and handed him a letter of introduction from the Viennese police official. The major read it and granted Friedman permission to enter the camp, but only for a few hours.

Donning a POW shirt, a pair of old khaki trousers, and an SS jacket with all the emblems and insignia removed, Friedman walked through the rows of barracks, "feeling like a stray dog in a pack of wolves," as he paused from time to time to glance into open doorways.[56] Finally Friedman spotted his prey, and managed to get a good look at Buchmayer as he entered barrack 11.

At camp headquarters, the major, with Friedman looking over his shoulder, thumbed through a prisoner list until he found Buchmayer's name and admission date. Within the hour Friedman had changed back to his own clothing and joined the major and several other officers in a large interrogation room. When the former German officer was brought in, the major spoke first. He asked the prisoner if he was Konrad Buchmayer—yes, he was. And had he been stationed in Radom during the war?—yes, he had been there.

"Do you remember, Buchmayer, how you pulled the young children from the Radom Ghetto into Bialla Street and shot them?" Friedman asked.[57]

Buchmayer looked stunned. "But that was an order from General Botscher," he protested. "I merely took the children into the street and the other SS men did the shooting. It wasn't I."[58]

After conferring with his fellow officers, the major ordered Buchmayer transferred to solitary confinement. Eventually, the SS officer was sent to Poland, where he was tried and sentenced to twelve years for war crimes.

Back in Vienna, Friedman was summoned to a meeting with Arthur Pier, the head of the Haganah in Austria, who had heard of Friedman's war crimes work in Danzig. Posing as a journalist, Pier, whose real name was Arthur Piernikraz, had arrived from Palestine in November 1945 carrying a briefcase with a false bottom, which contained a black notebook and gold coins to fund his operation. In the days to come Pier would change his name to Asher Ben Natan and, after the establishment of the Jewish state, serve as head of the Israeli Foreign Ministry's political department, one of the forerunners of Mossad. Like Friedman, Pier was fueled by a desire for revenge. "Vengeance is a means to do justice," he commented. "When I arrived in Vienna there were two words missing in my vocabulary: one was to forgive, the second was to forget."[59]

Pier's notebook contained the names of high- and low-ranking Nazis, all linked to war crimes. The Jewish Agency in Jerusalem, which functioned as the government of a nascent Israel, had compiled the list based on hundreds of interviews with concentration camp survivors who had arrived in Palestine over the previous year. Pier's task was to establish a special group to find the men listed and bring them to justice.

If Friedman stayed on in Vienna, Pier said, the Haganah would provide him with a monthly budget of $200 to run a Jewish documentation center, which would serve as a cover for a Nazi-hunting operation. As the meeting drew to a close, Pier asked Friedman if he'd ever heard of a high-ranking SS officer named Adolf Eichmann. Friedman shook his head, feeling somewhat stupid. That was understandable, Pier said; Eichmann had a murderous past, but he was an elusive fellow who took special care in covering his tracks. "Well, Friedman," Pier finally said with a chuckle before they parted, "You must find Eichmann."[60]

Friedman's first break in that case came in late 1946, when he received an anonymous tip that the former SS officer was being held in a POW camp near Nuremberg. Even so, finding him, Friedman realized, wouldn't be easy. Eichmann was a common surname in Germany, much like Smith in the United States or Britain, and the camp housed tens of thousands of prisoners. Without a photograph, it would be next to impossible. Fortunately, Arthur Pier had just returned from interviewing Dieter Wisliceny, Eichmann's right-hand man, who had recently testified about his superior at Nuremberg and was now in Bratsilava awaiting trial himself for war crimes.[61] Wisliceny's information led Pier and Friedman to Eichmann's former chauffeur, who in turn revealed the name and address of Eichmann's mistress, Maria Mösenbacher. She was an attractive, frivolous woman of forty who adored Eichmann, the chauffeur said. And he was sure she had a photograph of him—in fact, he had seen it with his own eyes.[62]

Pier dispatched Manus Diamant, a handsome Haganah agent, to befriend Fraulein Mösenbacher, who, it turned out, had moved to a small apartment near Linz. One afternoon as she was leaving the market, some groceries fell from her basket, and Diamant scooped them up. He introduced himself as a Dutchman named Henry van Diamant. Before long they were sharing coffee, evening strolls, and the occasional dinner at local restaurants. One night as Diamant sat next to her on the sofa flipping through a photo album, he paused at a snapshot of a man in his thirties with a sharp nose and a receding hairline. Noticing his hesitation, Mösenbacher explained that the man was one of her admirers, "her Adolf," but she hadn't seen him since the war.[63]

Diamant had found the prize he was looking for. Within weeks, hundreds of copies of the photo were being distributed to POW camps and Allied investigators across Europe.[64] Finally, the hunt for Adolf Eichmann was underway.

Friedman spent the next six years as director of the Jewish Historical Documentation Center in Vienna. The center gathered information on the Final Solution, with a view to securing the indictments of war criminals, but it also served as a cover for Friedman's own small team of Nazi-hunters. Before it was disbanded the team had tracked down over 200 Nazi war criminals in Austria and Germany. For Friedman, any former Nazi was fair game, though he took special delight in ferreting out those responsible for murders in his hometown: men like Herbert Bottcher, head of the SS in Radom, and his assistant Wilhelm Blum, an SS officer who had sent tens of thousands of Jews to the Treblinka extermination camp, both of whom he found and who were later tried, and hanged.[65]

During this time Friedman came to know Simon Wiesenthal, a fellow concentration camp survivor who, in early 1947, with thirty other volunteers, opened his own Holocaust documentation center in his apartment in Linz. At eye level on a wall across from Wiesenthal's desk was a large map of Europe bearing the names of hundreds of Nazi death and concentration camps. Wiesenthal had survived five of them, but barely. His closest call came during a forced march from a railroad station in Upper Austria to the Mauthausen-Gusen labor camp in early February 1945. On the four-mile uphill hike Wiesenthal and dozens of other inmates, famished and exhausted, collapsed in the snow. When lorries arrived to collect the dead, Wiesenthal was picked up and taken to the crematorium. When Jewish prisoners working there noticed that Wiesenthal wasn't quite dead they carried him to a shower-room and immersed him in cold water. When he was conscious they smuggled him into the "death barracks," where prisoners too weak to work were left to die. In the first four months of 1945, more than 30,000 perished at the labor camp, but somehow Wiesenthal managed to survive. When Mauthausen-Gusen was finally liberated that May, an emaciated Wiesenthal, weighing just ninety pounds, rose from his cot and walked out to greet the American soldiers.[66]

Wiesenthal claimed to have been prompted to start the documentation center by an anti-Semitic joke told by an American officer he had met in U.S. Army Occupation headquarters in Salzburg. The next day,

Wiesenthal declared to thirty concentration camp survivors who had come to his Linz apartment that they should form a center to document the Final Solution, and that he, at least, would have nothing more to do with the Americans. "Life is too simple to them," he said. "They think that in America they have cowboys and Indians and in Europe we have Nazis and Jews. I feel it is our duty to do this job with our own hands."[67]

Wiesenthal was the first to admit that his center was an amateur affair, lacking in money and in investigative skills. What it did have was a dedicated army of volunteers who were unyielding in their determination to see justice done. In just over a year, Wiesenthal and his volunteers administered over 3,000 questionnaires to concentration camp survivors in displaced persons' camps in Germany and Austria. Informants were asked about any brutality, torture, or killings that they had personally witnessed in the camps; exact names and dates were more important than gory details, and no hearsay evidence was accepted. Volunteers transferred the data to a card-filing system, categorized by geographical location, alleged perpetrators, and witnesses. As a system that worked from the ground up, it far surpassed anything the Allies had ever implemented.[68]

As word of the center's work spread, Wiesenthal's apartment began to look more like a post office sorting room than the nerve center of one of the greatest home-grown sleuthing operations in history. Virtually all of the correspondence came from concentration camp survivors scattered around the world who had heard that there was a man in Linz called Wiesenthal who was compiling evidence against Nazi criminals. Frequently letters arrived at Goethestrasse 63 addressed just "Wiesenthal, Austria."

Simon Wiesenthal and Tuviah Friedman kept in touch on an almost daily basis, exchanging historical documents, municipal registries, survivors' testimonies; they often asked each other to investigate or gather evidence on cases they were working on. They were also both obsessed with Eichmann's whereabouts and how they might facilitate his capture.[69] But for all their camaraderie, fissures developed in their relationship. "We were like 'twin spirits,'"[70] Friedman commented in his autobiography. "[Wiesenthal] was an embittered, ruthless, vengeful pursuer of Nazi criminals. I understood him perfectly."[71] But Friedman also berated his Linz colleague for being "a right-wing Zionist, a militant who admired the policies of extremists like Menachem Begin."[72] For his part, Wiesenthal found Friedman to be somewhat of "a nuisance"[73] who longed for recognition, constantly bombarding him with, in the words of his biographer, Tom Segev, "innumerable letters containing a mixture of adulation, self-abnegation, and most of all, a searing pain over Wiesenthal's refusal to share his glory with him."[74]

One might excuse these differences as merely the repressed acrimony of rivals who greatly depended on one another, but they also underscore the hazards of zealotry, especially in the case of the much-decorated Wiesenthal, who by the end of the twentieth century would be regarded as the consummate Nazi-hunter, having, by some accounts, helped expose the location of 1,100 Nazis.[75] But for all the honors and adulation, serious questions began to surface as early as the 1950s about Wiesenthal's tactics and his propensity to glorify his role as a Nazi-hunter. Historian Guy Walters, in a bruising critique of Wiesenthal and his need to take credit even where none was due, concluded: "From the end of the war to the end of his life in 2005, he would lie repeatedly about his supposed hunt for Eichmann as well as other Nazi hunting exploits. Wiesenthal would concoct outrageous stories about his war years and make false claims about his academic career. Indeed, there are so many inconsistencies between his three main memoirs, and between those memoirs and contemporaneous documents, that it is impossible to establish a reliable narrative from them alone."[76]

Walters places some of the blame for the "construction of the Wiesenthal legend" at the feet of the media in the 1950s and '60s, which were "hungry for the heroic tale of the lone Jew against the Nazis."[77] Nevertheless, Wiesenthal's megalomania, Walters shows, would result in wild goose chases, inflated figures on Holocaust deaths, and the mythologizing of a fictitious Nazi-escape organization.[78] Wiesenthal claimed repeatedly in his memoirs that his information led to Eichmann's "capture, conviction, and execution,"[79] but there is little evidence of that.

By late 1951, most surviving, displaced Jews in Germany and Austria had been settled in Western Europe, Israel, Australia, and North and South America, which slowed to a trickle the flow of witnesses into the documentation centers in Vienna and in Linz. At about this time, Wiesenthal learned that Eichmann's wife, Vera, and her sons had suddenly disappeared, leaving all their possessions behind. No one—neighbors, teachers, or officials—apparently knew they were leaving. There was speculation that she had left to remarry. But Wiesenthal didn't believe it. He had heard rumors that Vera had reunited with Eichmann and the family was living somewhere in northern Germany or had even fled overseas. Now that Vera was gone, Wiesenthal was in despair of ever finding Eichmann himself.

Friedman, meanwhile, was moving on. In the summer of 1952, he packed all of his files into two large trunks and gave up the ghost—in Austria at least—to join his bride-to-be in Israel. Before his departure, he paid a farewell visit to Wiesenthal in Linz. The two men spoke of many things, but their thoughts always drifted back to their failure to find Eichmann. Recalls Friedman: "We both felt that only the two of us cared about Eichmann. Everyone else had forgotten." Standing on the platform as Friedman's Vienna-bound trained approached, Wiesenthal couldn't resist giving his fellow Nazi-hunter one last piece of advice: "Go back to Israel and don't let them push you around. Keep reminding the Israelis about Eichmann. Don't let them tell you to forget about him. Let the Israel Government do everything it wants to do: build houses for immigrants, teach everybody Hebrew, make a strong army. Fine! Very good! But they must also start looking for Eichmann. And only you can nag at them and make them do something."[80]

SOUTH AMERICAN CONNECTIONS

By the time Friedman was settled in northern Israel, newly married and eking out a living as a police reporter in Haifa, Adolf Eichmann had embarked on a new life in South America, as had both Josef Mengele and Klaus Barbie. Mengele was the first to disembark at the Port of Buenos Aires, in June 1949, followed a year later by Eichmann, and then Barbie and his family in April 1951. Mengele and Eichmann set down roots in Buenos Aires, while Barbie and his brood stayed only for a month before taking a Pullman train to La Paz, Bolivia.

Eichmann, having spent most of his earnings on his passage over, arrived in Buenos Aires with 485 pesos (about 37 U.S. dollars) in his pocket. If he was prudent, that amount might keep him housed and fed for a few weeks; if not, he could easily fall into the squalor of the *villas miserias*, the cardboard-and-tin shantytowns that ringed the city. Fortunately for Eichmann, Carlos Fuldner, an Argentine operative who had helped him escape from Europe, took him under his wing, directing him to a German boarding house, Pension Jurmann, in the Partido Vicente Lopez. It was a favorite haunt of former Nazis, and he stayed there for several months before moving to an apartment north of the city. Fuldner also facilitated approval of his Argentine ID card in the name of Ricardo Klement by the Buenos Aires police.[81]

With this Argentine *cédula* in hand, Eichmann was now a permanent resident of Argentina and free to take a regular job. Fuldner hired him to work as a topographical engineer in his Argentine-German hydroelectric company, Compañía Argentina para Realizaciones Industriales—CAPRI for short—located in Tucuman Province, a rugged region in the northwest corner of the country. So many Germans like Eichmann were employed by CAPRI that it was jokingly referred to as the German Company for Recent Immigrants.

In August 1952, Eichmann's wife Vera and their three sons joined him in Tucuman. More than seven years had passed since their last meeting; the couple's eldest son, Klaus, was now sixteen, Horst twelve, and Dieter ten. Klaus knew that the man standing before him was his father, but his younger brothers, believing that their father had been dead for years, were told that he was their Uncle Ricardo. In April 1953, Eichmann lost his job at CAPRI and moved his family back to Buenos Aires. By then, Eichmann had revealed the truth about his identity to his sons, but he warned them to always refer to him as Uncle Ricardo, though he hubristically (and foolishly) refused to ask his sons to give up their Eichmann surname.[82]

In Buenos Aires, Eichmann and his family rented a modest bungalow on Chacabuco Street, an unpaved, gravel road in a dilapidated section of the Olivos suburb. It was about this time that he met Josef Mengele. The two men occasionally ran into one another at a popular German restaurant, but they never struck up a friendship. Eichmann looked every inch a man of little means, his clothes a bit shabby, his shoes worn and unpolished, while Mengele, who was receiving support from his family in Günzburg, exuded an air of confidence and invincibility. Mostly, Mengele disliked the downtrodden aura of fear that seemed to follow Eichmann around like a black cloud.[83]

In 1955, Vera Eichmann gave birth to a fourth son, who was officially registered as Ricardo Francisco Klement. The following year, Klaus, then in his early twenties, began dating Sylvia Hermann, a young German woman whose family had moved to Argentina in 1938. Sylvia's half-Jewish father, Lothar, had been imprisoned for two years as a political dissident in Dachau, where severe beatings had left him blind. After his release and the events of *Kristallnacht*, the Hermanns had left Germany and settled in Olivos, where, in an effort to fit into the German community there, they never mentioned their Jewish ancestry. Klaus regularly visited the Hermanns and on one occasion let slip that his father had served as a high-level German officer during the war and done his duty for the fatherland. When the conversation turned to the fate of the Jews, Klaus suddenly became animated, blurting out that in his view it would have been better if the Germans had finished their job of extermination.[84] Soon thereafter, Sylvia and Klaus ended their relationship, possibly because of the latter's anti-Semitic remark or because the Hermanns were moving to a town some 300 miles away.

The story might have ended there, but for Sylvia Hermann's discovery of an article in the *Argentinisches Tageblatt,* a German-language weekly published in Buenos Aires, about preparations for Germany's first major war crimes trial of its own. While reading the story to her father, she came across a reference to Adolf Eichmann and his role in the Final Solution. Recalling that her former boyfriend had always been vague about his father's fate and had refused to give her his address, Sylvia and Lothar began to suspect that the young Klaus was Eichmann's son. Aware that the German Embassy in Buenos Aires was staffed with former Nazis, Lothar decided to write to the Frankfurt prosecutor's office about his suspicions.[85]

Several weeks later, Lothar's letter landed on the desk of Frankfurt's attorney general, Fritz Bauer, a jurist in his early fifties whose desire to prosecute Nazi war criminals had already earned him many detractors in the German government. Bauer ordered his senior prosecutor to gather as much information as he could on Eichmann, including photographs, descriptions of his wife and children, and details about the former Nazi's last known whereabouts. Bauer then sent the dossier to the Hermanns with a request that they try to discover the address of the individual concerned.

According to Guy Walters, Sylvia made inquiries around Olivos and learned that her former boyfriend and his family lived at 4261 Chacabuco Street. One Sunday afternoon she traveled by bus to Olivos and found the address. The white one-story house, a short walk from the bus stop, was a drab affair, surrounded by a low picket fence and an unkempt garden. Sylvia knocked on the door and was greeted by a woman with a small blond boy cradled on her hip and a middle-aged man who identified himself as Klaus's uncle. The couple invited her in to wait for Klaus's return. Sipping coffee, Sylvia chatted with the couple about her studies and ambitions, her love of languages, and her dream of traveling to Europe one day. When Klaus returned, he was shocked to find his old girlfriend in the living room chatting with his parents. What happened next sealed Eichmann's fate. Feeling uncomfortable, writes Walters, "Klaus motioned to Sylvia that she should go, and Eichmann accompanied her and Klaus to the front door. Klaus then told his 'uncle' that he would see Sylvia to the bus, but Eichmann said that it

would be even more gentlemanly if Klaus escorted Sylvia back home....
'Thank you, Father,' he said. 'I'll take care of Sylvia and see to it that she
gets home.'"[86]

After receiving the address and details of Klaus's "uncle," Fritz Bauer
circumvented the West German judicial system, which he knew had no
hunger for hunting Nazis in far-off places like Argentina, and in a surreptitious meeting in September 1957 gave the information to the director of the Israeli Reparations Mission in Berlin, who then passed it on
to Isser Harel, the head of the Israeli secret service (Mossad). No one
terrified Israel's enemies like Harel, who was always alert for conspira-
cies and had a knack for getting things done, whether it was handing
the Americans the full text of Soviet leader Nikita Krushchev's famous
1956 "secret speech" denouncing Stalin, or convincing King Hassan to
allow tens of thousands of Moroccan Jews to leave for Israel in return
for valuable security information. Even his Mossad colleagues rued the
day that they crossed Little Isser, as he was known.[87]

But Harel, preoccupied with other security matters, let four months
pass before he finally asked an Israeli operative who was going to
Argentina on other business to check out Bauer's tip. The agent met
with Lothar and Sylvia Hermann and, somewhat baffled by the encounter, reported back that Lothar was nearly blind and seemed somewhat
unreliable, and while the daughter's description of her encounter with
Klaus's "uncle" was intriguing, he wasn't fully convinced that Ricardo
Klement and Adolf Eichmann were the same person.[88]

At this point, the hunt for Eichmann lost momentum. To make matters worse, Tuviah Friedman, who was now operating his own war
crimes documentation center in Haifa, had publicly announced that he
had reliable information indicating that Eichmann was living in Kuwait,
a report that generated headlines worldwide that were, of course, totally
misleading.

THE EICHMANN ABDUCTION

In December 1959, Bauer visited Israel and met with Harel and the
Israeli attorney general. The German prosecutor vented about Harel's
foot-dragging and then informed the two men that yet another informant had linked Eichmann to Klement. He insisted that the Israelis "were
the only people who could be relied upon to do anything with the information."[89] He couldn't trust the German Embassy in Buenos Aires as
there were too many former Nazis in key positions. If Harel now did

nothing, the German prosecutor warned, he would push for extradition proceedings in West Germany.

Days later, Israeli Prime Minister David Ben-Gurion gave Harel the go-ahead to kidnap Eichmann and, if his identity was confirmed, smuggle him back to Israel for trial. Harel acted quickly, dispatching Zvi Aharoni, then chief interrogator of Shin Bet (the Israeli FBI), to Argentina to confirm Eichmann's identity. Aharoni spent weeks watching the Klement house with a black briefcase tucked under his arm. There was a camera hidden in the briefcase. One day, Aharoni snapped several pictures of Klement as he stepped out of the house to hang some laundry. Back in Israel, two forensic experts compared the photographs to pictures taken of Eichmann during World War II, paying particular attention to the shape of the former Nazi's left ear. They found ten points in the photographs that matched and none that did not match. Without a doubt, they concluded, the bespectacled, balding man in the Argentine photographs was Adolf Eichmann.[90]

Harel and his second-in-command, Rafi Eitan, hurriedly assembled a team of ten "volunteers" to capture Eichmann and bring him to Israel. Most of the team members were Mossad agents, but several other Israelis were also enlisted because of their connections in Buenos Aires.[91] The operation would be extremely tricky. First, the team would have to establish a base in Buenos Aires, kidnap Eichmann, and keep him hidden, possibly for several weeks. The most difficult part would be smuggling him out of Argentina. If the agents were discovered, they could be imprisoned for violating Argentine sovereignty, leaving Mossad with a tarnished image and the Israeli government embroiled in a major diplomatic crisis.[92] But, as Rafi Eitan later recalled, the Israelis believed it well worth the risk. "We wanted to bring one of those Nazi fugitives to Israel for trial, as a symbol. And . . . as a way of bringing back the Holocaust to the Israeli public and to the whole world."[93]

Harel and Eitan spent weeks in Tel Aviv planning the operation. Harel, it was decided, would stay behind but remain in contact with the team in Buenos Aires, while Eitan would be the field commander with ultimate responsibility for Eichmann's kidnapping. "I had my instructions from Harel that if something went wrong I should chain myself to Eichmann and say to the police, 'Here, take me to the Israeli ambassador. This is the war criminal Adolf Eichmann and I'm an Israeli intelligence officer.'"[94]

The Israeli team entered Argentina from different places and at different times, with each member entering under a false identity. They carried leather suitcases with the necessary equipment for the operation: a kit for preparing false license plates for the vehicles to be used; a lathe for making keys; stationery and writing implements, including ink for forging documents; medical equipment; items to be used for disguises; and numerous maps and travel guides for Argentina and Buenos Aires. During the operation the team would rent ten cars, replacing their original license plates with false ones to conceal any connection between the operatives who rented the vehicles, the abduction team, and the hideouts where they were staying.[95]

Once in Buenos Aires, Harel's team quickly discovered that the Eichmann family had left Chacabuco Street and moved across town to San Fernando, an isolated neighborhood just north of the city. The cinderblock house, which they had built themselves, was set back on a hillock above Garibaldi Street, in one of the more secluded parts of the suburb. The house's front porch and living-room windows afforded unobstructed views up and down the street, enabling its residents to spot visitors well before they reached the chicken-wire fence surrounding the house.[96]

Lacking any other means of communication, the team met each day at a different coffee house, where they strategized the operation and fixed a new meeting place for the following day. They rented three safe houses, which were to be used to hold Eichmann and interrogate him until he could be smuggled out of Argentina.

Early in the evening of May 11, 1960, the Israeli team parked two cars facing one another near Eichmann's house on Garibaldi Street. One vehicle was stationed near a small bus kiosk, a short distance from the house where every weekday evening Eichmann descended from the bus he took home from work at a German-Argentine Mercedes Benz plant. The other car was parked closer to the house, with its hood up. Two agents were positioned in front of it, with their backs to the road, as if they were tinkering with the engine. Another agent stayed at the wheel, while a fourth lay in the back seat.

At about 8 P.M., the city bus pulled up to the bus stop. Eichmann appeared at the door and stepped onto the pavement. Immediately the first vehicle flashed its lights, signaling that the passenger was their target. When Eichmann reached the second vehicle, one of the agents, Zvi Malhin, turned to him and said, "Momentito, señor, una pregunta?" Eichmann looked up in surprise and Malhin leapt forward and tackled him. The two men tumbled into a ditch. Eitan and Malhin, along with another agent, dragged Eichmann to his feet and bundled him into the back seat of the car. As the car sped away, Eitan quickly checked Eichmann's head and belly for old scars that would help identify him, as another agent whispered into the German's ear, "Sit still and nothing will happen to you. If you resist, we will shoot you. Do you understand?"[97]

On their way to the safe house in the Florencio Varela district of Buenos Aires, the agents passed through two police checkpoints. "It was the time of Juan Perón and the police and army were everywhere," Eitan recalled. "But we had diplomatic passports and fake diplomatic license plates so they let us through." Once inside the house, the agents stripped and blindfolded their captive and began peppering him with questions. "At one point, Zvi Aharoni asked him his name," recalled Eitan. "And he said he was Otto Eckmann, the name he used when he was hiding in Germany after the war." Then he paused and said, "No, I'm Ricardo Klement," his alias in Argentina. Aharoni pressed him further, "Okay, what's your SS number?" He told the Israelis and then admitted he was Adolf Eichmann.[98]

The agents stayed in the safe house for ten days, anxiously awaiting the arrival of an El Al airliner at Ezeiza International Airport, just outside Buenos Aires. During this hiatus Harel instructed his men to go after another fugitive: Josef Mengele. "Mengele," he later recalled, "burned like a fire in my bones."[99] That may have been so, but Harel was also aware that the Eichmann operation was so costly it might benefit all concerned to pick up Mengele at the same time.[100] Harel had little to go on other than a report that the Nazi doctor was residing at a boarding house run by a German woman named Jurmann. Spanish-speaking agents were dispatched to watch the house. Late one morning one of the agents stopped the mailman in the neighborhood and asked if he had ever delivered mail to his "uncle," "a Dr. Mengele." The mailman replied that a man by that name had lived at the Jurmann boarding house but had moved away. Unbeknownst to the Israeli team, Mengele had fled Argentina a year earlier.

On the evening of May 20, the Mossad team began making its final preparations to whisk Eichmann out of the country. The team's doctor drugged Eichmann, leaving him groggy but compliant, and turned him over to another agent, who dyed his hair grey and dressed him in an El Al uniform. The final flourish was the cap—with a blue Star of David on the front.

The Israeli agents, also in El Al uniforms, escorted Eichmann to a car and drove him to Ezeiza, where the commercial jet stood ready to depart. Passing through Argentine immigration would prove tricky, but if anyone asked about the stumbling, glassy-eyed flight attendant with his arm draped over the shoulder of another flight attendant, they would be told he'd just had a few too many drinks. Just past midnight, the El Al plane rose from the tarmac and flew out of Argentine air space. After refueling in Dakar, the plane continued on to Tel Aviv, where it touched down at 7:35 on the morning of May 22.[101]

The following day, Isser Harel sent a Mossad agent in Germany a top-secret telegram, which read: "You are to go immediately to Tolstoy [the code name for Fritz Bauer] and inform him that Dybukk [Adolf Eichmann] has been captured and brought to Israel. The message should be delivered between 14:00 to 14:30 local time."[102] Ninety minutes after the message was delivered, Ben-Gurion stood at the speaker's podium in the Knesset and announced: "A short time ago, one of the greatest Nazi war criminals was found by the Israeli security services: Adolf Eichmann, who was responsible, together with the Nazi leaders, for what they called the 'Final Solution of the Jewish Problem'—that is, the extermination of six million Jews of Europe. Adolf Eichmann is already under arrest in Israel and he will shortly be brought to trial in Israel under the Nazis and Nazi Collaborators Law of 1950."[103]

Eichmann's capture, as Deborah Lipstadt relates in *The Eichmann Trial,* exploded like a bombshell on the international scene.[104] Soon after *Time* magazine published a lengthy exposé of the operation, including details the Israelis would have preferred to keep secret, a wave of anti-Semitism spread across South America. Scores of Jewish landmarks—synagogues, cemeteries, Hebrew schools, and restaurants—were desecrated, sprayed with bullets, or bombed. In Colombia, Nazis held a memorial service for the eleven major war criminals executed at Nuremberg.[105] In the United States, the *Washington Post* ran two editorials condemning Israel's use of what its editors curiously called "jungle law," predicting that an Israeli trial would be "tainted with lawlessness." The *New York Post* called on Israel to return Eichmann to Germany to face justice, while the *New York Times* characterized Israel's actions as "immoral" and "illegal." In contrast, German newspapers were relatively complimentary. The *Neue Ruhr Zeitung* declared that Israel had every right to try Eichmann, while the *Frankfurter Rudschau,* following the dictum *male captus, bene detenus* (badly captured, [yet] properly detained), found "any legal basis acceptable" so long as it "guarantees an orderly trial."[106]

Argentina, meanwhile, railed against Eichmann's kidnapping, describing the Israelis' actions as "typical of the methods used by a regime completely and universally condemned."[107] (Later, in what appears to have been a face-saving gambit, the Argentine government claimed that their intelligence services had actually been monitoring the Israeli operation from beginning to end, and that one intelligence officer had even witnessed the abduction on Garibaldi Street.[108]) Argentina's ambassador to the United Nations, Mario Amadeo, demanded that the world body launch an investigation and that Israel pay reparations, while Israel fulminated that Argentina had become a haven for Nazis, leaving Israel with no other choice but to carry out an "act of historic justice."[109] The feud made its way into the great rotunda of the UN Security Council, where Israel faced potential condemnation for its actions. But the world body dropped the matter after Ben-Gurion sent a personal letter to Argentine President Frondizi apologizing for Israel's violation of Argentina's sovereignty, followed by a public apology by Israel's foreign minister, Golda Meir.[110]

Mossad chief Isser Harel was largely praised for his role in the planning and execution of Eichmann's kidnapping. That said, he also had his detractors inside the Israeli government and military who felt it was foolish to deploy limited resources to track down Nazi fugitives given the increasing threats from the Soviet Union and Israel's Arab neighbors. Given these attitudes it was surprising that Ben-Gurion gave Harel carte blanche to set up a special Paris-based unit in early 1961 to track down other major Nazi criminals, with Mengele at the top of the list.[111] As Mossad agents fanned out across Europe and South America, elaborate and costly plans were hatched to flush Nazi fugitives from their hideaways. Eichmann's capture had sparked new life into the hunt for Nazi fugitives.

Meanwhile, back in Jerusalem, carpenters were working around the clock to ready the theater of Beit Ha'am, Jerusalem's brand-new cultural center, for the Eichmann trial. Unlike Nuremberg, where victims were a sidebar, this trial would foreground the Holocaust in public consciousness as much as it would pass judgment on a mass murderer.

EICHMANN IN JERUSALEM

On April 11, 1961, the trial of Adolf Eichmann commenced before the Jerusalem District Court. More than a hundred police and military guards with automatic weapons at the ready surrounded the white stone-and-marble building. Inside, over 700 people took their seats, falling silent as the accused, dressed in a dark-blue suit and tie and wearing thick horn-rimmed glasses, was brought into the courtroom and directed into a bulletproof glass booth. Unobtrusive cameras recorded every moment, allowing television networks to dispatch daily updates to their viewers worldwide. By the end of the seven-month trial, more reporters had travelled to Jerusalem to cover the Eichmann trial than had gone to Nuremberg and Tokyo combined.[112]

After the presiding judge, Moshe Landau, read the indictment, Israel's attorney general, Gideon Hausner, claiming that he would be the spokesman for all of Eichmann's victims, presented his case. Next, Eichmann's lawyer, Robert Servatius, took the stand. Servatius, a distinguished advocate from the Cologne bar, had defended three of the accused at Nuremberg. In recent weeks, he had met frequently with Eichmann in his cell, alone and out of earshot of the guards. Exuding confidence and an air of competence, Servatius turned to the judges and immediately challenged the proceedings. His client's alleged "crimes were committed prior to Israel's existence, on foreign soil, and against people who had no connection to Israel," he said.[113] Furthermore, Eichmann had been abducted and, finally, the judges, "as Jews, . . . were incapable of remaining impartial in a case that dealt with the Final Solution." In his rebuttal, the prosecutor, Gideon Hausner, argued that how an accused was brought to justice in no way negated the state's right to try him. Anyway, "the abduction had no bearing on the case, because Eichmann had been in Argentina illegally."[114]

Over a hundred prosecution witnesses (ninety of whom were concentration camp survivors) took the stand at Eichmann's trial, and dozens of defense depositions were delivered to the court by diplomatic couriers from sixteen different countries. At night, Eichmann stayed up late writing a 1,300-page memoir in which he vowed that he never hated Jews and never believed in Hitler's racial theories. Throughout the trial he insisted he had had no choice but to follow orders, as he was bound by an oath of loyalty—the same superior-orders defense some of his fellow SS officers had used in the Nuremberg trials. Servatius also argued that the decisions of the Nazi government were acts of state and therefore not subject to normal judicial proceedings, but this argument was for naught.

On Friday, December 15, 1961, Judge Landau delivered the court's 211-page judgment: Adolf Eichmann, he announced, was guilty of crimes against humanity, war crimes, crimes against the Jewish people, and membership in an outlawed organization.[115] Landau then asked Eichmann to rise to hear his sentence:

> For the dispatch of each train by the Accused to Auschwitz, or to any other extermination site, carrying one thousand human beings, meant that the Accused was a direct accomplice in one thousand premeditated acts of murder. . . . Even if we had found that the Accused acted out of blind obedience, as he argued, we would still have said that a man who took part in crimes of such magnitude as these over the years must pay the maximum penalty known to the law. . . . But we have found that the Accused acted out of an inner identification with the orders that he was given and out of a fierce will to achieve the criminal objective. . . . This Court sentences Adolf Eichmann to death.[116]

The eight-month trial captivated the world and generated an international debate about where, how, and by whom Nazi war criminals should be brought to justice. Some of its vicissitudes deeply affected the Jewish community, while others transformed how courts would view the role of victim-witnesses in future war crimes trials. According to French historian Annette Wieviorka, the trial marked the advent of an "era of testimony" that continues to this day.[117] She points to the pedagogical and commemorative role performed by the scores of prosecution witnesses, many of whom were Holocaust survivors, as having lit, in the chief prosecutor's words, "a spark in the frigid chamber which we know as history."[118] But perhaps the trial's greatest contribution was its effect on the broader public's understanding of the Holocaust, a term that only entered the lexicon of the non-Hebrew-speaking world during these proceedings, as it was repeated constantly by translators in the courtroom. Writes Deborah Lipstadt: "As a result of the trial, the story of the Holocaust, though it had previously been told, discussed, and commemorated, was heard *anew,* in a profoundly different way, and not just in Israel but in many parts of the Jewish and non-Jewish world. The *telling* may not have been entirely new, but the *hearing* was. . . . This new hearing of the history of the Final Solution would shape our contemporary understanding of this watershed event in human history."[119]

At midnight on May 31, 1962, Eichmann was hanged and his body cremated in a specially designed furnace. Early the next morning, an Israeli police boat scattered Eichmann's ashes over the Mediterranean, beyond Israel's territorial waters, to ensure that there would be no future memorial and that no country would serve as his final resting place.[120]

Eichmann's capture and execution helped catapult Simon Wiesenthal and Tuviah Friedman, now resentful rivals, back onto the world's stage. When asked by the *Times* of London if he had had anything to do with Eichmann's arrest, Wiesenthal correctly said he hadn't, though in later years he seemed to backpedal on this moment of humility, telling his daughter that the Eichmann case would guarantee his name in history. According to Friedman, Wiesenthal reportedly told an audience in Toronto that he had been "present at the capture of Eichmann in Argentina and actually fell into the ditch with him during the struggle."[121] When Friedman confronted him about the claim, Wiesenthal supposedly replied: "Journalists want sensations, so I told them and then repeated it in my speeches when I was questioned about the Eichmann operation. . . . People want heroes and leading actors, not extras."[122]

Friedman, meanwhile, was himself becoming something of a press darling, implicitly taking credit for instigating Eichmann's capture where again none was really due. Having little to show for recent years, Friedman often diverted the media's attention to his early attempts, in the postwar years, to track down Eichmann in Germany and Austria. At the same time, Friedman began receiving angry letters from Lothar Hermann, demanding to be paid the $10,000 reward the World Jewish Congress, at the behest of Friedman, had posted in 1958 for information about Eichmann's whereabouts. When the organization refused, citing the fact that the Israelis had never credited Hermann with a role in Eichmann's capture, Friedman turned without success to Mossad on the Hermanns' behalf. Twelve years later, in April 1972, after Harel had mentioned Hermann's role in a series of articles about the Eichmann operation, the Israeli government finally paid Hermann the reward he was due.[123]

If success has many fathers, then certainly Fritz Bauer, the tenacious German prosecutor who pressed Harel and Mossad into action, deserves to be among them. Bauer's involvement in Eichmann's capture remained a secret for two decades, but his pursuit of Nazi war crimes suspects, including several of Eichmann's deputies, in the German courts became front-page fare in Germany. Until his death in 1968, Bauer continued to prosecute Nazi war crimes, most notably with the 1963 Auschwitz trials, in which twenty-two former commanders and guards stood accused of grisly atrocities. The proceedings received considerable press coverage in Germany and, according to Guy Walters, forced a reluctant German public "to evaluate the horrors that had been committed in its name."[124] Six of the accused were given life sentences, five were released, and the remaining eleven were sentenced to three to fourteen years in prison. Yet, at the close of the trial, Bauer lamented the absence of Auschwitz's most notorious killer, Josef Mengele, the SS doctor who had stood most mornings at the death camp's railhead, closely scrutinizing the new arrivals. Rarely speaking, he simply tipped his thumb: death to one side, life to the other.

THE ELUSIVE ANGEL OF DEATH

As Eichmann's ashes slowly drifted into the depths of the Mediterranean, Josef Mengele was settling into his new home on a coffee and cattle farm, owned by Geta and Gitta Stammer, ninety-three miles north of São Paulo. Called Santa Luzia, the 111-acre farm was nestled on a high plateau in the Serra Negra, its open pastures bordered by tall eucalyptus trees, their crowns swaying gracefully in the sky. A month after his arrival, Mengele, just shy of his fifty-first birthday, recorded in his diary that the "beautiful landscape" provided "solace to a peaceless man."[125]

Mengele's journey to Santa Luzia began in May 1959 when he abruptly left Argentina for Paraguay. During the preceding ten years, he had lived in Buenos Aires, working at various jobs but mostly as a salesman for his family's farm-equipment business in Günzburg. In 1954, he divorced his wife, Irene, who was still in Germany, and four years later he married his older brother's widow in Uruguay, only to leave her a year later. In Paraguay, he settled in a region known as Nueva Bavaria, populated at the time with Nazi sympathizers who followed the teachings of a late-nineteenth-century anti-Semite, Bernhard Förster. Mengele lodged at the home of a farmer and one of Föster's diehard followers, Alban Krug, who helped his new lodger apply for Paraguayan citizenship under the name of Jose Mengele.[126]

Exactly what prompted Mengele's sudden departure from Buenos Aires remains a mystery.[127] Most likely, his family in Günzburg had informed him that an Auschwitz survivor named Hermann Langbein was snooping into the family's affairs and petitioning records from the state medical examination board in Munich, where Mengele had received his license to practice medicine. In fact, Langbein was compiling an impressive dossier against Mengele. Among the documents were several detailed interviews with Auschwitz survivors who had been sub-jected to Mengele's gruesome experiments, and a copy of Mengele's divorce papers bearing a Buenos Aires notarization stamp. Langbein first presented the dossier to the state prosecutor's office in Bonn, who on jurisdictional grounds declined to take it on. Undeterred, he approached a state court in Freiberg, which on June 5, 1959, a month after Mengele arrived in Paraguay, indicted the former Auschwitz doc-tor on seventeen counts of premeditated murder. The charges were shocking, if incomplete. They included "killing numerous prisoners with phenol, benzene and/or air injections; killing numerous prisoners in the gas chambers . . . killing several twins of Gypsy parents either with his own hands or by mixing lethal poison into their food, for the purpose of conducting specious medical studies on their bodies during autopsies."[128]

Two days later, the foreign office in Bonn cabled the West German embassy in Buenos Aires with instructions to begin an extradition request. From then on, the judicial pursuit of Josef Mengele would move slowly down a road pockmarked with delays and obfuscations. The first delay began at the West German embassy, where Ambassador Werner Junkers, himself a former high-ranking Nazi, sat on the request for a full nine months before sending it to the Argentine minister of foreign affairs, who passed it on to the president of the Senate, who, in turn, gave it to the procurator general. Finally, on June 30, 1960, twelve months after Bonn contacted the West German embassy, the extradition request was assigned to an Argentine judge.[129]

While West Germany's extradition request languished in Argentina, the Paraguayan government gave Mengele a precious gift: a Paraguayan naturalization certificate. While the country was internationally known as a haven for former Nazis, it had never naturalized anyone with so much blood on his hands. Nor could Paraguay claim it had no idea of Mengele's infamous past. A week before Mengele received his citizen-ship papers, Interpol, the world's largest law enforcement organization, acting on the Freiberg court's ruling, had asked the Paraguayan author-ities to forward a copy of Mengele's naturalization files to its headquar-ters in Lyon, France. At about the same time, the West German consul asked the Paraguayan minister of the interior if he might inspect Menge-le's immigration file.[130]

By September 1960, Mengele had caught wind of the inquiries being made by Interpol and the West German government. Six weeks later, he crossed the border into Brazil, with the help of a friend, Wolfgang Gerhard, a former corporal in the German army who had settled on a small farm just outside of São Paulo. A man who told his friends that he dreamed of "putting a steel cable to the leg of Simon Wiesenthal and dragging him to death behind my car,"[131] Gerhard introduced Mengele to Geza and Gitta Stammer, an Austrian-Hungarian couple who had moved to Brazil in 1948.[132] By then, Mengele had assumed the identity of Peter Hochbichler, a German-Swiss national who was looking for temporary work. The Stammers agreed to let Peter manage their small farm in the Austrian and German colony of Nova Europe in Araraquara, about 300 kilometers northwest of São Paulo. A year later, the Stammers and Peter Hochbichler moved to Santa Luzia.

It was there that the Stammers began to suspect that Peter wasn't the Swiss laborer he claimed to be. They noticed, for instance, that although he never indicated he'd had any medical training, he skillfully treated sick and injured farm animals. And his tastes were unusually sophisticated for a farm laborer—he read philosophy and history and in the evenings enjoyed listening to classical music.

One day Gitta opened the *Folha de Brazil* newspaper and saw a photograph of Mengele as he was in his late twenties at Auschwitz. Noticing the smile and the gap between the two front teeth, she showed her employee the picture and kidded him about the resemblance. "It made him pale," she said, and he fled the room. Later that evening he confessed: "I have been with you for two years, and you have a right to know," he told her. "I am Doctor Mengele."

When the couple confronted Gerhard with Peter's real identity, Gerhard told them they were lucky. "You used to be nobodies, unknown," he said. "Now a great thing has happened in your lives."

Mengele remained under the Stammers' protection for the next twelve years. He shunned most personal contacts, making an exception for sex. According to Gitta, Mengele had several affairs with housemaids and local farm girls during those years. "Men are men, you know, even in Hell," she said. "He could not get involved with women of his station, for fear of detection."[133]

Mengele's fear of being captured by the Israelis was almost realized in 1962, a year after his arrival in Brazil. After the Eichmann trial, Harel's team of Nazi-hunters began keeping close tabs on Willem Antonius Maria Sassen, the wartime SS officer who had recorded long interviews with Eichmann in Argentina. One day in 1962, Zvi Aharoni and a small team flew from Paris to Uruguay to recruit Sassen's help in finding Mengele. The Israelis already knew that Sassen, though still a

Nazi ideologue, had been shocked by some of the things Eichmann had told him about his participation in the Final Solution.

For two days, Aharoni and his men patiently educated Sassen about Mengele's crimes. They also added a sweetener of $5,000 a month should he cooperate. In the end, Sassen agreed, revealing that Mengele had indeed fled to Paraguay before moving on to São Paulo. Although Sassen didn't have the exact address, he knew that a man by the name of Wolfgang Gerhard was acting as his protector. Weeks later, Aharoni and two Brazilian operatives followed Gerhard as he drove into the hills to a farm outside of São Paulo. Later that afternoon, as the three agents sat by the road eating their lunch, a European-looking man and two Brazilians approached. Aharoni was unable to take a photograph, but prompted his Brazilian colleagues to engage with the three men. Later, Aharoni would describe to Mengele biographers Gerald Posner and John Ware what happened next: "I thought the man may well be Mengele. In fact I was sure of it. Our information was good. I said nothing because I didn't want to talk, so the two other guys did the talking. They just chatted away. The man I thought was Mengele didn't talk, though he didn't seem at all worried about us. They stayed talking about five minutes, so I got a good look at his face. He had a moustache [and] was the right height. There was a striking similarity with the photographs we had."[134]

Excited, Aharoni rushed back to Paris to share his discovery with Harel. Aharoni, with Harel's blessing, returned to Brazil to draw up a kidnapping plan. But when he returned again to Europe he found that Harel was no longer interested, his attention diverted by a different manhunt, one that didn't involve Nazis. He ordered Aharoni on to another operation. Months later, Harel says, he sent another team to Brazil, but they claimed that the farmhouse was heavily guarded with armed men and dogs. Unable to confirm the man inside as Mengele, and fearful of causing an incident, Harel called off the hunt, forever ending Israel's pursuit of the Angel of Death.[135]

It would later be revealed that Israel's Prime Minister David Ben-Gurion had pulled Harel and his agents off the Mengele case in mid-1962, soon after he learned, much to his surprise, that Egyptian President Gamal Abdel Nasser had launched a secret missile program. With the help of former Nazi rocket scientists, the Egyptian military had successfully test-launched four missiles capable of striking anywhere "south of Beirut"—that is, anywhere in Israel. Harel immediately launched a letter-bomb campaign against those German scientists who did not heed his anonymous letters warning them to return to Europe. A parcel sent to rocket scientist Wolfgang Pilz exploded in his Cairo office, seriously injuring his secretary. Another parcel, sent to the Heliopolis missile factory, killed five Egyptian workers. In the middle of 1963, Harel resigned, after a bitter clash with Ben-Gurion over whether Mossad should continue to target Germans working in Egypt.[136] Harel's replacement, Meir Amit, a young technocrat who had headed military intelligence, later harshly criticized Harel for diverting precious resources to tracking down Nazi fugitives rather than directing them to nipping Egypt's rocket program in the bud. "I wish we had had the money and manpower to have done it all," Amit recalled. "But we were fighting for the survival of the state of Israel. We didn't have the luxury of going after Nazis anymore."[137]

Some time in 1970, Wolfgang Gerhard introduced Mengele to his old friends Wolfram and Lisolette Bossert. Aware that tensions had developed between the Stammers and their boarder, Gerhard hoped that the Bosserts, Austrians like himself, might eventually take Mengele off the Stammers' hands. It was only a matter of time before the Bosserts would learn that Peter was in fact the Auschwitz doctor Josef Mengele, but it didn't make any difference. Mengele was already a regular guest at the Bosserts' home, where they spent evenings reminiscing about the prewar years. Mengele and Wolfram shared the same deep-rooted anti-Semitism and favored forced sterilization of "inferior races" to reduce the number of "primitive births."[138]

The following year Gerhard, before returning for good to his native Austria, gave Mengele his Brazilian identity card. Wolfram, an amateur photographer, took several passport-size photographs of Mengele, sliced open the laminated I.D. card, and slipped Mengele's photograph in over Gerhard's. What Wolfram couldn't change was Gerhard's date of birth, which transformed Mengele, then sixty, into a very old-looking forty-six-year-old, the age listed on the card.

Mengele had by this time increased his correspondence with his family in Günzburg and his childhood friend Hans Sedlmeier, who regularly sent him money and visited him on at least two occasions. In 1975, Mengele finally left the Stammers' house and moved into a bungalow by himself on Alvarenga Road in Eldorado, a suburb of São Paulo. Located in one of the poorer parts of town, the house consisted of a small living room, a gloomy bedroom, a bathroom, and a tiny kitchen. "My cage becomes more comfortable," he wrote to his friend Gerhard in Austria, "but it remains a cage."[139]

Mengele's health also began to deteriorate. His blood pressure was high, and he suffered from a variety of maladies, including migraines, insomnia, rheumatism, depression, and an enlarged prostate. In May 1976 he suffered a stroke and spent several days in the hospital. Although he eventually recovered, his stroke exacerbated his depression, leaving him in an acutely anxious state, fearful of many things but mostly in dread that the Israelis might knock down his door in the middle of the night.[140]

In February 1979 Mengele visited the Bosserts at a house they had rented for the weekend on a beach just south of São Paulo. At about five o'clock in the afternoon of the 7th, Mengele rose from his beach chair, next to where the Bosserts and their children were sitting, and dove into the breakers. Stroking vigorously, he broke through the surf to calmer water and began swimming parallel to the beach. Moments later, Lisolette noticed that he had stopped swimming and seemed to be thrashing about with one arm. She called to her husband, who immediately ran into the water and pulled Mengele to shore. Wolfram tried to revive his friend, but it was too late. Having almost drowned himself, Wolfram then collapsed.

The police took Wolfram to the hospital and Mengele's body to the local coroner, who issued a death certificate in the name of Wolfgang Gerhard. The next day, Lisolette hired a hearse and driver and drove Mengele's body to Our Lady of the Rosary Cemetery in Embu, where it was buried under a tombstone bearing Gerhard's name.[141] The trail had grown as cold as Mengele's decaying corpse.

Two events took place in early 1985 that would breathe new life into the hunt for Josef Mengele. In January, a group of concentration camp survivors held a vigil at the gates of Auschwitz in recognition of the fortieth anniversary of its liberation. Huddled together against the winter winds, the former inmates described Mengele's atrocities and expressed their outrage that he was still free. A week later, a mock trial of Mengele was held in Jerusalem before a distinguished panel chaired by Gideon Hausner, Israel's chief prosecutor at the Eichmann trial, Telford Taylor, an American prosecutor at Nuremberg, and Simon Wiesenthal.[142]

The politics of shame succeeded. Within days the American, Israeli, and German governments announced that a fresh attempt would be made to find Mengele. U.S. Attorney General William French Smith directed the Department of Justice's Office of Special Investigations to spearhead the hunt in cooperation with the U.S. Marshal's Service. Established in 1979 by the Carter administration, the Office of Special Investigations was already tracking down and deporting Nazis who had lied about their crimes in order to enter the United States at the end of the war. The Israeli justice minister, Moshe Missim, announced that a special panel of police, foreign affairs, and justice ministry officials would be set up to coordinate their effort and a million dollars would be offered for information on the Nazi doctor's whereabouts. The Germans followed suit by increasing their bounty to $330,000. The Simon Wiesenthal Center pledged an additional million, while the *Washington Times,* owned by the Reverend Sun Myung Moon, matched it with a million. Not to be outdone, Tuviah Friedman offered $100,000, and the Klarsfelds pledged $25,000, bringing the total on Mengele's head to a staggering $3,458,000.[143]

What happened next caught everyone by surprise, and revealed how little anyone—whether independent Nazi-hunter or Israeli agent—knew of Mengele's whereabouts. On May 31, 1985, without a word to their Israeli and American counterparts, the West German Federal Police, acting on a tip, raided the house of Mengele's childhood friend and family-company executive, Hans Sedlmeier. The police opened walls and pried up floorboards until they found a bundle of letters—all from Mengele—and an address book containing telephone numbers and addresses in code. One of the letters was from Wolfram Bossert announcing "with deep sorrow the death of our common friend." Later, referring to the letter, Sedlmeier fumed to a *New York Times* reporter, "Well, naturally I knew [Mengele was dead] because I got a letter from the Bosserts. My wife stupidly kept it. Stupid. I don't know why she did, but that's what got us in the end."[144]

Comparing the letters with the telephone numbers, the police quickly established that they were connected to various addresses in São Paulo and contacted the Brazilian authorities.[145] Within days, the São Paulo police had brought in Wolfram and Lisselotte Bossert for interrogation. The pair stonewalled at first, claiming they only knew a Peter Hochbichler from Switzerland. Finally, after two hours, Lisselotte broke. She told the police they should go to the Embu cemetery and look for the tombstone of "Wolfgang Gerhard."[146]

On the morning of June 21, 1985, a formidable team of German, American, and Brazilian forensic experts gathered in front of a podium on the third floor of the federal police headquarters in São Paulo. Behind the scientists stood two representatives of the U.S. Marshals Service and the head of the Nazi crimes section of Israel's police, Menachem Russek. For the past week, the scientists had huddled together in São Paulo's Medico-Legal Institute, examining a set of remains exhumed from the cemetery in Embu.

At the outset, the forensic experts had been highly skeptical of the Bosserts' story—it seemed to fit together too easily. But as the first round of forensic tests came in, the bones spoke for themselves. The skeleton's sex, race, and stature fit the description of Mengele's 1939 SS files. Counting osteons and osteon fragments in the blood-carrying canals of a femur, the scientists placed the age of the skeleton at between 64 and 74 years, and estimated the most probable age as 69. If the Bosserts' story was correct, Mengele would have been a month shy of his sixty-ninth birthday when he drowned. Other evidence also fell into place. X-rays of the skull showed that the nerve canal extending along the top of the mouth toward the upper central incisors was especially wide, a condition known as a diastema. This finding suggested that Mengele's front teeth, which were removed at some point in his sixties, had been widely spaced. It also explained why Mengele had a "gap-toothed smile" in his SS photograph. Pelvic X-rays revealed a hip fracture, consistent with an account in Mengele's SS files that he had been injured in a motorcycle accident in 1943. But the most compelling evidence came from West German pathologist Richard Helmer. Using a video-imaging process called skull-face superimposition, Helmer was able to match the Embu skull with a photograph taken of Mengele in the late 1930s. He repeated the process with other photographs, including several taken by Wolfram Bossert shortly before Mengele's death.[147]

At the press conference, an American forensic odontologist, Lowell Levine, read from a forensic report drafted the night before. The "exhumed remains are definitely not those of Wolfgang Gerhard," he said. "It is further our opinion that this skeleton is that of Josef Mengele within reasonable scientific certainty." Setting the statement aside, he added, "Our conclusion represents a very, very, very high degree of probability. Scientists never say anything is 100 percent. The odds are astronomical that another person on this earth could have the same characteristics as this skeleton."[148]

Despite the findings of the forensic experts, the Israeli and U.S. governments refused to close the Mengele case. In an attempt at final resolution, Hans Klein, the West German prosecutor in charge of the Mengele investigation, turned to a British geneticist, Alec Jeffreys, in

September 1989. Klein had heard about Jeffreys's extraordinary new technique, recently applied to questions of paternity or maternity and used in criminal investigations: DNA fingerprinting. Klein sent Jeffreys several bones from the Embu grave. Though reluctant at first, Mengele's first wife, Irene, and their son, Rolf, agreed to donate blood samples that were then matched with a 99.9-percent probability to the remains found in Brazil.[149]

With the positive conclusion of the DNA comparison, the Frankfurt State Prosecutor's Office announced on April 8, 1992, that it would formally ask the Hesse state court to close the Mengele case. The Israeli Justice Ministry followed suit later in the day by announcing that "all reasonable doubt was [now] removed, and it is possible to determine that Josef Mengele . . . died in 1979."[150] In October 1992 the U.S. Office of Special Investigations issued a long-delayed report on the Mengele case. The report faulted "the postwar American authorities, West Germans, and others for what it portrayed as ill-informed, sloppy and sporadic efforts to track down" the Nazi doctor and bring him to justice in a timely manner.[151] The report attempted to salvage some solace by concluding that "the many years [Mengele] . . . spent hiding in sheer squalor in Brazil, tortured by his fear that Israeli agents were on the verge of capturing him, arguably provided a kind of rough, albeit inadequate, 'justice.'"[152]

The notion that Mengele's victims, now deceased or entering their twilight years, have salvaged any sense of justice knowing that their Auschwitz tormentor spent many of his fugitive years decently housed, if penniless and fearful of capture, seems tenuous at best. Yet some solace might be taken in the fact that the Mengele investigation introduced a variety of procedures and techniques in the forensic identification of human remains that are still being applied in investigations of war crimes throughout the world today. Clyde Snow, a forensic anthropologist who helped identity Mengele's remains and those of hundreds of victims of massacres in Bosnia, Rwanda, and Iraq, noted that the Mengele case introduced "a certain analytical method . . . [that] set the procedural standards for . . . large-scale investigations of war crimes and crimes against humanity."[153] Mengele may have escaped justice, but his last legacy endures in the pursuit of justice for victims of oppression worldwide.[154]

Like the ebb and flow of tides, the search for Eichmann and Mengele surged forward and just as quickly pulled back, depending on the political exigencies of the governments of West Germany, Israel, and the

United States—not to mention the recalcitrance of several South American governments that had no desire to track down and expel Nazi war criminals from their shores. And had it not been for the combined efforts of Simon Wiesenthal and Tuviah Friedman, the tenacity of German prosecutor Fritz Bauer, and the obsession of Mossad chief Issel Harel, it is likely that Eichmann would have died, like Mengele, very much a free man in a distant land. Instead, his 1961 trial in Jerusalem stands as a watershed moment in the history of international justice, raising public awareness of the Holocaust and the suffering it caused to millions of our fellow human beings, and underscoring the need to hold those responsible for such crimes individually accountable.

CHAPTER 4

The Last Nazi War Criminals

Klaus Barbie cut a pathetic figure as he wandered the streets of La Paz after his arrival there in June 1951. Passersby would never have known that the slightly built man, dressed in a rumpled jacket and faded trousers, was once a former Gestapo captain in Lyon, France, and directly responsible for the deaths of up to 14,000 people, including many he tortured with his own hands. Having spent most of his savings in Buenos Aires and on the journey north to Bolivia, he settled his wife, Regine, and their two children into one of the capital's shoddiest hotels and started pounding the pavement in search of work. Like Argentina, Bolivia in the early 1950s boasted a large German community with lucrative business holdings, especially in the manufacturing sector, and strong ties to the country's military. Many Nazi sympathizers resided in the provinces, and Barbie naturally drifted in their direction. One of them, Hans Ertl, a recent immigrant and former cameraman who had worked with Leni Riefenstahl on several of her Nazi propaganda films, helped him get his first job, working as a manager of a sawmill high in the Yungas forest of the Andes. Barbie's family joined him, and his wife became the manager of the company store. In the late 1950s, Barbie was promoted to be the firm's representative in La Paz and returned with his family to the capital.[1]

In 1957, Barbie obtained Bolivian citizenship in the name of Klaus Altmann and struck out on his own, establishing sawmills in Cochabamba and La Paz. The timber business enabled his family to live comfortably and allowed the former Nazi officer to join La Paz's racially exclusive German Club, where he frequently waxed lyrical about the Third Reich, peppering stories with references to his time as a German officer. One night at the club, after imbibing a few too many of the Bolivian cocktails known as *chuflay*, Barbie gave a Nazi salute and shouted "Heil Hitler!" in the presence of the German ambassador, an act that got him expelled from the club for several months.[2]

Barbie's ascent in the Bolivian business world of the 1960s, where hands could be padded and pockets filled, was breathtaking. After the 1964 CIA-backed coup by René Barrientos, a conservative military officer who went on to quash political dissent, Barbie's relations with influential army officers tightened, helping him, in turn, to expand his own business ventures. First he turned to extracting quinine from chinin trees, which he imported from the Congo and cultivated outside of La Paz, to feed the growing Pentagon demand for the antimalarial for American soldiers serving in Vietnam. When the demand for quinine dropped off, Barbie billed himself as a maritime engineer and garnered a lucrative government contract to create the Transmartíma Boliviana, a transoceanic shipping company. The subterfuge was impressive given that Bolivia had been landlocked since 1879, when it lost its maritime Antofagasta Province in a war with neighboring Chile. Barbie rapidly expanded his business, appointing friends as managers and his son Klaus as a company representative in Hamburg.

For nearly a year, Barbie worked as a spy for West Germany's foreign intelligence agency, the Bundesnachrichtendienst (BND). In November 1965, a BND agent named Wilhelm Holm met Barbie during a four-week visit to La Paz and was impressed with his political leanings. Holm was a "tipper," a unique species in the shadowy world of postwar intelligence, who traveled the world scoping out potential agents and sending their names back to BND headquarters near Munich. The two men quickly became friends, so much so that Holm dined with the Altmann family almost every day at the German Club. Although Barbie appears not to have revealed his true identity to Holm, he did say that he had served with the SS and had fled to South America in 1951. Holm wrote in a cable to BND headquarters that his new friend was a staunch German patriot and a "committed anticommunist."[3]

The BND then hired Barbie as a "political source" under the code name Adler (Eagle) and instructed him to keep tabs on Bolivian officials and their overseas business interests. According to BND documents obtained by a German magazine, *Der Spiegel,* the former Gestapo captain delivered at least thirty-five reports to the agency before he was suddenly dropped from the payroll in late 1966 "to avoid later complications and difficulties." The BND documents suggest that Barbie's severance came soon after he refused to travel to Germany for a training program, but *Der Spiegel* suspected that some of the former SS men and Gestapo officials in the BND came to recognize the new agent from their days in the Third Reich. A 1964 BND document even states that Barbie was "possibly" living in La Paz.[4]

In 1969, the U.S. embassy issued Barbie a visa to conduct business for the Transmartíma Boliviana in the United States. He visited Miami, Houston, San Francisco, and New Orleans before traveling on to the Bahamas to deposit money in a secret bank account.[5] The City Council of New Orleans even presented him with keys to the Big Easy. As Transmartíma prospered, Barbie exploited his high-level contacts in the Bolivian army to import small arms and ammunition.[6] In one of his more daring and ironic ventures, he purchased small arms from Belgium, registered the shipment as bound for Bolivia, and then diverted it to Israel, which, at the time, was under an international arms embargo.[7]

While Barbie prospered in Bolivia, West German prosecutors, after a long hiatus, had begun to renew efforts to prosecute Nazi war crimes suspects. Even then, they pursued their investigations, as one German legal scholar put it, "wearily and without passion," largely limiting their investigations to charges made by survivors who saw their persecutors walking free in the streets. While statistics vary somewhat from source to source, of the 5,426 former Nazis tried in West Germany for past crimes between 1950 and 1962, only 1,399 were convicted. Of these, 155 were convicted of murder but, given the gravity of their crimes, received very lenient sentences.[8]

Why the lack of enthusiasm to vigorously pursue Nazi crimes? First, after the Nuremberg trials and Allied Occupation, the West German populace and the postwar government of Konrad Adenauer simply wanted to forget about the Nazi era. Most Germans, in historian Jeffrey Herf's words, were opposed to "any serious efforts at postwar judicial reckoning or frank public memory."[9] They were far more preoccupied with reconstruction and the expansionist interests of their communist neighbors to the east. Second, by the early 1950s, many former Nazi jurists, purged during the Allied denazification program, had returned to their judicial posts, while former Third Reich officials had taken over most of the leading positions in the Foreign Service. In 1952, Adenauer, reluctant to sweep them out, told the Bundestag, "I think we now need to finish with this sniffing out of Nazis."[10] Third, many of the few Holocaust survivors in West Germany had migrated to Israel or other countries, so no political or activist base existed to lobby for trials.[11] Finally, limitations in the West German penal code (coupled with the fact that the majority of crimes had been committed outside Germany proper) made it easier for individual courts to overlook or reject lawsuits involving Nazi crimes. After its founding in 1949, the Federal Republic of Germany chose not to apply the international charges contained in the Nuremberg charter—particularly genocide, crimes against humanity, and war crimes—to alleged Nazi crimes and decided instead to try such cases under the German penal code, established in 1871. The code contained several loopholes—including statutes of limitations for murder (twenty years) and manslaughter (fifteen years)—that allowed most Nazi criminals to get away scot-free. Defendants who were sentenced were mostly convicted as accomplices, because to convict them as perpetrators (earning an automatic life sentence) the prosecution had to prove their *inner motivations*, including lust for killing, sexual drive for killing, cruelty, treachery, or other base motives. As historian Rebecca Wittmann observes, these limitations

> made it easier for those who had the most power in the Nazi regime—the desktop murderers—to go free or escape trial, and in the end only the most sadistic—and exceptional—of Nazi criminals, usually camp guards, were tried and convicted of murder. On the one hand, there were thousands of trials. On the other hand, the continuities in the judicial personnel made the sentences and interpretation of the laws extremely favorable to the defendants. . . . The Law was not the setting in which Germans would come to recognize the wholesale complicity of an entire generation.[12]

Despite these restraints, prosecutions of suspected Nazi war criminals received a boost after the 1958 trial of ten Gestapo and SS officers in the southern German town of Ulm. The court convicted the defendants of killing more than 5,000 Lithuanian Jews during the Wehrmacht's initial invasion of the Soviet Union in June 1941. The month-long proceedings, which received widespread media coverage throughout Germany, revealed that many of the perpetrators responsible for gruesome crimes had continued to live normal lives in West Germany for years after the war. The trial also prompted a group of liberal jurists to push for the creation of a centralized body—the Zentralestelle der Landesjustizverwaltungen zur Aufklaerung der NS-Verbrechen (Central Office of the State Judicial Authorities for the Investigation of National Socialist

Crimes, or Central Office)—to investigate Nazi crimes, heretofore left solely to the discretion of individual prosecutors. Established in December 1958 and based in Ludwigsburg, the Central Office was initially restricted to investigating wartime crimes outside Germany, but in 1964 its jurisdiction was extended to crimes in German territory as well. As a fact-gathering institution, the Central Office could only refer its findings to a public prosecutor, who in turn determined whether a case merited a full investigation and prosecution. Despite this limitation, Ludwigsburg investigators amassed an extensive and compelling archive of documents and microfilms from the Nazi era that subsequently made it difficult for prosecutors to dismiss Nazi cases out of hand.[13]

One of the Central Office's first actions was to distribute a list of Nazi suspects, with Klaus Barbie at the top, to every police station in Germany. When approached by the Ludwigsburg investigators, the U.S. Army in Germany claimed that all contact with Barbie had been lost in 1951. Next, the police interrogated a relative of Barbie's wife, who revealed that she had received letters from Regine postmarked Bolivia, but knew nothing more about her whereabouts. By 1963, the German police, aware of Barbie's conviction *in absentia* by two French courts, had sent his file to the French secret service requesting that they look for him in La Paz, but the appeal went nowhere. Ironically, that same year, a Bolivian businessman, who had established that Klaus Altmann and Klaus Barbie were one and the same, went to the French Embassy in La Paz to complain that Barbie owed him a considerable sum of money. He hoped the French Embassy would apply pressure on Barbie to pay back the debt. The matter was referred to Paris, but French officialdom never managed to connect the German request with the inquiry from its embassy in La Paz; the Bolivian businessman's démarche was tucked away in a bureaucrat's file drawer.[14]

In the mid-1960s, a general amnesty for all Nazi war crimes suspects, known as the Law of Adjustment, was pending in the German Parliament. Although the bill was never adopted, it dampened the ardor of the Ludwigsburg investigations, and by the early 1970s the Germans had effectively shelved Barbie's case.[15]

THE KLARSFELDS AND THE POLITICS OF SHAME

The Butcher of Lyon may well have lived out his last years in South America had it not been for the daughter of a Wehrmacht soldier and the son of a man who died in Auschwitz. Born to a Christian family,

Beate Künzel grew up in postwar Berlin. A rather restless girl who longed to break away, in 1960, at the age of twenty-one, she traveled to Paris to work as an au pair, much to the distress of her father, who was sure she would end up a prostitute in the Bois de Boulogne. One afternoon, while riding the Metro to a class at the Alliance Française, Beate met a young French Jew named Serge Klarsfeld, who was studying to be a lawyer. Three years later, the couple married, and Beate was formally welcomed into the Klarsfeld family.[16]

Serge and his mother and sister had barely survived the German occupation of Nice. Late one night in September 1943, a few days after Serge's eighth birthday, the Gestapo, led by a member of Eichmann's deportation team, Alois Brunner, an SS *Hauptsturmführer* who had recently become the commander of the Drancy internment camp outside Paris and who by war's end would send at least 140,000 Jews to concentration and forced-labor camps, raided the apartment building where the Klarsfelds lived.[17] Serge's father, Arno, anticipating a Gestapo raid, had built a false front in a closet to hide his family. When the Germans burst into the apartment, Arno, fearing they would discover the hiding place, slipped out of the cupboard and surrendered. His family survived, but Arno was sent to Drancy and later to Auschwitz.

In 1965, at the age of thirty, Serge traveled to eastern Poland to visit Auschwitz while Beate, pregnant with their first child, stayed behind in Paris. Scouring through the archives, he discovered a document bearing his father's camp number—159683—and a cross indicating that he had died, most likely in a gas chamber. Serge later recalled that it was a pivotal moment in his life:

> Up until then I hadn't been involved in politics. But I recognized that I was about to become a father, and so I had a duty to reconstitute the last stage of my father's life. . . . What had happened that night in Nice had happened to many children and many families all over Europe. Germans were looking for Jewish families in order to kill them. . . . Many fathers tried to hide their children behind false walls, in basements, and in attics. Some were saved, but many were lost. . . . I understood that I belonged to a unique generation. My generation had seen the destruction of European Jewry and the resurrection after 19 centuries of a Jewish state. So we had a special duty to defend the memory of the Jews who were killed and also to defend the Jewish state.[18]

Like many young Germans growing up in the 1950s, Beate had remained ignorant of the history of the Third Reich—though this would change with subsequent generations. "There had been no revelations in my postwar generation," she later told the *International Herald Tribune.*

My parents were part of that silent majority of Germans who didn't want to take a position on the war. At school my history teacher would dodge questions that proved embarrassing. Serge played an essential role in helping me to come to grips with my own past. I always wanted my children to be proud of their half-German background, to never blush about their country. Anyway, one day they would have asked what my attitude was toward Nazi war criminals after the war. My children's grandfathers had two pasts: One died in Auschwitz, the other fought for the Wehrmacht. It's from this rather exceptional situation that my motivation sprang.[19]

The Klarsfelds faced social, ideological, psychological, and legal hurdles, both in France and in West Germany, as they set out to track down and expose surviving Nazi war criminals. Most of these impediments had been created during and immediately after the German occupation of France (1940–44). From 1940 to 1942, German forces occupied northern France, while southern France became a Nazi collaborationist, or Vichy zone libre ("free zone"), under the Nazi puppet regime of Philippe Pétain. In November 1942, the Nazis occupied the zone libre as well and disbanded what remained of the Vichy military forces. As in other occupied European countries, the Nazi occupation of France created deep societal fissures between "resisters," "collaborators," and "bystanders." These fractures left France deeply divided and influenced French policies on holding German war criminals legally accountable for their past crimes. On one side were French citizens who demanded justice for resistance fighters who had been captured and tortured by the Germans and summarily executed (but not necessarily for the tens of thousands of French Jews deported to death camps). On the other side were those, led by former officials of the Vichy regime, who preferred simply to forget.[20]

After the war, French officials estimated that the Nazis had committed 20,000 violent crimes, including war crimes, in France. These ranged from the execution of resistance fighters and their supporters during antipartisan operations to the deportation of French Jews to their deaths in the east. The Nazi occupiers, with the assistance of Vichy officials, also used several hundred thousand French civilians as forced laborers, while siphoning off much of the country's wealth. France's liberation in the summer of 1944 led to a wave of lynchings and other acts of revenge against many former occupation officials and their Vichy collaborators. But the vast majority of Nazi officers responsible for war crimes were able to return to West Germany, where they were absorbed into society, taking up positions as judges, university professors, and businessmen. As a result, the French had few prominent Nazis left in their custody.

By late 1947, with the onset of the Cold War, the Americans and British had not only begun to wind down their trials of suspected Nazi war criminals in postwar Germany but also established a policy of turning down extradition requests of German suspects to other countries once occupied by the Nazis. While the halt to extraditions was not targeted at the French per se, but more at Eastern European states, this abrupt change in policy eroded French aspirations of obtaining suspects for trial on their own soil. The French received a second blow in 1950, when officials in the British-administered zone of West Germany refused to extradite Kurt Lischka, a wartime Gestapo chief for Jewish affairs in France, who was accused of deporting 80,000 Jews to concentration camps during the German occupation. Spurned by the British, a Paris court sentenced Lischka *in absentia* to hard labor for life in September 1950 for his role in the Final Solution in France. Lischka meanwhile lived freely in Cologne, working for a time as a commercial employee and then becoming a judge, his French life sentence notwithstanding. Unable to compel the extradition of German residents, French military courts had to resort to *in absentia* trials of German suspects like Lischka, of which 1,314 defendants were eventually convicted.[21]

The Klarsfelds' first foray into the world of Nazi-hunting took place in 1967, just after the election of Kurt Georg Kiesinger, the leader of the Christian Democratic Union and a former Nazi official, as chancellor of West Germany. Beate, who at the time was working as a secretary for the French-West German Youth Service in Paris, was outraged. "It was unbelievable for my generation to have a former Nazi propagandist as the chief of the German government."[22] She wrote a series of articles for the leftist French newspaper *Combat,* revealing that during the war Kiesinger had been an outright supporter of Hitler and Nazi policies, including all of Himmler's anti-Jewish measures. "If Eichmann represented the banality of evil," she wrote, in reference to Hannah Arendt's analysis, "Kiesinger represents the respectability of evil." Later that year Beate was dismissed from her job.[23]

Undeterred, Beate travelled to Germany and mounted a public campaign against Kiesinger, calling for his resignation at student rallies and political gatherings. At one point, Beate posed as a reporter and infiltrated the Christian Democratic Union's congress in Berlin. Sweet-talking a guard, she managed to slip up to the podium and confront Kiesinger. Shouting "Nazi! Nazi!" at the top of her lungs, she drew back her right hand and slapped the politician's face.[24] "The gesture was symbolic," Beate recalled. "It was a slap of the German youth towards the Nazi generation. It was the German daughter slapping the Nazi father."[25] The following day, articles about the Kiesinger Slap were spread across the front pages of nearly every major newspaper in Europe, catapulting the Klarsfelds and their confrontational brand of activism into the spotlight.

Overnight, and without any training, the Klarsfelds had crafted a publicity strategy that would become their modus operandi for pursuing Nazi fugitives. "Attracting media attention was the key to the Klarsfeld campaign," writes Barbie biographer Tom Bower. "Newspaper and television journalists were lobbied either in person or by phone, and personally handed massive folders containing photocopies of original documents, which always provided seriously incriminating evidence against their target. The Klarsfelds either called their own news conference or infiltrated other people's; politicians were approached, called or harassed to win their support; speeches, demonstrations and 'incidents' were arranged to ensure maximum publicity; no day passed without considerable expenditure on telephone calls or photocopying machines."[26]

Recalled Beate: "What Serge and I learned early on was that we couldn't gain attention through pamphlets and articles. We had to do something spectacular. We had to create a small scandal, like slapping Kiesinger, to bring attention to a much bigger scandal." Although the slap landed Beate in jail for three months, it also gave her a moniker, one that would prove attractive to West Germany's growing counterculture. "Whenever I went to speak in Germany, I was known as the 'girl who slapped the chancellor.' This allowed me to unite a large following among young Germans."[27]

The Klarsfelds' activism often entailed a challenge to the law, as it had with the famous slap. On several occasions Beate chained herself in protest outside parliament buildings and courthouses in Eastern Europe and Latin America, while Serge drew up ingenious, if foolhardy, plans to abduct accused Nazi war criminals. In one such attempt, in 1973, Serge stopped Kurt Lischka on a Cologne street and pointed a pistol at his head. "I'm sure he thought he was going to die by the tortured look on his face," Serge recalled.[28] Serge's ploy with the gun was designed to persuade the West German government, which had been refusing calls to prosecute Lischka, to think again. "I didn't shoot, and escaped, and then wrote to the West German government to say that if they did not deal with this man, then we would. We told them to do their duty and apply the law."[29] Instead, a warrant was issued for the arrest of both Klarsfelds.

But the Klarsfelds' fortunes began to change in 1975 when a Franco–German agreement gave West German courts the authority to try ex-Nazis for crimes committed in France. Five years later a German court convicted Kurt Lischka and two fellow SS intelligence officers—Herbert-Martin Hagen and Ernst Heinrichson—of mass murder. Hagen received 12 years, Lischka 10 years, and Heinrichson 6 years. At trial, Serge Klarsfeld, who had amassed thirteen volumes of documents linking the defendants to individual deportations, represented the French victims.

Years later Jonathan Silvers, a New York–based filmmaker, posed the following hypothetical scenario to Serge Klarsfeld in his documentary *Elusive Justice: The Search for Nazi War Criminals*:

Question: If the law had not been passed [allowing German courts to try Nazi crimes committed in France] would you have gone back and killed Lischka?

Serge Klarsfeld: If not myself, another one would have done it. . . . But we didn't want that. We wanted something that was a great victory: to have the [German] children of the criminals sending their fathers to jail. So that's much more difficult to obtain than just to kill a criminal. To kill a criminal is an act of despair and not an act of hope.[30]

In the early 1970s, the Klarsfelds began focusing much of their attention on Klaus Barbie. Their interest was piqued in June 1971 when the Munich police officially announced they were closing the Barbie investigation. In September, Beate traveled to Munich with the mother of three young boys—Jacques, Richard, and Jean-Claude Benguigui—who had perished at Auschwitz. Mrs. Benguigui had herself been deported to Auschwitz, but lived in the hope that her three children, who had been left in the Izieu orphanage, in the mountains fifty kilometers outside of Lyon, were safe. It was Barbie who had ordered her sons and forty-one other Jewish children in the orphanage deported to Auschwitz in April 1944.[31] A month later, while walking through the camp, Mrs. Benguigui found the sweater of her eldest son, Jacques, in a pile of clothing near the entrance to the gas chambers.

As sheets of rain swept across Munich, Beate and Mrs. Benguigui stood on the steps outside the courthouse. Benguigui held a sign that read: "I am on hunger strike for as long as the investigation of Klaus Barbie, who murdered my children, remains closed."[32] Late that afternoon the prosecutor, Manfred Ludolph, summoned Beate and Mrs. Benguigui to his office and agreed to reopen Barbie's case, but on one condition: the two women must first find a man named Raymond Geissmann, a former wartime Lyon official and member of the Union Générale des Israélites de France, who had acted as an intermediary between the Jewish community and Barbie during his time in Lyon. According to Ludolph, Geissmann had been present at several meetings where Barbie had ordered the killing of Jews.

Beate and Serge swung into action. Geissmann, as it turned out, had a law office near the Place de Vôsges in Paris. The Klarsfelds laid out their case to him, and Geissmann agreed to provide a written statement. In it he described one particular encounter with the Gestapo chief: "I remember seeing Barbie froth at the mouth as he vented his hatred of Jews, and his remark—'Deported or shot, there's no difference'—was truly spoken by him. He said it in front of me and I reported it to my colleagues in Paris."[33]

The Klarsfelds returned to Munich and handed the prosecutor Geissmann's sworn affidavit. "Once he had [it], Ludolph completely changed his attitude," Beate recalled. Then, similar to Fritz Bauer's earlier enlistment of the Hermanns in the Mengele search, Ludolph gave the Klarsfelds two photographs reportedly of Barbie—one a portrait of the young Gestapo captain taken in 1943, and the other, taken in La Paz in 1968, of a group of Bolivian businessman and military officers standing in front of a microphone as if they were holding forth at a press conference. The German prosecutor pointed to one of the businessmen, a stocky man with a broad forehead and a receding hairline, and said, "We think this may be Klaus Barbie." He then asked Beate, "Why don't you help me identify this man?"[34]

Back in Paris, Beate pestered a government forensic anthropologist until he finally agreed to examine Ludolph's photographs. Using anthropometric measurements, the scientist scrutinized the facial features of the pictures and determined that there was "every likelihood" that they were of the same man, a view shared by experts in the anthropology department at Munich University. At about the same time, the Klarsfelds learned from a reliable source in Peru that Barbie was on an extended visit to Lima. They tried to persuade the French government to ask for Barbie's extradition. When that failed, they took their story to the newspaper *L'Aurore,* which had published Emile Zola's extraordinary 4,000-word open letter on the Dreyfus Affair under the headline

"J'Accuse...!" in January 1898. On January 19, 1972, the newspaper published the purported photographs of Barbie and, as the Klarsfelds had hoped, called on the French authorities to extradite him.

That evening, a world away, Barbie, fresh from a weekend on the Peruvian coast, answered a knock on his door in Lima. The man standing there, without identifying himself by name, explained that he was a French journalist and asked if he might step in. When Barbie refused, the man shrugged his shoulders and told him he should expect a surprise the next day. The following morning Barbie stopped at a local kiosk, bought his favorite newspaper, and, anticipating the worst, took a deep breath. "[T]here it was," he recalled in his memoir, spread out on "the whole front page," a warmed-over version of the *L'Aurore* story, with Ludolph's two photographs staring back at him.[35]

Over the next week, the press hounded Barbie and his wife. He steadfastly denied that he was anyone other than the Bolivian businessman noted in his passport: "I am not Klaus Barbie, but Klaus Altmann, a former lieutenant in the Wehrmacht. I've never heard of Klaus Barbie, and I've never changed my identity."[36] Then, on January 26, 1972, Peruvian policemen burst into his apartment and arrested him. Barbie managed to appease the officers by agreeing to accompany them to the Interior Ministry the following morning. When he arrived, an official warned him that Beate Klarsfeld was on her way and he'd better leave the country.[37]

Barbie, escorted by two Peruvian policemen, drove out of Lima in his Volkswagen Cabriolet that morning, heading for the Bolivian border, a two-day journey at best.[38] At about the same time, Beate Klarsfeld boarded a London flight bound for Lima. In her briefcase was a German dossier that would prove Altmann and Barbie were one and the same and copies of two extradition treaties signed by Peru and France in 1888 and 1924.

Late in the day of her arrival, after being stonewalled repeatedly by Peruvian officials, Beate learned that Barbie had already crossed the border into Bolivia.[39] She immediately returned to the airport and purchased a ticket to La Paz.

While Beate had an inkling that the Peruvian authorities were behind Barbie's escape, she had no way of knowing just how complicit they, as well as the Bolivian government, had been. For that we have to turn to Barbie's memoirs. "I spent [my last] night with the police escort getting terribly drunk, and then they took me through Puno to Desguadero, the frontier town. There they handed me a form to sign and said to me, 'Herr Altmann, you left Peru voluntarily, didn't you?' I replied, 'If it is voluntary, why would I have needed an escort?' But I agreed to sign in the end. I crossed the bridge into Bolivia . . . and there was a fifteen-man military squad under the command of Colonel Navarro waiting to greet me. They drove with me to La Paz."[40]

Barbie immediately went to the Ministry of the Interior, where an official assured him that he was regarded "as an honorable Bolivian citizen with all the rights that implied."[41] Still, the official continued, Beate Klarsfeld was coming, and it would be wise to stay out of sight. Barbie, as he recalls in his memoirs, checked into a hotel under a false name and was assigned twenty-four-hour police protection.[42]

Beate's time in La Paz was brief. While the Bolivian authorities begrudgingly met with the activist, the French ambassador, Jean Louis Mandereau, avoided her, although he did send an underling to see her in secret and photocopy her documents. On day three of her visit, the Bolivians arrested Beate and expelled her from the country, ostensibly for violating her tourist visa.

Although Beate's mission to confront Barbie was thwarted, her visit left little doubt that Altmann and Barbie were one and the same and impelled the French to submit a request to the Bolivian Supreme Court for Barbie's extradition.[43] The appeal was based on two *in absentia* trials, which had taken place in 1952 and 1954, in which the Permanent Military Tribunal in Lyon had convicted Barbie and sentenced him to death for murder and conspiracy to commit murder during his time as Lyon's Gestapo chief.[44] To add ballast to the extradition request, French President Georges Pompidou sent a personal letter to Bolivian President Hugo Banzer calling on the general to use all of his powers to expedite the process.[45]

The French embassy in Washington meanwhile asked the U.S. State Department to provide documentary evidence to support Beate's claim that Altmann and Barbie were the same person. State, joined by the Justice Department, turned to the Pentagon, arguing that it was in the "national interest" to support the French while coming clean about their employment of Barbie at the war's end. But the Pentagon refused to cooperate.[46]

Chastened by Washington, the French remained hopeful, though they were aware that the extradition request faced numerous legal and political impediments in Bolivia. To begin with, Bolivia and France had never signed an extradition treaty. Nor was Barbie a French citizen.

Lastly, and perhaps most importantly, Barbie had long curried President Banzer's favor and could rely on him to intervene even it meant defying the high court.

Beate, determined to strike while the iron was hot, returned to La Paz on February 24. She brought with her Itta Halaunbrenner, a sixty-eight-year-old former resident of Lyon who held Barbie responsible for ordering the execution of her husband and sending her eldest son, Leon, to his death in Auschwitz. Fearing for their safety, Itta had sent her two youngest daughters to the Izieu orphanage, from where Barbie had them dispatched, along with the other orphans and staff, to be gassed at Auschwitz.

It didn't take long for Beate to become impatient with the Bolivian authorities. Though they expressed their sympathy to Itta for the tragic story of her children's deaths, they made no promises to extradite Barbie. Early on the morning of February 28, despite having promised not to talk to the press, Beate began telephoning journalists from her room at the La Paz Hotel and inviting them to a press conference. Even after an arrest and another police warning, Beate held a press conference and Itta told her anguished story. The newspapers the next morning devoted several pages to Itta's story and ran a surprisingly detailed description of Barbie's role as a Gestapo chief in Lyon.[47]

As their stay in La Paz drew to a close, Beate and Itta decided to undertake one last action to draw attention to Barbie. After booking seats on the daily 8 P.M. flight to Lima, the two women walked from their hotel to the Prado, La Paz's main street, and chained themselves to a bench opposite Barbie's Transmartíma Boliviana offices. Itta held up a placard bearing a picture of her dead family. Underneath was written: *Bolivians. As a mother I only claim justice. I want Barbie-Altmann, who murdered my husband and three of my children, brought to trial.* Beate held up her own sign, which read: *In the name of millions of Nazi victims, let Barbie-Altmann be extradited.* Then, as dusk fell, the two women released themselves, gathered their bags at the hotel, and dashed to the airport to catch their flight.[48]

THE DECEPTION

For the next three years, France's extradition request languished in the offices of the Bolivian Supreme Court. Barbie, meanwhile, divided his time between his sawmill in Cochabamba and his shipping company in La Paz, where he and his wife maintained a simple fourth-floor apartment. At one end of the flat hung a large oil painting of Hitler, dressed in a black coat with the collar turned up.[49] Barbie, always insisting that his name was Altmann, lived openly, often giving interviews to foreign journalists. After his friend General Hugo Banzer, a member of the tight German circle in Bolivia, took power in 1971, Barbie had also found employment in Department 7 of the army in Cochabamba, a department notorious for what were euphemistically called "psychological operations." "The Bolivians used simply to beat people up," an Interior Minister official later recalled. "Under Barbie, they learned the use of techniques of electricity and the use of medical supervision to keep the suspect alive until they had finished with him."[50]

Such revelations about Barbie's "talents" keeping suspects alive during torture would surely have surprised many of his Jewish victims—and even his Gestapo colleagues—from his Lyon days. According to Jane Kramer, who later covered the Barbie trial for the *New Yorker*, "the few people in Lyon who survived his interrogations say that he always worked with a bullwhip or a blackjack, and that his rage betrayed his incompetence; once he started beating, he usually could not stop himself until his prisoner was either dead or dying."[51] One of his most famous victims was Jean Moulin, the resistance leader, who possessed information on every aspect of the underground. Barbie apparently beat him to death in a fit of rage.

Fate once again smiled on Barbie in December 1974. The Bolivian Supreme Court, under threat of dissolution by Banzer, rejected the French request on the grounds that the two countries had never signed an extradition treaty, that Barbie was a Bolivian citizen, and that the Bolivian penal code did not recognize war crimes.[52]

Six years later, on July 17, 1980, in what is often referred to as the Cocaine Coup, General Luis García Meza Tejada and a band of his supporters from the Santa Cruz region occupied the Palacio Quemado, Bolivia's presidential residence in La Paz, moments before the recently elected president, Hernán Siles Zuazo, was to take residence there. Fearing for his life, the president-elect fled to the residence of the French Ambassador, Raymond Césaire, who later helped him across the border to Peru via Lake Titicaca.

In the 1980s military coups were a common, though destructive, occurrence in Bolivia, but this one would prove to be particularly calamitous, in no small part because it had substantial backing from unsavory German nationals like Klaus Barbie. García Meza Tejada outlawed all political parties, exiled opposition leaders, repressed the unions, and muzzled the press.[53]

Barbie, though, fared well under the new regime. Given the rank of honorary colonel in the Bolivian army, he moved from Department 7 to a highly paid position in state security, where he consorted with the likes of Major Roberto D'Aubuisson, the Salvadorian death-squad leader, and other right-wing military officers who came hat in hand to Bolivia to obtain weapons and money for their "anti-guerrilla" forces. Using connections he had developed in the drug world, Barbie also helped García Meza Tejada and his cronies skim sizeable profits from Bolivia's lucrative cocaine trade. "For the first time in history," one U.S. official remarked, "the cocaine trade had bought itself a government."[54]

García Meza's drug trafficking and human rights record eventually led to his government's international isolation. Even the newly elected conservative U.S. president, Ronald Reagan, kept his distance, aware of the regime's unsavory links to criminal circles. In August 1981, with the Bolivian economy in ruins, García Meza Tejada resigned, only to be succeeded by a series of equally inept and unpopular military governments. Finally, in October 1982, President General Guido Vildoso Calderón, facing a staggering foreign debt, 44-percent unemployment, and a rash of national strikes, stepped aside to let Siles Zuazo return from exile to begin the four-year term he was to have started in 1980.[55]

While in exile, Siles Zuazo had met on several occasions with French Ambassador Césaire. On one such visit, the sixty-eight-year-old president-in-exile listened intently as Césaire told him about the arrest warrant for Barbie that had been filed by the Lyon public prosecutor. Barbie was now wanted not only for war crimes but for crimes against humanity, including the 1943 deportation to Auschwitz of forty-four Jewish children from the Izieu orphanage.[56]

Once in power, Siles Zuazo moved swiftly with plans to "solve the Barbie problem." On December 30, he had Bolivia's comptroller, Jamie Urcullo, issue a summons instructing Barbie to settle a sizeable government loan that his company, Transmartíma Boliviana, had received twelve years earlier or else face arrest. It was a shrewd move, as it gave Siles Zuazo the opportunity to hold Barbie legally without involving the courts, which could potentially delay his expulsion.

In Washington, Justice and State officials were nervously watching developments in La Paz.[57] Already French and American journalists were raising questions about Barbie's postwar connection to U.S. intelligence, leaving American policymakers to fret about how honest they had to be about an issue that the Soviets and other critics of U.S. foreign policy would surely seize upon. For years, the Soviets had claimed that Nazi war criminals were active in NATO countries, but the United States had concealed this as "a matter of state policy."[58] Despite pressure from the State and Justice departments, the Pentagon remained opposed to making its past relationship with Barbie public. Meanwhile, the CIA was indecisive. While the CIA station in Paris counseled CIA Director William Casey on ways to explain away Barbie's use by the Counter Intelligence Corps (CIC) in the late 1940s, CIA General Counsel Stanley Sporkin was warning his boss that it was in America's interest for the CIA and the U.S. government to come clean and distance themselves from events that took place thirty years earlier. "We must all recognize," he told Casey, "that it was the documented policy of the United States to make pragmatic intelligence collection use of ex-Nazis after World War II, because we were retooling our capabilities to deal with a new enemy, the Soviet Union."[59] Washington, at least for the time being, chose to remain silent.

At first, Barbie ignored the summons to pay back the government loan, but the sheer impertinence of the demand soon got the better of him. On January 25, 1983, Barbie and his long-time friend and bodyguard, Alvaro de Castro, strode into the comptroller's office and began arguing with a junior functionary over the debt. When the civil servant demanded that it be paid in Bolivian pesos at the regular rate, Barbie countered that he would only repay it at the black market rate. Exasperated, the functionary slipped out of his office and returned with two policemen, who promptly placed Barbie under arrest and took him to San Pedro Prison, where he was charged with fraud and contravening immigration regulations.[60]

The day after his arrest, the Bolivian cabinet voted unanimously to expel the Nazi fugitive. After the French Embassy notified Paris of the decision, President François Mitterrand's secretary-general formed an ad hoc "Barbie group" to track Bolivia's future actions and named France's justice minister, Robert Badinter, as its leader. In 1943, during a raid on the Jewish welfare office in Lyon, Barbie had arrested Badinter's father and deported him to Auschwitz. Like the German prosecutor Fritz Bauer, who had doggedly pursued Adolf Eichmann, Badinter would play a pivotal role in securing Barbie's delivery to French justice.[61]

The French, having been denied an extradition request in 1974, encouraged Germany to increase its pressure on the Bolivians. They soon learned, however, that Bonn was having second thoughts about bringing the former Gestapo chief back to Germany. It was a federal election year, and a trial could potentially become a public embarrassment, especially if it provoked pro-Nazi demonstrations. Further, should a German court hand down a lighter sentence than it was expected a French one would, it might provoke anti-German sentiments in France.[62] Bonn also wanted to avoid the kind of international outcry that had greeted a recent trial in Dusseldorf of fifteen former camp guards from the Majdanek extermination camp. According to Barbie's biographer, Tom Bower, defense lawyers repeatedly called victim-witnesses "liars" and claimed that the camp's gas chambers "were not used for killing people, but for cleaning clothes."[63]

Despite these political considerations, Bonn pressed the Bolivian Interior Ministry to expedite Barbie's extradition. But there was a problem: Bolivia's high court was conspicuously delaying a decision on the matter, and without it, the ministry's hands were tied. In an attempt to break the impasse, the interior minister, Mario Roncal, summoned the French and German chargés d'affaires to his office. Barbie, he told them, had to be expelled from Bolivia, but *not* officially *extradited* to Germany. If everyone agreed, Roncol would personally ensure that Barbie was on the next Lufthansa flight to Frankfurt via Lima.[64] When the German diplomat consulted with his superiors later that day, however, he learned that Bonn no longer wanted Barbie to return to Germany.[65]

With the Germans out of the picture, the Barbie group in Paris hastened to formulate a new strategy—albeit a quasi-legal one—to bring Barbie to France. Since no extradition treaty existed between France and Bolivia, they would have to find a way to transport him out of Bolivia in a manner that would respect Bolivian sovereignty and appear as if La Paz were expelling him. Bolivian public opinion would also have to be prepared for what could potentially be a diplomatically dicey event.

Curiously, the morning after the meeting in Roncal's office, the *Agence France-Presse* ran a wire story applauding Bolivia's decision "to detain the war criminal Klaus Barbie" and hinting that his delivery to an unspecified European country would greatly "improve its relations with Europe" and lead to substantial aid to debt-strapped Bolivia.[66]

Two days later, on the fiftieth anniversary of Hitler's assumption of power, a Bolivian television station began airing a short film about Nazi atrocities, strategically placed after Bolivia's most popular *telenovela*. The Israeli ambassador had personally loaned the station footage of Nazi rallies in Nuremberg as well as scenes of the ovens and piles of corpses on the grounds of Auschwitz. On the lower-right side of the screen appeared an inset of Barbie in his Gestapo uniform and cap. The documentary ended with a commentary declaring that Barbie would soon meet the same fate as Adolf Eichmann.[67]

Barbie, though supposedly in solitary confinement and without access to the outside world, was well aware that he could be deported at any moment. Never one to sit on his hands, he was using Alvaro de Castro and his lawyer Constantino Carrión as intermediaries to rally support among his military and drug-dealing friends. As the weekend approached, articles and editorials began to appear in Bolivian newspapers lambasting Siles Zuazo's motives for expelling a Bolivian citizen without due process when it was the government's duty to protect him. A group of right-wing politicians railed in one article that the president was in effect "selling a Bolivian citizen" to the highest bidder. Even Zuazo's coalition partners publicly criticized him for failing to try Barbie in Bolivia for crimes committed there.[68]

On the morning of February 3, 1983, Barbie, perhaps fearing deportation was imminent, decided to settle his debt at the official exchange rate. He sent de Castro on his behalf to the comptroller's office with a suitcase filled to the brim with fifty-peso notes. As a group of functionaries gathered in the room, de Castro confidently placed the valise on the comptroller's desk, unaware that his interlocutor had another card up his sleeve. "They made me sit there and count it out," de Castro recalled. "Then they made me count it again. Finally it was paid, but then they said it wasn't enough, they wanted interest."[69]

As the sun rose the next day on a wet and windy Friday, diplomats at the French Embassy were already at their desks frantically fielding phone calls from Paris. A French military C-130 Hercules aircraft, disguised as belonging to a privately owned Bolivian airline, had landed at La Paz's military airport and was waiting to whisk Barbie away. Still, the Elysée was nervous. Rumors circulated that Siles Zuazo was now vacillating. Some of his advisors were urging him to expel Barbie to Paraguay, Brazil, or Peru, where Barbie was due before a magistrate in connection with currency dealing and, of all things, ballpoint-pen trafficking. If the Bolivian president chose any of these options, France would end up looking like penny-ante amateurs. To make matters worse, journalists were starting to swarm outside the French Embassy and San Pedro Prison.

Just after sunset, an official from the Bolivian Interior Ministry slipped pass the press at the prison gates and entered Barbie's cell. With the help of a prison guard, he placed a blanket over Barbie's head and led him to an unmarked van waiting at the back entrance to the prison. The van sped to La Paz's military airport, where Barbie was led to a VIP lounge and told he was being sent to Germany. Startled at first, he then smiled faintly, patted his pockets, and asked: "I haven't any money. How will I pay for my hotel room?"[70]

On board the C-130 Hercules were several tight-lipped French agents disguised as crew, a Bolivian television team, and three Bolivian policemen. Having no possessions of his own with him and still believing he was bound for Germany, he jokingly asked one of the TV journalists if he knew the price of razor blades in Germany.[71]

After seven hours, the Hercules touched down at Rochambeau Airport, near Cayenne, French Guyana. French officials escorted Barbie to a hangar, where a judge read out five charges involving 341 separate counts of "crimes against humanity" for the torture or deportation to extermination camps, or both, of 737 Jews and other victims, including the 44 Jewish children hidden in the village of Izieu. The number of victims named in the indictment represented only a fraction of the 4,342 *maquisards*, or French resistance fighters, that Barbie murdered or ordered murdered, and 7,591 French Jews that he deported to concentration camps in the Reich.[72]

Even so, it was an unprecedented moment—both legally and historically. In 1964 France had become the first country in Europe to take the Nuremberg concept of "crimes against humanity" and give it binding legal definition within its own penal code. This was done, in part, because France wanted to settle on a principled rationale for keeping dossiers on Nazis like Klaus Barbie open. The Nuremberg Charter and later French law held that a crime against humanity was by its very nature universal. As such, French justice, as Jane Kramer notes, "could claim Klaus Barbie in Bolivia because French justice did not recognize a distinction between Bolivia and France where Barbie's crimes were concerned. And it could claim him in 1983—or in 1993, for that matter— because humanity did not die with Barbie's victims. Legally speaking, humanity was always there to represent them."[73]

When the formalities were finished, Barbie was ushered onto a French military DC-8. Now visibly angered by the ruse, Barbie spoke on camera as the plane was prepared for takeoff. His expulsion, he complained, was completely illegal, a "kidnapping," plain and simple. He was like Napoleon, he said, who was condemned for his tyranny but later praised as a hero—as he, Klaus Barbie, would be some day.[74]

When the DC-8 landed the following morning at a military base in southeastern France, Barbie, handcuffed and attached to a nylon cord, was hustled to a Puma helicopter, which took him to a small air base south of Lyon, where he was escorted to a van with its windows darkened. The police convoy proceeded to Lyon's Fort Montluc, the same prison where, forty years before, the young SS *Hauptsturmführer* Klaus Barbie had nonchalantly strolled through its cellblocks, his thin smile always present, signaling with a casual wave of his hand who would be sent to the interrogation rooms, or to the execution yard.[75]

Barbie's trial commenced on May 11, 1983 in Lyon's Palace of Justice, its interior temporarily refurbished to accommodate the hundreds of people who had come for the opening day. Among the bevy of attorneys gathered in the courtroom was Serge Klarsfeld, there to represent over 120 of Barbie's Jewish victims, including the 44 children from the Izieu orphanage. On the third day, Barbie refused to appear in court on the grounds that he had been "illegally" extradited. The Criminal Chamber of the Court of Cassation, France's court of last resort, later rejected Barbie's motion for dismissal, arguing, rather convolutedly, that his arrest by the French in Cayenne was not an unlawfully "disguised" extradition but simply the execution of an arrest warrant, issued by a French judge and carried out on French territory, for a set of international crimes that were bound not "solely to French Municipal Law, but also to an international penal order," to which the rules of extradition applicable in common crimes were "fundamentally foreign."[76] For the rest of his trial, Barbie appeared only three more times—twice for witnesses to identify him, and at the end for the summation and sentencing.

On July 4, 1987, after four years and 23,000 pages of testimony—much of it dedicated to the suffering of Barbie's victims[77] and to the expiations of Barbie's sixty-two-year-old lawyer, Jacques Vergès, a French-Algerian Maoist, de facto anarchist, and future defense attorney for leaders of the Khmer Rouge—Barbie was sentenced to life imprisonment.[78]

Handcuffed and flanked by armed guards, the former Gestapo chief was driven to Lyon Prison, where he remained until his death, in September 1991, at the age of seventy-seven.

Barbie's trial opened a Pandora's Box in France, as would the subsequent trials of two Frenchmen, Paul Touvier (leader of a Vichy-run paramilitary group under the direction of Barbie, convicted in 1994) and Maurice Papon (a police official in the prefecture of Bordeaux, convicted in 1998). Serge and Beate Klarsfeld's son, Arno, was a lead prosecutor in both.

"The Barbie trial was for France like an abreaction in psychoanalysis, a single relived piece of a trauma that brings the other buried pieces back to life," cultural historian Alice Y. Kaplan wrote in 1992.[79] The cathartic lid was first opened when victim-witnesses began taking the stand at Barbie's trial. Many told wrenching stories of the four years of German Occupation, and how their neighbors—French men and women like themselves—watched, fearful and silent, while the Gestapo and their Vichy collaborators broke into their homes or nabbed them on the street in broad daylight. Some had been sent to Fort Montluc and other prisons because they fought or supported the Resistance, while others had been packed into concentration camp convoys because they were Jews. Either way, much of the pent-up anger of these survivors, often expressed with mutterings of disbelief and head shaking, was directed not only at Barbie but at Vichy France and its hushed majority, the "bystanders" who were neither active collaborators nor active resisters.[80] Until then, Vichy had been a subject the French usually avoided, preferring instead to revel in a past that corroborated and confirmed an idea of France's collective resistance to the Occupation, one peopled with heroic resistance fighters and the brave and resourceful souls who hid and nurtured them.

Barbie's trial was a huge media event in France. Writes Kaplan: "If you went to the dentist in June or July 1987, you talked about the Barbie trial. If you went to the coiffeur, you talked about the Barbie trial, if you read the newspapers, you read about the Barbie trial; and if you sat at the family dinner table, chances are you talked about the Barbie trial, whether you lived in low income housing in the northern suburbs of Paris or in a chateau in Sologne."[81]

And, as trials often do, it brought out the best and the worst in the media. On the positive side, French editors and columnists finally began grappling with topics that hitherto had been taboo. In May 1983, days after the trial commenced, Le Monde reprinted the full text of the Jewish Statute of October 3, 1940, signed by Vichy head of state Philippe Pétain and his ministers, stripping Jews of their professions, their civil service positions, and their military status. One of the thorniest topics for discussion was the immediate postwar years and the difficulty many French had accepting the three thousand Jews who had survived the death camps and returned, penniless and dispossessed, to France.[82] Known as the "zebra men," they were welcomed, in Alice Kaplan's words, not "as heroes but as embarrassing reminders of France's shame and guilt during the Occupation."[83] Conversely, "revisionists" began holding press conferences and writing articles claiming, contrary to what the survivors were saying in the Lyon courtroom, that there had been no Holocaust, no camps or crematoriums, and that the so-called "extermination" of six million Jews was merely a Jewish invention intended to destabilize Europe and perform what one revisionist called "the circumcision of Aryan man."[84]

NAZI WAR CRIMINALS IN AMERICA

In the United States, the popular media, so often incapable of thinking historically, might not have paid much attention to the Barbie trial had it not been for a retired Wayne State University professor named Erhard Dabringhaus. The evening after Barbie's expulsion from Bolivia, Dabringhaus happened to be watching the *NBC Nightly News* when a familiar face from his past flickered across the screen. It took a minute, but then it came to him: Klaus Barbie was one of the paid informants he had known while he was a CIC officer stationed in Austria during the war. Dabringhuas immediately called the local NBC station in Detroit. At first, the reporters thought he was a crank, but after a day checking his bona fides, they took him seriously and punted the story to headquarters in New York, where it went national the following night.[85]

Dabringhaus's revelations caught the attention of Congresswoman Elizabeth Holtzman of New York, who had been elected to the House of Representatives in 1972 at the age of thirty-one. As the youngest woman to serve in the U.S. Congress and a Jew, Holtzman had encountered her share of discrimination, but it had also turned her into a tenacious fighter. Her position on the Immigration Subcommittee of the Judiciary Committee brought her into regular contact with staff at the Immigration and Naturalization Service (INS). On one such occasion, a middle-ranking official had made an offhand remark that the agency had a list of Nazi war criminals living in America and was doing nothing about them. Months later, in a hearing with the INS commissioner, Holtzman inquired whether the INS kept a list of Nazi war criminals living in the United States.

"Yes," he answered.

"How many names are on the list?" she asked.

"Fifty-three," he replied.

Days later, Holtzman went to the INS office and discovered that the agency had not only a list of Nazi criminals but *actual files* on each of the fifty-three fugitives, complete with details about the crimes they had reportedly committed.[86]

Holtzman remembers looking up from the stack of INS files and thinking: "So what does America stand for? If we stand for human rights and justice and respect for human life, then how [can we] allow mass murderers to come here and escape justice? And how can we tell another country in the world that we stand for human rights if we allow these people to stay here unpunished, giving them immunity and impunity? So I felt I had to do something about it."[87]

Perusing U.S. newspapers, Holtzman and her staff found that the pasts of only a handful of the fifty-three fugitives had been exposed in the United States, largely through the efforts of *Newsday* and the *New York Times*. Among them were a Manhattan housewife and former concentration camp guard who had been convicted of mass murder and later amnestied in Austria; a Catholic priest living in Michigan who had organized anti-Jewish pogroms in Bucharest; and the commander of an Estonian concentration camp, living in a Long Island suburb.[88]

In 1977, Holtzman, with the backing of Senator Edward Moore "Ted" Kennedy, succeeded in passing groundbreaking legislation that gave the INS authority not only to deport Nazis and their collaborators but also to refuse their admission to the United States. In pushing the legislation through, Holtzman relied on two Government Accounting Office studies, which had found that since the end of World War II only two Nazi war criminals had been expelled from the United States and that several federal agencies had even employed Nazi suspects. Known as the Holtzman Amendment, the bill required that those entering the United States declare whether they had been involved, in any way, "in persecutions associated with Nazi Germany and its Allies."[89]

Two years later, Attorney General Michael J. Egan announced that the INS unit with jurisdiction to pursue Nazi cases would be transferred to the Department of Justice and renamed the Office of Special Investigations (OSI). Based in the Criminal Division, the OSI began with a paltry annual budget of $2.3 million and "was assigned the responsibility for carrying out all of the investigative and prosecutorial activities of the Department involving individuals who, in association with the Nazi Government of Germany and its Allies, ordered, incited, assisted, or otherwise participated in the persecution of any person because of race, religion, national origin, or political opinion between 1933 and 1945."[90]

Shortly after Erhard Dabringhaus's February 1983 appearance on the NBC evening news, Holtzman, along with Judiciary Committee Chairman Peter Rodino, pressed the U.S. attorney general, William French

Smith, to open an official inquiry into U.S. involvement in the Barbie case. At first Smith objected, arguing that an investigation would be of only historic interest and thus not worth the time and cost. After substantial pressure, he relented and, in March 1983, appointed OSI director Allan Ryan Jr. to investigate the U.S. government's relationship with Barbie.[91]

Four and a half months later, Ryan presented Smith a 218-page report, together with a massive 680-page appendix of official documents. Ryan concluded that, as we saw in chapter 3, in 1951 agents from the CIC had paid the Croatian priest Krunoslav Draganovic to smuggle Barbie to South America so that he could avoid arrest by the French authorities. This was undertaken with the full knowledge that Draganovic, as a CIC memo notes, was "known and recorded as a Fascist, war criminal etc., and his contacts with South American diplomats of a similar class are not generally approved by US State Department officials."[92] Still, the CIC ignored these traits because it realized that Draganovic's so-called "welfare organization for displaced persons" was a perfect cover: "We will be able to state, if forced, that the turning over of a DP [displaced person, such as Barbie] to a Welfare Organization falls in line with our democratic way of thinking and that we are not engaged in illegal disposition of war criminals, defectees and the like."[93] Ryan also posited that the "CIC may have been involved in—at least it contemplated the possibility of—assisting Draganovic with the escape of Croatian war criminals."[94] Either way, Ryan noted, the money the CIC paid Draganovic for assisting with the escape of Barbie and others, in turn, paid for Croatian fugitives.[95]

The U.S. government could not "disclaim responsibility" for the actions of the CIC agents who helped Barbie escape to South America, Ryan argued in the report's cover letter. "It is a principle of democracy and the rule of law that justice delayed is justice denied. If we are to be faithful to that principle—and we should be faithful to it—we cannot pretend that it applies only within our borders and nowhere else. We have delayed justice in Lyon."[96]

Ryan's investigation of the Barbie case marked the first time that the postwar relationship between U.S. intelligence agencies and the defeated Nazis was explored officially and publicly. In Germany the *Stuttgarter Zeitung* observed that the United States showed "a powerful and impressive capacity of democratic self-purging,"[97] while the Moscow World Service called the U.S.–Barbie connection "a miserable and shameful spectacle."[98] On a more literary note, cultural historian Alice Y. Kaplan wrote: "Allan

Ryan's Department of Justice report on Barbie, neither apologetic nor vindictive, has a lucid calm and a sad wisdom one doesn't expect in a government document; the sadness it exudes, in particular, comes from the unveiling of an American intelligence bureaucracy that is not so much wrong as it is naïve and entirely ignorant of its own criminality."[99]

Yet for all its revelations, Ryan's limited mandate prevented him from going beyond the particulars of the Barbie case to probe the larger question: *how* was it possible that so many Nazi war criminals and their collaborators (Ryan himself believes that number could not be "less than 10,000 people"[100]) had managed to escape postwar justice and come to settle in the United States. In the late 1970s and the 1980s, a handful of investigative journalists (foremost among them Linda Hunt, Tom Bower, and Mike Wallace) had begun the process of unearthing U.S. and British intelligence records on the Nazi–American intelligence connection,[101] but it wasn't until the late 1990s that a fuller picture would evolve. Spurred on by Senator Michael DeWine of Ohio and Congresswoman Caroline Maloney of New York, in 1988 Congress passed the Nazi War Crimes Disclosure Act. The law obliged the CIA, the U.S. Army, and the FBI to declassify operational information on their recruitment of former Nazis and Axis collaborators in the early Cold War years. It also created a new organization, the Nazi War Criminal and Japanese Imperial Government Records Interagency Working Group (IWG), to implement and oversee what turned into the largest targeted declassification effort in American history.[102]

For five years, a small group of IWG consultant historians hunkered down in the U.S. National Archives in Maryland to examine a large portion of the eight million pages of newly declassified government records—on everything from Nazi espionage, to Vichy French investment funds in the United States, to Vatican policies toward the Ustasha. The IWG historians concentrated not on military intelligence (as most writers did) but on political intelligence, the seemingly prosaic information that often slipped by in the war and immediate postwar years but illuminates, in their words, "a different facet of American policy—a cold war where *Realpolitik* trumped idealism, where the primary aim was the acquisition of raw information, and where secrets often served the most practical of ends."[103] Their book, *U.S. Intelligence and the Nazis*, along with a shorter volume, *Hitler's Shadow: Nazi War Criminals, U.S. Intelligence, and the Cold War*, represents the most authoritative and comprehensive account to date of Allied protection and use of war criminals and their postwar activities.[104]

The IWS historians reached four major conclusions about the U.S. government's knowledge of Nazi atrocities and the relationship of its intelligence agencies to Nazi war criminals and their collaborators. First, the unclassified documents the historians examined revealed that American and Allied intelligence agencies were aware of the nature and scope of German atrocities against European Jewry as early as September 1941, and that by 1942 some senior American intelligence officers "grasped that Nazi measures amounted to a state policy of full-blown extermination."[105] While the British conducted some studies of concentration and extermination camps during the war years, the Americans chose not to examine the Final Solution or any of its components, from shooting operations to extermination camps. Priority was given instead to military information and analysis that, it was believed, could help shorten the war. The Soviets, in the meantime, amassed enormous amounts of witness testimony and physical evidence of bona fide Nazi crimes committed on their soil.[106]

Why did the U.S. intelligence community avoid, or fail to pay attention to, the Holocaust and other Nazi crimes? "American intelligence agencies," the IWS historians concluded, "did not view World War II and the Holocaust as closely related." While American spy networks gathered vast amounts of intelligence in the Nazi-occupied territories and satellite countries, they made no special efforts "to secure information about the fate of the Jews in occupied Europe until President Roosevelt established the War Refugee Board in January 1944." This failure, the historians said, had "less to do with the intelligence community's ability to collect information than with recognizing its significance."[107]

Still, the American intelligence community was not entirely in the dark about Nazi atrocities. Old and new documents of the U.S. Office of Strategic Services (OSS), the forerunner of the CIA, suggest that at least some high OSS officials comprehended the range of Nazi crimes but chose to downplay their significance because they believed Washington wasn't interested. Allen Dulles, the OSS station chief in Bern, Switzerland, during the war and later the first director of the CIA, received regular reports on Nazi crimes, from mass shootings to the creation of the Jewish ghettos. But Dulles never pressed for this information to be made public, largely because he knew that the State Department believed that too much attention to Nazi killings of Jews would increase the ardor of the World Jewish Congress and other Jewish organizations that were already pressing for rescue operations and relaxed immigration quotas for Jews, at a time when many Americans opposed increased immigration.[108]

Hindsight allows us to see that the U.S. intelligence community's failure to study the Final Solution in any significant way and its failure to encourage broadcast of what it knew of the Final Solution also undermined postwar investigations of Nazi war crimes suspects. With no clear understanding of the Third Reich's command structure and how it was intertwined with the organization of concentration and extermination camps, the SS *Einsatzgruppen* (mobile killing squads), and the German police brigades sent in to exterminate Jewish enclaves in rural Poland, Allied investigators were ill prepared for the task of linking specific suspects to massive crimes.

Second, the IWS historians concluded, the declassified files revealed "no overarching policy by American intelligence agencies [to target] known SS or Gestapo officers" for employment as Cold War spies. Instead, U.S. intelligence offices and CIC units opportunistically hired such Nazis and Nazi collaborators on a case-by-case basis. That said, the IWS historians rejected the notion that American use of actual or alleged war criminals was "limited to the infamous Klaus Barbie . . . or a few bad apples."[109]

The IWS historians, perhaps far too charitably, attributed American undercover operations to protect and, in some cases, help Nazi fugitives-cum-operatives escape from Europe as "blunders" and "misjudgments" made by individual intelligence officers in their overly zealous pursuit of Cold War intelligence. Eager to satisfy Washington's rapacious appetite for information, some intelligence officials "could not or did not want to" scrutinize the past activities of former SS officers and police and the non-German collaborators in their employ. Many Nazi war criminals exploited this susceptibility, successfully "casting themselves as highly knowledgeable intelligence men with caches of vital information rather than as thugs, killers, and incompetents."[110] Consider the former Nazi prosecutor Manfred Roeder, who as late as 1952 dazzled his CIC handlers with tales of hidden intelligence records that never materialized. Or Reinhard Gehlen, the Major General of the Wehrmacht, who in the postwar years hired, with U.S. funding, scores of former Gestapo and Waffen-SS into his CIA-backed intelligence-gathering organization but, according to the IWS historians, was "wrong on every prediction he made concerning the Red Army."[111]

Once ensconced in American intelligence organizations, these men generally found protection from criminal prosecution. In 1949, the CIC, as we have seen, refused to turn over Klaus Barbie to stand trial for war crimes in France. Army intelligence extended the same courtesy to Hermann Julius Höfle, a paid informant and former member of the murderous police auxiliaries (*Selbschutzführer*) and head of a labor camp for Jews near Belzec in southeastern Poland, who was wanted by the Polish government for war crimes. In the declassified CIA records the IWS historians found evidence of the agency's direct relations with at least thirty former Axis war criminals, including Sicherheitsdienst officer Otto von Bolschwing and Ukrainian nationalist Mikola Lebed, who were rewarded for their work with U.S. citizenship. FBI records revealed that J. Edgar Hoover ignored reports that several Eastern European informants his agency employed in the United States in the 1950s were war criminals. On the contrary, the FBI chief regarded them as useful assets "in the global struggle against Communism" because they were pressing an anti-communist line in their own émigré communities while reporting subversion from within those same communities.[112]

A third finding of the IWS historians was that American intelligence agencies had learned very little from the stable of Nazis and Nazi collaborators they hired. The CIC paid the Croatian priest Krunoslav Draganovic handsomely, but all it got in return were "sheaves of useless and false material." Reinhard Gehlen not only bilked the U.S. Army of half a million dollars during the American occupation, but he also had the habit of snarling at his handlers whenever they complained about their poor return on investment. All in all, it was the worst sort of Faustian bargain: so much given, so little gained.[113]

Fourth and finally, the IWS historians concluded that the embarrassment to the United States created by taking on these Cold War assets continued long after the intelligence relationships had ended. Barbie's removal to France in 1983 to stand trial for crimes against humanity, coupled with the revelation that the CIC had helped him escape to South America, was a massive blow to American prestige, as was news of the OSI discovery that two CIA assets-cum-war criminals, Otto von Bolschwing and Mykola Lebed, were residing comfortably in the United States. All of this, according to the IWG historians, "provided grist for active Communist propaganda mills while eroding much of the moral high ground that had been won by U.S. leadership in prosecuting Nazis" in the immediate postwar years. In hindsight, wrote the IWG historians, the government's use of Nazis was reprehensible, and "there was no compelling reason to begin the postwar era with the assistance of some of those associated with [the] worst crimes of the war."[114]

According to all accounts, however, the vast majority of Nazi and other Axis war criminals fleeing Europe in the immediate aftermath of World

War II had no connection to American or Allied intelligence agencies. Most simply emigrated as refugees to South America, the Middle East, and the four largest Anglo-Saxon democracies (the United States, Canada, Australia, and Great Britain), slipping through the receiving country's immigration vetting process, which was often lax, and beginning new lives for themselves and their families far from the scene of their crimes. It also helped that many were fleeing from Eastern European countries (Lithuania, Estonia, Belarus, Ukraine, Croatia) that had recently fallen under communist control. Many, if not most, kept their given names, largely because they assumed that their participation in crimes would never be discovered in their homelands, let alone investigated in their new countries of residence.[115]

And they were usually right on both assumptions, at least for a time. For example, in the thirty-four years between the end of World War II and the establishment of the OSI in 1979, only one Nazi war criminal was denaturalized (Hermine Braunsteiner-Ryan), and she and just one other Nazi war criminal (Ferenc Vajta) were removed from the United States. Moreover, a report released in 2015 by the Social Security Administration's inspector general revealed that during this same period more than 130 United States citizens linked to Nazi atrocities received millions of dollars in Social Security benefits.[116] Yet once the OSI was established and began working effectively, the situation changed dramatically.

By 2009, the OSI had opened over 1,500 investigations of suspected Nazi and other Axis war criminals. Of these, the office had won civil proceedings against 107 individuals, 86 of whom had been denaturalized and 66 removed from the United States. More than two-thirds of these proceedings were initiated by OSI investigators and not, as is commonly portrayed in novels and films, from tips from Nazi-hunters like Simon Wiesenthal or victims who encountered and recognized their former tormentors in the United States. All but a handful of the remaining proceedings were based on referrals from European governments and U.S. government agencies.[117]

Unlike the traditional "gumshoe" detective work conducted in domestic criminal cases, the OSI relied on a group of staff historians, who sifted through surviving fragments of Nazi documentation and related records to reconstruct the wartime whereabouts and activities of suspects under investigation. In the 1990s, as communist rule dissolved, the OSI was able to gain tens of thousands of archival records previously sealed by the former Soviet Union and its satellite countries. As a result, in 1994 the OSI filed civil proceedings against seven alleged Nazis and

Axis war criminals residing in the United States, the highest single-year total in a decade.[118]

Since 1979 the OSI has compiled a "watch list" for the Department of State and, later, the Department of Homeland Security, of nearly 70,000 "lookouts," men and women from former Axis countries who may have been involved in war crimes. The list contains fewer than 100 names of Japanese perpetrators, largely because the Japanese government has declined to provide the OSI access to pertinent information in its archives. As a result of their own research, the OSI has added the names of members of the Japanese Army's infamous Unit 731, which conducted lethal medical experiments on prisoners of war captured on China's Manchurian Plain, as well as Japanese military personnel implicated in the operation of "comfort women" stations, where non-Japanese women were forced into prostitution for Japanese soldiers.[119]

Kurt Waldheim, the former Austrian president and UN secretary-general, is one of the best-known names to have appeared on the OSI watch list. In 1987, five years after he concluded his term at the United Nations, Waldheim was banned from entering the United States because an OSI investigation revealed that he had lied about his wartime service in the German army. Waldheim had claimed that he had ceased active military service after being wounded in December 1941 and had spent the rest of the war as a law student. Yet the OSI discovered a photograph of Waldheim taken in Yugoslavia in May 1943 dressed in his German uniform and standing next to Artur Phleps, the commander of the notorious Prinz Eugen Division. Far from studying the law, Waldheim was serving as the head of the division's intelligence branch, which had participated in the extermination of tens of thousands of Sephardic Jews in northern Greece. The OSI's discovery led to a clash with Simon Wiesenthal, who, though aware of Waldheim's service in the Prinz Eugen Division, had deliberately avoided investigating his fellow Austrian's war conduct.[120]

Over the years, the Justice Department has petitioned for the deportation or denaturalization of dozens of former Nazis and their collaborators residing in the United States. In doing so, the department has had to meet a high standard of proof, demonstrating "clear, unequivocal and convincing evidence that does not leave the issue in doubt" that a person being deported is in fact guilty of war crimes, a standard that the Supreme Court has ruled is "substantially identical" to the beyond a reasonable doubt standard applied in criminal trials.[121]

Among the suspects pursued by the OSI in the United States was Arthur Rudolph, a former German rocket engineer and operations director of the V-2 missile factory at Dora-Nordhausen, for his treatment of slave labor. After World War II, he was brought to the United States under Operation Paperclip, the U.S. intelligence program, noted in chapter 2, which brought more than 1,600 German scientists and medical researchers to America under secret military contracts. Many of these scientists, like Rudolph, continued their weapons-related work for the U.S. government, developing long-range missiles, sarin gas cluster bombs, weaponized bubonic plague, aviation and space medicine (for enhancing pilot and astronaut performance), and many other armaments at a mind-boggling pace that came to define the Cold War. The rationale was that if America didn't recruit these scientists, the Soviets surely would.[122]

In late 1946, a week after the Nuremberg convictions were announced, the *New York Times* blew the cover on Operation Paperclip, revealing that 233 German scientists were already in the United States and more than a thousand more were on their way.[123] One of the program's most strident critics was former First Lady Eleanor Roosevelt, who urged the U.S. government to suspend visas for all Germans for twelve years.[124] In early February 1947, the Federation of American Scientists met in New York City to ask President Truman to terminate the program. One of its members, Albert Einstein, who had fled to the United States after Hitler came to power, wrote an impassioned letter on behalf of his colleagues in the federation, directly appealing to President Truman to stop Operation Paperclip. "We hold these individuals to be potentially dangerous," he wrote. "Their former eminence as Nazi Party members and supporters raises the issue of their fitness to become American citizens and hold key positions in American industrial, scientific and educational institutions."[125] But such appeals fell on deaf ears.

While in the United States, Rudolph worked for the U.S. Army and NASA, where he helped develop the Pershing missile and the Saturn V moon rocket, for which he received NASA's Distinguished Service Medal. In late 1983, Allan Ryan and another OSI prosecutor confronted Rudolph with evidence of his crimes at the Dora camp. Rudolph agreed to leave the United States and renounced his U.S. citizenship. He was never tried in Germany for his wartime activities; he died in Hamburg in January 1996, at the age of eighty-nine.[126]

Another Nazi war crimes suspect found residing in the United States was John Demjanjuk, whose case remains a *cause célèbre* of OSI opponents like American politician Pat Buchanan, who criticizes the expenditure of public funds to investigate aging Central European immigrants about their alleged participation in crimes committed over sixty years ago.[127] The Demjanjuk case also serves as a cautionary tale about the reliability of witness testimony decades after the commission of crimes.

A native Ukranian who became an Ohio autoworker after World War II, Demjanjuk was stripped of his U.S. citizenship in 1981 and deported to Israel, where witnesses and a Soviet-supplied identity card identified him as Ivan the Terrible, a sadist who murdered thousands of Jews at the Treblinka death camp. In 1988, an Israeli court, in its one and only Nazi war crimes proceeding since the Eichmann trial in 1961, convicted Demjanjuk of crimes against humanity and sentenced him to death. But five years later, the Israeli Supreme Court overturned the conviction when new evidence showed that the identity card was probably a KGB fake and that another Ukrainian—a larger and older man— was probably the notorious Ivan. Back in the United States, Demjanjuk regained his U.S. citizenship, only to have it revoked again when new allegations arose.[128]

Deported to Germany in 2009, Demjanjuk, eighty-eight and suffering from bone-marrow and kidney diseases, was tried and convicted in Munich in 2011 for having served as a guard at the Sobibór extermination camp in German-occupied Poland, where 27,900 Jews perished. The Munich court sentenced him to five years but, given his age and illnesses, ordered him sent to a nursing home, where he died a year later at the age of ninety-one.[129]

Demjanjuk spent most of the trial lying on a gurney or propped in a wheelchair, his eyes closed or idly staring into space. Duty rosters proved that he had served in Sobibór from March to September 1943 and that the SS had trained him for such service at the Trawniki concentration camp, a forced-labor camp and training center for auxiliary police guards near Lublin, Poland. However, not one surviving witness, including those shown photographs, could place Demjanjuk at the Sobibór camp. The trial evidence consisted of an SS card purported to be Demjanjuk's, and written orders of his superiors ordering him to work at the camp.

Prosecutors did not present evidence that Demjanjuk committed a specific crime. Instead, the case was based on the theory that Demjanjuk had been part of a "joint criminal enterprise" by acting as a guard. The fact that Demjanjuk wore a uniform and was armed with a rifle meant, in this legal doctrine, that he was as guilty as someone who threw the switch to turn on the gas. "Simply being where the killing took place [is] enough for a conviction," commented Kurt Schrimm of Germany's Central Judicial Office for the Investigation of Nazi Crimes.[130]

Not everyone supports applying "joint criminal enterprise" to past cases. D. W. de Mildt, a professor at the University of Amsterdam and co-editor of *Nazi Crimes on Trial*,[131] a compendium of trials in Germany, questions the assumption that "being part of a complex makes one automatically guilty." He also questions the German government's newfound ardor for targeting death-camp guards like Demjanjuk: "Why didn't they do anything before? Why now, all of a sudden?"[132]

Within days of the Demjanjuk ruling, Germany's Central Office for the Investigation of Nazi Crimes broadened the scope of its investigations of some 6,000 guards who served at the Auschwitz death camp between 1940 and 1945, most of whom are deceased. By late 2013, German prosecutors had located more than forty former Auschwitz guards and planned to recommend charges against most of them.[133] But by 2015 it became evident that, in light of their advanced age, no more than a few of the suspects would ever face trial.

Still, the legal opening made possible by this watershed conviction spurred the Simon Wiesenthal Center in 2013 to launch a poster campaign in major German cities to elicit information about other Nazi fugitives who, like Demjanjuk, have spent their lives hiding in plain sight. With the phrase "late, but not too late" standing out against a grim photograph of the railroad tracks leading to the entrance of Auschwitz, the posters appealed to the citizenry not to turn their backs on the pursuit of accountability for the Holocaust.

German prosecutors are in a race against time. And it is one they are losing. While the 2011 Demjanjuk verdict paved the way for future prosecutions of Nazi concentration camp guards and other lower-level functionaries, hardly any are still alive. "And this," writes Elizabeth Kolbert, "makes it difficult to know how to feel about the latest wave of investigations. Is it a final reckoning with German guilt, or just the opposite? What does it say about the law's capacity for self-correction that the correction came only when it no longer really matters?"[134]

"LATE, BUT NOT TOO LATE"

"Like mirrors of morality," writes Norman Goda, a former member of the IWS group of historians, "manhunts [of war crimes suspects] cast a poor light on nations that shelter criminals and a more benevolent glow on those that work for their capture. While satisfying an intrinsic need for judicial reckoning, manhunts also have a broader cultural meaning, which reflects their own time as well as a more painful past."[135]

Goda's insight takes on added meaning when we consider that the shadow of the Nazi period is quickly receding. Many Nazi and other Axis war criminals have died or are nearing the end of their lifetimes. So, too, are their pursuers: in September 2005, Simon Wiesenthal died in his sleep at the age of ninety-six. Five years later, his postwar collaborator and sometime sparring partner, Tuviah Friedman, died, at eighty-eight, at his home in Haifa, Israel. Still very much alive, but now in their late seventies, Serge and Beate Klarsfeld have begun to slow down. Gone are the days when Beate Klarsfeld mounted podiums to slap German politicians with unsavory Nazi pasts or traveled as a tourist to South American republics to harangue Nazi-harboring dictators.

Still, the pursuit of Nazi war criminals continues, through the work of the U.S. Department of Justice, German prosecutors, a number of government agencies around the world, and even some self-described Nazi-hunters, the most prominent being Efraim Zuroff, the Israeli director of the Simon Wiesenthal Center and a former OSI researcher. Based in Jerusalem, the American-born Zuroff helps prosecutors track down and try aging Nazi war criminals living freely around the world. Zuroff says it has now become "almost impossible" to see a case through from arrest to trial to conviction.[136] In an effort to console himself, he assesses effectiveness not only by the number of Nazi suspects brought to trial but also by how well the pursuit of suspects challenges Holocaust denial and keeps the memory of the Holocaust alive.

In 2002, Zuroff and the Wiesenthal Center launched Operation Last Chance, a program that offers cash rewards of $25,000 or more for information leading to the capture of the remaining Nazi war criminals and their Axis collaborators. Like the Klarsfelds', Zuroff's activism has been global in scope and often confrontational. When governments balk at arrests, he often goes on the offensive, exposing the identity and whereabouts of particular suspects and condemning state inaction. Zuroff has also sought to bolster his leverage by shaming uncooperative states (while recognizing cooperative ones) through issuing yearly grades, from A to F, to countries for their efforts in capturing and prosecuting World War II war crimes suspects.[137]

Since 2001, the center has consistently awarded the United States an A, its highest rating. Such progress notwithstanding, by late 2013 at least ten suspected Nazi war criminals ordered deported by the United

States remained there because their countries of origin have refused to accept them.[138] And even when countries accept deportees, domestic criminal prosecutions are by no means guaranteed.

On the other end of Zuroff's grading scale is Austria, which since 2001 has received D or F ratings. In the 1960s and '70s Austria held isolated trials, but the verdicts were criticized as a mockery of justice. Among those tried was Franz Novak, an SS member and aide to Adolf Eichmann who coordinated the railroad deportation of European Jews to concentration and extermination camps. After a series of trials, Austria's Supreme Court in 1972 finally sentenced Novak to seven years of imprisonment, but the verdict was appealed, during which time he was granted a pardon by Austrian President Rudolf Kirchschläger. Since then, more than twenty WWII cases have languished in the Austria courts, prompting Zuroff to call Austria "a paradise for Nazi war criminals."[139] This criticism was reinforced when Austria in 2008 refused to extradite to Croatia Milivoj Asner, who was implicated in the deportation of hundreds of Jews and Serbs.

In pursuit of Nazi suspects, Zuroff has closely scrutinized suspects from Eastern Europe, particularly from the Baltic and Balkan states, who participated directly in the mass murder of Jews. He has sought to expose those East European states, such as Lithuania, Latvia, Estonia, Croatia, and Hungary, that helped Hitler carry out the Final Solution. In Lithuania, as in its Baltic neighbors, Latvia and Estonia, national complicity in the effort to eradicate Jews led to the murder of more than 95 percent of their respective Jewish communities.[140] In Lithuania, the murdered Jews included Zuroff's great-uncle, his wife, and two sons. Bringing collaborationist war crimes suspects from the Baltics to justice has proved difficult, particularly in Lithuania, where the political establishment has trumpeted a national narrative of the World War II years that highlights the country's victimization at the hands of the Soviet occupiers while disavowing the state's direct role in massacring tens of thousands of Jews.[141] Lithuanian denial has even found expression in the state's post–Cold War campaign to rehabilitate the reputations of prominent Lithuanian citizens of the World War II era who were implicated in the murder of Jews.[142]

A crucial factor in the quest to bring war crimes suspects to trial is international pressure, Zuroff suggests. Not long after Lithuania, Latvia, and Estonia won independence from the Soviet Union in 1991, they sought membership in the European Union and other important Western institutions. That desire might have been—but wasn't—used as leverage by the West to compel prosecutions of Nazi collaborators, Zuroff points out.[143]

In contrast to the stonewalling Zuroff faced in the Baltics, further south, in the Balkans, he experienced his greatest success in helping to bring a Nazi collaborator to justice. In October 1999 in the Croatian capital of Zagreb, Dinko Sakic—a seventy-eight-year-old Croatian man implicated in the murder of thousands of Jews and Serbs while serving as a commandant at the infamous Jasenovac concentration camp, "the Auschwitz of the Balkans"—was found guilty and given the maximum sentence of twenty years in prison. The trial was the most important post–Cold War domestic effort to hold criminally accountable a Nazi war crimes suspect in a former Eastern European communist country.

Sakic's trial was the culmination of years of effort that began in June 1995 when Zuroff received a tip about Sakic's role in Jasenovac from a Serbian curator of the Museum of Genocide Victims in Belgrade. Zuroff eventually learned that Sakic was living in Santa Teresita, a seaside resort town on the Argentinian coast. The next hurdle was to persuade the right-wing Croatian President Franjo Tudjman to have Sakic extradited and prosecuted in Croatia. As a nationalist who led Croatia to independence in 1991, Tudjman had long maintained that Jewish prisoners had actually operated the Jasenovac concentration camp and that the six-million figure for the number of Jews murdered in the Holocaust had been grossly exaggerated.[144] But international pressure eventually prodded the Croatian president to seek Sakic's extradition. Tudjman proved to be susceptible to such pressure for two main reasons. First, Croatia's bid to establish diplomatic relations with Israel, which was also seen as a stepping-stone to improved relations with Europe, hinged on making amends for the state's treatment of Jews during World War II.[145] Second, Western diplomats had signaled that Croatia's emerging bid for membership in coveted institutions such as the EU might be enhanced not only by handing over war crimes suspects to the UN International Criminal Tribunal for the former Yugoslavia, but also by undertaking domestic prosecutions of those with blood on their hands from the World War II era.[146]

LOOKING BACK TO THE FUTURE

If the seven decades since the end of World War II have taught us anything, it is that governments must work collaboratively in their pursuit of war crimes suspects if large-scale success is to be achieved. This means changing antiquated extradition laws, allocating adequate law enforcement and judicial resources, and revealing past intelligence blunders, as well as remedying and apologizing for past mistakes. As the rigorous work of the IWS historians makes clear, it is also important to expose cover-ups by requiring full disclosure of government records as they pertain to war crimes, including those concerned with intelligence.[147] For example, German academic researchers and journalists played a critical role in forcing the BND, Germany's foreign intelligence agency, to examine its past links to remnants of the Third Reich. It has long been known that around 10 percent of BND staff once served under SS chief Heinrich Himmler in Nazi Germany. In 2011, historians conducting an internal study of the links between BND employees and former SS and Gestapo officers found that in 2007 the agency had destroyed the personnel files of around 250 BND officials. *Der Spiegel* discovered in the late 1990s, for example, that the agency had shredded a 581-page file on Alois Brunner, SS officer and commander of the notorious Drancy internment camp outside of Paris, who later fled to Syria, fueling speculation that he had worked for the BND and was being protected by senior German officials.[148]

Revealing past cover-ups, as the experience of the United States in the early 1980s underscores, can act as a political catalyst to tackle related challenges. Disclosure of the role of the CIC in protecting Klaus Barbie, for example, spurred Congress to establish the OSI.[149] Vatican records, if ever opened, could reveal the degree to which Church officials helped Nazi and Ustasha war criminals after the Second World War. The opening of official files still kept secret in Argentina, Bolivia, Brazil, Paraguay, and Chile could illuminate the role past regimes played in hiding Holocaust perpetrators. And there is still much to be learned from unreleased British records on its intelligence activities in postwar Germany. As history repeatedly reminds us, we must constantly reckon with the past to unravel the Gordian Knot of the present.

The successes as well as the failures in the long-running pursuit of World War II–era suspects point to the crucial role of the political determination of states, sometimes spurred on by specific individuals and institutions inside or outside of government, to bring perpetrators of war crimes to light, to order arrests, and to facilitate credible trials. In the aftermath of the Allied-run Nuremberg and Tokyo military tribunals, criminal accountability for World War II atrocities was left to individual states. In sharp contrast to the German government, which has made atonement for its Nazi past a priority, albeit belatedly, Japan has held no trials in the decades since the end of the U.S. occupation of the country in the early 1950s. Japanese leaders continue to sidestep moral responsibility for wartime atrocities. Moreover, in recent years, some Japanese prime ministers have turned visits to a Tokyo shrine honoring class A war criminals (see chapter 2 for definition) into a political rite of passage to assuage nationalists.

At the same time, the United States and other Allied states that engineered the post–World War II international tribunals often came to view activist campaigns by Nazi-hunters like Simon Wiesenthal and the Klarsfelds as an impediment to the Cold War imperative of cultivating valuable intelligence and scientific assets. Meanwhile, as we've seen, new opportunities to pursue Axis war criminals arose with the creation of the OSI in 1979, which provided a systematic American effort to denaturalize and deport Nazi suspects, though Washington eschewed actually holding criminal trials in the United States. Britain and Australia seemed to go one step further by passing legislation allowing for trials of Nazi suspects, but their commitment was short-lived. Australia, for example, shuttered its special investigation unit even before it had a chance to register any convictions of Nazi suspects in its jurisdiction.

The Soviet Union tried thousands of Nazi war criminals in the 1950s and '60s. Many of those convicted were executed, while others were sentenced to lengthy terms in prison camps. After the breakup of the Soviet Union, Russia opened its wartime archival materials in Moscow and other cities, helping U.S. investigators track down aging Nazi collaborators living in the United States.[150]

Holocaust memorializations have become commonplace, but the political will of states to consistently pursue criminal trials for the full range of World War II–era atrocities in Europe as well as in Asia and the Pacific has not followed suit. The rise of the international human rights movement and the emergence of the contemporary international criminal tribunals in the early 1990s granted renewed legitimacy to the norm of facing the past through retributive justice. However, these new institutional experiments in international law have only focused scrutiny on selected atrocities of the recent past, not on more distant ones. Meanwhile, with the main exception of Germany, few countries affected by World War II atrocities (committed by the Allied as well as the Axis powers) have taken any meaningful action to examine the participation of their own governments or societies in these crimes.

In this regard, the vicissitudes of political will—along with the operational challenges of identifying and tracking down war crime suspects, the legal complications of prosecuting suspects for crimes committed almost seventy years ago, and the unwillingness of societies to confront their own complicity in horrendous crimes—remain daunting obstacles for those few individuals still engaged in the pursuit. As the following chapters demonstrate, the creation of an international system of ad hoc tribunals and a permanent global court in the 1990s by no means transcended the enduring problems and politics of cultivating political will and garnering state cooperation to bring war criminals to justice.

PART TWO

CHAPTER 5

Balkan Fugitives, International Prosecutors

Late on the afternoon of July 11, 1995, an exuberant Ratko Mladic strode through the abandoned streets of Srebrenica savoring his finest hour as commander of the Bosnian Serb army. Relishing the capture of this strategic town on the eastern border of Bosnia-Herzegovina, the fifty-two-year-old general stopped to embrace some fellow Serb officers. Then, as he walked by a row of apartment buildings that had been gutted by Serb artillery, he turned to a Bosnian Serb television crew. Outfitted for the occasion with freshly laundered army fatigues, a pair of heavy field glasses dangling from his neck, and a 9 mm Heckler submachine gun in his hand, Mladic foretold the fate of the Bosnian Muslims fleeing toward a United Nations compound and nearby forests: "Here we are in Srebrenica . . . on the eve of yet another great Serb holiday. We present the city to the Serbian people as a gift. Finally, the time has come to take revenge."[1]

Srebrenica had been under siege by Mladic's troops for three long years. Since early in the Bosnian war, the town of 8,000, wedged in a narrow valley, had swelled to as many as 40,000 people with the arrival of Bosnian Muslims fleeing Serb attacks across the region. When Serb forces had threatened to overrun Srebrenica in 1993, the UN Security Council had promised protection, declaring it the first-ever UN safe area. But to back up that guarantee, the UN sent only a contingent of Dutch peacekeepers, lightly armed and with no clear mandate to halt any Serb advances from the surrounding hills.[2] Then, in early July 1995,

Serb forces began to shell Srebrenica and close in on the town. The "safe area" of Srebrenica soon became one of the most dangerous places on the planet.[3]

As the Serbs drew closer, Dutch peacekeepers reassured residents that NATO airstrikes would soon turn Serb military positions into "a zone of death."[4] The night of July 10, recalled Ilijaz Pilav, a thirty-one-year-old Srebrenica native who served as the town's chief surgeon, "nobody slept. Everyone looked at the sky. But that wretched July 11 arrived without any action. The morning was so deceitful. It was sunny, beautiful weather—and silence. But soon the terrible shelling of the city resumed, and the brutal attacks on all our positions."[5]

NATO, stymied by indecision and a complicated procedure for approving military strikes in tandem with the UN, dropped only two bombs, mid-afternoon on July 11, hardly enough to halt the Serbs. Bosnian Muslim soldiers and many other able-bodied men in the town set out through the forest for a grueling sixty-five-kilometer trek northwest to Tuzla, while thousands of desperate civilians streamed north toward the UN compound in Potocari a few kilometers away. When a thirty-year-old Bosnian Muslim man who stayed behind tried to surrender to Mladic's troops, Bosnian Serb Lieutenant Milorad Pelemis reportedly ordered a member of his unit to kill the man on the spot. The soldier obeyed without hesitation, slashing the man's throat.[6]

With some 5,000 people inside the UN compound and 30,000 more outside clamoring for protection, Mladic met with several representatives of Srebrenica's refugees to discuss removing women and children from Serb-held territory. But Mladic remained determined to hunt down the fleeing men, whom he held collectively responsible for attacks on nearby Bosnian Serb villages. "The ones who are guilty of crimes will answer for it," he said. "Whoever gives up their arms will be untouched. I am a professional soldier. I take no joy in killing either civilians or soldiers."[7]

David Rohde was a young American journalist whose investigative reporting would uncover the bloody aftermath of Srebrenica's fall. At Potocari, he wrote, thousands of exhausted and heat-stricken refugees anxiously awaited safe passage. From the columns headed to nearby buses, Serb soldiers stopped many teenagers and older men and led them away. Lieutenant Eelco Koster, a Dutch peacekeeper, prevented a Serb soldier from taking a Muslim teenage boy from his mother. Yet Mladic's forces enjoyed the upper hand. "The situation was out of control," wrote Rohde. "Other peacekeepers were being robbed of their helmets and flak jackets at gunpoint. . . . The Serbs were leading the Muslim men away with little or no resistance. A deep wave of depression washed over Koster. The Serbs were arresting, taunting and expelling the people the Dutch were supposed to be safeguarding."[8] In all, the Dutch peacekeeping force handed over nearly 300 Bosnian Muslims to Mladic's troops, including a UN employee and the father and brother of a UN translator. They would be among the 8,000 Bosnian Muslims murdered by Mladic's men.

A FRAGILE EXPERIMENT: INTERNATIONAL
JUSTICE IN THE HAGUE

As Mladic's forces hunted down their victims, UN lawyers 1,750 kilometers away in the Netherlands struggled to turn a newly launched experiment in international law into a functioning reality. In May 1993, just a month after the UN Security Council had designated Srebrenica a "safe area," the world body authorized the establishment of the first-ever UN international criminal tribunal. Based in the Dutch city of The Hague, the International Criminal Tribunal for the Former Yugoslavia was given jurisdiction over not only Bosnia and Herzegovina but the entire territory of the former Yugoslavia that had begun to splinter when Croatia and Slovenia each seceded from the Serb-dominated nation in June 1991 and Bosnia asserted its independence in early 1992. The UN endowed the Yugoslavia tribunal with extensive legal authority, enabling its chief prosecutor to bring cases against individual suspects—including heads of state—accused of committing war crimes, crimes against humanity, or genocide. On paper, the nascent tribunal's authority had precedence over state sovereignty: all UN member states faced a binding legal obligation to provide full and immediate cooperation with tribunal requests for evidence, access to witnesses, and the arrest of any indicted suspect.

For the first time since the Nuremberg and Tokyo military tribunals, an international court had been created to adjudicate violations of international humanitarian law codified over the previous century in various Geneva and Hague conventions. Yet, the UN-run Yugoslavia tribunal marked a significant departure from the post–World War II Allied-run military courts. Whereas the Nuremberg and Tokyo tribunals had been established by the victors with the explicit intention to punish only the losers, the UN Yugoslavia tribunal had been established, its founders pledged, to be a truly impartial international court.

Impartiality meant that the tribunal's chief prosecutor had the legal authority to indict suspects in the Yugoslav wars of secession regardless of which particular faction or ethnic group they came from. While ethnic Serb suspects were implicated in carrying out the majority of wartime atrocities in Bosnia, scrutiny of atrocities committed by ethnic Croats and Bosnian Muslims would highlight the importance of the tribunal's broad-based jurisdiction and impartial mandate.

Creation of the new tribunal captured the imagination of human rights activists around the world, who envisioned that holding war crimes suspects accountable before an impartial international court might provide a novel way to break cycles of violence and vengeance. Yet even the hopeful realized how fragile was this new experiment and wondered whether the seedling of an institution planted far off in The Hague as war raged in the Balkans could even take root. *New Yorker* writer Lawrence Weschler likened the challenge of establishing the tribunal to the difficulty of pitching camp on the "precarious slopes" of a figurative valley "where [the] Geneva and The Hague [conventions] and Nuremberg [trial] rose up tentatively out of the mayhem below."[9] Others suspected that the decision to create an international tribunal was a cynical move by the UN Security Council to claim the moral high ground by seeking justice for victims while diverting attention from the world's ongoing failure to deploy military force to stop the carnage in Bosnia.

In the beginning, this cynical view held sway, reinforced by the UN's own evident ambivalence toward supporting the tribunal. As the Bosnian war dragged on through 1993 and 1994, the Security Council failed to back the fledgling court it had authorized, most notably by not appointing a chief prosecutor for fourteen months. "There seemed a real possibility that the tribunal would flop," notes Madeleine Albright, the U.S. ambassador to the UN, who played a pivotal role in the tribunal's founding.[10] Even when UN support increased, the tribunal's future still appeared precarious: the court had no army or police force of its own to arrest war crimes suspects or to compel states to comply with their legal obligation to hand over suspects. To make matters worse, some of the most wanted suspects the tribunal would target were protected by armies or militias of their own.

Based in the offices of a former insurance building in The Hague, the initial tribunal staffers had to build an institution from scratch, a task made more frustrating because they had constantly to lobby UN headquarters in New York for resources, personnel, and relaxation of bureaucratic procedures that hampered their investigations. And even as the UN itself put these obstacles in the court's way, the first tribunal chief prosecutor, Richard Goldstone of South Africa, faced mounting UN and international pressure to deliver tangible results.

Goldstone, however, could hardly keep pace with the continuing revelations of wartime atrocities in Bosnia. Not long after his appointment as chief prosecutor in Summer 1994, Goldstone and his small team of investigators had begun collecting evidence against Ratko Mladic and Bosnian Serb leader Radovan Karadzic, though they did not vigorously pursue evidence against Serbia's president, Slobodan Milosevic, the man who many victims and analysts believed bore the greatest responsibility for wartime violations in Bosnia. Both Mladic and Karadzic seemed easier targets in evidentiary and political terms. Since early in the war, both men had been implicated in directing widespread ethnic cleansing attacks and the siege of the Bosnian capital, Sarajevo, which by war's end would claim the lives of some 10,000 residents, including thousands of children. And then there was Srebrenica.

By laying ambushes in the forests outside of town, Mladic's soldiers mowed down thousands of virtually defenseless Bosnian Muslim men in the days following Srebrenica's fall. Thousands of others who sought to escape the ambushes by surrendering met an equally grisly fate. In one gruesome massacre, Mladic's soldiers tortured captured Muslims in a warehouse before killing them with an axe.[11] In another warehouse massacre, Serb soldiers threw in hand grenades and then opened fire on their defenseless prisoners. On the Branjevo Farm near Srebrenica, Bosnian Serb Lieutenant Milorad Pelemis allegedly commanded his men to execute some 800 Bosnian Muslims brought there by the busload.

By late July 1995, the world began to learn of the disappearance of Srebrenica's men. Evidence of the massacres was substantiated by victim accounts as well as by American U-2 reconnaissance aircraft and drones, whose cameras detected large swaths of earth that had been moved, indicating the location of mass graves.[12] After U.S. Secretary of State Albright revealed satellite imagery of mass graves during an August Security Council meeting, Mladic's forces called in bulldozers to dig up bodies from some of the original mass graves and rebury them in smaller secondary gravesites in an attempt to hide evidence of the crimes. It was just as the initial revelations about the disappearance of Srebrenica's men were becoming known that Chief Prosecutor Goldstone indicted Mladic and Karadzic for atrocities committed earlier in the war. Goldstone's action in The Hague, however, did not stop the Bosnian Serb general from seizing Zepa, a UN-designated safe area southwest of Srebrenica. Mladic dismissed the criminal charges as "idiotic accusations."[13] And to a group of captured Bosnian Muslims from Zepa, Mladic bragged: "Not Allah, not the United Nations, not anything can help you. I am your God."[14]

WAR CRIMES ON THE CROATIAN FRONT

As evidence of the Srebrenica massacres was beginning to surface, a new front emerged in the ethnic war for territory in the former Yugoslavia, this time leading to Croatian atrocities. On the last day of July 1995, charismatic Croatian General Ante Gotovina gathered with other top military commanders and Croatian President Franjo Tudjman for a crucial strategy session. The aim of the meeting was to plan a military assault to retake the Krajina, a region of eastern Croatia comprising approximately one-third of the country. In the aftermath of Croatia's June 1991 independence declaration four years earlier, Serb militias backed by Slobodan Milosevic's Yugoslav National Army had taken up arms to carve out the Krajina region as an independent Serb state. Within months Serb forces routed the poorly armed Croats, deploying paramilitary units to ethnically "cleanse" towns and villages. In Vukovar, a multiethnic town along the Danube River in eastern Croatia, Serb forces under the command of the Yugoslav National Army laid siege, indiscriminately targeting trapped civilians. When the town fell, in November 1991, Serb forces hunted down Croat soldiers with the same brutality they would employ against Bosnian Muslims years later in Srebrenica.

With piercing eyes and striking features, the thirty-nine-year-old General Gotovina cut an impressive figure. His good looks later caught the attention of Carla Del Ponte, the tribunal chief prosecutor who would target him for indictment in 2001. In military uniform, she wrote, Gotovina looked "devastatingly handsome."[15] After leaving the country as a teenager, Gotovina had lived the life of an adventurer and mercenary, traits that would bolster his cult status in Croatia as the country's preeminent war hero after he returned home to fight for the dream of an independent Croatian state.[16] Croatia had previously known independence only briefly, as a fascist state allied with Nazi Germany during World War II.

For the July 31 strategy meeting, Gotovina, Tudjman, and top military brass gathered on Brioni, a serene island in the northern Adriatic

Sea that had once served as a retreat for the late Yugoslav leader Marshal Tito. Tito had coined the phrase "brotherhood and unity" to symbolize the cohesion of the modern Yugoslav state he and fellow Yugoslav partisans established after defeating German and Croatian Nazis during World War II. As a young man, Tudjman had been one of those partisans, but later ran afoul of Tito for criticizing the government's history of World War II:[17] Tudjman had greatly minimized widespread Croatian atrocities against Serbs and Jews during the Holocaust, particularly those that occurred at Jasenovac, the concentration camp known as "the Auschwitz of the Balkans."

Transcripts of the Brioni meeting suggest that Croatian leaders had two key objectives for what they termed Operation Storm: defeating the Croatian Serb military forces and driving out ethnic Serbs, who made up 12 percent of Croatia's prewar population and had lived in the Krajina for generations. In early August 1995, Gotovina's troops launched their attack, and in less than 100 hours routed the Serb forces, leading 150,000 to 200,000 ethnic Serbs to stream out of Croatia. Washington tacitly supported the military assault, but advised Tudjman to make it clean and quick.[18] The Croatian victory and the "mopping up" operations that followed were quick but not clean: they raised many red flags for violations of the Geneva Conventions, such as persistent shelling of the civilian population of Knin, the capital of Krajina, looting of villages, and the murder of approximately 150 ethnic Serbs, including many elderly who were unable or unwilling to leave their homes. While denying that the ethnic Serbs had been forcibly expelled, President Tudjman appeared nevertheless to revel at their departure from Croatia: "They were gone in a few days as if they had never been here. . . . They did not even have time to collect their rotten money and dirty underwear."[19]

THE QUESTION OF ARRESTS: "ONE OF THOSE
PROBLEMS WE HOPED WOULD GO AWAY"

Not long after the Serbian, Croatian, and Bosnian presidents signed the Dayton Accords, in December 1995, officially bringing an end to the Bosnian war, tribunal investigators traveled the snowy hills of Bosnia to find the mass graves of Srebrenica and to investigate other war crimes, such as those committed at the Omarska prison camp outside of Prejidor. With a U.S.-brokered peace agreement in place and 60,000 NATO soldiers on the ground in Bosnia, investigators had an army to provide protection from possible Serb retribution. But when it came to sending its troops to arrest indicted war crimes suspects, NATO balked. In contrast to the resolute Allied occupation of Germany half a century earlier, NATO peacekeepers arriving in Bosnia were ambivalent occupiers and reluctant guarantors of a fragile, negotiated peace. For the Allies, capturing high-level German Nazis was initially a top postwar priority; for NATO, making arrests was initially something to avoid at all costs.

On a rhetorical level, Western leaders and the UN embraced the tribunal as a moral and pragmatic means to confront the evil of mass atrocity. In 1995, U.S. President Bill Clinton insisted that "those accused of war crimes, crimes against humanity and genocide must be brought to justice."[20] But on the ground, political calculation drove NATO to inaction: fear abounded that arrests of suspected war criminals could trigger casualties, provoke a backlash from Serb nationalists, and imperil the Dayton Accords. In other words, the political interest of NATO states in sidestepping arrests clearly trumped their legal obligation and moral responsibility to confront the crimes of the Bosnian war. For the United States, the killing of eighteen U.S. Rangers in a botched 1993 attempt to arrest Somali warlord Mohammed Farrah Aidid had cast a long shadow over Washington's willingness to send troops into harm's way, either to arrest war crimes suspects or to keep atrocities from occurring in the first place. For Clinton, the approaching 1996 presidential elections magnified the potential domestic repercussions of an arrest operation should it fail. Indeed, caution prompted a U.S. policy of requiring its 20,000 troops in Bosnia under the auspices of NATO to wear flak jackets at all times, even in their dressing rooms.[21]

Richard Goldstone's indictments of Mladic and Karadzic had rendered them international pariahs, thereby preventing their attendance at the November 1995 peace talks in Dayton, Ohio. Both men initially clung to their leadership positions in Republika Srpska, the 49 percent of Serb-controlled Bosnia-Herzegovina carved out by wartime ethnic cleansing and granted autonomy by the Dayton Accords. Republika Srpska became a virtual safe haven for Bosnian Serb suspects following the agreement's signing, despite the presence there of tens of thousands of heavily armed NATO soldiers. A relaxed, tanned, and newly pensioned Mladic, for example, was spotted skiing at a resort in the mountains above Sarajevo that winter of 1996.[22] Later, he and his wife took up residence in a vacation home situated inside a well-fortified Bosnian Serb army headquarters, about twenty kilometers from a U.S. military base.

NATO announced that it would arrest tribunal suspects only if its peacekeepers happened to encounter them in the line of duty. It soon became clear, however, that NATO actively sought to avoid any such encounters with indictees, particularly Mladic and Karadzic. To avoid running into Mladic, U.S. soldiers reportedly warned of their impending visits to the army base where he resided.²³ When NATO forces actually did encounter suspects, they let them pass, no questions asked. In early 1996, Karadzic, riding in his tinted-window Mercedes, drove through several NATO checkpoints, two of which were staffed by U.S. troops. Italian soldiers reportedly turned their backs when Karadzic sped by them in the former Bosnian Serb capital of Pale.²⁴ "It became a popular media sport for journalists to stand near NATO checkpoints and take notes and pictures of the indicted criminals passing through," Canadian journalist Carol Off recalled.²⁵

With thousands of NATO troops deployed in the country, mounting arrest operations was by no means Mission Impossible. "I'm not uncatchable," Bosnian Serb suspect Blagoje Simic told American journalist Elizabeth Neuffer in late 1996.²⁶ Simic openly served as mayor of a Bosnian town, traveling back and forth to his office just down the road from an American military base. "The war crimes thing was easily passed over," William Nash, a U.S. general and head of NATO at the time, candidly acknowledged. "It was one of those problems we hoped would go away."²⁷

Back in Washington, a thirty-three-year-old State Department lawyer named David Scheffer worked to keep alive the question of apprehending war crimes suspects indicted by the Yugoslavia tribunal. Shortly after President Clinton's first inauguration in January 1993, Madeleine Albright had deputized Scheffer to spearhead U.S. efforts to draw up a blueprint for an international war crimes court for the former Yugoslavia. Over the next eight years, Scheffer became the point man for international justice within the U.S. government.²⁸ Scheffer and other like-minded administration officials pressed the war crimes agenda in Washington and abroad. Yet they faced an uphill battle to persuade even their own government that pursuing war crimes suspects served a vital national interest. As a result, Scheffer reported that he "often spent as much time fighting the Washington bureaucracy as I did negotiating in foreign capitals and with UN officials."²⁹

Scheffer and his Washington allies waged the battle for arrests on several fronts. In interagency meetings, he sought to underscore the importance of empathizing with victims of mass atrocities and the need for criminal accountability. But the logic of nonintervention, whether to halt atrocities or to bring justice in their aftermath, held sway. Distancing themselves from the plight of victims, Scheffer believed, made it easier for the White House and the Pentagon to justify to themselves not sending troops on arrest missions. NATO commanders on the ground in Bosnia also found ways to avoid confronting the legacy of wartime atrocities. A small but telling example, in Scheffer's view, was NATO's decision to refer to each tribunal indictee as a PIFWIC, a bureaucratic acronym for "person indicted for war crimes." To Scheffer's ear, the acronym sounded like something out of Winnie the Pooh, which in turn diminished the urgency of apprehending suspects wanted for mass murder.[30]

Scheffer and his allies also tried to counter the dominant U.S. government view that pursuing suspects would lead to "mission creep" and undermine what peace and stability had been achieved in Bosnia. Instead, they argued, the continued failure to capture high-profile suspects would fuel virulent nationalism and embolden Serbian resistance to NATO's continuing military occupation of Bosnia. Leaving Mladic and Karadzic in leadership positions could also dissuade refugees driven from their homes by wartime ethnic cleansing attacks from soon returning. Richard Holbrooke, the chief U.S. negotiator at Dayton, had warned President Clinton a day after the Dayton talks ended that the peace agreement could not be fully implemented without arresting Karadzic and Mladic.[31]

By late 1996, Clinton took action to curb the disruptive role of Karadzic in postwar Bosnia. He deputized Holbrooke to travel to Belgrade and press Serbian President Milosevic, who effectively controlled political events in Republika Srpska, to remove Karadzic from power or face U.S. sanctions. Milosovic complied, but this brought neither Karadzic nor Mladic any closer to custody. The threat of sanctions only applied to Karadzic's removal from power and not to his—much less to Mladic's—arrest and transfer to the Yugoslavia tribunal. "We were ambivalent about what we had done," Holbrooke recalled, since removing Karadzic from power drove him underground and relieved pressure on NATO to arrest him.[32]

Mounting criticism of international inaction on arrests finally prompted a grudging change in NATO policy. In late 1996, leading NATO governments set up a task force to carry out arrest operations. But problems remained, some a function of NATO's having divided Bosnia into three different jurisdictional zones, one controlled by American troops, one by British troops, and one by French troops. French peacekeepers controlled the areas that Mladic and Karadzic called home, but, particularly concerned about troop casualties, they were the most reluctant to authorize arrest missions.

RICHARD GOLDSTONE'S PROSECUTORIAL DIPLOMACY

Although without enforcement powers of its own, the Yugoslavia tribunal did possess a source of potential strength—a reservoir of moral authority, deriving from its status as an international criminal court mandated to adjudicate some of the world's gravest atrocities. If deployed strategically, this moral standing could bring pressure to bear on the entrenched defiance of targeted states in the Balkans and a passive international community. As the world's most prominent prosecutor and the tribunal's public face, Richard Goldstone became a new type of political actor on the international stage, with potentially far-reaching influence. His statements could carry weight. Not necessarily enough weight to overcome NATO resistance or the recalcitrance of Balkan states, but enough to galvanize activists and focus international media scrutiny on the fugitive problem.

Goldstone had walked into his new job in The Hague with no prior experience as a prosecutor and little knowledge of either the Balkans or international law. "To have described my knowledge of international humanitarian law as scanty would have been generous," Goldstone conceded.[33] In apartheid South Africa, he had earned a reputation for being an independent judge and gained prominence in the early 1990s heading an independent South African commission investigating state-sponsored violence.

Given his steep learning curve in The Hague, Goldstone relied heavily on Australian Graham Blewitt, the tribunal's deputy prosecutor. As the former head of a special domestic unit established to prosecute Australian citizens from Eastern Europe who were implicated in Holocaust crimes, Blewitt had experience running complex investigations of atrocities. His experience, however, was a cautionary tale as to how quickly a state can renege on its promised support of war crimes prosecutions: not long after establishing Blewitt's unit, the Australian government announced plans to shutter it.

To make his mark, Goldstone soon realized, he would have to move beyond the role of legal actor in the courtroom and take on the time-consuming and often delicate role of diplomat, navigating the rocky shoals of the UN system and international politics.[34] Although the UN Security Council had granted the tribunal sweeping legal authority to trump state sovereignty, conduct investigations in any UN member country, and insist on cooperation as a matter of international law, Goldstone felt that securing state support in the long run depended on being upfront with governments and obtaining explicit consent to conduct investigations. "Not to give prior notice," he remarked, "would be undiplomatic, especially if a mishap occurred or if government assistance was ultimately required."[35] Some of Goldstone's own investigators, however, found his by-the-book approach naive in view of the frequent necessity of conducting sensitive investigations without a government's knowledge.

Despite his penchant for diplomacy, Goldstone earned a reputation among justice advocates for firmly defending the tribunal's prerogative to prosecute war crimes suspects without political interference. During his tenure, Goldstone clashed repeatedly with UN Secretary-General Boutros Boutros-Ghali over matters as weighty as indicting Mladic and Karadzic prior to a peace agreement and as trivial as whether the prosecutor would be allowed to travel to international conferences to promote the tribunal's work. In one meeting at UN headquarters in New York, the Secretary-General told Goldstone he should remain in The Hague and focus on his prosecutorial tasks. Goldstone insisted that his frequent travels to Western and Balkan capitals were essential to building global support for the fledgling court.[36] Goldstone prevailed in this battle, and in the one over when to indict Mladic and Karadzic; and in doing so he helped enshrine the important principle of prosecutorial autonomy from external intrusion.

Adhering to diplomatic conventions rendered it difficult at times, as Goldstone himself admitted, "to get down to the nitty gritty"[37] of what was needed to facilitate tribunal investigations and make arrests. In a meeting in Zagreb with Croatian Deputy Foreign Minister Ivan Simonovic, for example, Goldstone forged a bond based on their common enjoyment of good wine and good food, but that did not override Croatian resistance to the court's indictment of its citizens or exposure of state-sponsored atrocities. On this score, Croatian politicians, Goldstone recalled, were more skillful diplomats than their counterparts in Serbia, who initially made no effort to cloak their obstruction of justice. "Belgrade said 'we don't recognize you.' Hence, zero cooperation. Croatia said, 'we recognize you and we'll give you all the cooperation we can.' Only they didn't. It was more shrewd and more . . . devious. . . . . They were happy to cooperate when it suited them, but if it got close to home they would shut up like clams."[38]

By the end of Goldstone's two-year term in 1996, few suspects were actually in tribunal custody, and only the trial of a comparatively low-level concentration camp commander, Dusan Tadic, was underway. Tadic, a young Bosnian Serb karate instructor, had been arrested and transferred to The Hague after one of his victims spotted him on the streets of Munich in February 1994. Skeptics still dismissed the tribunal as a public relations device of the Great Powers and questioned its capacity to hold significant trials. Yet Goldstone had bolstered the tribunal's international visibility by issuing dozens of indictments. "During Richard's tenure, the issuance of indictments was newsworthy, and that's what kept the tribunal alive," observed Louise Arbour, a Canadian appeals judge and his hand-picked successor.[39]

The signing of the Dayton Accords in December 1995 and the arrival of NATO troops in Bosnia the next month "introduced a new element of hope" in the tribunal's effort to hold trials, Blewitt recalled.[40] Nevertheless, Dayton yielded no agreement to ensure the actual handover of indicted Serb, Croat, and Bosnian Muslim suspects. In meetings in Washington, Goldstone took his case for arrests to the highest echelons of government, but to no avail. "They feared that if they started arresting people, then that would have triggered World War III," Blewitt recalled. For the deputy prosecutor, hope soon turned to "utter disappointment."

LOUISE ARBOUR AND THE SEALED-INDICTMENT STRATEGY

When Louise Arbour took over as chief prosecutor in Fall 1996, she quickly found herself dismayed by the situation facing the Yugoslavia tribunal and wondered why she had left her secure job as an appeals court judge in Québec. Arbour, like Goldstone before her, had no international law or prosecutorial experience. Only a handful of suspects were in tribunal custody, none of them high-ranking. Approximately seventy of those the court had indicted remained at large, most of them hiding in plain sight in Bosnia or in neighboring Serbia and Croatia. "The question of arrests was the number-one make-or-break deal during my tenure," Arbour recalled.[41] A few tribunal judges, frustrated with having virtually no courtroom work, broached the idea of allowing *in absentia* trials. Arbour, steeped in the common law's embrace of granting defendants the right to face their accusers, responded, "If the rules get changed, I'm telling you right now, I'll quit. I mean, I didn't come here for show trials."[42]

Arbour soon realized that the struggle to apprehend indictees had to be waged on several fronts. So far, the tribunal had focused on trying to persuade NATO troops to arrest suspects in Bosnia. Arbour feared that this Bosnia focus had the effect of relieving political pressure on the Serbian government in Belgrade and the Croatian government in Zagreb to hand over suspects under their protection. While many indictees roamed freely in Bosnia, others enjoyed government protection in Serbia, which had no international forces on its territory, and in Croatia, with only a limited number of UN peacekeepers on its soil.

To induce NATO to make arrests in Bosnia, Arbour issued indictments under seal, unlike Goldstone, who had quickly made his indictments public. The chief prosecutor's idea was not an original one. Law enforcement jurisdictions the world over often keep indictments and warrants secret to retain the element of surprise in arrest operations. In her estimation, sealed indictments could break NATO's resistance by giving it the element of surprise in making arrests, thereby countering its argument that such operations posed grave danger to its peacekeepers.

Arbour's sealed-indictment strategy took months to bear fruit, largely because of NATO's ongoing reluctance to apprehend suspects. And during this time she came under intense pressure from leaders of international human rights organizations that, not privy to her well-developed arrest strategy, criticized the appearance of prosecutorial inaction. Arbour remembers a particularly difficult meeting early in her tenure with NGOs in Washington: "It was so tense. Nobody dared say publicly, 'What the hell are you doing?' But I could tell, the question was, 'What the hell are you doing?'"[43]

Then, in June 1997, news broke of the tribunal's first international arrest operation, carried out not by NATO troops in Bosnia but by UN peacekeepers in Croatia. Acting on a sealed indictment of Slavko Dokmanovic, UN forces in the eastern Slavonia region made a stunning arrest that had been months in the making. Prosecution officials worked closely with Jacques Klein, a former American general and head of the UN transitional authority in eastern Slavonia. At the heart of operation lay an age-old law enforcement arrest tactic: using what Arbour described as tricks and lies, they induced Dokmanovic, on the pretense of a meeting that held out promise of real estate compensation, to leave the safety of Serbia, which was beyond the reach of any international peacekeeping force, and cross over into Croatia. Dokmanovic, the former ethnic-Serb mayor of Vukovar, was implicated in one of the more macabre atrocities of the Balkan wars, the removal in 1991 of 260 wounded Croat soldiers from their hospital beds and their massacre in Vukovar's outskirts.[44] UN authorities arrested Dokmanovic not long after he entered Croatia. While Arbour and her team did not have actual control over the operation, they demonstrated their capacity to work with UN peacekeepers to help plan arrests. The success showed up NATO for its own passivity, building momentum for a breakthrough a month later in Bosnia.

By summer 1997, the British NATO commanders operating in northwest Bosnia had begun to realize there might indeed be merit in arresting war crime suspects, many of whom were heavily armed and posed a growing challenge to the tenuous peace NATO was supposed to enforce. The May 1997 election of British Prime Minister Tony Blair and the promotion of what he characterized as an "ethical foreign policy" influenced London's change of heart. In Prijedor, Bosnian Serb police chief Simo Drljaca, who was implicated in playing a central role in two infamous concentration camps, Omarska and Keraterm, had become a persistent problem for NATO forces. He reportedly drove around fully armed, and at times shot over the heads of peacekeepers, as well as intimidated Bosnian Muslim refugees from returning home.[45] Eager to remove Drljaca, the local British commander reportedly told a tribunal investigator that if Drljaca were under international indictment, he would arrange his arrest.

When the tribunal investigator relayed this information to Blewitt back in The Hague, the deputy prosecutor realized that Drljaca, along with two alleged co-conspirators, were next in line to face indictment. Prosecutors quickly prepared three indictments, issuing them under seal to ensure that the suspects would not go underground. With the indictments in hand, Blewitt and Arbour traveled to Brussels to meet with high-level NATO officials. "We laid the arrest warrants on the table," Blewitt later recalled, "and said . . . we expect you to do what you said that you would [do and] arrest indicted war criminals. . . . If you don't, then we will go public and expose NATO for the fraud that it is."[46]

On a quiet summer day in July 1997, British SAS commandos, part of a group of 125 special forces troops, tracked Drljaca down to a reservoir, where he was fishing with his son. A British soldier tackled him, and Drljaca shot him in the leg. The British commandos killed the suspect with four shots. The second co-indictee was arrested at his workplace without incident, while the third suspect evaded arrest until years later.

For Arbour, the July arrest operation demonstrated that NATO could apprehend suspects without incurring major casualties themselves or sparking retribution. "So it proved, contrary to what they had always asserted, that if you pick up a PIFWIC, the Third World War will not start," she said. "When we did the first one on a secret indictment, the penny dropped," said Arbour. "And then the question [on the minds of suspects] was, how many of those does she have? Maybe she has three, maybe she has thirty." Worry over a surprise arrest by NATO troops persuaded some suspects to arrange their own surrender. The sealed indictment strategy, she concluded, "totally changed the dynamics. . . . A very big part of the issue [was] settled."[47]

PROGRESS ON THE CROATIAN FRONT

NATO's shift in strategy coincided with another welcome arrest, this time with the grudging assistance of Croatia's president. President Tudjman of Croatia and President Milosevic of Serbia were united in their opposition to a tribunal that threatened to derail their respective narratives of national virtue and victimization. Tudjman, however, appeared more susceptible to international pressure, given his deep interest in gaining membership in European and other Western institutions. With this in mind, strong American and European pressure first focused on Croatia, despite the fact that tribunal indictments focused greater attention on the more numerous Serbian atrocities.

In the spring of 1996, the United States and other Western countries pressed Tudjman particularly hard to hand over Tihomir Blaskic, a Bosnian Croat general implicated in the killing of Bosnian Muslim civilians in 1993. Initially, President Tudjman and other Croatian officials vowed not to capitulate to "immoral" pressure or "to trade people for loans."[48] Instead, he promoted Blaskic to a senior position in the Croatian army just one day after the tribunal had indicted him. Government protection for indictees also extended to Dario Kordic, another prominent suspect implicated in atrocities against Bosnian Muslims.[49] Despite his initial defiance, Tudjman did give Blaskic up in April 1996, and then in October 1997 facilitated the handover of Kordic and nine other Bosnian Croat suspects in response to the West's threats to withhold World Bank loans and block Croatia's membership in the Council of Europe. As with the handover of Blaskic, the Croatian president disavowed his decisive role in sending these ten suspects to The Hague, insisting that the suspects had voluntarily surrendered. "I think it was as voluntary as going to the electric chair," Goldstone commented. "They were told probably what would happen to them and to their families if they didn't hand themselves over."[50] The transfers were an important indication that conditioning economic aid and membership in international organizations on the handover of indicted war criminals could sometimes serve as an effective tool of compliance.

Progress on the arrest front solved one problem but created another. Many of the suspects arriving at the tribunal's detention center were not the "big fish" suspected of directing the carnage of the Bosnian and Croatian wars but "small fry" who bore much less political and criminal responsibility than those leaders. Arbour realized that coping with so many low-level defendants could clog the wheels of tribunal justice and divert limited resources away from investigating more important suspects. "The minute we started arresting people, it became obvious we had to drop the small fish," she said, referring to her decision to withdraw twenty indictments originally issued by Goldstone.[51]

During his tenure at the Yugoslavia tribunal, Goldstone had followed a classic criminal law approach toward organized crime wherein investigations initially focus on indicting lower-level perpetrators in the hopes of incriminating higher-level ones. Building the pyramid from the ground up in the case of suspects in the former Yugoslavia, however, looked to be an endeavor years in the making, in part because low-level suspects were not turning against their superiors. In Arbour's estimation, the Yugoslavia tribunal had to make its mark quickly by tracking responsibility for atrocities committed on the ground by Bosnian Serbs and Bosnian Croats back up the chain of command to their leaders in Belgrade and Zagreb. When Arbour took over as chief prosecutor, she was surprised to find that, despite the tribunal's having been in business for several years, the Office of the Prosecutor had not initiated serious investigations of either the Serbian or the Croatian president. This despite the fact that both Milosevic's and Tudjman's funding and direction of their respective proxy forces in Bosnia were a matter of detailed media reporting.[52]

KARADZIC AND MLADIC AT LARGE

With the July 1997 arrest raid in Bosnia of Simo Drljaca and a co-indictee, NATO had finally, in Arbour's view, "crossed the Rubicon."[53] But the pursuit of Karadzic and Mladic was proving to be another matter altogether. More than any others indicted up to that point, they held the greatest import for the tribunal and for many Bosnian Muslim victims.[54] Although World War III had not broken out when NATO moved to arrest a range of low-level Bosnian Serb and Bosnian Croat suspects, the military alliance remained fearful of troop casualties if and when they moved to take Karadzic and Mladic. An aura of untouchability surrounded Mladic, who, even more than Karadzic, was revered by Serbs on both sides of the Drina River, the border between Bosnia and Serbia. Mladic sought to raise the stakes by vowing to kill as many peacekeepers as he could if they came for him. Such threats were not always idle ones. In October 2000, another Bosnian Serb suspect, Janko Janjic, set off a grenade, killing himself and wounding four German NATO soldiers, during an attempted arrest.[55]

Fortunately for the two Bosnian Serb icons, the French, who controlled the region of eastern Bosnia where they resided, still balked at making arrests or cooperating with British or American forces. French foot-dragging was accompanied at times by public contempt for the tribunal, as seen in the French defense minister's dismissal of the court as a media circus. This prompted the chief prosecutor to go on the offensive. In an interview in *Le Monde,* Arbour sharply criticized the French government for coddling indicted war criminals. "In the French sector can be found lots of war criminals, and they feel absolutely secure there," Arbour said.[56]

Months turned into years. There were various failed attempts to bring the French around and an aborted attempt to launch a NATO expedition to apprehend Karadzic along with a number of other suspects.[57] Then, toward the end of 1999, the number-two official in the U.S. State Department, reportedly at Madeleine Albright's request, told David Scheffer, now the first U.S. Ambassador-at-Large for War Crimes Issues, to halt his ongoing efforts to bring Karadzic to The Hague. Scheffer believes that Albright sidelined him because he was so persistent in pressing for arrests that he had become a thorn in the side of the French and the Pentagon.[58] Albright often portrayed herself as the "mother of the war crimes tribunals,"[59] but now it seemed she was treating the Yugoslavia tribunal as an abandoned stepchild.

U.S. officials now favored a passive approach to gaining custody of the former Bosnian Serb leaders. In addition to offering a $5 million reward for information leading to their arrest, Washington hoped that the suspects' economic and political influence would weaken and they would somehow "drop like rotten fruit" into the hands of NATO peacekeepers.[60] But neither Karadzic nor Mladic had any intention of giving himself up.

THE HUNTING PARTY

By 2000, NATO had lost Karadzic's trail, or rather, stopped seriously trying to find it. Yet, as a group of veteran Western war correspondents vacationing in Bosnia soon realized, one did not need to be a secret agent to at least come close to tracking him down. The five journalists—Americans Scott Anderson, Sebastian Junger, and John Falk and Europeans Harald Doornbos and Philippe Deprez—had all covered the Bosnian war several years earlier. Now they had returned for a reunion in Sarajevo and would soon be off to a seaside vacation on the Croatian coast. Sitting in a cafe in the Bosnian capital they mulled over what they all considered to be the last great story of the Balkan wars: the unfinished pursuit of indicted war criminals. The conversation turned to why NATO countries had still been unable to arrest either Karadzic or Mladic.[61]

The journalists handed around the table a full-page ad in a Bosnian newsmagazine advertising $5 million U.S. bounties for the arrest of Karadzic, Mladic, and Slobodan Milosevic, who had come under tribunal indictment in May 1999 for war crimes and crimes against humanity committed in the Kosovo war. The U.S. government shouldn't go into the advertising business, opined Scott Anderson: the "wanted" photos of Karadzic and Mladic were out of date, and the toll-free hotline accepted calls only from the United States. The ad was only useful, Anderson joked, "should any of them be hiding out in Des Moines." Elsewhere in the same magazine, the journalists read a report that Karadzic was residing in the town of Celebici, near Bosnia's border with Montenegro.

Over sips of slivovitz, the Balkan brandy that British peacekeeping troops call "sleep in ditch," the five friends hatched a harebrained scheme that began in jest but slowly grew more serious. The next morning they would travel to Celebici, pinpoint Karadzic's whereabouts, notify the international authorities, and split the bounty money between them. "We'd give new meaning to the term advocacy journalism," wrote Anderson, whose *Esquire* article about their exploits became the basis of *The Hunting Party*, a $20 million Hollywood movie starring Richard Gere. Some in the group expressed reservations, but they all went along with the plan in the spirit of their enterprising war correspondent days. Anderson surmised that the group's "boldness largely stemmed from the conviction that our mission had absolutely zero chance of success."

The next day, the group headed toward the UN base near Celebici, where they asked an official whether there was any truth to the Bosnian newsmagazine story revealing Karadzic's whereabouts. "Sorry, guys," the man told the group. "You just missed him. He was in Celebici, but he left two days ago." Then the plot thickened. To its collective surprise, the group met a Ukrainian UN official named Boris who was willing to buck the inertia of the UN system and help the journalists track down Karadzic. Over coffee, they won Boris's trust and learned that because he spoke Serbo-Croatian and felt strongly about criminal accountability he had been able to build a network that informed him of Karadzic's presence in the area. Boris came to believe that the journalists were actually CIA agents out to nab the former Bosnian Serb leader. The group tried to set him straight, but to no avail. Their effort to convince Boris was complicated, Anderson sardonically observed, by the fact that "the sheer mindless incompetence we displayed so far—five guys blundering through eastern Bosnia in a very conspicuous car without a clue of what we're doing—bore uncanny resemblance to what a bona fide CIA operation would look like."

Boris put the journalists in touch with a Bosnian Serb who apparently served as a high-level secret policeman and had worked closely with Karadzic's associates smuggling cigarettes and liquor. The man was willing to cooperate with the journalists, who he too believed were CIA, because of a bitter falling out with Karadzic's men over the smuggling business. In exchange, he wanted a share of the bounty and help in relocating himself and his family out of the country.

The journalists' scheme hit a roadblock when Boris notified the group that he had been dismissed from his UN post because American forces had secretly taped their meetings and learned he was aiding their quest to have Karadzic arrested. Afraid that the Bosnian Serb informant's identity had been compromised, Boris advised him to go into hiding. A short time later, a U.S. lieutenant colonel ordered the journalists to stop meddling. For Anderson, the final twists in the bizarre story underscored the hypocrisy of the UN and the U.S. publicly committing themselves to arresting war crimes suspects only to punish an international civil servant who took this commitment seriously. As with Scheffer back in Washington, Boris, the Ukrainian UN official in Bosnia, had apparently been sidelined for showing too much interest in tracking down one of the tribunal's top war crimes suspects. Once again, the international effort to arrest Karadzic had been shelved.

THE ARREST OF SLOBODAN MILOSEVIC AND THE END OF THE AUTHORITARIAN ERA

While Karadzic kept a low profile, reportedly moving between the mountainous border region of eastern Bosnia and neighboring Montenegro, Mladic had opted for the protection of his paymaster, Serbian President Milosevic. As NATO made more and more arrests in the late 1990s, many of the Bosnian Serb officers and soldiers who faced tribunal indictment, and who had killed for Mladic in Srebrenica and elsewhere in Bosnia, sought the protective embrace of Mother Serbia and its state security apparatus. By the end of the 1990s the main theater for arrests had thus shifted from Bosnia to Serbia and Croatia.

Sometime after stepping down from his position as head of the Bosnian Serb army in late 1996, Mladic moved to Belgrade. Beyond the reach of NATO and close to the epicenter of Serbian political and military power, he had little reason to hide. Further, in Belgrade, he enjoyed around-the-clock protection from a team of fifty heavily armed bodyguards reportedly established at the direction of Milosevic. "We were tasked with protecting Mladic from criminals and bounty hunters," one member of the protection unit told a Belgrade court during a subsequent trial of ten Serbs accused of hiding Mladic and obstructing justice.[62] Mladic continued to collect his government pension and lived in a well-appointed stone house in one of Belgrade's tree-lined upmarket neighborhoods. He could often be spotted sipping coffee at sidewalk cafes and dining in expensive restaurants or decked out in his military uniform,[63] talking with neighbors on a park bench. But this life of relative unconcern would not last.

Although Slobodan Milosevic had been the source of protection for Mladic and scores of other war crimes suspects, a confluence of international and domestic events would soon push him from power and into the custody of a police force he had once controlled with an iron hand. After Milosevic's September 2000 electoral defeat and his insistence on remaining in power, a mass democratic protest movement forced him to abide by the results and step down, dramatically changing the Serbian political landscape. Milosevic's strident nationalism had gained him repeated victories at the polls since his coming to power in the late 1980s. But by 2000, voters were ready to throw out a leader who had mired the country in a series of losing wars. The 1998–99 Kosovo war proved the most humiliating for Serbia. NATO's seventy-eight-day bombing campaign to halt Serbia's ethnic cleansing of Kosovo's ethnic Albanian population placed Belgrade and other cities in the military alliance's crosshairs, forcing Milosevic's capitulation in Kosovo and further isolating Serbia. The loss proved symbolically devastating because the province of Kosovo was celebrated as the cradle of Serb civilization, though in modern times Serbs made up only a small minority of its population. The atrocities in Kosovo placed an added investigatory burden on the Yugoslavia tribunal's Office of the Prosecutor, which launched investigations leading to indictments of a number of Serbian officials and eventually some members of the Kosovo Liberation Army implicated in atrocities against Serbs.

At the end of March 2001, a force of hundreds of Serbian policemen descended on Milosevic's residence in a midnight operation. Milosevic's arrest and subsequent transfer to The Hague just months after his fall from power was by no means a foregone conclusion, however. The election of Vojislav Kostunica was hailed in the West as the beginning of a new democratic era in Serbia. A former constitutional law professor, Kostunica had played no direct role in Serbia's wars in the region. But as a committed nationalist he held the tribunal in contempt and contested the basis of his government's international legal obligation to cooperate fully with it. Nor did Serbia's celebrated "transition to democracy" suddenly sweep aside extremism or sideline members of the state security apparatus implicated in war crimes. Within weeks of taking power, Kostunica made it clear he had no intention of cooperating with The Hague. At first, Western leaders took no action to press Belgrade for suspects; they felt that forcing this controversial issue could derail Serbia's fragile democratic transition. But within months, international pressure mounted on Serbia to hand over Milosevic, the tribunal's prime suspect and now a pariah in the eyes of the Western powers.

Milosevic might well have remained a free man if not for two developments, one international and one domestic. On the international front, the George W. Bush administration, prodded by a bipartisan, pro-tribunal consensus in Congress, made Milosevic's arrest and transfer to The Hague worth Serbia's while. Driving the arrest and transfer of Milosevic to the tribunal were unambiguous American threats to withhold economic aid. But monetary incentives alone do not tell the whole story.

The emergence of a pro-Western political bloc in Serbia, led by Zoran Djindic, also played a critical role in altering the domestic politics of state cooperation. Several months after Kostunica's electoral victory as president of the rump Yugoslavia, Djindic won election as Serbia's prime minister. In sharp contrast to Kostunica, Djindic was more amenable to assisting the tribunal, as a pragmatic means to accelerate Serbia's acceptance in the international community after years of isolation. And as prime minister, Djindic had authority over Serbia's interior ministry. This gave him the power to authorize arrest operations.

A day before the March 31 U.S. deadline for the arrest of Milosevic, Djindic took action. On Friday night, March 30, state security forces under the prime minister's control surrounded Milosevic's villa in Belgrade. Yugoslav army soldiers, reportedly under the control of Kostunica, rebuffed the initial attempts to apprehend Milosevic. The standoff that ensued provided a stark illustration of the volatile domestic politics of arrests. Hours later, however, Kostunica's forces backed down, and Milosevic, who had vowed never to be taken alive, surrendered in the early morning hours of April 1.

For the president turned prisoner, incarceration by his own government proved particularly embittering. "If only I had been imprisoned by Albanians or Germans," Milosevic told a confidant who visited him in Belgrade's district prison. "I wouldn't have minded that. But by my own Serbs!"[64] Yet Milosevic's experience behind bars in Belgrade was not all bad, as prison warden Dragisa Blanusa documented in a diary.[65]

Following Milosevic's April 1 arrest, there was some doubt as to whether the prime minister would hand Milosevic over to the tribunal, because Djindic sought to prosecute him on corruption charges at home. After Milosevic's arrest, Chief Prosecutor Carla Del Ponte ruled out deferring the case to Belgrade and pressed the U.S. to intervene with Serbia. Finally, the U.S. warned Belgrade that failure to hand over Milosevic by the end of June would jeopardize Washington's participation in an upcoming donors' conference and $100 million in loans to Serbia.

As the weeks passed and international pressure mounted for his prosecution in The Hague, Milosevic feared a second betrayal. When transferred to a military hospital to treat his high blood pressure, Milosevic grew worried that he would be taken to the helipad on the roof and spirited out of the country. When a Serbian judge tried to serve him with his Yugoslavia tribunal indictment, Milosevic refused even to acknowledge it. "I won't even touch that pile of shit," he announced.[66]

The judge lodged the indictment between the prison cell's bars, leaving Milosevic grumbling to himself.

When the Djindic government initiated proceedings to send him to the tribunal, Milosevic's distraught family gathered at the prison. His daughter Marija blamed her father for ending up behind bars: "If only you had resisted arrest!" Shortly before his departure for The Hague, he and Blanusa had a goodbye drink of imitation whiskey, courtesy of the warden himself. The next day, June 28, Milosevic had lunch with his family at the prison and then spent the rest of the day feeding pigeons. That evening the former Serbian president was transported to a Belgrade helipad and formally placed under arrest by the tribunal. As he was escorted to the waiting helicopter, he reminded a number of Serbian law enforcement officials on the scene that June 28 was the 600th anniversary of a famous Serbian military defeat that had done much to shape the nation's sense of victimhood. As a parting shot, he derided his countrymen for sending him to an international court in exchange for international largesse. "Well done, you lot," he said. "You can take your money now."

In the days before the donors' conference, Djindic had worked up an elaborate plan to spirit Milosevic out of the country. Operationally, the plan worked to a T: the transfer provoked few street protests. Ironically, sending Milosevic to The Hague in the short run caused fewer headaches for the government than a gay pride parade in Belgrade several days later that was greeted by street riots. Djindic acknowledged that handing over Milosevic was an unpopular and painful move, likening it to "deciding to cut your finger off without anesthesia when you have gangrene."[67] Still, explained Djindic, the operation was a necessary one for the country's long-term health. It would not turn out to be politically so simple, though.

The grainy photograph of two UN security officers escorting Slobodan Milosevic to the tribunal's detention center that night of June 28, 2001, provided an indelible symbol of the tribunal's newfound power. Just a few years earlier, even getting low-level suspects into tribunal custody involved moving political mountains. But now the international spotlight moved to the court as it prepared to hold what promised to be one of the most important trials of the new century. Only a few years previously, Western leaders had thanked Milosevic for his crucial role at the Dayton peace talks, even praising him as a statesman. Now, following the NATO war against Serbia, Western leaders hailed his arrest, pointing to the trail of death he had left through the Balkans.

Its symbolic importance notwithstanding, the Milosevic trial itself would prove a cautionary tale regarding the many problems international courts can face when taking on a complex case that involves determining whether a head of state is criminally responsible for genocide and other atrocities committed far from his (or her) capital. The prosecution's decision to charge Milosevic in connection with crimes in Kosovo, Croatia, and Bosnia ensured that the trial would last years. In perhaps the tribunal's greatest setback, Milosevic suffered a fatal heart attack in March 2006, shortly before his more than four-year-long trial would have been completed. Revelations of lax procedures in his medical treatment while in custody proved a major blow to the tribunal's reputation. It was not the first time the tribunal had been denied a looming conviction. Just a week earlier, former Croatian Serb leader Milan Babic had committed suicide in his tribunal jail cell. And in 1998, Slavko Dokmanovic, the former mayor of Vukovar, had committed suicide by hanging himself in a tribunal jail cell shortly before a verdict could be rendered.

Tribunal officials and international human rights activists welcomed Milosevic's arrival at The Hague as a turning point in the struggle for state cooperation and arrests of those accused of war crimes. Yet in the years to come Serbia would hand over other suspects only in fits and starts, and usually only when key international actors applied strong pressure and offered attractive incentives. The only monetary rewards officially on offer were the ones available from the U.S. Department of State's war crimes office—up to $5 million for information leading to the arrest of Yugoslavia tribunal fugitives. In reality, the most effective rewards were much-needed loans and other material incentives that the West provided to the states of the former Yugoslavia for fulfilling their legal obligations. To downplay the unseemly appearance of a cash-for-suspects transaction, these were not officially designated as rewards, but the financial arrangements surely constituted a handsome payback.

Within a few years of Milosevic's arrest, the U.S., preoccupied by its post–September 11 wars in Afghanistan and Iraq, ceded its leadership role in the Balkans to the European Union. The EU dangled an even larger carrot than economic assistance to encourage the states of the former Yugoslavia to overcome their aversion to arresting their own nationals for international war crimes prosecution. The EU's mechanism became known as "conditionality" because it made handover of tribunal suspects a condition of a state's advancement toward European Union membership. The incentive was a particularly strong one because at the time many reformist leaders in the former Yugoslavia viewed EU membership as crucial for ameliorating their nation's political and economic woes.

If EU conditionality became indispensable to the tribunal's quest for suspects, it, too, was susceptible to negotiation and manipulation. Serbian and Croatian diplomats constantly pressed their case for leniency in implementation, sometimes quite successfully. The EU, in turn, at times diluted its conditionality policy when it perceived that pressuring Serbia and Croatia to make arrests would undermine the political standing of pro-European moderates. When the EU relaxed its conditionality policy, Serbia as well as Croatia predictably lost interest in making arrests.

In Serbia, the demise of Milosevic's rule did little to alter the deep-seated antipathy to an international court viewed as trampling on state sovereignty. In Croatia, which also moved away from authoritarian rule with the death of Tudjman in December 1999 and the election of a center-left coalition in early 2000, claims of tribunal persecution became a rallying cry. Nationalists argued that any indictments of ethnic Croats created an unfair moral equivalence between the lesser overall transgressions of Croat suspects and the greater overall culpability of Serb suspects. Serbian and Croatian leaders, therefore, carefully weighed the potential benefits of fulfilling their legal obligation to the tribunal against the palpable prospect of backlash at home.

CARLA DEL PONTE AND THE RISE AND FALL OF A SERBIAN MODERATE

With Milosevic in custody, Carla Del Ponte, who had taken over from Arbour as tribunal chief prosecutor in September 1999, trained her sights on Mladic, who, along with Karadzic, was now at the top of the tribunal's most wanted list. The Serbian government had proved skillful at staving off international pressure for his capture by instead arresting low-level suspects at strategic intervals. The EU, the U.S., and the UN Security Council bolstered this dynamic by not delivering an ultimatum for the arrest of Mladic and Karadzic, as the U.S. had for Milosevic in 2001.

Del Ponte, who had been involved in high-profile Mafia investigations during her tenure as Switzerland's attorney general, quickly earned a reputation for an effective no-holds-barred approach to dealing with uncooperative states. Taking a page out of the human rights activist playbook, Del Ponte, to a greater extent than either Richard Goldstone or Louise Arbour, employed the politics of shame, castigating politicians she perceived to be obstructing the course of justice. In private meetings with heads of state and in public speeches at the Security Council, Del Ponte said what was on her mind, devoting little attention to the diplomatic niceties that Goldstone felt were key to cultivating relationships. Critics charged that she relished confrontation at the expense of smart diplomacy. And there can be downsides to a prosecutorial strategy that brandishes shaming to the exclusion of less adversarial forms of persuasion: continual complaints of state noncooperation without tangible results can make an international criminal tribunal seem simply ineffectual.[68] For her part, Louise Arbour came to believe there was too much faith placed in the celebrated human rights strategy of shaming. "I never believed in shaming the Security Council," she said. "It is like whistling in the wind."[69]

Even as Del Ponte burnished her adversarial image, she remained mindful of cultivating allies in the former Yugoslavia as well as in the West. For Del Ponte and other chief prosecutors, making friends often provided the clearest path to garnering state cooperation and ensuring arrests. Given their lack of enforcement powers, uneven international support for their work, and the frequent defiance of targeted states, all of the contemporary chief prosecutors have realized the need to selectively compromise to advance the difficult quest for state cooperation, even as they rarely acknowledge their political maneuvering in order to uphold their moral authority as purely legal actors.

From her first meeting with Serbian Prime Minister Djindic in early 2001, Del Ponte sought to establish an alliance with this pragmatic, pro-Western politician. The prime minister's outlook, in Del Ponte's estimation, was far different from that of Kostunica, whom she publicly derided for his "incredible nationalism" and for being "a man of the past."[70] In contrast, Del Ponte treated Djindic as a trusted ally. How she later handled his request for lenience in the timing of Mladic's arrest is a case in point. In early 2003, when Djindic privately asked Del Ponte for some respite from her public calls for Mladic's capture so that he might overcome domestic opposition, Del Ponte obliged: after all, Djindic had already proven himself an invaluable tribunal ally in handing over Slobodan Milosevic. Further, Djindic's promise to crack down on organized crime groups, some of whose members faced tribunal indictment and maintained close ties to the state security services, further bolstered Del Ponte's confidence in the prime minister.

Djindic went on to tell Del Ponte that he was vulnerable to the Serbian organized crime–war criminal nexus he had vowed to target, she reported.[71] "He told me, 'They will kill me.' But he didn't believe it. He thought he was protected," Del Ponte recalled, and she had warned

Djindic that he actually was in grave danger, she said. Assassins had already made an unsuccessful attempt on his life by slamming a truck into his motorcade in late February 2003. A few weeks later, on March 12, 2003, the fifty-year-old prime minister was murdered by a sniper's bullet as he entered a government building in Belgrade.

In the aftermath of the assassination, some in Serbia harshly criticized the tribunal and the chief prosecutor for allegedly contributing to the domestic political backlash that ended the prime minister's life. Skeptics asked whether Del Ponte's crusading campaign for arrests was worth the high price of political instability in Serbia. This was a variation on the question frequently asked in Bosnia in the mid-1990s, when NATO feared that arrests of war crimes suspects would jeopardize the fragile peace. Now in Serbia a parallel debate arose as to whether the pursuit of suspects advanced or imperiled the country's democratic transition. After losing Djindic, it became increasingly difficult to argue that international justice was a risk-free endeavor. The tribunal and Del Ponte herself were thrown on the defensive.

Yet for Zoran Zivkovic, the former interior minister who became the next prime minister, Djindic's assassination at the hands of criminal gangs implicated in wartime atrocities imparted an urgent lesson. Given the threat posed to Serbian democracy, carrying out Djindic's planned crackdown was imperative, he concluded. Acting under emergency powers, Serbian police made mass arrests of those believed to be involved in the assassination or implicated in criminal networks, including high-level members of Milosevic's security apparatus. The operation resulted in the arrest or detention of more than 10,000 people.[72] Many suspects were denied access to lawyers, and accusations of widespread human rights violations, including torture, at the hands of the police followed.[73] Earlier in the year, prominent international NGOs such as Human Rights Watch had criticized Serbia's lack of resolve in arresting indicted suspects. Now these groups issued stinging criticisms of the government's overzealousness.[74]

DAMAGING LEAKS AND OTHER OBSTRUCTIONS OF JUSTICE

In February 2001, the Croatian government's decision to prosecute some of its own soldiers for war crimes triggered mass demonstrations in the Dalmatian port city of Split. Many of the 150,000 antigovernment protesters also rallied to block the government's rumored move to send another Croatian war crimes suspect to the Yugoslavia tribunal. That suspect, Milan Norac, a retired army general who had also participated in Operation Storm, was not yet subject to a tribunal indictment but had recently been named in a Croatian arrest warrant for his alleged role in the 1991 killing of approximately forty Serb civilians.[75]

Given the likelihood that public indictments would inflame the political situation in Croatia, Del Ponte opted for sealed indictments when Croatian generals Ante Gotovina and Rahim Ademi were targeted in June 2001. Six years after the Croatian military assault on the Krajina region in Operation Storm, these two generals now faced charges of war crimes and crimes against humanity.

Shortly after the tribunal handed Croatian officials the sealed indictments, however, the news was leaked to the Croatian media. The damaging leak underscored the downside of trusting a government where some officials had an interest in helping suspects evade accountability. Gotovina's fate in particular became a matter of rancorous public debate rather than a straightforward legal obligation smoothly executed by Croatian law enforcement. On July 7, the Croatian cabinet convened an emergency meeting to discuss whether to arrest Gotovina and Ademi, a Croatian general of Albanian ethnicity. Prime Minister Ivica Racan emerged from the six-hour meeting promising arrests (Ademi eventually turned himself in to tribunal authorities in Amsterdam). Racan's pledge played well in the international diplomatic arena, but not at home. Four cabinet ministers resigned in protest, and nationalists threatened to stage a repeat of the mass protest in Split earlier that year.[76]

Despite his promise of cooperation with the tribunal, Racan did not move to arrest Gotovina, and the latter did what any fugitive with little interest in trading liberty for a prison cell did: he went into hiding. Around the same time, a right-wing author held a book promotion event touting his new biography of Gotovina. It was an author's dream; 5,000 people assembled in Gotovina's hometown, the Dalmatian coastal municipality of Zadar, to celebrate the book and its hero.[77] That event marked Gotovina's "transformation from mere soldier, adventurer and ladies' man, into a potent political symbol," opined Croatian scholar Vjeran Pavlakovic.[78] Throughout the country, particularly in the nationalist strongholds along the breathtaking Dalmatian Coast, photographs of the general in military dress adorned billboards and posters. At the height of Gotovina's popularity, observed Pavlakovic, it was "practically impossible to travel in the country without encountering his image."[79]

Slogans printed alongside his image, which also adorned T-shirts, key-chains, wine bottles, and graffiti, reprised the nationalist defiance of the 2001 protest in Split. A popular nationalist slogan made creative use of the word *gotovina*, which means "cash" in Serbo-Croatian: "Don't pay for entry into the EU with Gotovina."[80] Gotovina's fugitive status only bolstered his image as a national icon, heightening the political risk of arresting him.

Prime Minister Racan tried to deflect international criticism of government inaction, telling journalists in summer 2001: "Don't ask me every day where Gotovina is; I told you I don't know."[81] Chief Prosecutor Del Ponte, meanwhile, felt betrayed by the leak of her sealed indictment. "My trust was misplaced," she told the Security Council in October 2002, adding that Gotovina "was allowed to evade arrest . . . [and] . . . he is now enjoying a safe haven in the territory of Croatia."[82]

Trusting national authorities with confidential information has proved a perennial challenge for tribunal chief prosecutors, as seen in the leaking of the Gotovina indictment. Two years later, for example, tribunal officials transmitted a sealed indictment to Serb authorities only to learn that the suspect had soon fled. The next time around, Del Ponte was prepared: she arranged to have the house of a Serb suspect put under surveillance to observe his actions immediately after tribunal officials handed a sealed indictment to the Serbian foreign ministry. The work of investigating war crimes had thus expanded to investigating a state's efforts to obstruct the course of justice.

At 9:30 A.M. on July 13, 2004, a tribunal official met with Serbian foreign ministry officials in Belgrade to deliver a sealed indictment and an arrest warrant for Goran Hadzic, an ethnic Serb wanted for war crimes in Croatia, including involvement in the infamous Vukovar hospital massacre.[83] The officials were also told exactly where they could find Hadzic: in his house in Novi Sad, Serbia's second-largest city.

Back at the stakeout in view of Hadzic's house, the suspect's every move was being tracked. A few hours after the indictment had been given to Serbian officials in Belgrade, Hadzic, working in his garden, was observed receiving a brief cell phone call. Immediately afterward he left the garden, and minutes later, walked out of his house carrying a briefcase and drove away. Two days later, Serbian police reported to a judge that they could not find him at his house and did not know his whereabouts.[84]

Only a week and a half before this tip-off, the Serbian foreign minister himself, Vuk Draskovic, had promised an end to government obstruction: "Our obligations toward The Hague court are something that must not be bargained with, they must be followed through. We don't want to be an isolated island in the sea of European democracies. All the excuses have been long spent."[85] Yet excuses still held currency with many of the European democracies he had in mind. When it came to failing to arrest high-level fugitives, the Serbian and Croatian governments could still win respites from international pressure and punishment. The most effective way for Belgrade and Zagreb to do so was to plead extenuating circumstances—their alleged inability to track down key suspects, or the specter of domestic instability if the suspects were actually found and then arrested.

THE POLITICS OF EU CONDITIONALITY

Ordering the arrest of war crimes suspects ultimately rested with decision-makers in the Balkans. But these decisions could be heavily influenced by officials in the corridors of EU headquarters in Brussels who wielded the instrument of "conditionality," the policy that made Serbia and Croatia's progress toward European membership contingent on the handover of war crimes suspects.[86] The EU, which had begun life in the 1950s as an economic union called the European Steel and Coal Community, had in recent years styled itself as a club of nations that placed the pursuit of human rights on an equal footing with the quest for material wealth and social welfare. Therein lay its promise to back a European-based tribunal with a mandate to determine individual criminal responsibility for atrocities that occurred on Europe's doorstep.

By 2005, EU leaders stipulated that *full cooperation* with the Yugoslavia tribunal would be a condition for Serbia's and Croatia's bids to move closer to EU membership. But the conditionality policy was still susceptible to interpretation and negotiation. The states of the former Yugoslavia as well as the tribunal each thus tried to gain the upper hand in influencing the twenty-seven-member EU to act in its favor. The political objective of the Croatian government focused on deflecting EU pressure to track down and arrest Gotovina while soliciting Brussels' invitation to become the Union's twenty-eighth member state. (Croatia would eventually enter the EU in 2013.) Zagreb sought to score points by handing over less important suspects. In 2004, for example, the new center-right Croatian prime minister, Ivo Sanader, facilitated the transfer of three Croatian generals implicated in Operation Storm crimes and six Bosnian Croats implicated in atrocities that occurred in the war in Bosnia. Sanader's HDZ (Croatian Democratic Union) government, in power since 2003, was the heir of President Tudjman's HDZ nationalist party. Even as Sanader's HDZ cultivated a more moderate image, its nationalist credentials insulated it from right-wing attacks portraying state cooperation as collaboration with a foreign enemy.

The Croatian government sought to capitalize on the 2004 surrenders of the three Croatian generals and the six Bosnian Croat suspects in the hopes of winning an invitation to become an official EU candidate country, though without first handing over Gotovina. Initially, Brussels handsomely rewarded Croatia that year by granting it candidate status, a move that opened the way for membership negotiations. Del Ponte played a crucial role in the EU's decision by giving Zagreb high marks for its recent upturn in cooperation. The prosecutor's glowing assessment was open to question, however, given Croatia's ongoing failure to help track down Gotovina, the most important Croatian suspect.[87]

Having cleared a major obstacle in the path toward Brussels, Croatian leaders now acted as if there were little reason to work toward Gotovina's arrest. But Zagreb sorely underestimated the EU's resolve to harden its conditionality policy. Del Ponte's conciliation turned to confrontation later in 2004, when she sharply criticized Croatia's lackluster cooperation in pursuing Gotovina. Under pressure from Del Ponte, EU officials turned up the pressure on Zagreb. Just one day before the scheduled opening of membership discussions with Croatia in March 2005, the EU called off the talks and vowed not to restart them until Zagreb delivered its prime suspect. Croatian law enforcement had to arrest Gotovina, or, if he was outside the country, it must mount a vigorous effort to help track him down.

For years, Croatian leaders had denied knowing where Gotovina was. Now they made it their business to find out. Del Ponte began to see a "can do" attitude on the part of a team of Croatian officials working under the direction of the Croatian state prosecutor and tasked with tracking down the fugitive. The Croatian efforts focused not only on the operational aspects of finding Gotovina but also on disrupting his network of support within and outside the Croatian government.[88] In spring 2005, the government also began to take some action to weaken his societal support by releasing details of his criminal past and taking down some banners extolling the retired general.[89]

In late September 2005, Del Ponte sensed that a major breakthrough might be near. By monitoring Gotovina's cell-phone calls to his family in Croatia, Croatian authorities had learned that the itinerant Gotovina had recently been in Spain's Canary Islands, off the northwest coast of Africa, and later had returned there. The authorities then traced him to a luxury hotel on the island of Tenerife, where he had registered under a false name and with a false passport. With this information in hand, Spanish special forces moved in to apprehend Gotovina on the evening of December 7, just after the celebrated fugitive had ordered dinner and wine and was settling in for a pleasant evening at his seaside hotel.

Gotovina's arrest and subsequent arrival in The Hague sparked nationalist demonstrations back in Zagreb and Split. But none of the protests approached the scale of those that had threatened to destabilize Croatia in early 2001. The nationalist claim that prosecuting Gotovina would tarnish the legitimacy of Operation Storm and undermine the foundations of the newly independent Croatian state still had currency. But a consensus had formed among the Croatian political elite that securing the country's European future trumped all. Moreover, the government's right-wing credentials protected it from later suffering significant losses at the polls from accusations of national betrayal. It helped, of course, that the government left few fingerprints on an arrest operation carried out by another country's police force and far from Croatia's Dalmatian shores.

KARADZIC AND MLADIC: THE TENACIOUS FUGITIVES

While Gotovina sat in a jail cell in The Hague, Mladic and Karadzic continued to elude the tribunal by staying on their home turf in the heart of the Balkans. Europe's two most wanted war crimes suspects still reaped the benefits of sophisticated support networks with ties to the Serbian security services. Yet by late 2005, a decade since the signing of the Dayton peace accords, their world had become a lot smaller. Long past were the days when the two former Bosnian Serb leaders could drive freely through NATO checkpoints and dine openly in Bosnian Serb cafes or in Belgrade's finest restaurants.

The gravitational pull of the EU had given new incentive to Serbian and Croatian leaders to turn against their wartime heroes. The imperative to make progress toward EU membership even influenced Vojislav Kostunica—who returned to power as the Serbian prime minister in 2004—to facilitate the "voluntary" arrest and handover of scores of other Serbian suspects. In Sarajevo, the Bosnian Muslim–dominated government, which also aspired to gain admission to the EU, stood out for its smooth handover of its own nationals and its strong support for an international tribunal that was shining a global spotlight on its wartime victimization.

With so many war crimes suspects captured and compelled to surrender in Serbia, both Mladic and Karadzic recognized that they were
living on borrowed time if they didn't make further moves to elude capture. For each man, this new chapter in their lives as fugitives from
international justice began around the same time.

Early in 2006, Mladic made his way to the home of an unmarried
second cousin whom he had not seen for years, Branislav Mladic, in the
village of Lazarevo, eighty kilometers north of Belgrade. In the middle
of the night, Mladic knocked on the door of Branislav's small house.
When his cousin opened the door, Mladic whispered, "Do you know
who I am?"[90] For the next five years, the two cousins, whose grandfathers were brothers and who both hailed from the mountainous
region of eastern Bosnia, were housemates.[91]

Living in close quarters, the cousins followed a daily routine that
began with an early-morning coffee together before Branislav began his
farm work. Mladic spent much of his time reading the Serbian press and
watching television shows. On the rare occasions when he would venture outside, it would usually be late in the evening, for a short stroll in
the farmyard. The family bond with his bachelor cousin, as well as a
Serbian law immunizing relatives of a wanted man from obstruction-of-
justice charges, apparently helped keep Mladic's whereabouts secret.[92]

While Mladic hid from the authorities out of sight, Karadzic chose to
hide disguised but in plain sight. When the psychiatrist turned political
leader moved to the Serbian capital in 2005 he reinvented himself again,
this time as a New Age healer. In one of the most elaborate ruses for a
war crimes fugitive in the annals of international justice, Karadzic began
by taking on the name Dragan Dabic, which actually belonged to a
working-class man from a small Serbian town.[93]

Dabic's old-fashioned appearance—accentuated by a top hat, long
overcoat, oversized glasses, and flowing beard—helped complete his
transformation from one of the world's most wanted war crimes suspects into an intriguing newcomer to Belgrade's burgeoning New Age
scene.[94] Karadzic also abandoned his Bosnian accent, adopting a Belgrade one instead, and lost a considerable amount of weight. "In the
end, Dragan Dabic inhabited a persona and a face that obscured every
physical, auditory and historical feature associated with Radovan Karadzic," journalist Jack Hitt wrote in a *New York Times Magazine* article
that revealed the bizarre story of how the former Bosnian Serb leader
forged a new life and did so with "such hippie panache."[95]

As he began to develop some familiarity with his new world, Dabic focused on becoming a "bioenergy" healer, which involved moving his hands near a patient's body in order, somehow, to regulate energy flows. On the side, he worked with a Belgrade sexologist trying to develop a new sperm-rejuvenation method. Dabic also developed his own website and soon began writing a regular column for a national alternative medicine magazine. To supplement his income, he added on work as a Belgrade sales representative for a Connecticut-based vitamin company. The ironies of Karadzic's midlife career turn were multifold. Indeed, aspiring to be a healer was a stunning turnaround for a man accused of causing so much suffering.

To the small circle of New Age healers with whom he interacted, there was no reason to doubt that Dabic was who he said he was. That said, Mina Minic, an established practitioner whom Dabic had befriended, suspected that Dabic was actually a spy: his multiple cell phones were perpetually ringing, and he would never speak for long in the presence of others. Dabic's evasive explanations of his professional past and family history also sparked suspicion. When asked why he did not have a certificate substantiating his claims to be a New Age healer, Karadzic blamed an estranged wife who lived in New York and refused to send it. Still, none of his New Age associates harbored the slightest suspicion that he was actually Radovan Karadzic. Nor did people he met and passed in the street, including an employee at Interpol's Belgrade office. Every morning on her way to work, she would pass Dabic and bid him a good day. And then a few minutes later she would turn on her computer and gaze at Interpol's most wanted list, which featured Karadzic. Never once did she wonder whether Dabic and Karadzic might be one and the same.[96]

INTERNATIONAL CAT AND MOUSE

Backed by leading international human rights organizations, Carla Del Ponte repeatedly claimed that Mladic was hiding in Serbia and within reach of the authorities, though she reported Karadzic was likely moving between the mountainous region of eastern Bosnia and western Montenegro. At risk of losing its prized reputation as a global human rights leader, the EU could ill afford to ignore Del Ponte's criticism of state noncooperation, especially because it had routinely turned to her as the authority best situated to assess state cooperation.[97]

Under growing international pressure, Serbian Prime Minister Vojislav Kostunica promised in early 2006 to apprehend Mladic within
months. The pledge held particular significance because he had earlier
denied that Mladic was in Serbia at all. In the clearest backing of the
tribunal to date, the EU established a March 31, 2006, deadline, later
extended by a month, by which pre-membership talks with Serbia
would be frozen if Mladic had not yet been apprehended. With Mladic
still at large in early May 2006, the EU held true to its word: the
country's path toward Brussels would remain blocked, EU officials said,
until Serbian authorities delivered the former Bosnian Serb general to
the tribunal.

International censure of Serbia's noncooperation intensified with a
historic decision handed down by another international court in The
Hague. In early 2007, the UN International Court of Justice (ICJ), which
hears civil suits between states, issued its long-awaited decision in the
genocide lawsuit that Bosnia had lodged against Serbia. Although the
ICJ ruled that Serbia was not responsible for the genocide in Srebrenica,
it declared that Serbia's failure to arrest Mladic and Karadzic constituted
a violation of the UN Genocide Convention of 1948, the international
treaty codifying states' obligations to prevent and prosecute genocide.
This marked the first and to date only time the ICJ has found a state in
violation of its duty to assist in the prosecution of genocide. In doing so,
the ICJ had validated Del Ponte's claim that Serbia had violated international law by effectively obstructing the course of justice.

The moral weight of the ICJ ruling had the potential to be a political
game changer compelling Belgrade to finally locate, apprehend, and
hand over the alleged architects of the Srebrenica genocide. Yet not long
after the ICJ ruling, EU member states reversed their course, reneging
on their commitment to keep the pre-membership talks with Serbia suspended as leverage to compel Mladic's arrest. With national elections
approaching in Serbia, EU officials grew worried that their decision to
halt the country's progress toward EU membership would bring to
power in Belgrade ultranationalists with sympathy toward Russia.
European diplomats felt that taking an uncompromising stance on
behalf of international justice could exact too high a political cost. Reo-
pening the talks, EU officials reasoned, would bolster the electoral fortunes of Serbian pro-Western moderates whose political popularity
relied on advancing the country closer to EU membership.

In Brussels, EU officials seeking political cover for relieving pressure
on Serbia changed the measuring stick by which to gauge Serbian gov-

ernment cooperation. The decision to reopen the pre-membership talks was made, they explained, because Serbia had, in their estimation, shown a clear commitment to be fully cooperative in its attempts to find and arrest tribunal fugitives. This despite the fact that Mladic remained at large and that evidence was compelling that only a few years earlier the Serbian government had protected him, even providing him with his retirement pension. Just as the EU engaged in the politics of compromise, so too did Chief Prosecutor Del Ponte. With the EU apparently set to weaken its conditionality policy, Del Ponte took a decidedly conciliatory step by positively evaluating Belgrade's cooperation despite its ongoing failure to arrest Mladic.

Seeking to fend off further criticism of betraying human rights values, EU officials made a new promise to the tribunal: Serbia would not be declared an EU candidate country until Mladic and Karadzic were actually sent to The Hague. Yet shortly afterward, EU officials again relieved pressure on Serbia, undermining the ICJ ruling on Serbia's violation of the genocide convention. In its newest diplomatic formulation, Serbia was told it could gain candidate status even if it did not hand over the few remaining fugitives—as long as the EU considered that its cooperation was sufficient to lead to future arrests. With the ultranationalist party ahead in the polls as elections loomed in 2008, the EU granted Serbia an early signing of a pre-membership agreement. Once again, the EU strategy was designed to bolster the political prospects of pro-European moderates. Still, some EU officials privately conceded that Belgrade had not arrested any tribunal suspects in almost a year. "It is stretching [it] a bit to say cooperation [was] satisfactory when it is not," remarked an EU official familiar with the negotiations with Serbia.[98] Nevertheless, Serbia's moderate Democratic Party, led by Boris Tadic, prevailed at the polls.

The EU's emphasis on encouraging efforts in lieu of delivering results gave Belgrade new incentive to showcase attempts to tighten the net around Mladic by staging well-publicized raids. At the same time, some Serbian officials downplayed the state's responsibility to arrest Mladic by repeating the old story that he was no longer in Serbia.[99] The Netherlands, still stung by the debacle at Srebrenica and feeling a special responsibility to the tribunal because it played host to the court in The Hague, remained skeptical of Serbian sincerity. "I will believe it when I see it," Dutch Foreign Minister Bernard Bot said in July 2006 when it came to the question of Serbia's actual commitment to arresting Mladic.[100] Most EU states, however, favored diluting the EU's conditionality policy to speed Serbia's path toward membership. Summing up the softening European approach, French Foreign Minister Bernard Kouchner publicly credited Serbian authorities for trying their best to capture Mladic and the remaining fugitives: "I believe they're doing what they can. They should keep going, that's key," he announced in October 2009.[101]

Even a number of EU officials who advocated a softer conditionality policy prior to the Serbian national elections in spring 2008 doubted whether the shifting political climate would actually prompt the authorities to arrest either Karadzic or Mladic. But soon after he took office in early July 2008, Boris Tadic did in fact intensify the state's efforts to track down and arrest Karadzic.

In late July, thirteen years after the Srebrenica massacre, Karadzic's life on the run came to an end when Serbian authorities arrested him on a bus in a Belgrade suburb. So, too, did the New Age adventure of Dragan Dabic, who was just gaining prominence as a bioenergy healer, vitamin salesman, and columnist for an alternative health magazine. Some mystery still surrounds the circumstances of his capture, particularly how Serbian authorities could have arrested Karadzic so soon after Tadic took office after years of government denial of knowing the whereabouts of the former Bosnian Serb president. Serbian officials explained that Karadzic had been under surveillance for several weeks after they had received a tip from a foreign intelligence agency.

SERGE BRAMMERTZ AND THE ENDGAME
OF SERBIAN NONCOMPLIANCE

Karadzic's arrival in The Hague accelerated Europe's political embrace of Serbia. Over the next two and a half years, Brussels rewarded Belgrade with political and economic concessions aimed at bolstering the Serbian moderates and keeping the prize of EU membership alive. But as more time passed hopes of finding and finally prosecuting Mladic—along with the other remaining tribunal fugitive, Croatian Serb Goran Hadzic, also believed to be hiding in Serbia—dimmed. Serge Brammertz, the tribunal's new chief prosecutor as of January 2008, was a former Belgian investigatory judge who had served briefly as International Criminal Court deputy prosecutor and then as head of the UN commission investigating the 2005 car-bomb assassination of former Lebanese Prime Minister Rafiq Hariri. He seemed the antithesis of the hard-charging Carla Del Ponte. "Brammertz is a Eurocrat," lamented a tribunal insider in 2010, suggesting that the Belgian would be unwilling to insist that Brussels pressure Serbia on the Mladic issue. With time running out in the tribunal's mandate, activists and victim groups in Bosnia feared that the campaign to capture Mladic was losing urgency not only in Belgrade but in Brussels and even in The Hague.

In his initial biannual speech to the UN Security Council in early June 2008, Brammertz had come across as lenient. Rather than remind the Security Council of Serbia's violation of the UN Genocide Convention, as underscored by the ICJ's unprecedented 2007 ruling, the prosecutor credited the new Tadic government with launching "a genuine but, alas, failed attempt" to arrest a Bosnian Serb suspect whom Serbian authorities ended up arresting later that month.[102] In his December 2008 speech, he again struck a conciliatory note by highlighting the potential of Belgrade's new action plan to find and arrest Mladic. Brammertz's 2009 speeches also credited the Serbian government for improving its hunt for Mladic and Hadzic.

With time running out, however, Brammertz grew more critical of Serbian efforts. In December 2010, he told the Security Council that results, not efforts, were the true litmus test for state cooperation.[103] The prosecutor and his small circle of advisers had also come to realize that Serbia and key EU states were selectively interpreting his Security Council reports in a bid to justify a weakening of the EU conditionality policy. Recognition of such manipulation, one well-placed prosecution official recounted, influenced Brammertz's shift to a more confrontational approach. "That was a triggering point when we saw how our words were twisted and turned and used for political goals," the official recalled. With that realization came the "the real fear that we were losing leverage."[104]

Brammertz did not need to brandish the politics of shame so freely used by his predecessor to make heads turn in Belgrade and Brussels. Because EU politicians regarded the tribunal chief prosecutor as the most authoritative evaluator of state cooperation, they could not simply ignore Brammertz's measured yet mounting criticism. Even before his critical turn, some diplomats considered Brammertz a shrewd practitioner of prosecutorial diplomacy, given his ability to safeguard the tribunal's influence over Europe's malleable conditionality policy without antagonizing Belgrade or alienating Brussels. Brammertz did so, according to U.S. war crimes ambassador Stephen Rapp, by acknowledging improvements in Serbian cooperation, but not declaring that the government had achieved full cooperation.[105]

For Brammertz, building trust and credibility in Belgrade and Brussels remained paramount. By doing so, he sought to inoculate himself against charges of being too aggressively political. Such accusations had dogged Carla Del Ponte even though she too reverted to conciliation as a means to elicit state cooperation. Brammertz realized, as the prosecution official said, that a chief prosecutor's assessments of state cooperation were political tools with far-reaching political consequences. It therefore behooved the prosecutor to craft his public statements with great care so as not to be seen as crossing the line from impartial legal actor to a partisan political one. Yet in strategically navigating the shoals of international affairs, Brammertz, no less than his predecessors, was engaged in the politics of prosecutorial diplomacy.

The primary function of a tribunal chief prosecutor is to investigate individual criminal responsibility for violations of international humanitarian law. But as Brammertz had come to learn, a no less important role is to investigate how targeted states may be impeding the course of international justice. Toward this end, Brammertz sent Bob Reid, his veteran chief of investigations, to Belgrade to work closely with Serbian law enforcement officials and to evaluate their plan to arrest Mladic.[106] In his Security Council reports, the prosecutor urged the Serbian authorities to intensify their hunt for the former Bosnian Serb general, including tracking the movements of Mladic's family. "They were not doing the basic investigatory steps," said the prosecution official, referring to what Reid had learned about the shortcomings of Serbia's efforts to track down Mladic. "We were convinced it was going nowhere."[107]

Serbia's full-court press to win designation as an official EU candidate country further bolstered the prosecutor's leverage. European foreign ministers had voted in October 2010 to move Serbia closer to this prize by requesting a formal study of its membership bid. But Brammertz's growing criticism pressed the EU again to condition Serbia's quest for candidate status on delivering Mladic. The Netherlands remained steadfast and, like one of its famous dikes, held back the European tide favoring Serbia. Just weeks before the prosecutor's June 2011 Security Council address, the Serbian press published the contents of Brammertz's forthcoming report criticizing the government's insufficient efforts to find Mladic. The impact of the report was reinforced by a May visit to Belgrade by Dutch Parliament members who said in no uncertain terms that the Netherlands would block Serbia's quest for EU candidacy status as long as Brammertz remained critical of Serbia's search for Mladic.

With the writing on the wall, the politics of delay that Serbian authorities had turned into an art form quickly approached its endgame. Now, Serbian officials intensified their efforts to catch Mladic, including stepped-up monitoring of Mladic's family members. Around the same time, Mladic, pining for a reunion with his son and grandchildren, arranged for them to visit his elderly cousin Branislav's farmyard. As his two young grandchildren petted the animals in the farmyard, Mladic watched from a distance, remaining out of sight in the house. "I told him it was a big mistake," Branislav recalled, "but he wouldn't listen."[108]

On May 26, 2011, Serbian authorities raided the small house in Lazarevo. Nearly sixteen years after the notorious massacre at Srebrenica, the former Bosnian Serb general, now sick and ailing from three recent strokes, surrendered to Serbian authorities without even trying to reach for the pair of pistols he kept nearby. The timing of the arrest, coming on the heels of Brammertz's decisive report, raised suspicions that Serbian law enforcement officials had long known of Mladic's whereabouts, but only moved to action when given no other alternative.

Following Mladic's transfer to The Hague in early June, Serbia moved to apprehend Goran Hadzic, the last remaining fugitive under tribunal indictment and the suspect who had fled his home in Novi Sad back in 2004 just after receiving a tip from a government insider. Wanted for his involvement in the Vukovar hospital massacre and other war crimes in Croatia, he was finally arrested by Serbian authorities in July 2011 and transferred to The Hague. Serbia's chief prosecutor, Vladimir Vukcevic, later acknowledged that Hadzic had actually been under surveillance for some time. Serbian authorities had held off on arresting him until after Mladic's capture, explained Vukcevic, in the belief that an earlier arrest would spark international criticism that Serbia still lacked the political will to arrest Mladic.[109]

INCOMPLETE JUSTICE

Seen from one perspective, the Mladic and Hadzic arrests marked the culmination of a protracted but remarkably successful quest for the scores of suspects indicted by the Yugoslavia tribunal. In all, the tribunal indicted 161 individuals, of whom 20 had their indictments withdrawn by Louise Arbour, 16 died before their arrest or completion of trial, and 13 were referred back to national courts in the former Yugoslavia. The resolution of the fugitive problem demonstrates that even an international tribunal lacking enforcement powers, and one that in its early days was dismissed as a toothless institution, can surmount the arrest challenge, though only when the political interests of key international actors and targeted states converge. Yet even after summer 2011, the pursuit of accountability both in The Hague and the former Yugoslavia was by no means over.

Throughout its tenure, the Yugoslavia tribunal registered many convictions of low- and mid-level defendants as well as a number of senior figures responsible for atrocities committed throughout the former Yugoslavia. By August 2015, the tribunal had sentenced a total of eighty defendants while acquitting eighteen. Ten cases had yet to be adjudicated by the tribunal's appeals chamber, while four cases had still not cleared the trial stage. Like the other contemporary international war crimes courts, but unlike the Nuremberg and Tokyo tribunals, the Yugoslavia tribunal does not hand down death sentences. To date, the tribunal has only delivered five life sentences. However, the numbers of trials and convictions and the lengths of sentences do not tell the whole story of the Yugoslav tribunal. The trials—with verdicts handed down after affording defendants extensive due process—have played an essential role in upholding the principal of the rule of law while substantiating legal responsibility and historical truth for many of the atrocities that occurred in Bosnia, Croatia, and Kosovo.[110]

The tribunal's Srebrenica judgments have played a particularly important historical role with their finding that the murder of 8,000 Bosnian Muslim men and boys in July 1995 constituted genocide. This legal imprimatur has rendered it more difficult for Serb nationalists to convince their brethren that genocide did not occur or that the killings at Srebrenica were simply collateral damage. Moreover, key tribunal judgments, such as those relating to the prosecution of rape, have helped reverse the inured neglect of gender crimes in international trials. Beyond that, the trials have produced landmark legal precedents that have advanced the global development of international humanitarian law. The first of the modern international criminal tribunals, the Yugoslavia tribunal has stood out among its contemporaries for its professionalism and precedents. "By most measures, the International Criminal Tribunal for the Former Yugoslavia is the gold standard for international justice," Kenneth Roth, executive director of Human Rights Watch, concluded in 2013.[111]

Yet the pursuit of justice at the Yugoslavia tribunal has also disappointed many victims, dashing their expectations of more timely and extensive criminal accountability. A key source of grievance has been the prosecution's difficulty in linking atrocities on the ground to those in the highest echelons of power alleged to be the masterminds. This particularly relates to the prosecution's struggle to substantiate the key roles played by Serbian and Croatian political and military leaders in engineering crimes beyond their borders. In the view of many historians and analysts, the ultimate responsibility for the Bosnian war and its ethnic cleansing campaigns lay with nationalist leaders in Belgrade and Zagreb who seized on the collapse of Yugoslavia as an opportunity for ethnic cleansing and territorial gain. Yet the Yugoslavia tribunal has largely failed to hold high-level leaders in Serbia and Croatia criminally responsible for atrocities in Bosnia. In several instances, the age, ailing health, or death of key leaders has allowed them to escape trial or judgment. For instance, Croatian President Tudjman and his defense minister, Gojko Susak, both died before tribunal prosecutors could indict them in connection with atrocities in Bosnia as well as in Croatia. Another major Croatian suspect, former Army Chief of Staff Janko Bobetko, charged in connection with alleged crimes in the 1995 Operation Storm offensive, died before he could face trial. Then there is the legendary failure of the Slobodan Milosevic case, which has cast a long shadow over the tribunal. The court's most important trial ended inconclusively when the former Serbian leader died shortly before the end of his long-running trial. Verdicts in the cases against Mladic and Karadzic, the next-most important suspects to face trial, had not been delivered by November 2015. Moreover, a verdict in the long-running and often delayed trial of Vojislav Seselj, which began in November 2007, had not been delivered by late 2015. Prosecutors had hoped that the Karadzic and Mladic cases would be less difficult to substantiate, as compared to their greater challenge in the Milosevic trial, because of the more direct chain of command linking these two Bosnian Serb leaders to crimes they allegedly committed against Bosnian Muslims. The prosecution has been confounded by other problems in its effort to hold the highest-level suspects criminally responsible: tribunal judges have set high evidentiary thresholds for substantiating genocidal intent as well as for convicting political and military leaders of aiding and abetting atrocities physically committed by others.

For many victims, disappointment has centered around a string of recent acquittals handed down by the tribunal's appeals chamber, which have overturned the convictions of a number of prime suspects, including Bosnian Muslim military commander Naser Oric, Croatian generals Ante Gotovina and Mladen Markac, and former Serbian Army Chief General Momcilo Perisic. In the joint Gotovina and Markac case, the trial judges issued a unanimous decision in April 2011 finding that these Croatian generals had conspired with the late President Tudjman in a joint criminal enterprise to permanently expel ethnic Serbs from the Krajina region in the 1995 Operation Storm military assault. But in November 2012, the tribunal's appeals chamber reversed the decision on a 3–2 vote, ruling that there was insufficient evidence that Gotovina's forces had deliberately attacked Serb populations to force their exodus. The appeals chamber action, described by the *International Herald Tribune* as "the most dramatic reversal in the history of the war crimes tribunal,"[112] led to bitter recriminations in Serbia, giving ammunition to nationalists' long-standing accusation that the tribunal is an anti-Serb institution. The reversal also sparked controversy from the two dissenting appeals chamber judges. In his dissent, one of the judges lambasted the ruling authored by tribunal Chief Justice Theodor Meron, criticizing an aspect of the majority's reasoning as "grotesque" and the judgment itself as contradicting "any sense of justice."[113]

The February 2013 appeals chamber acquittal of Perisic—the former Serbian army chief earlier convicted by tribunal judges for aiding and abetting atrocities carried out by Bosnian Serb forces—proved to be another public relations debacle for the tribunal.[114] The appeal chamber's acquittal, in which Justice Meron also presided, has sparked intense controversy for establishing a new legal standard that makes it considerably more difficult for prosecutors to prove that suspects like Perisic, high-level but far removed from the crime scene, bear culpability for causing atrocities by providing arms and other material support to direct perpetrators. The new legal standard introduced by Meron and his colleagues in that case required the prosecution to show evidence that suspects like Perisic "specifically directed" the crime in question. Previously, a suspect's liability for aiding and abetting a crime could be established if the prosecution could show that the suspect knew that his actions were likely to have a substantial influence on the crime in question.

Applying the more stringent legal precedent from the Perisic appeals judgment, a tribunal trial chamber in May 2013 acquitted Jovica Stanisic and Franko Simatovic, two former state security chiefs who worked for Slobodan Milosevic directing Serb paramilitary forces in Bosnia and Croatia. The two defendants had been accused of establishing, organizing, and funding paramilitary units to attack and permanently remove scores of non-Serbs from certain parts of Bosnia and Croatia. "Arguably, if Hitler were being judged for crimes arising out of the Holocaust on the basis of that aiding and abetting standard now being applied by the [tribunal], he might well have gotten off," opined Chuck Sudetic, a former wartime journalist who later co-authored Carla Del Ponte's memoir.[115] Taken together, the Gotovina and Perisic acquittals signaled a conservative turn in tribunal jurisprudence that deeply worried human rights activists and others opposed to limiting the bounds of criminal responsibility.[116]

An appeals chamber ruling in the Nikola Sainovic case in early 2014 suggests that the pendulum may have shifted toward a more liberal interpretation of the aiding-and-abetting doctrine at the Yugoslavia tribunal. In this ruling, the appeals chamber (this time without Judge Meron on the appeals bench) rejected the "specific direction" legal standard from the Perisic appeal and upheld the Sainovic trial judgment.[117] Nevertheless, the Perisic acquittal stands, despite Chief Prosecutor Brammertz's extraordinary appeal for a reconsideration. The existence of these two contradictory appeals judgments has sowed some confusion regarding the Yugoslavia tribunal's definitive stance on the proper legal standard that should apply when defendants are accused of aiding and abetting atrocities.

Sainovic, a former prime minister of Serbia and a close associate of Slobodan Milosevic, and several other co-defendants, were found guilty for their role in a joint criminal enterprise for atrocities committed in Kosovo in 1999. To date, however, not a single suspect from the Serbian power structure in Belgrade has been found guilty of aiding and abetting the atrocities carried out by ethnic Serbs in Srebrenica and elsewhere in Bosnia and Croatia. Nor has a single high-level Croatian political or military leader been convicted for violations of international humanitarian law committed in Croatia or in neighboring Bosnia. Ramush Haradinaj, the former Kosovo prime minister and highest-level Kosovar Albanian to face tribunal indictment, secured an acquittal. In light of an earlier acquittal of another high-ranking Kosovar Albanian, no one of political importance from this ethnic group has been convicted either. Yugoslavia tribunal chief prosecutors distinguished themselves for their indictment of suspects from all the major ethnic groups in the Yugoslav wars of secession. But from the tribunal's judges emerge a more one-sided narrative of the wars that significantly diminishes the culpability of key high-level non-Serb suspects.

JUSTICE DELAYED

As the Yugoslavia tribunal worked on completing its final cases, a growing number of domestic prosecutors across the Balkans continued their targeting of scores of low- and mid-level war crimes suspects. In the mid-1990s, diplomats and activists had argued that international war crimes courts were necessary because warring states implicated in mass atrocities were too bent on revenge to deliver impartial justice. Indeed, in the aftermath of ethnic wars, the pursuit of criminal accountability by former belligerent states can easily degenerate into witch-hunts of suspects belonging to opposing ethnic, religious, or political groups. But by the early 2000s, the tide had begun to shift in favor of domestic prosecutions. In 2005, the High Representative for Bosnia and Herzegovina, the international protectorate created after the signing of the Dayton peace accords in December 1995, established a domestic–international "hybrid" tribunal in Sarajevo to pursue domestic war crimes prosecutions. Known as the War Crimes Chamber of the Court of Bosnia and Herzegovina, the tribunal, or chamber, had a substantial international presence, with international judges and prosecutors working alongside their Bosnian counterparts. In an effort to streamline its own caseload, the Yugoslavia tribunal transferred ten cases to the war crimes chamber for prosecution. It also sent three cases to Croatia for domestic trial. The Bosnian war crimes chamber eventually evolved into a domestic court and, by the end of 2013, had completed almost 100 war crimes cases while district courts throughout the country had taken on numerous other war crimes cases.[118] The chamber aims to bring an end to domestic war crime cases by 2023.[119]

This domestic turn in the pursuit of alleged war criminals holds promise as well as peril. On the plus side, domestic courts can adjudicate scores of additional cases that neither the Yugoslavia tribunal nor states outside the Balkans are willing or able to handle. In contrast to the Yugoslavia tribunal, which lacks any police force of its own, domestic prosecutors can use their own law enforcement agencies to make arrests. And in contrast to the Yugoslavia tribunal—which is still viewed by many ethnic Serbs (as well as ethnic Croats) as an unwanted intrusion on state sovereignty—domestic courts have the potential of garnering and sustaining more societal acceptance.

On the negative side of the ledger, nationalist leaders who oppose war crimes trials can undermine the authority of domestic war crimes courts by sparking sharp societal discord and political backlash. In Bosnia, for example, numerous Serb politicians have sought to demonize the Bosnian war crimes chamber. According to the Organization for Security and Co-operation in Europe, this crusade has caused "undue pressure and interference regarding the processing of specific cases" before the chamber.[120] Meanwhile, chamber officials fear that Bosnian Serb politicians serving in the national government could potentially undermine the chamber by cutting back funding and logistical support. Despite these real threats, law enforcement agencies in Bosnia and neighboring states have carried out scores of arrests, though as many as 10,000 war crime suspects remain at large due to a lack of resources and a general unwillingness to extradite suspects across borders.[121]

Still, there is hope that some of the more heinous crimes will be prosecuted. In a major breakthrough, Bosnian and Serbian prosecutors agreed in late 2012 on a protocol to share case files on suspects residing in their respective jurisdictions. In another promising development, Bosnian police conducted coordinated raids in December 2014 netting a total of fifteen suspects wanted in connection with the massacre of more than twenty Bosnian Muslims who were taken off a train in a remote border town in eastern Bosnia and murdered by Bosnian Serb militia members in 1993. Three months later, in March 2015, Serbian authorities arrested eight suspects in Serbia implicated in the Srebrenica massacre—the first time ethnic Serbs directly involved in the killings had been arrested in Serbia.

Significant progress has been made in prosecuting war crimes in the former Yugoslavia since the signing of the Dayton Accords in 1995. Yet more should be done. The pursuit of suspects implicated in the Branjevo Farm massacre, which took place days after the fall of Srebrenica, is a telling example of what has been achieved and what remains to be achieved in the pursuit of criminal accountability in the Balkans.

Today all but one of the eight foot soldiers implicated in the gunning down of some 800 Bosnian Muslim men in a fallow field on the Branjevo Farm have been arrested and tried. The first was Drazen Erdemovic, who surrendered to the Yugoslavia tribunal in the mid-1990s. Four others were arrested in Bosnia and convicted for their role in the massacre in 2012. Another suspect, Marko Boskic, had fled to the United States in 2000 and settled in the small town of Peabody, Massachusetts.[122] But U.S. immigration officials soon caught up with him, and forty-five other suspects connected to the Srebrenica massacres, and deported them to Bosnia.[123] In 2010, the Bosnian war crimes chamber convicted Boskic for his involvement in the killings on the farm. As of early 2015, U.S. immigration officials were in the process of trying to deport about 150 Bosnians and had identified a total of about 300 Bosnians living in America who were suspected of hiding their role in atrocities.[124]

Still another suspect in the Branjevo Farm massacre, Aleksander Cvetkovic, fled to Israel. According to testimony given by a comrade in his former unit, at some point during the executions Cvetkovic proposed using automatic weapons to speed up the killings. When the Bosnian authorities learned that Cvetkovic had fled Bosnia they asked Interpol to issue a red notice, which is a request for any country to locate and arrest a criminal suspect. Cvetkovic meanwhile married a Jewish woman, which entitled him to Israeli citizenship, and lived a tranquil life in northern Israel. In 2011, Israeli authorities arrested Cvetkovic and later extradited him to Bosnia to stand trial before the war crimes chamber in Sarajevo.[125] Citing a lach of sufficient eyewitness testimony, judges acquittal Cvetkovic in July 2015.

Yet, at the time of writing, two of the field commanders—Milorad Pelemis and Dragomir Pecanac—who allegedly directed the mass killings at Branjevo and are wanted by the Bosnian authorities, remain at large in Serbia. Ironically, both men have played a role in two high-profile trials of Bosnian Serb military leaders in The Hague. In March 2015, Pelemis testified for the defense in the Ratko Mladic trial, and several years earlier Pecanac was called to testify in the case of Zdravko Tolimir. Tribunal judges jailed Pecanac for three months for failing to appear as a witness in that case, but the tribunal then let him return home. Today, Pecanac and Pelemis, as well as scores of other Serb suspects implicated in the Srebrenica genocide and other wartime atrocities, are living normal lives, as so many Germans and Nazi collaborators have in the decades since World War II.

"They are not hiding," a Bosnian war crimes prosecutor remarked in a June 2013 interview in Sarajevo. "You can find them in Belgrade."[126]

CHAPTER 6

Tracking Rwanda's
Génocidaires

In a span of less than twenty-four hours, Rwanda, a country of emerald
green hills and mist-shrouded mountains locked in the heart of central
Africa, was transformed into a slaughterhouse. At approximately 8:30
P.M. on April 6, 1994, Rwanda's Hutu president, Juvenal Habyarimana,
who for two decades had ruled over his country's two main ethnic groups,
the Hutu and the Tutsi, was returning from Tanzania when two surface-
to-air missiles shot his plane out of the sky over Rwanda's capital of Kigali.
Although it has never been determined who was truly responsible for the
assassination, Hutu extremists who carried out the ensuing genocide initially profited most from the president's death.

Eight months earlier, in what Hutu hard-liners saw as a capitulation
to the vilified Tutsi minority, Habyarimana had signed the Arusha
Accords, a peace agreement intended to end a three-year civil war
between the Hutu-led Rwandan government and the Rwandan Patriotic Front (RPF), a Tutsi rebel army that had launched an invasion of
the country from neighboring Uganda in October 1990. The RPF aimed
to take power in Kigali and by doing so to facilitate the return of hundreds of thousands of Tutsi refugees living in Uganda and neighboring
countries who had long been barred from returning home. Many of
these refugees had been forced to flee Rwanda following the 1959 Hutu
Revolution, which had empowered the majority Hutus after decades of
Tutsi domination. Belgian colonial rule, which had stretched from the
end of World War I to 1962, had long entrenched the ethnic domination

of the Tutsi group, but in 1959 the Belgians threw their support to the Hutus.

Within a day of the plane crash, Hutu extremists had taken political control of the country, installed an interim government, blamed the Tutsis for the assassination, butchered ten UN Belgian peacekeepers, and begun one of the fastest killing campaigns of the twentieth century, a slaughter that would last 100 days and claim the lives of approximately 800,000 Tutsis and Hutus accused of being political moderates and sympathetic to the Tutsi minority. The killing began in Kigali and spread like a cancer across Rwanda. As Hutu soldiers roamed neighborhoods looking for prominent Tutsis, gangs of Interahamwe ("those who strike as one"), an anti-Tutsi militia, set up roadblocks at crossroads. Passersby with government-issued identification cards marked as Tutsi would be taken aside and hacked to death with machetes.

As the violence spread, the Tutsi-dominated RPF launched a military offensive, leaving their encampments in the north and pressing south in the direction of Kigali. Another front opened up in the capital, where an RPF battalion stationed there under the terms of the Arusha Accords took up arms against the new Hutu interim government. Hutu extremists took to the radio to demonize Tutsis as *inyenzi* (cockroaches) and exhort their fellow Hutus to unite in killing them. The Interahamwe coerced ordinary Hutus to join the massacres, leading husbands to kill wives, teachers to kill students, and neighbors to turn on neighbors in a country where Hutus and Tutsis had often intermarried and lived side by side. While evidence points to extensive preplanning of atrocities, scholarship also suggests, in the words of political scientist and genocide scholar Scott Straus, "a dynamic of escalation" in which the RPF's significant military successes prompted Hutu extremists to order a "genocide as a desperate measure to win a war that they were losing."[1]

The genocide unfolded as 2,500 UN peacekeepers, sent to Rwanda to monitor possible violations of the Arusha Accords some months earlier, watched helplessly from the sidelines. No one from the UN felt the anguish of this impotence more than the forty-six-year-old French Canadian commander of the UN Assistance Mission for Rwanda (UNAMIR), General Roméo Dallaire, who in the months leading up to the genocide had repeatedly warned his superiors at UN headquarters in New York about the Hutu extremists' plans to launch a killing campaign to scuttle the Arusha Accords and its promise of a power-sharing government, to no avail. What affected him most were the anguished calls for help he received from Tutsis soon after the downing of the

President's plane. Recalled Dallaire: "It was terrifying and surreal to be talking to someone, sometimes someone you knew, listening to them pleading for help, and being able to do nothing but reassure them that help was on the way—and then to hear screams, shots and the silence of a dead line. You'd hang up in shock, then the phone would ring again and the whole sequence would be repeated."[2]

Even as the massacres in the streets of Kigali in early April shocked Dallaire and his fellow peacekeepers, he acknowledged that initially "it was unimaginable for us that we could be finding ourselves in the middle of a genocide."[3] As the carnage pressed in on him, he pled almost daily with his superiors in New York to send reinforcements. But UN officials downplayed the violence, and avoided designating it as genocide, which under the terms of the UN Genocide Convention of 1948 creates an expectation for UN member states to take action to prevent such atrocities and prosecute those responsible. UN officials and world powers clearly did not want to be sucked into the vortex of a civil war, genocidal or not, in an impoverished country in central Africa. Most of all, the Security Council, led by influential states such as the U.S. and Britain, feared suffering casualties reminiscent of the failed UN mission in Somalia a year earlier, in which militants killed eighteen U.S. special forces personnel during an attempt to arrest a Somali warlord.

Isolated and demoralized, Dallaire took on the fruitless diplomatic task of trying to negotiate a ceasefire between the RPF forces and officials in the new Hutu interim government installed after the president's plane crash—the same people, according to Dallaire, "that were conducting the slaughters."[4] As Dallaire recalled, he could neither "shoot them outright, which I wanted to do a couple times, nor actually slap them under arrest."[5] As the days wore on, he vowed to protect potential witnesses and "save every goddamn piece of paper so that someday we could incriminate" the killers in a modern-day reprise of the Nuremberg trials. As he recalled telling a reporter at the time: "If I could keep one witness, one Rwandan witness alive, this would be worth it and I'd be prepared to pay whatever price necessary to do that . . . to protect the last surviving Tutsi who could testify at some sort of an international tribunal."[6]

On the afternoon of April 21, fourteen days into the carnage, Daillare's hopes of decisive international intervention to halt the killings were all but dashed. In a move that revealed the UN's complete lack of resolve to stop the genocide, the Security Council passed Resolution

912, ordering the withdrawal of all but a skeletal force of peacekeepers from Rwanda.

In the days of slaughter, escape for Tutsis became exceedingly difficult, often impossible. Many sought refuge in churches or schools, traditionally places of safety in times of ethnic strife, only this time they had become death traps. One of the most horrific massacres took place in mid-April in the town of Nyarubuye, in eastern Rwanda near the border with Tanzania. The region's mayor, Sylvestre Gacumbitsi, a Hutu, promised to provide safety for Tutsis who took refuge in the Catholic Mission, a large brick complex of parishes, cloisters, and classrooms on the outskirts of town. Once the Tutsis were ensconced in the mission, Gacumbitsi directed the heavily armed local Interahamwe and communal police to storm the complex and massacre the 7,000 men, women, and children inside.

The slaughter at Nyarubuye reflected the logic of genocide that dominated the Hutu leadership and militarily would ultimately prove their undoing. As Hutu extremists focused on slaughtering Tutsis, the RPF rebel army was capturing more and more territory[7]—so much so that by late April, the tables had begun to turn, and it was now Hutus who were very much on the run. Among them were Gacumbitsi and his band of killers, who melded into a human stream of hundreds of thousands of Hutu civilians who, over a forty-eight-hour period, crossed the border to the east into Tanzania, one of the largest refugee flows in recent history. Once across the border, Gacumbitsi and thousands of other genocide perpetrators, along with many thousands of Hutu civilians fearful of possible RPF reprisals, sought refuge in hastily prepared UN refugee camps. UN aid officials even allowed Gacumbitsi to resume a position of authority inside the sprawling Banaco camp, delegating to him some control of food distribution to camp residents. Irish journalist Fergel Keane characterized Banaco at the time as "the province of the Hutu warlords," adding, "Gacumbitsi is king here."[8]

GÉNOCIDAIRES IN FLIGHT

In mid-June, the central Rwandan city of Gitarama, to which the Hutu interim government had retreated early in the genocide, fell to the Tutsi rebels, triggering another massive Hutu exodus, this time toward the country's western border with Zaire. The RPF now controlled the north and much of the central part of Rwanda, and was closing in on Kigali.

As the Kigali-based Hutu forces fled, they grabbed arms and other military equipment and emptied the national coffers of their cash reserves. In a matter of days in mid-July, over one million Hutus, with thousands of *génocidaires* in their mist, crossed into Zaire. "Old and young, men and women, ministers, bankers, teachers, students, pupils, delinquents, and criminals fled," recalled Marie Beatrice Umutesi, a Hutu sociologist and activist who was among the post-genocide refugees. "Rwanda was like a sinking ship that even the rats were leaving."[9] And so it was that nearly all those thought to be most responsible for planning and executing the genocide initially evaded capture by the advancing RPF.

As they fled, a number of high-level members of the Hutu government received the support of France, which in mid-June had dispatched its elite forces on a mission Paris dubbed Operation Turquoise and characterized as purely humanitarian.[10] The Security Council lent credence to this portrayal when, stung by its own inaction in halting the genocide, it authorized the belated French expedition. Dallaire believed that the French "were using a humanitarian cloak to intervene"[11] to forestall an RPF victory and resuscitate the beleaguered Hutu forces. In any case, the French did provide a lifeline for the escaping Hutu government, helping it to remain a cohesive entity in Zaire, keeping alive the possibility of fighting their way back to Rwanda or negotiating their way back into government under the power-sharing framework of the 1993 Arusha Accords.

France, an ardent ally of Hutu President Habyarimana, had on previous occasions since the RPF's 1990 invasion sent troops and provided weapons and technical support to hold back the Tutsi rebels.[12] And on April 8, a little more than a day after the Habyarimana plane crash, French special forces landed in Kigali, evacuating French nationals as well as scores of Hutus implicated in fomenting anti-Tutsi violence in the previous months.[13] Now in June 1994, the prospect of an RPF victory threatened French influence in an important client state and its prestige as leader of francophone Africa.

French troops that came as part of Operation Turquoise did not dismantle roadblocks, disarm militiamen, or arrest Hutus who had already been named as playing a role in massacres.[14] In key respects, the French zone in the southwest seemed to be geared more to enabling Hutus to flee to Zaire than to helping Tutsi civilians escape the Hutu militias. However, the French role in directly helping high-level political and military leaders escape Rwanda appears to have been limited, given that most of these leaders fled the country to the northwest, where the

French presence was minimal.[15] Once outside Rwanda, Hutu political and military leaders enjoyed the protection afforded by not only the international border but also French forces and the Zairian military.

The massive flow of Hutu refugees into Zaire in the summer of 1994, prompted by a relentless RPF advance and by Hutu extremist coercion and alarmist predictions of RPF retaliatory massacres, brought a strong though private rebuke of RPF tactics from the United States, which, following the RPF takeover of power after the genocide, had forged a strong political alliance with the Rwandan government. An internal U.S. State Department document reveals that in mid-July American officials sharply criticized RPF leader Paul Kagame's zealous pursuit of the fleeing Hutus. A U.S. official reportedly conveyed to RPF officials at the time that "it [makes] no sense to displace millions of innocent civilians in an attempt to capture a few hundred leaders of the genocidal campaign who could easily step across . . . into Zaire right before the RPF reaches [the border town of] Gisenyi. The RPF would then be faced with a hostile force across the border with a large refugee population possibly supporting it."[16]

While the Rwandan Tutsis stood out as the primary victims during the spring of 1994, their suffering was soon eclipsed that summer by the international media attention given to the dire predicament of the fleeing Hutus, who began to succumb to disease, dehydration, and exhaustion, and then to a massive cholera outbreak on the inhospitable volcanic terrain in and around Goma. The UN High Commission for Refugees and dozens of aid organizations quickly mobilized to respond to the humanitarian crisis. Dispatching international aid workers to rescue the desperate refugees proved politically easier and less risky for the international community than mobilizing military forces to stop the genocide would have been several months earlier. Amid this focus on victims of the humanitarian emergency, the presence of Hutu perpetrators received scant mention in the international media, as did the question of whether steps should be taken to identify and arrest suspects. Hutu fugitives in Zaire, as in Tanzania, were reaping the fruits of being welcomed as refugees.

The refugee camps not only provided a sanctuary for high-level Hutu *génocidaires* but also enabled the Hutu army and former government to remain essentially intact. At one point after the genocide, 21 former government ministers from the Hutu interim government, more than 50 former members of Parliament, and 126 former mayors lived in the refugee camps, according to a UN estimate.[17] The Hutu leadership took control of key aspects of camp management and reestablished the structures of governance that had existed previously in Rwanda, according to Sadako Ogata, who served as the UN High Commissioner for Refugees during this period.[18] The empowerment of high-level Hutus stemmed from a UN refugee policy of seeking assistance in running camps from those with leadership experience. "We didn't think this through, but it meant: Give the genocidal leaders more power," observed UNHCR special envoy Caroll Faubert.[19] In the camps, the extremists continued their coercion of the Hutu population, compelling them to contribute money to the war effort and intimidating and even killing Hutu refugees who sought to return to Rwanda. Now encamped in a seemingly secure sanctuary in eastern Zaire, the Hutu *génocidaires* were no longer fugitives on the run, but a government and army waiting in plain sight.

While the Hutu army in exile was not strong enough to retake power in Rwanda, their persistent cross-border attacks on both military and civilian targets raised the specter of a larger military conflagration with the RPF-controlled Rwandan government. As the attacks increased, Paul Kagame, the de facto Rwandan leader who had engineered the RPF's military victory, threatened to take matters into his own hands if the international community did not curb the violence. "Your relief workers are sheltering those who committed genocide in the refugee camps at our borders," Kagame told John Shattuck, the U.S. assistant secretary of state for democracy, human rights, and labor. "And you are doing nothing to bring these criminals to justice."[20]

Fearing an eventual RPF attack on the camps, Shattuck, in a cable back to Washington, called emphatically on the United States to take the lead in building an international tribunal and arresting the key perpetrators of genocide. In this impending-war context, justice and the arrest of suspects were cast as indispensable tools of conflict prevention. "If ever there was a case where justice was a precondition for peace, Rwanda was it," Shattuck said.[21]

THE UN RWANDA TRIBUNAL AND
THE PROBLEM OF ARRESTS

The UN Security Council's unanimous vote in 1993 to establish the International Criminal Tribunal for the Former Yugoslavia reinvigorated interest in the long-dormant idea of using international courts to respond to mass atrocities. According to David Scheffer, the first U.S. ambassador at large for war crimes issues (a post created in 1997), the end of the Cold War created "a very unique moment" of international cooperation among former Great Power adversaries.[22] When it came to authorizing UN criminal tribunals, now "there was a chance of getting the Russian and Chinese votes with us on these initiatives," Scheffer said.[23] The precedent of that first contemporary international tribunal played a role in prompting the Security Council to create a tribunal for the far more extensive atrocities in Rwanda.

In May 1994, the UN authorized a commission of experts, modeled on the body that had served as the institutional precursor for the Yugoslavia tribunal, to investigate reports of genocide and crimes against humanity in Rwanda. In mid-June, U.S. officials took the lead in drawing up blueprints for a second ad hoc international tribunal and, a month later, urged the UN to move quickly to establish it. Initially, the RPF supported the idea of the tribunal, especially as it would focus global condemnation on the genocide of Tutsis as well as increase prospects that high-level Hutu suspects would be apprehended and brought to trial. But the new RPF Rwandan government, which happened at the time to have a temporary seat on the Council, previously occupied by the Hutu extremist government, soon withdrew its support, unhappy over not having more say in shaping the contours of the new court's mandate and procedures. When the Security Council voted in early November to authorize the creation of the International Criminal Tribunal for Rwanda, Rwanda cast the sole dissenting vote.

Meanwhile, Rwandan authorities began arresting tens of thousands of mid- and lower-level Hutu suspects who remained in the country after the genocide. The combination of mass arrests, inadequate detention facilities, a devastated judicial system, and a dearth of international funding soon led to deaths in overcrowded jails and systematic violations of defendants' due-process rights. Meanwhile, the Rwandan government's most sought-after suspects—the high-level political and military leaders believed to have engineered the genocide—remained beyond its grasp. The government's lack of extradition agreements with many states made the prospect of prosecuting Hutu suspects in Rwanda who might be captured elsewhere particularly difficult. The Rwandan government remained determined to track down and prosecute some high-level Hutu suspects at home. At the same time, the Tutsi-led government's recognition that it could accrue political advantage by aiding the international tribunal's prosecution of its Hutu enemies prompted it to support the UN court, albeit with some reluctance.

The Rwandan government's support for the idea of an international tribunal did not mean it agreed with the UN's vision of international justice. The government particularly objected to the UN's plans to locate the tribunal outside Rwanda, bar capital punishment, and grant jurisdiction to court prosecutors to target not just Hutus responsible for massacres of Tutsis but also RPF officers implicated in massacres of Hutu civilians. After the RPF's July 1994 victory its forces had murdered thousands of Hutu civilians, sometimes after summoning families to public meetings, where they were shot en masse, sometimes going house to house to hunt down Hutus in hiding, leaving an estimated 25,000 to 30,000 dead.[24]

The Rwandan government pressed the UN to adopt a narrow temporal jurisdiction that would keep the tribunal focused only on the genocide. But UN negotiators held firm, in the belief that contemporary international justice should transcend the "victor's justice" of the Nuremberg and Tokyo military tribunals. In the end, the Security Council provided the nascent Rwanda tribunal with a temporal mandate that encompassed atrocities committed any time in 1994. Thus, the tribunal would potentially confront a twofold arrest challenge: tracking down and obtaining custody of Hutu genocide suspects as well as RPF officials who were implicated in revenge killings of Hutu civilians.

Establishing the tribunal and turning it into a functioning institution would prove to be a slow and frustrating task, made yet more difficult by poor senior leadership and lack of UN oversight. So too would be ensuring Rwanda's continued support. But the most vexing question the tribunal initially faced was how the leading Hutu suspects, all of whom had fled Rwanda, could ever be arrested and brought to trial. All UN member states had a legal obligation to provide full and immediate cooperation with the Rwanda tribunal, just as they did with the Yugoslavia tribunal. Yet without enforcement powers at their disposal to apprehend fugitives, the prospect of a stillborn tribunal remained palpable.

In the months between the end of the genocide in July and the UN's decision to establish the Rwanda tribunal in November, a handful of U.S. officials strategized on how to track down top genocide suspects and compel international troops in the region to apprehend them. David Scheffer, then a young State Department lawyer working with John Shattuck and Madeleine Albright, spearheaded these efforts. In Washington, Scheffer met with U.S. intelligence officials and with Alison Des Forges, the preeminent Rwanda expert and an adviser to

Human Rights Watch, to develop a list of top suspects and work on closing loopholes in the U.S. immigration system that might allow genocide suspects to arrive on American soil undetected.[25] With the prospect of a Security Council vote to authorize a tribunal still months off, Scheffer tried to build support that summer for apprehending top suspects before they disappeared deeper into Zaire or elsewhere in Africa and beyond.

Scheffer and his State Department allies initially confronted two interlinked problems: a weak legal foundation on which to detain suspects in the absence of criminal indictments from an international tribunal, and a lack of international will to make arrests. Without international tribunal indictments, key countries such as France, well positioned to deploy troops to make arrests, were reluctant to take action. Yet, as Scheffer observed, in the absence of detained suspects, it was initially difficult to build support for a tribunal. "In effect," Scheffer recalled, the Europeans initially "tried to have it both ways by saying, 'Well, we have no authority to go out and arrest these people.' So we said, 'Well, okay, then let's authorize the building of the tribunal.' And then they said, 'Well, wait a minute, you don't have anyone in custody, what's the point of this tribunal?'"[26] Scheffer well understood the legal and ethical problems in seeking the detention of suspects.[27] The American plan—though it never came to pass—was to authorize short-term detention of genocide suspects until the prospective tribunal could prepare their indictments. As Scheffer later put it: "You know, it's sort of similar to what we've [subsequently] experienced in the so-called war on terror, where we collect all these al-Qaeda people on the battlefield . . . [and] the whole idea is to corral them and detain them and then figure out, oh, [do] we have a basis for holding these people?"[28]

U.S. diplomats pressed France—which still had troops in the region from its Operation Turquoise intervention—and Zaire and Tanzania—home to vast refugee camps—to apprehend Hutu political and military leaders implicated in the genocide. In doing so, the Americans cited the Genocide Convention of 1948, which calls on UN member states to take action to prevent and prosecute genocide. But France balked, now claiming that ordering its soldiers to arrest Hutu extremists "could undermine our neutrality, the best guarantee of our effectiveness."[29]

Even the creation of the tribunal, Scheffer was disappointed to discover, did not initially persuade influential UN member states, such as France and the United States, to act. In early 1995, Scheffer crafted a

U.S.-sponsored Security Council resolution detailing the obligation to apprehend suspects even before the issuance of tribunal indictments. The French opposed the draft resolution, however.[30] Washington and Paris finally reached a compromise: there would be a Security Council resolution on arrests, but the resolution would only urge rather than require states to make arrests. "It was pathetic that it was taking so long to achieve so little," a frustrated Scheffer concluded. "One of our closest allies appeared determined to act as an accomplice in facilitating the genocidaires' freedom."[31]

However, it wasn't just Paris but also Washington and other influential governments that were reluctant to take steps to separate genocide suspects from the general refugee population in Zaire and Tanzania, and then make arrests. With the Hutu extremists firmly in control of the camps, the prospect of sending an international arrest force posed risks the UN and powerful states were unwilling to incur. Even Scheffer's own government, which, as he said, had pushed Paris "to buck up and get on board"[32] and agree to a strong Security Council resolution on arrests, was itself unwilling to send any troops of its own to undertake this task. The same political calculus that drove the Security Council to minimize the risk of casualties by removing most of its UN peacekeepers at the start of the genocide also drove the White House and the Pentagon to oppose sending an arrest force to the refugee camps following the genocide. For the U.S. and other states the memories were still fresh of the bungled U.S. arrest operation in Mogadishu in 1993. By summer 1995, a year after the genocide, and still without tribunal indictments in place, the prospect of apprehending key suspects and prosecuting them at the nascent tribunal in Arusha, Tanzania, seemed remote.

The RPF Rwandan government's attack more than a year later, in fall 1996, which was designed to dismantle the UN refugee camps in eastern Zaire that had been used to launch cross-border attacks on Rwanda, came as little surprise, given Kagame's repeated public and private threats. The lack of forceful international opposition to those threats and the lack of condemnation of the attack afterward suggest that the U.S. and some allied states had an interest in seeing the Rwandan military solve a problem they had little interest in tackling themselves. Some analysts, and even Kagame himself, contend that the U.S. gave tacit approval to the 1996 invasion. When Kagame met with U.S. officials in Washington and issued a veiled warning of his invasion plans if the refugee camps were not dismantled, he was pleased that he did not receive a red light. Said Kagame: "Their response was really no response."[33]

The Rwandan government trumpeted the operation as a legitimate act of self-defense, even as it sought to downplay its own involvement by contending that ethnic Tutsi rebels in eastern Zaire had taken the lead in the fighting. The 1996 invasion and a subsequent one in 1998 were not arrest missions to bring genocide suspects to trial in Arusha or Kigali, but operations to stop the cross-border raids and to exact a harsh kind of retribution by breaking up the refugee camps, forcing hundreds of thousands of refugees to return to Rwanda, and hunting down tens of thousands of Hutu militants, along with tens of thousands of civilians, deep into the forests of Zaire. These attacks triggered a long-running regional war and humanitarian crisis whose death toll over the next decade far exceeded the approximately 800,000 people who were killed in Rwanda in 1994. A 2010 UN report detailing atrocities in Zaire (renamed Democratic Republic of Congo in 1997) implicated Hutu militants as well as RPF forces in war crimes and crimes against humanity. The report found that RPF forces carried out "apparent systematic and widespread attacks" in their "apparently relentless pursuit and mass killing of Hutu refugees," which resulted in the deaths of "several tens of thousands." Moreover, the report stated that atrocities committed by the RPF and its Congolese allies, "if proven before a competent court, could be characterized as crimes of genocide."[34]

What happened to the hunted Hutu militants and civilians in the Congolese forests occurred largely off the world's radar screen. In the RPF's public pronouncements, the fleeing Hutus were castigated as criminal elements with blood on their hands from the genocide, a narrative amplified by many Western journalists who, in the aftermath of the genocide, came to regard the RPF as a victim government with the moral standing to vanquish the Hutu *génocidaires*. American journalist Philip Gourevitch stands out in this regard for his popular *New Yorker* articles that valorized the RPF's actions.[35]

Key supporters of the new Rwandan government, particularly the U.S., also seemed invested in accepting Kagame's virtuous portrayal of the intervention. Howard French, a former *New York Times* correspondent, recalls that U.S. officials, including David Scheffer, dismissed questions raised about the killing of Hutu refugees. "Almost across the board," French said, "American officials had written off the Hutu as a pariah population, and no one had time for questions about their fate."[36] By law, the newly created Rwanda tribunal could not consider the fate of Hutu victims in Zaire, because its purview was limited to crimes committed in Rwanda itself, and only during 1994.

The specter of a full-scale RPF invasion of the refugee camps had led many Hutus, from the higher echelons of the government in exile to innocent civilians, to seek protection elsewhere in advance. "It was very clear they were going to attack," said Filip Reyntjens, a prominent Rwanda and Congo scholar, in reference to the months leading up to the RPF's fall 1996 invasion. "So, then, if you are a Hutu suspect, even unindicted, and you're listening to this and [you're] thinking, is it a bluff or not, but you don't want to be caught up in this, you might think it's time to leave. . . . Even feeling totally innocent, this was a very dangerous situation for those people."[37]

Though the Hutu exodus from Rwanda in the summer of 1994 occurred in a matter of days, the exodus from eastern Zaire in 1995–96 took place steadily over a number of months. Some Hutus who could afford to do so sought safer ground even sooner to avoid the chaos and instability of the refugee camps. Those, such as the wealthy Hutu financier Felicien Kabuga, who was accused of playing a key role in bankrolling the genocide, fled the region relatively early, initially traveling to Switzerland and later seeking refuge in Kenya, a country whose president, Daniel arap Moi, was known for his close alliance with Hutu officials from the Habyarimana government. Others, such as the former minister of family and women affairs, Pauline Nyiramasuhuko, and her son, Shalom Ntahobali, and his wife fled to Zaire, but then quickly made their way to Kenya. Once there, Ntahobali and his wife applied for residency in the United States. Other high-level officials, such as Jean Kambanda, the former prime minister of the Hutu interim government, did not flee the camps for Kenya until August 1996, the eve of the Rwandan invasion.[38]

Hutu extremists traveled elsewhere as well. Many headed to West Africa, while others traveled south to Zambia, Zimbabwe, and South Africa. Those with the right connections and sufficient resources sought to leave Africa altogether, often drawn to Rwandan and francophone communities in Belgium, France, and Québec. Two years after the genocide, writes French journalist and tribunal expert Thierry Cruvellier, "the former regime's elites who had been ousted . . . were now scattered to the four corners of Africa and Europe."[39]

In the two years following the genocide and during the first days of the newly formed tribunal, some high-level Hutu officials maintained a high profile and gave interviews to the press. But many became more circum-spect, particularly after the arrest[40] of about a dozen Hutu suspects in Cameroon in March 1996. To lower their chances of ending up in tribu-nal custody, some potential suspects acquired fake passports and aliases. Word that the fledgling tribunal had begun to issue indictments set some potential suspects on edge. Georges Ruggiu, a Belgian-Italian who had spent the genocide as a broadcaster for a Hutu extremist radio station in Kigali, fled to Zaire, then to Tanzania, back to Zaire, and finally to Mom-basa, Kenya. He changed his name first to Trevor MacCusker and then, after embracing Islam, to Georges Omar Ruggiu.[41] Some potential sus-pects began to plan for their legal defense in the event they ended up in tribunal custody. Jean Kambanda, the former prime minister of the interim government, in June 1995 contacted a Belgian lawyer experi-enced with Rwanda. Another Belgian lawyer, Luc de Temmerman, assem-bled several of his colleagues in Nairobi in July 1996 to build a common defense strategy should high-level Hutu suspects ever become defendants. According to Thierry Cruvellier, de Temmerman's "insider's connection with the former regime's elites" enabled him to meet with scores of former Hutu officials in Africa and Belgium to obtain promises that they would come to his group for legal defense.[42] That the lawyer could locate and meet with so many high-level Hutus in exile suggested that it might not prove too difficult for the tribunal to track down Hutu fugitives.

THE TRIBUNAL'S EARLY DAYS

Arriving in Rwanda in early 1995, the tribunal's first investigators faced a daunting assignment. Initiating investigations in a devastated country and establishing the tribunal's headquarters in neighboring Tanzania proved far more challenging than the parallel task of building the Inter-national Criminal Tribunal for the Former Yugoslavia in the heart of Europe. The Rwanda tribunal's task was made more difficult early on by insufficient resources from the UN and poor senior leadership. Lack of in-depth knowledge of Rwandan politics, history, and the genocide itself also hampered the work of investigators, prosecutors, and judges. Before 1994, relatively few outside the region knew much about the small, landlocked Central African country beyond its being home to the endangered mountain gorilla, as depicted in *Gorillas in the Mist*, the 1980s movie starring Sigourney Weaver as Dian Fossey. The magnitude of the genocide and the sheer number of perpetrators posed yet another challenge for the tribunal's investigators and prosecutors.

When the Security Council authorized the creation of the Yugoslavia and Rwanda tribunals, in 1993 and 1994, respectively, it granted their chief prosecutor—the same person for both tribunals, for the first decade—considerable discretion as to who to target for investigation and indictment. The chief prosecutor had a mandate to prosecute individuals implicated in serious violations of international humanitarian law, namely genocide, crimes against humanity, and war crimes. There was no immunity granted to heads of state, and the chief prosecutor had the authority to target individuals from all sides of the armed conflict in question. That still left prosecutors, given time and resource constraints, with the difficult choice of determining who was most worthy of indictment and in what order to prioritize investigations. Taking a page from their predecessors at Nuremberg and Tokyo, some prosecutors thought it best to start from the top by building cases against those Hutus believed to be most responsible for the genocide, and then seek their arrest. Initially, however, the opposite of this top-down approach took place at both the Rwanda and the Yugoslavia tribunals.

In fall 1995 tribunal prosecutors working in their disheveled office in Kigali received an unexpected phone call from Zambia. Days earlier, the Zambian authorities had arrested several Hutus who, using their real names, sought to enter Zambia as refugees. Among them were Jean-Paul Akayesu, who had served as mayor of the town of Taba during the genocide, and Georges Rutaganda, a leader of the infamous Interahamwe militia. Another suspected *génocidaire*, Clement Kayishema, was already in Zambian custody. Given the dire detention conditions in Rwanda and the specter of the men facing execution back home, Zambia had no intention of sending them to Rwanda. But neither did the authorities want these and other potential suspects to make Zambia their new home. Zambia thus turned to the nascent international tribunal.

That the tribunal might gain custody of genocide suspects well before the completion of any investigations caught international prosecutors off guard. Sara Darehshori, an American prosecutor and one of the first tribunal employees sent to Rwanda, remembers how surprising it was that a foreign government even knew how to track down officials of the fledgling tribunal. "It was crazy even getting a call," she recalled, referring to the office's one landline. "The fact that the phone even rang [was] startling."[43] Even more surprising was that the tribunal suddenly had the opportunity to hold its first trials. Yet the opportunity presented the immediate problem of figuring out who these detained individuals in Zambia actually were and what crimes they were suspected of having committed during the genocide. It soon became apparent, though, that Zambian authorities also knew very little about the suspects. Recalls Darehshori: "Our investigator said, 'Well, what do you have in your files?' And they said, 'What do you have in your files?' And so nobody had anything."[44]

Although Akayesu, Rutaganda, and Kayishema were relatively low-level players, Richard Goldstone—then the chief prosecutor—decided to pursue indictments against the three men. In doing so, he followed the path he had taken as chief prosecutor of the Yugoslavia tribunal, when he indicted Dusan Tadic, the Bosnian Serb prison guard who became the first defendant tried by the Yugoslavia tribunal. In the early days of both tribunals, the arrest challenge loomed large. Goldstone feared that having no one to put on trial could derail the court before it even got off the ground. This led him to take advantage of situations in which suspects fell into the tribunals' lap, even if the suspects were relatively low-level. "There's a lot of pressure to have someone on trial because [if you don't] it looks like you're not doing anything," explained Darehshori.[45]

When the three suspects were transferred to Arusha in May 1996, it was unclear how soon scores of high-level Hutu genocide suspects would join them. There was in fact considerable doubt that many such high-caliber suspects would end up in tribunal custody, given the freedom that Hutu extremists enjoyed in the refugee camps in eastern Zaire and in the anonymity of large cities in Africa and Europe.[46] Not long afterward, however, a confluence of factors led to a dramatic change in the tribunal's fortunes.

As the tribunal staff multiplied and as investigators traveled the hills of Rwanda interviewing survivors to build their early cases, the new Rwandan government was pursuing its own brand of justice for the genocide. In 1996, the government adopted a law to facilitate prosecution of the more than 100,000 mid- and low-level genocide suspects languishing in detention in its overcrowded jails and communal lockups. The task for the Rwandan courts was overwhelming, given the destruction of its judicial system during the genocide and ensuing civil war.

Even as the Tutsi-led Rwandan government had a strong interest in seeing Hutu suspects prosecuted on the world stage afforded by the UN tribunal, the new Rwandan leaders had by no means relinquished their own desire to prosecute high-level suspects accused of masterminding the genocide. Toward that end, the RPF's intelligence services proved more resourceful than the better-funded tribunal in locating and quickly seeking the return of some high-level suspects abroad. Before the tribunal in Arusha even assembled an arrest tracking team, the Rwandan government had tracked down some senior and mid-level officials of the former Hutu interim government in Cameroon, in Zambia, and even one suspect in India. In one early case, the Rwandan authorities reportedly kidnapped the former Hutu minister of justice in Zambia and brought her to trial in Kigali.[47]

In March 1996, the Rwandan authorities learned that Theoneste Bagosora, the power behind the Hutu interim government, and several of his close associates were under arrest in Cameroon. Their presence in Cameroon came to Rwanda's attention when Belgium filed an international arrest warrant for Bagosora for purported involvement in the murder of the ten Belgian UN peacekeepers at the beginning of the genocide. The Rwandan government aimed to block Belgium's bid by filing an extradition request of its own with the Cameroon government. In the race to gain custody of the most valuable Hutu genocide suspects under arrest to date, the tribunal was the laggard.

After learning that Bagosora and his associates were in Cameroon, Chief Prosecutor Goldstone filed his own legal request to prosecute them. Although the tribunal played no role in tracking down the suspects and was last to file a request, international law was on its side. Under the Security Council–approved statute, the Rwanda tribunal (as with the Yugoslavia tribunal) enjoyed the right to override a state's own bid to prosecute. The tribunal's ensuing political struggle with the Rwandan government, however, underscores that for international tribunals winning the battle over the transfer of a suspect can be as difficult as executing an arrest.

Goldstone's insistence that he would invoke the tribunal's legal right to bring the suspects to Arusha outraged Rwandan officials, who invoked their own moral right to try Bagosora and his associates at home. In what Goldstone described as a "very tense" meeting, Rwandan officials pressed him to drop his bid for the suspects.[48] Ever since the Rwandan government had voted against establishing the tribunal at the November 1994 Security Council meeting, Goldstone had been aware that he needed to proceed diplomatically with Kigali lest it withhold crucial cooperation by barring investigators from working in the country and blocking Tutsi survivor-witnesses from leaving the country to testify in Arusha.

A break with the Rwandan government over the Bagosora case might have led Kigali to suspend cooperation, imperiling the tribunal's mandate even before it started its first trial. "The tribunal was in its greatest peril over Bagosora because I just wasn't prepared to give in on that one," recalled Goldstone in a 2003 interview. "I made it very clear to them that that wasn't negotiable."[49] Goldstone remained resolute, not only to defend the tribunal's right, under the principle of primacy, to decide what suspects it would select for prosecution, but also to target such an important suspect as Bagosora, whom he considered "the Milosevic of Rwanda." Said Goldstone: "I think they realized that I wasn't just threatening, that I meant it when I said that I prefer to suggest closing down the tribunal than to defer a major criminal involved in the genocide." After a number of delays and the diplomatic intervention of David Scheffer from the U.S. State Department, Goldstone prevailed. The Cameroon government thereupon sent Bagosora and three other suspects to Arusha, in January 1997.

The next confrontation with Rwanda, however, prompted Goldstone to take a different tack. Not long after the Bagosora incident, Goldstone learned of another opportunity to bring an important genocide suspect to trial in Arusha. In June 1996, the Ethiopian authorities had detained Froduald Karamira, who had been implicated in inciting Hutus to participate in the genocide. Rwandan officials successfully tracked him down in India and convinced authorities there to send the suspect back home for trial. When his plane landed for a stop in Addis Ababa, Karamira briefly escaped, before being detained by Ethiopian authorities. When the incident became public, Goldstone moved quickly to request that Ethiopia transfer Karamira to Arusha.

But obtaining custody of Karamira would not be so easy. Unbeknownst to Goldstone, Rwanda had already staked a claim to the suspect. Rwandan officials now threatened to play their political trump card of withholding cooperation if the prosecutor insisted on bringing Karamira to trial in Arusha. Goldstone quickly backtracked, allowing Rwanda to proceed with its bid to bring Karamira to trial in Kigali. Although law was on Goldstone's side, politics was not. Said Goldstone later: "Politically . . . I don't think I had any options. . . . It would have been the end of cooperation and the end of our relationship. . . . If they stopped cooperation the tribunal would have closed down."[50]

Taken together, the stories of the Hutu suspects in Zambia, Cameroon, and India revealed the new tribunal's strength and its weakness. On the one hand, the tribunal showed that it could prevail in competition over suspects because it had recognized legal authority to override Rwanda's own quest for accountability. On the other hand, that authority was constrained by politics. To Goldstone, maintaining a strong partnership with Rwanda, even at the cost of dropping the tribunal's legal claim to an important suspect, was smart politics. In Rwanda, as in the Balkans, Goldstone demonstrated that an effective chief prosecutor must be able to skillfully navigate not only the legal realm of the courtroom but also the political world beyond its walls. Yet if negotiation is part of the chief prosecutor's job, a question arises: At what point do prosecutorial concessions compromise the institution's leverage and principles?

Goldstone's concession averted a crisis with the RPF government. But his move opened the way for the suspect to be sent to Rwanda without guarantees of appropriate pretrial treatment, a fair trial monitored by the tribunal, or a reprieve should the sentence be execution, a penalty barred by the UN tribunal. After a three-day trial, Karamira was found guilty and executed by a firing squad, along with twenty-one other Rwandans implicated in the genocide, before a crowd of tens of thousands in a Kigali stadium. The execution of Karamira left Goldstone feeling "bloody awful,"[51] yet it did not prompt him to revise his political analysis of the situation or regret his decision. Goldstone's acquiescence to Rwanda over the threats issued in the Karamira case, however, appeared to sow a continuing dynamic of tribunal acquiescence to Kigali to ensure its continuing cooperation.[52] In the face of Rwandan noncooperation in 2002, for example, Chief Prosecutor Carla Del Ponte backed away from her promise to indict RPF officers implicated in nongenocidal atrocities of Hutu civilians in 1994. Doing so, especially in the absence of international political backing for the investigations, ensured that the only arrests sought by the tribunal would be of Hutu suspects.

PURSUIT IN KENYA AND WEST AFRICA

When Canadian jurist Louise Arbour took over as chief prosecutor of the Rwanda and Yugoslavia tribunals in fall 1996, the multiple crises facing both international courts became quickly evident to her. Among her top concerns in Arusha was the prospect of spending too much of the court's limited resources on investigating suspects who, after fleeing Rwanda, might already be dead, hiding in the forests of Zaire, or otherwise beyond the possibility of arrest. The handover of the three suspects from Zambia in 1996, and two other suspects from Belgium in 1995, showed that thanks merely to the tribunal's existing and invoking its legal primacy, some states were willing to transfer suspects to it for trial. This was particularly the case for states such as Zambia that regarded Hutus implicated in the genocide as a problem better dealt with elsewhere. But an "if you build it they may come" approach was not a reliable strategy for a young tribunal that needed to establish its credibility, secure UN funding, and develop a sustainable prosecutorial strategy that prioritized targeting high-level suspects. Moreover, filling the dock with suspects others had arrested by chance in one country or another could lead to a disproportionate focus on low-level suspects who didn't have the political connections and financial resources to evade arrest.

Arbour realized the importance of seizing the initiative. The first question to be answered about high-level Rwandan suspects, she recalled in a 2011 interview, was "Where the hell are they?"[53] This question, she said, was much easier to answer in the Balkans, where war crimes suspects were often hiding in plain sight under the protection of the Serbian and Croatian governments. By contrast, much less was known about the specific locations of suspects when Arbour came to the Rwanda tribunal in fall 1996. By then, many high-level Hutu fugitives had melded into the refugee camps of eastern Zaire and, according to Arbour, "were just too hard to find," or had now fled throughout Africa or to other continents in advance of the RPF's threatened attack.[54]

Tracking fugitives in Africa and beyond, Arbour came to realize, would require an arrest tracking team made up of experienced professionals. For that she turned to fellow French-Canadian Gilbert Morissette, a former Royal Canadian Mounted Police undercover detective, to head a team that would crisscross Africa and Europe to cultivate contacts and informants, track down suspects, and ultimately plan arrest operations to be carried out by domestic authorities.

Arbour's focus on tracking down and arresting suspects before completing investigations had the potential to solve the operational problem of effective capture, but at the same time it could create legal and logistical problems associated with being unprepared to charge and bring to trial multiple defendants in a timely manner. The emphasis on locating suspects, though, fostered urgency to plan arrest operations expeditiously lest fugitives catch wind that they were under surveillance. Explained Arbour: "This ended up being very risky . . . legally, because in the end, we were quite successful, and . . . [picked] up a lot of people where we hadn't done the investigation. We had . . . them on charts, we knew they were in the Interahamwe and so on, but [the cases were] not indictment-ready, never mind trial-ready."[55]

The tribunal's unexpected success in overcoming operational obstacles to bringing suspects into custody by the late 1990s created a bureaucratic logjam of cases that bedeviled the poorly run and otherwise dysfunctional tribunal. This delayed the trials of many defendants, leading to extensive pretrial detention and undermining the tribunal's claim of serving as an international legal role model for domestic judiciaries. Moreover, the expansive authority granted to the chief prosecutor—which initially granted her the extraordinary legal right to authorize an arrest warrant without the approval of a tribunal judge—did little to burnish the tribunal's rule-of-law credentials. Certain aspects of the rules of procedure and evidence, Arbour said, were "completely unconscionable" from a due-process perspective—"but they were to my benefit, so I didn't challenge them."[56]

Arbour's new investigative team did not have to look far when it came to identifying places to begin tracking high-level Hutu suspects implicated in the genocide. Kenya's capital city of Nairobi, just a four-hour drive from Arusha, had by 1996 earned a reputation as a sanctuary for Hutu fugitives. Moreover, President Daniel arap Moi of Kenya, who had enjoyed a close alliance with Hutu officials of the Habyarimana government, had implicitly extended a warm welcome to the fugitives when early on he had issued an ominous warning: instead of apprehending Hutu suspects, he would arrest any tribunal personnel found on Kenyan soil.[57]

While the prosecution's tracking team quietly began its work to locate suspects in Nairobi, Arbour and her deputy, Bernard Muna of Cameroon, began to address the political problem of turning a defiant Kenyan government, which Arbour described as initially "100 percent non-cooperative,"[58] into a helpful one.

Despite Moi's early defiance, he proved vulnerable to sustained international pressure to turn against his Hutu allies, who had been increasingly marginalized as stateless international pariahs. Kenya's heavy reliance on Western development aid also played a role in this belated cooperation, as did the international community's interest in avoiding the embarrassment of having Nairobi, a center of UN and diplomatic activities in eastern Africa, be known as a haven for genocide suspects. Arbour played a leading role in prodding influential states, particularly the U.S. and Canada, to apply pressure on the Moi government. But Western diplomatic intervention also took the less noticed form of facilitating tribunal meetings with Kenyan authorities that, in turn, opened the way for the tracking team's work in the country. The tracking team's Gilbert Morissette later recalled the vital role played by the Canadian High Commissioner to Kenya. "He would even come . . . sit with us in the hallway to wait for a meeting [with high-level Kenyan law enforcement officials] . . . to make sure that that meeting was going to happen."[59]

Lacking its own police powers and ultimately needing to respect state sovereignty, the tribunal would eventually have to turn to the Kenyan police to make arrests. But if the tracking team worked quietly and effectively, it could first develop its own capacity inside Kenya to track suspects and design an airtight arrest operation under its own direction. Then, according to Luc Côté, a French-Canadian tribunal prosecution official who worked closely with Morissette in Kenya, "at the very, very last moment" the tribunal would turn to the Kenyan police to honor its international legal obligation to make arrests.[60] Still, Côté and Morissette felt the imperative to closely monitor the Kenyan police. "We had to shadow people behind each police officer to be sure they were doing their job. That basically was our job there," Côté said, in reference to the major arrest operation that the tribunal's tracking team orchestrated in summer 1997.[61]

Just as Hutu suspects sought to blend into the big-city environment to evade notice, Morissette and his small team sought anonymity of their own. Because Nairobi was a bustling center of international activity, with many UN employees entering and moving about the country for work, transit, or R&R furloughs, that was relatively easy to do. Working out of Morissette's room in a major Nairobi hotel, the team began the delicate work of discreetly shadowing some of the world's most notorious mass murderers.

When Morissette and his tracking team began their search for genocide suspects in Kenya they were navigating the uncharted shoals of contemporary international justice. It was the kind of challenge relished by Morissette, who as a police detective had worked undercover to infiltrate Montréal biker gangs. Québec's largest city was a world away from the streets of Nairobi, and the suspects he targeted in Montréal were implicated in drug dealing, not mass murder. Yet, tracking down both types of suspects required a passion for working undercover as well as the skill and patience needed to gain access to criminal organizations and cultivate trusted insiders.

In Québec, Morissette had grown his hair and beard long to gain acceptance from a biker gang as a local businessman interested in making drug deals. In Kenya, absent any practical way he himself could gain access to the highest-level Hutu suspects, Morissette cultivated Hutu informants from the leadership of the Interahamwe militia who had blood on their hands but apparently did not belong to the inner circle of the former Rwandan Hutu interim government. Morissette, who previously had little international experience and none in Africa, soon demonstrated that his penchant for developing contacts and working undercover extended far beyond Canada's borders. "It was what Gilbert loved best and what he was the best at: schmoozing, developing the contacts and friendships with some shady characters that would enable him to" track down suspects, said Stephen Rapp, the U.S. ambassador-at-large for war crimes issues and a former prosecutor at the Rwanda and Sierra Leone tribunals.[62]

For Morissette and his team, a cornerstone of cultivating informants was fostering trust. "Whether it's on genocide or a drug case [it is critical to] build up confidence and, you know, [find a way to] help each other," he said. That, in turn, relied on patiently forging a bond with potential informants. Morissette points to his efforts to meet Hutus in the Kenyan coastal city of Mombasa as an illustration of this approach. "When we were in Mombasa, I remember spending two, three days on the beach, at the White Sands, meeting with these people and having a beer, and not taking notes, just talking, talking about what happened to them, what happened to their family [during 1994], to show that you care. And, I like beer and they like beer, you know, so that's how you build confidence with these people. . . . And then they'll tell you everything you want to know."[63]

Building confidence with informants also relied on offering incentives to cooperate with the tracking team. That was the case for Dieudonne Niyitegeka and Pheneas Ruhumuliza, two former leaders of the Interahamwe militia living illegally in Kenya. Both had a strong reason to work with the tribunal as well as enough information to be useful, given their considerable knowledge of the organizational structure of the genocide leadership and the high-level Hutus who had relocated to Nairobi and elsewhere. For former Interahamwe leaders, receiving limited financial support in exchange for information could ease the rigors of living in Kenya with little money and few prospects. Further, aiding the prosecutors might shield them from indictment and protect them from ending up in Rwanda's courts, where they could face execution, like Froduald Karamira. Significantly, the Rwandan government in November 1996 published a long list of genocide suspects it sought to prosecute, including six leaders of the Interahamwe leadership, among them Dieudonne Niy-itegeka and Pheneas Ruhumuliza.[64]

The former militia leaders' role as insiders, and even accomplices, to genocide proved indispensable to the tracking team's ability to find suspects as well as to identify the most important individuals among them to target for arrest and prosecution. The strategic advantage of working closely with insiders comes, however, with the ethical disadvantage of giving them favorable treatment, such as immunity from prosecution. The prosecution's reliance on members of the Interahamwe leadership as informants led to most of them evading tribunal prosecution, a result that some analysts believe has impoverished the tribunal's legacy.[65] Dieudonne Niyitegeka, considered the most valuable informant, fared the best. The Office of the Prosecutor arranged for him to enter a special witness protection program in Canada, where his identity was changed.[66] Former prosecution officials downplay the suggestion that informants were given immunity, arguing that the militia members they chose were never prime suspects. Said Côté: "They were not necessarily the ones who were carrying on the massacres, at least we didn't have that kind of evidence. . . . But if we had dug, quite probably, like most of them, they must've killed a few during the genocide because they were part of the Interahamwe."[67]

With vital intelligence gained from Dieudonne Niyitegeka, by July 1997 the tracking team possessed the detailed information necessary to carry out what they dubbed Operation Naki (an abbreviation for Nairobi-Kigali), designed to simultaneously apprehend a dozen high-level Hutu suspects in different parts of Nairobi. With the operation planned, prosecution officials then went to the Kenyan authorities asking them to perform arrests but without revealing the suspects' names. The Kenyan authorities agreed under one condition, Arbour recalled: "They said, 'Okay, we're ready to do that, but we want these guys out of the country instantly. We don't want them processed through our court system.'"[68] After its early defiance, in other words, the Moi government now indicated that it would make arrests as long as the tribunal quickly ushered the suspects out of the country to avoid the political complications of a legal battle that the suspects might wage in Kenyan courts.

Operation Naki proved to be the most complex arrest operation in the history of the contemporary international tribunals up to that time, in no small part because of the need to maintain secrecy and coordinate simultaneous arrests across Nairobi. To maintain secrecy, the tracking team even delayed telling tribunal investigators coming in to help with the operation the true nature of their mission.

Early in the morning of July 18, 1997, Morissette, Côté, and some twenty other members of the prosecutor's staff gathered with Kenyan police in a parking lot at national police headquarters and spread out their maps on the hood of a car. At 5 A.M., tribunal officials handed sealed envelopes to a dozen teams, each including at least one Kenyan police officer and one tribunal investigator. Each envelope contained the name and photograph of the targeted suspect, the house plan of the suspect's residence, and other information needed to carry out the arrest an hour later, just before sunrise. If the investigator was unsure of the identity of the suspect, Morissette would then dispatch one of the Hutu informants to confirm the identity in person.

By early morning, Kenyan police had arrested seven suspects, including Jean Kambanda, the former Rwandan prime minister, and Pauline Nyiramasuhuko, the former minister of family and women's affairs and the only female indicted by the tribunal. Kenyan police and tribunal officials moved quickly to put the arrested suspects on a bus to Arusha to honor Arbour's agreement with President Moi. Luc Côté, Operation Naki's legal advisor, insisted that they be read their rights immediately. According to Côté, Bernard Muna, the tribunal deputy prosecutor, argued that there was no time to do so. "I said, 'Hey, it's going to take ten minutes.'. . . I went on the bus and I read them their rights, one after the other." Suspects "needed to know why they were there and they had rights." Failure to follow legal protocol, he added, could "come back to bite you in court" by bolstering the suspects' inevitable claims of kidnapping and ill-treatment.[69]

While Côté's conscientiousness saved the prosecution trouble down the road, the tribunal administration's treatment of other suspects in the Kenya raids sparked controversy. One problem centered on the mistaken arrest of a Hutu man believed to be Shalom Ntahobali, a minister in the former interim government and the son of Pauline Nyiramasuhuko. Once in Arusha, the man, Esdres Twagirimana, revealed his true identity but begged not to be returned to Kenya, from where he might be extradited to Rwanda. After two months in tribunal custody, Twagirimana was nevertheless sent back to Kenya, where he was arrested and the compensation money he had received from the tribunal was confiscated.[70] The handling of his case drew sharp criticism from Amnesty International.

The tribunal received even more scrutiny for its treatment of Kambanda, the former Rwandan prime minister. With the exception of

214 I Chapter Six

Kambanda, the suspects arrested in Operation Naki traveled overland to Arusha and were held in the tribunal's detention center. But Kambanda was flown there and then quickly driven to a secret location in the Tanzanian city of Dodoma, a few hundred miles away. The secret location turned out to be a large and comfortable house that one tribunal investigator dubbed the Royal Palace.[71] There, investigators sought to negotiate an admission of guilt from Kambanda and to persuade him to testify against other defendants in exchange for relocation of his family, who were then refugees in West Africa. For nine months after his arrest, though, Kambanda was not brought to the tribunal for his initial appearance, and was denied the attorney of his choice; he was given legal representation only several weeks before his first court appearance. Moreover, he was given a lawyer who actually served as the legal advisor to the tribunal's deputy prosecutor's father. In the end, Kambanda confessed to genocide, but later tried unsuccessfully to retract the confession, blaming the prosecution for unduly pressuring him while in the Royal Palace. He was given a life sentence. The arrest and conviction of Kambanda was, as Thierry Cruvellier writes, "meant to be one of the [Rwanda tribunal's] major accomplishments for justice and for history," but by revealing the prosecution's lack of regard for the principles of due process, it turned into "a fiasco."[72]

In the days following the wave of arrests in Nairobi, several more suspects, including Georges Ruggiu and the real Shalom Ntahobali, were apprehended in Mombasa. However, several other suspects, including the high-profile Hutu financier Felicien Kabuga, eluded the Operation Naki dragnet, suggesting the possibility of a damaging leak. Still, it was, in Arbour's estimation, "our biggest breakthrough."[73] Many observers and diplomats echoed this assessment, though, like much else at the African-based tribunal, the arrests garnered few international headlines.

The unexpected success of the Kenya operation indicated that the tribunal, despite its lack of enforcement powers and the paucity of global attention it would receive, might become an effective instrument of accountability as well as a tool to marginalize former members of the Hutu regime who still hoped to return to power. The tribunal's early success in bringing suspects into custody, however, overwhelmed its fledgling legal bureaucracy, which had come under sharp international criticism for incompetence and corruption. This led to prolonged pretrial detention for a number of suspects, a problem that tribunal defense attorneys believed violated the guarantee to be tried without undue delay that is enshrined in the International Covenant on Political and Civil Rights.

Well before the July 1997 arrests in Nairobi, Morissette and his team began to plan another major arrest campaign, this time on the other side of Africa. This new operation would also entail intricate planning, because the arrests were to take place simultaneously in four different West African countries: Benin, Côte d'Ivoire, Mali, and Togo. Once again, the key informant, Dieudonne Niyitegeka, would use his close contacts with high-level genocide suspects to provide information to help the tracking team. To avoid suspicion that he was on the tribunal's payroll and might have played a role in the Nairobi arrests, prosecution officials moved him from Kenya to West Africa prior to the Operation Naki roundup. As in Nairobi, the team worked under the radar. Still, they managed to forge working relationships with trusted law enforcement officials in the four West Africa countries.

Early in the morning on June 5, 1998, the Ki-West Operation (an abbreviation for Kigali West Africa) went off without a hitch, yielding all five suspects the team had targeted. In Benin, Morissette himself accompanied a French-trained SWAT team that scaled a twelve-foot-high wall to gain entrance to the compound where Joseph Nzirorera, a genocide suspect who had served as president of the national assembly in the Hutu extremist government, resided. As they approached the house, Morissette recalls, he heard a woman screaming, "Joseph, there's somebody coming over the fence."[74] Inside the house, they also found Juvenal Kajelijeli, a former Hutu mayor implicated in the genocide but who had not been on the list of targets. Morissette called Deputy Prosecutor Bernard Muna and Luc Côté in Kigali for instructions. Invoking the sweeping powers to detain suspects on the Office of the Prosecutor's own authority, Muna reportedly ordered Morissette to authorize the Benin police to arrest Kajelijeli, despite having virtually no evidence against him at the time. Kajelijeli was later convicted of genocide and sentenced to life. Nzirorera, however, escaped judgment. He remained in detention for seven long years, from 1998 to 2005, and died in July 2010 before his lengthy trial concluded.

THE DOUBLE LIFE OF SIMEON NSHAMIHIGO

Juvenal Kajelijeli was not the only accidental suspect to end up in tribunal custody. In 2001, tribunal officials were shocked to discover several genocide suspects hiding in plain sight in the tribunal's own headquarters in downtown Arusha. Through an unlikely series of events, prosecutors learned that the court had actually been employing several genocide suspects as investigators working on behalf of Hutu defendants.

While many suspects fled far from the UN tribunal and the scene of the Rwandan genocide, these suspects-turned-defense-investigators apparently believed that the perfect hiding place would be inside the tribunal itself—and they'd collect a salary for it besides. Simeon Nshamihigo had worked for the tribunal as a diligent defense investigator for three years under the alias of a Congolese national named Sammy Bahati Weza. Nshamihigo might have continued his work on behalf of genocide defendants for the tribunal's duration had he not been spotted in the halls of the tribunal by a fellow Rwandan, who passed on the information. The news that Bahati Weza was actually Simeon Nshamihigo, the former deputy prosecutor of Rwanda's Cyangugu Prefecture, who was involved in planning massacres of the Tutsi minority, stunned many at the tribunal and beyond.[75] The revelation also caught others off guard. "Nobody would have ever [thought] a possible genocide suspect would hide under the wing of the ICTR," remarked a European diplomat based in Rwanda. "Imagine Klaus Barbie working for the defense at Nuremberg."[76] Half a year after Nshamihigo's arrest, another tribunal defense investigator, Joseph Nzabirinda, was apprehended in Belgium and subsequently handed back to the tribunal for prosecution. Nzabirinda, a former youth organizer and businessman, was sentenced to seven years in prison following a guilty plea for his role in the genocide. Nshamihigo was sentenced to life in prison.

These embarrassing revelations led the tribunal's registry, responsible for vetting the defense investigators, to scrutinize the approximately forty-five other Hutu investigators working on tribunal defense teams. The registry tried to downplay the tribunal's responsibility by maintaining that the defense investigators were actually "independent contractors recruited by defense counsel." The Rwandan government dismissed such attempts as damage control and used the incidents to sharpen its criticism that the tribunal had become a haven for genocide suspects. The government demanded action against other defense investigators whom it had placed on its own domestic list of wanted genocide suspects. Under pressure, the registrar announced that he would not renew the contracts of several defense investigators allegedly implicated in the genocide. These events, along with continuing RPF allegations of a tribunal cabal of *génocidaires*, cast a pall over the community of Hutu defense investigators.[77] Their concerns were heightened when the registrar, working quickly to assuage Rwandan government anger, mistakenly dismissed an investigator who had the same name as a man wanted by Rwanda but was thirteen years older. The tribunal reinstated the investigator, but the damage to his reputation had been done.

FELICIEN KABUGA AND THE FATE OF THE REMAINING TRIBUNAL FUGITIVES

Following Operations Naki and Ki-West, the prosecution broadened its search, giving more attention to locating suspects who had fled to Europe. France and Belgium became natural destinations for suspects, given the networks of support available in Hutu exile communities there. Indeed, the French government had flown a number of Hutu extremists back to France in the early days of the genocide. Most of them, including Habyarimana's wife and Eugene Mbarushimana, the former secretary-general of the Interahamwe militia, were reportedly implicated in the genocide, but never indicted by the tribunal. As in the earlier operations in Africa, the arrests in Europe required extensive tracking-team planning and coordination with local law enforcement officials. By the end of 2002, some sixty suspects, including most of the alleged masterminds of the genocide, had been arrested and transferred to Arusha.

Still, one group of Hutu suspects remained largely beyond the tribunal's reach. While many high-level Hutu suspects left the Democratic Republic of Congo (DRC) prior to the Rwandan 1996 invasion, some remained. Of these, former Rwandan Chief of Staff Augustin Bizimungu and some others had joined with Congolese forces battling the RPF in eastern DRC. In the Republic of Congo, several former Hutu fighters were also reportedly given state protection, ironically through their employment as close protection officers for key government ministers.[78] Whereas many Hutu genocide suspects elsewhere in Africa and Europe had become vulnerable to arrest, the suspects in the DRC and the Republic of Congo enjoyed direct state protection.

The 2002 Sun City, South Africa, peace accords that led to a hiatus in the devastating Congo conflict created a more favorable political climate for apprehending some of these high-level Hutu genocide suspects.[79] One outcome of the peace talks was an agreement that, in exchange for Rwanda's withdrawal from eastern Congo, the DRC government would arrest and turn over Hutu genocide suspects. DRC

President Joseph Kabila's decision to turn against his Hutu allies appeared to be motivated in part by an interest in avoiding international criticism and U.S. pressure for arrests. The changing political dynamic led to the arrest of two Hutu suspects in the DRC, one in 2002 and the other in 2004; two arrests in the Republic of Congo, in 2002 and 2003; and the arrest of Bizimungu in Angola, in 2002.[80] Several years later, two more suspects were arrested in DRC. But as the twentieth anniversary of the Rwandan genocide approached, in early 2014, nine indicted Hutu genocide suspects had still managed to evade capture, with most of these believed to be living in the DRC.

Felicien Kabuga, the wealthy Hutu businessman accused of financing the Interahamwe and the most notorious tribunal genocide suspect still at large, has reportedly spent much of his time in Kenya, where he evaded the Operation Naki dragnet back in 1997. For years, the Kabuga case has bedeviled tribunal and UN officials and American diplomats, who have devoted considerable energy to his capture. Kabuga has kept one step ahead of the authorities by deploying his fortune to buy himself protection and false passports. Midway through the genocide, in June 1994, Kabuga left Rwanda and sought refuge in Switzerland. In 1995, Swiss authorities expelled Kabuga, who had not yet been placed on a tribunal wanted list. He ended up in Nairobi, forging close ties with senior figures in the Kenyan government. He also established an import-export firm, working out of his house in a posh Nairobi neighborhood.

A key mystery in how Kabuga has eluded arrest for so long is why he was not in his residence when Operation Naki was launched the morning of July 17, 1997. During the operation, tribunal investigators found a note implicating a Kenyan law enforcement officer in warning Kabuga to leave the premises before the raid. Years later, Morissette, who took pains that morning to prevent such leaks, remains uncertain how Kabuga was able to flee. Although Morissette closely guarded the identity of the targeted suspects until just before the arrest operation, it is possible that at least one senior Kenyan law enforcement official knew the day before that a big raid would take place the next morning and passed word to Kabuga.

Even after Operation Naki, opportunities arose to apprehend Kabuga. In April 1998 tribunal investigators learned that he was hiding in various Nairobi residences, two of which were owned by President Moi's nephew. Kabuga was reportedly seen a number of times in public, including in Southeast Asia in 1998 and while transiting through Belgium in 2000. Following Operation Naki, an attempt was made to negotiate Kabuga's surrender, but the deal failed to materialize, reportedly in part because the tribunal's chief prosecutor would not agree to allow Kabuga to be released prior to trial.[81] The Rwanda tribunal has not allowed defendants out on court-supervised, pretrial release, though the Yugoslavia tribunal has found the carrot of provisional release effective in persuading a number of suspects to surrender.

The prosecution did try other tactics to bring Kabuga into custody. In the late 1990s, Chief Prosecutor Carla Del Ponte succeeded in having several European countries freeze $2.5 million in his bank accounts.[82] And in 2002, the U.S. State Department expanded its Rewards for Justice program, which had previously focused on terrorism suspects wanted by the U.S. and on Yugoslavia tribunal indictees, to also target Rwandan suspects, including an offer of up to $5 million for information leading to Kabuga's capture. In 2002, two informants contacted the U.S. Embassy in Nairobi with information on Kabuga's whereabouts and protection networks. This led the FBI, the U.S. Embassy in Nairobi, and U.S. war crimes ambassador Pierre-Richard Prosper to develop a plan to have Kenyan authorities arrest the elusive financier. But once again, a Nairobi arrest operation failed to apprehend him. One of the two informants who had disclosed information on Kabuga's whereabouts was later found murdered.[83]

THE RPF AND THE RETURN OF DOMESTIC
ACCOUNTABILITY

As the Rwanda tribunal began to wrap up its investigations in 2004 and streamline its operations to abide by the UN Security Council's plan to close the court's doors by the end of the decade, efforts to capture the remaining Hutu genocide fugitives seemed to lose steam. At the Yugoslavia tribunal, the same UN demand to wrap up its cases prompted concerted diplomatic pressure on Serbia and Croatia to hand over fugitives. But in the Rwanda context, there was no robust diplomatic imperative to do so. Carla Del Ponte's successor as chief prosecutor, Hassan Jallow, frequently called on states to provide cooperation in arrests. Yet, at no time did the Security Council take any punitive action against the DRC and Kenya, the two main states suspected of harboring the remaining fugitives. From November 2009 through the end of August 2015, none of the nine fugitives remaining on the tribunal's wanted list had been arrested. Most of the Rwanda tribunal's work was slated to come to an end in 2013, after the initial 2010 deadline proved too ambitious.

However, both the Rwanda and Yugoslavia tribunals would continue to function for at least a few more years in order to complete their last trials and appeal cases.

As international interest in the remaining tribunal fugitives faded, the RPF Rwandan government reinvigorated its drive to bring high-level Hutu genocide suspects to trial at home. In 2012, the tribunal referred the cases of six of the remaining fugitives to Rwanda. From the early post-genocide days, the RPF government had tried to convince third countries and the tribunal itself to allow Rwandan courts to prosecute high-level genocide suspects, generally without success. However, several developments had led the tribunal to rethink its position. Security Council pressure to close the tribunal and clear the backlog of genocide suspects languishing in pretrial detention gave the tribunal prosecution incentive to send suspects to Rwanda as well as to other states for prosecution. This created a golden opportunity for the RPF government, which had tens of thousands of low-level suspects in custody but virtually no high-level ones.

The original call for an international tribunal, both for Rwanda and the former Yugoslavia, was premised on the belief that governments ensnared in violent conflict would be unable to deliver justice impartially, or at all, and that such tribunals are best situated outside conflict zones.[84] Over time, this skepticism toward the credibility of domestic prosecutions began to soften and the attractiveness of shifting the growing financial burden of war crimes prosecutions to domestic courts increased. This trend has been furthered by the emergence of the International Criminal Court in 2002 and its principle of complementarity, which allows domestic courts to adjudicate war crimes cases unless they are unable or unwilling to do so.

To satisfy tribunal judges that its courts were in fact capable of meeting international trial standards, however, the RPF government first needed to make reforms in its legal system. An RPF decision to drop capital punishment in 2007 persuaded tribunal Chief Prosecutor Jallow to support the idea of transferring some Hutu genocide suspects. However, tribunal judges in 2009, citing ongoing concerns about due-process rights, rejected the prosecution's request to transfer any indicted suspects to Rwanda.

This rejection prompted Rwanda to implement further legal reforms. This time it granted immunity to witnesses who would testify in the trial of any suspect transferred from the tribunal. This move was designed to assuage the tribunal's concern that Hutu witnesses testifying on behalf of genocide defendants might themselves be later prosecuted under a controversial Rwandan law that criminalizes genocide ideology and denial of the genocide. Under this law, Hutus have even been jailed for calling attention to RPF atrocities, an act the RPF government equates with negating the genocide. The government invoked this legislation, for example, to jail American tribunal defense attorney Peter Erlinder in 2010 for questioning the RPF narrative that the genocide resulted from a carefully planned conspiracy.

Given Rwanda's repressive and highly politicized environment, Human Rights Watch and the tribunal's defense lawyers association sought to persuade tribunal judges that Hutu defendants were unlikely to receive a fair trial in Rwanda. They argued that many potential Hutu witnesses, still fearful of government retribution against themselves or their families, would stay away from participating in the domestic trials. Such fear has been stoked by an authoritarian regime that strictly controls political and civic life and uses courtroom prosecutions to punish not only Hutu opposition leaders and journalists but also Tutsi dissidents who have called attention to government abuses.[85]

Despite these deep human rights concerns, tribunal judges in June 2011 reversed their earlier decision regarding the transfer of tribunal defendants, ruling specifically that Jean Bosco Uwinkindi, a Pentecostal Hutu in tribunal custody, could be sent to Rwanda.[86] The tribunal assigned a regional African human rights court to monitor the trial and stipulated that if violations were found, as a last resort the case could be remanded back to the tribunal. The monitoring, however, was only to scrutinize the legal arena of the courtroom and not to examine the issue, equally important but more difficult to observe, of the state's possible role in influencing its judiciary and intimidating potential witnesses and their families. Nevertheless, the tribunal's June 2011 decision in the Uwinkindi case served as the long-awaited international seal of approval for the Rwandan judiciary. That quickly opened the way for other cases to be sent to Rwanda, both from the tribunal and from several states that had arrested genocide suspects. As of August 2015, the tribunal had sent one other Hutu defendant for trial in Rwanda and two other suspects for trial in France.

Since its inception the International Criminal Tribunal for Rwanda has indicted 93 suspects, including most of the high-level political and military officials implicated in the genocide. Yet this represents only a fraction of the total number of individuals implicated in mass atrocities in Rwanda during 1994. By mid-2015, the tribunal had convicted

56 suspects and acquitted 14. By mid-2006, some ten thousand genocide suspects had faced prosecution in Rwandan courts. Hundreds of
thousands of Hutus who allegedly played a far lesser role in the genocide have faced accountability in Gacaca, a quasi-legal proceeding
derived from a traditional form of Rwandan conflict resolution, which
has allowed quick action but provides few due-process protections and
no provision for the prosecution of RPF suspects implicated in non-
genocidal massacres. And there are many others implicated in the genocide who fled Rwanda unnoticed and have gone on to build new lives
elsewhere in Africa, in Europe, and in North America.

The presence of these Rwandans on foreign soil raises two challenges. The first centers on how states, NGOs, and individuals can
increase their capacity to track down and aid the arrest of these suspects, many of whom are unknown to national law enforcement agencies and not yet under criminal indictment. The second challenge centers on what states should do, once Rwandan genocide suspects have
been brought into national custody. Both challenges can be confound-
ing and have been faced before, particularly in regard to identifying the
crimes of German Nazis and their European collaborators.

In the wake of the Rwandan genocide, a handful of U.S. officials began
to anticipate the challenges of tracking down the multitude of Hutu suspects who might slip through the nation's federal immigration system.
The U.S. government's war crimes ambassador, David Scheffer, soon realized how easy it would be for Hutu leaders and lower-level suspects to
enter the United States undetected. He was astonished to learn that in
1994 U.S. visa application forms only asked applicants about any association with Nazi Germany. As Scheffer recalled: "We were certain to run
into trouble, and we did, with Hutu ringleaders who truthfully filled out
their visa applications and legally waltzed into the United States to visit
as tourists, some ultimately achieving green card status that would grant
them permanent residence."[87] Scheffer and his colleagues developed a
visa watch list of some 200 names and decided that all Rwandans seeking
entry into the U.S. should be asked about their possible role in the genocide, as a way to detect those implicated in committing atrocities. One
U.S. official even suggested excluding all Rwandan clergy from entering
the U.S. because of the high number implicated in mass atrocities. Despite
these precautions, an undetermined number of Rwandan suspects managed to slip past immigration gatekeepers, often doing so legally.

The best-known case is that of a Rwandan Hutu pastor who had
entered the U.S. after the genocide. Acting under a tribunal arrest war-

rant, federal marshals in September 1996 arranged a stakeout near Laredo, Texas, and arrested the pastor, Elizaphan Ntakirutimana, after stopping him on the Interstate.[88] He was transferred to the tribunal, but only after a contentious four-year-long battle in federal court that brought into question America's legal commitment to the very tribunal it had helped establish. The pastor was convicted for his role in the massacre of Tutsis who during the genocide had taken refuge in the hospital and church compound where his son worked. Tutsi representatives appealed to the pastor for rescue, writing a letter to him foretelling what would happen if there was no intervention to save them: "We wish to inform you that tomorrow, we will be killed along with our families," the letter of appeal read.[89] The pastor ignored the Tutsis' appeal and instead brought attackers to the compound who then massacred the unarmed civilians hiding inside. The pastor's son, Dr. Gerard Ntakirutimana, was arrested in Côte d'Ivoire in 1996 and was later convicted by the tribunal for crimes against humanity and genocide for his role in the massacre. The pastor was released following the completion of his ten-year sentence in 2006, while his son was granted early release in 2013 from his twenty-five-year sentence.

How to handle genocide, crimes against humanity, and war crimes suspects not under the indictment of an international tribunal or a domestic court in the country where the crimes occurred presents a vexing challenge for national court systems. Under the principle of universal jurisdiction, suspects implicated in mass atrocities committed anywhere in the world can be prosecuted in any national court. Since Spain's landmark 1998 attempt to obtain custody of former Chilean President Augusto Pinochet, activists have hailed universal jurisdiction as an important tool to ensure accountability regardless of where suspects may travel or live in the world. Western states with ample resources and well-trained legal professionals would seem to provide a robust forum for such trials. Yet, even these well-established legal systems have struggled to adjudicate appropriately cases of atrocity crimes that occurred a world away.[90] Legal actors in universal jurisdiction trials have been hampered by their relative lack of experience and knowledge about faraway countries and armed conflicts. These deficits have also hampered immigration proceedings that states such as the U.S. and Canada have held to determine whether to denaturalize and deport alleged war crimes suspects. In practice, states have been reluctant to devote the resources necessary to pursue a significant number of universal jurisdiction trials. European states, the Netherlands and Belgium in particular, have held several universal jurisdiction trials pertaining to atrocities in Rwanda and the former Yugoslavia. Canada has prosecuted two Hutu immigrants implicated in the genocide, including a 2012 trial in Ottawa Superior Court in which Rwandan witnesses testified by video link from Kigali. "It is a very good idea, but the problem is that the average prosecution costs four million dollars. It's too expensive," remarked a Canadian official in the country's war crimes program. "Universal jurisdiction prosecutions compete with other priorities . . . [and] after 9/11, terrorism became the big issue."[91]

In the United States, the preferred option for suspected Nazi war criminals and those implicated in atrocities in Rwanda and the Balkans is to initiate immigration proceedings that can result in deportation and denaturalization. These cases center on whether an alleged Nazi or a contemporary genocide or war crimes suspect lied on his immigration forms on entering the country. In Canada and other Western states, such deportation proceedings also constitute a common approach for dealing with suspected war criminals. However, "the big dilemma," as the Canadian war crimes official put it, "is what to do with people found to be war criminals in [national] refugee systems [when] you can't guarantee a trial if you deport them."[92] The other big dilemma is what to do when the deported suspect is likely to face an unfair, even rigged trial back home. That dilemma explains why states such as Canada, Britain, and Sweden did not hand over genocide suspects to Rwanda until the UN tribunal signaled that it was legitimate to do so.

Given the long-held reluctance both to send cases to Rwanda and to prosecute them at home, some states have kept suspected genocide suspects in legal limbo. Canada's handling of a Rwandan Hutu ideologue who resettled with his family in Québec City but never came under tribunal indictment is a case in point. Whereas many Hutu implicated in the genocide fled Rwanda in summer 1994, Léon Mugesera left a year and a half before the outbreak of the genocide, after a falling out with Hutu authorities. Mugesera had gained notoriety for a virulent anti-Tutsi speech he delivered in northwest Rwanda in 1992. Since then, the speech has become infamous for its coded exhortation to eliminate the Tutsi minority. Such incitement played an instrumental role in dehumanizing Tutsis and preparing the ground for mass murder in 1994, according to some scholars as well as the current Tutsi-led Rwandan government. For Mugesera, Québec City and its main educational institution, Laval University, were natural places to make a second home. "Dad had friends here. He had studied here. He felt it was a good place," explained his daughter. In the leafy suburbs of Québec City, Mugesera and his family lived openly, with little sense of the turn of events that would alter their lives. Then, one day in 1995, the Royal Canadian Mounted Police arrested him on immigration charges, following media reports that linked him to his 1992 speech. The arrest, recalled his daughter, "came as a total surprise. . . . [We] never thought he would be arrested" for a speech given well before the genocide.[93]

As it happened, Mugesera lived not far from a Canadian with first-hand experience of the consequences of hate speech that vilified the Tutsis of Rwanda. In the mid-1990s, Roméo Dallaire, traumatized and beleaguered from his months of witnessing the genocide, returned to his family in Québec City. One day in 1998, while he was walking with his wife back to their car in a shopping center, she spotted Mugesera several rows away. To avoid a direct encounter, she quickly ushered Dallaire to their car. Recalled Dallaire in a 2012 interview: "I was not well and real upset in those days and totally unpredictable. [My wife] hurried me into the car and said we have to go before I saw him. And that was probably the really wisest thing she might have done."[94]

Mugesera's contentious deportation battle lasted sixteen years. Initially, he denied making the 1992 speech. The case might have ended there, but Canadian forensic experts produced a composite tape of the speech after splicing together three partial recordings. In 2005, the Canadian Supreme Court ruled that he could be sent to Rwanda to face charges of incitement of genocide, but the decision was stayed because of concerns about the court system there. Soon after the tribunal's Uwinkindi decision was confirmed on appeal in December 2011, the Canadian government had the green light to move forward. The government rebuffed a last-minute appeal from the UN Committee against Torture to halt the deportation until it could guarantee that Mugesera would not face torture back in Rwanda. In late January 2012, the Canadian authorities put him on a flight to Rwanda, where he would face trial.

UNFINISHED JUSTICE AND RPF IMPUNITY

Legal proceedings against Hutu genocide suspects in Arusha, Kigali, Brussels, and Ottawa, even if all were adjudicated fairly, would not complete the circle of accountability for the mass atrocities that occurred in Rwanda during 1994. Unindicted genocide suspects abound. Moreover, the Rwanda tribunal's list of indictees is itself incomplete because it does not include Tutsi RPF military and political leaders or even low-level suspects implicated in crimes against humanity and war crimes against Hutu civilians which led, according to Human Rights Watch, to the killing of between 25,000 and 30,000 people during 1994. With few notable exceptions, neither has the question of the RPF's own culpability in atrocities come onto the radar for most national jurisdictions. Rwanda itself has handled only one RPF war crimes case, a trial sharply criticized by leading international human rights organizations for shielding the accused from serious punishment. Otherwise, the government has effectively immunized RPF suspects from criminal accountability.

The number of Hutus murdered in Rwanda in 1994 of course pales in comparison to the approximately 800,000 people who perished in the genocide. Tepid interest in seeking accountability for the atrocities of the RPF may also stem from the international community's quest for atonement in the wake of its failure to intervene to stop the genocide. RPF crimes have sparked little global attention in part, too, because early influential journalistic and scholarly accounts of the genocide either downplayed RPF culpability or failed to mention it altogether. Yet the death toll and evidence of wholesale massacres of Hutu families and communities underscore the severity of these crimes.

The genocide as well as the widespread and systematic nature of RPF atrocities led, as we have seen, to a tribunal whose temporal scope was limited to 1994 but not its ability to target both the genocide and RPF reprisal attacks that spiked in its aftermath.[95] Neutral mandates like this distinguish today's international tribunals from the Nuremberg and Tokyo military tribunals of the post–World War II era, which immunized the winners of the war. Yet, in sharp contrast to the Yugoslavia as well as the Sierra Leone tribunal, the Rwanda tribunal's indictments have been one-sided. That omission has fueled charges, from supporters and opponents of the tribunal alike, that international justice has become a political tool of the RPF Rwandan government. The tribunal's neglect of RPF crimes has led to what one leading human rights scholar calls "victor's justice and victor's history."[96] This, in turn, calls into question the impartiality of the tribunal's chief prosecutors and exemplifies how politics can shape who ends up on an international tribunal's most wanted list.

The story of the chief prosecutors' decisions to forego indicting any RPF suspects is a story of the enduring power of Rwandan state impunity, or of the logic of tribunal accommodation to this power, or both. All four chief prosecutors who served at the Rwanda tribunal feared confrontation with an RPF government that at various times threatened to bring the tribunal to a standstill. Carla Del Ponte attempted to tackle this volatile issue head-on, but she ran afoul of the Rwandan government when she laid down the gauntlet, warning that RPF indictments would be handed down by the end of 2002. In the Balkans, Del Ponte's boldness often worked to her advantage. But her penchant for confrontation proved a less strategic form of prosecutorial diplomacy in Rwanda, where she enjoyed significantly less international backing and spent less time cultivating it. By relinquishing the element of surprise, Del Ponte gave Rwandan government officials ample opportunity to cultivate diplomatic allies and thwart what they perceived to be a grave threat to the regime. When it came to Rwanda, "she simply did not approach the job as a diplomat [who] understands the significance of what one might say to the media," according to a former senior U.S. government official.[97] A former prosecution source with the Rwanda tribunal elaborated on the importance of keeping sensitive investigations close to the vest: "When you're doing this type of operation you keep your mouth shut and when it is time to go into action you do it. You don't advertise it in the newspapers."[98]

To counter Del Ponte's threat to issue indictments against RPF suspects, Kagame's government in June 2002 blocked Tutsi genocide survivors from traveling to Arusha to testify in ongoing genocide trials. Del Ponte and the tribunal president registered a formal complaint of noncooperation with the Security Council in July. The council took six months to address the issue, and when it did, it presented only a toothless reminder to Rwanda of its obligation to cooperate in the RPF investigations. In the face of Rwanda's recalcitrance, Del Ponte suspended her investigations. She later maintained that she did not drop the RPF investigations,[99] but sources close to the prosecution report she actually did.[100]

Worried that a determined Del Ponte might revive investigations, the Rwandan government did not let up. It targeted Del Ponte herself by successfully lobbying the Security Council not to grant her another term as chief prosecutor at the Rwanda tribunal. In a move publicly justified as a change to increase management effectiveness, the council in 2003 appointed Hassan Jallow of Gambia as the new chief prosecutor for the Rwanda tribunal but kept Del Ponte in her leadership post at the Yugoslavia tribunal. In its campaign to remove the chief prosecutor, Kigali had the support of its two closest international allies, the U.S. and Great Britain, who apparently feared the possible destabilizing effects of arrest warrants targeting RPF officials. The Rwandan leadership had some cause for personal concern as well, because the atrocities in question, which it publicly dismissed as only isolated revenge killings, apparently implicated high-level officials, possibly President Kagame himself. "It went all the way to the top," a well-placed former prosecution source said in regard to evidence that pointed to the role of the RPF leadership.[101]

Why did Del Ponte stop short of issuing RPF indictments? For the Swiss prosecutor, the answer boiled down to damaging interference from Rwanda and its Western allies that ultimately deprived her of the evidence needed to seek RPF indictments. "You are independent theoretically, but in reality you depend a lot on the international community," Del Ponte said in a 2003 interview in The Hague, several months after losing her post in Arusha.[102] An alternate explanation is that Del Ponte chose to back down in the face of intense pressure and perhaps to increase her prospects of becoming the first chief prosecutor of the International Criminal Court, a position she coveted in 2002 and had described as her "dream job."[103] The prosecution had ample evidence to seek judicial approval for indictments well before her departure from the tribunal in September 2003, according to sources close to the RPF investigation. Del Ponte insists that she lacked sufficient evidence to support "trial ready" indictments.[104] But one key source close to the prosecution contradicts this assertion. "We have the information," the source said in a 2005 interview. "We've got the reports, we've got the evidence, we've got . . . the statements of the witnesses [who] . . . were directly involved themselves."[105]

In contrast to Del Ponte, Jallow kept the RPF issue in the shadows, rarely tipping his hand. Some human rights activists hoped that the silence was a tactic to bide his time until close to the end of the tribunal's mandate, when the institution was less vulnerable to Rwandan retaliation. However, other observers believed that he had little appetite for sparking a confrontation with a regime he had publicly credited for having "waged a war of liberation . . . putting an end to the genocide."[106] In the end, Jallow relinquished his RPF investigations to the RPF government-controlled legal system, which then held a trial of several RPF suspects who had been under tribunal investigation. In so doing, Jallow heeded a plan long advocated by Kigali and Washington to keep the question of RPF atrocities under Rwandan control and out of the international limelight. The brief 2008 Rwandan war crimes trial of only one massacre, which steered clear of prosecuting senior RPF officials or bringing charges of crimes against humanity, resulted in the acquittal of two RPF officers and light sentences for two lower-level ones. Human Rights Watch, which closely monitored the trial, called it "a political whitewash."[107]

The pursuit of criminal accountability in the aftermath of the Rwandan genocide and civil war underscores the crucial factor of political protection in allowing suspects to evade indictment, arrest, and ultimately trial and imprisonment. In the waning days of the 1994 genocide, the Hutu extremist leadership fled Rwanda to seek the protection of UN refugee camps in neighboring Zaire and Tanzania. Once safely across the border, high-level political and military officials regrouped and initially remained beyond the reach of the Tutsi-led RPF government newly in power. The UN provided aid to hundreds of thousands of Hutu refugees, but took no interest in identifying and arresting the scores of high-level former political and military Hutu leaders who were implicated in the genocide but did not begin to come under tribunal indictment until the mid-1990s.

As the horrors of the Rwandan genocide became seared into global consciousness, the former Hutu extremist leadership, many members of which had sought refuge in comfortable urban environments in Africa and Europe, became widely tarnished as pariahs. No longer in power and effectively stateless, these pariahs had little to offer African leaders, the UN, or other diplomats around the world. As a result, their arrests did not stir opposition from world leaders who might have needed the suspects' cooperation when it came to signing and implementing a peace agreement or to being a good regional neighbor. In this political context, many of the political obstacles that blocked progress in making arrests in the former Yugoslavia did not exist when it came to pursuing Rwandan Hutu suspects.

The operational challenge of tracking down suspects who had dispersed across Africa and the world, however, often proved a daunting one for the tracking team the tribunal prosecution had established. In Africa, in particular, there was the challenge of securing the cooperation of law enforcement agencies. Of particular concern to the tracking team was the real prospect, in Kenya especially, of corrupt police officials sabotaging the tribunal by leaking details of arrest operations. The tribunal's vulnerability here is part and parcel of the larger problem of lacking arrest and other enforcement powers that all of the contemporary international criminal tribunals confront. Although little noticed, the Rwanda tribunal's tracking team largely overcame this enforcement deficit. As we've seen, this entailed skillfully planning arrest operations to limit the potential for damaging leaks by often involving domestic authorities only at the last moment. Despite the Rwanda tribunal's impressive arrest record in its early years, progress has stalled in recent years. Since the end of 2009, not one of the remaining nine suspects under tribunal indictment has been arrested. As the twentieth anniversary of the start of the Rwandan genocide approached in early 2014, the fate of these suspects, most of whom were believed to be in the Democratic Republic of Congo, received little media or diplomatic attention. International interest in justice for Rwanda waned as the world's focus turned to other international courts and global calamities.

Beyond the tribunal's list of indictees, there are scores of other suspects implicated in the Rwandan genocide and civil war who have been untouched. In France, for instance, a number of Hutu extremist ideologues live openly, having never faced indictment or arrest by an international or domestic court. And then, as we have seen, there are the numerous RPF Tutsi political and military officials implicated in non-genocidal massacres against Hutu civilians who have never faced indictment. The story of the tribunal's failed—and abandoned—attempts to prosecute suspects implicated in those mass atrocities demonstrates the strength of the protective shell that surrounds and immunizes key officials in the present-day RPF Rwandan government. Officially, senior RPF officials, including Rwandan President Paul Kagame, may not be classed as fugitives. But in another sense, these are men hiding in plain sight.

CHAPTER 7

Hybrid Tribunals

Thinking Globally, Acting Locally

On a bright May afternoon in 1982, twelve-year-old Nic Dunlop sat on a sofa in the living room of his parent's home in Dun Laoire, Ireland, fascinated by a *National Geographic* article about Angkor Wat, the vast complex of ancient temples in Cambodia built between the ninth and fifteenth centuries for the Hindu god Vishnu and his consort, Lakshmi.[1] He marveled at Angkor's vast stone waterways stretching as far as the eye could see, and its cathedral-like sanctuaries wrapped in the thick roots of enormous silk cotton trees, with towering stone walls decorated with images of churning sea serpents and leaping water spirits led by the monkey god, Hanuman. It was like no other world he had ever seen or imagined.

Dunlop turned the page. He paused, lingering on a photograph of a palm-lined hill, its tropical undergrowth split open by a large brown crater. On the crater's rim, embedded in brown mud, were shards of clothing and hundreds of human skulls and other skeletal remains, white-washed by the sun. "What struck me was how fertile and vibrant the countryside looked," Dunlop would recall decades later. "Amid this emerald landscape clothes and skulls were mixed in the chocolate earth, as though the countryside had melted away in the midday sun to reveal a terrible secret."[2]

The gruesome pit that had so absorbed young Dunlop's imagination was called Choeung Ek; it was one of thousands of mass graves that were dug when the Khmer Rouge ruled Cambodia, from 1975 to 1979.

In those 1,364 days nearly 2 million people, fully one quarter of Cambodia's population, were killed or died from some combination of starvation, exhaustion from slave labor, malnutrition, torture, or untreated diseases. Measured by the percentage of the national population killed, it was the worst mass murder of the twentieth century.[3]

In 1984, Dunlop and his family moved to London, where he repeatedly watched the recently released British film about the Khmer Rouge regime, *The Killing Fields*. He cut out newspaper stories about the region and scoured London's bookshops for books on Cambodia. He attended art school but "spent most of my time gazing out of the window dreaming of Cambodia, thinking that one day I would go there."[4] And in the summer of 1989, he did. Then nineteen, he flew to Ho Chi Minh City, where he joined a group of backpacking journalists making preparations to go to Cambodia. Within a week, they had rented an old Lada jeep and were driving through the Mekong Delta bound for the Cambodian capital. There Dunlop checked into a cheap hotel. The next morning, as storm clouds gathered over Phnom Penh, he flagged down a *cyclo* and went straight to Tuol Sleng, the former Khmer Rouge prison that the Vietnamese had turned into a museum after they occupied Cambodia in early 1979. For the next twenty years, Dunlop would make a special point of visiting Tuol Sleng on nearly every trip he made to Cambodia.

Code-named S-21, Tuol Sleng—"hill of poisonous trees" in the Khmer language—was a former secondary school, or *lycée*, in the center of Phnom Penh that the Khmer Rouge had converted into a secret torture and detention center. The S stood for Santebal, the security police. The number 21 identified the prison as one of dozens of detention and execution centers established throughout the country. The Khmer Rouge sealed off the neighborhood around the prison, with no one allowed in or out. Those who worked at S-21 lived, ate, and worked in the zone without leaving. Vehicles delivering prisoners usually arrived at night, stopping a few blocks from the prison to protect the secrecy of its location.[5]

Prison guards escorted newcomers from the arrival point to the prison itself, where they handed them over to their superior, Suor Thi, whose job it was to note down their "biography" and to register them in a prison log. "After I took their names, the prisoners were sent to the photographers," Thi recalled. "Then they were blindfolded again and taken to the cells. I had to keep a record of which rooms in which building they were being held, so that we could keep track of the number of prisoners per cell and to make it easier for the interrogators."[6] Some of the larger, lice-ridden cells could hold up to 1,500 prisoners. "I know they suffered a lot," he said. "They were extremely thin, malnourished, and the air circulation was terrible. But I didn't really worry about that. My job was to check them off the list and then hurry back to my office."[7]

The prisoners spent weeks, even months, in the cells waiting to be taken to the interrogation room. They were not allowed to stand or sit up but had to remain lying on their backs all day and night. Once in the interrogation room, prisoners were subjected to torture and forced to confess their "crimes." Some were accused of disobeying orders or of making disparaging remarks about the revolution. Others were accused of working as spies for the Vietnamese or of sending secret messages to the KGB or CIA. Of the 14,000 who passed through Tuol Sleng's gates, only 12 survived.[8]

Nic Dunlop's first visit to Tuol Sleng would haunt him for years to come. As he walked through the musty concrete corridors and empty cells, snapping photographs and jotting down notes, he struggled to comprehend the sheer horror of the place. "It was visceral," he recalled. "I had the feeling that I was in a time warp, as if the Khmer Rouge guards had just vacated the prison, leaving it frozen in time."[9] He found rows of iron shackles bolted to the walls of prison cells and, in one room, what appeared to be a large pool of dried blood below a metal bed frame. Hanging on a wall was a picture of the same bed with a corpse stretched across its frame.[10]

Toward the end of his tour, Dunlop entered a large room, a foyer of sorts, with tall windows and cracked terra cotta tiles. A monsoon raged outside and he could hear the rain pounding on the roof. It was as if he had stepped through a looking glass and entered another world. On all four walls were rows and rows of black-and-white photographs—mug shots, he assumed, that must have been taken soon after the prisoners had entered Tuol Sleng. Some of the prisoners had placards strung over their chests, bearing their names and dates of arrival at the prison. Some simply had numbers crudely fixed to their shirts or pinned to the skin of their chests.

Moving slowly around the room, Dunlop paused to snap photographs of a few of the portraits: a boy of eight or nine, his face bloodied and swollen; a woman cradling a sleeping baby, staring passively at the camera. Hearing the swish of morning traffic rushing past the prison gates, Dunlop peered at the faces through his viewfinder, struggling to reconcile *his* present with *their* past. He thought about what it must be like now for families who come to the prison looking for information about their loved ones, only to find their images in this stark room peering down at them through the lens of their executioners.

Walking to the far end of the room, Dunlop came upon a photograph of what appeared to be a group of prison guards standing shoulder to shoulder in front of the prison gates, with traditional Cambodian red-checkered scarves (*krama*) draped around their necks and their black uniforms neatly ironed. Next to the picture was a smaller photograph encased in a narrow wooden frame. In it, a man sat behind a bare table, holding a microphone, apparently speaking to an unseen audience, possibly the prison staff. Just below the picture a faded label read, in English: "Comrade Duch, Commandant, S-21."

Dunlop aimed his Nikon and snapped the shutter.

Nic Dunlop wasn't the only one interested in the man in the photograph. Cambodian refugees who had fled the Khmer Rouge often mentioned "Comrade Duch" in their testimony about the prison to Amnesty International and other human rights organizations. The newly formed Documentation Center of Cambodia, based in Phnom Penh, had begun gathering evidence on Duch and other officials who had overseen the Khmer Rouge's vast prison network. Documentation of Khmer Rouge atrocities, coupled with pressure from human rights organizations, led eventually to the formation of the Extraordinary Chambers in the Courts of Cambodia (ECCC).[11] Established in 2006 and based in a former military barracks on the outskirts of Phnom Penh, the ECCC would try senior Khmer Rouge leaders and other functionaries, like Duch, who were deemed to be most responsible for genocide and other crimes committed in Democratic Kampuchea (the state name during the Khmer Rouge government) from 1975 to 1979.

The ECCC was a new breed of international tribunal, born out of disenchantment with the ad hoc international criminal tribunals for Rwanda and the former Yugoslavia. By the late 1990s, several members of the United Nations Security Council had begun grumbling about the rapacious financial appetite of the ad hocs, which, after only a few years of operation, were already on their way to consuming over $2 billion in UN funds.[12] Victims groups also complained that the kind of justice meted out in The Hague and Arusha was too slow, too physically distant, and too psychologically removed from the daily lives of victims and their loved ones.[13] These groups wanted a judicial process that would take place in what Eleanor Roosevelt had once called "the small places, close to home": the towns and villages where justice can be seen to be done by those who often were the most victimized.[14]

What emerged from these debates was the concept of the *hybrid* or *mixed* court. Unlike the ad hoc tribunals, which are comprised of international employees, hybrid courts are staffed with *both* international and domestic personnel (judges, prosecutors, investigators, defense counsel, and support staff) working in tandem to apply a mixture of international and national law. Because hybrid courts are based in countries where the crimes actually occurred, they require less start-up funding than their predecessors and, at least in theory, are more accessible to surviving victims and witnesses.[15] They thus marry the best of two worlds—the experience and perspective of the international community, and the legitimacy of local actors in a local setting.[16] Or so it has been hoped.

Between 1999 and 2007, five hybrid courts, in addition to the ECCC, were created by the United Nations and the governments where they are located: the Regulation 64 Panels in Pristina, Kosovo; the Special Panels for Serious Crimes in Dili, East Timor; the Special Court for Sierra Leone in Freetown; the Court of Bosnia and Herzegovina in Sarajevo, Bosnia; and the Special Tribunal for Lebanon in The Hague, Netherlands.[17] In February 2013, the Extraordinary African Chambers, a special "hybrid" criminal court, opened in the West African nation of Senegal to prepare a case against former Chadian president Hissène Habré. Habré has been accused of responsibility for the deaths of more than 40,000 people and the torture of more than 20,000 during his eight-year rule of Chad, from 1982 to 1990.[18] And in August 2015, the Kosovo government announced that it would create a special court to prosecute crimes committed by former members of the Kosovo Liberation Army after the 1998–99 war. The court will operate under Kosovo law but with a chamber abroad and internationally appointed judges and prosecutors.[19]

No two hybrid courts are identical. The Cambodian and Sierra Leone tribunals are treaty-based courts—that is, they were developed through a series of negotiations between their respective national governments and the United Nations—but with different legal standing. The Cambodian court is embedded in that nation's domestic judicial system, while the Sierra Leone court is independent of the national judiciary, thus removing the obstacles of a prior amnesty law and the sovereign immunity of one of its most wanted suspects, Charles Taylor, then president of Liberia.[20] By comparison, the judicial panels in Kosovo and East Timor were established under the authority of UN international administrations, which had essentially taken over the sovereignty of these two conflicted countries and exercised *all* legislative and executive authority, including the administration of the judiciary. The panels were established to address war crimes because the local judicial systems had been virtually destroyed. To avoid the massive costs and delays that plagued the Yugoslavia and Rwanda tribunals, the framers of the hybrids imposed time limits on the courts' work and, in the case of Cambodia and Sierra Leone, limited prosecutions to those who were considered most responsible for the violence. Meanwhile, the Extraordinary African Chambers in Senegal is a rarity among hybrid tribunals. It is essentially a national court. However, being the result of a treaty between Senegal and the African Union and having two non-Senegalese Africans among its judges, it is also the first pan-African criminal tribunal to date. And, unlike other hybrid courts, it is possible that it may only prosecute a single individual.

Hybrid courts have confronted unique challenges when compared with ad hoc tribunals. Tensions have arisen between national and international staff members on a range of issues, including differences in investigation methods, witness management, and pay scales. Host governments also have tried to use their influence to promote or dissuade prosecutors from opening one or another investigation.[21] One of the greatest impediments for the hybrid courts, as compared to the ad hoc tribunals, has been their lack of Chapter VII powers. (As previously noted, the UN Charter's Chapter VII gives the UN Security Council the power—although it is rarely exercised—to oblige member states to assist in the execution of arrest warrants or else face censure or other coercive measures.) Without a Chapter VII pedigree, the hybrid tribunals have had difficulty gaining the cooperation and assistance of other states, especially neighboring states, to arrest and turn over suspects who have taken refuge in their territory.[22]

For a war crimes prosecutor, says David Scheffer, the former U.S. war crimes ambassador, cooperation is everything; it is "your daily lodestone,"[23] an Augean undertaking that requires superlative political and diplomatic skills. "Think of it this way," explains Brenda Hollis, a veteran war crimes prosecutor and at the time of writing a chief prosecutor at the Special Court for Sierra Leone. "I'm the prosecutor of a court. You're an official in the state where [the defendant] is now residing. You and I have a good relationship. You're amenable to helping me unless, of course, the political environment or the postwar environment in your country is such that you can't. Because if you hand over this person maybe there'll be a coup or maybe you'll even be assassinated. . . . But if our working relationship is good, there's a much better chance that we'll end up having a hand over."[24]

But diplomatic finesse and political acumen have their limits. Nowhere has this been more evident than at the hybrid courts in East Timor and Kosovo. Try as it did for nearly six years, the Special Panels in Dili failed to secure the transfer of hundreds of high- and middle-level defendants who had fled to Indonesia following that country's bloody retreat from East Timor in September 1999, after twenty-four years of occupation. Most notable among these defendants was the head of the Indonesian armed forces, General Wiranto, whom prosecutors and human rights organizations had singled out as bearing "ultimate responsibility" for the violence.[25] Indonesia's lack of cooperation made a mockery of the court, with 309 out of 391 accused, including General Wiranto, remaining outside the jurisdiction of East Timor by the time the panels closed down in 2006.[26] In the end, after 55 trials, 84 defendants were convicted and 4 were acquitted. Few of those convicted could be described as leaders or individuals with significant command authority. The upshot: powerful military officers in Indonesia evaded justice, whereas lesser Timorese offenders could not, leaving many Timorese victims with the impression that justice was just as selective as it had been under the Indonesian occupation.[27]

Kosovo's Regulation 64 Panels—named after the UN regulation that created them—faced a similar predicament in early 2000. A year earlier, Serbian troops had invaded the breakaway province of Kosovo in an unsuccessful attempt to quash the Kosovo Liberation Army. NATO responded with a relentless bombing campaign that sent thousands of Serb fighters back across the border into Serbia or into neighboring Montenegro and Macedonia. Among them were hundreds of ultra-nationalist Serb paramilitaries and policemen, who had orchestrated a campaign of terror against Kosovar towns and villages, displacing hundreds of thousands of Kosovar Albanians.[28]

Once NATO troops secured Kosovo, the UN set up the Regulation 64 Panels, a hybrid system of international and national judges working within Kosovo's regular courts, to prosecute war crimes and acts of genocide. Each panel consisted of two international judges, one local judge, and an international prosecutor.[29] But the Kosovo Panels were stymied in their efforts to secure the arrest and transfer of war crimes suspects from Serbia and neighboring countries. Belgrade was the principal stumbling block. Serbia's pro-Western president, Zoran Djindjic, agreed to ship some defendants—including Slobodan Milosevic—to stand trial in The Hague, but he dragged his heels when it came to sending Serbian suspects to Kosovo, which he still viewed as a Serbian province.[30]

At the time of writing, the hybrid courts in Kosovo, East Timor, and Sierra Leone have been shuttered, while their sister tribunals in Cambodia, Bosnia and Herzegovina, and Lebanon continue to try cases. All told, these courts have held proceedings against more than 200 defendants. Of these, the cases of two—the Cambodian prison commander, Duch, and the Liberian president, Charles Taylor—best illustrate the political and diplomatic machinations that often enable fugitives sought by hybrid tribunals to hide in plain sight for years—and even decades—after their crimes have been committed.

THE MAN IN THE PHOTOGRAPH

On his repeated trips to Cambodia, where he eked out a living as a free-lance photographer, Nic Dunlop carried the prison commander's photograph in his shirt pocket on the off chance that he might encounter him or, more likely, someone who knew of his whereabouts. Years later, Dunlop recalled why he had been so drawn to the picture of Duch and obsessed with finding Duch himself: "It was terribly upsetting seeing the pictures of the prisoners at Tuol Sleng, trying to imagine what they must have suffered. But I was also seized by a whole set of other questions: What about Duch and the torturers and the prison guards? Who were these people? Where did they come from? What led them to do the things they did? And where were they now?"[31]

Dunlop traveled throughout Cambodia, interviewing Duch's family members, S-21's few survivors, and former prison guards. He learned that Duch's real name was Kaing Guek Eav and that he had been a high school math teacher before joining the Khmer Rouge. On one trip, Dunlop tracked down the Tuol Sleng photographer, Nhem Ein, who lived in an apartment in Phnom Penh.

Nhem Ein spoke openly about his time with the Khmer Rouge. He first served as a messenger boy but was later sent to Shanghai to be trained in photography. In late 1975, after the Khmer Rouge had taken over, he returned to Cambodia and went to work at Tuol Sleng. His darkroom and studio were located next to Duch's home, a few minutes' walk from the prison. He admired Duch, whom he respectfully referred to as *Ta* (Uncle), and considered him "a clean leader who wasn't corrupt or partisan," though he was often bad-tempered with his staff. At home, Duch was relaxed and easygoing, but at work he could be chameleon-like, transforming himself into different characters depending on the situation. "He could be anybody," Ein said. "He could play the role of a giant, a cruel man, a gentle man, a sad man or a miserable man."[32]

Ein told Dunlop about the day Vietnamese troops arrived in Phnom Penh. As F-111 fighter jets swept across the skies and T-55 tanks rumbled down the boulevards of the city early that morning of January 7, 1979, Ein and other prison staff gathered in the prison courtyard, unsure of what to do. Duch suddenly walked through the front gates, armed with a pistol and, like Martin Bormann's call to arms in the Chancellery garden above the Fürherbunker in April 1945, ordered the staff to split into two groups. They were to fight their way to Amleang, a Khmer Rouge stronghold on the highway just north of the city.

Over the next three months, Vietnamese troops pushed the Khmer Rouge deep into the jungles of northwestern Cambodia, while hundreds of thousands of Cambodian refugees streamed across the heavily mined border into Thailand. At first, the massive movement of people caught the Thai government off guard. In one incident, panicked Thai soldiers drove more than 40,000 people back across the border, causing hundreds, if not thousands, of deaths as the refugees stumbled through mine fields or succumbed to starvation and disease. Facing a mounting human calamity, the Thais, with the assistance of the UN High Commissioner for Refugees, finally began building a complex network of camps in the jungle that covered much of the ill-defined frontier between the two countries. By the end of 1979, more than 650,000 people were living in over a dozen such border camps, with no running water or electricity, mounting sewage and trash, and spreading disease.

Journalists were drawn to the camps like filings to a magnet. Some wired sensational stories on the misery and squalor of the camps to their editors in London, Paris, and New York. *Time* magazine dedicated almost an entire issue to the humanitarian crisis. Splashed across the magazine's glossy cover, just above a photograph of a young mother cradling an emaciated baby, screamed the headline: "Starvation: Death Watch in Cambodia."[33]

Such lurid reportage kept relief dollars flowing into the camps but obscured what else was happening along the "hidden border" just inside Cambodian territory. It was here that the Khmer Rouge leader, Pol Pot, and his paladins had taken refuge in fortified enclaves where no journalists were allowed. With Pol Pot were his deputy prime minister and minister of foreign affairs, Ieng Sary; his head of state (and Sary's wife), Khieu Samphan; and Nuon Chea, the deputy secretary of the Communist Party of Kamphuchea. Their businesses in this shadowy no man's land were as sordid as they were lucrative, attracting a steady parade of dubious characters—among them Thai military operatives, Chinese arms dealers, and Cambodian timber and gem merchants. Despite widespread knowledge that the Khmer Rouge were responsible for nearly 2 million deaths, Pol Pot and his top leaders were able to live for decades relatively undisturbed in this jungle region of northwestern Cambodia, thanks mainly to the regional chess moves of the Cold War.[34]

Ever since the French had cast their protectorate over Cambodian in 1864, China and Thailand had regarded Cambodia as a bulwark against Vietnamese expansion in Southeast Asia. In early January 1979, soon after Vietnamese troops entered the deserted streets of Phnom Penh, Chinese and Thai officials held a top-secret meeting to discuss how to respond should Vietnamese troops cross the border into Thailand itself. A bargain was struck: China would end its support of the Thai Communist Party if Thailand would provide Cambodia's Khmer Rouge with a safe haven along the border and allow the Chinese to rearm them. Cambodia was thereby transformed into the frontline for the containment of Soviet expansion through its Vietnamese surrogates in Southeast Asia, a situation that would continue for another nineteen years.[35]

Soon after the meeting, Pol Pot appointed Ieng Sary to serve as principal intermediary between the Khmer Rouge and the Chinese. On January 11, Sary was flown to Bangkok in a Thai army helicopter and from there to China. When he reached Beijing, Sary met with Chinese leader Deng Xiaoping to discuss how to expel the Vietnamese from Cambodia.[36] The Chinese Ministry of Foreign Affairs issued Sary a Chinese passport, under the alias of Su Hao, that allowed him to travel extensively on Khmer Rouge business. He went to Sri Lanka for a meeting of the Non-Aligned Movement, to New York to attend numerous UN meetings, and to Hong Kong to check on his bank account, which at one point contained nearly $20 million, largely amassed from the Chinese government for Khmer Rouge use and from sales of huge amounts of timber and gemstones extracted from the Thai–Cambodian border areas he commanded.[37]

The Royal Thai Army meanwhile dispatched a task force to the border to work secretly with Pol Pot. Known as Unit 838, the task force set up bases adjacent to the Khmer Rouge enclaves. One Thai detachment took up residence in the village of Phnom Prak, less than a mile inside Cambodian territory, where it built a large wooden house for Pol Pot on a scrub-covered hillside with a panoramic view across the border.[38] For nearly a decade, Unit 838 provided money, Chinese weaponry, transportation, and medical care to the Maoist-inspired guerrillas. As an added perk, it arranged for Pol Pot and other Khmer Rouge leaders to spend holidays at the Thai beach resort of Pattaya. In return, Thai military operatives got rich from timber and gem deals with their Khmer Rouge charges.[39]

Duch, traveling mostly on foot, arrived at the Thai border in May 1979, several weeks after his superiors. He first went to Nuon Chea's compound, known as Camp 404, where he was reunited with his wife and children. The family encounter was interrupted by Chea, who excoriated Duch for having failed to destroy the prison files at Tuol Sleng, which had subsequently fallen into the hands of the Vietnamese. Years later, in a courtroom in Phnom Penh, those very documents would come back to haunt both men.[40]

Duch and his family eventually settled in Borai, ideologically the most hard-line of the Khmer Rouge camps. Located on an isolated patch of land near Thailand's eastern province of Trat and surrounded by malarial forests, Borai was home to some 4,000 Khmer Rouge and their families.

Duch taught math at the camp school, and, because of his proficiency in English, often served as an intermediary between the camp leadership, the United Nations, and the few NGOs who supplied the camp with food and clothing. In 1986, Son Sen, the head of the Santebal and Duch's immediate superior, sent Duch to China to teach Khmer to Chinese intelligence personnel and advisers who were to be stationed along the Thai–Cambodian border. When the Chinese learned that Duch had been head of Tuol Sleng, though, they canceled his visa and sent him back to the border.

Aware that his past was following him, Duch changed his name to Hang Pin and with his wife and their four children left the Borai camp and moved to Phkoam, a Khmer Rouge village located in a flat expanse of rice paddies near the Thai border. The family bought land and opened a small medical kiosk in front of their new home, while Duch found work in the school down the road and at Svay Chek college, an hour's bus ride away. His combined income enabled him to buy more land, a motorbike, and several cows.

The United States was well aware that Thailand and China were rearming the Khmer Rouge. Still smarting from its defeat in the Vietnam

War, the U.S. saw China as an indispensable regional ally against its former enemy and, by extension, the Soviet Union. In 1980, under U.S. pressure, the World Food Programme provided $12 million in food aid to the Thai army to pass on to the Khmer Rouge camps and enclaves. This assistance, according to U.S. Assistant Secretary of State Richard Holbrooke, helped to feed and clothe "20,000 to 40,000 Pol Pot guerrillas."[41]

In New York, U.S. diplomats, with full knowledge of the crimes of the Khmer Rouge, worked behind the scenes to ensure that the Khmer Rouge kept their seat in the UN General Assembly as the legitimate representatives of the Cambodian people. The Americans also spearheaded a campaign to have the United Nations declare the Vietnamese invasion illegal. As a result, the World Bank and the International Monetary Fund stopped providing development aid to the Vietnam-backed government in Phnom Penh, which further isolated Cambodia from its Asian neighbors and Western countries.[42]

Meanwhile, back on the Thai–Cambodian border, the Khmer Rouge and two other Cambodian factions formed the Coalition Government of Democratic Kampuchea with the objective of rolling back the Vietnamese and ousting their puppet regime in Phnom Penh. For the Khmer Rouge it was a major political and strategic coup: the coalition would provide the guerrilla force with respectability and serve as a cover for it to obtain more aid and training from Western countries. Before long, the United States and Britain were sending arms and other aid to the two non-communist factions fighting the Vietnamese, knowing full well that it would be impossible to prevent such assistance from reaching the Khmer Rouge, who were the best organized and military-ready of the three groups.[43]

A fragile peace finally came to Cambodia in late 1991. At a UN-brokered peace accord in Paris, Cambodia's warring parties agreed to form a national council with the aim of holding elections at some point in the near future. As part of the agreement, 70 percent of each faction's army was to disarm within a year. Drafted principally by China and the United States, the agreement made no mention of past Khmer Rouge crimes, let alone genocide and the importance of holding its perpetrators accountable. Instead, the treaty proclaimed rather euphemistically that "Cambodia's tragic recent history requires special measures to assure protection of human rights, and the non-return to the policies and practices of the past."[44] At least for the time being, then, Pol Pot and other Khmer Rouge leaders had no reason to fear they would ever be arrested and tried for their past crimes.

Soon after the signing of the Paris agreement, the United Nations sent 22,000 troops and police to Cambodia to secure the peace and prepare for elections. The blue helmets were soon followed by a legion of humanitarian organizations and a few human rights groups, which quickly turned downtown Phnom Penh into an alphabet soup of acronyms. Bars, brothels, and dance halls sprang up like mushrooms along the city's main boulevard next to the Mekong, attracting a nightly crowd of UN soldiers and office workers flush with U.S. dollars. Perhaps embarrassed by the seedier side of it all, the UN mission posted notices around the city instructing its staff not to park UN vehicles in front of "parlor houses."

As Phnom Penh roared back to life and the UN began busing refugees from the camps back to their destroyed villages, several Khmer Rouge leaders, including Pol Pot's right-hand man, Khieu Samphan, and Duch's former boss, Son Sen, left their border enclaves and took up residence in the capital. On his first attempt to return, in October 1991, an angry crowd chased Khieu Samphan out of town. But he came back a few months later without incident, and before long he was a regular at UN cocktail parties, often dressed in a neatly pressed safari suit, mingling with diplomats and foreign correspondents.

At one UN ceremony Samphan even received an embrace from then Secretary-General Boutros Boutros-Ghali. Then again, with his receding gray hairline and quick smile, Khieu Samphan must have seemed far removed from the iconic black-pajamas-and-checkered-scarves look associated with Khmer Rouge fighters of years past. When Reuters correspondent Angus MacSwan confronted him about Cambodia's bloody history, Samphan replied, "Yes, some mistakes were made but most of the accusations were just propaganda. Cambodia's real problem was Vietnam's plan to annex the country."[45]

From his base in Bangkok, Dunlop struggled to make a living as a freelance photographer and writer. News outlets gave paltry commissions, and there were no guarantees that they would publish your story or photographs in the end. "Every year I returned to the UK with my pictures and tried to interest magazines and newspapers," he would later write. "'Cambodia,' I was told, 'has been done.' The world had moved on."[46]

In early 1999, Dunlop received a commission to photograph landmine-clearance teams in Cambodia. The assignment took him to Battambang, where he met up with a group of Canadian sappers who were preparing to travel to Samlaut to negotiate a mine-clearing operation. He was excited, as he knew from interviews with Duch's relatives that the former Khmer Rouge commander was probably living somewhere in the area. He hitched a ride with the Canadians, and while they were in their meeting, he walked over to a Khmer Rouge soldier who was sitting on his motorbike, chatting with some children. He asked in his rudimentary Khmer if he could photograph them, and they agreed. A small, older man approached the group and, noticing Dunlop, introduced himself as Hang Pin. He had once been a math teacher and had recently worked in a refugee camp on the Thai border.[47] Dunlop could hardly believe his luck as he looked closely at the man. Before leaving, he surreptitiously snapped a photograph of him.

Back at his Bangkok apartment, Dunlop hurried to develop his film. The negative "was back lit, but clear enough," he recalled. "Emerging from the developer was Duch in [a] T-shirt, a coy grin on his face. Behind him was the Khmer Rouge soldier looking directly at the camera. I compared it to the creased picture that I had carried in my pocket for so long. There was no doubt in my mind. His hairline, although graying, remained the same and his stretched lips revealed identical teeth."[48]

Dunlop pitched the story to a group of editors at the *Far Eastern Economic Review*. They were intrigued, but wanted Dunlop to give Duch a chance to defend himself. Feeling slightly out of his depth and uneasy about security, Dunlop approached Nat Thayer, a correspondent with the *Review*, to accompany him to Samlaut. Thayer was the last Western journalist to interview Pol Pot and was known for his finesse in dealing with the Khmer Rouge.

The two journalists met Duch at his home and accompanied him to a nearby beer stall. "It was clear we had caught Duch completely unawares," Dunlop recalled. "But when he knew why we had come, he seemed to accept it. He was gregarious by nature, and once he started talking he couldn't stop himself. But Christianity also played a role: the act of confession followed by forgiveness. He thought he was safe, and that emboldened him. After all, he'd never been named as a Khmer Rouge likely to be tried by a tribunal, and he wasn't on a 'wanted list.' We can't rule out vanity either. He loved having an audience and being able 'to set the record straight.'"[49]

Dunlop began the conversation by asking Duch about his life in the district. He told of his conversion to Christianity and his time working as a volunteer for World Vision and the American Refugee Committee in one of the camps along the border, and how his wife had been killed and himself wounded by an intruder, lifting his shirt to show his own scars. Then, as Dunlop recalled, Nate spoke up: "'I believe that you . . . worked with the security services during the Khmer Rouge period?' Duch appeared startled and avoided our eyes. . . . He then glanced at Nate's business card. A concentrated expression appeared on his face; and he turned slowly to me, looking directly in my eyes. 'I believe, Nic, that your friend has interviewed . . . Monsieur Pol Pot?' 'Yes,' I replied. 'That's right.'"[50]

After a long pause, Duch sighed in resignation. "I have done very bad things in my life," he said. "Now it is time for *les représialles* [to bear the consequences] of my actions." The two journalists were stunned; it was almost as if the aging Khmer Rouge commander had wanted to be caught.

Duch told Dunlop and Thayer that it was his idea "to have the prisoners [at S-21] photographed on arrival. He did it to protect himself in case they escaped, making it easier to track the prisoner down." Anyway, it didn't matter, he said. No one ever escaped. As early as 1971, Pol Pot and the central committee had given verbal instructions to Duch and other prison commanders: whoever was arrested must die. But first they were to be interrogated and their confessions sent directly to the central committee. "Even children," Duch said. "This was the policy, the orders. No one could leave S-21 alive."[51]

Dunlop and Thayer's article on Duch's discovery and confession appeared in the *Far Eastern Economic Review* on May 6, 1999, and was soon picked up by news outlets around the world.[52] While their exposé was a revelation to many Cambodia watchers, it didn't surprise Cambodia's prime minister, Hun Sen, who, as Dunlop later discovered,[53] had known Duch's whereabouts for years but had had no desire to stir up the past by arresting him and other leading Khmer Rouge leaders. Hun Sen had himself served as a Khmer Rouge commander, but fled with his battalion to Vietnam in 1977, and was subsequently installed as prime minister after Vietnamese forces took control of Phnom Penh in January 1979.

On May 10, 1999, Hun Sen, sensing a scandal brewing at home and abroad, ordered the Cambodian police to arrest Duch. That afternoon Duch was apprehended and placed in a high-security prison, not far from Tuol Sleng. He stayed there until July 2007, when he was transferred to one of eight prison cells in a detention facility adjacent to the ECCC. Four other elderly Khmer Rouge leaders—Ieng Sary, Kheiu Samphan, Nuon Chea (Ieng Sary's wife), and former Khmer Rouge social affairs minister Ieng Thirith—would later join Duch at the detention center. (Absent was Pol Pot, the founder and leader of the Khmer Rouge, who had suffered a fatal heart attack at his home in western Cambodia in 1998, the same year his few remaining guerrillas agreed to finally abandon their fight.) Duch and his fellow inmates were well cared for—three meals a day, a television room, a visiting room—everything was in conformance with international rules, enough, according to one of Duch visitors, "to make the guards jealous."[54]

The Khmer Rouge tribunal, as the ECCC became known, was established in 2006, the product of over a decade of painstaking and often ill-tempered negotiations between the United Nations and the Cambodian government. Throughout these discussions, Hun Sen personally pushed for a tribunal controlled by Cambodians. The United Nations, along with most of the international human rights community, pressed for a tribunal controlled by UN-appointed "internationals." In the end, both sides agreed to a tribunal consisting of a majority of Cambodian judges appointed by Hun Sen, with all court decisions requiring a supermajority, effectively requiring the vote of at least one international judge for the will of the majority of Cambodian judges to become a decision of the court. It was also agreed that the Office of the Prosecutor would consist of two co-prosecutors, one appointed by the United Nations and the other by the Cambodian government.[55]

The ECCC decided to try the former prison commander first, and then his superiors. On the morning of February 16, 2009, he was driven by bulletproof car to the custom-built courtroom and charged with crimes against humanity and war crimes for "personally overseeing the systematic torture of more than 15,000 prisoners."[56] As at the opening day of the Eichmann trial, the courtroom in Phnom Penh was packed with people, many of them survivors of the Khmer Rouge or relatives of victims of the regime. After the presiding judge, Nil Nonn, read a statement, Duch rose to speak. Guided by his French defense lawyer, François Roux, he admitted his guilt:

> I joined the revolution to liberate my own people, including my parents, my relatives, myself. That's why I was compelled to accept the task. At that time, in that regime, I saw no other alternative to solve the matter except to respect the discipline of the party. Sometimes we have to do a job we do not like. I would like to emphasize that I am responsible for the crimes committed at S-21, especially the torture and execution of the people there.[57]

A year earlier, the Court had taken Duch, with his consent, to the scenes of his crimes, where he reportedly pled for his victims to forgive him: "I ask for your forgiveness—I know that you cannot forgive me, but I ask you to leave me the hope that you might."[58]

One of the trial's most riveting moments took place halfway through the proceedings when a fifty-two-year-old farmer named Neth Phally asked the presiding judge if he could show the court a photograph of his brother, who had died at S-21. With the judge's approval, Phally carefully took out an 8-by-11-inch photograph of a young man with black, short-cropped hair and held it upright on the witness table in front of him. "I would like to show a photo of my brother," he said. "It is like he is sitting here . . . next to me . . . [and] at peace, having learned that justice is achieved through this court."[59]

Phally later built a small shrine at the back of his house and placed the photograph, surrounded by incense sticks and a painting of the Buddha, above the altar. When asked what had led him to display the photograph in the courtroom, he replied: "There are many reasons. To begin with, I wanted to show Duch my brother so he would know I was not accusing him for no reason. I also wanted my brother to see the man who was responsible for his suffering. You see when my brother was taken to Toul Sleng, he was blindfolded and couldn't see anyone. But in the courtroom I could show him the accused. . . . I felt this would release his soul from wandering and help him find peace so he could be reborn again."[60]

Phally was one of ninety Cambodians and foreigners who participated in the Duch trial as "civil parties" (in French, *parties civiles*). Of these, twenty-two testified in court about their imprisonment at S-21 or about the loss of one or more of their relatives there. To be accepted by the court as a civil party, each of the ninety had to show evidence of "physical, material or psychological" injury as a "direct consequence" of the offences alleged in Duch's indictment.[61] Unlike regular witnesses, they testified without taking an oath, could participate at various stages of the proceedings, and could comment in court about the awarding of any reparations.

Thierry Cruvellier, a French journalist who observed and later chronicled the trial in his book *The Master of Confessions,* believes that the participation of civil parties "added a certain value to the trial of a kind that is said to be sorely lacking at other international tribunals. Civil parties ensured that an important and legitimate voice was heard, and facilitated a human, concrete understanding of the severe damage suffered by victims' families."[62] Their presence in the courtroom was a living rebuke of the Khmer Rouge slogan, "To keep you is no gain, to destroy you is no loss."

During the nine-month trial, Duch repeatedly admitted his guilt and, at times, acknowledged the harm he had done to his victims. Then, on the last day of the trial, something bizarre happened that confused everyone observing the proceedings. Duch's Cambodian lawyer, Kar Savuth, in an abrupt about-face that his co-counsel didn't see coming, made a last-minute request for an acquittal. Visibly confused, the presiding judge turned to Duch to clarify his stance. "I would ask that the chambers release me," he said, rising to his feet and pressing his palms together in a show of respect for the judges.[63]

Outside the court, Dara Chey, a student who lost four relatives during the Khmer Rouge years, told the *Guardian* that Duch's request for acquittal cast doubt on his earlier apology. "I do not believe him when he says he is sorry any more. He is just trying to get out of jail. He should never be allowed out. Cambodians will not be happy if he ever walks free."[64]

On the morning of July 26, 2010, hundreds of Cambodians crowded into the courtroom to hear the ECCC's verdict. After the judges filed into the chambers and took their seats, the presiding judge, Nil Nonn, pronounced Duch "criminally responsible" for crimes against humanity and grave breaches of the Geneva Conventions of 1949 and sentenced him to thirty-five years' imprisonment, which was reduced to nineteen years,[65] owing to time already served and to compensate for a period of illegal detention by a Cambodian military court.[66] An appeals chamber later overturned the sentence and resentenced the former prison commander to life imprisonment.[67]

The ECCC's second trial, featuring the four aging Khmer Rouge leaders, commenced in June 2011. Later that year, Ieng Thirith was found unfit to stand trial due to dementia and dropped from the case. Her husband, Ieng Sary, died of a heart attack in March 2013. The ECCC in the meantime tried Nuon Chea and Khieu Samphan, both octogenarians, separately. In August 2014 the court sentenced the two Khmer Rouge leaders to life in prison for masterminding mass evacuations of Cambodians from their homes during the Khmer Rouge takeover of Phnom Penh. Two months later, in October 2014, the ECCC opened a second trial against Chea and Samphan charging them with crimes against humanity and genocide for their role in the killing of ethnic Vietnamese and Muslim minorities. The trial is expected to last until 2017.[68] In March 2015, the ECCC charged Im Chaem, a Buddhist nun in her sixties and a former Khmer Rouge district commander suspected of running a forced-labor camp; Meas Muth, a former Navy chief in his eighties who allegedly oversaw the executions of Vietnamese and Thai prisoners of war at the S-21 prison; and Ao An, seventy-nine, a former Khmer Rouge cadre who allegedly committed "inhuman acts" at various detention centers. Days before the indictments were announced, Prime Minister Hun Sen warned that prosecuting further suspects would spark a civil war. Meanwhile, his deputy police chief, Mao Chandara, said that his force would not detain the three accused. "As our prime minister said, if we do this it leads to a break up of the country, and it won't be useful," he said. "I am a police officer and it is my duty to protect the Royal Government and the Constitution."[69] Since no other local justice mechanisms exist to prosecute surviving Khmer Rouge officials and their subalterns, it is likely that this trial, if it ever comes to pass, will end Cambodia's quest for historical justice.

BROTHERS IN ARMS, PARTNERS IN CRIME: SIERRA LEONE

One day in July 1999, half a world away from the beer stall where Duch had confessed his crimes to Nic Dunlop and Nate Thayer, Sierra Leone's president, Ahmed Tejan Kabbah, and the leader of the Revolutionary United Front (RUF), Foday Sankoh, sat down at a table in Lomé, Togo, to sign a U.S.-brokered peace agreement to end eight years of civil war. The conflict had begun in 1991 when the RUF, a band of Sierra Leonean rebels led by Sankoh and supported by Charles Taylor's National Patriot Front of Liberia, crossed into Sierra Leone to overthrow the government of Joseph Momoh. The fighting that ensued left 75,000 people dead and more than three million displaced.[70]

Standing behind the two men, eagerly watching the signing process, was Charles Taylor, president of Liberia. It was a chilling tableau of characters, especially with Foday Sankoh and Charles Taylor, the two men most responsible for some of the worst atrocities committed in Africa since the 1994 Rwandan genocide—killings, mutilations, amputations, sexual slavery, rape, and forced recruitment of child soldiers—at the table playing peacemakers.

Although the Lomé Peace Accord mandated the establishment of a truth and reconciliation commission, it also contained a provision granting "absolute and free pardon and reprieve to all combatants and collaborators . . . up to the time of the signing of the present Agreement"[71]—in effect, a blanket amnesty for anyone who had committed war crimes during the civil war. At the last minute, however, the UN envoy to the peace talks, Francis Okello, had appended a handwritten reservation to the agreement stating that the United Nations would not recognize any amnesties for "international crimes of genocide, crimes against humanity, war crimes, and other serious violations of international law" enacted by Sierra Leone and Liberia.[72] While Okello's note had no binding legal authority, leaving Sankoh and Taylor free to go about their dirty business without fear of legal censure or judicial restraint, it would serve as a palimpsest, a sort of shadow text that would come to have meaning some years later.

As the ink dried on the parchment, the United States and Great Britain issued statements congratulating the signatories and expressing their "support for the agreement, which will bring to an end the tragic war of Sierra Leone."[73] The Security Council, for its part, welcomed the accord and praised the Sierra Leone government for its "courageous efforts to achieve peace, including legislative and other measures already taken towards implementation of the Peace Agreement"—a reference to the blanket amnesty, seats in government, and other concessions to the rebels provided in the agreement.[74] At a news conference in Freetown the following October, U.S. Secretary of State Madeleine Albright defended the amnesty as "the price of a peace so desperately needed after a struggle for power in which severing limbs was a common rebel tactic."[75]

Both the accord and the laudations were yet another example of the triumph of hope over experience. The Lomé Peace Accord would bring neither peace to Sierra Leone nor security to her people. In contrast to his boss, Madeleine Albright, David Scheffer, then U.S. Ambassador for War Crimes, later said that the agreement "stank."[76] And, sure enough, within months the rebels, still intent on overthrowing the government in the capital of Freetown, had violated nearly every provision of the accord, and the country was again engulfed in violence.

Much of what was wrong-headed about the Lomé agreement can be traced to the back-door wheeling and dealing of president Bill Clinton's then Ambassador for Democracy in Africa, the Reverend Jessie Jackson. In the months leading up to the signing of the agreement, a U.S. delegation led by Jackson, who was said to be on good terms with Charles Taylor, had grappled with the conundrum of how to end the fighting and atrocities in Sierra Leone. In meetings in Freetown and Monrovia, Jackson struck a deal with all the parties. The RUF would agree to lay down its arms if President Kabbah would form a new coalition government with Sankoh as its vice president and extend amnesty to Sankoh and any member of his fighting forces.[77] It was, as one commentator put it, "a shotgun marriage."[78]

Any peace agreement should include a provision for retributive justice, David Scheffer says he argued. But in the end, Reverend Jackson and Scheffer's superiors consented to an agreement that included a blanket amnesty for all combatants and a token nod toward justice through the establishment of a truth and reconciliation commission, which some human rights activists called window dressing in a conflict where it was only too obvious what had been done. "As for the . . . pardon of Foday Sankoh," Scheffer later wrote, "the public line was that it would become the chance to transform the . . . rebel movement into a political party and advance the interests of reconciliation and reconstruction." Looking back on the Lomé talks, he wrote: "The priority for the African specialists in the State Department was a peace deal, apparently at whatever cost to justice. The moment exemplified years of confrontation that I typically had with the regional bureaus. The quest for accountability always complicated their work, which was the 'realism' of political negotiations and peace agreements. I spent much of my time lobbying all the regional bureaus to take international justice seriously."[79]

In the fifteen years prior to Lomé, Foday Sankoh and Charles Taylor had risen from rebels to formidable warlords and politicians in Western Africa. The son of a farmer, Foday Sankoh began his career as a corporal in the Sierra Leonean army and served briefly in the failed UN peacekeeping operation in Congo in the early 1960s, an experience during which he developed contempt for the United Nations. In the 1970s, he spent four years in jail in the capital city of Freetown for having participated in a coup attempt. In 1988, Sankoh attended one of Moammar Ghadafi's training camps in Libya, where he and other emerging African revolutionaries studied Gaddafi's *Green Book,* a 200-page collection of the Libyan leader's military stratagems and political diatribes against Western capitalism.[80] It was in one of Gaddafi's camps that Sankoh and Taylor became friends and reportedly signed a pact to support each other's struggles to liberate their respective countries from corruption.[81]

Charles Taylor's route to Libya was more circuitous. Born in 1948 to a family of Americo-Liberians, the elite group that grew out of the freed slaves who founded Liberia in the nineteenth century, Taylor became a lay preacher in the Baptist tradition and eventually landed a plum job in the Liberian government of Master Sergeant Samuel Doe, who took power in 1980. Taylor later fell out with Doe, after the Liberian leader accused him of embezzling almost a million dollars and depositing the money in a U.S. bank account. Exposed and disgraced, Taylor broke for the United States. In May 1984 two U.S. marshals, acting on a Liberian extradition warrant, arrested him in Somerville, Massachusetts. He was then transferred to the Plymouth County Correctional Facility, considered the most secure prison in New England.

What happened next is shrouded in mystery. By mid-September, the extradition hearing against Taylor was coming to a close. Then, like a scene from *The Shawshank Redemption*, Taylor and four other inmates, two car thieves and two petty thieves, staged a break from the Plymouth facility, the first in the prison's history. After sawing through the bars of a cell and shinnying down a rope made from bed sheets, they split up,[82] Taylor going on foot to a nearby hospital, where his wife and sister-in-law were waiting with a car and money to spirit him from the country. The two women were later arrested for driving the getaway car, but never brought to trial; Taylor meanwhile had made his way to Côte d'Ivoire.

Taylor would later tell a very different story: he did not "escape" from the Plymouth facility as originally reported, but walked out of the jail with the help of U.S. government agents, only days before his friend and Liberian military leader, Thomas Quiwonkpa, allegedly tried, with U.S. backing, to overthrow the Liberian government. "I'm calling it my release because I didn't break out," Taylor said.[83] According to Taylor, a guard escorted him from his cell to a minimum-security area. He then climbed out a window and over the prison fence, where a car containing two men was waiting to whisk him to New York. Taylor said he assumed that the car "had to be a [U.S.] government car" because his companions feared Taylor might be "picked up" if he changed cars to be with his wife and sister-in-law.[84]

Once in Côte d'Ivoire, Taylor formed a rebel army made up of Liberian exiles called the National Patriotic Front of Liberia (NPFL). In December 1989, Taylor and his NPFL rebels crossed into Liberia, marking the beginning of a brutal seven-year civil war that soon grew into a regional conflict engulfing Sierra Leone, Guinea, and eventually Côte d'Ivoire.[85] Taylor's aim was to seize control of Liberia, but he also had his eyes on controlling Sierra Leone's diamond-rich Kailahun District as a means of financing his rebel movement and lining his own pockets.

The better-equipped and better-armed NPFL was a magnet for Foday Sankoh and his ragtag group of Sierra Leonean freedom fighters. They called themselves the Revolutionary Union Front and claimed to seek political and economic power for Sierra Leone's impoverished rural population through the overthrow of the central government in Freetown. In March 1991, Sankoh and about 100 fighters trained by Taylor's NPFL invaded Kailahun District. From the onset, Taylor acted, in the words of African scholar Abdul Tejan-Cole, "as mentor, patron, banker, and weapons supplier for this motley collection of Sierra Leonean dissidents, bandits, and mercenaries."[86] To fund their insurgencies, Sankoh sent diamonds to Taylor in exchange for shipments of arms, artillery, radio sets, and other logistical materiel. According to the UN, Taylor profited handsomely from the arrangement.[87]

The RUF rebels and particularly their Liberian collaborators soon became notorious for their brutality. Both Sierra Leonean and Liberian fighters pillaged, razed entire villages and neighborhoods, and raped young girls and women, forcing many of them into sexual slavery. Thousands of children were abducted and turned into combatants. The rebels, typically stoked up on drugs, chopped off hands, arms, or feet as a means of terrorizing villagers.[88] They adopted a sinister vocabulary for their deeds: applying a "smile" meant cutting off the upper and lower lips of a victim, giving "long sleeves" meant hacking off the hands, and giving "short sleeves" meant cutting off the arm above the elbow. Most of the amputation victims, estimated by the International Committee of the Red Cross at 4,000, died from their injuries.[89] For every surviving victim who made it to a hospital, four or five died in the forests.

Sankoh personally ordered many of these operations, including one called Operation Pay Yourself that encouraged troops to loot anything they could find. Photographs were sent back to Sankoh to show him that they were doing their job. Some 180 photographs—images of torture sessions, executions, and amputations, some showing Sankoh directing the atrocities—fell into the hands of the journalist Sebastian Junger and were published by *Vanity Fair* in October 2000.[90]

During the 1990s, the Sierra Leone Army (SLA) split into various factional alignments, all of which were responsible for systematic war crimes. Soldiers often shed their uniforms at night and joined RUF rebels in looting and rape, earning the nickname "sobels," or soldier-rebels. In 1996 elections were held in Sierra Leone, and Ahmed Tejan Kabbah, who had spent the previous twenty years working for the UN Development Fund, emerged as the victor. A year later, a group of break-away SLA officers calling themselves the Armed Forces Revolutionary Council (AFRC) led a coup against Kabbah and installed Major Johnny Paul Koroma in his place.

In February 1998, a combination of Nigerian-led troops from the Economic Community of West Africa Monitoring Group (ECOMOG) and pro-Kabbah civilian militias forced a hugely unpopular AFRC/RUF coalition out of Freetown and restored Kabbah's government to power. Among the civilian militias, the Civilian Defense Forces (CDF) soon developed a reputation for mass killings and destroying homes and other property of civilians believed to be collaborating with the rebels. In one operation, known as Black December, CDF fighters killed and raped hundreds of civilians. Some people were ritually slaughtered, with parts of their bodies left in plastic buckets on their families' doorsteps.[91]

Then in January 1999, AFRC fighters and some RUF rebels quickly entered Freetown's city center and, facing little opposition, occupied several key government buildings. For two days, the 2,000-strong rebels easily outmaneuvered a much larger force of about 15,000 ECOMOG soldiers as they rampaged through neighborhoods, looting, raping, and killing indiscriminately. But on the third day, the AFRC began to lose ground. By nightfall, the Nigerian-led ECOMOG troops, using extremely brutal tactics, had driven the insurgents out of the city and into the bush. It was later estimated that 150,000 civilians fled Freetown during the siege, and that more than 7,000 people were killed, at least half of them civilians.[92]

Images of the AFRC's assault on Freetown—the executions, the amputations, buildings set ablaze—made their way into the international media, sending shivers throughout the region. Alarmed, Washington began working behind the scenes to bring the warring parties to the negotiating table. In a tense meeting in Monrovia, Liberia's capital, U.S. officials warned Charles Taylor that "he was suspected of being responsible for the commission of atrocities in Sierra Leone and that there would be a price to pay."[93] They pressed him to stop bankrolling and sending fighters to the RUF in Sierra Leone. Taylor ignored the plea, but still went to Lomé for the signing by Sankoh and Kabbah of the peace agreement.

Within weeks of the signing of the Lomé Peace Accord in July 1999, the whole peace process began to unravel, largely because of the blanket amnesty granted to the rebel leaders. Sankoh even began to speak publicly about his opposition to a truth and reconciliation commission because it would tarnish the "heroic" image of his fighters. In December 1999, the Nigerian-led ECOMOG troops left Sierra Leone and were replaced by nearly 18,000 blue helmets, the largest UN troop deployment ever. Sankoh and other rebel commanders, taking advantage of the amnesty and power-sharing agreement provided in the Lomé Peace Accord, moved back to Freetown. In a mind-boggling development that angered many Sierra Leoneans, President Kabbah, hoping to avoid future violence, appointed Sankoh chair of the Commission for the Management of Strategic Resources, National Reconstruction and Development, with the same status as vice president, and granted him formal authority over the country's diamonds and other natural resources.[94]

Sankoh lasted only ten months in his government post. One day in May 2000, an angry mob confronted the former rebel leader on the street in front of his house. They stripped him naked and dragged him to an SUV that sped off in the direction of Army headquarters. From there, Sankoh was handed over to British UN troops, who flew him by helicopter to a secret location.[95]

NO PEACE WITHOUT JUSTICE

Soon after Sankoh's capture, Kabbah, abandoning any pretense that the civil war could be solved through further peace talks and anxious to remove his rivals from the political scene, sent UN Secretary-General Kofi Annan a letter requesting his assistance in sponsoring a UN Security Council resolution that would create "a strong and credible" court to try Sankoh and other rebel leaders.[96] Kabbah's letter triggered seventeen months of intensive negotiations between the United Nations and the Sierra Leonean government. Leading those discussions were David Scheffer for the United States, Ralph Zacklin, the UN's deputy legal counsel, and Sierra Leone's attorney general, Solomon Berewa.

The group grappled with a surfeit of thorny issues. To begin with, they had to decide what kind of tribunal should be put in place. It was unrealistic to propose a conventional Security Council tribunal, as most council members had no interest in being compelled to pay for a new court along the lines of the Yugoslavia and Rwanda tribunals. Domestic trials were also out of the question. Security for the court, defendants and witnesses, Berewa argued, would be impossible to assure in war-torn Sierra Leone. Also, Sierra Leone's death penalty would make it impossible for European governments to provide expertise, funding, and logistical support, which were critical.

What emerged was an innovative idea: a "special court" that would be created through a treaty between the United Nations and the government of Sierra Leone. This agreement would avoid having to call on the

Security Council's enforcement authority, the use of which the British and other council members adamantly opposed, and it would place financial responsibilities for the court on the shoulders of the individual governments involved and not on the United Nations. A Security Council–sanctioned special court under both international law and Sierra Leone law gave the UN secretary-general the upper hand in staffing the court with international prosecutors, judges, and administrators, thus ensuring international control of the proceedings. Since the "special court" would exist outside of the national court system, it would also have no legal obligations to honor the blanket pardons provided to the rebel leaders in the Lomé agreement.

In January 2002, the United Nations and the Sierra Leone government signed the Special Court Agreement and Ratification Act establishing the Special Court for Sierra Leone to prosecute those persons who "bear the greatest responsibility" for crimes against humanity, war crimes, and certain crimes under Sierra Leonean law since November 1996.[97] The Special Court would be situated in-country, with a mixed staff, a narrow prosecutorial mandate, limited temporal jurisdiction, a tight budget, and what, in hindsight, was clearly an overly ambitious timeline for completion.[98] It would also be the most powerful judicial body in Sierra Leone, with "primacy" over the national courts.[99] Largely independent of the UN bureaucracy, the Special Court would be supervised by a Management Committee made up of representatives from the United States, Canada, the United Kingdom, Nigeria, and the Netherlands, who would be responsible for raising funds for the court from their own governments and overseeing all its non-judicial aspects.[100] Ultimately, this treaty model gave these representatives and their governments control over how the court would be administered, funded, and overseen.

Some commentators lauded the Special Court's "efficiency-minded, hybrid approach as a model for international justice worthy of replication."[101] Yet this neoliberal approach to "right-sizing" international justice also had its drawbacks. The court's low-budget, three-year timeline meant that staff were often forced to prioritize fiscal and political imperatives over core legal and procedural principles. One commentator, reviewing the Special Court's first two years of existence, called its "experiment with voluntary funding" a failure, quoting a senior court official's characterization of the court as not so much "mean and lean" as it was "anorexic."[102]

The voluntary nature of contributions to the Special Court also meant that simply by augmenting or revoking their funding individual states could gain undue influence over the direction and very existence of the court. During the court's first three years the United States, Netherlands, and United Kingdom provided more than 80 percent of the court's contributions, making them the top three "stakeholders." As such, the refusal by even one of these countries to make a contribution could undermine the court's functioning, even shutter it,[103] potentially leaving indictees without the chance to clear their names in a public trial.

There was a further problem. Unlike the Yugoslavia and Rwanda tribunals, but like the Cambodia hybrid tribunal established four years later, the Sierra Leone special court lacked Chapter VII powers and thus the ability to call on the UN Security Council to apply pressure on governments to hand over defendants and evidence. This meant that, short of a diplomatic miracle, Charles Taylor, then president of Liberia and the person largely responsible for the horrors that destroyed Sierra Leone, might never be brought to justice for his crimes.

During the first six months of 2002, the construction of the Special Court gradually took shape at UN headquarters in New York. Kofi Annan, in accordance with the relevant UN statute, appointed Robin Vincent of the United Kingdom as registrar and three trial and three appellate judges from various countries, three of whom had been nominated by the Sierra Leone government. The statute establishing the court called for an international prosecutor to lead the investigations and prosecutions in a manner that would "guarantee that the Prosecutor is, and is seen to be, independent, objective and impartial."[104] After considerable deliberation, Annan appointed David Crane of the United States to the post.[105]

Crane's appointment marked the first time since Nuremberg that someone from the United States had been chosen as chief prosecutor of an international court. Crane seemed an odd pick for an international prosecutor, though. A platoon leader in the U.S. Army and a law school graduate who had served in the Judge Advocate General's Corps of the Army, he had little if any courtroom experience. But the George W. Bush administration had aggressively promoted Crane's nomination at the United Nations. His only serious challenger—one favored by many UN representatives and human rights activists—was Ken Fleming, an Australian lawyer who had served as acting chief of prosecutions at the Rwanda Tribunal. Many human rights advocates had misgivings about an American's being appointed to such a prominent position in the court, although it provided a clear advantage in continued U.S. political and financial support for the court.[106]

As the court's first employees, Crane as chief prosecutor and Vincent as registrar were essentially responsible for developing a new organization from the bottom up,[107] a formidable task under any circumstances, but particularly so in a war-torn country, on a shoestring budget, and under tremendous pressure to complete the work quickly.

Crane's first task was to hire senior staff and develop a plan that would lay out the court's work for the next three to four years. He chose an old friend and colleague, Alan White, to serve as his chief investigator; White in turn hired Canadian investigator Gilbert Morissette, and Bobby Bridges as his legal administrator.[108]

Crane assembled his nascent staff in Washington, DC, to hash out their investigation strategies once they hit the ground in Freetown. White and Bridges had just returned from a reconnaissance trip to Sierra Leone with a grim assessment. Nothing was in place to support the court: no courthouse, no prison, no security, and no transport. Worst of all, UN peacekeeping officials were unwilling to provide any assistance to the new court. However, there was a silver lining. While in Freetown, White and Bridges had stayed at the home of the inspector general of the Sierra Leone National Police, Keith Biddle, and his wife, Sue. Biddle, who offered to do everything in his power to help the Special Court, was a globetrotting British policeman who had run police reform projects in South Africa, Ethiopia, Somalia, Indonesia, and the Democratic Republic of the Congo. He had retired in 1999, but, unable to resist the pull of a new challenge, he had accepted an offer to help President Kabbah rebuild Sierra Leone's beleaguered police force.[109]

Sue Biddle meanwhile helped White and Bridges find lodging for the prosecution staff in Freetown. They settled on a dilapidated villa called Seaview, a three-story building on a two-acre compound with boarded-up windows and walls pockmarked with bullet holes, a victim of a prolonged firefight between the rebels and ECOMOG troops in the late 1990s. The compound would have to serve, at least initially, as the Office of the Prosecutor's workplace and bunkhouse.

Back in Washington, Crane and his team developed a prosecutorial strategy with a ten-step process that included, in his words, "diplomatic initiatives, information operations, and military support [for the arrests] culminating in a complete tactical assault on the potential defendants using deception, surprise, and precision of action based on timely and actionable intelligence."[110] Crane believed that his mandate meant that the indictments should be restricted to the "twenty or less [with the greatest responsibility] . . . . If you change 'greatest' to 'most responsible,' it goes up to about 300, and the life of the court goes to fifteen or twenty years. If you want to prosecute everyone who bears responsibility, that is 30,000 people, and it can't be done."[111] Crane's team also debated the risks of contacting insider witnesses, who would be critical for establishing their case against top leaders. They already had the name of a potential informant in Burkina Faso that *Washington Post* correspondent Douglas Farrah claimed could link Charles Taylor to the RUF's guns-for-diamonds operation in eastern Sierra Leone.

Crane and his team agreed that the best course was to arrest most of their suspects in March of the following year. Operation Justice, as they called it, would be a risky maneuver, especially as they aimed to take down most of their "targets" in one fell swoop. Because the planning and execution of Operation Justice required the support of many nations and organizations, there was the added risk that it could spring a leak, and if it reached the ears of the indictees, the whole operation could fizzle as suspects slipped into the bush.[112]

In late July 2002, Crane left Washington for Freetown. En route, he stopped in London to brief Whitehall about Operation Justice and to ask for logistical support in making the arrests. He also briefed Dutch officials and paid a courtesy visit to Carla Del Ponte, then in her third year as chief prosecutor at the Yugoslavia and Rwanda tribunals in The Hague. Crane left Europe with a mixed feeling of success: the British, he later wrote, were "impressed but skeptical," while the "Dutch were polite yet held their cards close to their chest."[113]

Meanwhile, Robert Vincent scoured Freetown for a building to serve as a temporary courtroom and to house his staff (the official courthouse would not be finally inaugurated until March 2004). He also established internal procedures, including a security protocol and information management systems, and developed relationships with the diplomatic corps, civil society, and nongovernmental organizations. Vincent's task wasn't made any easier by the UN Mission in Sierra Leone (UNAMSIL), which, at least in the beginning, kept the fledgling court at arm's distance. It was yet another example, as we've seen in other chapters, of the peace-versus-justice conundrum. Some UNAMSIL officials believed that the Special Court would undermine a fragile peace and disrupt their mission to disarm the warring factions. According to a UN Special

Rapporteur's 2006 review, "UNAMSIL was uniquely situated to assist the Special Court in its early days, and its failure to help cost the Court valuable months."[114]

In early August, Crane and his staff moved into Seaview and a guesthouse nearby. For the first month, there was no electricity or running water; as a consequence, everyone showered in the rain. "It was very egalitarian," Crane recalled. "We shared our meals. I lived no differently than a junior trial counsel. I thought it was an important [message] to send: You know, we're all in this together. No one is any better than any other."[115]

The ground floor of Seaview was turned into an "operations center," with two bulletproof metal doors at the entryway. Court vehicles with tinted windows would pull up to the doors and witnesses would be whisked in and out for interviews. Keith Biddle seconded five of his top police officers to work with White and his international investigators. "My greatest worry were leaks," White said later. "So I vetted these five guys pretty thoroughly. One of them made me uncomfortable, so I cut him loose. But the other four were as good as you get."[116]

Crane tasked White with handling the Office of the Prosecutor's most sensitive "assets" outside of Sierra Leone, while White's deputy, Gilbert Morissette, the Canadian undercover policeman who had masterminded the Naki operation in Nairobi for the Rwanda tribunal, oversaw investigations inside the country.[117]

White traveled widely to find informants who could help the Office of the Prosecutor's infiltrate the inner circles of several West African leaders. Their objective: build a case around the theory that these leaders had conspired to enrich themselves and their armies by supporting the RUF's use of force to control the diamond mines in eastern Sierra Leone.[118] White contacted witnesses, took their statements, and negotiated deals on their behalf for relocation to countries outside Africa, along with support payments. Crane informed his senior staff and the registrar about these operations only on a need-to-know basis.

Within a relatively short time, White and Crane had their sights fixed on some very large game, including Charles Taylor of Liberia, Muammar Gaddafi of Libya, and Blaise Compaoré of Burkina Faso. It would also emerge later, in a confidential Office of the Prosecutor document Crane provided to the U.S. Congress, that White had been investigating reports that Charles Taylor had "facilitated access for al Qaeda operatives into Sierra Leone and Liberia in exchange for diamonds and weapons."[119] According to the document, White and Morissette made frequent undercover trips to Monrovia to interview potential insider witnesses about the Taylor–al-Qaeda connection. In February 2004, White also provided a visiting "FBI delegation with detailed information and names of witnesses in Sierra Leone and Liberia who could confirm the al Qaeda presence in West Africa as well as the purchase of conflict diamonds from Sierra Leone" and then "arranged for [the FBI delegation's] transport to Liberia in order to conduct their investigation."[120]

Back in Sierra Leone, Gilbert Morissette spent much of his time trying, in his words, to "roll over" or "flip" potential insider witnesses to testify against their superiors. It was an assignment he relished.[121] From Crane's perspective, flipping potential indictees to testify against their superiors was absolutely essential, especially if he was going to bring down those "bearing the most responsibility" for the atrocities. "It's an old prosecutorial trick," he said. "It's like taking on a drug cartel or taking on a mafia family, if you're going to go for the center of the circle, if you're going to go for the big guys, you have to take the people around them. . . . It has always been my experience that at the end of the day no one's going to go down for the big guy."[122]

In one undercover operation, Morissette sent two of his investigators to a refugee camp to "turn" an illicit diamond dealer who had once been an intermediary between Charles Taylor and the RUF. "We'd done our homework," Morissette recalled. "We knew our target was peddling blood diamonds and had received some serious threats, which meant he was vulnerable. So my guys, posing as diamond dealers, arrange for an informant to meet with this guy. The informant makes the connection and a meeting is set. Two days later, my guys go in without the informant. They talk, and when things are feeling comfortable, they reveal they're with the court and stick the deal right on the table: Testify and you'll be safe. In return, we'll take care of you and your family. So, the guy testifies and we move him and his family to Europe."[123]

OPERATION JUSTICE

David Crane knew that Operation Justice was going to need a lot of support from key international players in Sierra Leone.[124] With the assistance of Keith Biddle and the British High Commissioner, Alan Jones, Crane created the Security Group, a loose coalition of foreign diplomats and military attaches who gathered monthly to discuss the practical, political, and diplomatic aspects of Operation Justice. Crane never revealed the names of his targets to all the members of the group but, he says, everyone understood who the "local favorites" were.[125]

Of all Crane's confidants, Keith Biddle would be the key to the success or failure of Operation Justice. Following protocol, Biddle informed President Kabbah about his meetings with Crane. Kabbah replied that Biddle was free to work directly with the court and didn't need to report back to him. Getting Kabbah's blessing while also cutting him out of the information loop was critical: it would help staunch any leaks about the operation.

Not everyone in Freetown's diplomatic community supported Crane's aggressive pursuit of arrests. Crane commented:

> The American Ambassador at the time, Pete Chavez, was a reluctant player and largely unhelpful throughout his tenure there. I never understood why. I also did not trust the Secretary-General's Special Representative in Sierra Leone, Alieu Adenigi, who was blatantly trying to undercut the work of the Special Court and tried to secrete two of our potential indictees out of Sierra Leone on "agricultural scholarships" to Nigeria a month before Operation Justice was to be launched. I was told of this by a very senior deputy. I sent a note that simply stated that if he did what he was contemplating, I would have him arrested for obstruction of justice. This was passed on to senior officials at the United Nations. The two indictees, Issa Sesay and Morris Kallon, never left Sierra Leone.[126]

As 2002 drew to a close, Crane began meeting separately with the members of the Security Group to safeguard against leaks. He cut Adenigi out of the loop and began seeing the UN peacekeeping force's chief of staff, Brigadier James Ellery, on the sly. Like Crane, Ellery, a former aide-de-camp to Lord Mountbatten and a seasoned diplomat with years of service in Africa, didn't have much patience for what his American colleague called "UN hall walkers."[127] And, unlike many of his peacekeeping colleagues in Freetown, he supported the aims of the Special Court, just as some of his British and Canadian counterparts in the Balkans, contrary to the prevailing order, were willing to assist the Yugoslavia tribunal by enforcing arrest warrants and protecting mass grave sites.

The British soon became the biggest supporters of Operation Justice. Ellery promised Crane the support of a quick reaction force to transport the indictees to a temporary detention facility that the Special Court was building on Bonthe Island, 100 miles from Freetown. Sierra Leone's minister of the interior, Hinga Norman, had given the Special Court permission to build the prison as part of the court's legacy project for the Sierra Leone Police, when in reality the jail was to be the temporary detention facility for the defendants taken down in Operation Justice. Little did the minister know that in a few months' time, he would be cooling his heels in the Bonthe jail awaiting his own trial.

The British also told Crane they would send their Spear Point parachute battalion of Ghurkas to Sierra Leone weeks before the takedown. Every February, the elite battalion conducted a training program for the Sierra Leone Army near the Lungi International Airport outside of Freetown. Only this year, they would arrive a bit later to train the Sierra Leonean soldiers in maneuvers to seize their own airport. If the country melted down after the arrests, the British would then be in control of the airport and be able to evacuate court staff and other international players.[128]

In the weeks prior to the execution of Operation Justice, Crane launched what he called an "information operation" as a diversionary tactic. He met regularly with the media, openly discussing the general work of the court, tossing out sound bites like "the investigation is complex" and "my office won't be ready to go to trial for at least a year."[129] At the same time, somewhat paradoxically, he hinted in interviews with foreign journalists that he might be indicting a head of state or two.[130]

On March 3, 2003, Crane signed eight indictments and sent them to a duty judge for his review. The first was a sealed indictment against President Charles Taylor for seventeen counts (later reduced to eleven) covering a wide range of international crimes. The prosecutor charged that Taylor held a position "of superior responsibility and exercise[ed] command and control over subordinate[s]" who directly committed the atrocities, namely the RUF, AFRC, RUF/AFRC alliance, and Liberian fighters.[131] Indictment number two was for the RUF's director of military operations, Samuel "the Mosquito" Bockarie. Number three was for Foday Sankoh, who was already in the custody of the Sierra Leone government. The other indictments singled out the leadership of the warring factions that had destroyed Sierra Leone in the 1990s.

Absent from Crane's list of indictees were Gaddafi, Campaoré, and Kabbah. Crane had decided early on that the Sierra Leonean president was not among those who bore the greatest responsibility for the crimes that destroyed his country in the late 1990s. Gaddafi and Campaoré were another matter altogether. In fact, it was later revealed that Crane's deputy prosecutor, Desmond de Silva, had met with Gaddafi in Tripoli to inform him that he was under investigation by the Special Court. De Silva reportedly used that threat to solicit information from the Libyan leader about other high-level indictees.[132] Similarly, Alan White traveled to Ouagadougou to inform Compaoré of his potential indictment for his role in allowing weapons from Eastern Europe to pass through Burkina Faso to Liberia and Sierra Leone for rebel groups in violation of a UN embargo.[133] After Taylor, Crane considered Compaoré "the most indictable" of the three heads of state, but, like Gaddafi, the prosecutor chose not to indict him for both evidentiary and political reasons.[134] "When you [attempt to] take down a head of state, you have to have it beyond a reasonable doubt before you even indict," he said. "Because if you make a mistake, it's fatal. You are going to reap the whirlwind of an angry head of state who is falsely indicted. It makes the court look bad. Also he is going to come back with a vengeance and people will die, and so you have to be very careful."[135]

Crane also acknowledges that politics shaped his decision not to indict Gaddafi and Compaoré. "I realized that if I indicted three heads of state, then the international community would have ended political support for the court," he said. "As an international prosecutor, my power was absolute. I had the power to bring down governments. I could have indicted Gaddafi and the head of Burkina Faso. But I didn't because I didn't want to destroy the court. It's a naïve prosecutor who acts on law and facts without considering politics and culture."[136]

Crane also feared that the Special Court's main funders—the United States, the Netherlands, and the United Kingdom—would be angered by an indictment of Gaddafi because it would undermine the headway the West had made with the Libyan leader on a number of sensitive issues, including access to Libya's oil fields and his sponsorship of terrorism.[137] Beginning in the early 2000s, the Libyan leader had stopped funding terrorism, denounced the September 11 attacks, and surrendered the two Libyan suspects of the Lockerbie plane bombing. In response, the U.S. had removed Libya from its list of state sponsors of terrorism, opening the way for U.S., British, and Dutch oil companies to resume drilling in Africa's largest oil reserves. "I was very much aware of that all important three-letter word, 'oil,'" Crane told an audience at Brigham Young University in 2006. "Politics is the train that drives international courts, and oil is the grease."[138]

Once Crane received the signed indictments from the duty judge, he gave the green light for Operation Justice to commence on the morning of Monday, March 10, 2003. But he kept the specifics of the operation on a need-to-know basis, informing only Biddle, White, and the registrar, Robin Vincent. That Saturday, Crane gave a "diversionary speech" at the UN peacekeeping headquarters lamenting that his investigations were complex and could take years to complete.

As the weekend progressed, the United States readied helicopters to transport the indictees to Bonthe Island; Ellery put the quick reaction force on alert; Whitehall moved the British frigate HMS *Iron Duke* close to the shoreline to project a sign of force; and Biddle's officers tightened surveillance on the targets.[139] Still, Crane went to bed Sunday night unsure of what the next day would bring. He "had no idea whether this would be a day of triumph or disaster," he recalled. "I was concerned that we would miss someone who would promptly disappear into the bush and perhaps start the civil war all over again."[140]

At 5 A.M. on Monday, two hours before White's investigators were to gather in the Seaview compound, White and Crane went for their daily three-mile run, leaving the villa and jogging down the road to the beach, speaking in whispers as they reviewed each step of the operation and any conceivable repercussions.

At sunrise, Gilbert Morissette descended the stairs of the Seaview guesthouse to find the yard crawling with Gurkhas. During the night, they had slipped into the compound to protect the staff if things went south later in the day. He crossed the street to the Seaview, where he joined the other investigators—a mix of fellow Canadians, Australians, and Sierra Leonean police officers—in front of the operations center. The investigators split into three groups. Each group was given a cell phone and detailed instructions for their particular operation and sent into the city. Morissette and White, along with a Sierra Leonean police officer, took off in the direction of the headquarters of the Criminal Investigations Division (CID).[141]

At 11:15 A.M., the three men watched from their vehicle as three high-level RUF officers walked into the CID building. Two of the former rebel leaders—Morris Kallon and Issa Sessay—were targets. The third, Gibril Massaquoi, unbeknownst to his colleagues, was working hand in glove with Morissette and White. Little did Kallon and Sessay know they were walking into a sting operation of their own making.

The story goes something like this. Soon after the end of hostilities, several high-level RUF officials, including Kallon, Sessay, and Massaquoi, had occupied a house in Freetown. With funds from a government-run rehabilitation program, the group established an NGO. One day there was a break-in at the house, and money was stolen. Massaquoi convinced Kallon and Sessay that they should all go to the CID to file a complaint. It was a perfect ruse. The minute they walked into the building that Monday morning, CID officers handcuffed them and handed them over to White and Morissette. Kallon and Sessay were taken away, while Massaquoi was taken aside and released.[142]

Elsewhere in the city, the investigative teams were making similar arrests. In one of the more sensational captures, the head of the CID, Tom Gbekie, arrested his own boss, Minister of the Interior Hinga Norman, at his desk and "perp walked" him to a van waiting outside. "It was beautiful," Morissette said. "The SLP [Sierra Leone Police] guys were so happy to arrest their boss. I mean they really hated him."[143]

Operation Justice had unfolded in just fifty-five minutes and resulted in the arrests of six indictees.[144] Back at the Seaview, Crane paced the floor, waiting to hear from White. Finally, at 1 P.M., White called to report that all of the indictees, including Foday Sankoh, who was collected from his prison cell, were in helicopters on their way to Bonthe Island. Crane then called Kofi Annan's special representative to Sierra Leone, Alieu Adenige, who was sitting in a barber's chair having his hair cut. "I told him about the operation. He was stunned. He began to shout, and I hung up."[145]

All told, the Special Court issued arrest warrants for thirteen people for international crimes committed during the Sierra Leone conflict. The indictees were grouped into three trials—one for the Revolutionary United Front, and one each for the Armed Forces Revolutionary Council and the Civil Defense Forces—with a fourth trial reserved for Taylor alone, should he be apprehended.[146] Three of the accused—Foday Sankoh, Johnny Paul Koroma, and Sam Bockarie—died before the completion of their trials.[147] Sankoh died of complications arising from a stroke while awaiting trial; Johnny Paul Koroma, the leader of the Armed Forces Revolutionary Council, and Sam Bockarie of the Revolutionary United Front were killed in Liberia shortly after their indictments were made public but before they could be picked up. Three prosecution witnesses, including Taylor's former vice president Moses Blah, testified that while they did not witness Koroma's execution, Charles Taylor had told them about it.[148] Crane maintains that Taylor ordered Koroma's murder and then had "his body cut up and scattered in the jungle."[149] Bockarie met a similar fate in early May, allegedly killed by Taylor's men to prevent him from testifying. Taylor sent Bockarie's remains to Crane on the chief prosecutor's birthday that May.[150]

IN PURSUIT OF CHARLES TAYLOR

Over the first half of 2003 various rebel factions, backed by neighboring countries, fought to oust Charles Taylor from power. By early June, the largest rebel group, Liberians United for Reconciliation and Democracy, had arrived at the outskirts of the capital, Monrovia, and began shelling civilian areas of the city, killing dozens, if not hundreds, of people.[151] As the rebels closed in on the capital, regional and Western diplomats joined representatives from the African Union and the Economic Community of West African States (ECOWAS) in arranging for Taylor and the representatives of all the warring parties to meet in Accra, Ghana, to hammer out a peace treaty.[152]

On June 4, 2003, while Taylor was in Accra attending the first day of the peace talks, David Crane unsealed the Special Court's indictment against the Liberian leader and appealed to the Ghanaian authorities to arrest and transfer their guest to Sierra Leone to stand trial.[153] The unsealing of the indictment, Crane later said, was timed so as to maximize the "impact legally, diplomatically, and practically."[154] In effect, Crane wanted to embarrass Taylor in front of his West African colleagues and make it impossible for him to continue to play a role of significance in the peace talks.

Crane knew that unsealing the indictment was a big political gamble. Eight weeks earlier he had personally given copies of the indictment to both the U.S. ambassador to Sierra Leone and the ambassador-at-large for war crimes.[155] Soon thereafter, the U.S. assistant secretary of state for African affairs, Walter Kansteiner, had warned him that disclosing the indictment could foment unrest in the region and asked him to withdraw it. Crane refused.

Crane knew, of course, that the Ghanaian authorities were highly unlikely to arrest Taylor and transfer him to Sierra Leone, a move that would have been a flagrant violation of African protocol and hospitality.[156] Still, he pushed forward.

Caught unawares, Ghana's president, John Kufuor, reacted angrily to the timing of the indictment's release. He later told the magazine *New African*:

> Five African presidents were meeting in Accra to find ways of kick-starting the Liberian peace process, and Mr. Taylor had been invited as president of Liberia. We were not aware that a warrant had been issued for his arrest. Incidentally, the African leadership had taken the initiative to convince Mr. Taylor to resign and allow all the factions in Liberia to negotiate. It was when the presidents were leaving my office for the Conference Center where

Mr. Taylor was expected to make a statement that word came in that a warrant had been issued for his arrest. I really felt betrayed by the international community [and] I informed the United States of the embarrassment that the announcement caused.[157]

Taylor himself was reportedly stunned by the announcement, stating, "What do you mean indictment? It's not possible to indict a head of state."[158]

Within the hour, Taylor addressed the gathering in Accra. "Some people believe that Taylor is the problem," he said, speaking of himself in the third person. "If President Taylor removes himself from Liberia, will that bring peace? If so, I remove myself."[159] By nightfall, Taylor was on a Ghanaian presidential plane bound for Liberia.

With Taylor's departure, the chemistry of the peace talks changed radically. After seventy-six days of nonstop negotiations, the warring parties agreed to a comprehensive peace agreement that finally ended the conflict. They also pledged to establish a truth and reconciliation commission, initiate a massive campaign of disarmament and demobilization of troops fighting in Liberia, implement judicial reforms, and hold national elections in two years. In addition, they agreed to form a transitional Liberian government that would not include Charles Taylor.[160]

In the ensuing weeks, Nigerian President Olesegun Obasanjo—reportedly backed by the United States, the United Kingdom, the African Union, the United Nations, and ECOWAS—offered Taylor safe haven in Nigeria on the condition that he withdraw altogether from political activity in the region.

On August 11, Taylor officially resigned his presidency in a ceremony at Liberia's executive mansion. On stage with Taylor were three heads of state—South African President Thabo Mbeki; Mozambique's Joaquim Chissano, chair of the African Union; and Ghana's John Kufuor, the head of ECOWAS—who had come to see him off. That evening, as Liberians danced in the streets, Taylor and his family and aides flew to Nigeria's capital and then traveled to Calabar, a quiet town near the border of Cameroon, where they took up residence in three comfortable villas.[161]

Crane next went to work to build diplomatic and political support to pressure Nigeria into rescinding Taylor's asylum. It was a process that would consume Crane's entire last year as chief prosecutor.[162] In November 2003, Crane met with Interpol officials in Lyon, who later placed Taylor on their most wanted list, obligating countries to arrest him.[163] That same month the U.S. Congress tucked into an $87 million emergency-funding bill for Iraq and Afghanistan an appropriation of $2 million as a bounty for "an indictee of the Special Court for Sierra Leone"—everyone knew who the "indictee" was—which President Bush later signed into law.

Within days, a U.K.-based security firm, Northbridge Services Group, announced that it was looking for an investor to fund an operation to seize Charles Taylor in Nigeria. "We can split the profits" from the bounty, the firm's director, Pasquale Dipofi, said. He hinted that his company already had agents in Nigeria ready for the swoop. "We have everything in place . . . we can execute this and bring Mr. Taylor before the tribunal," he announced.[164] In the end, Dipofi's bounty scheme was overtaken by events.

In March 2004 the UN Security Council—having already placed a ban on Taylor's leaving Nigeria—voted to freeze his assets and those of his family, worth tens of millions of dollars.[165] Later that year, Crane's deputy prosecutor, Sir Desmond de Silva, a well-connected British national, travelled to Brussels and Strasbourg, where he lobbied successfully for a resolution in the European Parliament calling on Nigeria to send Taylor to the Special Court.[166] In the meantime Crane pressed his case for Taylor's arrest on key Democrats and Republicans in Washington, DC. The result was a joint congressional resolution—a signed copy of which hangs on Crane's office wall—urging the Nigerian government to "expeditiously transfer" Taylor to the jurisdiction of the Special Court.[167]

Crane next set his sights again on the thirteen-member Security Council. He calculated that of all the rotating council presidents slated to pick up the gavel in the first half of 2005, Denmark's ambassador, Ellen Margrethe Løj, would be the most supportive of Taylor's transfer to the Special Court. After a flurry of meetings in Copenhagen and New York, Løj agreed to place the issue on the council's agenda. Crane, in the meantime, met separately with the other council members in hopes of persuading them to accept the agenda. "It involved a lot of walking the hallways," he said. "A lot of lunches and teas and cocktails, saying 'Ambassador, here's why we need your assistance and support.'"[168]

On May 24, the Security Council considered the transfer of Taylor into the Special Court's custody. "It was a humbling experience," recalled Crane, who was in the audience, along with the court's registrar and the Special Court's president, Emmanuel Olayinka Ayoola, who addressed the chamber. At the end of the session, "every single member of the Security Council issued a public statement calling for Charles Taylor to be handed over. Some members pounded the table, saying it should happen immediately, some were a little more subtle, saying at the appropriate time, but all saying he should be handed over for a fair and just trial."[169]

By mid-2005, credible reports were emerging that the former Liberian warlord had violated the terms of his asylum, that he had been involved in an attempted assassination of Guinea's president, and that he had backed a coup plot in Côte d'Ivoire. These reports placed Nigeria's President Obasanjo in an uncomfortable position with other leaders in the region and could have tarnished Nigeria's image at the United Nations, where Obasanjo was lobbying to have his country named a permanent member of the Security Council.

But bringing Taylor to justice was certainly not a priority for Ellen Sirleaf-Johnson, the newly elected Liberian president. Liberia was on the brink of social and economic collapse, and with no standing army and Taylor loyalists still armed and in the bush, the new president was adamant about keeping Taylor out of the country. Some reports suggested that in her bid to win the presidency, Sirleaf-Johnson had promised Taylor's allies she would not request Taylor's surrender, in exchange for their financial support.[170]

Two events soon changed the situation, however. In November 2005, the Security Council expanded the mandate of the UN peacekeeping mission in Liberia to include both Taylor's arrest and detention in the event of his return to Liberia and his transfer to Sierra Leone for prosecution before the Special Court.[171] Two months later, in a clear shift of position, the Bush administration "suggested" to Sirleaf-Johnson that it was time for Taylor to be sent to Freetown to face justice. When she demurred, the United States and the European Union suggested they might withhold much-needed development assistance until Taylor was brought to justice.[172]

That threat seemed to do the trick. The following March, President Sirleaf-Johnson told the UN Security Council that she had made a formal extradition request to Nigeria, and that once Taylor arrived in Liberia he would be turned over to UN peacekeepers for transport to Sierra Leone.[173] Soon thereafter, Sirleaf-Johnson told an American news program: "We are facing . . . pressure—I must use that word—from the UN, from the US, from the European Union, who are all our major partners in development, on the need to do something about the Charles Taylor issue. . . . Three million people need to move on; they need to have their development needs met. One person should not [hold] up the progress of an entire nation."[174]

A week later, while President Obasanjo was en route to a much-anticipated meeting with President Bush in Washington, DC, Charles Taylor "disappeared" from the seaside villa in Calabar where he had been living in exile.[175] For the next twenty-four hours, Taylor was supposedly on the run, although the local press reported that Nigerian security forces were, in fact, helping him slip across the border into Cameroon in an attempt to save the Nigerian government the embarrassment of appearing to cave in to the West.

Taylor's apparent escape prompted Vermont Senator Patrick Leahy, an ardent supporter of the Special Court, in a Congressional hearing to urge Secretary of State Condoleezza Rice to cancel President Bush's meeting the following day with President Obasanjo.

But suddenly Nigeria reversed course. On March 29, hours before the meeting of the two presidents, Nigerian police apprehended Taylor near the Cameroon border and flew him on a presidential jet to Monrovia, where UN peacekeepers accompanied him by helicopter to Sierra Leone.[176]

On Taylor's arrival in Freetown, the president of the Special Court, Justice Raja N. Fernando, made a request to the Dutch government and the International Criminal Court to hold Taylor's trial in The Hague on the basis of "security concerns."[177] It was learned later that President Sirleaf-Johnson had handed Taylor over to the court with the precondition that his trial be held out of the region.[178]

On June 30, Taylor was transferred to The Hague and, a year later, proceedings against him commenced.[179] The change of venue was not without its critics. "It undermines the entire rationale for having the court in Sierra Leone in the first place," said a Sierra Leonean lawyer,[180] while the New York–based International Center for Transitional Justice argued that the trial in The Hague would be "less accessible . . . to the very people who were most affected by the crimes alleged."[181] Several African leaders condemned Taylor's arrest and transfer for entirely different reasons. They objected to Nigeria's unilateral decision to hand over one of its own to "a white man's Court" in The Hague, though the trial would be presided over by judges from the Special Court of Sierra Leone.[182] In a prescient comment, Libyan leader Muammar Gaddafi said Taylor's arrest and trial "means every head of state could meet a similar fate. This sets a serious precedent."[183]

In April 2012, after thirteen months of testimony and deliberation, a panel of three judges from Ireland, Samoa, and Uganda found Charles

Taylor guilty of eleven counts of crimes against humanity and war crimes, including murder, rape, slavery, and the use of child soldiers, and sentenced him to fifty years in prison. In their verdict, the judges said that the former Liberian leader had helped plan the capture of diamond mines in Sierra Leone and the invasion of Freetown. But in the eyes of the judges the prosecution failed to prove that Taylor had directly commanded the rebels responsible for the atrocities.[184]

Most Sierra Leoneans could only listen to the proceedings through BBC radio broadcasts. Still, according to Ibrahim Tommy, a prominent human rights activist in Freetown, the trial had brought "a sense of relief" to the country as a whole.[185] Another activist, Tiawan Gongloe, commented: "Taylor's removal from the scene had made it easier for people to be more outspoken and made them more willing to demand their rights. Now we won't close our mouths! And that is a hopeful sign for peace, stability, and the emergence of democratic values in West Africa."[186] The Taylor conviction, which was confirmed by an appeals panel in 2013,[187] was a success for David Crane and his successors, Desmond DeSilva, Stephen Rapp, and Brenda Hollis. Not since the International Military Tribunal at Nuremberg tried and sentenced Karl Dönitz—the German admiral who briefly succeeded Hitler on his death—had a head of state been convicted by an international court.[188]

The Special Court for Sierra Leone completed its work in December 2013. During its eleven-year tenure, the court indicted twenty-two people, sixteen of whom were convicted and given sentences ranging from eighteen months to fifty-two years' imprisonment; two were acquitted. Four indictees died before proceedings concluded. The United Nations and the Sierra Leonean government have established a Residual Special Court for Sierra Leone to oversee such matters as witness protection, supervision of prison sentences, and management of its predecessor's archives. Unlike the Special Court, which at its busiest employed more than 400 staff in Freetown and The Hague, the Residual Special Court is a small body with about a dozen staff.[189]

The Special Court for Sierra Leone has been hailed as an alternative model to the expensive and often unwieldy ad hoc tribunals for Yugoslavia and Rwanda and for its focused mandate to prosecute only "those bearing the greatest responsibility," which resulted in fewer and shorter trials at considerably lower costs. However, many Sierra Leoneans feel that the court's mandate was too limited and that without the prospect of domestic trials, many lower-level perpetrators have continued to walk free in their communities.[190]

The Special Court also struggled to survive under the system of voluntary contributions the United Nations imposed on its funding. Although voluntary contributions were sufficient to make a good start in the first two years, pledges were not redeemed, and in the second year the court had to borrow against third-year pledges, a process that tied up senior officials in fundraising. Despite these efforts, the court's coffers were nearly empty by the end of 2013, prompting the court's president, Shireen Avis Fisher, to appeal to the UN Security Council to encourage states to renew their funding. Without it, she said, the court faced a host of administrative, security, and legal problems, including its closure and the possibility that Charles Taylor would have to be "released, without ever receiving a final judgment" by the appeals chamber.[191]

UN insistence that the Special Court be efficient and timely resulted in serious shortcomings in addition to the funding problems. According to a study by the Berkeley War Crimes Studies Center, the Special Court's "budgetary and time constraints, including pressures to rapidly produce visible achievements, created an imperative for investigators to 'hit the ground running,' with minimal investment in training or education."[192] That led to some breaches of proper procedures during sensitive operations and in one case, according to the judges, misleading a potential insider witness.[193]

In the Special Court's early years, the voluntary funding scheme gave the court's three primary funders—the United States, the Netherlands, and the United Kingdom—considerable sway over its activities and, at times, its very existence. Sometimes the arrangement benefited the Office of the Prosecutor, as was the case in the planning and execution of Operation Justice, but at other times it ate away at both the reality and the public perception of the chief prosecutor's independence. While the influence was not always overt, it was certainly on the minds of many court officials as they struggled to set up the court and make ends meet.

Because war crimes investigations, by their nature, are politically controversial, it is paramount that war crimes prosecutors remain independent in all matters, especially when making decisions dealing with investigations and indictments. "A chief prosecutor, in the exercise of his or her functions and mandate, reports to nobody," believes Brenda Hollis, the chief prosecutor of the Special Court and a veteran of several international courts.[194] For her former boss, Richard Goldstone, the first prosecutor at the Yugoslavia and Rwanda tribunals, "the real point of independence is that the prosecutor should not be required to account to a political body for his or her policy or professional decisions. And, by the same token, a prosecutor should not have instructions from politicians on the exercise of prosecutorial discretion."[195]

Based on his experience as the Special Court's first prosecutor, David Crane frequently speaks and writes about the "bright red thread" of politics that runs through the pursuit of international justice. "The success or failure of . . . prosecutions," he writes, "hinges on a full understanding of politics and diplomacy to ensure justice at the end of the day. Ignore the role of politics, and there certainly is the possibility of failure, frustrating victims, and stunting the development of modern international criminal law."[196]

Yet, there is also the danger that if prosecutors become too preoccupied with politics or seek to play politics themselves, they run the risk of being pulled into the undertow of the very politics they are trying to navigate. Crane was swept into just such a slipstream in early 2003 when he claimed to have uncovered evidence that Osama bin Laden's al-Qaeda network was buying diamonds in Sierra Leone. These statements, according to the International Crisis Group, a Brussels-based NGO that monitors armed conflicts worldwide, fueled "the perception that the work of the Special Court [was] being used to gather intelligence on international terrorist networks unrelated to its mandate."[197] In explaining why he had repeatedly stated in the media that his team uncovered "very specific evidence of al-Qaeda ties to the blood diamonds of West Africa,"[198] Crane said that he wanted "to bring attention to the fact that if we don't pay attention to some parts of the world, it will cause terrible damage. What I want to tell Europe and the United States is that they cannot ignore this region because it will come and haunt them." He was "morally bound," he added, "to transmit whatever information he [found] to the international community."[199]

Yet Crane told the International Crisis Group that his office was "not looking at al-Qaeda" since there was "no link at all between al-Qaeda and the criminal enterprise [underlying the war in Sierra Leone]. It's just not there, not even close."[200] Why, then, did Crane raise the specter of al-Qaeda's presence in Sierra Leone? Was it, as he claims, to shine a light on a neglected region? Or perhaps to garner favor with and secure the court's continued funding by the United States as it sought to track down al-Qaeda terrorists? Or was the ultimate aim to soften the blow of his unsealing of the Taylor indictment, which he knew would anger the Bush administration? Or was it some combination of the above?

Whatever the answer, the International Crisis Group and other court monitors, as well as members of Crane's staff, worried at the time that his public statements on al-Qaeda, combined with the strong presence of U.S. personnel in the Office of the Prosecutor, were leaving an impression in Sierra Leone that the court was an "American instrument."[201] To his credit, Crane helped dispel such suspicions when he unsealed the Taylor indictment, annoying a number of U.S. officials in Sierra Leone and Washington, DC, and delaying the release of U.S. funds to the court.[202] Still, Crane's penchant for cooperating with American officials on matters that had little or nothing to do with the Special Court's mandate underscores why it is paramount for prosecutors not only *to remain* independent but, just as important, to *be seen as* independent.

The ad hoc and hybrid tribunals owe much of their existence over recent decades to the advocacy of human rights NGOs. During the 1990s, the number of such organizations grew tremendously, and both states and intergovernmental organizations, no longer stymied by superpower rivalries, opened up to them on a scale and in a manner qualitatively different from the preceding Cold War era.[203] But perhaps the greatest example of the newfound influence wielded by human rights NGOs took place at the United Nations Diplomatic Conference of Plenipotentiaries on the Establishment of an International Criminal Court held in Rome from June 15 to July 17, 1998. Eighteen months earlier, the UN General Assembly had requested that the Secretary-General invite NGOs to participate in the Rome Conference "on the understanding that their participation meant attending meetings of its plenary and . . . receiving copies of the official documents, making available their materials to [state] delegates and addressing, through a limited number of their representatives, its opening and/or closing sessions."[204] In the end, officially accredited NGOs outnumbered states 236 to 160.[205]

After five weeks of intense negotiations, the majority of the Rome delegates adopted the statute establishing a permanent International Criminal Court. Tyrants, said Secretary General Kofi Annan, "will no longer be beyond the reach of justice, humanity will be able to defend itself, responding to the worst of human nature, with one of [its] greatest achievements—the rule of law."[206]

Diplomats and human rights activists said that the creation of the International Criminal Court would usher in the end of impunity and launch a new age of accountability. If the jurisdiction of the ad hoc and hybrid tribunals had been restrained by temporal and geographical limitations, the International Criminal Court could potentially pursue war crimes suspects to the ends of the earth. Despite such largeness of vision, the new global court would soon face some sobering realities—not the least of which would be the arduous task of gaining custody of suspected war criminals. And in this regard, it would remain, just like its ad hoc and hybrid predecessors, inextricably bound to the mercy of states.

Following World War II, U.S. Army Counterintelligence Corps agents played a key role in tracking down suspected war criminals in counties occupied by the Allies, particularly Germany, Austria, and Japan. (Courtesy of National Archives and Records Administration)

Beate Klarsfeld insults Chancellor Kurt Georg Kiesinger during a parliamentary meeting on February 4, 1968, in Bonn. She was later arrested for slapping the chancellor. (DPA/LANDOV)

Former Nazi officer Klaus Barbie, handcuffed and surrounded by armed police, leaves the Lyon courthouse, July 4, 1987. Barbie was convicted of crimes against humanity and jailed for life for his actions during World War II. (© ROBERT PRATTA/Reuters/Corbis)

The Simon Wiesenthal Center hung this poster in major German cities in 2013 as part of its campaign to bring surviving Nazi war criminals to justice, almost seventy years after the end of World War II. (Courtesy of Simon Wiesenthal Center)

Louise Arbour is former chief prosecutor for the International
Criminal Tribunal for the Former Yugoslavia and the International
Criminal Tribunal for Rwanda. She indicted the Serbian leader
Slobodan Milosevic in May 1999. (Courtesy of Louise Arbour)

In this January 20, 2002, photo, a Bosnian couple in Sarajevo passes by a poster of Bosnia's two most wanted war crimes suspects, the leader of the Bosnian Serbs, Radovan Karadzic, and his wartime commander, General Ratko Mladic. (AP Photo/ Sava Radovanovic)

A combination of pictures shows former Bosnian Serb leader Radovan Karadzic (right to left) during the start of his initial appearance in the courtroom of the International Criminal Tribunal for the Former Yugoslavia in The Hague, July 31, 2008; in an undated portrait taken in Belgrade when he assumed the identity of a New Age Healer; and attending a parliamentary session in the Republika Srpska in Bosanski Samac, February 13, 1995. (Photo 1: Reuters/Jerry Lampen; photos 2 and 3: Reuters)

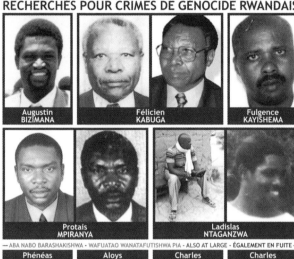

An International Criminal Tribunal for Rwanda poster with photographs of alleged perpetrators wanted for crimes committed during the genocide. (Courtesy of United Nations Mechanism for International Criminal Tribunals)

In 1987, during a visit to Tuol Sleng prison in Phnom Penh, photographer Nic Dunlop came upon a photograph of the prison's former commander Kaing Guek Eav, also known as "Duch." With his own camera, Dunlop snapped a picture of the photograph and carried it with him as he traveled throughout Cambodia in an effort to find the former Khmer Rouge commander. (Nic Dunlop/Panos Pictures)

Charles Taylor is arrested and brought to Sierra Leone to face charges of war crimes and crimes against humanity. (© 2006 United Nations Mathew Elavanalthoduka)

August 27, 2010: Sudan's president, Omar Hassan al-Bashir, arrives at Uhuru Park in Nairobi, Kenya, to celebrate the adoption of a new Kenyan constitution. (© NOOR KHAMIS/ Reuters/Corbis)

Fatou Bensouda is the current chief prosecutor of the International Criminal Court. (Max Koot Studio/Wikimedia Commons)

In November 2006, the leader of the Lord's Resistance Army, Joseph Kony, and his deputy, Vincent Otti, meet with UN humanitarian chief, Jan Egeland, at Ri-Kwamba in the Democratic Republic of the Congo, during the Juba peace talks. (© POOL/Reuters/Corbis)

A CIA secret prison or "black site," known as the "Salt Pit," northeast of Kabul, Afghanistan. (Trevor Paglen)

Newspapers announce the capture of Saddam Hussein in December 2003. (AP Photo/ Evan Vucci)

PART THREE

CHAPTER 8

International Criminal Court

At the Mercy of States

Shortly after 9 A.M. on August 27, 2010, a black limousine bearing Sudan's president, Omar Hassan al-Bashir, pulled into the parade grounds of Uhuru Park, a huge recreational reserve in the heart of the Kenyan capital of Nairobi, where tens of thousands of Kenyans had gathered to celebrate the signing of their country's new constitution, a ceremony presided over by President Mwai Kibaki and his prime minister, Raila Odinga.[1] Inauguration of a new constitution was no small accomplishment in a country that had been torn asunder only a few years earlier by widespread violence and by decades of authoritarian rule, ethnic favoritism, and corruption. Now, congratulatory messages were arriving from around the world.[2]

As al-Bashir stepped out of his limo, a loudspeaker announced his arrival, prompting the crowd to cheer and wave their hands in the air. The Sudanese leader lifted his walking cane triumphantly above his head. With his intelligence chief on one side and Kenya's tourism minister on the other, he strode toward the bleachers and took his place in a row of African dignitaries.[3]

Scenes of al-Bashir's unexpected arrival at Uhuru Park soon flickered on television screens across Kenya as commentators speculated on how a fugitive of the International Criminal Court (ICC), charged with genocide and crimes against humanity in the Darfur region of western Sudan, could be walking free in Nairobi.[4] By the time of al-Bashir's arrival in Nairobi, approximately 300,000 people had already been killed and about 2.5 million displaced from their homes in Darfur, and by the terms of the ICC statute to which Kenya had subscribed, Kenyan authorities were obligated to arrest and transfer the Sudanese president to the court in The Hague.[5]

As the story of his visit gained traction in Kenya and abroad, al-Bashir decided to skip a luncheon with President Kibaki and flew back to Khartoum that afternoon. Meanwhile, reporters with one of Kenya's leading dailies, the *Standard*, discovered that earlier that morning Kenyan officials had closed the country's airspace for al-Bashir's arrival in "a well-coordinated and guarded operation known to only a few."[6] When reporters confronted Kenya's foreign affairs minister, Moses Wetang'ula, about al-Bashir's visit, he was dismissive, suggesting that the government had no duty to arrest him. "He is here in response to our invitation to all our neighbors and the sub-region to attend this historic moment for Kenya," Wetang'ula said. "He is a state guest. You do not harm or embarrass your guest. That is not African."[7] In his responses to the press, Wetang'ula repeatedly referred to a resolution adopted at the 13th African Union summit, held in Sirte, Libya, in July 2009. It called on African leaders "not to cooperate with the ICC . . . in the arrest and surrender" of al-Bashir.[8]

Responses of Western governments to al-Bashir's visit, though swift, were only mildly critical. U.S. President Barack Obama expressed disappointment "that Kenya hosted al-Bashir in defiance of [an] International Criminal Court arrest warrant"[9]—though the United States itself had not ratified the agreement establishing the ICC. The European Union's foreign policy chief, Catherine Ashton, called on Kenya "to respect its obligations under international law to arrest and surrender those indicted by the ICC."[10] Such lukewarm advocacy underscored the West's desire not to appear too harsh toward one of its closest allies in Africa. Kenya, after all, was a base for many of the West's African endeavors, from running billion-dollar humanitarian aid programs to spying on agents of al-Qaeda in nearby Somalia.

In The Hague, ICC judges moved quickly to register their own consternation by filing a complaint against Kenya at the UN Security Council and at the Assembly of States Parties, the court's management and legislative body, of which Kenya is a member.[11] Such protestations, however, fell on deaf ears: neither the Security Council nor the Assembly of States Parties took any action to sanction Kenya.

Even after the commotion caused by his visit to Kenya, President al-Bashir continued to relish his role as an ICC fugitive.[12] An ICC arrest warrant did not get in the way of a three-day visit to China to meet with President Hu Jintao in June 2011, for example.[13] Within weeks of that visit, the 2005 Comprehensive Peace Agreement that had brought a tenuous end to Sudan's devastating north–south civil war was due to take effect, splitting Sudan into two countries.[14] The agreement would make South Sudan its own country, taking with it over two-thirds of Sudan's oil reserves, while the north, which included the Darfur region and remained under al-Bashir's authority, would retain the oil refining and export facilities. Since China purchased 60 percent of Sudanese oil and was Khartoum's top arms supplier, al-Bashir could ill afford to lose Beijing's business.[15]

Al-Bashir also traveled to Chad in May 2013, his fourth trip to that country while under an ICC arrest warrant, to visit a project aimed at fighting global warming. Chad, like Kenya, is a "state party" to the international court—that is, a state that formally accepted the ICC statute—and thus legally obligated to arrest and transfer the Sudanese leader to The Hague. After each of al-Bashir's visits, the ICC issued a finding of noncooperation against Chad. But, these, too, had little effect: neither the Security Council nor the ICC's own governing body, the Assembly of States Parties, took any measures to punish Chad for failing to live up to its legal obligations.[16]

This failure to deal decisively with recalcitrant states like Chad and Kenya points to the Achilles' heel that has afflicted the ICC since it was established in 2002. Writes Richard Dicker of Human Rights Watch:

> The Court, without is own police force, depends on state action for arrest, yet, ironically, it is blamed when governments fail to arrest. [This] paralysis generates an undercurrent of criticism that the Court is inefficient, expensive, and perhaps useless. In a word, the Court, rather than those states that have skirted their legal obligations to cooperate, takes the hit. The damage can be even more pernicious. A high profile suspect at liberty who continues to function in a senior position, ostentatiously conducting official visits to different capitals and hosting high level visitors, flouts the Court's writ in a way that is corrosive to its credibility.[17]

Such impunity, often perpetuated by the ICC's own member states as well as the UN Security Council's failure to act, belies the letter and spirit of the court's founding principle that no one, including a head of state, is above the law.

THE BIRTH OF THE ICC AND AMERICAN EXCEPTIONALISM

The birth of the ICC dates back to the thawing of the Cold War in the early 1990s. On November 22, 1992, the UN General Assembly adopted a resolution calling on the International Law Commission to draft a statute for a permanent world court with global jurisdiction over serious international crimes, including genocide and crimes against humanity. The emergence of the Yugoslavia and Rwanda tribunals in the mid-1990s gave further impetus to this idea. In 1998, with a draft statute in hand, representatives of governments from around the world met in Rome for five weeks to debate and adopt a multinational treaty that would pave the way for the ICC's formal inception in July 2002.[18] The move to create the ICC, its supporters argued, would extend the rule of law throughout the world; and, as a permanent body with a global reach, it would deter mass violence by sending a strong warning to would-be perpetrators. It would also encourage states to investigate and prosecute egregious crimes committed in their territories or by their nationals, for if they did not, the ICC could exercise its jurisdiction. The ICC's focus on individual criminality would also make it similar to the ad hoc international and hybrid tribunals but distinct from the International Court of Justice, which was established in 1945 to settle legal disputes between states and advise international agencies on legal questions. Moreover, the creation of the ICC would lessen but not entirely replace the need for ad hoc and hybrid tribunals, according to legal scholars Ronald Slye and Beth Van Schaack. They see three situations where ad hoc and hybrid tribunals may continue to be necessary. The first situation involves crimes committed before July 1, 2002, the date of the signing of the Rome Statute, establishing the ICC. The second involves "crimes committed within the territory of, and by nationals of, states that are not parties to the ICC (unless the UN Security Council refers the matter.)"[19] And the third involves crimes—such as terrorism—that are currently outside the purview of the ICC.

If the Nuremberg and Tokyo tribunals were the first modern courts overseen by "stern-looking white men in robes and military uniforms," then the ICC would be a "post-modern" court, legal scholars Luc Reydams and Jan Wouters have argued.[20] The work of its creation came not from the victors of war but from the efforts of a coalition of NGOs, some promoting gender justice and the rights of victims. The new court's jurisdiction would be "complementary," meaning that cases would be transferred to the court only if a state is unwilling or unable to meet certain due-process requirements. The ICC's aim would be not only punitive but also restorative. Victims, for example, would have unprecedented procedural rights, including their own legal counsel, and the right to receive reparations and to be heard by judicial authorities regarding the decision to authorize an investigation or admit a case.[21]

The creation of the ICC was fraught with controversy. While many human rights activists and diplomats viewed the new court as a revolutionary institution, a number of powerful states, including three of the five members of the UN Security Council (China, Russia, and the United States) balked at the notion that their own political and military leaders might fall under the court's jurisdiction. The United States, which had pioneered the establishment of international tribunals from Nuremberg to the contemporary ad hoc and hybrid tribunals, would, at various times over the next decade and more, openly try to sabotage the ICC, work to dilute its authority to accommodate American interests, or selectively support ICC investigations that targeted suspects Washington wanted to marginalize or put out of commission.

In his memoir, *All the Missing Souls*, David Scheffer, the United States' war crimes ambassador during the Clinton administration, provides a first-hand account of his role as Washington's chief negotiator at the Rome conference and how U.S. exceptionalism manifested itself in Washington's attempts to undermine the ICC's creation. Washington supported a global war crimes court, but only as long as it could ensure that the United States and its allies stood beyond the reach of prosecutorial scrutiny as perpetrators of war crimes. Scheffer writes:

> The siren of [U.S.] exceptionalism enveloped the entire enterprise of the International Criminal Court on my watch and dictated the far more extreme policies under the George W. Bush administration. By "exceptionalism" in the realm of international law, I mean that the United States has a tradition of leading other nations in global treaty-making endeavors to create a more law-abiding international community, only to seek exceptions to the new rules for the United States because of its constitutional heritage of defending individual rights, its military responsibilities worldwide requiring freedom to act in times of war, its superior economy demanding free trade one day and labor protection and environmental concessions the next day, or just stark nativist insularity. The [American] cynics of international law point to the realism of how nations act in their own self-interest. The United States, they argue, is a different nation of extraordinary attributes that simply cannot be lowered (or elevated) to the same level of performance as other nations.[22]

At the heart of the issue was the Pentagon's anxiety that an international court exercising its jurisdiction on the territory of any state that was party to the treaty might try to prosecute U.S. soldiers deployed to fight there. Traditionally, the United States enters into status of forces agreements, or SOFAs, with countries where it deploys soldiers. SOFAs ensure that U.S. military or federal courts handle all criminal investigations and prosecutions of soldiers and not the courts of the country where the alleged crimes have been committed. For the Department of Defense this arrangement was sacrosanct, which Scheffer contends left him little wiggle room for compromise with negotiators from other countries.

In the early 1990s President Bill Clinton had pledged support for a permanent war crimes tribunal, but as administration officials moved deeper into the weeds they began to carve out zones of impunity that would place American conduct beyond international legal scrutiny. In Rome, Scheffer, as instructed by Washington, sought to constrain the ICC's authority by allowing its chief prosecutor jurisdiction to launch investigations only when approved by the UN Security Council. This provision would give the United States and the other four permanent council members that enjoy veto powers (China, Russia, France, and the United Kingdom) the ability to preempt ICC investigations that were, in their eyes, undesirable. Human rights activists and pro-ICC states argued, successfully, that this prosecutorial restraint would emasculate the international court by putting it under the thumb of the dominant powers.

As a final vote on the Rome Statute neared, Scheffer stayed in constant touch with his superiors back in the State Department. During one phone call, Secretary of State Madeleine Albright told him that the administration had soured on the negotiations. Albright, who had been a driving force when it came to the creation of the Yugoslavia and Rwanda tribunals, now signaled her opposition to the very concept of the ICC. Frustrated with the United States' waning leverage in Rome, Albright blurted out to Scheffer: "What can we do to blow up the entire conference?" Scheffer was shocked. "I was so stunned I hesitated, but then told her that the U.S. delegation could simply walk out and return to Washington or I could try to stall the endgame by seeking an extension [of the negotiations]. . . . We chose the latter option, and I lobbied for resuming the conference in September or October so that I could reach a more accommodating position in Washington and structure some compromises with other delegations."[23] Scheffer's stalling maneuver failed, however, and on July 17, the Rome Statute of the International Criminal Court was adopted by a vote of 120 to 7, with 21 countries abstaining.

Although the United States eventually signed the Rome Statute in December 2000, President Clinton dragged his heels when it came to getting the treaty approved by the Senate—a prerequisite for U.S. ratification of international agreements.[24] After George W. Bush took office, his ambassador to the United Nations, John Bolton, announced that the United States had no intention of joining the ICC and ratifying the Rome Statute.[25]

The Bush administration's recalcitrance toward the ICC did not end there. At the prodding of Bolton, Washington threatened to cut off military assistance to dozens of states if they failed to guarantee U.S. citizens immunity from the court's jurisdiction, and required that they sign so-called Article 98 agreements. Also known as bilateral immunity agreements, these arrangements rest on Article 98 of the Rome Statute, which prohibits the court from proceeding with a request for surrender of a suspect if it would require the state in question "to act inconsistently with its obligations under international agreements."[26] The Bush administration interpreted this article to mean that its citizens cannot be transferred to the ICC by any state that has signed a bilateral agreement with the United States prohibiting such a transfer, even if the state is a member of the Rome Statute. By 2006, the Bush administration had managed to persuade more than 100 countries into signing such agreements.

In 2003 and 2004, the Bush administration also won Security Council resolutions immunizing American soldiers dispatched to UN peacekeeping operations from potential prosecution at the ICC. To anchor this exemption in law, the United States persuaded the Security Council to invoke Article 16 of the Rome Statute to discourage potential investigations into American activities related to the "war on terror." Article 16 allows investigations and prosecutions to be suspended for a year at a time. It was meant to provide UN diplomats with a tool to temporarily suspend ongoing cases deemed to threaten international peace and security. But U.S. diplomats at the UN successfully argued that Article 16 could and should be invoked preemptively to prevent, for at least a year, any investigation of American war crimes suspects. In 2004, Washington abandoned its effort to win another year-long exemption following strong UN opposition to such an act of American exceptionalism in the wake of the Abu Ghraib prisoner-abuse scandal.[27]

American distrust of actions the court might take hit its apex under the Bush administration and Republican Congress, which in August 2002 passed a bill, the American Service-Members' Protection Act, which authorized the president to use "all means necessary and appropriate to bring about the release of any US or allied personnel being detained or imprisoned by, on behalf of, or at the request of the

International Criminal Court."[28] The act was soon nicknamed the The Hague Invasion Act, since the freeing of U.S. citizens by force would require an invasion of The Hague, the seat of the court and of the Dutch government.

By the start of President Bush's second term, however, Washington's anti-ICC policy began to soften in significant and unexpected ways. Just months after an administration official vowed that the United States would take no steps to legitimize the ICC, it opted not to block a Security Council referral of the Darfur conflict that primarily implicated the Sudanese government of President al-Bashir. Later, Bush officials indicated that despite the constraints the American Service-Members' Protection Act placed on U.S. cooperation with the court, they would consider ICC requests for assistance when it came to Darfur. The Obama administration extended this kind of limited cooperation by aiding in the hunt for Lord's Resistance Army leader Joseph Kony, accused by the ICC of crimes against humanity in northern Uganda, and by sometimes leveling criticism against states that failed to live up to their obligation to arrest President al-Bashir, even as the United States accepted no responsibility to take action itself. Additionally, in January 2013, President Obama signed into law the Department of State Rewards Program and Technological Corrections Act, extending the State Department's existing rewards program, which applied to those indicted by the International Criminal Tribunal for the former Yugoslavia, International Criminal Tribunal for Rwanda, and Special Court for Sierra Leone, to include rewards leading to the arrest, transfer, or conviction of foreign nationals sought by the ICC. "To be clear," Secretary of State John Kerry later wrote about the initiative, "this is not a dead-or-alive bounty program. Information must lead to the secure arrest, transfer, or conviction of these [war crimes suspects] in a court of law. We want these men to look into the eyes of their victims and answer for their actions."[29]

If the U.S. government no longer issued scathing attacks against the court, Obama showed no interest in actually joining the court and thus subjecting U.S. nationals to its jurisdiction. On the other hand, if U.S. engagement with the ICC had the potential to aid the court's pursuit of suspects, it also promised political dividends for Washington.[30] A clear indication of this self-interested engagement occurred in June 2010 when President Obama sent a large delegation to the ICC's conference in Kampala, Uganda, to review the Rome Statute.[31] One of the United States' goals in Kampala was again to ensure that no American military or political leader would ever face charges before the court.

A major agenda item at the review conference was to negotiate a definition of the crime of aggression as an amendment to the Rome Statute. Sixty-five years earlier at Nuremberg, U.S. and Allied prosecutors made the crime of aggression, which criminalizes the illegal invasion of other countries, the central charge against leaders of the Nazi regime whose military rampage devastated Europe. Now the prospect of incorporating the crime of aggression in the Rome Statute sparked grave concerns for the United States (as well as some of its Western allies), in view of the country's penchant for overseas interventions. Although it was not a party to the Rome Statute, U.S. delegates nevertheless left their mark on the negotiations by securing compromises that effectively protected U.S. officials from future prosecution concerning the crime of aggression.

ICC backers, such as the broad-based Coalition for the International Criminal Court, hailed Obama's cooperation with the court and called his reelection for a second term "very significant for international justice."[32] Many observers have remained skeptical of U.S. intentions, however. "To use the court as an adjunct to soft power makes sense for the U.S.," Courtenay Griffiths, the defense attorney for former President Charles Taylor of Liberia, told the New York Times. "It's cost effective. If you can remove a warlord through the court, it's a lot cheaper and more acceptable than using force."[33] Or as Philippe Sands, author of Lawless World: America and the Making and Breaking of Global Rules, put it: "The U.S. wants to be at the table when the ICC doesn't touch on issues [it considers] of vital interest. I suspect the U.S. position would change direction rather quickly if issues of vital interest began to be investigated."[34]

THE FOUNDATIONS OF THE ICC

The ICC's founding document, the Rome Statute, sets out the legal framework for the court's operations, empowering it to investigate and prosecute allegations of war crimes, genocide, and crimes against humanity committed on the territory of any member state or by a national of any member state after July 1, 2002.[35] As a court of last resort, the ICC can only exercise its jurisdiction when national courts are unwilling or unable to investigate or prosecute serious international crimes. Like most contemporary ad hoc UN tribunals, it is not bound by amnesties granted at the national level. As an independent body, it is funded primarily by its member states.

288 I Chapter Eight

The Rome Statute details three trigger mechanisms enabling the ICC to open an investigation. Although the ICC is nominally independent of the UN, the Security Council was granted the authority to refer a particular armed conflict or country situation to the court under Chapter VII of the UN Charter. But much to the chagrin of the United States, the Security Council does not enjoy a monopoly here. A state party can refer to the ICC chief prosecutor crimes associated with an armed conflict on the territory of any other state party or on its own territory (the latter is called a self-referral). Under a Security Council or state referral, once the prosecutor has determined that crimes have taken place, he or she can proceed with a formal investigation and then request that the pretrial chamber issue either arrest warrants or summons for particular suspects. Unlike the ad hoc tribunals for Rwanda and the former Yugoslavia, the ICC does not "indict" suspects but moves directly to issuing arrest warrants or summons when the pretrial chamber accepts an application from the Office of the Prosecutor. Finally, the chief prosecutor can invoke *proprio motu* powers (that is, his or her own authority) by initiating an investigation on the territory of a state party.

The United States has long complained that the ICC prosecutor possesses far too much power, which could become a political weapon if wielded by a politically motivated or rogue prosecutor. Yet at Rome, pro-ICC countries accommodated state sovereignty concerns in four key ways. First, for the prosecutor to exercise *proprio motu* powers and formally open a new country situation investigation, he or she must secure approval from an ICC pretrial chamber that determines whether there is sufficient evidence to proceed. Second, a pretrial chamber must vet the evidentiary basis of any prosecutorial request for arrest warrants or summons. Third, the prosecutor's authority is further checked by the complementarity principle, which defers prosecutions to states unless they are unwilling or unable to carry out their own prosecutions. Fourth, under Article 16 of the Statute, the Security Council can suspend any ongoing investigation or trial for renewable one-year periods if they are deemed to threaten international peace and security.

ICC trials are conducted under a hybrid of common law, as practiced in the United States and the United Kingdom, and civil law, as practiced in many European countries. Eighteen judges organized in three chambers—a pretrial chamber, a trial chamber, and an appeals chamber—carry out the judicial functions of the court. They are elected for nine-year terms by the member-countries of the court. Candidates must be nationals of states party to the Rome Statute, and no two judges may be nationals of the same state. Trials are supposed to be public, but portions of proceedings are sometimes closed to guard the identity of protected witnesses or other confidential or sensitive evidence. Without the means to enforce arrest warrants themselves, the ICC and its chief prosecutor are at the mercy of states. When engaging with states, the ICC prosecutor must be a diplomat par excellence, appealing to their moral instincts to bring war crime suspects to justice, while at the same time not underestimating the political constraints that may hinder states from doing so.[36] It is on the shifting sands of state self-interest and vacillating international commitment that the ICC prosecutor must build global support for arrests. If this task has proven difficult for the Yugoslavia and Rwanda tribunal prosecutors, it is even more challenging for the ICC prosecutor, who must engage with many more global actors—a high-wire act with an uncertain ending. As the ICC's first chief prosecutor, Luis Moreno-Ocampo, put it: "For prosecutors political consensus is a real luxury—it is our champagne."[37]

The ICC chief prosecutor is the court's driving force and its face to the outside world. "It is the prosecutor," writes Luc Côté, a legal scholar who previously worked for the prosecution at the Rwanda and Sierra Leone tribunals, "who knocks on the door of various states, various international organizations, to request their aid. . . . It is the prosecutor the most notorious 'war criminals' have to fear. The prosecutor's power over individuals is considerable and, as a result, the . . . prosecutor has emerged as a major new figure in international politics."[38] Indeed, the ICC's reputation largely hinges on the chief prosecutor's judgments and behavior. "The decisions and public statements of the prosecutor will do more than anything else to establish the reputation of the court," then UN Secretary-General Kofi Annan opined, shortly before Moreno-Ocampo was appointed the court's first prosecutor in 2003.[39]

An Argentine lawyer who served as assistant prosecutor in his country's "Trial of the Juntas" in the mid-1980s and who later taught criminal law at the University of Buenos Aires, Moreno-Ocampo spent nine years at the ICC, stepping down when his term ended in June 2012. He was replaced by his deputy, Fatou Bensouda, a Gambian lawyer who had worked previously at the International Criminal Tribunal for Rwanda in Arusha, Tanzania. Moreno-Ocampo was a magnet for critics. His overbearing and erratic management style resulted in the resignations of a number of his senior lawyers and investigators, who felt that their own work was undervalued and found that his penchant for the limelight and extravagant claims chafed against their own more discreet work ethic.[40]

International human rights organizations and even ICC judges have often admonished the Office of the Prosecutor for its failure to get boots on the ground quickly enough to gather and preserve vital evidence, which, in turn, undermined a number of their cases.[41] In December 2012, for example, a trial chamber acquitted a Congolese militia leader, Matthieu Ngudjolo, after finding that the evidence presented by the prosecution did not support his guilt for the alleged crimes beyond reasonable doubt.[42] In early 2013, after a key witness recanted his earlier testimony, the ICC prosecutor withdrew charges against one of six officials charged with orchestrating post-election violence in Kenya in 2007–08. This setback followed an ICC pretrial chamber's early dismissal of charges against two other Kenyan officials because of insufficient evidence. The ICC's work in Kenya suffered its biggest blow when lack of sufficient evidence compelled the ICC prosecutor to withdraw the case against Kenyan President Uhuru Kenyatta in December 2014.

African leaders, meanwhile, have argued that the ICC and its chief prosecutor have eyes only for African crimes and a blind spot for crimes committed elsewhere in the world. "Africans," write Sudan experts Julie Flint and Alex de Waal, "were once the passionate supporters of the ICC: half of the countries that first ratified the Rome Statute were African. Now, they, too, are having second thoughts. They don't see the Court dealing with cases outside of Africa. They worry that warrants like those against al-Bashir and the Congolese opposition leader Jean-Pierre Bemba . . . may be turning criminal prosecution into a selective political instrument."[43]

Speaking in Ocampo's defense, then Deputy Prosecutor Fatou Bensouda took issue with this criticism in an interview with *New African* magazine in 2012: "What offends me the most when I hear criticism about this so called African bias is how quick we are to focus on the words and propaganda of a few powerful, influential individuals, and to forget about the millions of anonymous people who suffer from their crimes."[44] Still, even ardent ICC supporters like Aryeh Neier, former president of the Open Society Foundations, questioned the wisdom of the prosecutor's tunnel vision when it came to African prosecutions: "By not initiating prosecutions elsewhere during the Court's early years, Moreno-Ocampo provided inadvertent ballast to those Africans intent on provoking resentment against an institution they perceived as fostering disproportionally on African malfeasance."[45] The ICC's singular focus on African atrocities would in turn form the key line of attack that several African leaders would use against the court for years to come. At the time of writing, all of the cases before the ICC still involve defendants from African countries, although the chief prosecutor has initiated preliminary investigations in other parts of the world. In the pages ahead we examine the ICC's investigations of serious international crimes in Uganda, Sudan, Libya, Côte d'Ivoire, Democratic Republic of the Congo, and Kenya. Some states have cooperated, while others have been openly hostile or ambivalent to ICC jurisdiction. Still others have refused, or found it difficult in light of internal political realities, to cooperate voluntarily with the court or to appear to be doing so.

UGANDA AND THE ELUSIVE JOSEPH KONY

January 29, 2004, was a seminal day for the ICC and its chief prosecutor, Luis Moreno-Ocampo. With Ugandan President Yoweri Museveni by his side, the prosecutor announced at a press conference in London that the target of the court's inaugural investigation would be the Lord's Resistance Army (LRA), a notorious Ugandan rebel group.[46] Since the ICC formally began operations in July 2002, it had focused on the institutional challenges of building a court from scratch. Now, a year and a half later, Moreno-Ocampo was eager to demonstrate the ICC's relevance by moving quickly in pursuit of criminal accountability. "For the ICC, the Uganda referral appeared to be a great first opportunity," writes Benjamin Schiff in *Building the International Criminal Court*. "The conflict situation had produced massive casualties and civilian displacement, the alleged suspects were internationally reviled, and the friendly government's request for help avoided a clash with sovereign prerogatives."[47] But, as the nascent court would soon discover, the Uganda referral arrived with baggage bulging with political and procedural conundrums the ICC hadn't anticipated.

Uganda's conflict in its north extends back to colonial times, when southern and northern tribal groups clashed over ethnic prerogatives, religion, and economic interests. In the mid-1980s, with the backing of the Sudanese government, a group of disaffected government officials and soldiers formed a rebel organization, initially called the Holy Spirit Movement, under the leadership of Alice Lakwena, who called for President Museveni's demise and the overthrow of the Ugandan government. Lakwena eventually amassed thousands of followers and led them south on a marauding campaign to capture the Ugandan capital of Kampala. Government forces in 1987 defeated the rebel group in swamplands some 130 kilometers from the capital, but Lakwena escaped.[48]

Soon after that defeat, Joseph Kony, a self-proclaimed messianic prophet who claimed to be related to Lakwena, began to build the Lord's Resistance Army, a highly structured rebel group that would terrorize northern Uganda for more than two decades.[49] As a young man, Kony invented his own belief system and rituals, drawing on a mix of Christianity, Islam, and animist beliefs. He claimed to have apocalyptic visions, and declared himself the liberator of the Acholi people, the principal tribal group in northern Uganda.

Early on, Kony experienced jarring rejections from Acholi leaders. The first LRA operations against the Ugandan army failed, largely because Kony failed to muster popular support from the very people he wished to liberate. Lacking a popular base and resources, Kony fled to southern Sudan in 1994, where he received food, medical supplies, and weapons from the Khartoum government of Omar al-Bashir.[50] Operating from base camps there, LRA fighters struck fear in the civilian population of northern Uganda by carrying out mutilations, killings, and forced recruitment of child soldiers. Once abducted, children were made to serve as fighters, porters, and sex slaves. New conscripts were often forced to commit atrocities as soon as they were abducted to make it more difficult for them to contemplate return. Between 1994 and 2007, the LRA abducted more than 20,000 children, who constituted up to 80 percent of the rebel group's membership.[51]

Throughout most of the conflict, the Ugandan government's response to the LRA fluctuated between military action—which often resulted in serious violations of human rights, including killings, torture, and rape—and a promise of amnesty as an incentive for LRA members to surrender, which met with some limited success.[52] Then, in late 2003, Museveni tried a new tack. Having no feasible way of capturing the rebel leader and his top commanders, the Ugandan president instructed his staff to begin informal conversations with ICC prosecutors.[53] They found a receptive audience. Not only would a self-referral help the prosecutor avoid a *proprio motu* proceeding, it would also offer an opportunity, in ICC scholar Benjamin Schiff's words, to "help build the credibility of the Court, since critics often wondered what the chances were that the ICC would gain necessary cooperation from situation states."[54] Museveni later sent a confidential letter to the ICC chief prosecutor officially referring the situation in northern Uganda to the court.[55]

Once the referral was announced, Moreno-Ocampo and his small staff confronted a series of complex and bedeviling issues. The first problem was raised by some of the ICC's greatest backers: the dangers of cultivating too close a relationship with the Ugandan government. International human rights organizations hailed the Ugandan referral as a breakthrough, but expressed concern that the joint public appearance of the prosecutor with President Museveni presented a troubling image of the ICC's dependence on state power and deference to a leader whose troops had also committed war crimes during their two-decade pursuit of the LRA. After calling the referral a "first step" toward ending injustice worldwide, Amnesty International went on to warn that the prosecutor's investigation "must be part of a comprehensive plan to end impunity for such crimes regardless of which side committed them,"[56] while Human Rights Watch urged the ICC prosecutor not to "ignore the crimes that Ugandan government troops allegedly have committed."[57]

Underlying these criticisms was concern that if the court failed to investigate alleged government atrocities it could potentially undermine its own legitimacy in the eyes of victims and others as an institution of impartial justice. That a clear majority of people in northern Uganda wanted Ugandan army officers investigated and prosecuted for their crimes was confirmed in each of three population-based surveys conducted in the area in 2005, 2007, and 2010 by University of California, Berkeley, researchers.[58]

The likelihood that the ICC under Moreno-Ocampo would ever bring charges against Ugandan army officers for crimes committed in the north grew increasingly remote, however. In the court's defense, some in the prosecutor's office argued that the worst government abuses took place before the court's temporal jurisdiction began on July 1, 2002, and those violations that occurred *after* that date did not appear to be of sufficient gravity to warrant prosecution. What may have been a legitimate legal reason not to charge army officers was not sufficiently explained by Moreno-Ocampo; nor would it have been likely to persuade skeptics who viewed the prosecutor's sole focus on rebel wrongdoing as a *quid pro quo* for the government's referral and cooperation.

Many Ugandans were also highly suspicious of President Museveni's motives in referring the Ugandan situation to the ICC. Some saw the referral as a strategic move to reassert the president's international credentials after a failed 2002 military offensive that was supposed to drive the LRA from its bases in southern Sudan, capture Joseph Kony, and rescue thousands of abducted children. In reality the year-long operation made matters worse, displacing hundreds of thousands of people and prompting the LRA to *increase* their abductions of civilians, which climbed to nearly 10,000 by the end of that year.[59] Ultimately, Museveni would play the court both ways, alternately calling for the prosecution of the LRA leadership in The Hague and then letting the LRA know that he might end his cooperation with the court if the rebel group would negotiate an end to hostilities.[60]

Some Ugandan and international aid organizations were also critical of the ICC's intervention in Uganda for another reason. They claimed that the court's pursuit of the rebel group would provoke new LRA atrocities and doom any hope for peace. James Otto, a human rights activist in the northern town of Gulu, railed against the court: "The timing of the ICC is bad. It has no protection mechanism [for victims]. We have our own traditional justice system. The international system despises it, but it works. There is a balance in the community that cannot be found in the briefcase of the white man."[61] Other activists argued that even the specter of issuing arrest warrants against the LRA leadership could derail an amnesty process that had already lured over 6,000 LRA fighters out of the bush and undermine peace negotiations underway between Joseph Kony and Betty Bigombe, a Ugandan government representative who, like Kony, was an Acholi.

Meanwhile, children's rights groups feared that the ICC's presence in northern Uganda could jeopardize the safety of children in LRA captivity or heighten the risk of further abductions.[62] In a press release issued shortly after the referral, the Kampala office of Save the Children worried that arrest warrants might prompt "the LRA leadership [to] apply even more strict discipline to prevent [children] from escaping."[63] But some of the harshest criticism came from Father Carlos Rodriguez, a Spanish priest and activist who had engaged in private peace negotiations with LRA commanders since the later 1990s. "The issuing of . . . international arrest warrants," he said, "would practically close once and for all the path to peaceful negotiation as a means to end this long war, crushing whatever little progress has been made during these years. Obviously, nobody can convince the leaders of the rebel movement to come to the negotiating table and at the same time tell them that they will appear in court to be prosecuted."[64]

Whatever the merits of these accusations—and history, as we'll see, did not bear many of them out—such antipathy placed Moreno-Ocampo in a difficult position in his bid for political consensus both from the Ugandan state and from the victims of the war in northern

Uganda, whom he often invoked as key constituencies of the ICC. On an operational level, he risked losing the support of local leaders and organizations, entities that would normally act as his intermediaries, quietly assisting his investigators to secure evidence and speak to potential witnesses. From a public relations standpoint, he had to tread carefully lest he completely alienate the local community and religious leaders who doubted his motives. Sensing these perils, the prosecutor chose to mollify his detractors by hosting a series of meetings with Acholi leaders at the ICC headquarters in The Hague. After one such meeting, he suggested that if the right conditions prevailed he could suspend the planned prosecutions. "As soon as there is a solution to end the violence and if the prosecution is not serving the interest of justice, then my duty is to stop investigation and prosecution," he said.[65]

Meanwhile, behind the scenes, Moreno-Ocampo was presenting evidence of LRA atrocities to the pretrial chamber and requesting sealed arrest warrants for Joseph Kony and his top four commanders. The prosecutor elected to pursue sealed warrants to protect potential witnesses from possible retaliatory attacks by the LRA, and to avoid undermining ongoing investigations. On July 8, 2005, the pretrial chamber issued the warrants, asserting that the court had "reasonable grounds to believe" that Joseph Kony and four of his top commanders—Vincent Otti, Raska Lukwiya, Okot Odhiambo, and Dominic Ongwen—had ordered the commission of numerous crimes against humanity and war crimes in Uganda since July 1, 2002, the starting date for ICC jurisdiction.[66]

Though the warrants were sealed, a high-level UN bureaucrat named Ibrahim Gambari broke ranks and told a news conference in Nairobi that the ICC had issued a warrant for Kony's arrest. A week later, the Ugandan defense minister, Amama Mbabazi, made a similar announcement in Kampala. With the information now public, the pretrial chamber formally unsealed the warrants that October, a move that triggered a firestorm of protests in northern Uganda. "This is like a blow to the peace process," said Archbishop Odama of the northern Uganda's Gulu Catholic Archdiocese. "The process of confidence-building has been moving well, but now the LRA will look at whoever gets in contact with them as an agent of the ICC."[67] Museveni's chief mediator, Betty Bigombe, complained, "There is now no hope of getting them to surrender. I have told the court that they have rushed too much."[68] Justice Onega, the chair of the Ugandan Amnesty Commission, was equally outraged. The arrest warrants, he said, would only encourage the LRA leadership to act as "desperately as a wounded buffalo."[69]

Nevertheless, in late 2005, in a move that surprised many observers, the LRA withdrew its forces from southern Sudan, crossed the Nile, and reassembled in the remote Garamba National Park in the Democratic Republic of the Congo, some 500 miles from northern Uganda. The retreat was due to several factors. Over the previous year, Ugandan forces had launched several attacks on Kony's bases in southern Sudan, which had weakened the LRA's military capabilities inside Uganda. More significantly, when hostilities ceased between Khartoum and the Sudanese People's Liberation Movement (SPLM), al-Bashir's forces withdrew from southern Sudan, depriving the LRA of the steady flow of weapons and materiel it had enjoyed for years.[70] At the same time, the SPLM increased pressure on the LRA to leave its territory. The final inducement for the LRA departure came that October, the same month in which the warrants were unsealed, when Khartoum signed a memorandum of understanding with the ICC agreeing to cooperate with arrest warrants issued against LRA commanders.[71]

Now isolated in the jungles of northeastern Congo, facing mounting defections, and cut off from a steady supply of weapons, training, and transport, the LRA leadership finally capitulated—or so it appeared. In December 2005, Kony's second-in-command and spokesperson, Vincent Otti, told the BBC that he and his fellow commanders wanted to end their rebellion and were willing to cooperate with the ICC so long as Ugandan army officers also faced justice in The Hague.[72] This turn of events prompted Father Carlos Rodriguez to backtrack on his earlier denunciation of the court's presence in northern Uganda. Referring specifically to the high level of LRA defections, he suggested that "the ICC might not be so discouraging as we thought. . . . The LRA will only reduce violence out of pressure and Sudan has changed its attitude because of the ICC. They are concerned about being prosecuted. It gives a powerful signal. . . . Now that Sudan is not involved, it forces the LRA to talk about peace."[73]

Sensing the LRA's vulnerability, Museveni held out both a stick and a carrot to the rebel leaders. In April 2006, he announced that those individuals subject to ICC warrants would not be entitled to amnesty. But a month later, he raised the stakes, offering the LRA leaders "safety" if they agreed to participate in peace negotiations within sixty days.[74] This comment sparked a clear response from Moreno-Ocampo, who reminded the governments of Uganda, Sudan, and Democratic Republic of Congo that they were legally obligated to execute the arrest warrants against Kony and his top commanders. "The defendants could challenge the admissibility of the arrest warrants," he said. "But the prosecutor can do nothing. The case is in the hands of the judges."[75]

Moreno-Ocampo's reminder to Uganda and its neighbors of their legal duty to arrest Kony and his commanders was an early indication that the chief prosecutor was slowly moving toward a more adversarial stance in pressing for state cooperation. The politics of conciliation, explained a prominent human rights NGO official who had watched Moreno-Ocampo since he began his ICC tenure, was damaging "the prosecutor in the eyes of a lot of human rights organizations because it is like you are not acting like a prosecutor, you are acting like a diplomat."[76] In the eyes of many pro-ICC NGO representatives, Moreno-Ocampo appeared particularly ineffective when compared to the hard-charging Carla Del Ponte, who had served as the chief prosecutor of the Yugoslavia and Rwanda tribunals.

But such comparisons sometimes missed the mark as they ignored the institutional and political constraints that were placed on the nascent court and its chief prosecutor in the early years. Operating from a less robust legal foundation than the Yugoslavia and Rwanda tribunals, Moreno-Ocampo had a strong incentive, at least initially, to avoid alienating states whose cooperation he would need to facilitate his investigations and execute arrest warrants. Indeed, what was ostensibly given to the ad hoc tribunals, by virtue of the Security Council mandate that binds all UN members to support these tribunals, had to be earned by the ICC through its campaign for universal ratification of the Rome Statute. At times, Moreno-Ocampo's conciliatory approach was not only a strategic, non-threatening way to cultivate state party support, it also served to encourage support from influential states that had not yet ratified the agreement, such as the United States, that were wary of a crusading prosecutor too eager to challenge state authority.[77]

If Museveni faced difficulties arresting Kony, then Moreno-Ocampo's challenge was far greater. The enduring problem was his lack of enforcement powers, coupled with the ability of LRA suspects to elude capture by simply decamping and slipping deep into the rainforests of northeastern Congo. In mid-2006, Moreno-Ocampo's prospects of capturing Kony were further eroded by Museveni's decision to open peace talks with the LRA rather than redouble his efforts to track down the rebel leaders. As the International Crisis Group wrote at the time: "Bereft of a stick long enough to reach Kony, Museveni saw little choice but to opt for a carrot."[78]

In fact, Museveni's overture gave Kony an added incentive to return to the bargaining table, especially given the LRA's loss of support from the Sudanese government. For Kony, negotiating with Museveni also offered hope of winning a formal amnesty, even if the Ugandan president had no legal right to usurp the ICC's arrest warrants. Meanwhile, Kony and his top commanders, with the help of legal counsel provided by their supporters in the Acholi diaspora, had been boning up on the ICC's rules and procedures, looking for "escape clauses" that could apply to them as well as for ways to turn the ICC threat to their advantage. To begin with, a provision in the Rome Statute provided that a pretrial chamber could withdraw arrest warrants and defer cases back to a domestic judiciary if it were determined that the latter was genuinely able and willing to prosecute. Similarly, the chief prosecutor could, under Article 53, halt a case if doing so was found to be "in the interests of justice."[79] Finally, the LRA leaders knew that the Security Council could always invoke its authority to suspend the Uganda investigation or prosecution for renewable one-year periods.[80] Kony and Museveni thus had several incentives to give the chief prosecutor the cold shoulder and work together to pursue a negotiated peace.

Formal peace talks between the LRA and the Ugandan government began in the southern Sudanese city of Juba in July 2006[81] and sputtered on and off for the better part of a year. On some occasions the LRA delegation stormed out of meetings, claiming that the Ugandan army had attacked their forces. On others, they refused to sign specific agenda items or agreements until the ICC warrants were dropped.[82] During one of these interludes, UN Under-Secretary-General for Humanitarian Affairs and Emergency Relief Coordinator Jan Egeland met with Kony and Otti in hopes of pushing the talks forward. Flanked by Kalashnikov-toting fighters in T-shirts and Wellington boots, Kony walked out of the jungle and shook hands with the UN envoy. Egeland pressed the LRA leader to free the women and children, and the sick and wounded, in his ranks. Kony, speaking through an Acholi interpreter, insisted he didn't have anyone who fit that description and instead pressed Egeland to intervene to cancel the ICC arrest warrants.[83]

Back in The Hague, Moreno-Ocampo watched as events unfolded in Juba, trying neither to interfere with the peace talks nor to relinquish the court's prerogative to prosecute the LRA suspects one day. It was certainly not helpful having high-level officials like Egeland engaging with Kony and Otti, and potentially undermining the ICC's legitimacy.

But in his public statements, the prosecutor balanced reminders that the arrest warrants remained in effect with hints that they could be suspended or withdrawn consistent with the Rome Statute.[84]

By appearing to remain above the fray of the Juba talks, Moreno-Ocampo took a very different approach from that taken by the Yugoslavia tribunal Chief Prosecutor Richard Goldstone during the Dayton peace talks that brought an end to the Bosnian war in 2005. For both Moreno-Ocampo and Goldstone, the respective peace talks potentially threatened their nascent tribunals. While Goldstone sought to safeguard the Yugoslavia tribunal's authority by strategically issuing indictments of Serb and Croat suspects during the three-week Dayton talks and by criticizing a potential amnesty for some indicted suspects,[85] Moreno-Ocampo initially tried to protect the ICC's standing by remaining in the background, apparently in the hopes that a collapse of the fragile Uganda peace negotiations would not be blamed on an overreaching prosecutor.[86]

But that stance changed noticeably in June 2007 when Moreno-Ocampo delivered a forceful keynote address on the role of justice in promoting peace at an international conference in Nuremberg, Germany. He publicly abandoned his diplomatic demeanor and openly called for the immediate arrest of Kony and his top commanders. As one veteran international human rights activist observed, the prosecutor had come to "the realization that the softy approach wasn't really getting anywhere."[87]

Symbolically, Nuremberg, as the seat of the post-WWII trials, served Moreno-Ocampo's purposes well. In his address he embraced prosecutions as a key to lasting peace, rejected any compromise on accountability, and criticized the tepid support he was receiving from states party to the Rome Statute. In response to the claim that the ICC was threatening the peace, he shifted the blame to fugitives, such as Kony, and the lack of international commitment to arrest them. That failure, he said, "is the real threat to enduring peace." Lifting the LRA warrants, the prosecutor warned, would be a capitulation to blackmail, given Kony's threat to resume violence if he did not get his way. Most notably, Moreno-Ocampo argued that "if States Parties do not actively support the court [in pressing for arrests] then they are actively undermining it."[88]

What had led to Moreno-Ocampo's shift in strategy? To begin with, the slow, drawn-out nature of the Juba talks was beginning to legitimize the LRA suspects as peacemakers. Nothing underscored the saliency of this transformation better than Jan Egeland's visit to Kony's jungle redoubt in November 2006, just two months after Egeland had hinted to reporters that the ICC was a barrier to peace in northern Uganda. "I have been told by the people [at the Juba talks] that the ICC indictment is a stumbling block to the peace process," Egeland had said at the time. "The predominant feeling among all the stakeholders in the peace process is that the ICC warrant of arrest should be dropped against the LRA leaders so that a peaceful conclusion to the talks can be reached."[89] This perspective had even led some Ugandan officials and European pro-ICC diplomats to begin playing down the rebels' atrocities. As Stig Barlying, the Danish ambassador to Uganda, said: "If the process requires us to momentarily put aside our strong stance on the inhumane and degrading way the LRA have behaved . . . I am not the one to oppose this."[90]

There was a further reason why Moreno-Ocampo felt he needed to sharpen his rhetoric at Nuremberg. Back in Juba, the LRA and government delegates appeared on the verge of agreeing on one of the most sensitive issues on the agenda: how justice and reconciliation would be handled under the peace agreement. Indeed, five days after the prosecutor's speech—on June 29—the LRA and government representatives emerged from an all-night meeting to sign an Agreement on Accountability and Reconciliation.[91] The agreement specified that for nonstate actors such as members of the LRA a special regime of penalties would be introduced that would take into account the gravity of the crimes but also the need for reconciliation. The agreement also stipulated that traditional justice—namely, *matu oput*, an elaborate reconciliation ceremony of the Acholi people—would play a "central role" in the accountability process. Finally, under the agreement the Ugandan government promised to deal "conscientiously" with the issue of the ICC arrest warrants. In effect, this meant that once a final peace agreement was signed the Ugandan government would most likely petition the court to suspend or drop the LRA arrest warrants in favor of a domestic accountability process.

As 2007 wore on, Moreno-Ocampo frequently asserted that international food aid given to the LRA while its representatives negotiated peace in Juba was being sold by the rebels to finance their rearming, increasing Kony's prospects of evading arrest if the peace talks collapsed.[92] He singled out the humanitarian aid agency Caritas and several European states—Denmark, Sweden, Austria, and Switzerland—for violating both the spirit and the letter of the Rome Statute and called for vigilant monitoring of how the LRA used the aid. "It must be recalled that any assistance that can help the sought individuals abscond from the court would be illegal," he told diplomats in an October 2007 briefing in The Hague.[93]

In February 2008, Ugandan government and LRA representatives agreed in principle that a special chamber of Uganda's High Court would be established to prosecute Kony and his top commanders while lower-level suspects would face traditional justice. The Ugandan government saw the domestic war crimes court as serving three purposes. First, it would demonstrate to the ICC that the Ugandan judiciary was willing and able to take over the LRA prosecutions. Second, it would provide the groundwork for the Ugandan government to call on the Security Council to suspend the arrest warrants under Article 16. And, finally, the domestic war crimes court would serve as a way to entice Kony—who was said to especially fear an international trial—into concluding a peace agreement.

But the specter of facing justice, even in Uganda, was unpalatable to Kony. In March, the rebel leader failed to show up to sign the final peace deal. The onus, he said, was on the Ugandan government to write first to the Security Council demanding that the ICC warrants be lifted. The Ugandan government responded that first the rebels must demobilize. A new date was set in April, but Kony failed to appear, claiming that he was suffering from diarrhea. Four weeks later, the Ugandan government announced that its own High Court's special war crimes chamber would soon be operational, hoping the move would convince the ICC to withdraw the arrest warrants. But then, on June 5, LRA rebels attacked a camp belonging to the Sudan People's Liberation Army, killing twenty-one soldiers and civilians. Three days later, after the BBC reported that the rebels were digging up arms caches and resuming their past practice of abducting civilians, the government of South Sudan announced that it would no longer mediate the peace talks.[94] Nearly two years of mediation had finally collapsed.

With the Juba talks over and reports of renewed LRA atrocities in northeastern Congo, Moreno-Ocampo intensified his campaign for the arrests of Kony and the surviving LRA suspects—Kony having disposed of his second-in-command, Vincent Otti, by firing squad.[95] In a rare act of self-criticism for a chief prosecutor, Moreno-Ocampo faulted his previous conciliatory approach to the peace negotiations. He particularly regretted his support for a UN decision not to authorize its peacekeeping mission in the Democratic Republic of the Congo to pursue Kony during the Juba talks.[96] Addressing a meeting of the ICC states parties in July 2008, he asked: "How many times will Kony . . . use negotiations to regain power and attack again?"[97] The prosecutor's rhetorical question underscored a lethal if unintended consequence of the drawn-out Juba peace process: it had given the LRA time to bolster its operational capacity and threaten stability in the border region of northeastern Congo, southern Sudan, and the Central African Republic. By the end of 2008, according to an International Crisis Group report, the Ugandan rebel group had become "a much harder force to disarm . . . than a few years ago."[98]

After Kony failed to respond to one more Ugandan overture, Museveni in November 2008 turned to the American Embassy in Kampala for help. His request was kicked up the chain of command to President Bush, who, to help a regional ally, personally authorized the deployment of seventeen military advisers and analysts to northeastern Congo, to join Ugandan troops on a mission to raid Kony's compound. The American advisers and Ugandans used satellite imagery and field intelligence reports to locate Kony's jungle base in Garamba National Park. The plan, known as Operation Lightning Thunder, was for the Ugandan army to bomb the rebel leader's stronghold and then cut off his 700 or so fighters with more than 6,000 Ugandan and Congolese ground troops. On December 13, 2008, the day before the attack, several American advisers traveled to a staging site near the Uganda-Congo border for a final coordination meeting. The next morning, as Ugandan helicopters idled in a clearing waiting for the go-ahead, a heavy fog descended, forcing the attack to be delayed by several hours. By the time Uganda helicopters bombed Kony's compound it was empty.[99]

In retaliation for the attack, LRA fighters scorched Congolese villages, slaughtered hundreds of civilians, and abducted Congolese children as new recruits as they fled toward the vast expanse of the Central African Republic.[100] Kony's most horrific act of revenge occurred in a forty-eight-hour period over Christmas in several villages in the Haut-Uele district near the DRC's border with the Central African Republic. LRA fighters struck quickly and quietly as villagers gathered for festivities, surrounding villagers as they ate their Christmas meal or settled in to listen to a Christmas Day concert. In Mabando village, according to Human Rights Watch, "the LRA sought to maximize the death toll by luring their victims to a central place, playing the radio and forcing their victims to sing songs and to call to others to come join the party. . . . [The LRA rebels] bound their victims, stripped them of their clothing, raped the women and girls, and then killed their victims by crushing their skulls."[101]

In 2010, President Obama signed the Lord's Resistance Army Disarmament and Northern Uganda Recovery Act. It would now be U.S. policy to "work vigorously" to "eliminate the threat posed by the Lord's

Resistance Army to civilians and regional stability."[102] A year later, Obama put teeth into the law by dispatching more than 100 Special Forces advisers to Africa to assist 3,000 African Union troops, mostly from Uganda, in tracking and apprehending Kony.[103] While the Obama administration's newfound willingness to pursue Kony cannot be attributed to one single factor, there is little doubt that U.S.-based human rights organizations played a significant in role in pressing the White House and Congress to take action. Among them was Invisible Children, an advocacy group based in Southern California that used social media to galvanize young people to lobby for Kony's capture through letter-writing campaigns to Washington.[104]

To bolster the U.S. initiative, Shannon Sedgwick Davis, an American philanthropist and CEO of the Texas-based Bridgeway Foundation, hired South African mercenaries to train more than 300 Ugandan elite troops in the specialized tactics she believed were needed to pursue fugitives who had successfully evaded their pursuers for over twenty years. The South Africans trained their Ugandan counterparts to travel silently, lightly, and in small units of six men. They learned how to plait their hair in the style favored by the LRA, dress like them, and behave like them so as to infiltrate their encampments undetected. Late one night in September 2011, a special-operations team trained by the South Africans slipped into Sudan and raided one of Kony's camps. The rebel leader escaped, however, fleeing with one of his wives into the bush.[105]

In an August 2012 visit to Uganda, Secretary of State Hillary Clinton added a new twist to the search for the ICC fugitives. After visiting President Museveni, she traveled to a Ugandan military base on Lake Victoria to inspect twelve Raven unmanned aircraft, or drones, that the United States had given to the Ugandans to track al-Qaeda-linked militants in Somalia. As one of the drones circled overhead, Clinton said she hoped drones would be used in the hunt for the LRA.[106]

Spooked by recent raids, the LRA, which numbered no more than 250 fighters by late 2012, had scattered into small groups and stopped using radios and mobile phones to avoid leaving an electronic trail.[107] That December a commander close to Kony defected, bringing with him a GPS unit containing a virtual constellation of the LRA's movements.[108] The Americans used the coordinates to capture satellite images of Kony's new camp in South Sudan. Three days later, Ugandan troops raided the camp—only to find that Kony had fled a week earlier.[109]

Although, at the time of writing, the hunt for Kony continues, it remains anyone's guess whether he and his surviving top commanders will ever be captured—dead or alive. But the militarized pursuit of Kony, who is heavily armed and highly determined to evade capture, raises the likelihood that he may never end up facing trial in The Hague. As one American official involved in the search put it: "There's only one way this is going to end, and that's with Kony shot in the back, running for his life, deep in the forest."[110]

SUDAN AND THE FAILURE TO ARREST OMAR AL-BASHIR

Moreno-Ocampo adopted the same conciliation-to-confrontation approach in Sudan that had characterized his earlier pursuit of Joseph Kony. In Sudan, however, he possessed a seeming advantage—a Security Council referral, issued in 2005—that at the time he did not have in the other ICC situation countries. On paper, at least, a Security Council referral gives the ICC authority to press for UN sanctions and enforcement measures to ensure compliance with its resolutions. Thus in the Darfur situation, the ICC possessed nearly the same level of legal authority to demand state cooperation as the Yugoslavia tribunal has had over the government of the former Yugoslavia and the Rwanda tribunal has had in Rwanda. But when it came to Darfur, as in the case of the former Yugoslavia and Rwanda, the Security Council would be reluctant to wield its enforcement powers on behalf of international justice.

Nevertheless, for Moreno-Ocampo the benefits of this Security Council referral were multifold. First, the council's decision to refer the Darfur situation to the ICC was based largely on a January 2005 report by the UN International Commission of Inquiry on Darfur that would give him valuable fodder for his own investigations. Led by a former Yugoslavia tribunal president, Antonio Cassese, the report focused the lion's share of blame on the Sudanese government security forces and their proxy militias—the Janjaweed—for their campaign of terror against civilians in Darfur, resulting in mass murder, rape, and the forced displacement of over two million people. In a confidential addendum, the commissioners provided a list of fifty-one potential suspects, reaching to the highest levels of government, and recommended that the ICC further investigate their alleged involvement in these crimes.[111] Second, the Security Council referral provided the ICC—and, by extension, the chief prosecutor—the authority to open an investigation in a state (Sudan) that had not ratified the Rome Statute and therefore would not have been legally obligated to cooperate with the court. Third, the council's referral, by requiring the prosecutor to report to the world body biannually on the progress of his investigations, gave Moreno-Ocampo a high-profile forum from which to expose any noncompliance, perhaps with an eye toward pressing the council to take punitive action.[112] Finally, the fact that the United States did not oppose or veto the referral marked a surprising turnabout for the Bush administration. It also sparked hope among justice advocates that Washington might be softening its attitude toward the ICC and might even consider applying diplomatic pressure to help bring in Sudanese war crimes suspects.

In theory, the Security Council's Darfur referral could have emboldened Moreno-Ocampo to deal strongly with the al-Bashir government from the start. Yet from mid-2005 until mid-2007, the ICC prosecutor was decidedly cautious in his approach to Sudan, much to the dismay of some international human rights activists. There are several reasons why his approach to Khartoum was conciliatory. First, a pressing issue for the prosecutor was getting Khartoum to sign a memorandum of understanding with the ICC, agreeing to aid in the capture of LRA fugitives, which the Sudanese finally did in October 2005.

Second, with the ICC as a court of last resort, the prosecutor needed to establish whether Sudan's judicial system was genuinely able and willing to undertake war crimes cases being pursued by the court. Toward that end, the ICC Office of the Prosecutor undertook a rigorous evaluation of the Darfur Special Criminal Court, which had been hurriedly established by the Khartoum government, purportedly to prosecute suspects implicated in the Darfur atrocities.

Third, Moreno-Ocampo needed Sudan to divulge evidence that could aid his investigations of Darfur atrocities. In the face of security threats, the prosecutor had decided not to send investigators to Darfur but rather to interview refugees from the conflict who had fled to camps in Chad and further afield. Still, Moreno-Ocampo's case would be strengthened if he could secure "insider witnesses" and documentary evidence linking potential suspects to specific crimes, information that could be best acquired from Sudanese officials willing to cooperate with his office. Finally, the prosecutor hoped to rely on the Sudanese government to hand over suspects to the court, especially if the Security Council might be unlikely to exercise its enforcement powers.

In early 2007, following eighteen months of investigatory work, Moreno-Ocampo determined that his cases against Sudanese government official Ahmad Harun and Janjaweed militia leader Ali Kushayb were admissible for ICC prosecution. He requested that the pretrial chamber issue summons—a legal measure provided to the ICC but not to the ad hoc tribunals for Rwanda and the former Yugoslavia—rather than arrest warrants for the two suspects. Whereas an arrest warrant is unmistakably confrontational, a summons is in effect a legal request to appear before a court, with an expectation that a suspect will voluntarily surrender. Even so, the Sudanese justice minister spurned Moreno-Ocampo's overtures, calling them "an execution of a political agenda" and rejecting "the trial of any Sudanese outside the Sudanese judicial system."[113] Citing the government's obstinacy, the pretrial chamber in late April issued warrants instead.[114]

Moreno-Ocampo later said that the Sudanese authorities had indicated some interest in surrendering the suspects after the arrest warrants were issued. It was at this point, he insisted, that international pressure on Khartoum could have played an important role in the arrest and transfer of Harun and Kushayb to The Hague. But the UN and European Union declined to make arrests a priority. "The international community preferred to deny the facts and the need to enforce the judges' decision," Moreno-Ocampo said, in a stinging rebuke of UN and European acquiescence.[115]

Undeterred, the prosecutor decided to take action. In December 2007, he hatched an audacious plan, in conjunction with several third-party states, to divert an airplane that was expected to carry Ahmad Harun to the *hajj* pilgrimage in Saudi Arabia.[116] However, the plan flopped: Harun was tipped off and deplaned. Still, Moreno-Ocampo used the disclosure of the arrest attempt to project his determination and the long shadow of the ICC's global reach. "As soon as Harun leaves Sudan he will be arrested," the prosecutor said in June 2008. "He is a fugitive. Inside Sudan he can have his freedom. Outside Sudan he will be in jail."[117] Khartoum responded to the news by denouncing the prosecutor's action as "piracy," calling for his ouster, and announcing that it had filed domestic terrorism charges against him.[118]

Since its 2005 referral, the Security Council has, as of this writing, taken no punitive steps against Sudan despite its blatant noncooperation and its public declarations that it will not cooperate with the court. The council's reluctance to pressure Sudan to cooperate with the court has been linked to its significantly greater interest in finding a negotiated peace settlement in Darfur, in holding Khartoum to its promise to allow the full deployment of an expanded joint African Union–UN peacekeeping force in Darfur, and in ensuring that Sudan and South Sudan do not slide back into a devastating armed conflict. Moreover, the international community continued to rely on the Sudanese government to permit the unfettered delivery of humanitarian relief to civilians displaced by the violence in Darfur. At times, this dependence led even strong ICC supporters such as the European Union to avoid applying sustained pressure on Sudan to cooperate with the court. As a senior EU diplomat with first-hand knowledge of Sudan explained in May 2008, the ICC fits in the diplomatic landscape "like a stone in a shoe." He added: "It would require robust pressure on the government to [hand over suspects] to the ICC, robust pressure we're not inclined to put because of the need to engage" on several other agendas.[119]

By June 2008, Moreno-Ocampo had become openly adversarial toward a defiant Sudanese government and an indifferent international community. In a speech to the Security Council, he called "the entire Darfur region a crime scene," implicated the "entire state apparatus" in atrocities, and excoriated Khartoum for a cover-up. He also laid blame for Sudan's noncompliance at the feet of the international community, invoking its previous failures in Rwanda and Srebrenica. "It takes a lot to commit massive crimes," he said. "It takes commanders and many executioners. But mostly, it requires the rest of the world to look away and do nothing."[120] In seeking to shame the Security Council into taking action, the prosecutor also tried to preempt the predictable accusations that the ICC threatened peace in Darfur—accusations that would grow more intense after his request, in July 2008, that the pretrial chamber issue an arrest warrant for President al-Bashir himself.

Moreno-Ocampo's newly confrontational approach caught many observers off guard. Targeting a head of state and charging him with genocide is the boldest and riskiest act a tribunal chief prosecutor can take. Where ICC advocates had once criticized Moreno-Ocampo for being too conciliatory and aiming too low in the caliber of targeted suspects, ICC opponents in Sudan and elsewhere were now accusing him of being too adversarial and aiming too high. ICC critics Julie Flint and Alex de Waal, for example, warned that the arrest warrant could bring about "the very sorts of atrocities that the ICC is meant to deter."[121]

As an ICC pretrial chamber deliberated over the legal merits of the prosecutor's application, Sudan called on the Security Council to heed the disastrous consequences that might ensue were the ICC allowed to proceed. However, by the end of 2008, there were no signs that key council members were planning to formally give al-Bashir a get-out-of-jail-free card by invoking an Article 16 suspension of the case. Still, the Sudanese president pressed on with his fear campaign, with Khartoum skillfully playing the "instability card,"[122] painting grim scenarios of an unaccountable ICC reigniting the Darfur crisis and perhaps even the dissolution of Sudan. This argument, along with allegations of an ICC anti-African bias, became Sudan's most potent tools for discrediting the ICC and recruiting African leaders to oppose any future effort by the court to arrest the Sudanese president.

On March 4, 2009, the ICC charged President Omar al-Bashir of Sudan with seven counts of war crimes and crimes against humanity over the conflict in Darfur.[123] A pretrial chamber rejected Moreno-Ocampo's request to also charge al-Bashir with genocide, ruling that there was insufficient evidence. But the ICC appeals chamber reversed that decision in July 2010, a month before al-Bashir flew to Nairobi to attend the signing of Kenya's new constitution, finding the standard of proof set by the pretrial chamber to be too demanding at the arrest-warrant stage, amounting to an "error of law."[124] Momentous though it was for international justice advocates, the ICC's indictment had no immediate impact on gaining custody of al-Bashir or easing the plight of Darfur's 2.7 million displaced people.

Given the dramatic power imbalance between a court without any direct enforcement powers and a head of state with an army of his own, gaining custody of a serving head of state poses no small challenge to an international criminal court. Being perched atop a state's hierarchy of political and military power provides a built-in safeguard against arrest. It is when leaders fall from power, as with Slobodan Milosevic of Serbia, that they are most susceptible to capture. Yet, the ICC prosecutor, like his counterparts at the Yugoslavia and Rwanda tribunals, is not powerless when it comes to the arrest of a sitting head of state. The tactic of issuing a sealed indictment or arrest warrant to catch unsuspecting indictees by surprise can land a head of state in custody. Issuing a sealed warrant for the Sudanese president might have led to his arrest had he traveled to a state party willing to apprehend him outside of Africa. Yet Moreno-Ocampo chose not to take the sealed-warrant route, perhaps to avoid an even greater Sudanese and African backlash against the ICC and a splintering of the political consensus needed from participating African states to sustain the court. Nevertheless, the very act of indicting the Sudanese president rendered Moreno-Ocampo's quest to build international support for the court yet more elusive.

Within hours of the arrest-warrant announcement in March 2009, al-Bashir was standing on a balcony before a throng of onlookers in the heart of Khartoum and denouncing the ICC. Stabbing the air with his walking stick, he called the ICC a throwback to the worst days of colonialism and its issuing of an arrest warrant a naked grab for Sudanese oil. "Here in Sudan," he shouted, "we are a liberation movement against this new colonization and we are ready for any battle."[125] As a group of young men set ablaze a crude papier mâché effigy of Moreno-Ocampo, the Sudanese president announced that he was expelling thirteen international and three domestic relief groups from Darfur, claiming they were spies for the court.[126]

At the time, the aid effort in Darfur was the largest in the world, with outlays reaching more than $1 billion a year and requiring more than 10,000 workers from the United Nations and private organizations. The Sudanese government's expulsions were carried out swiftly and ruthlessly. Troops arrived at the offices of Doctors Without Borders and the International Rescue Committee, among other charities, and ordered workers to leave. They then ransacked the premises, seizing valuable equipment like computers, cars, and generators. "This was in the works a long time," a senior aid official later opined. "They had been waiting for a chance to strike out at these organizations."[127]

Al-Bashir's expulsion of the aid workers—and the humanitarian threat their departure posed to over one million Darfuris in displaced-persons camps[128]—appeared to be a calculated attempt to drive a wedge between the ICC and the United Nations. By creating a greater humanitarian emergency, al-Bashir apparently hoped to pressure the Security Council into invoking an Article 16 suspension of the ICC investigation, or, if that failed, to diminish international pressure for his arrest. In the "battle of the narrative"[129] over whether international justice actions are a benevolent or a malevolent force, the Sudanese president sought to gain the upper hand by manufacturing a conflict between not only peace and justice but also between survival and justice.[130]

Back in The Hague, Moreno-Ocampo assailed al-Bashir, deploying incendiary rhetoric of his own by calling the expulsion of the aid groups a further confirmation that the Sudanese president was "exterminating his people."[131] Yet, as hard as he pressed his case before the Security Council and in press conferences, the ICC prosecutor's voice seemed to be drowned out by the high-profile attacks leveled against the ICC by al-Bashir and his African and Arab allies.[132] A case in point was the extensive media coverage given to the Arab League's decision to oppose the ICC warrant in a late-March summit meeting in Qatar, which al-Bashir attended. The Sudanese president further sought to flout the ICC and foster an image of an untouchable leader by traveling to Eritrea, Egypt, Libya, and Saudi Arabia, none of which were ICC states parties.

In early June 2012, just weeks before his departure from the court and after three years of a rhetorical war with no winner, Moreno-Ocampo delivered his last statement on the Darfur situation to the Security Council. He enumerated the strategies President al-Bashir had used "to ensure his own impunity and the impunity of those who follow his orders."[133] Among them, the ICC prosecutor said, was the Sudanese leader's success at "forcing the international community into a never-ending negotiation in order to gain access to [the] displaced [in Darfur]" and "offering the permanent promise of a peace negotiation."[134] The international community, meanwhile, was chasing "promises of peace agreements that [were] systematically ignored while President Bashir's forces [committed] more attacks and [created] the conditions for new promises of peace agreements."[135] Summing up the message he had been delivering to the Security Council for years, the ICC prosecutor called on the UN to arrest the Sudanese fugitives.[136]

Finding a way to somehow spirit the Sudanese president out of Sudan and to The Hague could produce the dramatic change on the ground that ICC chief prosecutors have long sought. But absent al-Bashir's arrest on the territory of a state party, or a homegrown insurrection leading to his arrest—a scenario which itself could trigger further bloody conflict—the Security Council would likely confront an enormous challenge if it heeded Moreno-Ocampo's and Fatou Bensouda's calls to forcefully stand up to al-Bashir's challenge to the council's authority. Under the UN Charter's Chapter VII powers, the Security Council could legally authorize a military intervention to apprehend al-Bashir and the three other ICC suspects implicated in state-sponsored atrocities in Darfur. But launching a mission to arrest the head of state of a sovereign country could well dwarf the high military and much higher civilian body count suffered in the disastrous 1993 U.S. raid in Somalia by triggering a wider war.

Absent Security Council support, a coalition of willing states could launch an arrest mission of its own. But such an intervention would fly in the face of the UN Charter's prohibition on military interventions without Security Council authorization. Indeed, the preamble to the Rome Statute reaffirms a fundamental aim of the UN Charter that binds states to "refrain from the threat or use of force against the territorial integrity or political independence of any State," except in self-defense.[137]

Taken together, the ICC's travails in Sudan and Uganda highlight how the court's quest for cooperation can founder—and often has—on the shifting sands of state and international politics. Receiving invitations to conduct investigations—through a state or Security Council referral—is an implicit promise of forthcoming cooperation because key political actors have signaled a strong interest in advancing the ICC's work. But the story of the Ugandan government and the Security Council's ambivalent relationship with the ICC in the Darfur situation shows how quickly initial demonstrations of support for international justice can turn into indifference and even obstruction. This, in turn, has thrown the ICC on the defensive, undermining the court's mission in northern Uganda and in Darfur by rendering the quest for crucial political support from avowed ICC allies frustratingly elusive. The pattern of external actors deputizing the court to open a country-situation investigation only to undercut it when the pursuit of justice is perceived as impeding the pursuit of what are deemed more important goals would soon be on display again, this time in Libya.

LIBYA AND THE DEATH OF MUAMMAR GADDAFI

On February 26, 2011, by a vote of 15 to 0, the UN Security Council adopted Resolution 1970 referring the rapidly deteriorating situation in Libya to the ICC.[138] Less than two weeks earlier, protesters—inspired by the Arab Spring revolutions in neighboring Tunisia and Egypt that quickly toppled their two authoritarian leaders—had taken to the streets in Benghazi, Libya's second-largest city, demanding an end to Colonel Muammar Gaddafi's forty-two-year dictatorial rule. Libyan government troops opened fire on demonstrators and, within days, the peaceful protest movement had turned into a full-fledged uprising.

Gaddafi appeared atop the ramparts of Tripoli's Red Castle fortress vowing to annihilate his foes. During one of his tirades he pledged to track down and crush the "cockroaches" that had taken up arms against him "inch by inch, room by room, home by home, alleyway by alleyway, person by person."[139] He ordered his forces to break the opposition by arresting thousands of protesters and their supporters, holding many in secret detention, and carrying out summary executions. Despite the crackdown, the resistance soon expanded into a broad coalition of opposition forces loosely coordinated under the banner of the National Transitional Council, the "interim government" formed by insurgent leaders in Benghazi the day after the council's referral.[140]

Resolution 1970 condemned the Libyan regime's use of lethal force and set out a robust set of punitive measures, including an arms embargo, a travel ban against sixteen Libyan officials, and asset freezes for Gaddafi and his immediate family. It also instructed the ICC prosecutor to report to the Security Council within two months, and every six months thereafter, on the status of his investigation into the crimes enumerated in the resolution.[141] As with the 2005 Darfur referral, the Libya referral did not restrict the prosecutor to investigating only state-sponsored atrocities. But to the chagrin of many human rights activists and diplomats, the Libya resolution, similar to the Darfur resolution, contained a proviso, included at the insistence of the United States, which effectively shielded from the court's jurisdiction the members of any future international military force in Libya that had not joined the ICC.[142] And, as with the Darfur referral, the Security Council had added a new country situation to the ICC's docket without allocating any funds to supplement the court's already strained budget.

Less than a month later, amid fears of an imminent large-scale massacre as Gaddafi's troops approached the opposition stronghold of Benghazi, the Security Council authorized a NATO military intervention to take "all necessary measures" to safeguard threatened civilians. Soon the NATO-led "humanitarian" intervention unfolded into a full-fledged war to oust Gaddafi, a development that sparked the ire of Russia and China, which charged NATO with manipulating the Security Council's implicit curbs on the use of force. U.S., French, and British planes bombed Libyan government installations, and rebels fought on the ground, to turn the tide against Gaddafi. In Sudan, as in the Yugoslavia tribunal's early years, the Security Council's call for accountability through international courts acted as a moral substitute for military intervention. But in Libya, the actions of the ICC quickly became an adjunct to military intervention. Initially a convergence of interests existed between the NATO-led coalition, the Libyan rebels, and the ICC prosecutor—all of whom sought Gaddafi's removal. Still, it was by no means clear that NATO or the Libyan rebels wanted to see the vilified Libyan leader stand trial in The Hague.

Moreno-Ocampo opened a preliminary investigation only days after receiving the February 26 referral. On May 4 he reported to the Security Council that in just over two months his office had conducted more than fifteen missions in ten countries, where investigators interviewed forty-five individuals with direct knowledge of the alleged crimes in Libya and reviewed more than 569 documents, including videos and photographs.[143] Two weeks later, the ICC prosecutor announced that he was "almost trial-ready" and, in a matter of weeks, would seek arrest warrants for Colonel Muammar Gaddafi, his son Saif al-Islam, and his intelligence chief and brother-in-law, Abdullah al-Sanussi.[144] Moreno-Ocampo's alacrity in seeking warrants was met with disbelief among seasoned international prosecutors: they found it incredible that any prosecutor could reach such an advanced stage in his investigation in less than three months. Louise Arbour, for example, expressed dismay that Moreno-Ocampo conducted his preliminary investigation in just a few days, a process that ordinarily would take some months.[145] Some critics saw this unprecedented zeal in the Libyan case as an example of Moreno-Ocampo's mission to show the world that the ICC could be a formidable force for preventing violence in unfolding conflicts. Others, however, echoing a long-standing criticism of international tribunals, questioned Ocampo's pursuit of suspects in conflict situations, notably Uganda and Sudan and now Libya, on the grounds that the pursuit of arrests would undermine peace and could encourage further atrocities.[146]

Still, the ICC prosecutor's rush to judgment played well internationally, propelling him and the ICC's accountability mission onto the front pages and lending legitimacy to the widening war against Gaddafi. For Moreno-Ocampo, the unanimous Security Council Libya referral, further backed by military intervention to halt ongoing atrocities, provided an unparalleled opportunity to score a victory in the continuing "battle of the narrative" over the value of the ICC. Even as the war raged on, the prosecutor repeatedly claimed that his pursuit of Gaddafi and the two other suspects would prevent further atrocities.

On June 27, 2011, an ICC pretrial chamber issued warrants against the three Libyans for crimes against humanity (murder and persecution) committed from February 15 until at least February 28. The warrants claimed that Gaddafi had ordered his security forces to "deter and quell by all means the civilian demonstration against his regime," while his Western-educated son Saif had managed the logistics of the crackdown. "His contributions were essential," the warrant said, adding that Saif was "the most influential person within [Muammar Gaddafi's] inner circle and, as such, he exercised control of crucial parts of the state apparatus."[147]

The unified Security Council coalition backing the ICC in Libya began to splinter as the conflict dragged on during the spring and summer of 2011. Even after the war ended that fall, a different political imperative—bolstering the fragile sovereignty of the post-Gaddafi government—would trump the legal imperative to bring the indicted Libyan suspects to trial in The Hague.

Initially, however, the ICC prosecutor's targeting of Gaddafi was enthusiastically received not only by ICC states parties but also by other parties, particularly the United States. In another sign that Washington recognized the value of the ICC in select circumstances, the Obama administration welcomed the warrants. "It's another indication that [Muammar Gaddafi] has lost his legitimacy," said White House spokesman Jay Carney. "It is another step in the process of holding him accountable."[148] Carney's remarks, however, masked behind-the-scenes maneuverings aimed at ending the Libyan conflict as swiftly as possible. Since early March, the United States and some Western nations had been quietly seeking a country, most likely in Africa, which might be willing to provide refuge to Gaddafi if he were forced out of Libya. Administration officials told the *New York Times* that one possibility was to find a country that was not a state party to the Rome Statute, which requires countries to turn over anyone under indictment to the jurisdiction of the ICC. "What we're simply trying to do is find some peaceful way to organize an exit, if the opportunity arises," said one U.S. official.[149]

Such machinations to short-circuit justice in the interest of peace were riddled with ironic connotations.[150] How could the United States, which was not a state party to the Rome Statute, vote in the Security Council to refer the Libyan situation to the ICC and then later seek a place of exile for Gaddafi where he could potentially live out his days without fear of standing trial in The Hague? Wasn't this similar to what American diplomats had done with Charles Taylor as rebel groups laid siege to Monrovia in 2003? And once ensconced in sybaritic splendor in his seaside villa in southern Nigeria, hadn't Taylor worked to destabilize his two successors—Moses Blah and Ellen Johnson Sirleaf—in Liberia, as well as other West African leaders, until the United States finally reversed course and used its diplomatic clout to have him expelled from Nigeria? Still, the prospect of facilitating Gaddafi's passage out of Libya might have had the short-term benefit of bringing the costly war to a speedy conclusion while also achieving the U.S. goal of regime change.

No exile deal came to pass, however, and in August 2011, NATO airstrikes and anti-Gaddafi militias had forced the Libyan leader to flee his stronghold in Tripoli for refuge in the coastal city of Sirte, his hometown. It was in Sirte two years earlier that the Libyan leader had scored a stinging political victory against the ICC by winning African Union support for a noncooperation resolution. From Sirte on the morning of October 20, the besieged dictator and members of his inner circle fled in a convoy of some fifty heavily armed vehicles.[151] Before the convoy had traveled several kilometers, an American Predator drone, originating in Sicily and controlled via satellite from a base outside Las Vegas, let loose a fusillade of Hellfire anti-tank missiles, striking the front of the convoy. In a matter of minutes the rest of the convoy came upon anti-Gaddafi militiamen and was struck by airburst bombs fired from a NATO warplane, incinerating dozens of Gaddafi fighters. As militia fighters descended on Gaddafi and his inner circle, who had fled to a culvert, one of his bodyguards threw a hand grenade, which bounced off the concrete wall and exploded in their midst, spraying shrapnel into the group and killing Libya's defense minister, Abu Bakr Younis. Militiamen immediately set upon Gaddafi, pummeling him with punches and kicks. Blood gushed from the shrapnel wounds on his face. As he was led onto the main road, a militiaman ran up and stabbed him in the buttocks with a bayonet, causing another rapidly bleeding wound. A militia commander later admitted to Human Rights Watch that Gaddafi's capture was out of control: "The situation was a mess. There were so many fighters around. He was alive when I saw him, so he must have been shot later, not when we saw him. But it was a violent scene, he was put on the front of a pickup truck that tried to drive him away, and he fell off. It was very confusing. People were pulling on his hair and hitting him. We understood there needed to be a trial, but couldn't control everyone."[152]

Photos of Muammar Gaddafi's grisly end ricocheted around the world. The Arab Twittersphere glittered with gleeful comments, many of them hinting that a similar fate awaited other Arab dictators—most notably President Ali Abdullah Saleh of Yemen and President Bashar al-Assad of Syria. In the Afghan capital of Kabul, U.S. Secretary of State Hillary Clinton received the news of Gaddafi's death while preparing for an interview with CBS News. While the camera was rolling, an aide handed Clinton a BlackBerry with photos of the Libyan leader's gruesome capture. Looking up from the cell phone, Clinton laughed and told a TV reporter "we came, we saw, he died."[153] Other Western officials were more reserved. The British defense secretary, Philip Hammond, said the circumstances of Gaddafi's death had placed a stain on the Libyan uprising. "It's certainly not the way we do things," he added. "We would have liked to see Colonel Gaddafi going on trial to answer for his misdeeds."[154]

Gaddafi's apparent torture and execution provides a cautionary tale of what can happen when the hot pursuit of war crimes suspects takes place amid the fog of armed conflict, though of course this was not an ICC-orchestrated endeavor. Gaddafi was apparently not killed accidentally in crossfire but deliberately after capture, pointing to a clear violation of the laws of war. Regardless of the exact circumstances of his death, however, since the fall of Sirte a defining feature of the postwar period in Libya has been a pattern of violent retribution against captured Gaddafi loyalists. During this new era, vengeance—unchecked by a weak Libyan government with little enforcement powers of its own and the absence of an international peacekeeping mission—has triumphed. Whether or not the ICC contributed to the prevention of violence during the Libyan war, as Moreno-Ocampo repeatedly asserted, the prosecution's avoidance of the abuses of the anti-Gaddafi forces has rendered the ICC vulnerable to charges that it has not acted to prevent violence committed by the victors.

Muammar Gaddafi's death left the ICC chief prosecutor with outstanding arrest warrants for two suspects on the run in a country the size of Alaska and with scores of militias eager to get their hands on them. In late August 2011, Saif al-Islam Gaddafi and Abdullah Senussi fled Tripoli for different destinations. Saif, once his father's heir apparent and a graduate of the London School of Economics, escaped to the loyalist town of Bani Walid, where he hunkered down for several weeks. On the move again in mid-October 2011, he made his way to Sirte, then turned south, heading deeper into the desert, hoping to reach the border of Niger. But militiamen caught up with him outside of the oasis town of Obari, and incarcerated him in the town of Zintan in the Nafusa Mountains.[155]

The other ICC suspect was Abdullah Senussi, Libya's former spy chief and one of the world's most wanted men. France wanted to question him in connection with the bombing of a UTA passenger plane in 1989, while prosecutors in Britain and the United States wanted to interrogate him about his role in the bombing of Pan Am flight 103, which had claimed the lives of 270 people over Lockerbie, Scotland, in 1988. After joining Gaddafi in Sirte following the fall of Tripoli, Senussi had traveled to Sebha, 500 kilometers to the south. Soon thereafter, he disappeared into the desert, only to reemerge in Morocco in March 2012, where he was detained for twelve days before being put on a plane to Mauritania. Senussi later told a Human Rights Watch investigator that the Mauritanians held him in solitary confinement for six months. His captors repeatedly interrogated him and allowed officials from Saudi Arabia, Lebanon, Great Britain, and the United States to do the same. He said his treatment was "reasonable" and that the Mauritanian authorities allowed him access to lawyers, as well as some family visits.[156] Then in early September 2012, in defiance of the ICC arrest warrant and without a subsequent murmur of protest from the UN Security Council, the Mauritanians placed Senussi on a plane bound for Tripoli.[157] Four months later, Reuters reported that in exchange for Senussi the Libyans had given Mauritania a "donation" of $200 million, equivalent to about 5 percent of Mauritania's gross domestic product.[158]

Senussi's arrival in the Libyan capital intensified a tug of war between Libya's government and the ICC over who would try him and Saif al-Islam. The stakes were high for both sides. With Gaddafi dead, Kony on the run, and al-Bashir hiding in plain sight in Khartoum, the ICC needed a success story. But so did the fledgling Libyan government. Holding high-profile trials of Saif al-Islam and Abdulla Senussi at home, the Libyans argued, was not only their sovereign right but a "matter of the highest national importance, not only . . . for the Libyan people but also in demonstrating that the new Libyan justice system is capable of conducting fair trials in complex cases."[159] But in the view of a number of observers, the Libyan court system, in tatters following the war and decades of Gaddafi's dictatorial rule, hardly seemed capable of upholding fair trials in even simple cases.[160]

The most contentious battle was over Saif. The ICC repeatedly requested that Saif be turned over to the court. Yet, perhaps in a bid to diffuse the gathering confrontation, Moreno-Ocampo left the door open for Libya to hold a domestic trial under the ICC's principle of complementarity, which allows states to make a case for trying ICC suspects in their national courts.[161] Moreno-Ocampo's successor as ICC chief prosecutor, Fatou Bensouda, also painted an optimistic scenario in which domestic accountability could prevail. Whether the trials took place in The Hague or in Tripoli, the new chief prosecutor told the Security Council in May 2013, they could be "Libya's Nuremberg moment, one that will endeavor to seal the primacy of the rule of law, due process and human rights for future generations."[162] Powerful international players, such as the United States, weighed in on what had now become an overtly political question: Did the ICC or the Libyan government possess the legal right to prosecute the suspects? For the United States, the need to bolster Libya's fragile central government and its sense of sovereignty and to do what it could to maintain Washington's limited leverage with the new Libyan leadership meant supporting the government's bid for domestic trials, despite the highly compromised state of the domestic court system. In early June, U.S. war crimes ambassador Stephen Rapp commented, "Our preference is to try cases in the national system if you can have a process there that meets minimal standards of fair justice. The Libyan government says they can do that."[163]

Yet just a day later, Zintan authorities dropped a fly in the ointment by arresting Melinda Taylor, an ICC staff member and defense attorney, midway through a meeting with Saif, thus violating the immunity of ICC staff. The authorities claimed that Taylor had conspired against the state by smuggling spying devices (a video-camera pen and a watch with the same function) and a coded letter into Saif's cell. Taylor was released some weeks later, but only after ICC President Sang-Hyun Song traveled to Zintan and, in a gesture of acquiescence that troubled some international human rights advocates, apologized for the "difficulties" caused by the defense attorney's trip.[164] The Taylor episode starkly illustrated the power of the Libyan militias and the powerlessness of the ICC. In May 2012, the Libyans filed an "admissibility challenge" to the ICC case against Saif al-Islam, claiming he would receive a fair trial in Libya, and a year later made a claim for Abdullah Senussi on the same grounds.[165] Admissibility challenges, as defined by the Rome Statute, involve a two-stage process.[166] First, for a state to bring a successful challenge, it must provide the court with "concrete, tangible and pertinent evidence that proper investigations are currently undergoing" for the conduct that is the subject of the ICC case. Second, if the court determines that such national investigations exist, it considers whether the state is genuinely willing and able to conduct appropriate judicial proceedings. Ultimately it is up to the ICC judges to determine whether national proceedings exist that meet the criteria for a successful admissibility challenge.[167]

In May 2013, an ICC pretrial chamber rejected Libya's challenge to the ICC's case against Saif. According to the jurists, the central government in Tripoli lacked "the capacity to obtain the necessary testimony" required to conduct a proper investigation and prosecution.[168] The judges also remained unconvinced that the central government would be able to secure Saif's transfer to Tripoli from the formidable Zintan militia, which regarded Gaddafi's son as a bargaining chip in its fraught relations with the government.[169] The Libyans responded by filing a 91-page appeal, which the ICC appeals chamber soon thereafter also rejected.[170] Having lost its appeal, the Libyan government balked at its legal obligation to transfer Saif into ICC custody.

Libya's admissibility challenge over the Senussi case yielded a very different ICC judicial outcome. For the first time in the court's history, an ICC pretrial chamber allowed a state to pursue a prosecution that had been under ICC investigation. In an October 2013 ruling, the pretrial chamber found that the Libyan judicial system's "concrete and progressive steps" in its ongoing investigation of Senussi substantiated the Libyan government's claim that it was genuinely able to conduct an adequate domestic trial.[171] Months after the ICC's complementarity decision, however, Senussi had still not been given legal defense. Nevertheless, in July 2014, the ICC appeals chamber unanimously confirmed the earlier pretrial decision, allowing Libya to prosecute Senussi for the crimes outlined in the ICC's arrest warrant.[172] The ruling, which came as various militia groups battled for control of the country, drew a sharp reaction from Human Rights Watch's Richard Dicker: "As the country enters another month of chaos, where judges, lawyers, and prosecutors are being killed, it is hard to imagine that Libya can hold any fair trial, much less a trial of this sensitivity and significance."[173]

In the meantime, Britain, France, and the United States—the most powerful Security Council states inclined to support international justice—have shown little inclination to press the now fractured Libyan government to take steps to compel the Zintan to hand over Saif. The unprecedented unanimous Security Council referral in February 2011 signaled a new global embrace of the principal of international criminal accountability. But both during the war and in its aftermath, international and Libyan political imperatives have held the trump card over compliance with the Rome Statute.

Fortunately for the ICC, such priorities have proven less of a hindrance in its pursuit of war crimes suspects in Côte d'Ivoire.

CÔTE D'IVOIRE AND THE ARRESTS OF LAURENT AND SIMONE GBAGBO

On March 30, 2011, just two weeks after NATO pilots launched their first bombing raids to halt Gaddafi's advance on Benghazi in eastern Libya, the UN Security Council approved an international intervention against another authoritarian leader implicated in ongoing atrocities against his own people. In the West African nation of Côte d'Ivoire, President Laurent Gbagbo clung to power after losing a long-delayed presidential election in late 2010 that international observers certified as fair and free. Days after a national election commission declared Alassane Ouattara, a former senior International Monetary Fund official, the winner, with 54 percent of the vote, Gbagbo's security forces and pro-government militias unleashed a wave of terror against opponents. In the commercial capital, Abidjan, Gbagbo's forces abducted political opponents from their homes, torturing and killing many of them. Individuals were burned alive, beaten to death with bricks, or simply executed. Gbagbo's forces also gang-raped women who had been active in getting out the vote for Ouattara. By late December, Navi Pillay, the UN High Commissioner for Human Rights, had found "growing evidence of massive violations of human rights" in Côte d'Ivoire.[174]

International efforts to broker a diplomatic solution and ease Gbagbo from power failed. A former history professor who had studied at the Sorbonne, Gbagbo rebuffed President Obama's personal offers in late 2010 to secure him a soft landing by facilitating his appointment as a distinguished fellow at a prestigious American university. In early March 2011, full-scale war broke out as pro-Ouattara forces launched a military offensive from their northern stronghold with the aim of taking the capital and driving Gbagbo from power. On March 30, the Security Council called on the intransigent Gbagbo to step down and unanimously authorized sanctions against him, his wife Simone, and his close associates. The Council authorized a UN peacekeeping force based in the country as part of a cease-fire agreement following a civil war nearly a decade earlier "to use all necessary means to protect civilians under imminent threat of physical violence" but stopped short of referring the situation in Côte d'Ivoire to the ICC.[175] It did, however, appear to implicitly back an ICC intervention by noting that the ongoing crimes could amount to crimes against humanity. Côte d'Ivoire would not become an ICC state party until early 2013. Yet the court could investigate atrocities that occurred up to a decade earlier there because, following the 2002–2003 civil war, President Gbagbo had submitted Côte d'Ivoire to the ICC's jurisdiction under a provision in the Rome Statute that allowed states not party to the statute do so.

By early April 2011, Ouattara's forces had swept through much of the country and were closing in on Gbagbo's presidential compound in Abidjan. The UN peacekeeping mission and a separate French force—Côte d'Ivoire had once been a prized French colony—provided military backing to Ouattara's offensive, strafing Gbagbo's compound with helicopter gunships. But resistance from Gbagbo's loyalists ground the advance to a halt. As the standoff persisted, a pro-Ouattara television station sought to demoralize Gbagbo, who had holed up in an underground bunker in the presidential compound, by playing parts of *Downfall*, the grim 2004 movie that recreates Adolf Hitler's last days in a Berlin bunker at the end of World War II.[176] But Gbagbo had no intention of becoming a martyr, and Ouattara officials signaled an interest in seeing him stand trial. "He must be alive and he must answer for the crimes against humanity that he committed," said Ali Coulibaly, who served as Ouattara's ambassador to France.[177] When, on April 11, Ouattara's forces, along with French troops, successfully stormed the presidential residence, they were able to arrest Gbagbo, his wife, and his inner circle.

The UN-authorized military interventions in Côte d'Ivoire and in Libya would be held up by proponents as models of limited yet effective international action to halt atrocities. But the fact that international forces took sides—working closely with rebels on the ground to corner Gbagbo and Gaddafi and force regime change—generated sharp criticism, particularly from Russia, regarding the realpolitik aims of the Western-led "humanitarian interventions." The ICC's judicial interventions would face a parallel criticism for only issuing indictments against members of the fallen regimes in Côte d'Ivoire and in Libya.

The defeated Gbagbo did not suffer the same fate as Gaddafi, but hundreds of the former Côte d'Ivoire president's political supporters suffered fatal retribution at the hands of the victors,[178] with the scale of atrocities committed by pro-Ouattara forces appearing to have approached the scale of those committed by Gbagbo forces. In the far western part of the country, for example, pro-Ouattara forces executed elderly villagers, raped women, and "burned entire villages to the ground," according to Human Rights Watch.[179] Human Rights Watch also documented scores of executions that pro-Ouattara forces carried out against their opponents, some of which occurred after their capture. In the aftermath of a decisive military victory, the new Ivorian president turned to the ICC to consolidate his power. In May, Ouattara called upon Moreno-Ocampo to initiate an investigation of the postelection violence.

Laurent Gbagbo was informed by Côte d'Ivoire authorities in late November 2011 that the ICC had issued a warrant for his arrest. Within a day, he was sent to The Hague to face charges of crimes against humanity in the postelection violence. Coming just a month after the murder of Gaddafi at the hands of Libyan executioners, the 2011 arrest and handover of the former Côte d'Ivoire leader signaled an important victory in the ICC's quest to uphold the rule-of-law paradigm. However, the prosecutor's decision not to target suspects tied to massacres committed by Ouattara's forces sparked growing concern that the ICC had bartered its principles to increase the prospects of securing ongoing state cooperation. "The fact that only Gbagbo has been transferred to the ICC, while a positive step, reinforces the perception in Côte d'Ivoire of victor's justice," Human Rights Watch opined in early 2013.[180]

As in Uganda, however, the decision of the ICC chief prosecutor not to seek arrest warrants in Côte d'Ivoire against suspects linked to the political and military leadership of the ruling government did not actually buy a guarantee of unlimited state cooperation. This point became evident in September 2013, when the Ouattara government announced that it would not send Laurent Gbagbo's wife, Simone, who had been under ICC indictment since early 2012, to the ICC. Like her husband, Simone—once called the Iron Lady and known for her fiery speeches—faced four counts of crimes against humanity for being an indirect co-perpetrator in murder, rape, and other sexual violence, as well as a range of other inhumane acts. The Côte d'Ivoire government's assertion that it had the legal capacity to prosecute Simone signaled its intention to seek to prosecute her, as well a third Ivorian suspect indicted by the ICC.

Not long after the government announced its intention to prosecute Simone, the ICC unsealed a crimes-against-humanity indictment against Charles Ble Goude, a former pro-Gbagbo militia leader who had been under arrest in Côte d'Ivoire since his extradition from Ghana in January 2013. Initially, the government maintained that Ble Goude too should be tried before a domestic court. But in March 2014 the government sent him to the ICC. Some analysts believe that Ble Goude was sent to the ICC to stem a domestic controversy sparked by photographs revealing that he had suffered poor treatment during his incarceration in Côte d'Ivoire.[181]

Laurent Gbagbo's and Ble Goude's joint trial was scheduled to begin in The Hague in late 2015. A court in Côte d'Ivoire meanwhile tried and sentenced Simone Gbagbo to twenty years' imprisonment in March 2015 for her alleged role in the post-election violence five years earlier. During the trial, several witnesses accused her of personally distributing arms to death squads that operated in the capital of Abidjan during the five-month conflict. Still determined to try Simone Gbagbo for separate crimes, ICC judges ruled in May 2015 that the former president's wife must be handed over to face trial in The Hague. If Côte d'Ivoire continues to refuse to hand her over, ICC judges could refer the matter to the court's member states.[182]

KENYA AND THE COLLAPSE OF THE
UHURU KENYATTA CASE

Several days before Alassane Ouattara's forces stormed into the presidential residence and arrested Laurent Gbagbo and his wife in April 2011, six of Kenya's most powerful men walked through the doors of the ICC following a long flight from Nairobi. The suspects, who included cabinet ministers Uhuru Kenyatta and William Ruto, had abided by a court-issued summons and made the trip to The Hague to enter pleas of not guilty to charges of orchestrating massacres after that East African country's contested presidential election in late 2007. Gbagbo's arrest in April 2011 and arrival at the ICC later that year demonstrated the sometimes indispensable role of force in bringing suspects to book. In contrast, the appearance of the Kenyan suspects—as with the voluntary surrenders of scores of Serb and Croat suspects at the Yugoslavia tribunal—illustrated that under certain circumstances simple persuasion can play an indispensable role in bringing suspects to court.

When it came to Kenya, the ICC chief prosecutor for the first time initiated a country investigation at his own behest rather than through the usual route of a state's request or a Security Council referral. Kenya, as a state party, had an obligation to provide full cooperation; yet, as we've seen, such state obligations have often remained unfulfilled. The Kenyan government, however, faced strong international expectations to make amends for the postelection violence that had claimed at least 1,100 lives, driven hundreds of thousands of people from their homes, and brought the country, once a bulwark of stability in East Africa, to the brink of civil war. In the eyes of the international community, making amends entailed either undertaking genuine domestic trials or cooperating with an ICC investigation. Delivering criminal accountability was a cornerstone of the peace agreement that former UN Secretary-General Kofi Annan brokered in early 2008. A joint domestic–international commission of inquiry—led by Kenyan judge Philip Waki and authorized by the government-approved peace agreement—called on the ICC to intervene if Kenya's leaders failed to initiate domestic trials for the postelection violence. Accordingly, Moreno-Ocampo took action when Nairobi made no move to initiate domestic trials.

In light of his past diplomatic engagements with Kenyan leaders, the ICC prosecutor hoped that issuing summons for the six suspects would bear fruit. Few suspects relish facing international trial, of course. But appearing voluntarily is preferable, even advantageous, to some, given the alternative of living under the long shadow of an international arrest warrant. Particularly for Kenyatta—who had served as Kenya's deputy prime minister and as its finance minister—living the life of a fugitive held little appeal. Kenyatta's Western orientation—he received his bachelor's degree from Amherst College in the United States—may have been a factor in his decision to abide by the summons and thereby retain his freedom to travel to Europe and beyond. Kenyatta, and Ruto as well, had another reason to appear voluntarily: their budding plans to run for high office placed a premium on public visibility. As long as the suspects appeared for occasional ICC pretrial hearings they could carry on with life in Kenya and devote themselves to politics.

On top of that, the odds of these Kenyans' besting the prosecution in court were not bad, given the defendants' high-powered defense teams, the ICC prosecution's organizational travails, and a string of botched court investigations. In the Kenya situation, the beginnings were certainly not propitious for the prosecution: the cases against three of the six Kenyan suspects—Francis Muthaura, a close presidential aide who served as head of the civil service; Hussein Ali, the former police commissioner; and Henry Kosgey, the industrialization minister—were either thrown out by the pretrial chamber or dropped by the prosecution for lack of evidence. That left only the case against Kenyatta and the one against Ruto and his codefendant, Joshua arap Sang, an influential radio announcer accused of inciting violence.

Kenyatta and Ruto's outwardly cooperative stance—marked by their appearances at pretrial hearings—was belied by their efforts to undermine their upcoming trials and the ICC as an institution. In this, Kenyatta, Ruto, and their surrogates borrowed from al-Bashir's anti-ICC playbook. Like al-Bashir, the Kenyan suspects sought to delegitimize the court by casting it as a political tool wielded by former colonial powers to undermine African sovereignty. Kenyatta and Ruto's attacks gained steam as they launched their high-profile campaigns for higher office. During the 2007 electoral campaign some years earlier, Kenyatta, who belongs to the Kikuyu ethnic group, and Ruto, a Kalenjin, were bitter political rivals. According to their ICC indictments, each bore criminal responsibility for killings that targeted members of the other's ethnic group. But in the 2013 campaign, the two men had struck a deal to run on a single ticket, with Kenyatta as the presidential candidate and Ruto as his running mate.

On the stump, Kenyatta, whose father had led Kenya's independence movement and had been the country's founding president, cast the upcoming election as "a referendum against the ICC" and portrayed the court's intervention as an attack on the Kenyan nation driven by former colonial powers. One month before the election, U.S. diplomat Johnnie Carson, anticipating a potential Kenyatta victory, added fuel to the fire by warning Kenyan voters that "choices have consequences."[183] That warning apparently backfired as pro-Kenyatta pundits seized the opportunity to question American motives at that critical juncture in Kenya's history.

In March 2013, the Kenyan electoral commission declared Kenyatta the winner of the presidential election, with 50.07 percent of the vote, narrowly avoiding a runoff. The second-place finisher, Prime Minister Ralia Odinga, who had lost the 2007 election under fraudulent circumstances, again cried foul and petitioned Kenya's Supreme Court to have the elections nullified. But the Supreme Court upheld Kenyatta's victory, making him the second sitting African head of state, after Omar al-Bashir of Sudan—the very same leader welcomed at the high-profile 2010 celebration of the new Kenyan constitution—to face ICC indictment. And as we saw in the Nairobi scene that opens this chapter, Kenyan leaders further flouted the ICC's authority by hosting the indicted Sudanese president. Kenyan commentators meanwhile opined that the ICC indictments against Kenyatta and his running mate had actually worked to their advantage. Writing for the *Daily Nation*, Rasna Warah argued that both men had taken control of the "national narrative" by associating opposition to the ICC with Kenya's struggle to free itself from its colonial past.[184]

Now at the helm of the Kenyan state, Kenyatta and his supporters enjoyed an ideal position from which to take the obstruction of international justice to a new level. As the Ruto and Kenyatta trials approached, in September and November 2013, respectively, witness intimidation surged. ICC Chief Prosecutor Fatou Bensouda alleged that the scale of interference with witnesses in the Kenyan cases was "unprecedented." Over the previous year, relatives of witnesses had been approached repeatedly with bribes and threats to disclose the whereabouts of witnesses. Two key witnesses withdrew on the eve of the Ruto trial. Meanwhile, at an African Union summit, African leaders called on the ICC to refer the cases against Kenyatta and Ruto to a Kenyan court, while African Union

Chair and Ethiopian Prime Minister Hailemariam Desalegn attacked the court for turning the judicial process into a "race hunt."[185]

Controlling the presidency conveniently handed Kenyatta the power to deal the ICC a devastating blow, given the Rome Statute provision allowing states parties to withdraw their membership. On the eve of Ruto's trial in fall 2013, Kenyatta secured a preliminary parliamentary vote to withdraw Kenya from ICC membership. The final decision to withdraw now rested with the same two men charged by the court with crimes against humanity. A few weeks later the African Union called for a special summit in October to consider the possibility of a mass withdrawal for all thirty-four African states parties. At the summit, the African Union refrained from that drastic measure, but ended up calling on the ICC not to prosecute any African head of state.

In November, the African Union took its bid for immunity for African heads of state to the Security Council, asking the UN body to invoke Article 16 to suspend the ICC cases against President Kenyatta and Vice President Ruto. ICC trials of Kenyatta and Ruto, the Union argued, would undermine peace and security because the Kenyan leaders needed to attend full-time to the aftermath of the September terrorist attack on Nairobi's Westgate Mall. In the wake of the Westgate attack by Somali Islamist fighters, Kenya's main Western allies, the United States and Britain, reacted cautiously to Kenyatta and Ruto's bid for impunity. Although they opposed invoking Article 16, they abstained—as did France—from taking a formal position when it became clear that the move to suspend the cases would fall short by two votes.[186]

The Kenyan leadership had been dogged in its campaign to win African Union support for a possible mass withdrawal. "The Kenyans have been crisscrossing Africa in search of support for their cause, even before their parliament voted to withdraw from the ICC," an African Union official said. In their campaign to thwart the ICC, Kenyan leaders welcomed the support of Rwanda, a state that a decade earlier had honed the art of undermining a UN tribunal while evading international censure for doing so. Rwanda now took a leading role among African states in charging the ICC and the Security Council with inequitable treatment of Africa and pushing for the mass-withdrawal plan. Although Rwanda is not a state party to the Rome Statute, its high-level military and political leaders, and possibly its head of state, President Paul Kagame, could come under ICC scrutiny for their alleged involvement in repeated atrocities in neighboring Democratic Republic of Congo, which is a member of the court. As the long-awaited trials of Kenyatta and Ruto were set to begin in fall 2013, the ICC—perhaps as much as the Kenyan leaders themselves—found itself on trial in the court of African and international public opinion.

By December 2013, it was clear that the Kenyan leadership had gained the upper hand in its sophisticated campaign to undermine the ICC trials. Although Kenya came away empty-handed at the Security Council in November 2013, it scored an important victory the next month during a meeting of the ICC's Assembly of States Parties. In the face of strong pressure from Kenya and other African states parties, the assembly approved a change to its rules to afford special treatment to any defendant who carries out "extraordinary public duties at the highest national level."[187] The new rule was geared toward mollifying Kenyatta and Ruto by granting them more leeway in attending all of their respective trials. "This is what we do at home, bending the courts for the sake of the powerful," commented Kenyan human rights lawyer Abdul Noormohamed. "It's painful to see an international court now changing the rules for the sake of the ego of one powerful man."[188]

In the wake of the Assembly of States Parties meeting, things went from bad to worse for the ICC prosecutor's case against President Kenyatta. In mid-December 2013, ICC prosecutor Bensouda signaled the near-collapse of her case against Kenyatta. Citing the withdrawal of a crucial witness in the fall and an early-December revelation that a second witness now claimed to have provided false testimony, Bensouda announced that her "case against Mr. Kenyatta [did] not satisfy the high evidentiary standards required at trial."[189] Her decision to seek an indefinite adjournment, she insisted, was based on the legal merits of the case and not on political considerations.[190] But worse was yet to come. A year later, on December 5, 2014, the same day Bensouda suspended her investigations in Darfur because of the Security Council's lack of support, she dropped her case against Uhuru Kenyatta. The evidence, she said, could no longer prove beyond a reasonable doubt that Kenya's president had been responsible for crimes against humanity as charged. Bensouda had long accused the Kenyan government of trying to outmaneuver the court by creating an atmosphere of fear that included harassing potential witnesses and threatening others, who then refused to testify. While the collapse of the Kenyatta case was neither the death knell of the ICC nor a testament to the impossibility of prosecuting a head of state, it showed, like the repeated failure to arrest al-Bashir, the limits of the court's power when faced with formidable actors who can bend the legal system to their will.[191]

A MIXED RECORD

Not long after Uhuru Kenyatta declared victory in the Kenyan elections in March 2013, a few hundred miles away in Rwanda, a tall, boyish-looking man in his late thirties approached a guard at the American Embassy in the capital city of Kigali. Introducing himself as Bosco Ntaganda, the man said he wanted to turn himself in to the International Criminal Court. Baffled by the request, the guard telephoned his superiors, who instructed him to let the man into the embassy. "It was a walk-in in the truest sense of the world," State Department spokeswoman Victoria Nuland later told reporters in Washington, DC, adding that the United States had no prior contact with the notorious Tutsi rebel leader nor advance notice that he would turn up at the embassy.[192]

In The Hague, Fatou Bensouda greeted the news with enthusiasm. "This is a good day for victims in the Democratic Republic of the Congo and for international justice," she said. But it was also a very good day for the court. Not only was the United States readily cooperative in passing on to the ICC a notorious suspect, but Ntaganda's surrender would mark the first time that a suspect facing an arrest warrant—as opposed to a summons, as in the case of the Kenyan defendants—had voluntarily turned himself into the court.[193]

Nicknamed the Terminator, General Ntaganda had been a major player in Central Africa, a ruthless militia leader who had formed an army of child soldiers in the eastern Congolese province of Ituri and profited handsomely from smuggling illicit "conflict minerals," natural resources like cassiterite (for tin), wolframite (for tungsten), and coltan (for tantalum), which are used by electronics companies to make mobile phones, laptops, and MP3 players. One of the most hideous crimes attributed to him was the slaughter of at least 800 ethnic Lendus in November 2002 that occurred when his forces attacked the gold-mining town of Mongbwalu. Four years later, the ICC had indicted Ntaganda for conscripting children under the age of fifteen into his militias. A second ICC warrant, issued in July 2012, accused him of a range of crimes, including murder, rape, sexual slavery, and pillaging.[194] During this time, Ntaganda lived openly, playing tennis at exclusive Ituri clubs in the Democratic Republic of Congo and dining at lakeside restaurants in full view of foreign diplomats and UN peacekeepers.[195]

Ntaganda's surrender to the ICC was a curious affair. In November 2012, with the backing of Rwanda, Ntaganda's M23 rebel movement had seized the eastern Congolese city of Goma. That Rwanda had bankrolled the M23 movement, including sending four companies from Rwanda's 305th brigade to oversee and participate in the siege of the city, was later confirmed as "credible and compelling" by a UN investigation.[196] In any case, after a dispute with Ntaganda over the management of the rebel movement, his powerful military chief, Sutani Makenga, withdrew his forces from Goma. In early March 2013, Makenga's fighters overran Ntaganda's compound, forcing the Tutsi leader to flee on foot to Rwanda and thence to Kigali. Once in the city he learned that the Rwandan government had arrested another senior M23 figure, placing him between two very unattractive options and perhaps raising the allure of safety in The Hague.

By early 2014, five out of the six suspects publicly charged by the court for atrocities in Congo had either been arrested or turned themselves in. In this respect, the ICC had been relatively successful in gaining custody of Congolese suspects. International and domestic civil society organizations credited the ICC prosecutor for this progress, yet urged her to expand the pursuit of justice, particularly for ongoing atrocities in the Kivu region of eastern Congo. In a March 2014 declaration, 134 human rights and civil society organizations called on the ICC chief prosecutor to turn her attention to senior political and military officials from Congo, Rwanda, and Uganda "responsible for grave human rights violations by providing . . . [Congolese armed groups] with weapons, funding, recruits and training."[197] The ongoing Rwandan intervention in this conflict, along with the earlier Ugandan intervention, plus the role of the Congolese government and a range of rebel and militia groups, combined to make the war in eastern Congo the deadliest conflict since World War II.

By late September 2015, the ICC had, all told, ten suspects in custody from its various country investigations, another nine defendants having appeared under summons. From one perspective, this record is an encouraging one that speaks to the capacity of the ICC and its international backers to build support for arrests. In addition to the arrest and transfer of the suspects from Côte d'Ivoire and the suspects from Congo, the ICC has also gained custody of three others through arrest operations. In 2008, Belgian authorities arrested Jean-Pierre Bemba, on a sealed warrant issued by the ICC. Bemba, a former high-level Congolese politician, is at the time of writing awaiting judgment on charges of war crimes and crimes against humanity as leader of a militia fighting on behalf of the Central African Republic government earlier in that decade. In January 2015, one of Joseph Kony's co-conspirators, Dominic

Ongwen, was arrested in the Central African Republic and transferred to The Hague.

In late September 2015, authorities in Niger arrested an Islamic extremist wanted on a sealed ICC warrant for allegedly directing the destruction of religious buildings in the historic city of Timbuktu in the West African country of Mali. Following his arrest, the suspect, Ahmad Al Faqi Al Mahdi, was transferred to the ICC. This marked the first arrest in the Mali situation and the first time that the court had brought war crimes charges for the deliberate destruction of religious and historical monuments. During their takeover of northern Mali in 2012, Islamic extremists destroyed most of Timbuktu's famous mausoleums, which they condemned as symbols of idolatry.[198] UNESCO, which lists Timbuktu as a World Heritage Site, recently reconstructed the destroyed mausoleums. A French military intervention pushed the extremists out of northern Mali in 2013. The ICC prosecution initiated a formal investigation in Mali after receiving a referral from the Malian government.

Still at large at the time of writing are nine publicly charged suspects, including Joseph Kony. The three other LRA suspects indicted by the ICC, Vincent Otti, Raska Lukwiya, and Okot Odhiambo, are believed to have been killed. Otti was reportedly executed on Kony's orders, while the other two reportedly died in battles with the Ugandan army. Five Sudanese remain fugitives: President Omar al-Bashir, his minister of defense, Abdel Raheem Muhammad Hussein, his former minister of state for humanitarian affairs and governor of South Kordofan State, Ahmad Muhammad Harun, a government-backed Janjaweed militia leader in Darfur, Ali Kushayb, and a Darfuri rebel leader, Abdallah Banda Abakaer Nourain.

The court's overall record has been decidedly mixed. At the time of writing, several trials, including Ntaganda's, are underway at the ICC. But in more than a decade, the court has convicted just two Congolese militia leaders. Thomas Lubanga was sentenced to fourteen years' imprisonment for the war crime of enlisting and conscripting children under the age of fifteen and using them to participate in hostilities, while Germain Katanga was sentenced to twelve years' imprisonment for crimes against humanity including attacks on civilian populations and destruction of property and pillaging. Another Congolese militia leader, Mathieu Ngudjolo Chui, was acquitted of war crimes and crimes against humanity charges in December 2012. In addition, the cases against six ICC suspects (out of a total of thirty-two publicly charged in connection with violations of international humanitarian law since the court began operations) have been dismissed or withdrawn prior to trial because of a lack of sufficient incriminating evidence presented by the prosecution.

As we have seen, the institutional foundations of the ICC are decidedly weak, especially when it comes to the prosecutor's ability to conduct investigations without state obstruction. Even when investigations are opened, the prosecutor often lacks the resources to do a proper job. And then there are the political maneuverings and obstructions of states that hinder arrests. In cases where a state petitions the court for an investigation of alleged atrocities within its own borders, state cooperation can often be highly unpredictable, waxing and waning depending on state interests and political circumstances. A "self-referring" state can change its mind about cooperating with the ICC at any time, leaving the prosecutor high and dry, as has been the case in Uganda. Or the accused can flee to a state that is not a party to the Rome Statute and is thus not legally bound to arrest and transfer the suspect to the court. States, as well as the UN Security Council, can also use referrals to brand their political opponents as international pariahs by asking the court to determine whether their forces have committed serious crimes. A self-referring state may then threaten to withhold cooperation if the ICC prosecutor decides to target state criminality.

On the positive side, select ICC member states have aided the court in vital ways: providing funding, promoting universal jurisdiction of the Rome Statue, and combatting the Bush administration's early anti-ICC campaign. Yet the withdrawal of crucial support for the ICC in apprehending suspects by many African and European states parties—and by the Assembly of States Parties as a whole—shows that even those states legally bound to provide cooperation often fail to do so when larger political or economic interests hang in the balance. Consequently, the ICC chief prosecutors have often had to maneuver on their own within the political and legal parameters of each situation country. This dynamic means that the chief prosecutor must become an agile strategic actor beyond the courtroom, urging both targeted states and key international community actors to fulfill their legal obligations to the court.

As of September 2015, only two of the five permanent members of the Security Council—France and the United Kingdom—are members of the ICC. Nor are there any prospects that the other three—Russia, China, and the United States—will join in the foreseeable future. While

Russian and Chinese attitudes toward the court are less open and pronounced than those of the United States, their behavior toward it similarly varies according to the policy interest at play. As we shall see in the next chapter, the prospects of the United States' joining the ICC any time soon grew increasingly remote after the terrorist attacks of September 11, 2001. Yet, with or without the support of the great powers, the ICC arguably remains a vital force in international affairs as an increasing number of states turn to it to address international crimes committed in their midst.

CHAPTER 9

The "War on Terror" and Its Legacy

When a plane hit the second tower of the World Trade Center the morning of September 11, 2001, President George W. Bush was in Sandra Kay Daniels's second-grade classroom in Saratoga, Florida, to publicize his education policy. He sat at the head of the class, next to Ms. Daniels, in front of a sign declaring "Reading makes a country great!" Off to his right, his chief of staff, Andrew Card, and three other White House staffers stood smiling, while in the back, reporters scribbled notes and adjusted their cameras to peer over the rows of boys in white shirts and girls with their hair neatly braided and beaded. It was the perfect media moment.

As Ms. Daniels rapped a pencil on her desk like a metronome and exhorted her students to open their books and begin reading a story—"The Pet Goat"—in unison, Card left the line of staffers and walked over to the president. "Sir," he whispered, "the second tower of the World Trade Center has been struck. We are under attack."[1]

Bush listened intently, nodded, and after a moment, reached for a copy of the students' text. Cradling the open book, he remained seated, his body oddly frozen. For the next seven minutes, his eyes moved from the book, to the students dutifully reciting their lines, to some unseen image floating high above their heads.

Although he was hotly criticized for his inaction in the classroom that morning, the president's response, when it came, was fierce. On September 20, 2001, nine days after the attacks, he addressed a joint

333

session of Congress. The United States, he said, had entered a "war on terror" unlike any conflict it had ever faced. "Our grief has turned to anger, and anger to resolution. Whether we bring our enemies to justice, or bring justice to our enemies, justice will be done. . . . Our war on terror begins with Al Qaeda, but it does not end there. It will not end until every terrorist group of global reach has been found, stopped, and defeated."[2]

A cornerstone in fighting this new war would be securing information from known and suspected terrorists. As Vice President Dick Cheney put it in an interview on NBC's *Meet the Press* a few days earlier, to defeat America's new enemy, "We . . . have to work . . . the dark side. . . . We're going to spend time in the shadows in the intelligence world. A lot of what needs to be done here will have to be done quietly, without any discussions, using sources and methods that are available to our intelligence agencies, if we're going to be successful. That's the world these folks operate in. And so it's going to be vital for us to use any means at our disposal, basically, to achieve our objective."[3]

Cheney's cloak-and-dagger pronouncement heralded the erection of an extensive scaffolding of legal rationales over the next two years that the Bush administration would use to justify, in Jane Mayer's words, "a new, ad hoc system of detention and interrogation that operated outside of any previously known coherent body of law."[4] The central feature of the New Paradigm, as the administration referred to this system, was the manufacture of extensive executive authority to use harsh methods of interrogation—including torture—on suspected terrorists, tactics they believed would yield higher-value intelligence. As former U.S. Undersecretary of Defense for Policy Douglas Feith bluntly put it: "Intelligence is in the heads of these people. We need to extract it."[5]

Distinguished American historian and former Kennedy-administration official Arthur Schlesinger Jr. called the New Paradigm "the most dramatic, sustained, and radical challenge to the rule of law in American history."[6] While the United States had banded together with other nations after World War II to ensure accountability for mass atrocities by developing shared international legal norms and procedures, the Bush administration was taking the United States in a quite different direction, one motivated by vigilante justice and adherence to the cowboy credo of "going it alone."[7] In some instances, the administration would nod toward traditional, due-process means of pursuing and arresting suspects; in others it would abandon the rule of law and "go rogue," preferring to "shoot first and ask questions later." Along the way, it would co-opt new players and technologies to hunt down those it deemed terrorists, persuade foreign governments to open secret detention centers, "render" suspects to third countries to be tortured,[8] and authorize cyber-dragnets to spy on U.S. citizens. By the end of the decade, the United States, long considered the human rights leader of the twentieth century, was making headlines as one of the most notorious human rights abusers of the twenty-first.

In this chapter, we scrutinize the post-9/11 actions of the United States to illustrate the path the Bush and later the Obama administrations took in pursuit of their own brand of international justice. In the decade and a half following the attacks, the United States would start two wars as part of the hunt for two men, Osama bin Laden and Saddam Hussein; backtrack from its global position on human rights and its push to promote the Geneva Conventions; attempt to ensure that no high-level American would ever be arrested for crimes committed as part of the response to the 9/11 events; and engage in numerous actions that many would see as direct violations of domestic law and international agreements the nation once supported. As one high-level administration official put it in a September 2002 interview, "All you need to know is that there was a before 9/11 and there was an after 9/11."[9]

This fundamental shift is demonstrated in the United States' post-9/11 refusal to support the evolution of the International Criminal Court; its trading of the dream of human rights for the paradigm of "capture or kill"; and its turn away from a courts-based approach to international criminal law to a military/CIA/intelligence–oriented emphasis on investigations and targeted killings. Such a fundamental transition notably moved power out of the hands of the judiciary, and to some extent the legislature, toward the executive branch. It also moved the government's response to 9/11 out of the media and legal spotlights into an undercover world, where the law could be not only stretched but in some cases broken in pursuit of a newer, rawer form of "justice."

After 9/11, the Bush administration in effect decided that the conventional method of fighting terrorism as a criminal act—which requires due process before a court of law—was obsolete. Michael Rolince, a high-ranking terrorism expert in the FBI, told the *New Yorker* that the prevailing attitude in the White House was "rule-of-law be damned."[10] Or as John Yoo, a law professor at the University of California, Berkeley, and a former attorney in the Office of Legal Counsel of the Department of Justice from 2001 to 2003, put it: "The United

States used to treat terrorism as a criminal justice problem. The September 11th attacks showed that the struggle with al-Qaeda had moved into warfare. And I think when a foreign entity, for political purposes, can kill 3,000 Americans, and cause billions of dollars of damage, and try to eliminate the leaders of the American government, that sounds like war to most people. It doesn't sound like crime."[11]

From now on, a new enemy would require new tactics, most of which would have been considered illegal and politically untenable before September 11. This declaration of exemption from the rule of law—while insisting that other nations adhere to its dictates—became yet another example of American exceptionalism in the aftermath of the 9/11 attacks, a pattern that would recur in multiple ways in the years ahead.

"THE GLOVES ARE OFF"

On September 17, 2001, Cofer Black, the head of the CIA's terror-fighting operation known as the Counterterrorist Center, presented to President Bush and Vice President Cheney a detailed memo setting out a series of covert CIA operations that would be hidden from the American public and require the oversight of only four members of Congress, who themselves would be sworn to secrecy. By late afternoon, Bush had signed off on Operation Greystone, a top-secret directive instructing the CIA to render al-Qaeda suspects to secret detention facilities known as "black sites" outside the United States, and to employ "an alternative set of interrogation procedures" for suspected terrorists taken into its custody.[12] Suspects would be captured with the assistance of foreign intelligence agencies and then flown in an unmarked plane to countries around the globe, where they would be kept incommunicado and subjected to torture.[13] To distance himself from the directive, the president gave CIA Director George Tenet blanket authority, in Jane Mayer's words, "to decide on a case-by-case basis whom to kill, whom to kidnap, whom to detain and interrogate, and how."[14] Gary Schroen, one of the first CIA officers to be dispatched to Afghanistan under Operation Greystone, recalled in his memoir *First In* a meeting he attended in Cofer Black's office in Langley. "Your mission is to find Osama Bin Laden and his senior lieutenants, and kill them," Schroen recalled Black as saying. "I don't want Bin Laden and his thugs captured, I want them dead. Alive and in prison here in the United States and they'll become a symbol, a rallying point for other terrorists. . . . I want to see photos of their heads on pikes. I want Bin Laden's head shipped back in a box filled with dry ice. I want to be able to show Bin Laden's head to the President. I promised him I would do that."[15]

Cofer Black's "hang 'em high" bravado reflected the CIA's updated mission. For those targets not marked for assassination, however, there was a problem: the agency was nearly devoid of expertise in detention and interrogation. A. B. Krongard, the number-three official in the CIA from March 2001 until 2004, recalled his reaction when he learned of Operation Greystone. "I asked, 'What are we going to do with these guys when we get them?' I said, 'We've never run a prison. We don't have the languages. We don't have the interrogators.'"[16] With relatively little research or reflection, as the world later learned, CIA staff hired two psychologists to glean new interrogation practices from a military training program known as Survival, Evasion, Resistance, and Escape (SERE).[17] SERE had initially been developed at the end of the Korean War to expose American military personnel to abusive practices and torture tactics—including stress positions, grueling forced exercise, sensory deprivation, sensory overload, sleep deprivation, extended isolation, and other forms of physical and psychological duress—that had been used by the Communists during the war, to prepare soldiers for possible abuse should they ever be captured by an enemy force.[18] Instead, such practices were now being extracted for use on detainees by the United States.

Greystone was kept secret until late October 2001, when a senior U.S. official told the *Washington Post* that the CIA had been directed to "undertake its most sweeping and lethal covert action since the founding of the agency in 1947." "The gloves are off," the official said. "The president has given the agency the green light to do whatever is necessary."[19]

That same month, on October 7, the United States began bombing Afghanistan, the nation that was believed to be housing the masterminds of 9/11. One month later, Bush signed a military order authorizing the detention of al-Qaeda members and other terrorist suspects who were being swept up in Afghanistan "at an appropriate location designated by the Secretary of Defense," and stipulating that suspects should be tried by military commissions overseen by the executive branch, and not by federal courts. The military commissions would be exempt from applying either the "ordinary rules of military law . . . [or] the laws of war."[20] The detention facility had to be located in a place where detainees could be interrogated for indefinite periods far from the reach of civilian courts, with their more exacting standards of evidence and their concern for defendants' rights. Eventually Defense Secretary Donald

338 | Chapter Nine

Rumsfeld chose the U.S. naval base at Guantánamo Bay, Cuba, a refueling station and a center for processing Cuban and Haitian refugees. The first detainees, transferred from U.S. custody in Afghanistan, arrived at Guantánamo on January 11, 2002, and were locked in a facility called Camp X-Ray, a series of small, outdoor cages. After three months, as the number of detainees swelled beyond X-Ray's capacity, the detainees were moved to a larger, newly-built supermax prison, Camp Delta.[21]

While Guantánamo's physical infrastructure was being expanded to house scores of "the worst"[22] suspected terrorists, attorneys in the Office of Legal Counsel, a division of the U.S. Department of Justice, were scrambling to develop a legal infrastructure to govern conditions of confinement and interrogation at Guantánamo and other U.S. military detention facilities. One of their overarching objectives was to find a way to appear to be adhering to the rule of law, yet remain relatively unhampered by its constraints.

Despite John Yoo's ruminations, the heart of the Bush administration's strategy was to blur the boundary between war and terrorism—two bodies of law that have historically been distinct, albeit overlapping—so that the executive branch could use its discretion to apply each body of law as it saw fit.[23] Notably, acts of war have been subject to one set of laws, best signified by the Geneva Conventions, while terrorism has been subject to criminal legal frameworks, and is primarily domestic. The marriage of—and blurring between—the two frameworks is evident in the title the United States assigned to the conflict in which it was engaged: the "war on terror."[24]

Lawyers in the Office of Legal Counsel also quickly began drafting memoranda designed to circumvent domestic and international laws established to protect prisoners of war from torture and ill-treatment. Beginning with the Lieber Code in the American Civil War, the U.S. military had championed the concept of humane and responsible behavior toward captured combatants and toward civilians in times of war. Since 1950, the United States had adhered to the Third Geneva Convention, also known as the Geneva Convention Relative to the Treatment of Prisoners of War, which it both signed and ratified in the aftermath of World War II. The convention sets forth an elaborate regime for how prisoners of war are to be treated during confinement, and prohibits "physical or mental torture" and "any other form of coercion . . . to secure from them information of any kind whatever." The convention also stipulates that prisoners who refuse to divulge information "may not be threatened, insulted, or exposed to any unpleasant or disadvantageous treatment of any kind."[25] Much of this language was reflected in the U.S. Army's field manual on interrogation, adopted in 1956, and its subsequent revisions, which warn of the perils of torture and ill-treatment: "Use of torture is not only illegal but also . . . is a poor technique that yields unreliable results, may damage subsequent collection efforts, and can induce the source to say what he thinks the [interrogator] wants to hear. Use of torture can also have many possible negative consequences at national and international levels."[26]

Government lawyers in the Office of Legal Counsel argued that the Third Geneva Convention did not apply to members of al-Qaeda or the Taliban captured in Afghanistan or elsewhere. Alberto Gonzales, then White House Counsel, sent a memorandum to the president claiming that the "war on terror" had "render[ed] obsolete Geneva's strict limitations on [the] questioning of enemy prisoners."[27] He explained that a key advantage in declaring Taliban and al-Qaeda operatives outside Geneva's protective gambit would be that it "substantially reduces the [eventual] threat of domestic criminal prosecution under the War Crimes Act" for the impermissibly harsh treatment of detainees.[28] He recommended that the president declare al-Qaeda and Taliban prisoners exempt from the protection of the Third Geneva Convention, a move that would "preserve flexibility" and "reduce the threat" that administration officials and military personnel would later be prosecuted for war crimes.[29]

President Bush formally endorsed Gonzales' recommendation and announced that persons of interest who were taken into U.S. custody during the "war on terror" would not be considered prisoners of war and were therefore not subject to the protections set forth in the convention.[30] On January 19, 2002, Secretary of Defense Donald Rumsfeld ordered the U.S. Joint Chiefs of Staff to inform military commanders in Afghanistan that Taliban and al-Qaeda captives should only be treated humanely "to the extent necessary and appropriate with military necessity."[31]

These directives ran counter to the development of domestic and international law over the previous six decades. In wartime, the Geneva Conventions apply to the CIA as much as to any branch of the military. In effect, all prisoners of war must be treated humanely, no matter which agency is the detaining authority.[32] But if, as the president had declared, in the new "war on terror" the Third Geneva Convention did not apply to the U.S. military, then it would not apply to the CIA— or so the administration reasoned.[33] In August 2002, in an attempt to provide a veneer of legality to the new use of "enhanced interrogation techniques," Office of Legal Counsel Director Jay S. Bybee and his colleague John Yoo drafted a memorandum putting their own spin on the international convention. They asserted that institutionalized abuse did not descend into torture unless such abuse inflicted pain "equivalent in intensity to the pain accompanying serious physical injury, such as organ failure . . . or even death,"[34] a standard that makes little sense given the lack of clear correlation between either organ failure, or death, and pain; further, by this standard, any "evidence" of torture would come too late to protect the detainee, as it would emerge only after the detainee was at dire risk of dying, or had already died. The lawyers wrote that torture could only occur where that harm was a "precise objective" of an abusive act, and not a by-product of interrogation, an absurd standard that would have condoned even the torture methods used by the Nazi regime during World War II, so long as the abusers' intention was primarily to extract information. In effect, these lawyers were using the law not as a means to prevent torture and cruel treatment but as an instrument to expand the permissibility of the "enhanced interrogation techniques" in which CIA interrogators were already engaged.[35]

While the administration was busy explaining why international— and even domestic law, in some cases—shouldn't apply to their treatment of detainees, they were, according to Jess Bravin, the Supreme Court correspondent for the *Wall Street Journal,* also attempting to expand the universe of offenses that they could classify as "war crimes" in order to import military law into historically civilian arenas.[36] By laboring to make crimes like conspiracy and material support for terrorism war crimes, U.S. officials could assert that those crimes should be tried not in U.S. courts but by the executive branch's military commissions. In such a way they could mitigate—if not eliminate—the judicial branch's oversight, and thus its ability to act as a check on executive power. Under the New Paradigm, terrorist suspects captured on and off the battlefield would never have access to the U.S. judiciary. Such a move would prevent future terrorist suspects from arguing to judicial courts that they had been subjected to "harsh interrogation practices" and therefore torture or cruel, inhuman, and degrading treatment.

This new legal paradigm conveniently provided the administration with the added bonus of expanded executive-branch authority, and thus advanced its efforts to realize the "unitary executive theory," of which many members of the Bush administration had long been ardent proponents. The theory asserts that Congress should have only limited ability to constrain the actions of the president when it comes to setting policy for the executive branch, particularly during times of war and especially with regard to issues of national security.[37]

Office of Legal Counsel lawyers also crafted the term "enemy combatant," a classification that does not exist in international law, to categorize terrorist suspects brought into U.S. custody. This new classification represented an attempt to further strip detainees of any protections under the Geneva Conventions, something that would—if it rendered the Conventions' protections moot—constitute a violation of the United States' international obligations. Writes law professor Peter Jan Honigsberg: "Enemy combatant sounds like a legal term, but it is not. . . . The term did not meaningfully exist . . . before the administration introduced it in spring 2002. Until then, the universe of combatants . . . consisted of two categories: lawful combatants—those entitled to prisoner of war (POW) status—and unlawful combatants [someone who fights illegally and thus may be prosecuted for his or her actions under domestic law], who were not so entitled. That is all."[38] By late 2002, hundreds of "enemy combatants" were being held and interrogated at Guantánamo and at CIA black sites around the world.[39]

The aim of these efforts revolving around the New Paradigm, the Bush administration repeatedly said, was to win the "war on terror." As part of that struggle, they were determined to find and neutralize the person they held most responsible for the 9/11 attacks: Osama bin Laden.

AN UNWANTED MAN

A Saudi national born to Yemeni parents, Osama bin Mohammed bin Awad bin Laden helped found al-Qaeda ("the Base") in 1988 in part to support Afghan resistance against the Soviet occupation of Afghanistan.[40] By the early 1990s, while still a relatively young man, bin Laden and his operatives had turned their focus toward ridding the Islamic world of all "occupiers," including Americans.[41]

By the mid-1990s, Osama bin Laden's organization was suspected of involvement in a series of terrorist activities, including the failed 1993 bombing of New York's World Trade Center and the financing of terrorist training camps in Sudan and, later, Yemen.[42] In May 1996, in the wake of al-Qaeda's attempted assassination of Egyptian President Hosni Mubarak, Sudan's president, Omar al-Bashir, expelled bin Laden from

Sudan. Bashir had originally offered to turn him over to the Saudis if they would guarantee bin Laden's freedom and safety,[43] but Saudi Crown Prince Abdullah refused. As one observer noted, "Bin Laden wasn't yet a wanted man, but he certainly was an unwanted one."[44] Bin Laden eventually left Sudan aboard a chartered flight and travelled to Jalalabad, Afghanistan, where he forged a close relationship with Mullah Mohammed Omar, the spiritual leader of the Taliban. On August 23, 1996, the al-Qaeda leader released a video statement declaring a religious war against the United States and excoriating Saudi leaders for exchanging *shari'ah* law for civil law and for allowing American crusaders to occupy Saudi Arabia[45]—an occupation he linked to the United States' desire to control oil prices for its own benefit in the aftermath of the first Gulf War.

In 1998 bin Laden expanded his call to action: "We . . . . call on Muslim *ulema,* leaders, youths and soldiers," he announced, "to launch the raid on Satan's U.S. troops and the devil's supporters allying with them, and to displace those who are behind them so that they may learn a lesson."[46] In June of that year, a lengthy U.S. grand jury investigation produced a sealed indictment charging bin Laden with "conspiracy to attack defense facilities of the United States."[47] Two months later, al-Qaeda operatives carried out bombings of U.S. embassies in Nairobi, Kenya, and Dar es Salaam, Tanzania, killing more than 200 people and injuring more than 5,000 others. And two years later, al-Qaeda bombed the USS *Cole,* a destroyer harbored for refueling in the Yemeni port of Aden. By this time, various countries had issued indictments against bin Laden for numerous crimes.

Against this background, the Bush administration seized the opportunity presented by 9/11 to attack Afghanistan as a safe haven for al-Qaeda and ferret bin Laden from his lair. The bombing of bin Laden's redoubt in the Tora Bora Mountains in December 2001 and an associated raid carried out by forty elite special operations forces were triggered when bin Laden spent "a couple seconds too long on his radio," enabling the CIA to locate him within a ten-meter range.[48] Given the attack's ferocity and bin Laden's subsequent silence, many U.S. officials surmised that he had died. But in November 2002, Al Jazeera received an audiotape, hand-delivered by a courier from bin Laden, celebrating a recent series of terrorist successes.[49] With evidence emerging that bin Laden had slipped out of Tora Bora just as the bombing began, the key question for the U.S. government shifted from whether he was dead or alive to where in the world he was.

THE ACE OF SPADES

Bin Laden wasn't the only person in the Bush administration's sights after the 9/11 attacks. Since the first Gulf War, under President George H. W. Bush, the United States had welcomed—if not actively encouraged—attempts to overthrow Saddam Hussein, the Iraqi dictator known as the Butcher of Baghdad, who had gassed Kurdish villages, was rumored to have attempted the assassination of the first President Bush, and had once threatened to "burn half of Israel."[50]

The search to find and arrest Hussein demonstrates a second approach the United States used in the wake of 9/11—a "good cop" approach that hewed more tightly to the traditional rule-of-law path than the more vigilante approach of the New Paradigm that characterized the search for bin Laden and others behind the 9/11 attacks. The hunts for both bin Laden and Hussein, however, stand in contrast to the search for Nazi fugitives, such as Eichmann, in the wake of World War II. In Eichmann's case, one man paid the price for the killing of millions, whereas in the twenty-first century, thousands have paid the price—due to fighting in Afghanistan and Iraq—as part of the quest for two. The cruel irony of these later stories is that in going after the two despots, the United States destroyed thousands more American lives and countless Afghani and Iraqi ones, and helped decimate two countries. Further, while Eichmann's capture led to a monumental trial, bin Laden and (to a lesser extent) Hussein met their fates largely outside of courts.

On March 17, 2003, eighteen months after the 9/11 attacks, President Bush announced that the United States was preparing to attack Iraq because of its alleged possession of weapons of mass destruction (an allegation later found to be false) and the related threat that Saddam and his government ostensibly posed to the security of the United States. The true rationale, however, according to several commentators, was to open Iraq to western oil companies and eliminate Saddam as a barrier to their expansion in the region.[51] "Saddam and his sons," Bush warned, "must leave Iraq within 48 hours. Their refusal to do so will result in military conflict commenced at a time of our choosing."[52] Two days later, tens of thousands of U.S. and coalition ground forces swept into Iraq as American forces dropped a hailstorm of 2,000-pound bombs on the capital, Baghdad. "In this conflict," President Bush told the nation on the eve of the invasion, "America faces an enemy who has no regard for conventions of war or rules of morality.... We have no ambition in Iraq, except to remove a threat and restore control of that country to its own people."[53]

Today, the trillion-dollar, eight-year war in Iraq, which would claim the lives of approximately 4,500 American soldiers and at least 165,000 Iraqis, is remembered not for what President Bush said he would accomplish but for the botched (if not fabricated) intelligence that preceded it; torture and abuse at the U.S. military prison at Abu Ghraib; and the tenacity of an insurgency that bedeviled U.S. and coalition forces. Amidst all that calamity, the pursuit, capture, and trial of Saddam Hussein stands out as a relative success story.

The search for the Iraqi leader, however, was not without its challenges. Historically, the U.S. military has preferred to leave the pursuit of fugitives to law enforcement. Just as the CIA was unprepared to house detainees, the military was unprepared to conduct a manhunt. According to a 2005 report by researchers at the Naval Postgraduate School in Monterey, California, "the U.S. military's limited experience conducting manhunts has created a doctrinal, legal, and procedural void. No established set of systems or procedures has been formalized to specifically address man hunting within the confines of military operations. Consequently, the U.S. military approaches man hunting according to established processes created for conventional battle—find, fix [lock in on], and destroy. Yet, the very nature of finding individuals differs considerably from finding a unit on the battlefield."[54]

Although "know thy enemy"—a phrase originally coined by Sun Tzu, the great Chinese military general and author of *The Art of War*—is one of the first principles of warfare, American military operations and national security decision-making have consistently suffered from limited knowledge of foreign cultures, their political history, and their organizations. As former Secretary of Defense Robert McNamara noted in his autobiography *In Retrospect* about his time in office during the 1960s, "I [had] never visited Indochina, nor did I understand or appreciate its history, language, culture, or values. When it came to Vietnam, we found ourselves setting policy for a region that was terra incognita."[55] McNamara's admission underscores how easily American leaders have been blinded by their own ethnocentrism and biased assumptions. In more recent years, this myopia has been reinforced by the misplaced belief that technical solutions—from satellite imagery to "surgical strikes" and drones—can provide quick fixes to national security problems. Moreover, until recently, American military officers have received little formal training in anthropology or sociology—disciplines whose purview is understanding the interests, habits, intentions, beliefs, and interconnections of groups of people.

In preparation for the 2003 invasion of Iraq, U.S. commanders had developed three simple tools to help them identify and ferret out key officials in Saddam's government, with the ultimate objective of apprehending Saddam himself. The first was a diagram depicting the hierarchal structure of Saddam's regime—who reported to whom and in what capacity. In form, the chart was almost identical to a diagram of the Nazi command that U.S. soldiers had carried into Germany in April 1945. The second tool was a catalog of hundreds of lower-ranking targets, known as the Black List—a list later discovered to be populated with the names of many people who were misidentified, innocent, or both, and based on a misunderstanding of Iraqi name conventions. And the third was a deck of cards containing the names of the fifty-five most wanted Iraqi officials, mostly high-ranking members of Saddam's Baath Party and his Revolutionary Command Council. Such playing cards— each of which typically contains the name of a wanted person, his address, and, if available, his job—had been used as far back as the American Civil War and later in both World War II and Korea.[56] Seeing the names, faces, and titles of targets as they pass the time playing cards is supposed to help soldiers identify their prey during field operations. In the Iraqi deck, Saddam Hussein was the ace of spades, and his sons Qusay and Uday the aces of clubs and hearts.[57]

The ace of diamonds was Saddam's trusted personal secretary, Abid Hamid Mahmoud al-Khatab. He was caught relatively quickly, but he had some bad news for his American interrogators: soon after the fall of Baghdad, his former boss had become convinced that he could survive only if he severed contact with his inner circle, including his two sons.[58] Hussein had then vanished. If Abid was telling the truth, the other men in the deck of cards might have little or no reliable information to contribute on Saddam's whereabouts.

Saddam's strategy caught the Americans by surprise, as Chris Wilson noted in *Slate*: "The war's architects had failed to account for the fact that Iraqi society functions completely differently than our own. Saddam's regime had been built on top of the country's ancient tribal traditions—a heritage that he either suppressed or tried to co-opt, depending on how much he needed the backing of the sheikhs at the moment. . . . When Baghdad fell, the institutions of Saddam's regime fell along with it."[59]

So where had Saddam gone?

According to Jerrold Post, a former CIA analyst who in 1991 had written a psychological profile of the dictator, Hussein would almost certainly have taken refuge in a place where he had always felt protected, surrounded by people he could trust. Post also noted that the former Iraqi leader was a huge fan of *The Godfather* and its fictitious Mafia boss, Don Vito Corleone. As any film buff knows, Corleone always turned to his family for support in times of crisis. So it made perfect sense: "Saddam went where he always did when he was in trouble. He went home."[60]

OPERATION RED DAWN

When the 1st Brigade Combat Team of the U.S. 4th Infantry Division rolled into Saddam's hometown of Tikrit in mid-April 2003, there were no Tikritis on the streets waving American flags and blowing kisses to the tired GIs. The city and surrounding farms, though quiet on the outside, were bristling with insurgents armed with rocket-propelled grenades and other weapons left behind by Saddam's elite guards. By late May, the insurgents had become a persistent threat, sniping at GIs and ambushing U.S. vehicles, often in broad daylight.

In June, Colonel James Hickey, a 1982 graduate of the Virginia Military Institute with advanced degrees in linguistics and international public policy, took command of the 1st Brigade. Hickey was impressed by his intelligence unit's database of more than a thousand names of known and suspected insurgents, but couldn't make heads or tails of it. He ordered his chief intelligence officer, Major Stan Murphy, to adopt a new approach, one that highlighted connections between everyone they had captured or wanted to capture.

Over the next five months, Murphy and his team mapped a network of Saddam's family, bodyguards, associates, and most trusted companions— many of whom had not been included in the infamous deck of cards or on the Black List. Murphy's team worked in tandem with a task force, headed by Lieutenant Steve Russell, that raided houses and farms to arrest suspected insurgents and gather photographs and documents.

In constructing their network diagram, Murphy's team was using the same tools that marketers employ to sell diet pills on the Internet and that epidemiologists use to map the spread of a virus. The concept—referred to as network analysis or social network theory—charts social relationships and prompts consideration of how such relationships might influence individual and group behavior. As Murphy's diagram grew, the soldiers began to connect the dots of familial and tribal allegiances not only in Tikrit but also in other regions of Iraq. Eventually, the intelligence team created a sprawling color-coded diagram containing the names, physical descriptions, whereabouts, and relationships of over 300 of Saddam's top aides, military officers, and other supporters. The diagram was basically an extensive family tree, with Saddam's picture in the center, and lines connecting his tribal and blood ties to five Tikriti families: the Hasans, Majids, Musslits, Hadooshis, and Heremoses.[61]

Acting on a tip that Saddam had broken with his inner circle and likely returned to Tikrit, Murphy's team looked more closely at his long-term relationships with the five Tikriti families and how they interacted. In network terminology, the team was looking for *multiplexity*— cases in which two or more individuals were connected in multiple ways.[62]

In the coming months, Russell's unit increased the frequency of its raids on the five Tikriti families, gathering more photographs and documents. The information they collected was added, piece by piece, to the diagram.[63] As U.S. personnel pored over this information, rumors of Saddam's whereabouts spread like wildfire. "We called these ruminations 'Elvis sightings,'" Russell recalled. "We often joked that he was probably pumping gas in Auja."[64] Others claimed he was using body doubles, or that he had undergone radical plastic surgery.[65]

Despite the far-fetched nature of these rumors, the Americans began to pay close attention to the men who were in Saddam's innermost circle and thus most likely concealing his whereabouts. Russell was sure the network revolved around the Musslit family in particular. "The problem," Russell recalled, "was getting to them and, once that was accomplished, how to move in on Saddam swiftly enough before the information decayed. We had [often] been so close yet always a step or two behind."[66]

One day a teenage boy came to see Hickey.[67] The boy claimed to know of a farm nearby where "some important people were hiding." Convinced that the boy was telling the truth, Hickey ordered Russell to raid the farm. The raid led to the capture of Thaier Amin Ali, a member of one of the five families. In 1959, Thaier's father had helped Saddam escape capture after his failed attempt to assassinate Iraq's prime minister, Abd al-Karim Qasim. Thaier hid Saddam on his farm, which adjoined the east bank of the Tigris River across from Auja and near the village of Ad Dawr. As Iraqi forces closed in, Saddam slipped into the river, mounted a horse on the other side, and "rode off into the sunset to become the future tyrant of Iraq."[68] Despite Saddam's annual reenactment of that swim with his cronies, as Russell writes, "little could we know in just a few days the significance of that very location."[69]

As successful captures mounted in Iraq, the military found that each "new vein seemed to be connected to the same families. Once again, the enemy was hidden in plain sight until we could unravel 'the big ball of yarn,' as Colonel Hickey . . . put it."[70] Within a day, however, the yarn would begin unraveling at a startling pace: as Russell recalls, with the captures that followed in Thaier's wake, by December 10 "we had plowed through almost more information than we could handle."[71]

Repeatedly, the focus returned to the Musslit family and two brothers, Rudman and Mohammed al-Musslit. Intelligence reports, based largely on interrogations of suspected insurgents, indicated that the Musslit family was heavily involved in the insurgency and thus likely to be in close touch with Saddam. On Murphy's diagram, Rudman and Mohammed played the role of "connectors": their names emerged frequently during interrogations as key intermediaries between Saddam and various factions within the insurgency.

Rudman was captured in November, but died of a heart attack shortly after his arrest. Then, on the evening of December 12, 2003, forces apprehended Mohammed, known to be Saddam's most trusted bodyguard. Under "pressure," Musslit revealed that Saddam was on a farm near Ad Dawr, on the east side of the Tigris River.[72] Colonel Hickey set a raid for later that night. Without being told who the target was, soldiers readied for the raid with Musslit in tow. Hickey reviewed Musslit's interrogation report and ordered his men to narrow their target to three locations, two of which were dubbed Wolverine 1 and Wolverine 2, after the movie *Black Hawk Down*, an epic memorial to the failed battle at Mogadishu. The sites were located in an orchard just three kilometers from the U.S. military's headquarters.[73]

Operation Red Dawn was set for approximately 8:00 P.M. so that it could take place under cover of darkness. Special forces units were called in to assist Hickey's forces, bringing the total to around 800 soldiers. The large number was needed to create an outer cordon around each farm and lessen the prospects for failure. As noted by Russell, "Saddam had eluded his would-be captors by swimming away once before from this exact location in 1959. A repeat performance was entirely possible."[74]

At 7:45 P.M., supposedly unplanned but "almost providential," the power went out across the town of Ad Dawr, providing the night- and thermal-vision-equipped forces with a clear advantage as they approached the first farm. As American troops closed in on Wolverine 1, helicopters betrayed their approach. Two men, "squirters," who turned out to be a cook and his brother, tried to flee but were quickly captured.

Hickey ordered his men to fan out across the farm. One group of soldiers headed to the house with Musslit, who had earlier told his interrogators that Saddam would probably be hiding in a "bunker" or an "underground facility." Musslit, looking increasingly distressed at the Americans' inability to locate Saddam, suddenly stopped in the middle of a small patio, looked around, walked to an innocuous-looking patch of earth, and tapped it with his shoe. A soldier kicked at the soft earth, quickly revealing a cloth rug. Soldiers lifted the rug, unveiling a rubber mat, and finally a hatch made of Styrofoam. They gently lifted the hatch, scattering dirt into the hole, and spotted a ragged-looking man with a long beard kneeling next to a small electric fan in the darkness below. As the soldiers trained their weapons on the opening, a translator leaned over and shouted for the man to reveal himself.

"I am Saddam Hussein, the duly elected president of Iraq," the man shouted back. "I am willing to negotiate."[75]

HOUSE OF HORRORS

Around the time that Saddam Hussein was being pulled from his "spider hole" in Tikrit, a twenty-four-year-old Army Reservist by the name of Joe Darby was in his office at a sprawling complex some twenty miles west of Baghdad. The day before, a buddy, Corporal Charles Graner, also a member of the 372nd Military Police Company, had given him a CD holding hundreds of images and video clips that he and other guards had taken of their colleagues and the surrounding countryside. Scrolling through the CD, Darby laughed when he came across a picture of a pyramid of naked men.[76] Then he arrived at a photograph of a young woman, a cigarette dangling from her mouth, giving a thumbs-up sign and pointing at the genitals of a young Iraqi detainee, who was naked except for a green plastic bag over his eyes. And then there were others: a video of a uniformed American soldier sodomizing a female detainee; an image of a corpse, its face battered and bruised, bundled in a cocoon of ice.

The more Darby looked, the more horrified he became. "It didn't sit right with me," he recalled. "I know, in the heat of the moment, in a war, things happen. You do things you regret . . . but this crossed the line to me."[77]

By that time, Darby had served as a military policeman at Abu Ghraib for several months. Built by British contractors in the 1960s, the 280-acre complex of cell blocks and guard towers first served as an insane asylum for severely disturbed inmates in the pre-Thorazine era. After Saddam took over the prison, the Western media dubbed it Saddam's Torture Central, because it was where he arranged for the torture and murder of dissidents in twice-weekly public executions overseen by his son, Uday. When ropes failed to kill the prisoners, Uday would have them gassed. Uday was especially fond of the women's prison: he would select a female prisoner to be brought into his office at Iraq's Olympics headquarters, rape her, then order her shot or hung from a nearby tree.[78] "If Iraq under Saddam Hussein was hell," one American commander recalled, "then Abu Ghraib was the furnace. . . . Of all the ghosts in Baghdad, none wailed louder than those at Abu Ghraib."[79]

When Saddam's regime collapsed, the prisoners at Abu Ghraib had looted whatever could be stolen—doors, wiring, iron bars, plumbing, light fixtures. Bob Bauer, a former CIA chief, visited the prison two days after it closed. "It was the most awful sight I've ever seen," he told CBS's 60 Minutes. "If there's . . . a reason to get rid of Saddam Hussein, it's because of Abu Ghraib. There were bodies that were eaten by dogs, torture. You know, electrodes coming out of the walls. It was an awful place."[80]

Senior U.K. officials recommended that the prison be demolished. However, after touring the facility, Lieutenant Paul Bremer III, the chief American administrator in Iraq—desperate for somewhere to hold the military's rapidly growing population of criminals, suspected insurgents, and other detainees—instead decided to rebuild it as quickly as possible. In late June, Janis Karpinski, an officer in the Army Reserve, was placed in charge of eight battalions of U.S. soldiers and more than twenty jails throughout Iraq, including Abu Ghraib.[81] Karpinski was the first female general ever assigned to command troops in a war zone and had no previous experience running a prison system. To make matters worse, her boss, General Ricardo Sanchez, wasn't pleased that a woman had been assigned to be the senior military officer in his theater. Recalled Karpinski: "The message I got was: Over my dead body is this female going to be in charge of all the police operations in this country."[82]

In her autobiography, One Woman's Army, Karpinski describes how Abu Ghraib became the dumping ground for suspected insurgents during the first six months of the war: "The rule around Iraq seemed to be, if in doubt, send 'em out to Abu Ghraib."[83] By late summer 2003, Abu Ghraib was packed with nearly 3,000 prisoners. Many of the detainees were Iraqi civilians who had been picked up in random military sweeps or at checkpoints for "suspicious activities." Most were men, but there were also women, adolescents, and even children as young as ten, the majority of whom were deemed not a threat to society but who were not immediately released due to orders from above.[84]

The prison's sewage system consisted of holes in the ground and portapotties that overflowed and, in the extreme summer heat, caused a horrible stench. Water was rationed, and electricity regularly went down, cloaking the prison in an eerie darkness. Shelling of the prison was so frequent that the guards, huddling against walls, would make wagers on the size of an incoming round—was it a 60, an 80, or the one they dreaded most, the 120 mm—and where it might explode.[85]

Three agencies interrogated prisoners at Abu Ghraib. The first was the CIA-directed Iraqi Survey Group, which had been set up to find weapons of mass destruction and to interrogate "high-value detainees" suspected of having links to international terrorist organizations. Then there was a Special Operations covert fusion group—Task Force 121— that included the CIA, Army Delta Force, and Navy SEALs. Task Force 121 was a hybrid of Special Forces that had tried unsuccessfully to capture Osama bin Laden in Afghanistan and was later deployed to pursue Saddam Hussein in Iraq. The Iraqi Survey Group and Task Force 121, which operated in the prison's secret dark site, kept the names of their detainees off the books to hide them from the International Committee of the Red Cross and thus international oversight.[86] Finally, there was the military's own intelligence unit.[87]

In late August 2003, General Geoffrey Miller—previously commander at Guantánamo—visited Iraq to consider ways of improving "the quality of intelligence [being] extracted from detainees" so as to gain the upper hand on the insurgents.[88] A two-star general from Texas with an "air of supreme confidence,"[89] Miller, with the help of psychologists, had made intelligence gathering the organizing principle at Guantánamo. During his tenure there he had developed specialized interrogation teams that integrated military intelligence personnel with military police, blurring a previously impermeable line.[90]

During his visit, Miller commanded military interrogators to, in Karpinski's words, "treat these prisoners like dogs." He reportedly declared, "if they ever get the idea that they're anything more than that, you've lost control of your interrogation." Miller brought with him a CD and a manual on the "advanced interrogation techniques" that military and CIA interrogators had developed at Guantánamo. Before leaving, he gave them to General Sanchez, thus extending the global migration of these techniques to Iraq.[91]

Days after Miller's departure, General Sanchez authorized a new interrogation plan, which included procedures that had been banned as too harsh, just months earlier, in Guantánamo.[92] The new regime allowed military police, reservists like Joe Darby and Charles Graner, to "set conditions" to soften up prisoners for interrogation by Military Intelligence and the CIA.[93]

On the night of November 4, 2003, Navy SEALs brought a wanted man—Manadel al-Jamadi—to Abu Ghraib and turned him over to the CIA. Al-Jamadi was a former Iraqi military officer suspected of involvement in an earlier bomb attack that had destroyed the Red Cross headquarters in Baghdad. The following morning, he died of asphyxiation while hooded and subjected to a form of torture known as Palestinian hanging. The technique, first practiced during the Spanish Inquisition, involves hanging the victim by his arms from the wall. As the victim hunches forward, his breathing restricts, which can cause severe stress and panic.[94]

It was later revealed that CIA officials tried to cover up al-Jamadi's death by packing his body in ice and binding it in plastic to retard decomposition. The next morning the corpse was taken out of the prison with a fake IV rig attached and driven to an undisclosed location. Military pathologists later ruled the death a homicide caused by "blunt force trauma to the torso complicated by compromised respiration."[95]

A "ghost prisoner," al-Jamadi's detention had taken place off the books. Nevertheless, his case would become the first publicly known homicide at CIA hands in the post-9/11 era.

INCOMPLETE JUSTICE

After weeks of soul-searching, Joe Darby placed a copy of Graner's CD and an anonymous note in a manila envelope and slipped it under the door of the U.S. Army's Criminal Investigation Division, where soldiers can report anything from sexual harassment to theft. Darby later admitted to a division special agent that he was the one who had delivered the package. The agent assured the young reservist that his name would be kept confidential. But it wasn't.

Four weeks later, Darby was sitting in a mess hall with the other guys in his unit. CNN was on, and a clip appeared of Defense Secretary Donald Rumsfeld reporting on Iraqi prisoner abuse to a congressional committee. Suddenly, Rumsfeld said he wanted to thank and extend his appreciation to Joe Darby "for his courage and his values" in alerting the world to the abuses. Darby dropped his fork mid-bite. "I was like, 'Oh, my God!' And the guys at the table just stopped eating and looked at me. . . . I got up and got the hell out of there."[96]

Rumsfeld's "outing" turned Darby's world upside down. When he returned to the United States, his wife was already in hiding due to threats. Some of Darby's family members called him a traitor; his brother stopped talking to him; and Darby, fearing recriminations from his former high school classmates and neighbors, kept away from his hometown of Cumberland, Maryland.[97]

Several investigations followed Darby's whistle-blowing on Abu Ghraib's "little shop of horrors." Of these, Major General Antonio M. Taguba's fifty-three-page report[98] detailing the Army's failure to uphold the Geneva Conventions at Abu Ghraib was the most devastating. Taguba lamented to Seymour Hersh of the *New Yorker* that his investigation was limited to the military police at Abu Ghraib and did not include those above them in the chain of command. "These M.P. troops were not that creative," he told Hersh. "Somebody was giving them guidance, but I was legally prevented from further investigation into higher authority. I was limited to a box."[99] Still, Taguba's inquiry, which revealed extensive evidence of wrongdoing, angered high-ranking officials in the Department of Defense. In January 2006, the two-star general received a telephone call from General Richard Cody, the Army's vice chief of staff, telling him he was to retire within a year. "They always shoot the messenger," Taguba recalled. "I was being ostracized for doing what I was asked to do."[100]

In his report, Taguba concluded that the 372nd Military Police Company had committed "sadistic, blatant, and wanton" criminal acts that included keeping detainees naked for days at time, threatening them with weapons and dogs, and forcing them to perform sexual acts on one another. He also found that Military Intelligence interrogators and those from "other government agencies" (OGA, a military euphemism for the CIA) "set . . . physical and mental conditions for favorable interrogation of witnesses."[101] Another investigation, this one led by Major General George Fay, concluded that "CIA detention and interrogation practices led to a loss of accountability, abuse, reduced interagency cooperation, and an unhealthy mystique that further poisoned the atmosphere at Abu Ghraib."[102]

Secretary of Defense Donald Rumsfeld and other high-level U.S. officials maintained that what happened at Abu Ghraib was abuse, not torture. Conveniently overlooking the Bybee and Yoo memo of August 2002 justifying certain forms of torture for interrogation purposes, Rumsfeld claimed that the abuses at the prison were at odds with what the president wanted. "The president from the beginning had a policy of humane treatment and torture was not allowed," said Rumsfeld. "We had a policy that reflected the president's policy."[103] Such protestations belied the fact that the International Committee of the Red Cross had written the administration as early as November 2003 about various forms of ill-treatment at the prison.[104] According to the Red Cross, detainees "under supervision of Military Intelligence were at high risk of being subjected to a variety of harsh treatments ranging from insults, threats and humiliations to both physical and psychological coercion, which in some cases was tantamount to torture, in order to force cooperation with their interrogators."[105]

In the end, few people were sanctioned for the cruelties at Abu Ghraib. Among them were seventeen Army Reservists. Karpinski received a court-martial, becoming the highest-level official to receive formal sanctions.[106] She was demoted from general to colonel for "dereliction of duty," misleading investigators, and, oddly, shoplifting,[107] the last a purported misunderstanding that had taken place years before.[108] Six other soldiers from the 800th were also sanctioned, with several doing prison time. Specialist Charles Graner, "the night-shift ringleader [infamously] photographed grinning beside piles of naked detainees,"[109] was sentenced to ten years via court-martial. Staff sergeant and night-shift leader Ivan Frederick received eight years, while three others received a year or less. Perhaps the most publicized reservist, Lynndie England—widely recognized as the woman holding a leash tethered to a detainee and hotly criticized for having an affair and a child with Graner—received three years and a dishonorable discharge.[110]

While the arrests of these particular individuals weren't difficult to effectuate, those at the highest levels of command remained shockingly immune from legal scrutiny. Although the reservists clearly committed crimes and deserved recrimination, as Karpinski notes in her memoirs, "Officers like me . . . do not make policies. We implement them."[111] Her higher-ups, by contrast, were rewarded for their time in Iraq. By the time of Karpinski's writing, General Sanchez—holder of the top military position in Iraq during the scandal—was awaiting a fourth star, and General Barbara Fast—the most senior military intelligence officer in Iraq—had been promoted to commanding general of the U.S. Army Intelligence Center at Fort Huachuca in Arizona.[112]

Also evading punishment for any role they may have played in either explicitly or implicitly condoning the abuse were the Bush Six: the six U.S. officials who authored the legal framework that had enabled torture. They include David Addington, former chief of staff for Vice President Dick Cheney; Jay Bybee, a prominent lawyer who served as head of the Office of Legal Counsel at the Department of Justice from 2001 through March 2003; Douglas Feith, Bush's former undersecretary of defense for policy; Alberto Gonzales, who served as both White House Counsel and U.S. Attorney General; William Haynes II, chief counsel for Secretary of Defense Donald Rumsfeld and former Department of Defense general counsel; and John Yoo, a deputy in the Office of Legal Counsel from 2001 to 2003.

Soon after his forced retirement from the Army, Antonio Taguba wrote in a preface to a human rights report that U.S. detention and interrogation practices in the war on terror had damaged "America's institutions and our nation's founding values, which the military, intelligence services, and our justice system are duty-bound to defend." He added: "After years of disclosures by government investigations, media accounts, and reports from human rights organizations, there is no longer any doubt whether the [Bush] administration has committed war crimes. The only question that remains to be answered is whether those who ordered the use of torture will be held to account."[113]

UNIVERSAL JURISDICTION IN ACTION

In the aftermath of the Abu Ghraib revelations, as the spotlight swiveled toward the dire condition of detainees in Guantánamo (many of whom, it was increasingly revealed, had been wrongly captured and should have never been incarcerated), human rights lawyers around the world strategized how to indict, arrest, and try various configurations of the Bush Six. The political, legal, and pragmatic hurdles loomed large. Though finding the individuals in question wouldn't be hard, claims of sovereign immunity and the political challenges of maneuvering into custody some of the most powerful people in the world would be difficult to overcome. When it became clear that U.S. officials would do nothing to ensure accountability for the torture and indefinite detention of detainees, the question became: Which institution or country would take the detainees' cases, and how?

One option was to request accountability through the International Criminal Court (ICC) for torture conducted by American citizens in countries that are signatories to the Rome Statute ("states parties").[114] Almost immediately after 9/11, however, the United States had begun strategizing how to undercut the possibility that members of the Bush administration would someday be called before the ICC for torture and other illegal treatment. One tactic was to push for bilateral immunity agreements with countries that were party to the ICC. As noted in chapter 8, such agreements—which raised accusations that the United States was "bullying" states parties[115]—required foreign nations to refrain from handing over "current or former Government officials, employees (including contractors), or military personnel or nationals of one Party" to the court.[116] The United States reportedly conditioned military and economic aid, as well as support for entry into NATO, on entering into the agreements. By 2007, 102 such agreements had been concluded,[117] despite the European Union's warning that entering into them would violate the states parties' obligations under the Rome Statute.

Another option for law firms and human rights organizations was to file cases in foreign domestic courts.[118] The most promising answer to the question of how to do this was to employ *universal jurisdiction*, a centuries-old doctrine—originally aimed at piracy[119]—that had languished unused for years until it was revived in 1980 with the landmark case of *Filartiga v. Pena-Irala*.[120] In that case, the United States' second district court had decided that the United States had jurisdiction over a case involving the kidnapping, torture, and murder of a seventeen-year-old boy even though the wrongs had all been committed outside the United States and neither the plaintiff (the boy's sister) nor the defendant were U.S. citizens. In assuming jurisdiction, the court noted that "the torturer has become—like the pirate and slave trader before him—*hostis humani generis*, an enemy of all mankind,"[121] and thus an enemy of the United States.

While courts will usually try cases only if the people involved or the places where the wrongs occurred are from or within their territorial borders, as law professor Máximo Langer, an expert on universal jurisdiction, explains, the doctrine makes it possible for "any state in the world [to] prosecute and try the core international crimes—crimes against humanity, genocide, torture and war crimes—without any territorial, personal, or national-interest link to the crime in question when [it] was committed."[122] The underlying rationale is that these crimes are so horrific that they are offenses against all mankind, and thus should be triable anywhere. Writes Langer: "Defenders of universal jurisdiction claim that it is a crucial tool for bringing justice to victims, deterring state or quasi-state officials from committing international crimes, and establish a minimum international rule of law by substantially closing the 'impunity gap' for international crimes. However, critics argue that universal jurisdiction disrupts international relations, provokes judicial chaos, and interferes with political solutions to mass atrocities."[123] During the 1990s, the doctrine of universal jurisdiction gained some traction as a tool to be used against Rwandan and Yugoslav war crimes suspects living abroad, and had been most visibly used in Spain as a means to charge and arrest former Chilean dictator Augusto Pinochet.

While universal jurisdiction is widely perceived as one of few means to ensure accountability for state officials who are unlikely to face prosecution in their home countries, as Langer notes, there are severe costs to the exercise of such authority: "The political branches of the prosecuting states must be willing to pay the international relations costs that the defendant's state of nationality [will] impose if a prosecution and trial take place."[124] This is a price many countries find too steep—especially when the defendants are powerful representatives of one of the world's major funders. This helps explain the critical role of international tribunals such as the ICC, which can provide nations with crucial diplomatic cover.

In the post-9/11 context, recognizing the unlikeliness of successfully bringing a case at the ICC, human rights lawyers deemed testing the doctrine's limits in various national courts their best shot for legal accountability. In November 2004, four Iraqis living in Germany filed a criminal complaint against eleven high-ranking U.S. officials, including then Secretary of Defense Donald Rumsfeld and Attorney General Alberto Gonzales. The complaint set out detailed accounts of torture suffered by the plaintiffs while in U.S.-run detention facilities in Iraq. The Iraqis were joined by a fifth plaintiff, the New York–based Center for Constitutional Rights, a nonprofit legal organization which represents current and former detainees held at various locations, including Abu Ghraib and Guantánamo, in civil and habeas corpus proceedings in the United States. The plaintiffs argued that they were seeking redress through the German judicial system because the United States was unwilling to investigate, let alone prosecute, high-ranking officials for the torture detainees endured in U.S. custody. To buttress this claim, the plaintiffs had international legal scholar Scott Horton append an expert opinion to their complaint in which he posited that no "criminal investigation would occur in the near future in the United States for the reason that the criminal investigative and prosecutorial functions are currently controlled by individuals who are involved in the conspiracy to commit war crimes."[125]

The U.S. government dismissed the case in Germany as a "frivolous lawsuit" that, if accepted by the German courts, would have a negative impact on U.S.–German relations. However, in January 2005, three months after the complaint was filed, the U.S. Embassy in Germany announced that Rumsfeld would not attend the Munich Conference on Security Policy, which suggested to many human rights advocates that Rumsfeld was trying to evade complications that might arise from the case. In February, Germany's chief federal prosecutor, Kay Nehm, decided not to open an investigation against Rumsfeld and the others, as none of the victims were German and all of the defendants American. He added that such a finding was consistent with "the framework of noninterference in the affairs of foreign countries."[126] The following day, Rumsfeld travelled to Munich. Undeterred, an alliance of international human rights organizations filed another complaint in Germany in 2006 on behalf of eleven Iraqi torture survivors and Mohammed al-Qahtani, a citizen of Saudi Arabia, who had been detained in Guantánamo since January 2002. The plaintiffs alleged that al-Qahtani had been subjected to interrogation techniques that amounted to torture. Years later, after a German federal prosecutor rejected the complaint, Susan Crawford, a Pentagon official in charge of deciding whether to bring detainees before military commissions, concluded that the techniques used on al-Qahtani over a fifty-day period from November 2002 to January 2003 in Guantánamo amounted to torture. "Shocked" and "embarrassed" by the discovery, Crawford nevertheless chose not to refer al-Qahtani's case to a military commission for prosecution.[127]

The 2006 German complaint alleged that five U.S. government attorneys were involved in formulating the detention and interrogation policies that resulted in the torture and other forms of serious abuse of al-Qahtani and his fellow plaintiffs. Among those cited in the complaint were Bybee and Yoo, authors of the infamous 2002 "torture memos" that condoned the use of interrogation techniques such as waterboarding and prolonged sleep deprivation. Strikingly, former Brigadier General Janis Karpinski, who had been a *defendant* in the 2004 case, submitted seventeen pages of testimony in support of the prosecution's complaint and offered to appear as a witness.

However, Karpinski never had her day in court. On April 27, 2007, the German prosecutor dismissed the complaint, claiming that any future prosecution would be "purely symbolic," as the defendants were not in Germany. The prosecutor chastised the complainants for "forum shopping" by bringing their case to Germany simply because the country was generally favorable to international claims. He also found it objectionable that resources would be wasted on "complicated but ultimately unsuccessful investigations."[128]

As time wore on, official support for the principle of universal jurisdiction headed into a tailspin: French and U.K. prosecutors and Spanish judges methodically shot down cases involving American defendants. In 2007, a Paris prosecutor quashed a complaint against Rumsfeld for torture and other serious abuses, claiming that under the jurisprudence of the International Court of Justice, immunity from criminal jurisdiction for heads of state and ministers of foreign affairs continues to apply after termination of their time in office. According to the prosecutor, Rumsfeld was immune for any criminal acts he had carried out while in office "in the exercise of his functions" as a government official. In a mind-boggling feat of reasoning, the prosecutor further ruled that the argument in the *Pinochet* case mentioned in the introduction to this book was inapplicable to the *Rumsfeld* complaint because the assassinations and kidnappings that Pinochet committed "did not fall under the exercise of his functions as [a government official] but were marginal to them."[129] In Great Britain, prosecutors also refused to take a case against George W. Bush on grounds of immunity.[130]

Spanish courts similarly threw out a string of universal jurisdiction cases involving alleged torture by American defendants. In 2009, the Spanish Parliament passed legislation, by an overwhelming 342 to 2, to restrict the future scope of universal jurisdiction litigation to cases involving Spanish victims. The bill also stipulated that the alleged perpetrators had to be in Spain, and some clear link to Spain demonstrated. Soon after the vote, Carlos Dívar, the chief justice of the Spanish Supreme Court, reasoned, "We cannot turn ourselves into the judicial gendarmes of the world."[131]

Based on this gutting of the principle of universal jurisdiction, the likelihood of legal accountability—let alone arrests—of any of the Bush Six or other high-level government officials in national courts remains small, at least at this point in history. As Langer notes, universal jurisdiction cases seem to work best when there is a pairing of "low-cost defendants"—that is, those defendants who "impose low international relations costs"—with prosecuting states that have relatively low degrees of executive branch control (and thus political control) over criminal proceedings.

In a study of 1,051 universal jurisdiction cases filed since the trial of Adolf Eichmann in 1961, Langer found that universal jurisdiction–prosecuting states, such as Germany, France, Belgium, Spain, and the United Kingdom, have strong diplomatic incentives not to concentrate on big fish, such as former President George W. Bush or former Secretary of Defense Donald Rumsfeld, because such prosecutions bring high international relations costs. According to Langer, between 1961 and 2010 only a handful of universal jurisdiction defendants—thirty-two—were ever brought to trial. Of these, twenty-four—amounting to three-quarters of all defendants tried under universal jurisdiction defendants—were Nazis, citizens of the former Yugoslavia, and Rwandans. Such defendants, writes Langer, were "the type of defendants that the international community has most clearly agreed should be prosecuted and punished and that their own states . . . have not defended."[132] In other words, prosecutions of these defendants posed little if any international relations costs to the prosecuting states. By contrast, all nineteen cases that had been filed in Germany by 2011 against members of the Bush Six were ultimately dismissed,[133] often on the basis of complementarity—a lack of evidence that the defendants would escape trial in the United States for their alleged activities—and the pragmatic difficulty of German prosecutors gathering sufficient evidence of criminal activity in the United States and Iraq.

Oddly enough, at the time of writing, the most promising forum for any kind of legal accountability for post-9/11 U.S. actions seems to be the ICC. In late 2014, the court revealed that it had commenced a preliminary investigation into the alleged torture of detainees in Afghanistan by U.S. personnel.[134] Interestingly, the announcement came just weeks before the public release of a Senate subcommittee's finding that CIA agents and their contractors had tortured detainees, and President Obama's repeated assurance that the CIA would continue to enjoy domestic immunity from criminal prosecution. Obama is, however, rumored to be cooperating with the ICC, whose temporal jurisdiction extends from 2003 to 2008 and thus excludes Obama's presidency.[135]

As the quest for justice continues, accountability proponents can perhaps take some small comfort from the fact that despite the lack of arrests, suspects may face other ramifications from any wrongs they committed.[136] That can be seen, for example, in the relatively limited international mobility of various members of the former Bush administration, as exemplified by Bush's aborted trip to Switzerland in 2011, which many claim was cancelled because of his fear of arrest due to a universal jurisdiction case that had recently been filed in that country.[137] Even when immunity has been flaunted—as with Rumsfeld's trip to France in 2007 and al-Bashir's trips to Kenya in 2010 and China in 2011—that decision has had to be well thought out. At the very least, such cases generate a potential vulnerability—a visibility—that didn't previously exist.

THE TORTURE PSYCHOLOGISTS AND
THE SEARCH FOR BIN LADEN

As human rights activists were exploring options for bringing the Bush Six to trial, the CIA was pulling out all the stops in its effort to determine Osama bin Laden's whereabouts. In the agency's headquarters in Langley, Virginia, analysts were scouring the files of earlier manhunts for clues about how fugitives behave. They scrutinized the hunts for Adolf Eichmann, the Nazi escapee captured by Israeli agents in Argentina in 1960; Pablo Escobar, a notorious Latin American drug lord, who was gunned down by police in Colombia in 1963; and Eric Rudolph, the "homegrown terrorist" who bombed downtown Atlanta during the 1996 Olympics.[138] Family members, the analysts learned, could be key to locating fugitives—whether it be a son confiding information about his father to a girlfriend, or a just-slightly-too-long check-in with a beloved child. They also found that fugitives tend to become sloppier and overconfident with time—perhaps contacting someone they know, sharing their secrets, or just becoming too comfortable or complacent— which can result in "lucky breaks" for investigators.

Taking a page from the Army's capture of Saddam Hussein, CIA analysts also dabbled for a while with social network theory, but soon declared it ineffectual. Their reasoning was fairly straightforward: Saddam fell back on ancient tribal structures for protection, but bin Laden had no such established network. Following the United States' initial response to the events of 9/11, al-Qaeda had metamorphosed from a structured organization into a loose, amorphous collection of cells and affiliated organizations without a clear central command. Finding a fugitive inside a terrorist group that had splintered required a different strategy than finding a deposed dictator who had used his family connections to foster an urban insurgency.[139]

One of the CIA's first real breakthroughs had come in March 2002, when they acquired cellphone information belonging to Abu Zubaydah, operations commander of al-Qaeda, in Faisalabad, Pakistan. Armed with his cellphone number, CIA operatives working out of the U.S. Embassy in Islamabad had attempted to track Zubaydah's movements. But Zubaydah was careful about security, turning on his phone only briefly to collect messages—not long enough for trackers to get a fix on his whereabouts. The CIA eventually sent a thirty-six-year-old analyst named Deuce Martinez to Islamabad to join the Zubaydah tracking team.[140] Martinez was a soft-spoken data-cruncher who worked in the agency's Counternarcotics Center. In a relatively short period of time, he had gained a reputation for tracking down drug traffickers by sifting through masses of phone numbers, travel records, and credit card transactions.

In his office in Islamabad, Martinez posted a large piece of paper on the wall and wrote Zubaydah's phone number on it. Over several weeks, Martinez created a spiderweb of more and more phone numbers linked to Zubaydah's cellphone, each gleaned from the eavesdropping files of the National Security Agency and Pakistani intelligence. Martinez and his colleagues were eventually able to reduce Zubaydah's likely hiding places to fourteen addresses in Lahore and Faisalabad. These locations were placed under surveillance. Then, similarly to the International Criminal Tribunal for Rwanda's Operation Naki in Nairobi, Kenya— during which Kenyan authorities pulled off the stunning simultaneous arrest of seven people—joint teams of Pakistani and American agents hit all fourteen locations at once.

One of the SWAT teams found Abu Zubaydah, protected by Syrian and Egyptian bodyguards, at an upscale house on Canal Road in Faisalabad. The house was bristling with bomb-making equipment and contained a safe loaded with $100,000 in cash. Zubaydah was flown to a secret CIA jail near Bangkok and then to a "black site" near Warsaw, Poland, where he became the first prisoner in the "war on terror" to undergo "enhanced interrogation."[141] During these interrogation sessions, he revealed that Khalid Sheikh Mohammed (known as "Mukhtar" to Zubaydah) was the mastermind of the 9/11 attacks. A year later, a combined force of members of the CIA and the Inter-Services Intelligence agency of Pakistan stormed a private villa in Rawalpindi, Pakistan, and captured Khalid Sheikh Mohammed. Soon after, the CIA brought in other important targets, one being Mohammed Neem Noor Khan, a computer and communications specialist who was reportedly the conduit for messages from Osama bin Laden to operatives in the West. These raids netted hard drives and memory sticks containing the names of dozens of potential terrorists. CIA investigators used this information to identify and track their cellphones, while experts known as "targeters" siphoned information from the phones' "digital exhaust."[142] Though this information helped CIA operatives locate still more suspects, because of al-Qaeda's fragmentation such successes weren't leading them any closer to Osama bin Laden himself.

Along with the scandal at Abu Ghraib, the CIA's interrogation of Abu Zubaydah and Khalid Sheikh Mohammed would blow the lid off Operation Greystone.[143] While brief reports of their torture appeared in the media, details wouldn't be revealed until a report, entitled the *ICRC Report on the Treatment of Fourteen "High Value Detainees" in CIA Custody*, was leaked to the press in 2009. The report was based on interviews by doctors with the International Committee of the Red Cross of Zubaydah, Mohammed, and twelve other "high-value detainees" shortly after they were transferred from overseas black sites to Guantánamo in 2006. The report gives remarkably uniform accounts of abuse, including waterboarding, confinement in a black box, prolonged stress positions, sleep deprivation, forced nudity, and beatings. These accounts led the Red Cross to conclude that "the ill treatment to which [many of the fourteen detainees] were subjected while held in the CIA program, either singly or in combination, constituted torture. In addition, many other elements of the ill treatment, either singly or in combination, constituted cruel, inhuman, or degrading treatment."[144]

Shortly after Abu Zubaydah was captured, CIA officers briefed the National Security Council's principals committee—including Vice President Dick Cheney, National Security Advisor Condoleezza Rice, and Attorney General John Ashcroft—on the interrogation plans for the al-Qaeda prisoner. As the interrogations proceeded, so did briefings with George Tenet, the CIA's director. Senior officials were provided almost daily reports of the applied techniques. "It wasn't up to individual interrogators to decide, 'Well, I'm going to slap him. Or I'm going to shake him,' said John Kiriakous, a CIA officer who helped capture Abu Zubaydah, in an interview with ABC News." Every interrogation technique used with Zubaydah, according to Kiriakous, "had to have the approval of the deputy director for operations. So before you laid a hand on him, you had to send in the cable saying, 'He's uncooperative. Request permission to do X'. . . . The cable traffic back and forth was extremely specific. . . . No one wanted to get in trouble by going overboard."[145] But they did go overboard, subjecting Abu Zubaydah, according to the ICRC report, to cold temperatures, confinement in a small box, loud music, wall slamming, and waterboarding—all tactics that can amount to torture or ill-treatment.

In 2009, an FBI agent named Ali Soufan, who was part of a joint FBI–CIA team, was sent to interrogate Zubaydah at a black site in Thailand. Soufan—who had a reputation at being so good at his job that the former head of the FBI's National Security Division had been known to refer to him as his "secret weapon"[146]—told Congress that he and his team had used standard rapport-building interrogation techniques on Zubaydah. However, Soufan's team was later replaced by a CIA team headed by a former military psychologist named James Mitchell, whom the intelligence agency had hired on a contract shortly after the 9/11 attacks.[147] Mitchell was an odd choice to be put in charge of such a sensitive mission. He had never been an interrogator. He spoke no Arabic and had no background in the Middle East or in Islamic terrorism. He had, however, spent much of his career studying the supposed terrorist mindset, first as a bomb specialist, then as a hostage negotiator and a clinical psychologist, and then as an instructor at the Air Force's SERE program, which trained pilots and other personnel to resist torture should they fall into the hands of an enemy, as noted earlier.[148]

Once on a CIA contract, Mitchell, and another Air Force psychologist, Bruce Jessen, "reverse-engineered" the SERE techniques to produce harsh interrogation tactics, including torture, to help CIA interrogators break terrorist suspects and gain information that could be used to thwart further terrorist attacks against the United States and its interests abroad.[149] Many of their techniques became standard methods of interrogation used against the high-value detainees in CIA custody in early 2002, including not only Abu Zubaydah but also Khalid Sheikh Mohammed, as well as other detainees held at Guantánamo and prison facilities in Iraq and Afghanistan.[150] The CIA ultimately paid the two psychologists' company $81 million to conduct these efforts, offering the funds along with a multi-year indemnification agreement "to protect the company and its employees from legal liability arising out of the program."[151]

In 2011, one of Mitchell and Jensen's colleagues, Captain Michael Kearns, spoke publicly about his outrage that the two psychologists had used SERE techniques to design the Bush administration's torture program. "I think it's about time for SERE to come out from behind the veil of secrecy if we are to progress as a moral nation of laws," Kearns told *Truthout*. "To take this survival training program and turn it into some form of nationally sanctioned, purposeful program for the extraction of information, or to apply exploitation, is in total contradiction to human morality, and defies basic logic. When I first learned about interrogation, at basic intelligence school, I read about Hanns Scharff, a Nazi interrogator who later wrote an article for *Argosy Magazine* titled 'Without Torture.' That's what I was taught—torture doesn't work."[152]

On arriving at the Thai black site in 2002, Mitchell announced that Abu Zubaydah, who was still recovering from wounds sustained during his abduction, must be treated "like a dog in a cage."[153] He and Jessen were put in charge of Zubaydah's waterboarding and other "enhanced" interrogation.[154] Soufan, with his tradition working within the U.S. criminal legal framework, was appalled. Fearful that he and his FBI colleagues would be implicated, and adamantly opposed to what Mitchell was proposing, Soufan left. He reported to his FBI superiors that the CIA's interrogation practices, which included placing Zubaydah in a coffin-like box, constituted "borderline torture," and argued that Mitchell should be arrested.[155] Soon thereafter, FBI director Robert Mueller barred the bureau's personnel from participating in the CIA's coercive interrogations.

Soufan later told *Newsweek* that Mitchell's harsh techniques were useless. By employing rapport-building techniques, Soufan said, "We were able to get the information about Khalid Sheikh Mohammed in a couple of days. We didn't need to do any of this [torture]. We could have done this the right way."[156] Ultimately, in March 2009, the *Washington Post* reported that, according to senior U.S. officials, "not a single significant [al-Qaeda] plot was foiled as a result of Abu Zubaydah's tortured confessions. . . . Nearly all of the leads attained through harsh measures quickly evaporated, while most of the useful information from Abu Zubaydah—chiefly names of al-Qaeda members and associates—was obtained before waterboarding was introduced."[157]

The executive summary of the U.S. Senate Select Committee's $40 million investigation into the CIA's detention and interrogation program, which was publicly released in December 2014, echoed this conclusion.[158] The report also emphasized the prominent role that psychologists had played in the creation and implementation of the torture program. In response, the board of the American Psychological Association ordered an independent investigation into psychologists' involvement in the program. The investigation confirmed that a number of prominent psychologists, including several of the association's officers, had "colluded" with Bush administration officials to ensure that the association's policies would not prevent psychologists from supporting the work of the administration. In August 2015, in light of this finding and abundant evidence of psychologists' complicity in torture, association members "overwhelmingly" voted to ban psychologists from ever again participating in national security investigations.[159]

BY THE HANDS OF OTHERS

Members of the military and the CIA were not the only actors involved in the hunt for bin Laden and Hussein. Like most armed conflicts, the wars in Afghanistan and Iraq attracted a menagerie of fortune seekers, including contractors such as Mitchell and Jessen, bounty hunters, and mercenaries, each of whom would play a role in tracking, apprehending and/or killing individuals believed to be a threat to national security interests.[160]

The United States has historically relied on contracts with private companies and individuals to supplement its military forces for a wide range of services, but the practice has expanded in recent decades. There are special legal, political, and operational advantages to doing so when carrying out pseudo-military objectives.[161] They enable the executive branch to outsource culpability and accountability for their actions, circumvent Congress's oversight authority, and bypass national and international laws.[162] As the Contractor's Creed published in Robert Young's *Licensed to Kill* puts it: "I look out for myself, the operators to my left and right, and no one else. I will always take advantage of the fact that I can finally tell military officers to pound sand, and will do so at every opportunity. I am my country's scapegoat, the 'plausible deniability' warrior, and I love it."[163]

In the post-9/11 context, security companies like Blackwater USA, started by Erik Prince, a former Navy SEAL and heir to an immense family fortune, and SCG International Risk, started by Jamie Smith, a former Blackwater employee,appeared in Baghdad and Kabul to provide security to heads of state, diplomats, and the occasional Saudi prince. The contracts they entered into were worth millions. Such contractors walk a wobbly line between offensive military operations and defensive security objectives. In the 1970s, for example, a Pentagon official described the privately owned Vinnel Corporation, a U.S.-based military training and logistics company, as the United States' "own little army in Vietnam," which did "things we either didn't have the manpower to do ourselves, or because of legal problems."[164]

America's hunt for Osama bin Laden also attracted "bounty hunters" determined to take on manhunts of their own in the hope of some promised reward. In early 2003, American helicopters dropped thousands of flyers along the fifteen-hundred-mile border between Afghanistan and

Pakistan. The flyers featured an image of bin Laden's face behind bars and offered a $25 million reward to anyone who could hand him to the authorities. In 2005, the United States increased the bounty to $50 million.[165] The extraordinary bounty on Osama bin Laden's capture lured a handful of ideologically or monetarily inspired privateers—operators who typically work in isolation or with small, private militias—to take on manhunts of their own. Tim Morris, a war correspondent for *Soldier of Fortune* and *Rolling Stone* magazines, notes that a privateer or bounty hunter "doesn't have to get permission from some bureaucrat, scared to death that he will ruin his career, to make his move. . . . A privateer doesn't have the resources of the government, but he can move fast and take chances no bureaucrat would ever countenance."[166]

One such privateer was Jonathan Keith ("Jack" or "Keith") Idema, a former Green Beret and journalist who in November 2001 traveled to Afghanistan to hunt for bin Laden.[167] Idema formed a paramilitary group, known as Task Force Saber 7, by employing former U.S. soldiers. By 2004, in his search for the al-Qaeda leader, Idema had begun sweeping up possible terrorists throughout Afghanistan and detaining them in his Kabul home. Contrary to later U.S. claims that Idema was working solo, NATO forces apparently assisted his raids on at least three occasions.[168]

Idema claimed that his work was condoned by although not contracted by the U.S. government.[169] However, the U.S. military distanced itself from Idema once graphic photos surfaced of his abusive treatment of detainees.[170] In its efforts to disassociate itself from Idema—who once claimed to have as many as nine wives[171]—the Bush administration hung wanted posters for Idema around Kabul and warned Americans in Afghanistan to steer clear of the "rogue operator." In 2004, the Afghan police raided Idema's house. He was later convicted of "having a personal jail, taking hostages, and torture" and was sentenced to ten years (later reduced to five) in an Afghan prison.[172]

Around the same time as Idema was scooping up presumed terrorists in Afghanistan, another bounty hunter, Gary Faulkner—also known as Rocky Mountain Rambo[173]—joined the hunt for bin Laden. A fifty-something former construction worker and ex-con from Colorado—purportedly driven more by his patriotism and Christian faith than by the cash award—Faulkner traveled to Pakistan and Afghanistan six times in search of the terrorist fugitive. With no military or other specialized training, and only limited knowledge of Urdu, he was a "self-taught terrorist tracker" with strong hunting and foraging skills. In June 2010, the

Pakistani police arrested Faulkner as he was trying to cross into a remote part of Afghanistan in search of bin Laden. He was reportedly carrying a pistol, a forty-inch sword, a dagger, night-vision goggles, handcuffs, hashish, and Christian literature. Faulkner was deported from Pakistan and subsequently went on a media tour, appearing on the *Late Show* with David Letterman, *The View*, and the *Early Show*. "This is not about me," he told an interviewer. "What this is about is the American people and the world. We can't let people like [bin Laden] scare us. We don't get scared by people like this, we scare them . . . that's what this is about."[174]

While bounty offers can—quite literally—pay off, they can also lead to the capture and violation of the human rights of innocents or suspects of little security value.[175] In Afghanistan, for example, the U.S. government's bounty payments created an indiscriminate dragnet that resulted in the detention of thousands of people, many of whom appear to have had little or no connection to al-Qaeda or the Taliban and posed little or no threat to U.S. security.[176] Of those given over to U.S. custody, screening procedures frequently failed to distinguish civilians from combatants. Instead of holding battlefield hearings, as mandated by the Geneva Conventions, to determine detainees' combat status,[177] President Bush had unilaterally determined that all prisoners captured in the "war on terror" could be held indefinitely, something that exacerbated the overcrowding experienced in Iraq.[178] Ultimately, capturing suspected members of al-Qaeda and the Taliban—and showing that something was being done about 9/11—became a higher priority than the diligence and investigation necessary to discern whose detention was justified.

As early as September 2002, several U.S. officials within military and intelligence circles grew concerned about the ineffectiveness of the bounty system in Afghanistan. A senior CIA analyst with extensive Middle East experience assessed the detainees at Guantánamo in summer 2002 and concluded in a top-secret report that approximately a third of the population—200 of the 600 detainees at that time—had no connection to terrorism.[179] Many, he said, had been "caught in the dragnet. They were not fighters, they were not doing jihad. They should not have been there."[180] Guantánamo's commander, Major General Michael Dunlavey, agreed with him and later estimated that half of the camp population was mistakenly detained.[181] An FBI counterterrorism expert went even further and told a committee of the National Security Council that there were at most only fifty detainees worth holding at Guantánamo.[182]

Mercenaries are the third group that has played a critical role in the search for suspected terrorists in the post-9/11 era. Largely independent—

much like bounty hunters, but more controversial—mercenaries have been described by journalist Robert Young Pelton as "men who fight for money instead of . . . a cause."[183] A mercenary is also defined as "an individual who fights abroad in combat motivated by private gain and paid substantially more than standing army combatants and is not a national or resident of the state and neither a member of its armed forces nor on official duty from a third party's armed forces."[184] The use of highly paid mercenaries to support military objectives extends back, at least in America, to the Revolutionary War, when various soldiers of fortune supported American efforts to defeat the British Army.

Their flexibility of movement and relative freedom from political and diplomatic constraints possibly explains why, as bounty hunters were penetrating Pakistan and Afghanistan in the search for bin Laden, mercenaries and private security teams were simultaneously multiplying in Iraq. Indeed, many men who sought fortune in the search for wanted terrorists ultimately operated as both. However, much like bounty hunters, mercenaries' relationship to the U.S. military and other official institutions can be opaque. As former special forces "legend" and CIA paramilitary operations officer William (Billy) Waugh has explained regarding individuals who have crossed over from "the 'white' side of military operations to the 'black' side of warfare—deniable TOP SECRET-level covert and clandestine operations that were never intended to be revealed to the American public"—"the license to kill once accorded special operations has been finessed or outsourced to avoid direct liability. 'We don't pull the trigger but we sure as hell give them a gun, bullets, show them the target, and teach them how to pull that trigger.'"[185] Indeed, mercenaries have often been the mechanism that the United States has used to conduct targeted assassinations when the United States politically, legally, or operationally could not.

TARGETED ASSASSINATIONS

Officially, the United States banned targeted assassinations in 1976 with President Ford's Executive Order 1190—an order prompted when secret CIA plots to assassinate foreign leaders were revealed through a series of exposés published in the *New York Times* by investigative journalist Seymour Hersh.[186] The ban was later expanded by President Carter in 1978, and reaffirmed by President Reagan in 1981.[187] However, the clear prohibition against assassinations became subject to creative administration reinterpretation toward the end of the twentieth century. In 1998, in the wake of attacks on American embassies in Kenya and Tanzania, President Clinton's legal team interpreted the prohibition as permitting exceptions for terrorists when the assassinations were committed in the nation's defense.[188] Also key to establishing some degree of legality was claiming that such assassinations were military operations, since the military are allowed to kill in some instances, for example as presumptive self-defense in the form of preemptive strikes.[189] In this way such assassinations were framed as legal exceptions to the general rule against extrajudicial killings.

In the twenty-first century, the reliance on mercenaries for assassinations has increasingly been augmented by the use of emerging technologies, such as robots and drones. The First Gulf War (1990–91) has often been referred to as the world's first "technology war," because of the use of smart bombs, which now seem relatively crude. However, technological advancements that followed in the wake of that war, including the ability to equip unmanned vehicles with GPS sensors and onboard computers, launched a new era in warfare.[190] First tested in the Balkan wars, drones—officially known as "unmanned aerial vehicles"—were used to document the flow of refugees and monitor Serb air defenses.[191] From there, the United States' use of technology for surveillance exploded, starting with land-based robots. When U.S. forces entered Iraq in 2003 in the Second Gulf War, they had no robotic systems. By the end of 2004, there were nearly 150 robots helping U.S. soldiers dismantle bombs and improvised explosive devices. By the end of 2006, almost 5,000 robots were scuttling around Iraq.[192]

Drones were not far behind. Bush's authorization of Operation Greystone in 2001 not only instigated the use of "enhanced" interrogation techniques but also empowered the CIA to use drones to kill members of al-Qaeda and allied groups.[193] Originally, drones were conceived as a replacement for the U-2 spy planes of the 1950s. While pilots on spy planes are limited by physiological factors such as operator fatigue and biological stresses brought on by traveling at extremely high speeds, drones suffer no such ailments.[194] Most importantly, drones can greatly reduce American casualties in war zones and pass clandestinely into territories outside the reach of conventional forces.

Several times in 2000 and early 2001, drones had located bin Laden, but they were not yet armed. After 9/11 that would change. Within a year after drones were adapted to carry missiles, they had killed more than 115 Afghanistan-based targets.[195] Drones quickly proved so "successful" compared to ground troops that General Tommy Franks, then

U.S. commander in Afghanistan, declared that drones are "my most capable sensor in hunting down and killing Al Qaeda and Taliban leadership and [are] . . . critical to our fight."[196]

The political pressure on the Bush administration—and later the Obama administration—to end the United States' renditions and indefinite detention of terrorist suspects made the use of Predator drones for assassination increasingly appealing to the government. Indeed, indefinite detention and targeted assassinations have a complementary policy history. The argument is often that if nations can't permanently neutralize individuals and groups perceived as security threats by capturing and holding them indefinitely, the most expedient policy alternative is to kill them.

By 2007, relations between Pakistan and the United States had begun to sour. Until then, Pakistan had largely viewed al-Qaeda as a common enemy due to the network's earlier targeting of Pakistan's president, Pervez Musharraf. As part of this collaboration, the Pakistani government handed over more than 300 suspected militants to the United States between 2001 and 2006. But as time passed, tensions increased between the two nations, and U.S. officials found it more and more difficult to use Pakistan to fill essential information gaps and apprehend suspected terrorists. This new reality prompted a ramping-up of the nation's nascent—and still secret—Predator drone program.

Of all the drone models, the Predator, each of which costs taxpayers about $4.5 million,[197] seemed to the U.S. military the best suited for hunting down suspected terrorists in Pakistan. Made of a lightweight composite, Predator drones can patrol over an area and launch Hellfire missiles when a designated target—such as a pickup truck fitted with a .50–caliber gun and loaded with fighters—emerges from a hiding place or a crowded urban area. And by Pentagon standards, it is relatively cheap. Writes P. W. Singer in *Wired for War:* "For the price of an F-22, the air force's latest jet, you can buy eighty-five Predators. More important, the low price and lack of a human pilot means that the Predator can be used for missions where it might be shot down, such as traveling low and slow over enemy territory."[198] The Predator's infrared camera, stationed on a swiveling device under the nose, enables it to transmit images day and night, while radar facilitates imaging through smoke, dust, and clouds. The drone is flown out of bases in war zones, but its pilot and sensor operator are often located thousands of miles away—frequently in the United States—and rely on satellite communications to guide the drone to the target.[199]

By 2006, President Bush had stepped up drone attacks in Pakistan's tribal areas. At first, U.S. officials alerted their Pakistani counterparts to each potential strike, a process that could take as long as seven hours. After the United States stopped such notifications, the strikes could be carried out within an hour, greatly increasing the ability to hit targets. In 2008, a drone attack that killed mostly women and children further strained Pakistan's relationship with the United States. Increasingly, it was revealed that while hundreds of targets had been taken out, such strikes had also resulted in the deaths of thousands of civilians.[200] However, the fact that drones mitigated the need for large numbers of special operations forces on the ground made them politically expedient, especially as U.S. ground engagement in the region declined in popularity back in the States, thanks to mounting costs and the relatively large number of American dead.[201]

Another development designed to lessen the need for large numbers of ground troops has been the increased use of the Navy's SEAL Team 6 to take out the United States' enemies. As reported in 2015 by the *New York Times,* "Once a small group reserved for specialized but rare missions, the unit best known for killing Osama bin Laden has been transformed by more than a decade of combat into a global manhunting machine . . . tracking those the United States wants to kill or capture."[202] According to the *Times,* the team steadily evolved during the wars in Afghanistan and Iraq from rescuing hostages to taking on missions that "blurred the traditional lines between soldier and spy," often cooperating with the CIA through a special initiative known as the Omega Program that offered increased flexibility in terms of the tactics they could use to track their targets.[203]

The team—which operates under the cover name Naval Special Warfare Development Group—enjoys little to no oversight from outside the Joint Special Operations Command, a fact that has proved expedient when administration officials conduct invisible operations that "bend the rules of international law."[204] According to the *Times,* one of the most concerning developments has been the administration's increased reliance on the team to go after not only high-level terrorists but "street thugs," sometimes resulting in the deaths of as many as twenty-five people at a time.[205]

Ultimately, with the greatly expanded use of Predator drones and largely invisible units such as SEAL Team 6 to track and/or take out opponents, the United States' post-9/11 path veered even more sharply away from the international rule of law and its deference to trials, in favor of a more expedient form of government-proclaimed "justice."

THE COURIER AND THE DOCTOR

As an increasing number of drones took to the skies, a shrinking number of CIA analysts continued the hunt for bin Laden from the ground. By 2005, the CIA had largely dismantled its bin Laden unit and had established a new counterterrorism center to track the increasingly globalized al-Qaeda movement.[206]

While the official narrative of what played out next has been contested by investigative journalist Seymour Hersh[207] and the operator of the national security blog *The Spy Who Billed Me*,[208] according to most authorities it was one agent in particular who continued a dogged pursuit of al-Qaeda's head from her office in the United States. That agent, known only as "Rebecca," supposedly developed a four-pillared strategy that would become the basis for the hunt for Bin Laden for the next several years. As Peter L. Bergen explains in *Manhunt*, his book on the search for bin Laden, "The first pillar was locating al-Qaeda's leader through his courier network. The second was locating him through his family members, either those who might be with him or anyone in his family who might try to get in touch with them. The third was communications [in which he might engage with other al-Qaeda leaders]. The final pillar was tracking bin Laden's occasional outreach to the media."[209] The courier route was eventually deemed most promising, and sights were set on finding bin Laden's personal aid, Abu Ahmed al-Kuwaiti.

One day, according to the official narrative, a CIA "asset" tracked the courier's car to a compound in the Pakistani town of Abbottabad and relayed that information back to Washington, D.C. Rebecca and her fellow analysts were intrigued by the compound's fortress-like design and scale—it was three stories tall, in a neighborhood of one- and two-story houses, with an estimated value of several hundred thousand dollars—as well as its lack of any phone or Internet service. Also intriguing were reports that children on the property occasionally spoke of a mysterious "uncle" who had lived there for six years, yet never left the compound. According to the asset, the man would take daily walks around the garden under a tarp that seemed designed to block any clear view by satellites.

The CIA, writes Bergen, was "familiar with the idea of 'hiding in plain sight,' but the Abbottabad compound seemed to take that concept to a new level."[210] Why had this "uncle" apparently not left the compound in so many years? And why had the Pakistani government apparently not run at least a routine check on the compound's twenty or so inhabitants? Little by little, the CIA's skepticism about whether bin Laden would truly be "hiding" in such plain sight turned to astonished belief that he just might be.

In contrast, Hersh has asserted that the locating of this mysterious man was not the result of careful investigative work but was triggered by a tip-off from a former senior Pakistani intelligence officer, who offered information on bin Laden's whereabouts in exchange for the bounty on the terrorist mastermind's head.[211] In Hersh's version of the story, the mystery man—who the officer claimed was bin Laden—was not hiding in plain sight but being held as a hostage by Pakistan's Inter-Services Intelligence as leverage against al-Qaeda and the Taliban, the threat being that Pakistan would turn bin Laden over to the Americans if either organization stepped out of line.

Either way, as suspicion mounted that this "uncle" could be bin Laden, CIA assets needed proof of the man's identity to convince President Obama to act. They monitored the compound by satellite and surveillance from a safe house in Abbottabad, while U.S. officials back in Washington considered four potential courses of action should bin Laden's identity be confirmed: a bombing run, a special ops swoop, a drone strike, or a joint US–Pakistani raid.[212] There were drawbacks to all four, including the potential destruction of valuable intelligence, further eroding of diplomatic relations with Pakistan, and the potential deaths of American soldiers. Above all, everyone wanted to avoid another Mogadishu.

Ultimately, the CIA needed to find a way to penetrate the Big House to confirm whom it was sheltering, and why. Sometime in late 2010, the agency hatched an elaborate ruse to obtain DNA from bin Laden's family. What happened next is also contested. According to the official narrative, the CIA approached Shakil Afridi, a health official in charge of Khyber, part of the tribal area that runs along Afghanistan's border, for help with implementation. A CIA asset since 2008, Afridi had ties to the West and family roots reflecting heroism in World War I, and was motivated by money. His assignment was to obtain DNA from the children in the compound. Samples would then be compared to a sample taken from bin Laden's sister, who died in Boston in 2010. For his services, Afridi would receive approximately $55,000, about nine times what he could make as a high-end doctor.[213]

According to the *Guardian,* which broke the story in July 2011, Afridi appeared in Abbottabad in March, saying that he had procured funds to give free vaccinations for hepatitis B.[214] Bypassing the management of the Abbottabad health services, Afridi paid generous sums to two nurses, who took part in the vaccination campaign without knowing that their ultimate target was vaccination of what were thought to be bin Laden's children, injected in such a way as to aspirate droplets of blood that could then be tested for DNA. Reportedly, the nurses had gained access to the Big House in the past, administering polio drops to some of the children.

Accounts vary as to whether Afridi was successful in obtaining blood from anyone at the compound. According to the *Guardian,* he waited outside the compound while one of the nurses, Mukhtar Bibi, went inside, carrying with her "a handbag that was fitted with an electronic device. It is not clear what the device was, or whether she left it behind. It is also not known whether the CIA managed to obtain any Bin Laden DNA."[215] The agency refuses to comment on the operation. In recounting the vaccination ruse in *Manhunt,* Bergen claims that Afridi failed to obtain any DNA. Yet, according to one reporter, relying on Pakistani court records, Afridi may have gathered a sample and passed it to the CIA in Islamabad.[216] If that is true, then based on the timeline for rapid DNA testing and travel, President Obama may have received the results of the tests as early as the night before he made his decision as to how to proceed.[217]

In contrast, according to Hersh's account, the narrative about Afridi is a cover for the man who *actually* secured bin Laden's DNA: Amir Aziz, a major in Pakistan's army and a doctor. According to Hersh, two of Pakistan's "most senior military leaders—General Ashfaq Parvez Kayani, chief of the army staff, and General Ahmed Shuja Pasha, director general of the ISI [Inter-Services Intelligence agency]" ordered Aziz to provide bin Laden with medical treatment, and through that secure his DNA. According to Hersh, that DNA sample provided the confirmation Obama needed to act.[218]

On Friday, April 29, Obama privately announced his decision: a small circle of Navy SEALs would raid the compound.[219] Hoping to avoid another Mogadishu, American officials had considered the operation from every possible angle. Contingency plans had been developed, and a model of the compound was built in Nevada's high desert to simulate conditions as closely as possible to what the Navy SEALs would encounter in the field.[220] The stakes were reportedly high: not only (according to the official narrative) was the United States' relationship with Pakistan stormy—and Pakistan was the supply route critical to keeping American troops in Afghanistan adequately supplied—but Obama's reputation was on the line. As White House aide Tony Blinken remembers, when he heard the news of the planned operation: "I thought, 'Man, that is a gutsy call.' First, we don't know for sure Bin Laden is there; the evidence is circumstantial. Second, most of [Obama's] most senior advisors had recommended a different course of action."[221] Obama, according to Bergen, was himself riven with doubts. Recalled Obama: "Obviously I knew that if we were unsuccessful, there was the potential for not only loss of life . . . but also there would be huge geopolitical ramifications. [And] what if the mysterious pacer was a prince from Dubai just keeping a low profile?"[222] Ultimately, Obama approved Operation Neptune Spear,[223] to take place on Sunday, May 1. The SEALs were given the command to kill bin Laden if they found him.

Just as had occurred during the capture of Saddam Hussein, the lights that night in the Abbottabad neighborhood went out, thanks to someone's taking the "sensible precaution"[224] of cutting electricity to the area, a practice that gave members of SEAL Team 6 a distinct advantage.[225] The raid almost began in disaster, as SEAL team member Matt Bissonnette (using the pen name Mark Owen) recalls in his book *No Easy Day*,[226] when one of their two Black Hawk helicopters crashed into the wall of the compound, thrown off by the tremendous heat emanating from the wall even well after midnight, and alerting those inside to their presence. Once on the ground, the team was allotted thirty minutes to recoup, and to find and kill their target. Still supposedly unknown was whether the shadowy pacer was, in fact, bin Laden. A handful of team members—including Bissonnette and another Navy SEAL, Robert O'Neill, among others—breached the main building and began making their way up the internal staircase. They met a young man on the stairs—later determined to be bin Laden's twenty-three-year-old son, Khalid[227]—shot him, and continued up the tile staircase, now slick with blood, toward the pacer's room on the third floor.[228]

Another Navy SEAL, the team's point man, neared the third-floor landing first, and quickly fired at a man who had peeked out of the door on the right side of the hall, then disappeared.[229] As they landed on the third floor, the point man tackled two women to absorb the blast of any suicide vest they might be wearing.[230] At this point, the narratives provided by Bissonnette and O'Neill conflict. According to Bissonnette, he and another SEAL breached the room to find two women wailing over a man on the floor. Per Bissonnette, as one of the women rushed the SEALs, a Navy SEAL grabbed her and the other woman and pushed them toward the corner, covering them with his body to absorb the impact should they be wearing suicide vests.[231] According to O'Neill, however, he entered the room alone, and shot bin Laden twice in the forehead. He was quickly followed by his teammates.[232] Children huddled nearby, wide-eyed and stunned, as the incoming SEALs shot additional rounds into the mortally wounded, but still twitching, man. The SEALs quickly took DNA samples, then cleaned away the blood to get a good look at his face.[233]

When the women in the room refused to divulge the dead man's name, one of the SEALs went to the balcony where the terrified children had been herded and asked one of the girls, "Who is the man?" As Bissonnette reports, "The girl didn't know to lie. 'Osama bin Laden.'"[234] They had him. The SEALs secured a second confirmation from one of the women, then radioed their commander in Jalalabad, who was keeping President Obama updated: "For God and Country, I pass Geronimo. . . . Geronimo E.K.I.A. [enemy killed in action]."[235]

When the Western world awoke to the news of bin Laden's death, they also awoke to Pakistan protesting that it had no idea bin Laden had been living within its borders, and that its sovereignty had been invaded.[236] On May 24, 2012, three weeks after bin Laden's death, the Pakistani police arrested Shakil Afridi—the doctor who may have led the phony vaccination campaign aimed at helping the Americans locate bin Laden. A Pakistani court later sentenced him to thirty-three years' imprisonment for treason (a sentence later reduced by ten years), purportedly for acts unrelated to the search for bin Laden. No members of the media were permitted to witness the closed-door trial.[237]

Meanwhile, the Obama administration's use of a sham vaccination program to hunt for bin Laden produced a lethal backlash in Pakistan. Dozens of public health workers were murdered by the Taliban, who call the war on polio—the longest, most expensive disease-eradication effort in history—a Western plot to sterilize Muslim children and spread HIV/AIDs.[238] "There could hardly have been a more stupid venture, and there was bound to be a backlash, especially for polio," said Dr. Zulfiqar A. Bhutta, a vaccine specialist at Pakistan's Aga Khan University, shortly after the ruse was revealed.[239]

In January 2013, as polio cases in Pakistan began rising at an alarming rate, public health deans from twelve major American universities sent a letter to President Obama calling on him to stop using vaccine campaigns as a cover for spy operations. The medical leaders compared the use of such ruses to the CIA's early infiltration of the Peace Corps: in both cases, the practice had to be stopped to protect volunteers and gain access where people are most vulnerable to disease.[240] A year later, the Obama administration announced that the CIA would no longer use vaccination campaigns in its operations or seek to obtain or exploit DNA or other genetic material acquired through vaccination programs.[241]

THE LEGACY

In May 1998, Osama bin Laden declared that "in today's wars, there are no morals."[242] One question that must be grappled with when considering the evolution of international law and its ability to produce arrests during the first decade of the twenty-first century is whether bin Laden was right.

The Pandora's Box that opened with the September 11, 2001 attacks and the United States' response has proved a significant challenge to attempts to further the rule of law in cases of crimes against humanity and war crimes, which had reached its culmination just a few years earlier with the 1998 passage of the Rome Statute, the founding treaty of the International Criminal Court. The events of 9/11—and the courses that the Bush and then Obama administrations blazed in its aftermath—significantly undermined the international effort to develop a worldwide legal order to help ensure peace during the new millennium.

Ultimately, the evils released from that box—which have persistently bedeviled the international effort—have assumed many forms. Among them are passage of the American Service-Members' Protection Act, which bars U.S. government actors from assisting ICC investigations; bilateral immunity agreements designed to ensure impunity for U.S. officials and their collaborators from prosecution at the ICC; the near-global watering-down of the universal jurisdiction doctrine; the blurring of "the traditional lines between soldier and spy;"[243] desperate attempts to inflate the power of the U.S. presidency and keep detainees out of courts run by the U.S. judiciary; a massive expansion of the U.S. intelligence community, whose voracious appetite for information would trample civil liberties and produce, in its first decade, what the *Washington Post*[244] branded a veritable "fourth branch" of the U.S. federal government, with 854,000 vetted security officials, 263 security organizations, over 3,000 private and public intelligence agencies, and 33 new security complexes, at a cost of more than $400 billion; the move from *capture and try in a court of law* to simply *kill*; and manipulation of legal definitions to broaden the tactics at the administration's disposal to fight terrorism—including distortions of the definitions of torture and the attempted reclassification of certain practices from criminal acts to acts of war—all of which became key components of the post-9/11 New Paradigm.

Indeed, the "war on terror" prefigured a shifting role for the United States on the global stage: from a vocal proponent of the international rule of law to a vocal proponent of American exceptionalism.

CHAPTER 10

Epilogue

The Future of Global Justice

"At its best," writes legal scholar David Cole, "law is about seeking justice, regulating state power, respecting human dignity, and protecting the vulnerable. Law at its worst treats legal doctrine as infinitely manipulatable, capable of being twisted cynically in whatever direction serves the client's desires."[1]

Cole's admonition captures the central tension in this book: on the one hand, the international community calls for justice and a greater respect for human rights, but on the other, the shifting political interests of states often lead them to be fair-weather friends to the pursuit of international justice, providing support when it suits their interests and just as easily withdrawing support when it does not.

Throughout this book we have documented the waxing and waning of state commitment to international and domestic war crimes prosecutions across different time periods and political contexts, ranging from post–World War II Germany and Japan to the recent emergence of international ad hoc and hybrid tribunals and the International Criminal Court (ICC). Even as many diplomats and human rights advocates have hailed the post–Cold War era as a renaissance of criminal accountability, international indifference and state obstruction of justice remain vexing problems for today's international tribunals. And then of course there are the many crimes of the major powers that the tribunals are constrained from investigating.

A telling example of fair-weather-friend behavior took place in the mid-1990s, soon after the United Nations established the International Criminal Tribunal for the Former Yugoslavia: within a year of its creation, the United Nations and some Western governments, out of indifference and neglect, had virtually abandoned the tribunal. Such "buyer's remorse" left many observers perplexed, while leading others to conclude that the UN had only created the tribunal as a means to deflect criticism for its failure to stop atrocities in Bosnia. It also left the tribunal's first chief prosecutor, Richard Goldstone, in a desperate situation. Initially, the tribunal was funded in six-month cycles, with an inadequate amount of funding for its first six months of operation.[2] This proved a serious impediment to its recruiting investigators and prosecutors, since no one could be promised a contract for more than half a year. To make matters worse, NATO troops on the ground in the former Yugoslavia were reluctant to arrest war crimes suspects under indictment by the new tribunal.

Without police forces of their own to ensure compliance with warrants, today's international tribunals have to depend on the cooperation of a range of external political actors, especially states. But despite their binding legal obligations, states often balk at tracking down and arresting suspects. Reluctance has frequently turned into outright obstruction when international tribunals ask governments complicit in atrocities to arrest and hand over suspects from their own political, ethnic, or religious groups. As one commentator noted in the context of the former Yugoslavia, having Croatian and Serbian officials make arrests "was like instructing the 'Untouchables' to cooperate with Al Capone and his henchmen in their mission to fight the bootleggers."[3]

The ICC has been especially vulnerable to this phenomenon. Since the establishment of the court in 2002, the Security Council has repeatedly ignored its requests to apply pressure on states to fulfill their legal obligations to carry out its arrest warrants. Even when it has come to the mass atrocities in the Darfur region of Sudan, which the Council referred to the ICC in 2005, the fifteen-member body has failed to issue a single statement supporting the ICC's findings of noncooperation against numerous states that have failed to arrest President Omar al-Bashir of Sudan when he has crossed into their territories.[4] In addition, the council, despite recommendations from the Panel of Experts of the UN Sanctions Committee, has opted not to include al-Bashir and his co-defendants on a list of Sudanese officials facing UN sanctions, including travel bans and the freezing of assets. This standoff came to a head in December 2014 when the court's chief prosecutor, Fatou Bensouda, announced that she was stopping her investigations in Darfur because the Security Council had taken no measures to enforce the Sudanese warrants.[5] Three months later, the ICC, clearly frustrated with Sudan's long-standing refusal to arrest and deliver its leader for trial in The Hague, repeated its request to the Security Council to take "necessary measures" to enforce the court's arrest warrant. Without such action, the ICC said, the council's decision a decade ago to refer Sudan to the court would "never achieve its ultimate goal, namely, to put an end to impunity."[6]

The Security Council is not alone in its failure to help secure the arrest of Omar al-Bashir. Since 2009, when the ICC issued an arrest warrant for crimes against humanity, the Sudanese leader has traveled to numerous countries, including Kenya, Mali, and Nigeria, always evading arrest. In June 2015, he traveled to South Africa—a founding member of the ICC and, in the past, one of its strongest supporters—to attend a summit meeting of the African Union. Soon after his arrival, South Africa's High Court, acting on a petition by a Johannesburg-based human rights group, ruled that the government was legally required to arrest the Sudanese leader. But South African officials ignored the order, letting al-Bashir slip out of the meeting and fly back to Khartoum, where thousands of supporters greeted him with patriotic and traditional songs, carrying flags, placards, banners, and even a makeshift coffin with the words "laying the International Criminal Court to its final resting place" written on its side.[7]

While states have often impeded the wheels of justice, they have not always derailed the process. The stories of the Yugoslavia and Rwanda tribunals in chapters 5 and 6 demonstrate that changing political circumstances, along with the strategic action of chief prosecutors and activists, can prompt once-recalcitrant states to provide robust backing for international justice, leading to numerous arrests and trials.

UNBOUND BY THE LAW

While we have paid close attention to the myriad ways in which the waxing and waning of political will has hampered the arrest of fugitives, we have also focused on a different but equally pernicious challenge to upholding international justice. This second challenge arises when states and other actors pursue suspected war criminals and terrorists with unchecked fervor, at times outside of any legal framework. Such pursuits may trigger new cycles of violence and human rights abuses and violate fundamental principles of due process. Witness the Rwandan government's invasion of eastern Zaire in pursuit of Hutu *génocidaires* in 1996, an intervention that resulted in the deaths of tens of thousands of refugees.[8] Or the United States' use of what it called "extraordinary rendition" soon after the attacks on the World Trade Center on September 11, 2001 to abduct suspected terrorists and transfer them to secret detention facilities, known as "black sites," in countries where they were often subjected to torture. In a 6,700-page report published in December 2014, the U.S. Senate Select Committee on Intelligence blasted the Central Intelligence Agency for its use of so-called "enhanced interrogation techniques," which the senators concluded were tantamount to torture.[9]

States have many tactics at their disposal to aid in the search and capture of suspects, several of which can be employed ethically and legally, and others which may be activated in more dubious ways. These include financial measures (such as sanctions), financial incentives (such as loans, economic aid, and bounties), and technology-based tactics (such as drones for tracking suspects)—and of course raids, abductions, renditions, and various exercises of police or military force.

Such tactics, when operating outside the bounds of law and commonly understood standards of humane treatment, have fostered a fierce debate in diplomatic and academic circles and among the public at large. Particularly at issue is an increased reliance on military and paramilitary force (as opposed to state cooperation and diplomacy) to capture or kill suspected war criminals. On one side are those who favor increased military intervention to capture fugitives—and their ill-treatment once in custody—even if the means used could result in the death of suspects and bystanders. On the other side are those who insist that such coercive measures violate the very principles of due process, fairness, and transparency that form the bedrock of international criminal law and, ultimately, justice.

One of those deeply troubled by the ethical and legal implications of pursuing fugitives is Louise Arbour, the highly regarded Canadian jurist who served as the second chief prosecutor of the Yugoslav and Rwanda tribunals, from 1996 through 1999, and later as the United Nations High Commissioner for Human Rights. In July 2001, at a time when human rights activists were calling on states to introduce more robust strategies to pursue and capture war criminals, Arbour asked in a speech in Melbourne, Australia: "Is the increased [demand for] accountability for war crimes inevitably going to require reduced accountability for law enforcers? And, if so, is this a dangerous development that could erode the rule of law by fostering tolerance for crime control at all costs?"[10]

In February 2006, four years into the Bush Administration's "war on terror," Arbour raised the topic again in a speech in London.[11] Only this time she argued that the pursuit of suspected terrorists, primarily by the United States, was running roughshod over the due-process protections enshrined in international human rights treaties. "The entire system of abductions, extra-legal transfers and secret detentions is . . . a complete repudiation of the law and of the justice system," she said. "No State resting its very identity on the rule of law should have recourse or even be a passive accomplice to such practices."[12]

Arbour compared the CIA's use of abductions and secret detention to the practice of forced disappearance, a tactic used by ruthless Latin American regimes in the 1970s and '80s as a convenient way of dealing with those seen as "undesirable." "Disappearing alleged terrorists, regardless of how dangerous they may be presumed to be," she said, "amounts to officials taking the law into their own hands, asserting themselves at once as secret accusers, adjudicators, and, in the worst cases, torturers, accountable to no one."[13]

Such tactics, Arbour said, create "a vicious circle of illegality."[14] Indeed, as we now know, many of those involved in the CIA's clandestine detention and interrogation program recognized its potential criminality early on and took steps to cover up their activities. In one incident in early July 2002, CIA agents working at a black site in Thailand cabled their superiors in Washington, DC, asking for advice on how to proceed with the interrogation of a "high-value detainee." Fearful that the interrogation techniques could potentially cause "a heart attack or another serious condition," the agents sought reassurances that the detainee "would remain in isolation and incommunicado for the remainder of his life." Several days later, their superiors responded that the interrogation process took precedence over any medical conditions. They also assured the agents that the detainee "will never be placed in a situation where he has any significant contact with others and/or has the opportunity to be released."[15]

Such clandestine practices of course shield the behavior of government agents from judicial and ultimately public scrutiny. And without such oversight, they offer no incentive to avoid illegality, and thus prevent the judiciary from exercising part of its proper function. "The role of the judiciary vis-à-vis law enforcement," as Arbour told her audience in London, "is a multifaceted expression of the rule of law. Judges play a part in the application of norms of prohibited conduct. They do so while keeping law enforcers in check against their own possible unlawful practices and, ultimately, they vindicate the judicial role as the supreme expression of the meaning of rights."[16]

The Bush administration's secret detention and interrogation program strikes at the heart of the modern-day arrest conundrum: how can the international community's demands for justice for serious international crimes be balanced with the need to respect the due-process protections of those it wishes to hold accountable? How we untangle this Gordian knot will ultimately influence the course of international justice for decades to come.

BOUND BY LAW

For those diplomats and human rights activists who lobbied for their creation, the contemporary international tribunals, and especially the ICC, represented the end of the idea that states were free to do anything they wanted inside their own borders—an assumption that had been the mainstay of international relations since the Peace of Westphalia in the seventeenth century. In joining the ICC, states have pledged to ensure that their domestic laws are consistent with the court's statute. They also have agreed to investigate and prosecute serious international crimes in their territories or by their nationals, for if they do not, the ICC can exercise jurisdiction and demand the arrest and handover of suspects for trial in The Hague. By pledging their support to this new global court, states parties have committed themselves to be bound by international humanitarian law.

At the time of this writing, nearly a decade and a half since the Rome Statute went into effect, the faith many human rights activists have put in the ICC to deliver justice effectively and equitably might seem naive. As with the other contemporary international tribunals, the ICC is at the mercy of states, because it has no enforcement arm of its own. Several of its current targets are well resourced and enjoy the benevolence of the very states obligated to arrest them, while many of the states that have committed to supporting the ICC continue to back the court when it suits them and undermine it when competing security, diplomatic, or economic objectives take precedence. State manipulation and outright obstruction are likely to threaten the effectiveness and legitimacy of the

ICC for years to come. The problem of state obstruction is readily seen in the ICC's failure to obtain the handover of several highly visible accused persons, particularly its most notorious and elusive defendants: Sudanese President Omar al-Bashir and Ugandan rebel leader Joseph Kony. Still, there have been some bright spots when it has come to the challenge of arrests: Congolese warlord Bosco Ntaganda's surrender to the U.S. embassy in Kigali, Rwanda, in 2013, for example, and the capture of both former president Laurent Gbagbo of Côte d'Ivoire in 2011 and Ugandan rebel commander Dominic Ongwen in 2015, all of whom were transferred to the court's custody.

Given its potentially global reach, the ICC has been hailed as an improvement over the ad hoc and hybrid tribunals whose jurisdictions have been limited to particular countries or regions. However, the promise of effective and equitable international justice has been belied by the current reality of a two-tiered system of justice. Since the Rome Statute is largely based on state consent, it effectively allows a range of states, especially powerful ones, such as the United States, Russia, and China, to remain immune from ICC scrutiny. At the same time, some of these states have attempted to use the court as a political instrument to support their friends and undermine their enemies.

Though the United States is highly unlikely to join the ICC in the foreseeable future, it has slowly moved from being one of the court's sharpest critics to being a fair-weather friend.[17] The Obama administration has not only walked back Bush-era policies but has actively sought out selective opportunities to help the court. U.S. officials regularly attend meetings of the Assembly of States Parties, the ICC's governing body, and no longer seek bilateral immunity agreements to shield U.S. government officials from prosecution. In early 2013, Chief Prosecutor Fatou Bensouda even lauded Washington for bolstering the court's efforts to bring war criminals to justice.

ICC supporters have welcomed these developments, but some long-time court watchers are less sanguine.[18] Political scientist Ben Schiff, for example, believes that the Obama administration's on-again, off-again attitude has been an awkward exercise in self-interest that has undermined the ICC's credibility: "Over time, the U.S. has figured out that the Court isn't that big a threat and, in fact, could potentially be an asset. So U.S. officials have begun picking and choosing how to use it. That sort of behavior doesn't enhance the Court's legitimacy."[19]

Even in the cases it supports, the United States could be more proactive in its cooperation with the court. As one high-level staff member in

the Office of the Prosecutor (OTP) said in 2010: "The American government first has to lead on one particular issue, the arrest of sought
war criminals . . . [then other countries] will follow. But we need the US
in the lead."[20] In this regard, the United States could do more to provide
technical advisors, legal and military training, and equipment to states
working to secure the arrest of ICC fugitives. It could also do more to
help states develop their capacity to prosecute serious international
crimes in their domestic courts and thus help make the international
community's conception of the ICC as a court of last resort a reality.[21]

Meanwhile, existing ICC states parties need to uphold their legal
obligations by acting decisively to secure the arrest and transfer of suspects to The Hague. The failure of the Assembly of States Parties to take
a strong stand against states like Kenya that have flouted the court's
authority renders the ICC increasingly vulnerable to state manipulation
and obstruction. And needless to say, the ICC's quest for cooperation
and arrests would have greater traction if the Security Council took
action against states like Sudan that harbor ICC fugitives.

The ICC's prosecutor's office also needs to enhance its operational
effectiveness and thereby increase leverage for international support. A
major problem lies with the uneven quality of OTP investigations. At
first blush, investigations and arrests might not appear linked, but they
are. According to Alison Cole, a former OTP investigator, the prosecution's early investigatory strategy "resulted in cases with limited evidence," which in turn prompted ICC judges to dismiss charges against
a number of defendants.[22] To improve this record, the judges suggested
that the OTP should be on the ground sooner, employ greater use of
forensic technologies, conduct fuller inquiries and do more thorough
crime scene analysis, negotiate greater access to insider witnesses, and
appreciate the cultural context.[23] This state of affairs has one clear
implication: If the OTP doesn't improve the quality of its investigations
and thereby improve its conviction rate, it may never persuade states
parties to be more proactive on the crucial issue of arrests. After all,
what state wants to subject its police or military personnel to a potentially risky arrest mission only to see the suspect acquitted years later
for lack of evidence?

And, finally, the ICC prosecutor, as the public face of the court, must
do more to maintain the court's *independence* from states while being
politically strategic enough to obtain the *state cooperation* needed to
advance investigations and bring suspects into custody. In a perfect world,
an international prosecutor would have both, rendering international

justice legitimate as well as effective. In a worst-case scenario, however, the prosecutor's office may be left with neither. Key to safeguarding the appearance and the reality of prosecutorial independence lies in not exhibiting bias for or against any region of the world, any particular state, or any specific political faction or ethnic group. Time will tell how well the ICC and its successive chief prosecutors balance the pursuit of independence with the quest for state cooperation.

Nongovernmental organizations have played an invaluable role in lobbying states to arrest and prevent visits of ICC fugitives. Even Sudan's peripatetic leader *cum* international fugitive, Omar al-Bashir, has felt the heat generated by African human rights advocates intent on stopping him in his tracks. From Kenya to Mali to Nigeria to South Africa, dedicated activists, operating out of makeshift offices and with little funding, have successfully petitioned their national courts to issue arrest warrants for al-Bashir should he ever step onto their territory. If African activists are able to resort to their own domestic laws to pursue al-Bashir, surely their governments—as ICC states parties—can do the same. Yet, most African states parties have stood in solidarity with the Sudanese leader, flouting their legal obligation to the ICC. The lesson here is clear: if the ICC is ever to fulfill its mandate, states must be prepared to subordinate their political and economic objectives to the interest of the international court.

Since the fall of the Berlin Wall, the international community has been collectively engaged in an unprecedented effort to promote human rights and advance the rule of law. This newfound willingness to end state impunity for mass atrocities is embodied in today's international criminal courts and in state efforts to strengthen the capacity of their domestic courts to do the same. But though the legal and operational regimes needed to apprehend and deliver suspected war criminals to justice are largely in place, the political will to make arrests happen in a consistent manner remains elusive. And until this situation is rectified, murderers will get away with murder, and torturers will retire with pensions.

Notes

CHAPTER 1. INTRODUCTION: THE PROMISE OF
INTERNATIONAL JUSTICE

1. Sarah Kneezle, "Official E-Mails Detail Osama bin Laden's Sea Burial," *Time,* November 22, 2012, http://newsfeed.time.com/2012/11/22/official-e-mails-detail-osama-bin-ladens-sea-burial/.

2. Vivienne Walt, "How Did Gaddafi Die? A Year Later, Unanswered Questions and Bad Blood," *Time,* October 18, 2012, http://world.time.com/2012/10/18/how-did-gaddafi-die-a-year-later-unanswered-questions-and-bad-blood/.

3. See e.g. Lawrence Weschler, "International Humanitarian Law: An Overview," in *Crimes of War 2.0: What the Public Should Know,* ed. Roy Gutman, David Rieff, and Anthony Dworkin, 22–26 (New York: W. W. Norton, 2007).

4. Ronald C. Slye and Beth Van Schaack, *International Criminal Law: Essentials* (New York: Aspen, 2009), 34–38. Also see Gary Jonathan Bass, *Stay the Hand of Vengeance: The Politics of War Crimes Tribunals* (Princeton, NJ: Princeton University Press, 2000), 203–05.

5. Convention on the Prevention and Punishment of the Crime of Genocide, https://treaties.un.org/doc/Publication/UNTS/Volume%2078/volume-78-I-1021-English.pdf.

6. Slye and Van Schaack, *International Law,* 209–11.

7. Eleanor Roosevelt, "Address to the United Nations General Assembly on the Adoption of the Universal Declaration of Human Rights," December 9, 1948, www.kentlaw.edu/faculty/bbrown/classes/HumanRightsSP10/CourseDocs/2EleanorRoosevelt.pdf.

8. Steven R. Ratner, "Categories of War Crimes," in *Crimes of War 2.0: What the Public Should Know,* 420–22.

9. See e.g. Alfred W. McCoy, *A Question of Torture: CIA Interrogation, from the Cold War to the War on Terror* (New York: Metropolitan Books, 2006).

10. Quoted in Eric Stover, "International Criminal Justice," in *World at Risk: A Global Issues Sourcebook* (Washington, DC: CQ Press, 2002), 374.

11. For an overview of hybrid tribunals and the challenges they have faced, see Lindsey Raub, "Positioning Hybrid Tribunals in International Criminal Justice," *New York University Journal of International Law and Politics* 41, no.4 (2009):1013–53.

12. Gavin Ruxton, "Present and Future Record of Arrest of War Criminals: The View of the Public Prosecutor of the ICTY," in eds. W.A.M. van Dijk and J.L. Hovens, *Arresting War Criminals* (Nijmegen: eds. Wolf Publishers, 2001), 19.

13. Interestingly, especially in light of its later prohibitions on cooperation with the International Criminal Court, the United States is the only state to have a specific suspect transfer law, known as the U.S. Surrender Agreements, with the ad hoc tribunals.

14. See Jorge A. F. Godinho, "The Surrender Agreements between the U.S. and the ICTY and ICTR: A Critical View," *Journal of International Criminal Justice* 1, no.2 (August 2003): 502–16.

15. For a discussion of *male captus, bene detentus,* see Christophe Paulussen, *Male Captus, Bene Detenus? Surrendering Suspects to the International Criminal Court* (Antwerp, Netherlands: Intersentia, 2010), 3–16.

16. Slye and Van Schaack, *International Law,* 82–83.

17. See e.g. Kenneth C. Randall, "Universal Jurisdiction under International Law," *Texas Law Review* 66, no.4 (1988), 785–88; Slye and Van Schaack, *Essentials,* 72–77; Máximo Langer, "The Diplomacy of Universal Jurisdiction: The Political Branches and the Transnational Prosecution of International Crimes," *American Journal of International Law* 105, no.1 (2011): 2–49; Mary Robinson, "Foreword," in *The Princeton Principles on Universal Jurisdiction* (Princeton, NJ: Princeton University Press, 2001), 16.

18. Larry Rohter, "Colonel's Death Gives Clues to Pinochet Arms Deals," *New York Times,* June 19, 2006.

19. Michael Ignatieff ed., *American Exceptionalism and Human Rights* (Princeton, NJ: Princeton University Press, 2005), 1–26.

20. Alfred W. McCoy, "The Real American Exceptionalism: From Torture to Drone Assassination, How Washington Gave Itself a Global Get-Out-of-Jail-Free Card," *TomDispatch.com,* February 24, 2015, www.tomdispatch.com /post/175960/tomgram%3A_alfred_w._mccoy,_the_unwritten_american_ rules_of_the_road_/.

21. Committee Against Torture, Consideration of Reports Submitted by States Parties under Article 19 of the Convention, Conclusions and Recommendations of the Committee Against Torture (United States), U.N. Doc. No. CAT/C/USA/CO/2, 36th Sess. (July 25, 2006).

22. See e.g. Manfred Nowak, "U.N. Covenant on Civil and Political Rights," *CCPR Commentary* (Arlington, VA: N.P. Engel, 1993), 31: "Also considered manifestly arbitrary are kidnappings by secret service agents abroad . . . in so far as these can be attributed to the State."

23. Open Society Institute, *Globalizing Torture: CIA Secret Detention and Extraordinary Rendition*, February 2013, www.opensocietyfoundations.org /reports/globalizing-torture-cia-secret-detention-and-extraordinary-rendition.

24. Jonathan S. Landay, "U.S. Allowed Italian Kidnap Prosecution to Shield Higher Ups, Ex-CIA Officer Says," *McClatchy Newspapers*, July 27, 2013, www .mcclatchydc.com/2013/07/27/197823/us-allowed-italian-kidnap-prosecution .html.

25. Richard J. Goldstone, "The Role of the United Nations in the Prosecution of International War Criminals," *Washington University Journal of Law and Policy* 5 (2001): 124, http://law.wustl.edu/harris/documents/p119_Goldstone.pdf.

26. Antonio Cassese, "On the Current Trends towards Criminal Prosecution and Punishment of Breaches of International Humanitarian Law," *European Journal of International Law* 9, no.1 (1998), 3.

27. Interview with Roméo Dallaire, July 17, 2012.

CHAPTER 2. TO NUREMBERG AND BEYOND

1. François Genoud, ed., *The Testament of Adolf Hitler: The Hitler-Bormann Documents, February – April 1945* (London: Cassell, 1961), 104. Also see Richard Overy, *Interrogations: The Nazi Elite in Allied Hands, 1945* (New York: Viking, 2001), xvii.

2. "Aufruf und die Soldaten der Ostfront (15 April [1945])," in *Kriegstagebuch des Oberkommandos der Wehrmacht (Wehrmachtführungsstab), Vol. 4: 1. Januar 1944–22. Mai 1945*, ed., Percy E. Schramm (Frankfurt am Main: Bernard & Graefe Verlag für Wehrwesen, 1961), 1589–90.

3. Expert assessment in the matter of Adolf Hitler, Berchtesgaden District Court, 1 August 1956 (Ref.: Z.: II 48/52), copy, Gb 05.01/2, pp. 34f., Institut für Zeitgeschichte, Munich.

4. Steven Rosenberg, "I Was in Hitler's Suicide Bunker," BBC News, September 3, 2009, http://news.bbc.co.uk/2/hi/europe/8234018.stm.

5. Heike B. Görtemaker, *Eva Braun: Life with Hitler* (New York: Alfred A. Knopf, 2011), 236–39.

6. Quoted in V. K. Vinogradov, J.F. Pogonyi, and N.V. Teptzov, *Hitler's Death: Russia's Last Great Secret from the Files of the KGB* (London: Chaucer Press, 2005), 154.

7. Vinogradov et. al., *Hitler's Death*, 56.

8. Guy Walters, *Hunting Evil: The Nazi War Criminals Who Escaped and the Quest to Bring Them to Justice* (New York: Broadway Books, 2010), 32–33.

9. Walters, *Hunting Evil*, 32–33.

10. Walters, *Hunting Evil*, 34.

11. Anthony Beevor, *Berlin: The Downfall 1945* (London: Penguin Books, 2002), 382–83.

12. Hugh Trevor-Roper, *The Last Days of Hitler* (London: Papermac, 1995), 193.

13. Walters, *Hunting Evil*, 157–58. Also see Hugh Thomas, *Doppelgängers: The Truth about the Bodies in the Berlin Bunker* (London: Fourth Estate, 1995), 215.

14. Charles Whiting, *The Hunt for Martin Bormann* (New York: Ballantine, 1973).

15. Gerald L. Posner and John Ware, *Mengele: The Complete Story* (New York: Dell, 1986); Christopher Joyce and Eric Stover, *Witnesses from the Grave: The Stories Bones Tell* (Boston: Little, Brown, 1991), 149–75.

16. Posner and Ware, *Mengele*, 65.

17. Posner and Ware, *Mengele*, 66–67.

18. Richard Bessel, *Germany 1945: From War to Peace* (New York: Harper-Collins, 2009), 246–49.

19. M. Cherif Bassiouni, "World War I: 'The War to End All Wars' and the Birth of a Handicapped International Criminal Justice System," *Denver Journal of International Law and Policy* 30 (Summer 2002): 244–91.

20. *Report Presented to the Preliminary Peace Conference by the Commission on the Responsibility of the Authors of the War and on Enforcement of Penalties* (March 29, 1919), www.firstworldwar.com/source/commissionwarguilt.htm.

21. *Memorandum of Reservations Presented by the Representatives of the United States to the Report of the Commission on Responsibilities* (April 4, 1919), www.firstworldwar.com/source/commissionwarguilt.htm.

22. Bassiouni, "World War I," 17–18.

23. Bassiouni, "World War I," 17–18.

24. Tom Bower, *The Pledge Betrayed: America and Britain and the Denazification of Postwar Germany* (New York: Doubleday, 1982), 17.

25. Bower, *The Pledge Betrayed*, 16–18.

26. John Loftus, *America's Nazi Secret: An Insider's History* (Walterville, OR: Trine Day, 2010), 56–57; President Roosevelt's statement on the "Execution of Hostages by the Nazis," www.ibiblio.org/pha/policy/1941/411025a.html. Also see Jewish Virtual Library, "War Crimes Trials: Crystallization of the Principles of International Criminal Law," www.jewishvirtuallibrary.org/jsource/judaica/ejud_0002_0020_0_20618.html.

27. Quoted in Bower, *The Pledge Betrayed*, 21.

28. Bower, *The Pledge Betrayed*, 22.

29. Inter-Allied Information Committee, "Aide-Memoire from the United Kingdom," in *Punishment for War Criminals: The Inter-Allied Declaration Signed in St. James's Palace, London, on 13 January 1942*, 4, www.ibiblio.org/pha/policy/1942/420112a.html.

30. Public Record Office, Kew, London, Prime Minister's Papers 4/100/10, note by Prime Minister, 1 November 1943, 1–4.

31. Overy, *Interrogations*, 8.

32. Moscow Declaration, www.ibiblio.org/pha/policy/1943/431000a.html.

33. Walters, *Hunting Evil*, 44.

34. Walters, *Hunting Evil*, 44.

35. Walters, *Hunting Evil*, 47–48.

36. Walters, *Hunting Evil*, 47–48.

37. Telford Taylor, *The Anatomy of the Nuremberg Trials: A Personal Memoir* (New York: Alfred A. Knopf, 1992), 28.

38. Bradley F. Smith, *The American Road to Nuremberg: The Documentary Record, 1934–1945* (Stanford, CA: Hoover Institution Press, Stanford University, 1982), 10–11; Taylor, *Anatomy of the Nuremberg Trials*, 33–39.

39. Murray C. Bernays, "Memorandum: The Subject: Trial of European War Criminals," September 15, 1944, in Smith, *The American Road to Nuremberg*, 33–37.

40. Murray C. Bernays, "Memorandum."

41. Smith, *The Road to Nuremberg* (New York: Basic Books, 1981), 36–37. The text of the Morgenthau Plan is available at http://docs.fdrlibrary.marist.edu /psf/box31/t297a01.html. Appendix B of the Morgenthau Plan addressed the "Punishment of Certain War Crimes and Treatment of Special Groups": http:// docs.fdrlibrary.marist.edu/psf/box31/t297a06.html.

42. Quoted in Smith, *The Road to Nuremberg*, 37.

43. National Archives and Records Administration II, College Park, MD, Record Group 107, McCloy Papers, Box 1, UNWCC, Report by Dr. Ečer, November 11, 1944.

44. Overy, *Interrogations*, 10–11.

45. Quoted in Bower, *The Pledge Betrayed*, 99.

46. Smith, *The Road to Nuremberg*, 133.

47. Overy, *Interrogations*, 13–15.

48. Overy, *Interrogations*, 13–15.

49. Harry S. Truman, *Year of Decisions: 1945* (London: Hodder and Stoughton, 1955), 206.

50. Overy, *Interrogations*, 14–15.

51. Walters, *Hunting Evil*, 52–54.

52. On CROWCASS, see United Nations War Crimes Commission, *History of the UNWCC and the Development of the Laws of War* (London: HMSO, 1948), 360–80.

53. Quoted in Brendan Murphy, *The Butcher of Lyon: The Story of Infamous Nazi Klaus Barbie* (New York: Empire, 1983), 230.

54. Christopher Simpson, *Blowback: America's Recruitment of Nazis and Its Effects on the Cold War* (New York: Collier, 1988), 66–79.

55. For descriptions of conditions at the Bergen-Belsen concentration camp see Raymond Phillips, ed., *The Trial of Josef Kramer and Forty-Four Others: The Belsen Trial* (London: William Hodge, 1949); Michael Berenbaum, *The World Must Know: The History of the Holocaust as Told in the United States Memorial Museum* (Washington, DC: United States Memorial Museum, 1993).

56. Bower, *The Pledge Betrayed*, 108.

57. Interview with Ben Ferencz in *Elusive Justice: The Search for Nazi War Criminals*, a PBS documentary film produced and directed by Jonathan Silvers, Saybrook Productions, September 2011, 6–7, transcript on file at the Human Rights Center, University of California, Berkeley, School of Law.

58. Ben Ferencz in *Elusive Justice*, 7.

59. *The Last Days of Ernst Kaltenbrunner* (CIA Library Center for the Study of Intelligence, 2007), https://www.cia.gov/library/center-for-the-study-of-intelligence/kent-csi/vol4no2/pdf/v04i2a07p.pdf. Although the CIA does not cite the author of this account, it is by Robert E. Matteson, the Counter Intelligence Corps officer who arrested Kaltenbrunner.

60. *Last Days of Ernst Kaltenbrunner*.

61. Walters, *Hunting Evil*, 198.

62. Quoted in Walters, *Hunting Evil*, 62.

63. Quoted in Walters, *Hunting Evil*, 200.

64. Quoted in Walters, *Hunting Evil*, 205.

65. Walters, *Hunting Evil*, 201.

66. Walters, *Hunting Evil*, 56.

67. Quoted in Walters, *Hunting Evil*, 64. Also see Ben Ferencz in *Elusive Justice*, 14–15.

68. Ian Cobain, "The Interrogation Camp That Turned Prisoners into Living Skeletons," *The Guardian*, December 16, 2005, www.theguardian.com /uk/2005/dec/17/secondworldwar.topstories3.

69. Cobain, "Interrogation Camp."

70. Ian Cobain, "The Secrets of the London Cage," *The Guardian*, November 11, 2005, www.guardian.co.uk/uk/2005/nov/12/secondworldwar.world.

71. Ian Sayer and Douglas Botting, *America's Secret Army: The Untold Story of the Counter Intelligence Corps* (New York: Franklin Watts, 1989), 2.

72. Sayer and Botting, *America's Secret Army*, 201–36.

73. Sayer and Botting, *America's Secret Army*, 201–36.

74. Nazi War Criminal Records Interagency Working Group (IWG), *Implementation of the Nazi War Crimes Disclosure Act: An Interim Report to Congress*, October 1999, www.archives.gov/iwg/reports/nazi-war-crimes -interim-report-october-1999.

75. Clarence Lasby, *Project Paperclip: German Scientists and the Cold War* (New York: Atheneum, 1971), 77–79.

76. Simpson, *Blowback*, 36–37.

77. Simpson, *Blowback*, 36–37.

78. Quoted in Simpson, *Blowback*, 37.

79. Quoted in Simpson, *Blowback*, 37.

80. IWG, *Implementation of the Nazi War Crimes Disclosure Act*. Also see Linda Hunt, *Secret Agenda: The United States Government, Nazi Scientists, and Project Paperclip, 1945 to 1990* (New York: St. Martin's Press, 1991), 1.

81. "Directive to Commander-in-Chief of United States Forces of Occupation Regarding the Military Government of Germany, April 1945," available at the website of the Avalon Project, Yale Law School, http://avalon.law.yale.edu /wwii/ger02.asp.

82. IWG, *Implementation of the Nazi War Crimes Disclosure Act*.

83. Sayer and Botting, *America's Secret Army*, 276–77.

84. Sayer and Botting, *America's Secret Army*, 278.

85. Communiqué issued at the end of the Yalta Conference, printed in *Foreign Relations of the United States: Diplomatic Papers—The Conferences of Malta and Yalta 1945* (Washington, DC, 1955), Document 497, https://history .state.gov/historicaldocuments/frus1945Malta/d497.

86. Bessel, *Germany 1945*, 193–94.

87. Sayer and Botting, *America's Secret Army*, 293.

88. Bessel, *Germany 1945*, 195.

89. Bessel, *Germany 1945*, 198–99.

90. Jewish Virtual Library, "War Crimes Trials."

91. Bessel, *Germany 1945*, 206.

92. Rebecca Wittmann, *Beyond Justice: The Auschwitz Trial* (Cambridge, MA: Harvard University Press, 2005), 19.

93. For a detailed account of the Dresden attack and its aftermath, see Marshall DeBruhl, *Firestorm: Allied Airpower and the Destruction of Dresden* (New York: Random House, 2006). Telford Taylor, one of the American prosecutors at Nuremberg, notes: "The great city air raids of the war—Hamburg, Berlin, Dresden, Tokyo, Hiroshima, and Nagasaki—had been conducted by Britain and the United States, which made it most unlikely that the prosecution would make a big thing out of the Germans' earlier raids which, destructive as they were, paled by comparison" (*Anatomy of the Nuremberg Trials*, 325–26).

94. Geoffrey Roberts, *Stalin's Wars: From World War to Cold War, 1939–1953* (New Haven, CT: Yale University Press, 2006), 170–72. Also see George Sanford, *Katyn and the Soviet Massacre of 1940: Truth, Justice and Memory* (New York: Routledge, 2005).

95. "Charter of the International Military Tribunal," in Smith, *American Road to Nuremberg*, 215–16.

96. Taylor, *Anatomy of the Nuremberg Trials*, 89–90.

97. Overy, *Interrogations*, 60–63.

98. Taylor, *Anatomy of the Nuremberg Trials*, 131–132.

99. Quoted in Taylor, *Anatomy of the Nuremberg Trials*, 167–168.

100. *Report of Robert H. Jackson, United States Representative to the International Conference on Military Trials, London, 1945* (Washington, DC: Department of State, Division of Publications, 1949), 433.

101. Rebecca West, *A Train of Powder* (New York: Viking, 1955), 5.

102. Bruce M. Stave and Michael Palmer, *Witness to Nuremberg: An Oral History of American Participants at the War Crimes Trials* (New York: Twayne, 1998), 72–73.

103. Wittman, *Beyond Justice*, 21–22; Jörg Friedrich, "Nuremberg and the Germans," in *War Crimes: The Legacy of Nuremberg*, ed. Belinda Cooper, 87–106 (New York: TV Books, 1998); Adlabert Rückerl, *The Investigation of Nazi Crimes, 1945–1978: A Documentation* (Heidelberg: C. F. Müller, 1979), 36.

104. Ben Ferencz in *Elusive Justice*, 7.

105. John W. Dower, *Embracing Defeat: Japan in the Wake of World War II* (New York: W. W. Norton, 1999), 36.

106. Dower, *Embracing Defeat*, 36.

107. Dower, *Embracing Defeat*, 445.

108. Yuma Totani, *The Tokyo War Crimes Trial: The Pursuit of Justice in the Wake of World War II* (Cambridge, MA: Harvard University Press, 2008), 20–21.

109. Totani, *Tokyo War Crimes Trial*, 262.

110. Herbert Bix, *Hirohito and the Making of Japan* (New York: HarperCollins, 2000), 545.

111. "Roster of 40 Ordered Arrested as War Criminals by MacArthur," *New York Times*, September 12, 1945.

112. Dower, *Embracing Defeat*, 475.

113. Totani, *Tokyo War Crimes Trial*, 65.

114. Dower, *Embracing Defeat*, 443.

115. Totani, *Tokyo War Crimes Trial*, 22.

116. Fifty of the death sentences were commuted on appeal (Dower, *Embracing Defeat*, 447).

117. "Road Show," *Time*, May 20, 1946, 24. Also see Richard H. Minear, *Victors' Justice: The Tokyo War Crimes Trial* (Ann Arbor, MI: Center for Japanese Studies, University of Michigan, 2001), 3.

118. Dower, *Embracing Defeat*, 453.

119. Totani, *Tokyo War Crimes Trial*, 41.

120. Dower, *Embracing Defeat*, 39.

121. Neil Boister and Robert Cryer, *The Tokyo International Military Tribunal: A Reappraisal* (Oxford: Oxford University Press, 2008), 51.

122. George H. Johnston, "MacArthur's Round Up of Criminals," *Argus*, September 25, 1945, 20.

123. Laura Hillenbrand, *Unbroken: A World War II Story of Survival, Resilience, and Redemption* (New York: Random House, 2010), 334–36.

124. Hillenbrand, *Unbroken*, 308.

125. Hillenbrand, *Unbroken*, 334.

126. Hillenbrand, *Unbroken*, 357.

127. Hillenbrand, *Unbroken*, 355.

128. Hillenbrand, *Unbroken*, 358–60.

129. Hillenbrand, *Unbroken*, 360–61.

130. "Finally, the Ordeal Is Over," *CBS News*, February 11, 2009.

131. "Finally," *CBS News*.

132. George F. Jones, "Tojo 'Botches' Suicide: Story of Eyewitness," *Chicago Daily Tribune*, September 12, 1945.

133. Chris Carola, "Veteran Who Caught Japan's Tojo Finally Breaks His Silence," *Deseret News*, September 10, 2010.

134. "Tojo's Futile Bid to Evade Arrest; Recovery after Suicide Attempt Likely," *Times of India*, September 12, 1945.

135. Jones, "Tojo 'Botches' Suicide."

136. Jones, "Tojo 'Botches' Suicide."

137. Hillenbrand, *Unbroken*, 195.

138. Dower, *Embracing Defeat*, 38.

139. Dower, *Embracing Defeat*, 39.

140. "Tojo's Futile Bid."

141. Jones, "Tojo 'Botches' Suicide."

142. Carola, "Veteran Who Caught Japan's Tojo."

143. Carola, "Veteran Who Caught Japan's Tojo."

144. "Tojo Eats Good Breakfast and Wants to Live," *Chicago Daily Tribune*, September 13, 1945.

145. Sierra Countis, "The Message on Tojo's Teeth: Remembering a Prank Pulled on Japan's Most Notorious War Criminal," *Chico News and Review*, September 12, 2002.

146. Countis, "Message on Tojo's Teeth."

147. Countis, "Message on Tojo's Teeth."

148. Charles Burress, "The Emperor as Warlord: An American Historian Charges that Hirohito Took an Active Part in World War II," *San Francisco Chronicle*, October 3, 2000.

149. Burress, "Emperor as Warlord."

150. Burress, "Emperor as Warlord."

151. Bix, *Hirohito*, 583.

152. Bix, *Hirohito*, 585.

153. Bix, *Hirohito*, 586.

154. Totani, *Tokyo War Crimes Trial*, 4.

155. Dower, *Embracing Defeat*, 281.

156. Dower, *Embracing Defeat*, 281.

157. Dower, *Embracing Defeat*, 281.

158. Bix, *Hirohito*, 6.

159. Sheldon Harris, "Japanese Biological Warfare Experiments and Other Atrocities in Manchuria, 1932–1945, and the Subsequent United States Cover Up: A Preliminary Assessment." *Crime, Law and Social Change* 15 (1991): 173.

160. Harris, "Japanese Biological Warfare Experiments," 174.

161. Harris, "Japanese Biological Warfare Experiments," 175.

162. Harris, "Japanese Biological Warfare Experiments," 175.

163. Harris, "Japanese Biological Warfare Experiments," 181.

164. Harris, "Japanese Biological Warfare Experiments," 181.

165. John W. Powell, "A Hidden Chapter in History," *Bulletin of the Atomic Scientists*, October 1981, 50.

166. Christopher Reed, "The United States and the Japanese Mengele: Payoffs and Amnesty for Unit 731 Scientists," *Asia-Pacific Journal: Japan Focus*, August 1, 2006, http://japanfocus.org/-Christopher-Reed/2177.

167. Harris, "Japanese Biological Warfare Experiments," 185, cites extracts from *Allied Translator and Interpretor Section Southwest Pacific Area*, Interrogation Report No. 449, 16 September 1944, Army Intelligence Document File, ID919284, Targets-BW-Japan, National Archives.

168. Harris, "Japanese Biological Warfare Experiments," 186.

169. Powell, "Hidden Chapter in History," 45.

170. Powell, "Hidden Chapter in History," 47.

171. Powell, "Hidden Chapter in History," 47.

172. Harris, "Japanese Biological Warfare Experiments," 191.

173. Harris, "Japanese Biological Warfare Experiments," 194.

174. Reed, "United States," 5.

175. Harris, "Japanese Biological Warfare Experiments," 194. For more on Shiro Ishii and Unit 731, see Morimura Seiichi, *Akuma no hosōhku: "Kantōgun saikinsen butai"* [Devil's Insanity: The Bacteriological Unit of the Kwantung Army] (Tokyo: Kōbunsha, 1981); Sheldon Harris, *Factories of Death: Japanese Biological Warfare 1932–45 and the American Cover-Up* (New York: Routledge, 1994).

176. Minear, *Victors' Justice*, 5–6.

177. Dower, *Embracing Defeat*, 449.

178. Totani, *Tokyo War Crimes Trial,* 190–217.
179. Totani, *Tokyo War Crimes Trial,* 247–50.
180. Quoted in Totani, *Tokyo War Crimes Trial,* 249.
181. Totani, *Tokyo War Crimes Trial,* 249–50. Also see Dower, *Embracing Defeat,* 486–511.

CHAPTER 3. THE HUNTERS AND THE HUNTED

1. Gerald L. Posner and John Ware, *Mengele: The Complete Story* (New York: Dell, 1986), 67.
2. Posner and Ware, *Mengele,* 67.
3. *In the Matter of Josef Mengele: A Report to the Attorney General of the United States* (US Department of Justice, October 1992), 2, www.justice.gov /sites/default/files/criminal-hrsp/legacy/2011/02/04/10–01–92mengele-rpt.pdf.
4. Posner and Ware, *Mengele,* 68–69.
5. Michael Phayer, *The Catholic Church and the Holocaust, 1930–1965* (Bloomington: Indiana University Press, 2000).
6. Christopher Joyce and Eric Stover, *Witnesses from the Grave: The Stories Bones Tell* (Boston, MA: Little, Brown), 154.
7. Neal Bascomb, *Hunting Eichmann: How a Band of Survivors and a Young Spy Agency Chased Down the Most Notorious Nazi* (Boston, MA: Houghton Mifflin Harcourt, 2009), 33–34.
8. Eichmann's life is described in his autobiography and numerous books. See e.g. Adolf Eichmann, *Meine Flucht: Bericht aus der Zelle in Jerusalem,* National Archives and Records Administration, Bethesda, Maryland, RG 263 (CIA), War Crimes, CIA name files, IWG, box 14, Eichmann, Adolf; Bascomb, *Hunting Eichmann;* Gerald Steinacher, *Nazis on the Run: How Hitler's Henchmen Fled Justice* (Oxford: Oxford University Press, 2011); David Cesarani, *Eichmann: His Life and Crimes* (New York: Vintage, 2004).
9. Bascomb, *Hunting Eichmann,* 17–18.
10. *The Last Days of Ernst Kaltenbrunner* (CIA Library's Center for the Study of Intelligence, 2007). Although the CIA does not cite the author of this account, it is by Robert E. Matteson, the CIC officer who arrested Kaltenbrunner.
11. *Last Days of Ernst Kaltenbrunner,* 22. Also see the Wilhelm Höttl interview in Ladislas Farago, *Aftermath: Martin Bormann and the Fourth Reich* (New York: Simon & Schuster, 1974), 252.
12. Bascomb, *Hunting Eichmann,* 22–25.
13. Quoted in Guy Walters, *Hunting Evil: The Nazi War Criminals Who Escaped and the Quest to Bring Them to Justice* (New York: Broadway, 2010), 12. Walters took the quote from "How I Escaped by Eichmann," *The People* (London, UK), May 7, 1961, 2–4. The London newspaper *The People* published a four-week serialization of Eichmann's memoirs.
14. "How I Escaped by Eichmann," 4.
15. *Elusive Justice: The Search for Nazi War Criminals,* a documentary produced and directed by Jonathan Silvers, Saybrook Productions, September 2011, 5 (transcript on file at the Human Rights Center, University of California, Berkeley, School of Law).

16. Bascomb, *Hunting Eichmann,* 30–31.

17. *Elusive Justice,* 5–6.

18. Bascomb, *Hunting Eichmann,* 31.

19. Walters, *Hunting Evil,* 71.

20. Quoted in Walters, *Hunting Evil,* 72.

21. Walters, *Hunting Evil,* 72. Dieter Wisliceny's affidavit to the International Military Tribunal can be found at www.phdn.org/archives/www.ess.uwe .ac.uk/genocide/Wisliceny.htm.

22. Bascomb, *Hunting Eichmann,* 48–50; Walters, *Hunting Evil,* 72–73.

23. "How I Escaped by Eichmann," 2.

24. Quoted in Walters, *Hunting Evil,* 182.

25. Quoted in Uki Goñi, *The Real Odessa: Smuggling the Nazis to Peron's Argentina* (London: Granta Books, 2002), 298.

26. Bascomb, *Hunting Eichmann,* 69.

27. Quoted in Bascomb, *Hunting Eichmann,* 70.

28. Steinacher, *Nazis on the Run,* 214. Also see Federica Bertagna and Matteo Sanfilippo, "Per una prospettiva comparata dell'emigrazione nazi-facista dopo la seconda Guerra mondiale," *Studi Emigrazione/Migration Studies* 41 (2004): 527–53.

29. Ronald C. Newton, *The "Nazi Menace" in Argentina, 1931–1947* (Stanford, CA: Stanford University Press, 1992), 374.

30. Bascomb, *Hunting Eichmann,* 70.

31. Alois Hudal, *Romishce Tagebücher: Lebenberichte eines alten Bischofs* (Graz-Stutgart: Leopold Stocker, 1976), 21; quoted in Walters, *Hunting Evil,* 126.

32. Steinacher, *Nazis on the Run,* 233–34.

33. Goñi, *Real Odessa,* 300. Also see Bascomb, *Hunting Eichmann,* 72–73.

34. Quoted in Mark Aarons and John Loftus, *Unholy Trinity: How the Vatican's Nazi Networks Betrayed Western Intelligence to the Soviets* (New York: St. Martin's Press, 1991), 81.

35. For differing views see Steinacher, *Nazis on the Run;* Walters, *Hunting Evil;* Michael Phayer, *Pius XII, the Holocaust, and the Cold War* (Bloomington: Indiana University Press, 2007); Richard Breitman, Norman J. W. Goda, and Timothy Naftali, *U.S. Intelligence and the Nazis* (Cambridge: Cambridge University Press, 2005).

36. Breitman et al., *U.S. Intelligence and the Nazis,* 211–13.

37. Breitman et al., *U.S. Intelligence and the Nazis,* 212.

38. *Elusive Justice,* 13.

39. Walters, *Hunting Evil,* 207–19.

40. Quoted in Christopher Simpson, *Blowback: America's Recruitment of Nazis and its Effects on the Cold War* (New York: Weidenfeld & Nicholson, 1988), 188.

41. Walters, *Hunting Evil,* 218.

42. Tom Bower, *Klaus Barbie: The Butcher of Lyon* (New York: Pantheon Books, 1984), 168.

43. Quoted in Tom Bower, *Klaus Barbie,* 163.

44. Bower, *Klaus Barbie,* 163.

45. Bower, *Klaus Barbie*, 176–78.

46. Breitman et al., *U.S. Intelligence and the Nazis*, 212.

47. Bower, *Klaus Barbie*, 180–181.

48. Bower, *Klaus Barbie*, 181. For more about Klaus Barbie's associations with the CIC, see Allan A. Ryan, Jr., *Klaus Barbie and the United States Government: A Report to the Attorney General of the United States* (Washington, DC: U.S. Department of Justice, Criminal Division, August 1983).

49. Quoted in *Elusive Justice*, 11.

50. Tuviah Friedman, *The Hunter* (Garden City, NY: Doubleday, 1961), 72–73.

51. Friedman, *Hunter*, 95.

52. Interview with Tuviah Friedman by Jonathan Silvers for *Elusive Justice*.

53. Friedman, *Hunter*, 104.

54. Friedman, *Hunter*, 104.

55. Tom Segev, *Simon Wiesenthal: The Life and Legends* (New York: Doubleday, 2010), 14.

56. Friedman, *Hunter*, 113.

57. Friedman, *Hunter*, 115–16.

58. Friedman, *Hunter*, 115–16.

59. Interview with Asher Ben Natan by Jonathan Silvers for *Elusive Justice*.

60. Friedman, *Hunter*, 118–19.

61. Moshe Pearlman, *The Capture and Trial of Adolf Eichmann* (New York: Simon & Schuster, 1963), 11.

62. Bascomb, *Hunting Eichmann*, 51–61.

63. Walters, *Hunting Evil*, 98–99.

64. Bascomb, *Hunting Eichmann*, 61; Walters, *Hunting Evil*, 99. Exactly how the image was captured is not clear. One version claims that the Austrian police, acting on Diamant's tip, raided Mösenbacher's apartment the following morning and seized the photo album, while another claims that Diamant, who always carried a camera, surreptitiously snapped a picture of the photograph.

65. "Tuviah Friedman," *The Telegraph*, February 16, 2011, www.telegraph.co.uk/news/obituaries/military-obituaries/8329295/Tuviah-Friedman.html.

66. Alan Levy, *The Wiesenthal File* (London: Constable, 1993), 64–65.

67. Levy, *Wiesenthal File*, 80.

68. Levy, *Wiesenthal File*, 80. Also see Walters, *Hunting Evil*, 98.

69. Segev, *Simon Wiesenthal*, 108–09.

70. Friedman, *Hunter*, 208.

71. Quoted in Levy, *Wiesenthal File*, 121.

72. Quoted in Levy, *Wiesenthal File*, 122.

73. Quoted in Levy, *Wiesenthal File*, 122.

74. Segev, *Simon Wiesenthal*, 326.

75. Walters, *Hunting Evil*, 77.

76. Walters, *Hunting Evil*, 77–78.

77. Walters, *Hunting Evil*, 267.

78. Walters, *Hunting Evil*, 78–100; Deborah E. Lipstadt, *The Eichmann Trial* (New York: Schocken Books, 2011), 5–10.

79. Simon Wiesenthal, *The Murderers Among Us* (New York: McGraw-Hill, 1967), flyleaf; Simon Wiesenthal, *Justice Not Vengeance* (New York: Grove Weidenfeld, 1989), 70; Walters, *Hunting Evil*, 332.

80. Quoted in Levy, *Wiesenthal File*, 80. Also see Walters, *Hunting Evil*, 122.

81. Pearlman, *Capture and Trial*, 38–39.

82. Bascomb, *Hunting Eichmann*, 80.

83. Posner and Ware, *Mengele*, 109.

84. Isser Harel, *The House on Garibaldi Street: The First Full Account of the Capture of Adolf Eichmann, Told by the Former Head of Israel's Secret Service* (New York: Viking Press, 1975), 17. Also see Walters, *Hunting Evil*, 268–69.

85. Goñi, *Real Odessa*, 312.

86. Walters, *Hunting Evil*, 269–70. There are numerous other accounts of Sylvia Hermann's encounter with the Eichmann family in Olivos and the former Nazi's kidnapping. Most agree on the basic story, while the details may vary—see e.g. Bascomb, *Hunting Eichmann*, 95–97; Lipstadt, *Eichmann Trial*, 12–13; Goñi, *Real Odessa*, 312–13.

87. Lawrence Joffe, "Isser Harel: The Israeli Intelligence Chief Who Brought in the Nazi Mass Murderer Adolf Eichmann," *The Guardian*, February 19, 2003, www.theguardian.com/news/2003/feb/20/guardianobituaries.israel.

88. Walters, *Hunting Evil*, 270–71.

89. Quoted in Posner and Ware, *Mengele*, 144.

90. From *Operation Finale*, brochure for the exhibit "Operation Finale: The Story of the Capture of Eichmann," at the Museum of the Jewish People, Tel Aviv, 2012 (in the files of the Human Rights Center).

91. Museum of the Jewish People, *Operation Finale*, 115.

92. Bascomb, *Hunting Eichmann*, 152–53.

93. Interview with Rafi Eitan by Jonathan Silvers for *Elusive Justice*.

94. Interview with Rafi Eitan by Jonathan Silvers for *Elusive Justice*.

95. Museum of the Jewish People, *Operation Finale*, 44.

96. Museum of the Jewish People, *Operation Finale*, 115.

97. Quoted in Bascomb, *Hunting Eichmann*, 227.

98. Interview with Rafi Eitan by Jonathan Silvers for *Elusive Justice*.

99. Quoted in Posner and Ware, *Mengele*, 156.

100. Gerald Posner, "The Man Who Let Mengele Get Away," *The Daily Beast*, July 25, 2009, www.thedailybeast.com/articles/2009/07/25/the-man-who-let-mengele-get-away.html.

101. For a detailed description of Eichmann's exit from Argentina, see Bascomb, *Hunting Eichman*, 276–96.

102. Museum of the Jewish People, *Operation Finale*, 127.

103. Quoted in Harel, *House on Garibaldi Street*, 288.

104. Lipstadt, *Eichmann Trial*, 22–26.

105. Posner and Ware, *Mengele*, 156.

106. Lipstadt, *Eichmann Trial*, 24–26.

107. Quoted in Lipstadt, *Eichmann Trial*, 21.

108. Posner and Ware, *Mengele*, 154.

109. Tom Segev, *The Seventh Million: The Israelis and the Holocaust* (New York: Henry Holt, 1993), 326.

110. Golda Meir, *A Land of Our Own: An Oral Autobiography* (New York: Putnam, 1973), 134; Lipstadt, *Eichmann Trial*, 22.

111. At least one of Mossad's Nazi-hunting expeditions resulted in the target's capture and murder. It involved Herbert Cukurs, a former member of the Arajs Komando, a unit of the Latvian Auxiliary Police, who was personally in charge of killing thousands of Jews, Roma, and mental patients. After the war, Cukurs acquired safe-conduct documents in France and settled in Interlagos, Brazil, where he ran a successful seaplane charter business. In 1965, Mossad agents lured Cukurs to a secret location in Uruguay, where they killed him and left a note on his body that read: "Accused was executed by those who can never forget" (*Elusive Justice*, 26–27).

112. Lipstad, *Eichmann Trial*, 58.

113. Lipstad, *Eichmann Trial*, 58.

114. Lipstad, *Eichmann Trial*, 58.

115. For a detailed analysis of the judgment, see Pearlman, *Capture and Trial*, 560–691.

116. Quoted in Bascomb, *Hunting Eichman*, 316–17. Eichmann appealed the verdict, but Israel's Supreme Court, sitting as a Court of Criminal Appeal, rejected it and upheld the District Court's judgment on all accounts.

117. Annette Wieviorka, *L'Ère du témoin* (Paris: Plon, 1998), 97.

118. Wieviorka, *L'Ère du témoin*, 97.

119. Lipstadt, *Eichmann Trial*, 193–94.

120. Allan Hall, "Eichmann Memoirs Published," *The Guardian*, August 11, 1999, www.guardian.co.uk/world/1999/aug/12/2/print.

121. Quoted in Walters, *Hunting Evil*, 302.

122. Quoted in Walters, *Hunting Evil*, 302–03.

123. Walters, *Hunting Evil*, 300–303.

124. Walters, *Hunting Evil*, 314.

125. Josef Mengele diary, entry for August 19, 1962, in possession of the Mengele family. Also see Posner and Ware, *Mengele*, 184.

126. Joyce and Stover, *Witnesses from the Grave*, 178–79; Posner and Ware, *Mengele*, 131–32.

127. Mengele's diary omits any discussion of his time in Argentina from 1949 to 1959. Posner and Ware speculate that his family in Günzburg may have deliberately destroyed the sections on his Argentine years "in order to protect the reputations of Karl Sr. and Alois, who, contrary to the family's indignant denials, employed Mengele as a salesman for much of this time" (*Mengele*, 102).

128. West German arrest warrant for Josef Mengele, dated June 5, 1959, Court Number 22, issued by Judge Robert Müller.

129. Posner and Ware, *Mengele*, 159–60.

130. Posner and Ware, *Mengele*, 138–39.

131. Posner and Ware, *Mengele*, 138–39.

132. Interview with Gitta Stammer at the Medico-Legal Institute in São Paulo, June 18, 1985, by Eric Stover and forensic specialists sponsored by the Simon Wiesenthal Center and the governments of Brazil, the United States, and West Germany. Also see Joyce and Stover, *Witnesses from the Grave*, 178–85.

133. Gitta Stammer interview.

134. Posner and Ware, *Mengele*, 196.

135. Gitta Stammer interview. Also see Joyce and Stover, *Witnesses from the Grave*, 183–85.

136. When Harel left, many of his loyal Mossad operatives joined him. Aside from a brief stint in the Knesset, he spent the years before his death in 2003 on a kibbutz, writing books and advising on security matters. See Ronen Bergman, "Killing the Killers," *Newsweek*, December 13, 2010, www.newsweek.com /killing-killers-69081; Posner, "Man Who Let Mengele Get Away."

137. Quoted in Posner, "Man Who Let Mengele Get Away."

138. Posner and Ware, *Mengele*, 240–41.

139. Letter from Josef Mengele to Wolfgang Gerhard, circa 1976, in possession of the Gerhard family, quoted in Posner and Ware, *Mengele*, 275.

140. Posner and Ware, *Mengele*, 284–85.

141. Interview with Lisolette and Wolfram Bossert at the Medico-Legal Institute in São Paulo, June 18, 1985, by one of the authors, Eric Stover, and the forensic specialists sponsored by the Simon Wiesenthal Center and the governments of Brazil, the United States, and West Germany (in the files of the authors).

142. Joyce and Stover, *Witnesses from the Grave*, 151.

143. Joyce and Stover, *Witnesses from the Grave*, 151.

144. "Go-Between Tells of Trips to Brazil," *New York Times*, June 13, 1985, 1.

145. Posner and Ware, *Mengele*, 336.

146. Interview with Lisolette and Wolfram Bossert.

147. Joyce and Stover, *Witnesses from the Grave*, 176–211.

148. Joyce and Stover, *Witnesses from the Grave*, 176–211.

149. Office of Special Investigations, Criminal Division, U.S. Department of Justice, *In the Matter of Josef Mengele: A Report to the Attorney General of the United States*, October 1992, 191; A. J. Jefferys, M. J. Allen, E. Gabelberg, and A. Sonnberg, "Identification of the Skeletal Remains of Josef Mengele by DNA Analysis," *Forensic Science International* 56 (1992): 65–76.

150. Quoted in Office of Special Investigations, *In the Matter of Josef Mengele*, 191.

151. Ralph Blumenthal, "U.S. Report on Mengele Reaffirms His Death," *New York Times*, October 9, 1992, 9.

152. Office of Special Investigations, *In the Matter of Josef Mengele*, 196.

153. Quoted in Thomas Keenan and Eyal Weizman, *Mengele's Skull: The Advent of Forensic Aesthetics* (Berlin: Sternberg Press, 2012), 55.

154. Posner, "Man Who Let Mengele Get Away."

CHAPTER 4. THE LAST NAZI WAR CRIMINALS

1. Several books have documented Klaus Barbie's life in Boliva. See e.g. Magnus Linklater, Isabel Hilton, and Neal Ascherson, *The Fourth Reich: Klaus Barbie and the Neo-Fascist Connection* (London: Hodder and Stoughton, 1984); Tom Bower, *Klaus Barbie: The Butcher of Lyon* (New York: Pantheon Books, 1984); Jean Beattie, *The Life and Career of Klaus Barbie: An Eyewitness Record* (London: Methuen, 1984); Ladislas de Hoyos, *Klaus Barbie: The Untold Story* (New York: McGraw-Hill, 1985).

2. Linklater et al., *Fourth Reich*, 223.

3. Georg Bönisch and Klaus Wiegrefe, "From Nazi Criminal to Postwar Spy: German Intelligence Hired Klaus Barbie as Agent," *Spiegel Online*, January 20, 2011, www.spiegel.de/international/germany/from-nazi-criminal-to-postwar-spy-german-intelligence-hired-klaus-barbie-as-agent-a-740393.html.

4. Bönisch and Wiegrefe, "From Nazi Criminal to Postwar Spy."

5. Allan J. Ryan, Jr., *Klaus Barbie and the United States Government: A Report to the Attorney General of the United States* (Washington DC: U.S. Department of Justice, Criminal Division, August 1983), 180–81. Barbie, under the alias of Klaus Altmann, entered the United States with an A-2 visa, which is reserved for accredited diplomats. At the time, the U.S. Embassy in La Paz "routinely" issued A-2 visas "to holders of Bolivian diplomatic passports, when so requested by the Bolivian Foreign Ministry, and the Foreign Ministry routinely requested them, using a form letter containing the passport holder's name." This further confirms Barbie's connections within the Bolivian government.

6. Bower, *Klaus Barbie*, 191.

7. Bower, *Klaus Barbie*, 191.

8. Rebecca Wittmann, *Beyond Justice: The Auschwitz Trial* (Cambridge, MA: Harvard University Press, 2005), 15.

9. Jeffery Herf, *Divided Memory: The Nazi Past in the Two Germanys* (Cambridge, MA: Harvard University Press, 1997), 203. Herf also states that Adenauer wanted at all costs "to avoid a renewal of German nationalism and Nazism" and to promote "economic recovery and political democratization" and that those goals should "take priority over a judicial confrontation with the crimes of the Nazi past."

10. Quoted in Deborah E. Lipstadt, *The Eichmann Trial* (New York: Schocken Books, 2011), 27.

11. Nancy Wood, "The Papon Trial in an 'Era of Testimony,'" in *The Papon Affair: Memory and Justice on Trial*, ed. Richard J. Golsan, 96–114 (New York: Routledge, 2000).

12. Quoted in Harry Reicher, "War Crimes Trials: Crystallization of the Principles of International Criminal Law," *Jewish Virtual Library*, www.jewishvirtuallibrary.org/jsource/judaica/ejud_0002_0020_0_20618.html.

13. "Landmark Trial Pushed Germany to Tackle Nazi Past," *DW Germany*, May 20, 2008, http://www.dw.de/landmark-trial-pushed-germany-to-tackle-nazi-past/a-3349537.

14. Linklater et al., *Fourth Reich*, 224.

15. *Elusive Justice: The Search for Nazi War Criminals*, a documentary produced and directed by Jonathan Silvers, Saybrook Productions, September 2011, 26. The transcript, on file at the Human Rights Center, University of California, Berkeley, School of Law, includes interviews not aired in the final film.

16. Peter Hellman, "Stalking the Last Nazi," *New York Magazine*, January 13, 1992, www.klarsfeldfoundation.org/press/92/stalking/stalking.pdf.

17. Interview with Serge Klarsfeld for *Elusive Justice*, 27. This reference is taken from parts of the interview not aired in the documentary.

18. Interview with Serge Klarsfeld for *Elusive Justice*, 6.

19. Charles Greenfield, "The Klarsfeld Saga," *International Herald Tribune*, March 6, 1983.

20. For background on the Vichy regime, see e.g. Eric Conan and Henry Rousso, *Vichy: An Ever-Present Past* (Hanover, NH: University Press of New England, 1998); Michael Curtis, *Verdict on Vichy: Power and Prejudice in the Vichy France Regime* (New York: Arcade, 2002).

21. Frank Buscher, book review of Claudia Moisel, *Frankreich und die deutschen Kriegsverbrecher: Politik und Praxis der Strafverfolgung nach dem Zweiten Weltkrieg* (Göttingen: Wallstein, 2004), https://networks.h-net.org /node/35008/reviews/43986/buscher-moisel-frankreich-und-die-deutschen-kriegsverbrecher-politik.

22. Interview with Beate Klarsfeld for Elusive Justice, 1–5. This reference is taken from parts of the interview not aired in the documentary. The interview is on file at the Human Rights Center, University of California, Berkeley, School of Law.

23. Greenfield, "Klarsfeld Saga."

24. Beate Klarsfeld was arrested and received a one-year sentence, which was later suspended. She continued her protests against Kiesinger until he was voted out of office in 1969. Beate Klarsfeld, *Wherever They May Be!* (New York: Vanguard Press, 1975), 11.

25. Interview with Beate Klarsfeld for *Elusive Justice*, 10.

26. Bower, *Klaus Barbie*, 200.

27. Interview with Beate Klarsfeld for *Elusive Justice*, 10.

28. Interview with Serge Klarsfeld for *Elusive Justice*, 11. This reference is taken from parts of the interview not aired in the documentary.

29. Mario Cacciottolo, "The Hunt for the Last Nazis," *BBC News,* March 23, 2009, http://news.bbc.co.uk/2/hi/7858822.stm.

30. *Elusive Justice*, 30.

31. More information about the Izieu orphanage and the children who were deported to Auschwitz can be found at www.auschwitz.dk/Star/Izieu.htm. See also Serge Klarsfeld's website dedicated to the memory of the French children who perished during the Holocaust, http://www.holocaust-history.org/klarsfeld /French%20Children/html&graphics/F005.shtml.

32. Klarsfeld, *Wherever They May Be*, 235–41. Also see Guy Walters, *Hunting Evil: The Nazi War Criminals Who Escaped and the Quest to Bring Them to Justice* (New York: Broadway Books, 2010), 351–52.

33. Quoted in Klarsfeld, *Wherever They May Be*, 241.

34. Bower, *Klaus Barbie*, 203.

35. Bower, *Klaus Barbie*, 204.

36. Bower, *Klaus Barbie*, 204.

37. Bower, *Klaus Barbie*, 204.

38. Walters, *Hunting Evil*, 352–53.

39. Walters, *Hunting Evil*, 352–53.

40. Quoted in Bower, *Klaus Barbie*, 205.

41. Linklater et al., *Fourth Reich*, 258.

42. Linklater et al., *Fourth Reich*, 258–59.

43. Leila Sadat Wexler, "The Interpretation of the Nuremberg Principles by the French Court of Cassation: From Touvier to Barbie and Back Again," *Columbia Journal of Transnational Law* 32, no.2: 332.

44. Jean-Olivier Voit, "The Klaus Barbie Trial and Crimes against Humanity," *Hofstra Law and Policy Symposium* 3 (1999): 155–57.

45. Linklater et al., *Fourth Reich*, 258.

46. Norman J. Goda, "Manhunts: The Official Search for Notorious Nazis," in Richard Breitman et al., *U.S. Intelligence and the Nazis*, 428 (Cambridge: Cambridge University Press, 2005), 428.

47. Beattie, *Life and Career*, 200–01.

48. Beattie, *Life and Career*, 202–03.

49. Bower, *Klaus Barbie*, 211.

50. Linklater et al., *Fourth Reich*, 267.

51. Jane Kramer, "Letter from Europe," *The New Yorker*, May 16, 1983, 50.

52. Bower, *Klaus Barbie*, 209–10.

53. Council on Hemispheric Affairs, "Guatemala and El Salvador: Latin America's Worst Human Rights Violators in 1980," press release, January 5, 1981, Washington, DC.

54. Linklater et al., *Fourth Reich*, 289.

55. "Bolivian President Takes His Oath of Office," *Associated Press*, October 11, 1982.

56. Judgment of 6 October 1983, Cass. crim., 1984 D.S. Jur. 113, G.P. Nos. 352–54, at 710 (18–20 Dec. 1983), 1983 J.C.P. II G, No,107, J.DI. 779 (1983).

57. Goda, "Manhunts," 429–30.

58. Goda, "Manhunts," 429. The reference is to a communiqué from the U.S. Embassy in Moscow to the U.S. Secretary of State, No. 03410, March 22, 1983, National Archives, RG 59, N-66.

59. Goda, "Manhunts," 430. The reference is to "Memorandum for the General Counsel from [CIA Associate General Counsel]," February 16, 1983, National Archives, RG 263, Klaus Barbie File, vol. 2.

60. Linklater et al., *Fourth Reich*, 312–13.

61. de Hoyos, *Klaus Barbie*, 236; Walters, *Hunting Evil*, 237.

62. Linklater et al., *Fourth Reich*, 315.

63. Bower, *Klaus Barbie*, 220.

64. Bower, *Klaus Barbie*, 221.

65. Bower, *Klaus Barbie*, 221.

66. de Hoyos, *Klaus Barbie*, 236; Walters, *Hunting Evil*, 242–43.

67. Bower, *Klaus Barbie*, 222–23.

68. Linklater et al., *Fourth Reich*, 222–23.

69. Linklater et al., *Fourth Reich*, 317.

70. de Hoyos, *Klaus Barbie*, 247.

71. Walters, *Hunting Evil*, 379.

72. Kramer, "Letter from Europe," 131.

73. Kramer, "Letter from Europe," 141.

74. Bower, *Klaus Barbie*, 224.

75. de Hoyos, *Klaus Barbie*, 251.

76. Wexler, "The Interpretation of the Nuremberg Principles," 334–35.

77. "Klaus Barbie: Women Testify to Torture at His Hands," *Philadelphia Inquirer*, March 23, 1987, www.writing.upenn.edu/~afilreis/Holocaust/barbie .html.

78. Walters, *Hunting Evil*, 398.

79. Alice Y. Kaplan's introductory remarks in Alain Finkielkraut, *Remembering in Vain: The Klaus Barbie Trial and Crimes against Humanity* (New York: Columbia University Press, 1992), xvii.

80. See e.g. Kramer, "Letter from Europe," 141. Also see Patricia Heberer and Jürgen Matthäus, eds., *Atrocities on Trial: Historical Perspectives on the Politics of Prosecuting War Crimes* (Lincoln: University of Nebraska Press, 2004). For a discussion of bystanders in the Bosnian and Rwanda contexts, see Eric Stover and Harvey M. Weinstein, eds., *My Neighbor, My Enemy: Justice and Community in the Aftermath of Mass Atrocity* (Cambridge: Cambridge University Press, 2004).

81. Kaplan's introductory remarks in Finkielkraut, *Remembering in Vain*, xxix.

82. Kaplan's introductory remarks in Finkielkraut, *Remembering in Vain*, xv; Michael Marrus and Robert Paxton, *Vichy France and the Jews* (New York: Basic Books, 1981), 344.

83. Kaplan introductory remarks in Finkielkraut, *Remembering in Vain*, xv.

84. Kramer, "Letter from Europe," 134–35.

85. Walters, *Hunting Evil*, 380.

86. Elizabeth Holtzman, *Who Said It Would Be Easy? One Woman's Life in the Political Arena* (New York: Arcade, 1996), 90–93. Also see Walters, *Hunting Evil*, 362–64.

87. *Elusive Justice*, 36–37.

88. *Elusive Justice*, 36–37.

89. Comptroller General of the United States, *Widespread Conspiracy to Obstruct Probes of Alleged Nazi War Criminals Not Supported by Available Evidence: Controversy May Continue* (Washington, DC: Government Accounting Office, May 15, 1978).

90. Eli M. Rosenbaum, "An Introduction to the Work of the Office of Special Investigations," *United States Attorneys' Bulletin* 54, no. 1, U.S. Department of Justice, January 2006, 2. Also see Efraim Zuroff, *Operation Last Chance: One Man's Quest to Bring Nazi War Criminals to Justice* (New York: Palgrave Macmillan, 2009), 36–37; Bower, *Klaus Barbie*, 232–32; Walters, *Hunting Evil*, 364–65.

91. Bower, *Klaus Barbie*, 232.

92. Allan A. Ryan, Jr., *Klaus Barbie and the United States Government: A Report to the Attorney General of the United States* (Washington, DC: U.S. Department of Justice, Criminal Division, August 1983), 138–40.

93. Ryan, *Klaus Barbie*, 138–40.

94. Ryan, *Klaus Barbie*, 138–40.

95. Ryan, *Klaus Barbie*, 138–40. Also see Norman J. W. Goda, "The Ustacha: Murder and Espionage," in Breitman et al., *U.S. Intelligence and the Nazis*, 211–12.

96. Ryan, *Klaus Barbie*, 1. Also see Kaplan in introductory remarks in Finkielkraut, *Remembering in Vain*, xxxi.

97. Quoted in Alan A. Ryan Jr., *Quiet Neighbors: Prosecuting Nazi War Criminals in America* (New York: Harcourt Brace Jovanovich, 1984), 323.

98. Commentary by Yuriy Soltan, "Washington's 'Hypocritical Apology to France over Barbie Affair,'" Moscow World Service, August 17, 1983.

99. Kaplan in Finkielkraut, *Remembering in Vain*, xxxii.

100. *Elusive Justice*, 36.

101. Linda Hunt, *Secret Agenda: The United States Government, Nazi Scientists, and Project Paperclip, 1945 to 1990* (New York, St. Martin's Press, 1991); Tom Bower, *The Pledge Betrayed: America and Britain and the Denazification of Postwar Germany* (Garden City, NY: Doubleday, 1982).

102. "Introduction," in Breitman et al., *U.S. Intelligence and the Nazis*, 4.

103. Norman J. W. Goda and Richard Breitman, "Conclusion," in Breitman et al., *U.S. Intelligence and the Nazis*, 445.

104. Breitman et al., *U.S. Intelligence and the Nazis*; Richard Breitman and Norman J. W. Goda, *Hitler's Shadow: Nazi War Criminals, U.S. Intelligence, and the Cold War* (Washington, DC: National Archives and Records Administration, 2010).

105. Goda and Breitman, "Conclusion," 444.

106. Goda and Breitman, "Conclusion," 444–45.

107. "Introduction," in Breitman et al., *U.S. Intelligence and the Nazis*, 6.

108. Goda and Breitman, "Conclusion," 444–45.

109. Goda and Breitman, "Conclusion," 449.

110. Goda and Breitman, "Conclusion," 449.

111. Goda and Breitman, "Conclusion," 450–51.

112. Goda and Breitman, "Conclusion," 453.

113. Goda and Breitman, "Conclusion," 454–55.

114. Goda and Breitman, "Conclusion," 454–55. Also see Annie Jacobsen, *Operation Paperclip: The Secret Intelligence Program That Brought Nazi Scientists to America* (Boston: Little, Brown, 2014), 431.

115. Zuroff, *Operation Last Chance*, 53.

116. Eric Lichtblau, "U.S. Paid Residents Linked to Nazi Crimes $20 Million in Benefits, Report Says," *New York Times*, May 30, 2015.

117. Rosenbaum, "Introduction," 1–3.

118. Rosenbaum, "Introduction," 4.

119. Elizabeth B. White, "Barring Axis Persecutors from the United States: OSI's 'Watch List' Program," *United States Attorneys' Bulletin* 54, no. 1 (January 2006), 20–21.

120. Walters, *Hunting Evil*, 384–87. Also see Eli M. Rosenbaum and William Hoffer, *Betrayal: The Untold Story of the Kurt Waldheim Investigation and Cover-up* (New York: St. Martin's Press, 1993), 461–62.

121. *Klapprott v. United States*, 335 U.S. 601, 612 (1949). Also see Rosenbaum, "Introduction", 5; Walters, *Hunting Evil*, 382.

122. Jacobson, *Operation Paperclip*, ix–x.

123. "U.S., Britain Hold German Experts, Berlin Communist Papers Charge," *New York Times*, October 27, 1946.

124. Jacobsen, *Operation Paperclip*, 250.

125. Jacobsen, *Operation Paperclip*, 262–63.

126. Linda Hunt, *Secret Agenda*, 57–77.

127. Patrick J. Buchanan, "The Persecution of John Demjanjuk," posted on LewRockwell.com, May 14, 2011, http://buchanan.org/blog/the-persecution-of-john-demjanjuk-4743.

128. Robert D. McFadden, "John Demjanjuk, 91, Dogged by Charges of Atrocities as Nazi Camp Guard, Dies," *New York Times*, March 17, 2012.

129. McFadden, "John Demjanjuk."

130. "Former Auschwitz Nazi Guard Hans Lipschis Found in Germany," *BBC News*, April 25, 2013, www.bbc.com/news/world-europe-22277866.

131. C. F. Ruter and D. W. de Mildt, eds., *Nazi Crimes on Trial: German Trials Concerning National Socialist Homicidal Crimes, 1945–1999* (Amsterdam: University of Amsterdam Institute of Criminal Law, 2002).

132. Katie Englehart, "Closing the Books: Should the World's 'Last Nazi Hunter' Give Up the Chase?" *Foreign Policy*, January 16, 2014.

133. "Germany's Auschwitz Investigation Finds More Than 40 Suspected Guards Still Alive," *Associated Press*, August 26, 2013.

134. Elizabeth Kolbert, "The Last Trial: A Great-Grandmother, Auschwitz, and the Arc of Justice," *New Yorker*, February 16, 2015, www.newyorker .com/magazine/2015/02/16/last-trial.

135. Goda, "Manhunts," 419.

136. Interview with Efraim Zuroff, May 5, 2013.

137. In the yearly grades, issued since 2001, an A rating indicates that a given country has instituted a "highly successful investigation and prosecution program." B ratings are given to countries that have "at least one conviction and/or filed one indictment, or submitted an extradition request during the period under review," while a C means countries have "failed to obtain any convictions or indictments . . . but have either advanced ongoing cases in . . . litigation or have opened new investigation." Category D is given to those countries "which have made at least a minimal effort to investigate Nazi war criminals but which failed to achieve any practical results." Category E indicates countries where "there are no known suspects and no practical steps have been taken to uncover new cases." An F-1 rating is given to countries "which refuse in principle to investigate, let alone prosecute, suspected Nazi war criminals because of legal (statute of limitation) or ideological restrictions," while an F-2 is awarded to countries where there are no legal barriers but where efforts to pursue suspects have been absent because of a lack of political will "and/or a lack of the requisite resources and/or expertise." Finally, an X rating goes to countries that fail to respond to the center's questionnaire and "clearly did not take any action whatsoever to investigate suspected Nazi war criminals during the period under review." The Simon Wiesenthal Center's rankings are available at www.operationlastchance.org. Also see Zuroff, *Operation Last Chance*, 69–79.

138. "AP Impact: American Limbo Was Fate of 10 Suspected Nazis Ordered Deported; 4 Alive in US," *Associated Press*, July 30, 2013.

139. "Closing in on Dr. Death: Germany Steps Up Hunt for Nazi War Criminal," *Spiegel Online*, July 30, 2007, www.spiegel.de/international/europe /closing-in-on-dr-death-germany-steps-up-hunt-for-nazi-war-criminal-a-497187 .html.

140. Goda and Breitman, "Conclusion," 457–58.

141. Klaus Wiegrefe, "Obscuring the Past: Intelligence Agency Destroyed Files on Former SS Members," *Spiegel Online,* November 30, 2011, www .spiegel.de/international/germany/obscuring-the-past-intelligence-agency-destroyed-files-on-former-ss-members-a-800809.html.

142. In March 2010, the OSI merged with a new Department of Justice section, Human Rights and Special Prosecutions (www.justice.gov/criminal-hrsp /about-hrsp), and expanded its brief to prosecute human rights violators from other countries who attempt to cross U.S. borders or are already residing in the United States. A year later, U.S. Immigration and Customs Enforcement opened a similar office called the Human Rights Violators and War Crimes Center, made up of historians, investigators, and legal experts whose job it is to identify and track human rights violators and war criminals around the world. By 2012, the center had more than 200 people in custody, and had deported more than 400, while pursuing another 1,900 cases involving suspects from 95 countries. The center's work has led to several high-profile arrests, among them a California martial arts instructor accused and later convicted of massacring at least 160 people during the Guatemalan civil war; a Georgia man who was allegedly part of a Serbian paramilitary group that killed thousands during the Bosnian war; and a Chicago-area grocery store owner wanted in Rwanda on charges of genocide and war crimes. In 2015, immigration officials announced that they had identified 300 Bosnian immigrants who they believe concealed their involvement in wartime atrocities when they came to the United States as part of a wave of war refugees in the 1990s. Of these, as many as half may have played a part in Europe's worst massacre since World War II: the 1995 genocide at Srebrenica, where Bosnian Serb forces executed some 8,000 Muslim men and boys.

143. Reicher, "War Crimes Trials."

144. Zuroff, *Operation Last Chance,* 131–41.

145. Zuroff, *Operation Last Chance,* 140–41.

146. Interview with Efraim Zuroff, May 5, 2013.

147. Goda and Breitman, "Conclusion," 457–58.

148. Klaus Wiegrefe, "Obscuring the Past."

149. Rosenbaum, "Introduction," 2.

150. Reicher, "War Crimes Trials."

CHAPTER 5. BALKAN FUGITIVES, INTERNATIONAL PROSECUTORS

1. The description of Mladic in Srebrenica is drawn from Eric Stover and Gilles Peress, *The Graves: Srebrenica and Vukovar* (Zurich: Scalo, 1998), 122.

2. David Scheffer, *All the Missing Souls: A Personal History of the War Crimes Tribunals* (Princeton, NJ: Princeton University Press, 2012), 88.

3. Laura Silber and Allan Little, *Yugoslavia: Death of a Nation* (New York: Penguin Books, 1997), 274.

4. David Rohde, *Endgame: The Betrayal and Fall of Srebrenica, Europe's Worst Massacre since World War II* (New York: Farrar, Straus & Giroux, 1997), 132.

5. Silber and Little, *Yugoslavia,* 348.
6. Rohde, *Endgame,* 169–70.
7. Rohde, *Endgame,* 187.
8. Rohde, *Endgame,* 205.
9. Lawrence Weschler, *Vermeer in Bosnia* (New York: Pantheon Books, 2004), 40.
10. Madeleine Albright, *Madame Secretary: A Memoir* (New York: Miramax Books, 2003), 231.
11. Rohde, *Endgame,* 253.
12. Christian Jennings, *Bosnia's Million Bones: Solving the World's Greatest Forensic Puzzle* (New York: Palgrave Macmillan, 2013), 49–50.
13. Michael Dobbs, "General Mladic in The Hague," *Foreign Policy,* August 2012.
14. Rohde, *Endgame,* 330.
15. Carla Del Ponte and Chuck Sudetic, *Madame Prosecutor: Confrontations with Humanity's Worst Criminals and the Culture of Impunity* (New York: Other Press, 2009), 243.
16. Vjeran Pavlakovic, "Croatia, the International Criminal Tribunal for the Former Yugoslavia, and General Gotovina as a Political Symbol," *Europe-Asia Studies* 62, no. 10 (2010): 1711.
17. Efraim Zuroff, *Operation Last Chance: One Man's Quest to Bring Nazi War Criminals to Justice* (New York: Palgrave Macmillan, 2009), 134–35.
18. Silber and Little, *Yugoslavia,* 360.
19. Prosecutor vs. Ante Gotovina and Mladen Markac Appeals Judgment, Dissenting Opinion of Judge Fausto Pocar, Case No. IT-06-90-A, 115.
20. Elizabeth Neuffer, *The Key to My Neighbor's House: Seeking Justice in Bosnia and Rwanda* (New York: Picador, 2001), 166.
21. Chuck Sudetic, "The Reluctant Gendarme," *Atlantic Monthly,* April 2000.
22. Neuffer, *Key to My Neighbor's House,* 176.
23. Rohde, *Endgame,* 391.
24. Neuffer, *Key to My Neighbor's House,* 178.
25. Carol Off, *The Lion, the Fox and the Eagle: A Story of Generals and Justice in Rwanda and Yugoslavia* (Toronto: Random House Canada, 2000), 296.
26. Neuffer, *Key to My Neighbor's House,* 165.
27. Sudetic, "Reluctant Gendarme."
28. Scheffer, *All the Missing Souls,* 29.
29. Scheffer, *All the Missing Souls,* 9–10.
30. Scheffer, *All the Missing Souls,* 136.
31. Richard Holbrooke, *To End a War* (New York: Random House, 1998), 315–16.
32. Holbrooke, *To End a War,* 44.
33. Richard J. Goldstone, *For Humanity: Reflections of a War Crimes Investigator* (New Haven, CT: Yale University Press, 2000), 75.
34. Scheffer, *All the Missing Souls,* 33.
35. Goldstone, *For Humanity,* 92–93.

36. Goldstone, *For Humanity*, 101–02.
37. Interview with Richard Goldstone, April 2003.
38. Interview with Richard Goldstone, April 2003, as quoted in Victor Peskin, *International Justice in Rwanda and the Balkans: Virtual Trials and the Struggle for State Cooperation* (New York: Cambridge University Press, 2008), 94.
39. Interview with Louise Arbour, May 30, 2011.
40. Interview with Graham Blewitt, July 25, 2011.
41. Interview with Louise Arbour, May 30, 2011.
42. Interview with Louise Arbour, May 30, 2011.
43. Interview with Louise Arbour, May 30, 2011.
44. Neuffer, *Key to My Neighbor's House*, 306.
45. Interview with Graham Blewitt, July 25, 2011; Neuffer, *Key to My Neighbor's House*, 303.
46. Interview with Graham Blewitt, July 25, 2011.
47. Interview with Louise Arbour, May 30, 2011.
48. Quoted in Peskin, *International Justice*, 113.
49. Samantha Power, "Croatia's Threat to Peace," *New York Times*, July 18, 1996, A23.
50. Interview with Goldstone, as quoted in Peskin, *International Justice*, 106.
51. Interview with Louise Arbour, May 30, 2011.
52. Interview with Louise Arbour, May 30, 2011.
53. Interview with Louise Arbour, May 30, 2011.
54. Address to the Security Council by Carla Del Ponte, June 18, 2007.
55. David Chuter, *War Crimes: Confronting Atrocity in the Modern World* (Boulder: Lynne Rienner, 2003), 198–99.
56. Charles Trueheart, "A New Kind of Justice," *Atlantic Monthly*, April, 2000.
57. Human Rights Watch, *"Safe Areas" for Srebrenica's Most Wanted*, briefing paper, June 29, 2005, 7.
58. Scheffer, *All the Missing Souls*, 155.
59. Scheffer, *All the Missing Souls*, 8.
60. Human Rights Watch, *"Safe Areas,"* 7.
61. The story of the journalists' quest for Karadzic and the quotes that appear in this section of the chapter are drawn from Scott Anderson, "What I Did on My Summer Vacation," *Esquire*, October 2000.
62. Robert Mackey, "Bosnian TV Airs Ratko Mladic Home Movies," *New York Times*, June 11, 2009.
63. Mackey, "Bosnian TV."
64. Dragisa Blanusa, "Milosevic in Prison," *Granta*, Autumn 2002, 242.
65. Blanusa, "Milosevic in Prison," 243.
66. Blanusa, "Milosevic in Prison," 245.
67. Quoted in Victor Peskin, *International Justice*, 70.
68. On the role of the chief prosecutor as strategic actor, see Peskin, *International Justice*, 238–46.
69. Interview with Louise Arbour, May 30, 2011.
70. Quoted in Victor Peskin, *International Justice*, 66.

71. Interview with Carla Del Ponte, December 2003.

72. International Crisis Group, "Serbian Reform Stalls Again," Balkans Report no. 145, July 17, 2003, 13.

73. International Crisis Group, "Serbian Reform Stalls Again," 13–14.

74. Daniel Simpson, "Serbia Arrests Man Suspected of Assassinating Prime Minister," *New York Times*, March 26, 2003.

75. For an account of state cooperation during the Tudjman years, see Peskin, *International Justice*, 92–118.

76. Peskin, *International Justice*, 119–48. Also see Jelana Subotic, *Hijacked Justice: Dealing with the Past in the Balkans* (Ithaca, NY: Cornell University Press, 2009), 83–121; Chrisopher Lamont, *International Criminal Justice and the Politics of Compliance* (Burlington, VT: Ashgate, 2010).

77. Pavlakovic, "Croatia," 1710.

78. Pavlakovic, "Croatia," 1710.

79. Pavlakovic, "Croatia," 1719.

80. Pavlakovic, "Croatia," 1719.

81. Quoted in Peskin, *International Justice*, 130.

82. Address to the Security Council by Carla Del Ponte, October 29, 2002.

83. Carla Del Ponte, press conference, The Hague, July 19, 2004.

84. Del Ponte and Sudetic, *Madame Prosecutor*, 306.

85. Quoted in Carla Del Ponte press conference, The Hague, July 19, 2004.

86. Victor Peskin and Mieczyslaw Boduszyski, "Balancing International Justice in the Balkans: Surrogate Enforcers, Uncertain Transitions, and the Road to Europe," *International Journal of Transitional Justice* 5, no. 1 (March 2011).

87. Interview with European Commission official, December 2006.

88. Pavlakovic, "Croatia," 1736.

89. Pavlakovic, "Croatia," 1731.

90. Dobbs, "General Mladic in The Hague."

91. Dobbs, "General Mladic in The Hague."

92. Dobbs, "General Mladic in The Hague."

93. Nick Hawton, *Europe's Most Wanted Man: The Quest for Radovan Karadzic* (London: Arrow, 2010), 179–80.

94. Jack Hitt, "Radovan Karadzic's New-Age Adventure," *New York Times Magazine*, July 22, 2009.

95. Hitt, "Radovan Karadzic's New-Age Adventure."

96. Hitt, "Radovan Karadzic's New-Age Adventure."

97. Interviews with EU officials, May 2008.

98. Interview with EU official, May 2008.

99. Peskin and Boduszyski, "Balancing International Justice in the Balkans," 69, n72.

100. "Serbians Propose 'Mladic Plan' in Plea to EU," *Financial Times*, July 17, 2006.

101. "Kouchner: Serbia Should Be in EU," *B92*, October 9, 2009.

102. Address to the Security Council by Serge Brammertz, June 4, 2008.

103. Address to the Security Council by Serge Brammertz, December 6, 2010.

104. Interview with tribunal official, June 3, 2011.

105. Interview with Stephen Rapp, May 23, 2011.

106. Interview with prosecution official, June 3, 2011.

107. Interview with tribunal official, June 3, 2011.

108. Dobbs, "Mladic in The Hague."

109. Interview with Vladimir Vukcevic, June 24, 2013.

110. The tribunal prosecution also handed down indictments of two suspects, in connection with the 2001 armed conflict in the former Yugoslav province of Macedonia.

111. Kenneth Roth, "A Tribunal's Legal Stumble," *New York Times,* July 9, 2013.

112. Marlise Simons, "Hague Court Overturns Convictions of 2 Croatian Generals Over a 1995 Offensive," *International Herald Tribune,* November 16, 2012.

113. Prosecutor vs. Ante Gotovina and Mladen Markac Appeals Judgment, Dissenting Opinion of Judge Fausto Pocar, Case No. IT-06–90-A, 115, 121, November 16, 2012.

114. Ian Traynor, "Hague Tribunal Acquits Serbian State Security Chiefs of War Crimes, *The Guardian,* May 30, 2013.

115. "Two Puzzling Judgments in The Hague," *The Economist,* June 1, 2013.

116. On the issue of extending the bounds of responsibility for wartime atrocities, though not at the level of international courts, a Dutch court in July 2014 ruled that the Netherlands government was liable to pay compensation because of the decision made by the Dutch peacekeeping force outside Srebrenica in 1995 to hand over almost 300 Bosnian Muslim men and boys to Bosnian Serb forces. According to the ruling, the Dutch peacekeepers "should have taken into account the possibility that these men would be the victim of genocide." Dan Bilefsky and Marlise Simons, "Netherlands Held Liable for 300 Deaths in Srebrenica Massacre," *New York Times,* July 17, 2014.

117. Leila Nadya Sadat, "Can the ICTY Sainovic and Perisic Cases Be Reconciled?" *American Journal of International Law* 108, no. 3 (July 2014): 475–85.

118. Human Rights Watch, *World Report 2014: Bosnia and Herzegovina,* New York, 2014.

119. *Delivering Justice in Bosnia and Herzegovina: An Overview of War Crimes Processing from 2005 to 2010,* Organization for Security and Co-operation in Europe (OSCE), Mission to Bosnia and Herzegovina, Sarajevo, 2011, 31.

120. OSCE, *Delivering Justice in Bosnia and Herzegovina,* 85.

121. Lara S. Nettelfield and Sarah E. Wagner, *Srebrenica in the Aftermath of Genocide* (Cambridge: Cambridge University Press, 2014), 202.

122. Nettelfield and Wagner, *Srebrenica,* 189–91.

123. Nettelfield and Wagner, *Srebrenica,* 203.

124. Eric Lichtblau, "US Seeks to Deport Bosnians over War Crimes," *New York Times,* February 28, 2015.

125. Adiv Sterman, "Israel Extradites Alleged Genocidaire to Bosnia," *Times of Israel,* August 15, 2013.

126. Interview with Bosnian court prosecution official, June 2013.

CHAPTER 6. TRACKING RWANDA'S *GÉNOCIDAIRES*

1. Scott Straus, *The Order of Genocide: Race, Power, and War in Rwanda* (Ithaca, NY: Cornell University Press, 2006), 226–27.

2. Roméo Dallaire, *Shake Hands with the Devil: The Failure of Humanity in Rwanda* (New York: Carroll & Graff, 2014), 231.

3. Interview with Roméo Dallaire, July 17, 2012.

4. Interview with Roméo Dallaire, July 17, 2012.

5. Interview with Roméo Dallaire, July 17, 2012.

6. Interview with Roméo Dallaire, July 17, 2012.

7. Straus, *The Order of Genocide*, 50.

8. Fergel Keane, *Season of Blood: A Rwandan Journey* (London: Viking, 1995), 107.

9. Marie Beatrice Umutesi, *Surviving the Slaughter: The Ordeal of a Rwandan Refugee in Zaire* (Madison: University of Wisconsin Press, 2004), 69.

10. Daniela Kroslak, *The French Betrayal of Rwanda* (Bloomington: Indiana University Press, 2007), 228.

11. Dallaire, *Shake Hands with the Devil*, 425.

12. Kroslak, *French Betrayal of Rwanda*, 124–52.

13. Kroslak, *French Betrayal of Rwanda*, 220–22.

14. Kroslak, *French Betrayal of Rwanda*, 265.

15. Interview with Filip Reyntjens, May 2012.

16. Luc Reydams, "Let's Be Friends: The United States, Post-Genocide Rwanda, and Victor's Justice and Arusha," discussion paper, University of Antwerp/Institute of Development Policy and Management, 2013, 17–18.

17. Samantha Power, *Chasing the Flame: One Man's Fight to Save the World* (New York: Penguin Press, 2008), 192.

18. Sadako Ogata, *The Turbulent Decade: Confronting the Refugee Crises of the 1990s* (New York: W. W. Norton, 2005), 200.

19. Power, *Chasing the Flame*, 193.

20. John Shattuck, *Freedom on Fire: Human Rights Wars and America's Response* (Cambridge, MA: Harvard University Press, 2003), 63.

21. Shattuck, *Freedom on Fire*, 63.

22. Interview with David Scheffer, April 4, 2012.

23. Interview with David Scheffer, April 4, 2012.

24. Ogata, *The Turbulent Decade*, 191–92; Alison Des Forges, *Leave None to Tell the Story: Genocide in Rwanda* (New York: Human Rights Watch and the International Federation of Human Rights Leagues, 1999), 734.

25. David Scheffer, *All the Missing Souls: A Personal History of the War Crimes Tribunals* (Princeton, NJ: Princeton University Press, 2012), 75.

26. Interview with David Scheffer, April 4, 2012.

27. Interview with David Scheffer, April 4, 2012.

28. Interview with David Scheffer, April 4, 2012.

29. Des Forges, *Leave None to Tell the Story*, 519.

30. Scheffer, *All the Missing Souls*, 110.

31. Scheffer, *All the Missing Souls*, 110.

32. Scheffer, *All the Missing Souls*, 110.

33. Power, *Chasing the Flame*, 198.

34. "DR Congo: Q&A on the United Nations Human Rights Mapping Report," Human Rights Watch, October 1, 2010, New York.

35. Tristan McConnell, "One Man's Rwanda," *Columbia Journalism Review,* January/February 1, 2011.

36. Howard W. French, *A Continent for the Taking: The Tragedy and Hope of Africa* (New York: Vintage, 2005), 142.

37. Interview with Filip Reyntjens, May 2012.

38. Thierry Cruvellier, *Court of Remorse: Inside the International Criminal Tribunal for Rwanda* (Madison: University of Wisconsin Press, 2010), 39.

39. Cruvellier, *Court of Remorse*, 33.

40. Cruvellier, *Court of Remorse*, 33.

41. Cruvellier, *Court of Remorse*, 61.

42. Cruvellier, *Court of Remorse*, 33.

43. Interview with Sara Darehshori, May 26, 2011.

44. Interview with Sara Darehshori, May 26, 2011.

45. Interview with Sara Darehshori, May 26, 2011.

46. Interview with Sara Darehshori, May 26, 2011.

47. Cruvellier, *Court of Remorse*, 11.

48. Interview with Richard Goldstone, April 2003, quoted in Victor Peskin, *International Justice in Rwanda and the Balkans: Virtual Trials and the Struggle for State Cooperation* (Cambridge: Cambridge University Press, 2008), 173.

49. Quoted in Peskin, *International Justice*, 173.

50. Quoted in Peskin, *International Justice*, 175–76.

51. Quoted in Peskin, *International Justice*, 176.

52. This argument is made by Victor Peskin in *International Justice* and by Cruvellier in *Court of Remorse*.

53. Interview with Louise Arbour, May 30, 2011.

54. Interview with Louise Arbour, May 30, 2011.

55. Interview with Louise Arbour, May 30, 2011.

56. Interview with Louise Arbour, May 30, 2011.

57. James C McKinley Jr., "Rwanda War Crimes Tribunal Indicts 2 Men in Jail in Zambia," *New York Times,* February 20, 1996.

58. Interview with Louise Arbour, May 30, 2011.

59. Interview with Gilbert Morissette, July 11, 2012.

60. Interview with Luc Côté, July 11, 2012.

61. Interview with Luc Côté, July 11, 2012.

62. Interview with Stephen Rapp, May 23, 2011.

63. Interview with Gilbert Morissette, July 11, 2012.

64. Cruvellier, *Court of Remorse*, 50; interview with Thierry Cruvellier, April 2012.

65. Interview with Thierry Cruvellier, April 2012.

66. Cruvellier, *Court of Remorse*, 53.

67. Interview with Luc Côté, July 11, 2012.

68. Interview with Louise Arbour, May 30, 2011.

69. Interview with Luc Côté, July 11, 2012.

70. Carol Off, *The Lion, the Fox and the Eagle: A Story of Generals and Justice in Rwanda and Yugoslavia* (Toronto: Random House Canada, 2000), 321.

71. Cruvellier, *Court of Remorse*, 40.

72. Cruvellier, *Court of Remorse*, 41.

73. Interview with Louise Arbour, May 30, 2011.

74. Interview with Gilbert Morissette, July 11, 2012.

75. Interview with tribunal official, April 2002, as quoted in Victor Peskin, "Rwandan Ghosts," *Legal Affairs*, September/October 2002, 21–25.

76. Interview with diplomat, April 2002, as quoted in Peskin, "Rwandan Ghosts."

77. Interview with tribunal defense investigator, April 2002, as quoted in Peskin, "Rwandan Ghosts."

78. "International Criminal Tribunal for Rwanda: Justice Delayed," International Crisis Group (ICG), June 7, 2001, 15.

79. Kingsley Moghalu, *Rwanda's Genocide: The Politics of Global Justice* (New York: Palgrave Macmillan, 2005), 173.

80. Moghalu, *Rwanda's Genocide*, 173.

81. ICG, "International Criminal Tribunal for Rwanda," 16, n31.

82. ICG, "International Criminal Tribunal for Rwanda," 16.

83. Moghalu, *Rwanda's Genocide*, 169–71.

84. Richard J. Goldstone, *For Humanity: Reflections of a War Crimes Investigator* (New Haven, CT: Yale University Press, 2000), 110.

85. Human Rights Watch, *World Report 2013: Rwanda*, New York, 2013.

86. Prosecutor vs. Jean Uwinkindi, Decision on Prosecutor's Request for Referral to the Republic of Rwanda, Case No. ICTR-2001–75-R11bis, June 28, 2011.

87. Scheffer, *All the Missing Souls*, 76.

88. Scheffer, *All the Missing Souls*, 119.

89. "Rwandan Genocide Pastor Released," *BBC News*, December 6, 2006.

90. The term *atrocity crimes* was coined by David Scheffer.

91. Interview with Canadian war crimes official, July 10, 2012.

92. Interview with Canadian war crimes official, July 10, 2012.

93. Interview with Mugesera family members, 2012.

94. Interview with Roméo Dallaire, July 17, 2012.

95. Scheffer, *All the Missing Souls*, 81.

96. Richard Ashby Wilson, *Writing History in International Criminal Trials* (Cambridge: Cambridge University Press, 2011) 173.

97. Interview with former U.S. government official, September 2004.

98. Interview with former Rwanda tribunal official, March 2005.

99. Carla Del Ponte and Chuck Sudetic, *Madame Prosecutor: Confrontations with Humanity's Worst Criminals and the Culture of Impunity* (New York: Other Press, 2009), 229.

100. Peskin, *International Justice*, 219–20.

101. Peskin, *International Justice*, 220.

102. Peskin, *International Justice*, 222.

103. Del Ponte and Sudetic, *Madame Prosecutor*, 230.

104. Peskin, *International Justice*, 223.

105. Interview with former Rwanda tribunal official, March 2005.

106. Hassan B. Jallow, "Prosecutorial Discretion and International Criminal Justice," *Journal of International Criminal Justice* 3, no. 1 (March 2005): 156.

107. "Rwanda: Tribunal Risks Supporting 'Victor's Justice'," Human Rights Watch press release, June 1, 2009.

CHAPTER 7. HYBRID TRIBUNALS: THINKING GLOBALLY, ACTING LOCALLY

1. *National Geographic* 161, no. 5 (May 1982), 547–622.

2. Nic Dunlop, *The Lost Executioner: A Story of the Khmer Rouge* (London: Bloomsbury, 2005), 3. Dunlop's recollections are also based on a Skype interview by one of the authors on August 7, 2012, and other personal communications noted below.

3. Estimates of the number of deaths vary; Craig Etcheson, *After the Killing Fields: Lessons from the Cambodian Genocide* (Westport, CT: Praeger, 2005), 107–28.

4. Interview with Nic Dunlop, August 7, 2012.

5. Thierry Cruvellier, *The Master of Confessions: The Trial of a Khmer Rouge Torturer* (New York: HarperCollins, 2014), 17–18.

6. Cruvellier, *Master of Confessions*, 18

7. Cruvellier, *Master of Confessions*, 21.

8. Dunlop, *Lost Executioner,* 5.

9. Interview with Nic Dunlop, August 7, 2012.

10. Dunlop, *Lost Executioner,* 18–19.

11. Law on the Establishment of the Extraordinary Chambers in the Courts of Cambodia for the Prosecution of Crimes Committed during the Period of Democratic Kampuchea, NS/RKM/1004/006, October 27, 2004, www.eccc.gov.kh /sites/default/files/legal-documents/KR_Law_as_amended_27_Oct_2004_Eng .pdf.

12. Stuart Ford, "How Leadership in International Criminal Law is Shifting from the United States to Europe and Asia: An Analysis of Spending on and Contributions to International Criminal Courts," *Saint Louis University Law Journal* 55, no. 953 (2011): 960–61.

13. See e.g. Adam M. Smith, *After Genocide: Bringing the Devil to Justice* (Amherst, NY: Prometheus Books, 2009), 146–55.

14. Smith, *After Genocide*, 96.

15. Ronald C. Slye and Beth Van Schaack, *International Criminal Law: The Essentials* (New York: Aspen, 2008), 61.

16. James Cockayne, "The Fraying Shoestring: Rethinking Hybrid War Crimes Tribunals," *Fordham International Law Journal* 28, no.3 (2004): 616–17.

17. Of the hybrids, the Special Tribunal for Lebanon is the least like the others as it is the first international court to investigate charges of terrorism. Established by the United Nations and the government of Lebanon in 2007, its mandate is to prosecute those responsible for an attack that killed the former Lebanese prime minister, Rafik Hariri, and twenty-two others on February 14, 2005. So far, the STL has indicted four Lebanese Shi'a Muslims connected to Hezbollah, an Islamic militant group and political party based in Lebanon. A fifth suspect was indicted in 2013 but, at the time of writing, has not been added to the case. In January 2014, the tribunal tried the four accused *in absentia,* the

first time in an international tribunal since Nuremberg. Meanwhile, the Lebanese government, which is made up of Hezbollah members, has been unable— or, as some have charged, unwilling—to arrest the four suspects. Somini Sengupta, "Mideast Strife Turns Trial on Beirut Assassination into Another Fault Line," *New York Times,* January 14, 2014; Vatican Radio, "Special Tribunal for Lebanon Readies for Trial," December 11, 2012. For an overview of hybrid tribunals and the challenges they have faced, see Lindsey Raub, "Positioning Hybrid Tribunals in International Criminal Justice," *International Law and Politics* 41, no.4 (2009): 1013–53.

18. Human Rights Watch, *The Case of Hissène Habré before the Extraordinary African Chambers in Senegal: Questions and Answers,* New York, April 27, 2015, www.hrw.org/news/2012/09/11/qa-case-hiss-ne-habr-extraordinary-african-chambers-senegal.

19. Human Rights Watch, "Kosovo: Special Court Step Toward Justice: Witness Protection Required," New York, August 4, 2015.

20. Office of the United Nations High Commissioner for Human Rights, *Rule-of-Law Tools for Post-Conflict States* (Geneva: United Nations Publications, 2008), 12.

21. Slye and Van Schaack, *International Criminal Law,* 59–60.

22. Hybrids also need state cooperation and assistance in conducting investigations and the collection of evidence, as well as enforcement of sentences. Göran Sluiter, "Legal Assistance to Internationalized Criminal Courts and Tribunals," in *Internationalized Criminal Courts: Sierra Leone, East Timor, Kosovo, and Cambodia,* ed. Cesare P. R. Romano, André Nollkaemper, and Jann K. Kleffner, 397– 406 (Oxford: Oxford University Press, 2004).

23. Interview with David Scheffer, October 7, 2011.

24. Interview with Brenda Hollis, June 12, 2011.

25. Commission for the Investigation of Violations of Human Rights in East Timor, *Report on the Investigation of Human Rights Violations in East Timor,* Jakarta, January 31, 2000, http://hass.unsw.adfa.edu.au/timor_companion/documents/KPP-HAM.pdf.

26. Slye and Van Schaack, *International Criminal Law,* 71.

27. Marieke Wierda and Catlin Reiger, *The Serious Crimes Process in Timor-Leste: In Retrospect,* International Center for Transitional Justice, New York, March 2008, 36.

28. Fred Abrahams, Gilles Peress, and Eric Stover, *A Village Destroyed: May 14, 1999, War Crimes in Kosovo* (Berkeley: University of California Press, 2001), 9.

29. Slye and Van Schaack, *Essentials,* 69–70.

30. Philip Kearney, *Under the Blue Flag: My Mission in Kosovo* (Beverly Hills, CA: Phoenix, 2008), 96–97.

31. Interview with Nic Dunlop, August 7, 2012.

32. Dunlop, *Lost Executioner,* 155–77.

33. "Starvation: Death Watch in Cambodia," *Time,* November 12, 1979.

34. William Shawcross, *The Quality of Mercy: Cambodia, Holocaust and Modern Conscience* (London: Andre Deutsch, 1984), 65.

35. Dunlop, *Lost Executioner,* 186.

36. Shawcross, *Quality of Mercy*, 76.

37. Dene-Hern Chen, "Ieng Sary's Chinese Passport Shows Bejing's Support of KR," *Cambodia Daily*, April 3, 2013, 19.

38. Philip Shenon, "Pol Pot & Co.: The Thai Connection," *New York Times*, December 19, 1993.

39. Angus MacSwan, "Cocktails with Khmer Rouge Killers," *Reuters*, July 30, 2010.

40. Dunlop, *Lost Executioner*, 198–99.

41. Shawcross, *Quality of Mercy*, 289, 345, 395.

42. Dunlop, *Lost Executioner*, 190.

43. John Pilger, ed., *Tell Me No Lies: Investigative Journalism and its Triumphs* (London: Vintage, 2005), 142.

44. United States Institute of Peace, "Peace Agreements: Cambodia," www.usip.org/publications/peace-agreements-cambodia.

45. MacSwan, "Cocktails with Khmer Rouge Killers."

46. Dunlop, *Lost Executioner*, 246.

47. Interview with Nic Dunlop, August 7, 2012.

48. Dunlop, *Lost Executioner*, 267–68.

49. Interview with Nic Dunlop, July 24, 2014.

50. Dunlop, *Lost Executioner*, 271.

51. Dunlop, *Lost Executioner*, 274.

52. Nic Dunlop and Nate Thayer, "Duch Confesses," *Far Eastern Economic Review*, May 6, 1999, 76.

53. Interview with Nic Dunlop, July 24, 2014.

54. François Bizot, "My Savior, Their Killer," *New York Times*, February 17, 2009.

55. Slye and Van Schaack, *International Criminal Law*, 62–63.

56. "Landmark Khmer Rouge Trial Starts," *BBC News*, February 17, 2009, http://news.bbc.co.uk/2/hi/asia-pacific/7893138.stm.

57. Quoted in Thierry Cruvellier, "Cambodia: Reflections on the Duch Trial," *Crimes of War*, February-March 2009, www.crimesofwar.org/commentary/regions/cambodia-reflections-on-the-duch-trial/. Cruvellier notes: "The Duch trial was unique in the history of international justice in that a guilty plea evolved into a full trial (thanks to the civil law procedure that applies before the ECCC and that does not contemplate plea bargaining). At other international tribunals, a guilty plea concludes with an agreement between the prosecutor and the accused, reached after lengthy and confidential talks, and endorsed by a Trial Chamber in a one-day hearing. It has the benefit of judicial economy, but it has little value to the public and in truth telling."

58. Quoted in Bizot, "My Savior, Their Killer."

59. ECCC, Transcript of Trial Proceedings—Kaing Guek Eav "Duch," Case File No. 001/18-07-2007-ECCC/TC, August 18, 2009, Trial Day 60, 109–10.

60. Interview with Neth Phally, Kampong Cham Province, Cambodia, November 13, 2009. Also see Eric Stover, Mychelle Balthazard, and K. Alexa Koenig, "Confronting Duch: Civil Party Participation in Case 001 at the

Extraordinary Chambers in the Courts of Cambodia," *International Review of the Red Cross* 93, no. 882 (June 2011), 503–46.

61. ECCC, Internal Rules (revision 3), as revised March 6, 2009, Rule 23(2).

62. Cruvellier, "Cambodia: Reflections."

63. Julia Wallace, "Duch Defense Victim of Teamwork's Complications," *Cambodia Daily*, November 30, 2009, www.cambodiadaily.com/archives /duch-defense-victim-of-teamworks-complications-1473/. Also see ECCC, Transcript of Trial Proceedings—Kaing Guek Eav "Duch," Case File No. 001/18–07–2007-ECCC/TC.

64. Ben Doherty, "Cambodia Torturer Duch—killer of 12,380—asks Court to Set Him Free," *The Guardian*, November 27, 2009, www.theguardian.com /world/2009/nov/27/cambodia-duch-asks-court-freedom.

65. Case 001, ECCC Trial Chamber, Judgment, Case File No. 001/18–7–2007/ECCC/TC, para. 568, Judgment (Trial Chamber), 26 July 2010, www .eccc.gov.kh/en/documents/court/judgement-case-001.

66. Ibid., paras. 679–81. The prosecution had asked for a forty-year sentence *after* taking into consideration mitigating factors and Duch's earlier illegal detention.

67. Associated Press, "Khmer Rouge Jailer Duch's Sentence Increased by Cambodian Court," February 3, 2012.

68. Julia Wallace, "Genocide Trial Begins for Khmer Rouge," *New York Times*, October 17, 2014, www.nytimes.com/2014/10/18/world/asia/khmer-rouge-leaders-genocide-trial.html.

69. Reuters, "Hun Sen Hostility Puts Decade-Old U.N. Khmer Rouge Tribunal in Doubt," as reported in the *New York Times*, April 21, 2015.

70. For general background on the civil war in Sierra Leone, see John L. Hirsch, *Sierra Leone: Diamonds and the Struggle for Democracy* (Boulder, CO: Lynne Rienner, 2001). Also see Human Rights Watch, *"We'll Kill You If You Cry": Sexual Violence in the Sierra Leone Conflict*, New York, January 2003; Tom Perriello and Marieke Wierda, *The Special Court for Sierra Leone under Scrutiny*, International Center for Transitional Justice, 2006; Thierry Cruvellier, *From the Taylor Trial to a Lasting Legacy: Putting the Special Court Model to the Test*, International Center for Transitional Justice, New York, 2009.

71. Lomé Peace Agreement between the Government of Sierra Leone and the Revolutionary United Front, July 7, 1999, Article IX.

72. An official version of the Lomé Peace Agreement with this reservation does not exist, but there is general consensus that these are the terms used.

73. David Scheffer, *All the Missing Souls: A Personal History of the War Crimes Tribunals* (Princeton, NJ: Princeton University Press, 2012), 312.

74. United Nations Security Council Resolution 1260 (1999).

75. Karl Vick, "Sierra Leone's Unjust Peace: At Sobering Stop, Albright Defends Amnesty for Rebels," *Washington Post*, October 19, 1999.

76. Scheffer, *All the Missing Souls*, 312.

77. Luc Reydams and Jan Wouters, "The Politics of Establishing International Criminal Tribunals," in *International Prosecutors*, ed. Luc Reydams, Jan Wouters, and Cedric Ryngaert (Oxford: Oxford University Press, 2012), 66.

78. James Traub, "The Worst Place on Earth," *New York Review of Books,* June 29, 2000, www.nybooks.com/articles/archives/2000/jun/29/the-worst-place-on-earth/.

79. Scheffer, *All the Missing Souls,* 312.

80. "Foday Sankoh: Foday Saybana Sankoh, an African Revolutionary, Dies on July 29th, Aged 65," *The Economist,* August 7, 2003.

81. Stephen Ellis, *The Mask of Anarchy: The Destruction of Liberia and the Religious Dimensions of an African Civil War* (New York: New York University Press, 2001), 70–71.

82. Bradford Randall, "Charles Taylor: Plymouth's War Criminal," *Kingston Journal,* November 8, 2012.

83. "Accused War Criminal Charles Taylor Says He Had Help in Plymouth Jailbreak," *Patriot Ledger,* July 17, 2009.

84. Tracey Gurd, "Taylor Alleges US Govt Helped Him Escape from US Prison," Open Society Justice Initiative, July 15, 2009, www.ijmonitor .org/2009/07/taylor-alleges-us-govt-helped-him-escape-from-us-prison/. Sheriff Peter Flynn, who ran the Plymouth prison at the time, told a local newspaper, the *Patriot Ledger,* in 2010 that Taylor's incarceration had become problematic for the federal government. "The feds didn't know what to do with Taylor," Flynn said. "They couldn't ship him back to Liberia because he would have been shot the minute he was on the ground, creating a diplomatic problem. They left him at our jail for months. I think they were almost relieved when he escaped." Other prison officials, however, have disputed Taylor's account; see "Accused War Criminal."

85. Abdul Tejan-Cole, "A Big Man in a Small Cell: Charles Taylor and the Special Court for Sierra Leone," in *Prosecuting Heads of State,* ed. Ellen L. Lutz and Caitlin Reiger, 205–32 (Cambridge: Cambridge University Press, 2009).

86. Tejan-Cole, "Big Man in a Small Cell," 208–09.

87. Lansana Gberie, *War and Peace in Sierra Leone: Diamonds, Corruption and the Lebanese Connection,* Partnership Africa Canada, November 2002.

88. Scheffer, *All the Missing Souls,* 303.

89. Perriello and Wierda, *Special Court for Sierra Leone,* 9.

90. Sebastian Junger, "Terror Recorded," *Vanity Fair,* October 2000, www .vanityfair.com/politics/features/2000/10/junger200010.

91. See, generally, Human Rights Watch, *"We'll Kill You If You Cry."*

92. Human Rights Watch, *"We'll Kill You If You Cry."*

93. Scheffer, *All the Missing Souls,* 302.

94. Ryan Liza, "Where Angels Fear to Tread," *New Republic,* July 23, 2000.

95. "The Strange Tale of Sankoh's Capture," *BBC News,* May 18, 2000; Norimitsu Onishi, "Neighbors Grab Fugitive Rebel in Sierra Leone," *New York Times,* May 18, 2000.

96. Ahmad Tejan Kabbah, President of Sierra Leone, "Letter to Kofi Annan, United Nations Secretary-General," S/2000/786, annex, June 12, 2000. This letter is quoted in Scheffer, *All the Missing Souls,* 326–27.

97. Agreement between the United Nations and the Government of Sierra Leone on the Establishment of a Special Court for Sierra Leone, January 16, 2002.

98. Penelope Van Tuyl, *Effective, Efficient, and Fair? An Inquiry into the Investigative Practices of the Office of the Prosecutor at the Special Court for Sierra Leone,* War Crimes Studies Center, University of California, Berkeley, September 2008, 16. Van Tuyl notes (80) that during the court's first fiscal year in operation (July 2002–June 2003) it operated on a budget of USD 19 million (First Annual Report of the President of the Special Court for Sierra Leone, p. 21). The budget in subsequent fiscal years has been between USD 32 million and USD 36 million per year (Second Annual Report of the President of the Special Court for Sierra Leone, p. 41; Fourth Annual Report of the President of the Special Court for Sierra Leone, p. 11). By comparison, the ICTY's two-year budget was USD 223 million for 2002–03, USD 271 million for 2004–05, USD 276 million for 2006–07, and USD 310 million for 2009–10 ("Regular Budget" statistics posted electronically at www.un.org /icty.glance-e/index.htm). The ICTR has operated on a similar budget, with USD 280 million allotted for the two-year period between 2008 and 2009 ("Budget and Staff" data posted electronically under "General Information" at www.ictr.org).

99. Special Court for Sierra Leone, *Statute of the Special Court for Sierra Leone,* Article 8.

100. Agreement between the United Nations and the Government of Sierra Leone on the Establishment of a Special Court for Sierra Leone, January 16, 2002.

101. Van Tuyl, *Effective, Efficient, and Fair?,* 17.

102. Beth K. Dougherty, "Right-Sizing International Criminal Justice: The Hybrid Experiment at the Special Court for Sierra Leone, *International Affairs* 80, no. 2 (2004): 312.

103. During the first three years of the operation of the Special Court, the United States provided $22 million, the Netherlands $14,597,172, and the United Kingdom $10,393,280. See Chad I. Losee, "Trustees as Agents: Prosecutor Behavior at the Special Court for Sierra Leone," International Studies Association Annual Conference, San Francisco, March 26–29, 2008, 22–23.

104. Report of Secretary-General on the Establishment of a Special Court for Sierra Leone, UN Doc S/2000/915, October 4, 2000, para 47.

105. Tim Kelsall, *Culture under Cross-Examination: International Justice and the Special Court for Sierra Leone* (Cambridge: Cambridge University Press, 2009), 31–33.

106. Perriello and Wierda, *Special Court for Sierra Leone,* 21.

107. Van Tuyl, *Effective, Efficient, and Fair?,* 7.

108. David Crane, personal communication, May 23, 2011; also see David Crane, "The Bright Red Thread: The Politics of International Criminal Law— Do We Want Peace or Justice? The West African Experience," in *Forging a Convention for Crimes against Humanity,* ed. Leila Nadya Sadat, 59–77 (Cambridge: Cambridge University Press, 2011).

109. Keith Biddle, *Building Strategic Capacity in the Police Force: Sierra Leone, 1998 to 2008,* Innovations for Successful Societies, Princeton University, http://successfulsocieties.princeton.edu/interviews/keith-biddle.

110. David M. Crane, "The Take Down: Case Studies Regarding 'Lawfare' in International Criminal Justice: The West African Experience," *Case Western Reserve Journal of International Law* 43 (2010): 206.

111. "David Crane: The Righteous Sword of the Law, Part 1," interview by Chris Tenove, *Radio Netherlands,* May 24, 2005.

112. Crane, "Bright Red Thread," 73.

113. Crane, "Bright Red Thread," 68.

114. Antonio Cassese, *Report of the Special Court for Sierra Leone,* December 12, 2006, para 70, www.rscsl.org/Documents/Cassese%20Report.pdf.

115. Interview with David Crane, May 23, 2011.

116. Interview with Alan White, February 25, 2013.

117. Interview with Gilbert Morissette, February 2, 2012.

118. Van Tuyl, *Effective, Efficient, and Fair?,* 11–12. Much of the information contained in this section of the report is based on an interview Van Tuyl conducted with David Crane in 2008.

119. Special Court for Sierra Leone, Office of the Prosecutor, Confidential Document, "Presence of al-Qaeda in West Africa: Independent Source Findings," www.douglasfarah.com/pdfs/stonesUN.pdf.

120. Ibid.

121. Van Tuyl, *Effective, Efficient, and Fair?,* 19–38.

122. Interview with David Crane, May 23, 2011.

123. Interview with Gilbert Morissette, July 11, 2012.

124. Interview with David Crane, May 23, 2011.

125. Crane, "Bright Red Thread," 70.

126. Crane, "Bright Red Thread," 70.

127. Interview with David Crane, May 23, 2011. Also see Charles Moore, "The Very British Gentleman Helping to Put Southern Sudan Back on Its feet," *The Telegraph,* September 25, 2006.

128. Interview with David Crane, May 23, 2011.

129. Crane, "Bright Red Thread," 71.

130. Eric Pape, "A New Breed of Tribunal," *Newsweek,* March 3, 2003.

131. *Prosecutor v. Charles Ghankay Taylor,* Special Court for Sierra Leone, SCSL-03–01-I-001, Indictment, March 7, 2003; *Prosecutor v. Charles Ghankay Taylor,* Special Court for Sierra Leone, SCSL-03–01-I-75, Amended Indictment, March 16, 2006. See also *Prosecutor v. Charles Ghankay Taylor,* Special Court for Sierra Leone, SCSL-03–01-PT, Second Amended Indictment, May 29, 2007.

132. Losee, "Trustees as Agents," 32; interview with Alan White, February 25, 2013.

133. David Pratt, *Sierra Leone: The Forgotten Crisis, A Report to the Canadian Minister of Foreign Affairs,* April 23, 1999.

134. Losee, "Trustees as Agents," 34.

135. Interview with David Crane, May 23, 2011.

136. Quoted in Losee, "Trustees as Agents," 25.

137. In 2011, *Awoko,* a newspaper in Sierra Leone, reported that several British officials were surprised at the suggestion that the British Government had sought

to influence the investigations at the Special Court for Sierra Leone. In the article Jack Straw—Britain's foreign minister between 2001 and 2006—said he had "absolutely no recollection of knowing [of] any involvement by the UK in putting pressure of any kind on anyone" at the court. He added: "And given our approach to international tribunals I would be very surprised if it turned out that anyone acting on behalf of the UK did so." Sir Malcom Rifkin, former foreign secretary under John Major, was also surprised: "If this is true then I am appalled because, first of all, it's been kept pretty secret until now." He was doubtful, however, that oil was behind any decision-making process. Soraya Kishtwari, "Gaddafi Instrumental in Sierra Leone Conflict David Crane," *Awoko*, February 28, 2011, www.awoko.org/2011/02/28/gaddafi-instrumental-in-sierra-leone-conflict-david-crane/.

138. David Crane, "Dancing with the Devil: Taking on West Africa's Warlords," speech at the David M. Kennedy Center for International Studies, Brigham Young University, April 5, 2006.

139. Interview with Gilbert Morissette, July 11, 2012.

140. Crane, "Bright Red Thread," 73.

141. Interview with Gilbert Morissette, July 11, 2012; Interview with Allan White, February 25, 2013.

142. Interview with Gilbert Morissette, July 11, 2012.

143. Interview with Gilbert Morissette, July 11, 2012.

144. Two days later, another three suspects were brought into custody.

145. Interview with David Crane, May 23, 2011. Also see Crane, "Bright Red Thread," 74.

146. See, generally, Human Rights Watch, *"Even a 'Big Man' Must Face Justice,"* New York, 2012.

147. "Foday Sankoh: The Cruel Rebel," *BBC News*, July 30, 2003, http://news.bbc.co.uk/1/hi/world/africa/3110629.stm.

148. Open Society Justice Initiative, *Charles Taylor Monthly Trial Report: October and November 2010*, 3 January 2011, www.ijmonitor.org/2011/01/charles-taylor-monthly-trial-report-october-november-2010/.

149. Crane, "Bright Red Thread," 73.

150. Crane, "Bright Red Thread," 73.

151. Tejan-Cole, "Big Man in a Small Cell," 212.

152. Tejan-Cole, "Big Man in a Small Cell," 213.

153. Statement of Chief Prosecutor for the Special Court for Sierra Leone, David Crane, June 5, 2003, www.rscsl.org/Documents/Press/OTP/prosecutor-060503.pdf.

154. Crane, "Take Down," 209.

155. Crane, "Take Down," 211.

156. Priscilla Hayner, *Negotiating Peace in Liberia: Preserving the Possibility of Justice*, Centre for Humanitarian Dialogue and International Center for Transitional Justice, November 2007, 8.

157. Lansana Gberie, Jarlawah Tonpoh, Efam Dovi, and Osei Boateng, "Charles Taylor: Why Me?" *New African*, May 2006, 3.

158. As recounted by a close adviser to Charles Taylor, in Hayner, *Negotiating Peace*, 8.

159. Hayner, *Negotiating Peace*, 8.
160. Tejan-Cole, "Big Man in a Small Cell," 215.
161. Stephan Faris, "Charles Taylor Leaves Liberia," *Time*, August 11, 2003.
162. Interview with David Crane, May 23, 2011.
163. Interview with David Crane, May 23, 2011.
164. "Firm Seeks Charles Taylor Bounty," *BBC News*, December 11, 2003.
165. UN Security Council Resolution 1532, 12 March 2004, UN Doc. S/RES/1532 (2004).
166. Interview with David Crane, May 23, 2011. See also European Parliament, *European Parliament Resolution on the Special Court for Sierra Leone: The Case of Charles Taylor*, P6_TA(2005)0059, February 24, 2005.
167. *Charles Ghankay Taylor—Transfer to the Special Court for Sierra Leone*, 109th Cong., 1st sess., H.Con.Res. 127, May 10, 2005.
168. Interview with David Crane, May 23, 2011.
169. Interview with David Crane, May 23, 2011.
170. Tejan-Cole, "Big Man in a Small Cell," 216–17.
171. UN Security Council Resolution 1638, 11 November 2005, UN Doc. S/RES/1638 (2005).
172. Tejan-Cole, "Big Man in a Small Cell," 216–17.
173. Warren Hoge, "Liberian President Seeks Extradition of Predecessor for Atrocities Trial," *New York Times*, March 18, 2006.
174. Transcript of interview, "Johnson-Sirleaf Describes Attempts to Come to Terms with Liberia's Violent Past," *NewsHour with Jim Lehrer*, March 23, 2006, www.pbs.org/newshour/bb/africa/jan-june06/liberia_3-23.html.
175. "Nigeria Faces Anger over Taylor," *BBC News*, March 29, 2006.
176. Tejan-Cole, "Big Man in a Small Cell," 218–19.
177. Special Court for Sierra Leone, "Special Court President Requests Charles Taylor Be Tried in The Hague" (press release), March 30, 2006.
178. Craig Timberg, "Liberian President Backs Bid to Move Taylor Trial to The Hague," *Washington Post*, March 31, 2006, A15.
179. Human Rights Watch, *"Even a 'Big Man' Must Face Justice,"* 18–19.
180. Thierry Cruvellier, "Why Try Taylor in The Hague?" *International Justice Tribune*, April 10, 2006.
181. International Center for Transitional Justice, "Taylor Should Be Moved from Sierra Leone as a Last Resort" (press release), New York, April 3, 2006.
182. Olenka Frenkiel, "Africa's Test for International Justice," *BBC News*, February 26, 2008.
183. Quoted in Sarah Grainger and John James, "Head Hunted," *Focus on Africa*, October-December 2006, 16.
184. Marilise Simons, "Liberian Ex-Leader Convicted for Role in Sierra Leone War Atrocities," *New York Times*, April 27, 2012, A6.
185. Simons, "Liberian Ex-Leader," A6.
186. Human Rights Watch, *"Even a 'Big Man' Must Face Justice,"* 54.
187. Marlise Simons and Alan Cowell, "Court Upholds 50-Year Jail Term in Sierra Leone War Crimes Case," *New York Times*, September 26, 2013.
188. Rapp and Hollis were also successful in prosecuting many of the surviving leaders of the Revolutionary United Front, Armed Forces Revolutionary

Council, and the Civil Defence Forces, who received prison sentences ranging from fifteen to fifty-two years.

189. For more information about the residual court, see www.rscsl.org.

190. Perriello and Wierda, *Special Court for Sierra Leone,* 43–44.

191. Special Court for Sierra Leone, "Summary of Final Tasks for the Special Court for Sierra Leone," October 2012. Also see Edith M. Lederer, "Sierra Leone Tribunal to Wrap Up Business Soon," *Bloomberg Businessweek News,* October 9, 2012, http://cnsnews.com/news/article/sierra-leone-tribunal-wrap-business-soon.

192. Van Tuyl, *Effective, Efficient, and Fair?,* 40.

193. Van Tuyl, *Effective, Efficient, and Fair?,* 42.

194. Interview with Brenda Hollis, July 12, 2011.

195. Richard J. Goldstone, *For Humanity: Reflections of a War Crimes Investigator* (New Haven, CT: Yale University Press, 2000), 132.

196. Crane, "Bright Red Thread," 77.

197. International Crisis Group, *The Special Court for Sierra Leone: Promises and Pitfalls of a "New Model,"* Brussels, August 4, 2003, 16.

198. Douglas Farah, "Sierra Leone Court May Offer Model for War Crimes Cases: Hybrid Tribunal, with Limited Lifespan, Focuses on Higher-Ups," *Washington Post,* April 15, 2003.

199. International Crisis Group, *Special Court for Sierra Leone,* 16. The Bush administration was obligated to release USD 10 million in Fiscal Year 2003 Economic Support Funds, to bring the total U.S. contribution to the Special Court to USD 20 million, as provided by the Consolidated Appropriations Act of 2003. On June 13, 2003, several U.S. representatives from both parties sent a letter to U.S. Secretary of State Colin Powell calling for the funds to be released.

200. International Crisis Group, *Special Court for Sierra Leone,* 15.

201. International Crisis Group, *Special Court for Sierra Leone,* 15. The ICG notes that a number of Sierra Leone journalists and NGO representatives complained in private and publicly about the overtly American cast of the Special Court in its first year of operations.

202. International Crisis Group, *Special Court for Sierra Leone,* 16.

203. Mary Kaldor, *Global Civil Society: An Answer to War* (Cambridge: Polity Press, 2003), 115.

204. UNGA Res 52/160 (1999), para 9.

205. Reydams and Wouters, "Politics," 74–75.

206. For statements welcoming the establishment of the ICC, see "The New International Criminal Court is Hailed as a Landmark Achievement in Human Rights but Scorned by the United States," *Reuters,* April 12, 2001, www.itnsource.com/shotlist//RTV/2002/04/12/2041100l4/.

CHAPTER 8. INTERNATIONAL CRIMINAL COURT: AT THE MERCY OF STATES

1. This chapter draws on two articles published previously by one of the authors: Victor Peskin, "Caution and Confrontation in the International Criminal Court's Pursuit of Accountability in Uganda and Sudan," *Human Rights*

Quarterly 31, no.3 (2009): 655–91; and Victor Peskin, "The International Criminal Court, the Security Council, and the Politics of Impunity in Darfur," *Genocide Studies and Prevention* 4, no. 3 (December 2009), 304–28.

2. Jeffrey Gettleman, "Kenyans Approve New Constitution," *New York Times*, August 5, 2010, www.nytimes.com/2010/08/06/world/africa/06kenya.html.

3. Walter Menya, "Bashir Surprise Guest in Kenya," *The Daily Nation*, August 27, 2010, www.nation.co.ke/News/Bashir%20surprise%20guest%20 in%20Kenya/-/1056/998008/-/wo3i5sz/-/index.html.

4. James Ratemo, "Bashir's Visit to Kenya Stirs Anger," *Standard Digital*, August 27, 2010, www.standardmedia.co.ke/business/article/2000016961/bashir-s-visit-to-kenya-stirs-anger.

5. "Kenyans Approve New Constitution."

6. "How Bashir Was Sneaked into Kenya," *The Standard*, August 28, 2010, www.standardmedia.co.ke/business/article/2000017088/how-bashir-was-sneaked-into-kenya.

7. "Bashir Surprise Guest in Kenya."

8. "Decisions and Declarations," Assembly of the African Union, 13th Ordinary Session, 1–3 July 2009, Sirte, Libya, Assembly/AU/Dec. 243–267 (XIII) Rev.1, Assembly/AU/Decl.1–5 (XIII). Also see African Union, "Decision on the Meeting of African States Parties to the Rome Statute of International Criminal Court (ICC)" (press release), July 14, 2009.

9. "Obama Criticizes Kenya over Bashir's Visit, Local Divisions Emerge in Nairobi," *Sudan Tribune*, August 28, 2010, www.sudantribune.com/spip .php?iframe&page=imprimable&id_article=36078.

10. "Obama Criticizes Kenya."

11. International Criminal Court, The Prosecutor v. Omar Hassan Ahmad Al Bashir, "Decision Informing the United Nations Security Council and the Assembly of the States Parties to the Rome Statute about Omar Al-Bashir's Presence in the Territory of the Republic of Kenya," August 27, 2010, ICC-02/05-01/09, 3.

12. Peskin, "Caution and Confrontation," 677.

13. Malcolm Moore, "Sudan's al-Bashir Given Red Carpet Treatment by China," *The Telegraph*, June 29, 2011, www.telegraph.co.uk/news/worldnews /asia/china/8605319/Sudans-al-Bashir-given-red-carpet-treatment-by-China .html.

14. Peskin, "International Criminal Court," 308.

15. "Sudanese Leader's Visit Emphasizes China's African Agenda," CNN, June 28, 2011, http://articles.cnn.com/2011-06-28/world/china.sudan.albashir_ 1_al-bashir-sudanese-president-liu-guijin.

16. "Darfur Victims Ignored as Chad Hosts Al-Bashir Yet Again," Coalition for the International Criminal Court, New York, May 10, 2013.

17. Richard Dicker, "Ramping Up Strategies for ICC Arrests: A Few Lessons Learned," *ICC Forum*, February-June 2014, http://iccforum.com/arrest#Dicker.

18. Eric Stover, "International Criminal Justice," in *World at Risk: A Global Issues Sourcebook* (Washington, DC: CQ Press, 2010), 524.

19. Ronald C. Slye and Beth Van Schaack, *International Criminal Law: Essentials* (New York: Aspen, 2008), 61.

20. Luc Reydams and Jan Wouters, "The Politics of Establishing International Criminal Tribunals," in *International Prosecutors*, ed. Luc Reydams, Jan Wouters, and Cedric Ryngaert (Oxford: Oxford University Press, 2012), 77–78.

21. Reydams and Wouters, "Politics," 77–78.

22. David Scheffer, *All the Missing Souls: A Personal History of the War Crimes Tribunals* (Princeton, NJ: Princeton University Press, 2012), 165.

23. Scheffer, *All the Missing Souls*, 207.

24. On January 1, 2001, in a White House press release, President Clinton stated: "I will not, and do not recommend that my successor, submit the Treaty to the Senate for advice and consent until our fundamental concerns are satisfied." Quoted in Rebecca Hamilton, *Fighting for Darfur: Public Action and the Struggle to Stop Genocide* (New York: Palgrave Macmillan, 2011), 220.

25. Quoted in Carla Anne Robbins, "Disarming America's Treaties," *Wall Street Journal*, July 19, 2002.

26. Georgetown Law Library, "International Criminal Court: Article 98 Agreements Research Guide," www.law.georgetown.edu/library/research/guides /article_98.cfm.

27. Warren Hodge, "The Reach of War: War Crimes; U.S. Drops Plan to Exempt G.I.'s from U.N. Court," *New York Times*, June 24, 2004, www .nytimes.com/2004/06/24/world/the-reach-of-war-war-crimes-us-drops-plan-to-exempt-gi-s-from-un-court.html.

28. American Service-Members' Protection Act of 2002, http://legcounsel .house.gov/Comps/aspa02.pdf.

29. John Kerry, "More Work to Bring War Criminals to Justice," *Huffington Post*, April 3, 2013, www.huffingtonpost.com/johnkerry/war-crimes-rewards-program_b_3007049.html. Also see War Crimes Rewards Program, U.S. Department of State, www.state.gov/j/gcj/wcrp/.

30. On the politics of U.S. engagement with the ICC, see David Bosco, *Rough Justice: The International Criminal Court in a World of Power Politics* (Oxford: Oxford University Press, 2014).

31. Marlise Simons, "U.S. Grows More Helpful to International Criminal Court, A Body It First Scorned," *New York Times*, April 2, 2013.

32. Simons, "U.S. Grows More Helpful."

33. Simons, "U.S. Grows More Helpful."

34. Simons, "U.S. Grows More Helpful."

35. Benjamin N. Schiff, *Building the International Criminal Court* (Cambridge: Cambridge University Press, 2008), 3.

36. Cedric Ryngaert, "Arrest and Detention," in *International Prosecutors*, ed. Luc Reydams, Jan Wouters, and Cedric Ryngaert (Oxford: Oxford University Press, 2012), 662.

37. Interview with Luis Moreno-Ocampo, May 31, 2011.

38. Luc Côté, "International Criminal Justice: Tightening Up the Rules of the Game," *International Review of the Red Cross* 88, no. 861 (March 2006), 135, www.icrc.org/eng/resources/documents/article/review/review-861-p133.htm.

39. See David Kaye, "Who's Afraid of the International Criminal Court? Finding the Prosecutor Who Can Set It Straight," *Foreign Affairs* 90, no. 3 (May 1, 2011).

40. William Wallis, "Lunch with the FT: Luis Moreno-Ocampo," *Financial Times*, September 23, 2011. See also Julie Flint and Alex de Waal, "Case Closed: A Prosecutor without Borders," *World Affairs*, Spring 2009, www.worldaffairs journal.org/article/case-closed-prosecutor-without-borders; Human Rights Watch, letter to the Office of the Prosecutor, International Criminal Court, September 15, 2008, www.innercitypress.com/hrw091508iccotp.pdf.

41. Peggy O'Donnell, *Using Scientific Evidence to Advance Prosecutions at the International Criminal Court*, research paper presented at Beyond Reasonable Doubt: Using Scientific Evidence to Advance Prosecutions at the International Criminal Court, convened in The Hague by the Human Rights Center, University of California, Berkeley, October 23–24, 2012, 10–14.

42. International Criminal Court, "ICC Trial Chamber II Acquits Mathieu Ngudjolo Chui" (press release), December 18, 2012, www.icc-cpi.int/en_menus /icc/press%20and%20media/press%20releases/news%20and%20highlights /Pages/pr865.aspx.

43. Flint and de Waal, "Case Closed," 129.

44. Quoted in Rick Gladstone, "A Lifelong Passion Is Now Put to Practice in The Hague," *New York Times*, January 18, 2013.

45. Aryeh Neier, *The International Human Rights Movement: A History* (Princeton, NJ: Princeton University Press), 274–75.

46. See e.g. Tim Allen, *Trial Justice: The International Criminal Court and the Lord's Resistance Army* (London: Zed, 2006), 53–71; Schiff, *Building the International Criminal Court*, 198–99.

47. Schiff, *Building the International Criminal Court*, 209.

48. Allen, *Trial Justice*, 34–36.

49. Phuong Pham, Patrick Vinck, Eric Stover, Andre Moss, Marieke Wierda, and Richard Bailey, *When the War Ends: A Population-Based Survey on Attitudes about Peace, Justice, and Social Reconstruction in Northern Uganda*, Human Rights Center, University of California, Berkeley, Payson Center for International Development, and International Center for Transitional Justice, December 2007, 14–17.

50. Philip Lancaster, Guillaume Lacaille, and Ledio Cakaj, *Diagnostic Study of the Lord's Resistance Army*, International Working Group on the Lord's Resistance Army, World Bank, June 2011, www.c-r.org/resources/lra-diagnostic-study-lords-resistance-army-philip-lancaster.

51. Pham et al., *When the War Ends*, 14–17.

52. Michael Otim and Marieke Wierda, *Uganda: Impact of the Rome Statute and the International Criminal Court*, Briefing Paper of the International Commission for Transitional Justice, Rome Statute Review Conference, June 2010, 1–2. See also "Uganda: Forgiveness as an Instrument of Peace," *IRIN News*, June 9, 2005; Human Rights Watch, *Selling Justice Short: Why Accountability Matters for Peace*, New York, July 2009, 28. Two years later, Justice Onega called for an end to the blanket amnesty because "former rebels granted amnesty were going back into rebel activities and committing greater crimes against humanity."

53. Schiff, *Building the International Criminal Court*, 198–99.

54. Schiff, *Building the International Criminal Court*, 199–200.

55. International Criminal Court, Presidency, letter from Chief Prosecutor Moreno Ocampo to President Kirsch, ICC-02/04-1 06-07-2004 (2004), appendix to "Decision Assigning the Situation in Uganda to Pre-Trial Chamber II" (2004), 4.

56. Amnesty International, *Uganda: First Steps to Investigate Crimes Must Be Part of Comprehensive Plan to End Impunity*, AFR 59/001/2004, January 30, 2004. Statute Article 42 (1) states: "The Office of the Prosecutor shall act independently as a separate organ of the Court. It shall be responsible for receiving referrals and any substantiated information on crimes within the jurisdiction of the Court, for examining them and for conducting investigations and prosecutions before the Court. A member of the Office shall not seek or act on instructions from an external source."

57. Human Rights Watch, *ICC: Investigate All Sides in Uganda—Chance for Impartial ICC Investigations into Serious Crimes a Welcome Step*, New York, February 4, 2004.

58. Phoung Pham and Patrick Vinck, *Transitioning to Justice: A Population-Based Survey on Attitudes about Social Reconstruction and Justice in Northern Uganda*, Human Rights Center, School of Law, University of California, Berkeley, December 2010, 39-43.

59. World Vision, "Northern Uganda: Not Another 'Iron Fist' Debacle," June 23, 2008.

60. Schiff, *Building the International Criminal Court*, 199-200.

61. Quoted in Allen, *Trial Justice*, 87.

62. Human Rights Watch, *ICC: Investigate All Sides*.

63. Quoted in Allen, *Trial Justice*, 85-86.

64. Quoted in Allen, *Trial Justice*, 85-86.

65. Quoted in "Court Rules Out Kony Immunity," *New Vision*, April 17, 2005, www.newvision.co.ug/D/8/12/429736.

66. International Criminal Court, "Statement by the Chief Prosecutor on the Ugandan Arrest Warrants," October 14, 2005, www.icc-cpi.int/en_menus/icc /situations%20and%20cases/situations/situation%20icc%200204/related% 20cases/icc%200204%200105/press%20releases/Pages/statement%20by% 20the%20chief%20prosecutor%20on%20the%20uganda%20arrest% 20warrants.aspx. Lukwiya died in 2006 and Otti in 2007.

67. "Uganda: ICC Issues Arrest Warrants for LRA Leaders," *IRIN News*, October 7, 2005, www.irinnews.org/Report/56630/UGANDA-ICC-issues-arrest-warrants-for-LRA-leaders.

68. "LRA Talks Over, Says Bigombe," *New Vision*, October 10, 2005, www .newvision.co.ug/D/8/12/460057. Also see Schiff, *Building the International Criminal Court*, 206.

69. "ICC Indictment to Affect Northern Peace Efforts, Says Mediator," *IRIN News*, October 10, 2005.

70. The Comprehensive Peace Agreements are a set of agreements culminating in January 2005 that were signed between the Sudan People's Liberation Movement and the Government of Sudan (http://unmis.unmissions.org/Portals /UNMIS/Documents/General/cpa-en.pdf). Also see Nick Grono and Adam O'Brien, "Justice in Conflict? The ICC and Peace Processes," in Nicholas Wad-

dell and Phil Clark (eds.), *Courting Conflict? Justice, Peace and the ICC in Africa* (London: Royal African Society, 2008), 23.

71. Payam Akharan, "The Lord's Resistance Army Case: Uganda's Submission of the First State Referral to the International Criminal Court," *American Journal of International Law* 99 (April 2005), 404.

72. Allen, *Trial Justice*, 191.

73. Quoted in Tim Allen, *War and Justice in Northern Uganda: An Assessment of the International Criminal Court's Intervention*, Crisis States Research Centre, Development Studies Institute, London School of Economics, February 2005, http://r4d.dfid.gov.uk/Output/173656/Default.aspx.

74. Henry Mukasa, "Museveni Gives Joseph Kony Final Peace Offer," *New Vision*, May 16, 2006, www.newvision.co.ug/D/8/12/498862.

75. Quoted in Schiff, *Building the International Criminal Court*, 207.

76. Quoted in Peskin, "Caution and Confrontation," 670.

77. Peskin, "Caution and Confrontation," 670.

78. International Crisis Group, *Peace in Northern Uganda?*, Africa Briefing no. 41, September 13, 2006, 11.

79. Article 53[2][c], Rome Statute, available at www.icc-cpi.int/nr/rdonlyres/ea9aeff7-5752-4f84-be94-0a655eb30e16/0/rome_statute_english.pdf.

80. Article 16, Rome Statute.

81. After independence on July 9, Southern Sudan became known as the Republic of South Sudan.

82. For background on the Juba Peace Process, see International Crisis Group, *Northern Uganda: Seizing the Opportunity for Peace*, African Briefing no. 124, April 26, 2007.

83. Jeffrey Gettleman, "U.N. Envoy Meets with Ugandan Rebel," *New York Times*, November 13, 2006, www.nytimes.com/2006/11/13/world/africa/13uganda.html.

84. Peskin, "Caution and Confrontation," 670.

85. Elizabeth Neuffer, *The Key to My Neighbor's House: Seeking Justice in Bosnia and Rwanda* (New York: Picador, 2001), 168–70.

86. Peskin, "Caution and Confrontation." 683–84. Also see Victor Peskin, *International Justice in Rwanda and the Balkans: Virtual Trials and the Struggle for State Cooperation* (Cambridge: Cambridge University Press, 2008), 41–45; Richard J. Goldstone, *For Humanity: Reflections of A War Crimes Investigator* (New Haven, CT: Yale University Press, 2000), 108.

87. Quoted in Peskin, "Caution and Confrontation," 664.

88. Luis Moreno-Ocampo, Chief Prosecutor, International Criminal Court, address at Nuremberg International Conference, Building a Future of Peace and Justice, June 25, 2007.

89. Grace Matsiko, Frank Nyakairu, and Paul Harera, "Kony Charges a Stumbling Block, Says U.N. Chief," *The Monitor*, September 13, 2006.

90. Quoted in Katy Glassborow, *LRA Accused of Selling Food Aid*, Africa Update no. 140, Institute for War and Peace Reporting, October 26, 2007.

91. Agreement on Accountability and Reconciliation, www.amicc.org/docs/Agreement_on_Accountability_and_Reconciliation.pdf.

92. Glassborow, *LRA Accused of Selling Food Aid.*

93. Luis Moreno-Ocampo, Prosecutor, International Criminal Court, Statement of Eleventh Diplomatic Briefing on the International Criminal Court, October 10, 2007.

94. "Ugandan Rebels 'Prepare for War,'" *BBC News*, June 6, 2008, http://news.bbc.co.uk/2/hi/africa/7440790.stm.

95. Out of the five original suspects, only two were reportedly alive as of August 2015.

96. Peter Eichstaedt, *ICC Chief Prosecutor Talks Tough*, Africa Update no. 169, Institute for War and Peace Reporting, April 29, 2008, http://iwpr.net/report-news/icc-chief-prosecutor-talks-tough.

97. Luis Moreno-Ocampo, Chief Prosecutor, International Criminal Court, Statement at Informal Meeting of the Assembly of State Parties to the Rome Statute, July 17, 2008, 7.

98. International Crisis Group, *The Road to Peace, With or Without Kony*, African Report, December 10, 2008, 14.

99. Jeffrey Gettleman and Eric Schmitt, "U.S. Aided a Failed Plan to Rout Ugandan Rebels," *New York Times*, February 6, 2009, www.nytimes.com/2009/02/07/world/africa/07congo.html.

100. "Push on LRA Rebels 'Catastrophic,'" *BBC News*, February 10, 2009, http://news.bbc.co.uk/2/hi/africa/7880755.stm.

101. Human Rights Watch, *The Christmas Massacres: LRA Attacks on Civilians in Northern Congo*, February 2009, 4–5, www.hrw.org/en/reports/2009/02/16/christmas-massacres-0.

102. Lord's Resistance Army Disarmament and Northern Ugandan Recovery Act of 2009, H.R. 2478, 111th Cong. (May 19, 2009), https://www.govtrack.us/congress/bills/111/s1067/text.

103. Beth Van Schaack, "ICC Fugitives: The Need for Bespoke Solutions," *ICC Forum*, February–June 2014, http://iccforum.com/arrest#/VanSchaack.

104. The authors interviewed Invisible Children CEO Ben Kessey on May 8, 2012. Also see "Invisible Children's Kony Campaigns Get Support of ICC Prosecutor," *BBC News*, March 8, 2012, www.bbc.co.uk/news/world-africa-17303179.

105. Elizabeth Rubin, "How a Texas Philanthropist Helped Fund the Hunt for Joseph Kony," *New Yorker*, October 21, 2013.

106. Mathew Lee, "U.S. Secretary Clinton Endorses Use of Drones to Hunt for Warlord Kony," Associated Press, August 4, 2012.

107. "Central African Republic Hunt for Kony Suspended," *The Guardian*, April 3, 2013, www.guardian.co.uk/world/2013/apr/03/central-african-republic-troops-suspend-hunt-kony.

108. Van Schaack, "ICC Fugitives."

109. Rubin, "How a Texas Philanthropist."

110. Jeffrey Gettleman, "In Vast Jungle, U.S. Troops Aid in Search for Kony," *New York Times*, April 20, 2012, www.nytimes.com/2012/04/30/world/africa/kony-tracked-by-us-forces-in-central-africa.html.

111. Report of the International Commission of Inquiry on Darfur to the United Nations Secretary-General, January 25, 2005, www.un.org/news/dh /sudan/com_inq_darfur.pdf.

112. Flint and de Waal, "Case Closed," 129.

113. "Sudanese Justice Minister Rejects ICC Indictments on Darfur," *Sudan Tribune*, March 8, 2007, http://www.sudantribune.com/spip.php?article20669.

114. Prosecutor v. Harun, Case No. ICC-02/05–01/07, Warrant for Arrest for Ahmad Harun, April 27, 2007, www.icc-cpi.int/iccdocs/doc/doc279813 .pdf.

115. Luis Moreno-Ocampo, "The Rome Statute and the International Criminal Court," speech at the International Center for Transitional Justice, May 20, 2008, on file at the Human Rights Center, University of California, Berkeley, School of Law.

116. Alis Wasil, "ICC Planned to Divert Plane of Darfur War Crimes Suspect," *Sudan Tribune*, June 25, 2008, www.sudantribune.com/spip .php?article27422.

117. Louis Charbonneau, "International Prosecutor Is 'Terrorist': Sudan Envoy," Reuters, June 11, 2008.

118. "Sudan to Press Terrorism Charges against the ICC Prosecutor," *Sudan Tribune*, June 19, 2008, www.sudantribune.com/spip.php?article27581.

119. Interview with European Union diplomat, May 2008.

120. Luis Moreno-Ocampo, Chief Prosecutor, International Criminal Court, address to the United Nations Security Council, June 5, 2008.

121. Flint and de Waal, "Case Closed," 129.

122. Peskin, *International Justice*, 91.

123. Pre-Trial Chamber I, International Criminal Court, Warrant for Arrest for Omar Hassan Ahmad Al Bashir, ICC-02/05–01/09, March 4, 2009, www .icc-cpi.int/iccdocs/doc/doc639078.pdf.

124. "Darfur: ICC Charges Sudanese President with Genocide," UN News Centre, July 12, 2010, www.un.org/apps/news/story.asp?NewsID=35293.

125. Xan Rice, "Sudanese President Bashir Charged with Darfur War Crimes," *The Guardian*, March 4, 2009, www.guardian.co.uk/world/2009 /mar/04/omar-bashir-sudan-president-arrest.

126. See e.g. Neil MacFarquhar and Marlise Simons, "Sudan's Leader Scolds the West and Assails Aid Groups," *New York Times*, March 6, 2009, A10.

127. Lynsey Addario and Lydia Polgreen, "Aid Groups' Expulsion, Fears of More Misery," *New York Times*, March 23, 2009, www.nytimes .com/2009/03/23/world/africa/23darfur.html. In July 2010, the ICC issued a second arrest warrant for al-Bashir—this time for the crime of genocide. Soon thereafter, the Sudanese authorities expelled several more aid workers from Darfur, including two staffers employed by the International Organization for Migration.

128. "UN Agencies Warn of Devastating Implications for Darfur," *Sudan Tribune*, March 8, 2009, www.sudantribune.com/spip.php?article30423.

129. Interview with Luis Moreno-Ocampo, May 31, 2011.

130. Peskin, "Caution and Confrontation." 676.

131. Louis Charbonneau, "Sudan Says to Never Reverse Decision to Expel NGOs," Reuters, March 20, 2009, www.reuters.com/article/2009/03/20 /idUSN20521830.

132. See e.g. MacFarquhar and Simons, "Sudan's Leader."

133. Luis Moreno-Ocampo, Statement to the United Nations Security Council on the Situation in Darfur UNSCR 1593 (2005), June 5, 2012, www.icc-cpi .int/NR/rdonlyres/CBAD6E54–6C8D-4F43-BE64–74A91C49275D/o/Statement UNSCdarfur5June2011.pdf.

134. Luis Moreno Ocampo, Statement to the United Nations Security Council on the Situation in Darfur UNSCR 1593 (2005).

135. Luis Moreno Ocampo, Statement to the United Nations Security Council on the Situation in Darfur UNSCR 1593 (2005).

136. Luis Moreno Ocampo, Statement to the United Nations Security Council on the Situation in Darfur UNSCR 1593 (2005).

137. Charter of the United Nations, www.un.org/en/documents/charter /chapter1.shtml.

138. United Nations Security Council, Resolution 1970 (2011), February 26, 2011, www.icc-cpi.int/NR/rdonlyres/081A9013-B03D-4859–9D61–5D0B0 F2F5EFA/o/1970Eng.pdf.

139. Quoted in Human Rights Watch, *Death of a Dictator: Bloody Vengeance in Sirte*, October 17, 2012, www.hrw.org/reports/2012/10/16/death-dictator-0.

140. Human Rights Watch, *Death of a Dictator.*

141. United Nations Security Council, Resolution 1970 (2011).

142. United Nations Security Council, Resolution 1970 (2011).

143. Luis Moreno-Ocampo, Prosecutor of the International Criminal Court, Statement to the United Nations Security Council on the situation in the Libyan Arab Jamahiriya, pursuant to UNSCR 1970 (2011), May 4, 2011, www.icc-cpi.int/NR/rdonlyres/oBDF4953-B5AB-42E0-AB21–25238F2C2323/o /OTPStatement04052011.pdf.

144. Louise Arbour, "The Rise and Fall of International Human Rights," lecture at the British Museum, April 27, 2011, on file at the Human Rights Center, School of Law, University of California, Berkeley.

145. Arbour, "Rise and Fall."

146. See e.g. Allen, *Trial Justice*, 72–95.

147. ICC arrest warrants, www.icc-cpi.int/iccdocs/doc/doc1099321.pdf and www.icc-cpi.int/iccdocs/doc/doc1099329.pdf.

148. Matt Steinglass and Michael Peel, "ICC Issues Arrest Warrant for Gaddafi," *Financial Times*, June 28, 2011, www.ft.com/intl/cms/s/o/97974bb4-a0b7–11e0-b14e-00144feabdco.html.

149. David E. Sanger and Eric Schmitt, "U.S. and Allies Seek a Refuge for Qaddafi," *New York Times*, April 16, 2011, www.nytimes.com/2011/04/17 /world/africa/17rebels.html.

150. Richard Dicker, "Handing Qaddafi a Get-Out-of-Jail-Free Card," *International Herald Tribune*, August 1, 2011.

151. This account is compiled from several sources, including Human Rights Watch, *Death of a Dictator*; Kareem Fahim, Anthony Shadid, and Rick Gladstone, "Violent End to an Era as Qaddafi Dies in Libya," *New York Times*,

October 20, 2011, www.nytimes.com/2011/10/21/world/africa/qaddafi-is-killed-as-libyan-forces-take-surt.html; Thomas Harding, "Col Gaddafi Killed: Convoy Bombed by Drone Flown by Pilot in Las Vegas," *Telegraph*, October 20, 2011, www.telegraph.co.uk/news/worldnews/africaandindianocean/libya/8839964/Col-Gaddafi-killed-convoy-bombed-by-drone-flown-by-pilot-in-Las-Vegas.html.

152. Quoted in Human Rights Watch, *Death of a Dictator*.

153. Video available on YouTube: www.youtube.com/watch?v=Fgcd1ghag5Y.

154. Quoted in Andrew Malone, "Libya's Most Gruesome Tourist Attraction," *Daily Mail*, October 24, 2011.

155. Human Rights Watch, *Death of a Dictator*.

156. Human Rights Watch, "Libya: Ensure Abdallah Sanussi Access to Lawyer," April 17, 2013, www.hrw.org/news/2013/04/17/libya-ensure-abdallah-sanussi-access-lawyer.

157. Human Rights Watch, "Libya: Ensure Abdallah Sanussi Access to Lawyer."

158. Thomas Escritt and Ali Shuaib, "Libya Paid Mauritania $200 Million to Extradite Ex-Spy Chief: Lawyer," Reuters, January 15, 2013, www.reuters.com/article/2013/01/15/us-libya-icc-senussi-idUSBRE90E1062013o115.

159. Quoted in Laura Smith-Spark and Nic Robertson, "ICC orders Libya to Hand Over Gadhafi's Former Spy Chief," CNN, February 7, 2013, http://edition.cnn.com/2013/02/07/world/africa/libya-icc-spy-chief/.

160. Vivienne Walt, "Libya's Disaster of Justice: The Case of Saif al-Islam Gaddafi Reveals a Country in Chaos," *Time*, June 28, 2013, http://world.time.com/2013/06/28/libyas-disaster-of-justice-the-case-of-saif-al-islam-gaddafi-reveals-a-country-in-chaos/.

161. "Libya Appeals ICC Order to Hand Over Saif," CNN, April 10, 2012, www.cnn.com/2012/04/10/world/africa/libya-saif-gadhafi-appeal.

162. Address to the Security Council by Fatou Bensouda, May 8, 2013, www.icc-cpi.int/en_menus/icc/situations%20and%20cases/situations/icco111/reports%20to%20the%20unsc/.

163. Chris McGreal, "US Backs Libya in Dispute over Trial Location for Saif al-Islam Gaddafi," *The Guardian*, June 6, 2012.

164. "Libya ICC Lawyer Melinda Taylor and Colleagues Fly Out," *BBC News*, July 2, 2012, www.bbc.co.uk/news/world-africa-18683786.

165. Walt, "Libya's Disaster of Justice."

166. Human Rights Watch, "ICC: Libya's Bids to Try Gadddafi, Sanussi," May 13, 2013, www.hrw.org/news/2013/05/13/qa-libya-and-international-criminal-court.

167. Article 17, Rome Statute of the International Criminal Court.

168. International Criminal Court, Decision on the Admissibility of the Case against Saif Al-Islam Gaddafi, May 31, 2013, www.icc-cpi.int/iccdocs/doc/doc1599307.pdf.

169. Ibid.

170. International Criminal Court, Decision on the Request for Suspensive Effect and Related Issues, July 18, 2013, www.icc-cpi.int/iccdocs/doc/doc1620847.pdf.

171. International Criminal Court, Summary of ICC Decision on the Admissibility of the Case against Mr. Abdullah Al-Senussi, www.icc-cpi.int/en_menus /icc/press%20and%20media/press%20releases/Documents/pr953/Summary%20 AL-Senussi%20English.pdf.

172. Human Rights Watch, "Libya: ICC Judges Reject Sanussi Appeal," July 24, 2014, www.hrw.org/news/2014/07/24/libya-icc-judges-reject-sanussi-appeal.

173. Human Rights Watch, "Libya: ICC Judges Reject Sanussi Appeal."

174. Colum Lynch, "Ivory Coast: UN Rights Chief, Navi Pillay Cites Night Abductions," *Foreign Policy*, December 19, 2010, http://blog.foreignpolicy .com/posts/2010/12/19/ivory_coast_un_rights_chief_navi_pillay_cites_night_ abductions.

175. Security Council Resolution 1975, March 30, 2011, www.refworld .org/docid/4d9ac4ea2.html.

176. "Ivory Coast: Laurent Gbagbo Standoff," *The Guardian*, April 6, 2011.

177. Xan Rice and Nicholas Watt, "Ivory Coast's Laurent Gbagbo Arrested: Four Months On," *The Guardian*, April 11, 2011.

178. Human Rights Watch, *"They Killed Them Like It Was Nothing": The Need for Justice for Côte d'Ivoire's Postelection Crimes*, New York, October 2011, 90–102.

179. Human Rights Watch, *"They Killed Them Like It Was Nothing."*

180. "Q&A: Laurent Gbagbo and the International Criminal Court," Human Rights Watch, February 12, 2013.

181. "Ivory Coast and the ICC: Will Justice Ever Be Evenhanded?" *The Economist*, March 25, 2014.

182. "Ivory Coast's Former First Lady Simone Gbagbo Jailed," *BBC News*, March 10, 2015.

183. Gabe Joselow, "US Official Says Kenya's Elections Have 'Consequences,'" Voice of America, February 7, 2013.

184. Rasna Warah, "How the ICC Helped, Rather Than Hindered, the Uhuru-Ruto Election," *Daily Nation*, March 10, 2013, www.nation.co.ke/oped /Opinion/How-the-ICC-helped-the-Uhuru-Ruto-election/-/440808/1716336/- /133pteb/-/index.html.

185. Press reports of Hailemariam Desalegn's exact words vary, but the implication remains the same. See e.g. Gabe Joselow, "AU Requests ICC Allow Kenya to Try Kenyatta," *Voice of America*, May 27, 2013, www.voanews.com/article-printview/1669074.html; "African Union Accuses ICC of 'Hunting' Africans," *BBC News*, May 27, 2013, http://www.bbc.co.uk/news/world-africa-22681894; Jehron Muhammad, "Kerry's Mystery Speech and Other News from the OAU/ AU Summit," *FinalCall.com News*, June 8, 2013.

186. Rick Gladstone, "African Call to Delay Kenyans' Trials Fails at UN," *New York Times*, November 16, 2013.

187. Marlise Simons, "A Less-Equal Court, in the Name of Stability," *New York Times*, December 4, 2013.

188. Simons, "A Less-Equal Court."

189. Statement of the Prosecutor of the International Criminal Court, 19 December 2013, www.icc-cpi.int/en_menus/icc/press%20and%20media/press% 20releases/Pages/otp-statement-19-12-2013.aspx.

190. Ibid.

191. Marlise Simons and Jeffrey Gettleman, "International Court Ends Case against Kenyan President in Election Unrest," *New York Times*, December 5, 2014.

192. "Congo Warlord Bosco Ntaganda, Wanted by the ICC Since 2006, Remains Ensconced at US Embassy," Associated Press, March 18, 2013.

193. Jeffrey Gettleman, "Rebel Leader in Congo is Flown to The Hague," *New York Times*, March 22, 2013, www.nytimes.com/2013/03/23/world/africa/war-crimes-suspect-bosco-ntaganda-leaves-congo-for-the-hague.html.

194. See the ICC charge sheet at www.icc-cpi.int/en_menus/icc/situations%20and%20cases/situations/situation%20icc%200104/related%20cases/icc%200104%200206/Pages/icc%200104%200206.aspx.

195. "Congo Warlord Bosco Ntaganda"; Michelle Nichols and Louis Charbonneau, "Exclusive: Fearing Death, Congo's Terminator Fled with Help of Family," Reuters, June 28, 2013.

196. Chris McGreal, "Obama Accused of Failed Policy over Rwanda's Support of Rebel Group," *The Guardian*, December 11, 2012.

197. "134 NGOs Call on ICC Prosecutor to Continue Investigations in Congo," Human Rights Watch, March 13, 2014.

198. "Suspect Arrested in Destruction of Monuments in Mali," *New York Times*, September 27, 2015, A14.

CHAPTER 9. THE "WAR ON TERROR" AND ITS LEGACY

1. "Bush's Seven Minutes of Silence," *YouTube*, www.youtube.com/watch?v=5WztB6HzXxI.

2. George W. Bush, "Address to a Joint Session of Congress Following 9/11 Attacks," September 20, 2001, www.americanrhetoric.com/speeches/gwbush911jointsessionspeech.htm.

3. Vice President Dick Cheney's discussion of the attack on America and the United States' response to terrorism is documented in *NBC News Transcripts (September 16, 2001)*, www.washingtonpost.com/wp-srv/nation/specials/attacked/transcripts/cheney091601.html.

4. Jane Mayer, *The Dark Side: The Inside Story of How the War on Terror Turned Into a War on American Ideals* (New York: Doubleday, 2008), 52.

5. Quoted in Philippe Sands, *Torture Team: Rumsfeld's Memo and the Betrayal of American Values* (New York: Palgrave Macmillan, 2008), 188.

6. Quoted in Mayer, *Dark Side*, 8.

7. See e.g. the interview with Vice President Dick Cheney on NBC's *Meet the Press*, transcript for March 16, 2003 (www.cheneywatch.org/speeches-and-interviews/cheney-interviews/interview-with-vice-president-dick-cheney-nbc-meet-the-press-transcript-for-march-16–2003), where Tim Russert explains the international view of President Bush as a "a cowboy, [someone who] wants to go it alone," when it comes to effectuating foreign policy.

8. See e.g. Open Society Foundations, *Globalizing Torture: CIA Secret Detention and Extraordinary Rendition*, New York, February 2013; Associated Press, "Italy: Guilty Verdicts in Rendition Case," *New York Times*, March 12, 2014.

9. "Top Secret America," *PBS Frontline*, September 2011, www.pbs.org /wgbh/pages/frontline/topsecretamerica/#original-report-(sept.-2011).

10. Quoted in Mayer, *Dark Side*, 34.

11. Quoted in *Taxi to the Dark Side*, documentary written and directed by Alex Gibney, X-Ray Productions, 2008.

12. According to a 2013 report by the Open Society Justice Initiative (*Globalizing Torture: CIA Secret Detention and Extraordinary Rendition*), at least fifty-four governments took part. Those nations span the continents of Africa, Asia, Australia, Europe, and North America and include Afghanistan, Albania, Algeria, Australia, Austria, Azerbaijan, Belgium, Bosnia-Herzegovina, Canada, Croatia, Cyprus, Czech Republic, Denmark, Djibouti, Egypt, Ethiopia, Finland, Gambia, Georgia, Germany, Greece, Hong Kong, Iceland, Indonesia, Iran, Ireland, Italy, Jordan, Kenya, Libya, Lithuania, Macedonia, Malawi, Malaysia, Mauritania, Morocco, Pakistan, Poland, Portugal, Romania, Saudi Arabia, Somalia, South Africa, Spain, Sri Lanka, Sweden, Syria, Thailand, Turkey, United Arab Emirates, United Kingdom, Uzbekistan, Yemen, and Zimbabwe.

13. Dana Priest, "Covert CIA Program Withstands New Furor," *Washington Post*, December 30, 2005; Peter Jan Honigsberg, *Our Nation Unhinged: The Human Consequences of the War on Terror* (Berkeley: University of California Press, 2009).

14. Mayer, *Dark Side*, 39.

15. Gary C. Schroen, *First In: An Insider's Account of How Seven CIA Officers Spearheaded the War on Terror in Afghanistan* (New York: Presidio, 2005), 40.

16. Scott Shane, "Inside a 9/11 Mastermind's Interrogation," *New York Times*, June 22, 2008, www.nytimes.com/2008/06/22/washington/22ksm.html.

17. Senate Select Committee on Intelligence, *Committee Study of the Central Intelligence Agency's Detention and Interrogation Program*, December 10, 2014, 9–10, https://web.archive.org/web/20141209165504/http://www.intelligence .senate.gov/study2014/sscistudy1.pdf.

18. For a description of SERE techniques, see "Appendix B: Physical Pressures Used in Resistance Training and against American Prisoners and Detainees," in Laurel E. Fletcher and Eric Stover, *The Guantánamo Effect: Exposing the Consequences of U.S. Detention and Interrogation Practices* (Berkeley: University of California Press, 2009), 134–38.

19. Bob Woodward, "CIA Told to Do 'Whatever Necessary' to Kill Bin Laden," *Washington Post*, October 21, 2001.

20. Jill Lepore, "The Dark Ages," *New Yorker*, March 18, 2013.

21. Fletcher and Stover, *Guantánamo Effect*, 4–5.

22. Statement ascribed to Dick Cheney; see "History: Guantánamo Bay Timeline," *Washington Post*, http://projects.washingtonpost.com/Guantánamo /timeline.

23. For a discussion of this distinction, see Ronald C. Slye and Beth Van Schaack, *International Criminal Law: The Essentials* (New York: Aspen, 2009), 195–208.

24. Interview with Jess Bravin, April 7, 2014.

25. International Committee of the Red Cross, *Geneva Convention Relative to the Treatment of Prisoners of War* (Third Geneva Convention), August 12, 1949, 75 UNTS 135, section 1, art. 17.

26. Department of the Army, *Field Manual FM 2–22.3: Human Intelligence Collector Operations* (2006), 5–21. The manual was first adopted in 1956 and has been updated several times since then.

27. See e.g. "Politics and Economy: The Geneva Conventions," PBS, www .pbs.org/now/politics/geneva.html, citing the memo drafted by Gonzales.

28. Michael Isikoff, "Memos Reveal War Crimes Warnings," *Newsweek*, May 16, 2004.

29. Quoted in Mayer, *Dark Side*.

30. Convention (III) relative to the Treatment of Prisoners of War. Geneva, art. 3, 12 August 1949.

31. Message from Chairman, Joint Chiefs of Staff to Unified Commands and Services, "Status of Taliban and Al Qaida," January 21, 2002, http://nsarchive .gwu.edu/NSAEBB/NSAEBB127/.

32. Stephen Grey, *Ghost Plane: The True Story of the CIA Rendition and Torture Program* (New York: Saint Martin's Griffin, 2006), 166–67.

33. Text of order signed by President Bush on Feb. 7, 2002, http://lawofwar .org/bush_torture_memo.htm.

34. Memorandum from Jay S. Bybee, assistant secretary general, to Alberto R. Gonzales, White House counsel, "Regarding Standards of Conduct for interrogation under 18 U.S.C §§ 2340–2340A," August 1, 2002, http://news .findlaw.com/hdocs/docs/doj/bybee80102ltr6.html.

35. K. Alexa Koenig, Eric Stover, and Laurel E. Fletcher, "The Cumulative Effect: A Medico-Legal Approach to United States Torture Law and Policy," *Essex Human Rights Review* 145, 6 (2009), 148–49.

36. Interview with Jess Bravin, April 7, 2014. See also Jess Bravin, *The Terror Courts: Rough Justice at Guantanamo Bay* (New Haven, CT: Yale University Press, 2013).

37. For an overview, see e.g. Lawrence Lessig and Cass R. Sunstein, "The President and the Administration," *Columbia Law Review* 94, no. 1 (1994).

38. Honigsberg, *Our Nation Unhinged*, 15.

39. "History: Guantánamo Bay Timeline."

40. "Osama bin Laden: A Chronology of His Political Life," *Frontline*, PBS, www.pbs.org/wgbh/pages/frontline/shows/binladen/etc/cron.html; Lawrence Wright, *The Looming Tower: Al-Qaeda and the Road to 9/11* (New York: Vintage, 2007), 139–64.

41. "Osama bin Laden: A Chronology."

42. "Osama bin Laden: A Chronology."

43. Wright, *Looming Tower*, 251.

44. Wright, *Looming Tower*, 251.

45. "Osama bin Laden: A Chronology."

46. Osama bin Laden, February 22, 1998, reprinted at "Osama bin Laden v. the U.S.: Edicts and Statements," *Frontline*, PBS.org (www.pbs.org/wgbh/pages /frontline/shows/binladen/who/edicts.html). This was approximately a year and

a half after bin Laden's "Declaration of War against the Americans Who Occupy the Land of the Two Holy Mosques."

47. See e.g. "Osama bin Laden: A Chronology."

48. See e.g. "How Bin Laden Escaped in 2001: The Lessons of Tora Bora," *Daily Beast*, December 15, 2013.

49. Peter L. Bergen, *Manhunt: The Ten-Year Search for Bin Laden from 9/11 to Abbottabad* (New York: Crown, 2012), 60–61.

50. Benjamin Runkle, *Wanted Dead or Alive: Manhunts from Geronimo to bin Laden* (Palgrave Macmillan, 2011), 180.

51. Antonia Johasz, "Why the War in Iraq Was Fought for Big Oil," CNN, April 15, 2013.

52. "Bush: 'Leave Iraq within 48 Hours,'" *CNN*, March 17, 2003, www.cnn.com/2003/WORLD/meast/03/17/sprj.irq.bush.transcript/.

53. "Bush Declares War," *CNN*, March 19, 2003, www.cnn.com/2003/US/03/19/sprj.irq.int.bush.transcript/.

54. Steven Marks, Thomas Meer, and Matthew Nilson, *Manhunting: A Methodology for Finding Persons of National Interest*, master's thesis, Naval Postgraduate School, Monterey, California, June 2005, 6, www.phibetaiota.net/wp-content/uploads/2012/02/2012–02–20-Manhunting-A-Methodology-for-Finding-Persons-of-National-In.pdf.

55. Quoted in Montgomery McFate, "The Military Utility of Understanding Adversary Culture," *Joint Forces Quarterly* 38 (2005), 42. Also see Robert S. McNamara, *In Retrospect: The Tragedy and Lessons of Vietnam* (New York: Random House, 1995), 42.

56. Lisa Burgess, "Buyers Beware: The Real Iraq 'Most Wanted' Cards Are Still Awaiting Distribution," *Stars and Stripes*, April 17, 2003, www.stripes.com/news/buyers-beware-the-real-iraq-most-wanted-cards-are-still-awaiting-distribution-1.4525.

57. Chris Wilson, "Searching for Saddam: The Social Network That Caught a Dictator," *Slate*, February 22, 2010, www.slate.com/articles/news_and_politics/searching_for_saddam/2010/02/searching_for_saddam_5.html.

58. Hussein's two sons would be captured later, in 2003, when a regional tribal leader led U.S. troops to their hideaway in the mountains of Iraqi Kurdistan, an effort for which he would be paid $30 million through the United States' Rewards for Justice program. See e.g. "White House Approves $30 Million Payment to Uday, Qusay Tipster," *Fox News*, July 31, 2003.

59. Wilson, "Searching for Saddam."

60. Wilson, "Searching for Saddam."

61. Wilson, "Searching for Saddam." Also see Farnaz Fassihi, "Two Novice Gumshoes Chartered the Capture of Saddam Hussein," *Wall Street Journal*, December 18, 2003.

62. Wilson, "Searching for Saddam."

63. Steve Russell, *We Got Him! A Memoir of the Hunt and Capture of Saddam Hussein* (New York: Pocket Books, 2012), 43–45.

64. Russell, *We Got Him*, 258–59.

65. "How We Got Saddam," *Newsweek*, December 21, 2003.

66. Russell, *We Got Him*, 259.

67. Russell, *We Got Him*, 294.

68. Russell, *We Got Him*, 294, 295.

69. Russell, *We Got Him*, 295.

70. Russell, *We Got Him*, 295.

71. Russell, *We Got Him*, 297.

72. Russell, *We Got Him*, 312.

73. "How We Got Saddam."

74. Russell, *We Got Him*, 314.

75. Russell, *We Got Him*, 321.

76. Dawn Bryan, "Abu Ghraib Whistleblower's Ordeal," *BBC News*, August 5, 2007.

77. Darby's quotes are from his first interview about his role in exposing the abuses, in Wil S. Hylton, "Prisoner of Conscience," *GQ*, September 2006, www.gq.com/news-politics/newsmakers/200608/joe-darby-abu-ghraib.

78. Janis Karpinski, *One Woman's Army: The Commanding General of Abu Ghraib Tells Her Story* (New York: Miramax, 2005), 29–30.

79. Karpinski, *One Woman's Army*, 27–28.

80. CBS, *60 Minutes*, April 27, 2004.

81. Karpinski, *One Woman's Army*, 31–32. Karpinski was criticized for comments she made to the press about conditions at Abu Ghraib. Susan Taylor Martin, "Her Job: Lock Up the Bad Guys," *St. Petersburg Times*, December 14, 2003, www.sptimes.com/2003/12/14/Worldandnation/Her_job__Lock_up_Iraq.shtml.

82. Karpinski, *One Woman's Army*, 160.

83. Karpinski, *One Woman's Army*, 190.

84. Antonio Taguba, *Article 15-6 Investigations of the 800th Military Police Brigade*, May 2, 2004, 8–9.

85. Philip Zimbardo, *The Lucifer Effect: Understanding How Good People Turn Evil* (New York: Random House, 2007), 334.

86. J. White, "Some Abu Ghraib Prisoners 'Ghosted,'" *Washington Post*, March 11, 2005.

87. Grey, *Ghost Plane*, 160–61.

88. Douglas Jehl, Eric Schmitt, and Kate Zemike, "The Reach of War: Detainee Treatment; US Rules on Prisoners Seen as a Back and Forth of Mixed Messages to GI's," *New York Times*, June 22, 2004.

89. James Yee, *For God and Country: Faith and Patriotism under Fire* (New York: PublicAffairs, 2005), 55.

90. Zimbardo, *Lucifer Effect*, 414.

91. *Taxi to the Dark Side*.

92. Jehl et al., "Reach of War."

93. Grey, *Ghost Plane*, 161.

94. Zimbardo, *Lucifer Effect*, 410.

95. In 2012, National Public Radio consulted Dr. Edmund Donoghue, chief medical examiner of Cook County, Illinois, on the military's autopsy report. The forensic pathologist said that he agreed with the military's findings. He added that the way al-Jamadi was shackled "makes it very difficult to breathe

because you are suspended in a very awkward position. When you combine it with having the hood over your head and broken ribs, it's fairly clear that his death was caused by asphyxia because he couldn't breathe properly." John McCheseney, "The Death of an Iraqi Prisoner," National Public Radio, October 27, 2005, www.npr.org/templates/story/story.php?storyId=4977986.

96. Hylton, "Prisoner of Conscience."

97. Hylton, "Prisoner of Conscience."

98. Taguba, *Article 15–6 Investigation,* 6–7.

99. Seymour M. Hersh, "The General's Report," *New Yorker,* June 25, 2007, www.newyorker.com/reporting/2007/06/25/070625fa_fact_hersh.

100. Hersh, "General's Report."

101. Taguba, *Article 15–6 Investigation.*

102. Major General George R. Fay, *AR 15–6 Investigation of the Abu Ghraib Detention Facility and 205th MI Brigade,* 52–53, www.npr.org /documents/2004/abuse/fay-jones_report.pdf.

103. Grey, *Ghost Plane,* 157.

104. Douglas Jehl and Eric Schmitt, "The Struggle for Iraq: Abu Ghraib; Officer Says Army Tried to Curb Red Cross Visits to Prison in Iraq," *New York Times,* May 19, 2004.

105. *Report of the International Committee of the Red Cross (ICRC) on the Treatment by the Coalition Forces of Prisoners of War and Other Protected Persons by the Geneva Conventions in Iraq during Arrest, Internment and Interrogation,* February 2004, http://cryptome.org/icrc-report.htm.

106. See e.g. Dave Moniz, "Gen. Karpinski Demoted in Prison Scandal," *USA Today,* May 5, 2005.

107. Hala Shah, "Backgrounder: Janis Karpinski," *Bullpen NYU Journalism,* http://journalism.nyu.edu/publishing/archives/bullpen/janis_karpinski/back grounder/.

108. Karpinski, *One Woman's Army,* 144. Allegations that she had misled investigators were never substantiated. See e.g. Moniz, "Gen. Karpinski Demoted in Prison Scandal."

109. Karpinski, *One Woman's Army,* 233.

110. "Iraq War 10 Years Later: Where Are They Now? Lynndie England (Abu Ghraib)," *NBC News,* March 19, 2013.

111. Karpinski, *One Woman's Army,* 229.

112. Karpinski, *One Woman's Army,* 231.

113. Physicians for Human Rights, *Broken Laws, Broken Lives: Medical Evidence of Torture by US Personnel and Its Impact,* June 2008, Cambridge, MA.

114. Michael Pizzi, "If Obama Won't Prosecute CIA Torture, Can the ICC?" *Al Jazeera America,* December 17, 2014.

115. See e.g. "Letter to US Secretary of State Colin Powell on US Bully Tactics against the International Criminal Court," from Kenneth Roth, executive director of Human Rights Watch, July 1, 2003, www.hrw.org/news/2003/06/29 /letter-colin-powell-us-bully-tactics-against-international-criminal-court.

116. See e.g. American Non-Governmental Organizations Coalition for the International Criminal Court, "A Campaign for US Immunity from the ICC,"

www.amicc.org/usicc/biacampaign; Memo drafted by the General Secretariat of the Council of the European Union, "Re: Draft Council conclusions on the International Criminal Court, 12386/02 COJUR 9 USA 35 PESC 369," September 30, 2002.

117. Lucia DiCicco, *The Non-Renewal of the "Nethercutt Amendment" and its Impact on the Bilateral Immunity Agreement (BIA) Campaign*, American Non-Governmental Organizations Coalition for the International Criminal Court, New York, April 30, 2009, www.amicc.org/docs/Nethercutt2009.pdf.

118. Katherine Gallagher, "Universal Jurisdiction in Practice: Efforts to Hold Donald Rumsfeld and Other High-level United States Officials Accountable for Torture," *Journal of International Criminal Justice* 7 (2009): 1087–1116.

119. See e.g. Máximo Langer, "The Diplomacy of Universal Jurisdiction: The Political Branches and the Transnational Prosecution of International Crimes," *American Journal of International Law* 105 (2011), 3 n4.

120. 630 F.2d 876 (2d Cir. 1980).

121. 630 F.2d 876 (2d Cir. 1980).

122. Langer, "Diplomacy," 1.

123. Langer, "Diplomacy," 1.

124. Langer, "Diplomacy," 2.

125. Quoted in Gallagher, "Universal Jurisdiction," 1104.

126. Quoted in Gallagher, "Universal Jurisdiction," 1105.

127. "Guantanamo Agents 'Used Torture,'" *BBC News*, January 14, 2009.

128. Gallagher, "Universal Jurisdiction," 1108.

129. Gallagher, "Universal Jurisdiction," 1111.

130. Langer, "Diplomacy," 18.

131. Soeren Kern, "Spain Steps Back from Universal Jurisdiction," *World Politics Review*, July 3, 2009.

132. Langer, "Diplomacy," 2–3.

133. Langer, "Diplomacy," 14–15.

134. See e.g. Pizzi, "If Obama Won't Prosecute."

135. Ryan Goodman, "International Criminal Court's Examination of US Treatment of Detainees Takes Shape," *Just Security*, December 3, 2014.

136. Malcolm M. Feeley, *The Process is the Punishment: Handling Cases in a Lower Criminal Court* (New York: Russell Sage Foundation, 1992).

137. Chege Mbitiru, "Bush No Longer a Free Man Amid Torture Charges," *Daily Nation*, February 13, 2011; see also James Risen, "Protest Threats Derail Bush Speech in Switzerland," *New York Times*, February 5, 2011 (claiming the talk was canceled by the event's organizer due to security concerns in the face of threatened protests).

138. Bergen, *Manhunt*, 84.

139. Wilson, "Searching for Saddam."

140. Shane, "Inside a 9/11 Mastermind's Interrogation."

141. Darius Rejali, *Torture and Democracy* (Princeton, NJ: Princeton University Press, 2007), 504–07; Shane, "Inside a 9/11 Mastermind's Interrogation."

142. Bergen, *Manhunt*, 63–65.

143. Mohammed Neem Noor Khan reportedly agreed to cooperate with the CIA and was released in August 2007 without being charged.

144. International Committee of the Red Cross, *ICRC Report on the Treatment of Fourteen "High Value Detainees" in CIA Custody*, February 2007, 26, http://assets.nybooks.com/media/doc/2010/04/22/icrc-report.pdf.

145. Mark Danner, "Tales From Torture's Dark World," *New York Times*, March 15, 2009, www.nytimes.com/2009/03/15/opinion/15danner.html.

146. Lawrence Wright, "The Agent: Did the CIA Stop an FBI Detective from Preventing 9/11?" *New Yorker*, July 10, 2006.

147. Jennifer G. Hickey, "Ex-CIA Interrogator: Senate Democrats 'Issued a Fatwa on Me,'" *Newsmax*, December 16, 2014; Megyn Kelly, "The Kelly File," Fox News, December 15, 2014; Senate Select Committee on Intelligence, *Committee Study of the Central Intelligence Agency's Detention and Interrogation Program* (referring to Mitchell and his colleague Bruce Jessen by pseudonyms).

148. Jason Leopold, "CIA Torture Architect Breaks Silence to Defend 'Enhanced Interrogation,'" *The Guardian*, 18 April 2014, www.theguardian.com/world/2014/apr/18/cia-torture-architect-enhanced-interrogation.

149. Senate Select Committee on Intelligence, *Committee Study of the Central Intelligence Agency's Detention and Interrogation Program*, 9–12.

150. Jason Leopold and Jeffrey Kaye, "CIA Psychologist's Notes Reveal True Purpose behind Bush's Torture Program," *Truthout*, March 22, 2011, http://truth-out.org/index.php?option=com_k2&view=item&id=205.

151. Senate Select Committee on Intelligence, *Committee Study of the Central Intelligence Agency's Detention and Interrogation Program*, 11.

152. Leopold and Kaye, "CIA Psychologist's Notes."

153. Mayer, *Dark Side*, 175–76.

154. Shawn Vestal, "More Details on 'Psychologist' Thugs Who Devised CIA Torture," *Spokesman-Review*, December 10, 2014.

155. Mayer, *Dark Side*, 156–57.

156. Michael Isikoff, "Ali Soufan Breaks His Silence," *Newsweek*, April 24, 2009, www.newsweek.com/ali-soufan-breaks-his-silence-77243.

157. Peter Finn and Joby Warrick, "Detainee's Harsh Treatment Foiled No Plots," *Washington Post*, March 29, 2009, www.washingtonpost.com/wp-dyn/content/article/2009/03/28/AR2009032802066_pf.html.

158. See e.g. Siobhan Gorman, Devlin Barrett, Felicia Schwartz, and Dion Nissenbaum, "Senate Report Calls CIA Interrogation Tactics Ineffective," *Wall Street Journal*, December 9, 2014.

159. James Risen, "Psychologists Approve Ban on Role in National Security Interrogations," *New York Times*, August 7, 2015. See also Editorial Board, "Psychologists Who Greenlighted Torture," *New York Times*, July 10, 2015.

160. Martin Brass, "U.S. Bounty Hunter on Trial in Afghanistan," Military.com, 2004, www.military.com/NewContent/0,13190,SOF_0804_Idema,00.html; see also Robin Moore, *Task Force Dagger: The Hunt for bin Laden* (New York: Random House 2003).

161. Saad Gul, "The Secretary Will Deny All Knowledge of Your Actions: The Use of Private Military Contractors and the Implications for State and Political Accountability," *Lewis & Clark Law Review* 10, no. 2 (2006), 287, 303.

162. Gul, "Secretary Will Deny," 298 (quoting Steven L. Schooner, "Contractor Atrocities at Abu Ghraib: Compromised Accountability in a

Streamlined, Outsourced Government," *Stanford Law & Policy Review* 16 (2005), 549, 553).

163. Excerpted from the full "creed."

164. Gul, "Secretary Will Deny," 303 (quoting William D. Hartung, "Mercenaries, Inc.: How a U.S. Company Props up the House of Saud," *The Progressive*, April 1996, 26).

165. Elise Labott, "U.S. Mulls $50 Million bin Laden bounty: Ad Campaign Launches in Pakistan to Assist Search," CNN.com, January 24, 2005.

166. Martin Brass, "U.S. Bounty Hunter on Trial in Afghanistan," *Military .com*, 2004.

167. Moore, *Task Force Dagger*; Stacy Sullivan, "Operation Desert Fraud: How Keith Idema Marketed His Imaginary Afghan War," *New York Magazine*, May 21, 2005.

168. Sullivan, "Operation Desert Fraud."

169. See e.g. Brass, "U.S. Bounty Hunter."

170. Sullivan, "Operation Desert Fraud."

171. Douglas Martin, "Jonathan Idema, Con Man and Afghan Bounty Hunter, Dies at 55," *New York Times*, January 29, 2012.

172. Sullivan, "Operation Desert Fraud."

173. Holly Quinn, "Gary Faulkner, Osama bin Laden Hunter: Where Is He Now?" AOL News, December 17, 2010; Tim McGirk, "Inside One American's Hunt for Bin Laden," *Time*, June 19, 2010; Sabrina Tavernise and Dan Frosch, "American Detained in Pakistan Had Sights on bin Laden," *New York Times*, June 15, 2010; Dexter Filkins, "Call Him Crazy, but bin Laden Bounty Hunter May Have Been Close," *New York Times*, June 15, 2010; John Johnson, "Remember This Osama Hunter? He Wasn't That Far Off: Gary Faulkner Was about 270 Miles Away on His One-Man Hunt," *Newser*, May 3, 2011.

174. *"Colorado Man Gary Faulkner, on Solo Mission to Hunt Down Osama Bin Laden, Returns Home to U.S.,"* Associated Press, June 23, 2010.

175. Joseph Margulies, *Guantanamo and the Abuse of Presidential Power* (New York: Simon & Schuster, 2007), 69; Pervez Musharraf, *In the Line of Fire: A Memoir* (New York: Free Press, 2006), 237.

176. Fletcher and Stover, *Guantánamo Effect*, 19.

177. Geneva Conventions III, Article 5.

178. President George W. Bush, "Military Order of November 13, 2002, 2001: Detention, Treatment, and Trial of Certain Non-Citizens in the War against Terrorism."

179. Mayer, *Dark Side*, 183.

180. Mayer, *Dark Side*, 183.

181. Mayer, *Dark Side*, 184.

182. Mayer, *Dark Side*, 187.

183. Robert Young Pelton, *Licensed to Kill: Hired Guns in the War on Terror* (New York: Broadway, 2007), 253.

184. Protocol Additional to the Geneva Conventions of 12 August 1949, and Relating to the Protection of Victims of International Armed Conflicts, art. 47, June 8, 1977, 1125 UNTS 3 (as quoted in Gul, "Secretary Will Deny," 293). A definition is also provided in the U.N. Mercenary Convention. While

the United States is not a party to either the Mercenary Convention or the Additional Protocol, it does accept them to the extent that they reflect customary international law.

185. Pelton, *Licensed to Kill*, 20.

186. Uri Friedman, "Targeted Killings: A Short History," *Foreign Policy*, August 13, 2012.

187. Jeremy Scahill, "The Democrats' Selective Amnesia on Assassination: Clinton Did It and Obama Does It Too," *Truthout*, July 15, 2009.

188. See e.g. Gorden L. Bowen, "Targeted Killings: US Policy toward Use of Covert Operations Involving Assassination," http://aldeilis.net/english/qtargeted-killingsq-us-policy-toward-use-of-covert-operations-involving-assassination/ (providing a timeline of U.S. assassination policy).

189. Bowen, "Targeted Killings."

190. P. W. Singer, *Wired for War: The Robotics Revolution and Conflict in the 21st Century* (New York: Penguin, 2009), 58.

191. Singer, *Wired for War*, 58.

192. Singer, *Wired for War*, 32.

193. Bergen, *Manhunt*, 59.

194. Of course, drones and drone operators are also susceptible to stressors. For example, drones experience physical stress, and operators can suffer from boredom, PTSD, and other ailments.

195. Singer, *Wired for War*, 35.

196. Singer, *Wired for War*, 34. Domestically, predator drones have been flown over the U.S.–Mexico border to assist with drug arrests and the capture of "illegal aliens" (40).

197. Christopher Drew, "Drones Are Weapons of Choice in Fighting Qaeda," *New York Times*, March 16, 2009.

198. Singer, *Wired for War*, 33.

199. Singer, *Wired for War*, 33.

200. See e.g. Spencer Ackerman, "41 Men Targeted but 1,147 People Killed: US Drone Strikes—the Facts on the Ground," *The Guardian*, November 24, 2014.

201. Bergen, *Manhunt*, 71–73.

202. Mark Mazzetti, Nicholas Kulish, Christopher Drew, Serge F. Kovaleski, Sean D. Naylor, and John Ismay, "SEAL Team 6: A Secret History of Quiet Killings and Blurred Lines," *New York Times*, June 6, 2015.

203. Mazzetti et al., "SEAL Team 6."

204. Mazzetti et al., "SEAL Team 6."

205. Mazzetti et al., "SEAL Team 6."

206. Bergen, *Manhunt*, 89.

207. Seymour M. Hersh, "The Killing of Osama bin Laden," *London Review of Books*, May 21, 2015, 3–12.

208. Matthew Rosenberg, "Seymour Hersh Article Alleges Cover-Up in Bin Laden Hunt," *New York Times*, May 11, 2015.

209. Bergen, *Manhunt*, 90; see also Dina Temple-Raston's review of *Manhunt* in the *Washington Post*, May 4, 2012.

210. Bergen, *Manhunt*, 130.

211. Hersh, "Killing of Osama bin Laden."

212. Bergen, *Manhunt,* 173–74.

213. Matthieu Aikins, "The Doctor, the CIA, and the Blood of Bin Laden," *GQ,* January 2013.

214. Saeed Shah, "CIA Organized Fake Vaccination Drive to Get Osama bin Laden's Family DNA," *The Guardian,* July 11, 2001, www.theguardian.com /world/2011/jul/11/cia-fake-vaccinations-osama-bin-ladens-dna; Donald G. McNeil Jr., "CIA Vaccine Ruse May Have Harmed the War on Polio," *New York Times,* July 9, 2012, www.nytimes.com/2012/07/10/health/cia-vaccine-ruse-in-pakistan-may-have-harmed-polio-fight.html.

215. Shah, "CIA Organized Fake Vaccination."

216. Aikins, "The Doctor, the CIA."

217. Aikins, "The Doctor, the CIA."

218. Hersh, "Killing of Osama bin Laden."

219. Bergen, *Manhunt,* 93.

220. Bergen, *Manhunt,* 185

221. Bergen, *Manhunt,* 205.

222. Bergen, *Manhunt,* 203.

223. Bergen, *Manhunt,* 208

224. Bergen, *Manhunt,* 211.

225. See e.g. Peter Bergen, "Who Really Killed bin Laden?" *CNN World,* March 27, 20013.

226. Mark Owen and Kevin Maurer, *No Easy Day: The Firsthand Account of the Mission that Killed Osama bin Laden* (New York: Penguin Books, 2012).

227. Phil Bronstein, "The Man Who Killed Osama bin Laden . . . is Screwed," *Esquire,* 11 February 2013. (The article refers to Rob O'Neill only as "the Shooter.")

228. Owen, *No Easy Day,* 230, 233.

229. Owen, *No Easy Day,* 235.

230. Bronstein, "The Man Who Killed Osama bin Laden."

231. Owen, *No Easy Day,* 236; Bergen, "Who Really Killed bin Laden?"

232. Bronstein, "The Man Who Killed Osama bin Laden"; "The Man Who Killed Usama bin Laden," *Fox News,* November 12, 2014 (two-part documentary film on the shooting of Bin Laden).

233. Owen, *No Easy Day.*

234. Owen, *No Easy Day,* 245.

235. Owen, *No Easy Day,* 246–47.

236. Luke Harding and Zofeen Ebrahim, "Pakistan's PM Denies Authorities Knew Osama bin laden Was Living in Country," *The Guardian,* May 9, 2012; Helene Cooper and Ismail Khan, "US Demands More from Pakistan in Bin Laden Inquiry," *New York Times,* May 6, 2011. See also Dexter Filkins, "What Pakistan Knew about Bin Laden," *New Yorker,* May 2, 2011.

237. "Pakistani Doctor Who Helped Find bin Laden Gets 33 Years in Prison," *Los Angeles Times,* May 24, 2012. See also Aikins, "The Doctor, the CIA"; Jill Reilly, "Brave Doctor Helped CIA Track Down bin Laden Is on Hunger Strike in Pakistani prison," *Daily Mail,* May 21, 2013.

238. By May 2014, as many as sixty polio vaccinators had been killed in Pakistan since December 2012, according to Rotary International, which has helped lead eradication programs. See Peter Robison, "The CIA Stops Fake Vaccinations as Real Polio Rebounds," *Bloomberg Businessweek,* May 21, 2014, www.businessweek.com/articles/2014–05–21/the-cia-stops-fake-vaccinations-as-real-polio-rebounds.

239. McNeil, "CIA Vaccine Ruse."

240. Letter to President Obama, January 6, 2013, available at www.jhsph .edu/news/news-releases/2013/Klag%20letter%20to%20President%20Obama .pdf.

241. Bill Chappel, "CIA Says It Will No Longer Use Vaccine Programs as Cover," National Public Radio, May 20, 2014, www.npr.org/blogs/thetwo-way /2014/05/20/314231260/cia-says-it-will-no-longer-use-vaccine-programs-as-cover.

242. Interview with Osama bin Laden, *Frontline,* PBS, May 1998.

243. Mazzetti et al., "SEAL Team 6."

244. Dana Priest and William M. Arkin, "A Hidden World, Growing beyond Control," *Washington Post,* July 19, 2010.

CHAPTER 10. EPILOGUE: THE FUTURE OF GLOBAL JUSTICE

1. David Cole, "The Torture Memos: The Case against the Lawyers," *New York Review of Books* 56, no. 15, October 8, 2009, 14.

2. Guy Lesser, "War Crime and Punishment: What the United States Could Learn from the Milosevic Trial," *Harper's Magazine,* January 2004, 37–52.

3. Mirko Klarin, "The Tribunal's Four Battles," *Journal of Criminal Justice* 2 (2004): 548.

4. Beth Van Schaack, "ICC Fugitives: The Need for Bespoke Solutions," *ICC Forum,* February–June 2014, http://iccforum.com/arrest#Van-Schaack.

5. Associated Press, "ICC Prosecutor Stopping Darfur Investigations," December 12, 2014.

6. Pre-Trial Chamber II, International Criminal Court, "Decision on the Prosecutor's Request for a Finding of Non-Compliance against the Republic of Sudan," ICC-02/05–01/09, March 5, 2015, www.icc-cpi.int/iccdocs/doc /doc1919142.pdf.

7. Norimitsu Onishu, "South Africa High Court Says Allowing Bashir to Leave Violated the Constitution," *New York Times,* June 15, 2015.

8. "DR Congo: Q&A on the United Nations Human Rights Mapping Report," Human Rights Watch, New York, October 1, 2010.

9. "Prosecute Torturers and Their Bosses" (editorial), *New York Times,* December 21, 2014, www.nytimes.com/2014/12/22/opinion/prosecute-torturers-and-their-bosses.html.

10. Louise Arbour, "The Rule of Law and the Reach of Accountability," *The Rule of Law Series,* Melbourne University, July 5, 2001, 5.

11. Louise Arbour, "In Our Name, and On Our Behalf," Chatham House and the British Institute of International and Comparative Law, February 15, 2006, 1,

https://www.chathamhouse.org/sites/files/chathamhouse/public/Research
/International%20Law/ilparbour.pdf.

12. Arbour, "In Our Name," 14.

13. Arbour, "In Our Name," 15–16.

14. Arbour, "In Our Name," 15–16.

15. Senate Select Committee on Intelligence, *Committee Study of the Central Intelligence Agency's Detention and Interrogation Program*, Washington, DC, December 10, 2014, 34.

16. Arbour, "In Our Name," 22.

17. Mark Kersten, "Obama and the ICC: Four Reasons Not to Hold Your Breath," *Justice in Conflict*, November 7, 2012, http://justiceinconflict.org/2012/11/07/obama-and-the-icc-four-reasons-not-to-hold-your-breath/.

18. Kersten, "Obama and the ICC." A prominent blogger on the ICC, Kersten posits four reasons that Washington is hesitant to join the court. First, the White House has not shown any indication that it wants to dismantle the American Service-Members' Protection Act, which, among other things, prohibits the transfer of classified national security information and law enforcement information to the court and prohibits ICC investigators from conducting investigations in the Untied States. Second, with any ICC investigation of alleged international crimes in Palestinian territory, "Israel will predictably be enraged and the US will just as predictably take sides with Israel." Third, the United States' increasing use of drones in the "global war on terror" has prompted high-level UN officials, including the special rapporteurs on counter-terrorism and extrajudicial killings, to declare strikes that kill civilians a war crime. "In this context," writes Kersten, "the US could reasonably calculate that joining the ICC would put its practices of targeted killing under the microscope of international criminal justice." Finally, if the U.S. were to become an ICC state party and accept the court's jurisdiction back to 2002, it would be vulnerable to an ICC investigation for alleged crimes, including torture, committed by the CIA in ICC member states, including Afghanistan, Poland, and Romania, as well as by American troops in Afghanistan and Iraq.

19. Interview with Benjamin Schiff, July 24, 2013.

20. Interview by Christiane Amanpour of Beatrice Le Fraper, special advisor to the ICC prosecutor, *CNN*, March 24, 2010, http://transcripts.cnn.com/TRANSCRIPTS/1003/24/ampr.01.html.

21. Scott A. Exner, "Mending the Fences: Strengthening the International Criminal Court's Arrest Apparatus through Renewed US Partnership," *ICC Forum*, February 17, 2014, http://iccforum.com/forum/permalink/93/4047.

22. Alison Cole, "Justice Doesn't Come Cheap. Can the ICC Afford It?" Open Society Foundations, August 7, 2013, www.opensocietyfoundations.org/voices/justice-doesn-t-come-cheap-can-icc-afford-it.

23. Cole, "Justice Doesn't Come Cheap."

Selected Bibliography

Aarons, Mark, and John Loftus. *Unholy Trinity: How the Vatican's Nazi Networks Betrayed Western Intelligence to the Soviets.* New York: St. Martin's Press, 1991.

Abrahams, Fred, Gilles Peress, and Eric Stover. *A Village Destroyed, May 14, 1999: War Crimes in Kosovo.* Berkeley: University of California Press, 2001.

Albright, Madeleine. *Madam Secretary: A Memoir.* New York: Miramax Books, 2003.

Allen, Tim. *Trial Justice: The International Criminal Court and the Lord's Resistance Army.* African Arguments. London: Zed Books, 2006.

Anderson, Scott. "What I Did on My Summer Vacation." *Esquire,* October 2000.

Bascomb, Neal. *Hunting Eichmann: How a Band of Survivors and a Young Spy Agency Chased Down the World's Most Notorious Nazi.* New York: Houghton Mifflin Harcourt, 2009.

Bass, Gary Jonathan. *Stay the Hand of Vengeance: The Politics of War Crimes Tribunals.* Princeton Studies in International History and Politics. Princeton, NJ: Princeton University Press, 2000.

Bassiouni, M. Cherif. "World War I: 'The War to End All Wars' and the Birth of a Handicapped International Criminal Justice System." *Denver Journal of International Law and Policy* 30 (Summer 2002): 244–91.

Beattie, Jean. *The Life and Career of Klaus Barbie: An Eyewitness Record.* London: Methuen, 1984.

Beevor, Anthony. *Berlin: The Downfall 1945.* London: Penguin Books, 2002.

Bergen, Peter L. *Manhunt: The Ten-Year Search for Bin Laden from 9/11 to Abbottabad.* New York: Crown, 2012.

Bix, Herbert P. *Hirohito and the Making of Modern Japan.* New York: HarperCollins, 2000.

451

Blanusa, Dragisa. "Milošević in Prison." Translated by Vanessa Vasic-Janekovic and Peter Morgan. *Granta,* Fall 2002, 237–54.

Boister, Neil, and Robert Cryer. *The Tokyo International Military Tribunal: A Reappraisal.* Oxford: Oxford University Press, 2008.

Bosco, David. *Rough Justice: The International Criminal Court in a World of Power Politics.* Oxford: Oxford University Press, 2014.

Bower, Tom. *Klaus Barbie: The Butcher of Lyons.* New York: Pantheon Books, 1984.

———. *The Pledge Betrayed: America and Britain and the Denazification of Postwar Germany.* Garden City, NY: Doubleday, 1982.

Bravin, Jess. *The Terror Courts: Rough Justice at Guantanamo Bay.* New Haven, CT: Yale University Press, 2013.

Breitman, Richard, and Norman J. W. Goda. *Hitler's Shadow: Nazi War Criminals, U.S. Intelligence, and the Cold War.* Washington, DC: National Archives and Records Administration, 2010.

Breitman, Richard, Norman J. W. Goda, Timothy Naftali, and Robert Wolfe. *U.S. Intelligence and the Nazis.* Cambridge: Cambridge University Press, 2005.

Cassese, Antonio. "On the Current Trends towards Criminal Prosecution and Punishment of Breaches of International Humanitarian Law." *European Journal of International Law* 9, no. 1 (1998): 2–17.

Cesarani, David. *Eichmann: His Life and Crimes.* New York: Vintage, 2005.

Chuter, David. *War Crimes: Confronting Atrocity in the Modern World.* IISS Studies in International Security. Boulder, CO: Lynne Rienner, 2003.

Cole, David. "The Torture Memos: The Case against the Lawyers." *New York Review of Books,* October 8, 2009.

Côté, Luc. "International Criminal Justice Tightening Up the Rules of the Game." *International Review of the Red Cross* 88, no. 861 (March 2006): 133–44.

Crane, David M. "The Take Down: Case Studies Regarding 'Lawfare' in International Criminal Justice: The West African Experience." *Case Western Reserve Journal of International Law* 43, no. 1–2 (Spring-Fall 2010): 201–14.

Cruvellier, Thierry. *Court of Remorse: Inside the International Criminal Tribunal for Rwanda.* Translated by Chari Voss. Madison: University of Wisconsin Press, 2010.

———. *The Master of Confessions: The Making of a Khmer Rouge Torturer.* Translated by Susanna Lea Associates. New York: HarperCollins, 2014.

Dallaire, Roméo. *Shake Hands with the Devil: The Failure of Humanity in Rwanda.* Toronto: Random House Canada, 2003.

de Hoyos, Ladislas. *Klaus Barbie: The Untold Story.* Translated by Nicholas Courtin. New York: McGraw-Hill, 1985.

Del Ponte, Carla, and Chuck Sudetic. *Madame Prosecutor: Confrontations with Humanity's Worst Criminals and the Culture of Impunity.* New York: Other Press, 2009.

Des Forges, Alison. *"Leave None to Tell the Story": Genocide in Rwanda.* New York: Human Rights Watch and the International Federation of Human Rights Leagues, 1999.

Dobbs, Michael. "General Mladic in The Hague." *Foreign Policy*, August 2012.

Dower, John W. *Embracing Defeat: Japan in the Wake of World War II*. New York: W.W. Norton, 1999.

Dunlop, Nic. *The Lost Executioner: A Story of the Khmer Rouge*. London: Bloomsbury, 2005.

Eichmann, Adolf. *Meine Flucht: Bericht aus der Zelle in Jerusalem*. Records of the Central Intelligence Agency (CIA) RG 263. National Archives and Records Administration, Bethesda, MD.

Ellis, Stephen. *The Mask of Anarchy: The Destruction of Liberia and the Religious Dimension of an African Civil War*. New York: New York University Press, 2001.

Etcheson, Craig. *After the Killing Fields: Lessons from the Cambodian Genocide*. Westport, CT: Praeger, 2005.

Feeley, Malcolm M. *The Process Is the Punishment: Handling Cases in a Lower Criminal Court*. New York: Russell Sage Foundation, 1992.

Finkielkraut, Alain. *Remembering in Vain: The Klaus Barbie Trial and Crimes against Humanity*. Translated by Roxanne Lapidus and Sima Godfrey. European Perspectives. New York: Columbia University Press, 1992.

Fletcher, Laurel E., and Eric Stover. *The Guantánamo Effect: Exposing the Consequences of U.S. Detention and Interrogation Practices*. With Stephen Paul Smith, Alexa Koenig, Zulaikha Aziz, Alexis Kelly, Sarah Staveteig, and Nobuko Mizoguchi. Berkeley: University of California Press, 2009.

French, Howard W. *A Continent for the Taking: The Tragedy and Hope of Africa*. New York: Vintage, 2005.

Friedman, Tuviah. *The Hunter*. Translated by David C. Gross. Garden City, NY: Doubleday, 1961.

Gell, Annie. *"Even a "Big Man" Must Face Justice": Lessons from the Trial of Charles Taylor*. New York: Human Right Watch, July 2012.

Genoud, François, ed. *The Testament of Adolf Hitler: The Hitler-Bormann Documents, February-April 1945*. Translated by R.H. Stevens. 2nd ed. London: Cassell, 1961.

Goda, Norman J.W. "Manhunts: The Official Search for Notorious Nazis." In *U.S. Intelligence and the Nazis*, by Richard Breitman, Norman J.W. Goda, Timothy Naftali, and Robert Wolfe, 419–42. Cambridge: Cambridge University Press, 2005.

Goldstone, Richard J. *For Humanity: Reflections of a War Crimes Investigator*. Castle Lectures in Ethics, Politics, and Economics. New Haven, CT: Yale University Press, 2000.

———. "The Role of the United Nations in the Prosecution of International War Criminals." *Washington University Journal of Law and Policy* 5 (2001): 119–29.

Goñi, Uki. *The Real Odessa: Smuggling the Nazis to Peron's Argentina*. London: Granta Books, 2002.

Görtemaker, Heike B. *Eva Braun: Life with Hitler*. Translated by Damion Searls. New York: Alfred A. Knopf, 2011.

Grey, Stephen. *Ghost Plane: The True Story of the CIA Rendition and Torture Program*. New York: St. Martin's Griffin, 2006.

Gutman, Roy, David Rieff, and Anthony Dworkin, eds. *Crimes of War 2.0: What the Public Should Know.* New York: W. W. Norton, 2007.

Hamilton, Rebecca. *Fighting for Darfur: Public Action and the Struggle to Stop Genocide.* New York: Palgrave Macmillan, 2011.

Harel, Isser. *The House on Garibaldi Street: The First Full Account of the Capture of Adolf Eichmann, Told by the Former Head of Israel's Secret Service.* New York: Viking Press, 1975.

Harris, Sheldon. "Japanese Biological Warfare Experiments and Other Atrocities in Manchuria, 1932–1945, and the Subsequent United States Cover Up: A Preliminary Assessment." *Crime, Law and Social Change* 15, no. 3 (1991): 171–99.

Hawton, Nick. *Europe's Most Wanted Man: The Quest for Radovan Karadžic.* London: Arrow, 2009.

Hayner, Priscilla. "Negotiating Peace in Liberia: Preserving the Possibility of Justice." New York: International Center for Transitional Justice, November 2007.

Heberer, Patricia, and Jürgen Matthäus, eds. *Atrocities on Trial: Historical Perspectives on the Politics of Prosecuting War Crimes.* Lincoln: University of Nebraska Press, 2008.

Herf, Jeffrey. *Divided Memory: The Nazi Past in the Two Germanys.* Cambridge, MA: Harvard University Press, 1997.

Hillenbrand, Laura. *Unbroken: A World War II Story of Survival, Resilience, and Redemption.* New York: Random House, 2010.

Hirsch, John L. *Sierra Leone: Diamonds and the Struggle for Democracy.* International Peace Academy Occasional Paper Series. Boulder, CO: Lynne Rienner, 2001.

Hitt, Jack. "Radovan Karadzic's New-Age Adventure." *New York Times Magazine,* July 22, 2009.

Holbrooke, Richard. *To End a War.* New York: Random House, 1998.

Holtzman, Elizabeth. *Who Said It Would Be Easy? One Woman's Life in the Political Arena.* New York: Arcade, 1996.

Honigsberg, Peter Jan. *Our Nation Unhinged: The Human Consequences of the War on Terror.* Berkeley: University of California Press, 2009.

Hunt, Linda. *Secret Agenda: The United States Government, Nazi Scientists, and Project Paperclip, 1945 to 1990.* New York: St. Martin's Press, 1991.

Ignatieff, Michael, ed. *American Exceptionalism and Human Rights.* Princeton, NJ: Princeton University Press, 2005.

International Crisis Group. *International Criminal Tribunal for Rwanda: Justice Delayed.* ICG Africa Report, no. 3. Brussels: International Crisis Group, June 7, 2001.

———. *Serbian Reform Stalls Again.* ICG Balkans Report, no. 145. Brussels: International Crisis Group, July 17, 2003.

———. *The Special Court for Sierra Leone: Promises and Pitfalls of a "New Model."* ICG Africa Briefing. Brussels: International Crisis Group, August 4, 2003.

Jacobsen, Annie. *Operation Paperclip: The Secret Intelligence Program That Brought Nazi Scientists to America.* New York: Little, Brown, 2014.

Jallow, Hassan B. "Prosecutorial Discretion and International Criminal Justice." *Journal of International Criminal Justice* 3, no. 1 (March 2005): 145–61.

Jennings, Christian. *Bosnia's Million Bones: Solving the World's Greatest Forensic Puzzle*. New York: Palgrave Macmillan, 2013.

Joyce, Christopher, and Eric Stover. *Witnesses from the Grave: The Stories Bones Tell*. Boston, MA: Little, Brown, 1991.

Kaldor, Mary. *Global Civil Society: An Answer to War*. Cambridge: Polity Press, 2003.

Karpinski, Janis. *One Woman's Army: The Commanding General of Abu Ghraib Tells Her Story*. New York: Miramax, 2005.

Keane, Fergal. *Season of Blood: A Rwandan Journey*. London: Viking Press, 1995.

Kearney, Philip. *Under the Blue Flag: My Mission in Kosovo*. Beverly Hills, CA: Phoenix Books, 2008.

Keenan, Thomas, and Eyal Weizman. *Mengele's Skull: The Advent of a Forensic Aesthetics*. Berlin: Sternberg Press, 2012.

Kelsall, Tim. *Culture under Cross-Examination: International Justice and the Special Court for Sierra Leone*. Cambridge Studies in Law and Society. Cambridge: Cambridge University Press, 2009.

Koenig, K. Alexa, Eric Stover, and Laurel E. Fletcher. "The Cumulative Effect: A Medico-Legal Approach to United States Torture Law and Policy." *Essex Human Rights Review* 6, no. 1 (December 2009): 203–34.

Kroslak, Daniela. *The French Betrayal of Rwanda*. Bloomington: Indiana University Press, 2007.

Langer, Máximo. "The Diplomacy of Universal Jurisdiction: The Political Branches and the Transnational Prosecution of International Crimes." *American Journal of International Law* 105, no. 1 (January 2011): 1–49.

Lasby, Clarence G. *Project Paperclip: German Scientists and the Cold War*. New York: Atheneum, 1971.

Levy, Alan. *The Wiesenthal File*. London: Constable, 1993.

Linklater, Magnus, Isabel Hilton, and Neal Ascherson. *The Fourth Reich: Klaus Barbie and the Neo-Fascist Connection*. London: Hodder & Stoughton, 1984.

Lipstadt, Deborah E. *The Eichmann Trial*. New York: Schocken Books, 2011.

Loftus, John. *America's Nazi Secret: An Insider's History*. 2nd ed. Walterville, OR: Trine Day, 2010.

Lutz, Ellen L., and Caitlin Reiger, eds. *Prosecuting Heads of State*. Cambridge: Cambridge University Press, 2009.

Marks, Steven, Thomas Meer, and Matthew Nilson. "Manhunting: A Methodology for Finding Persons of National Interest." Master's thesis, Naval Postgraduate School, Monterey, CA, 2005.

Marrus, Michael R., and Robert O. Paxton. *Vichy France and the Jews*. New York: Basic Books, 1981.

Matteson, Robert E. *The Last Days of Ernst Kaltenbrunner*. Center for the Study of Intelligence, CIA Library, McLean, VA, 2007.

Mayer, Jane. *The Dark Side: The Inside Story of How the War on Terror Turned Into a War on American Ideals.* New York: Doubleday, 2008.

McCoy, Alfred W. *A Question of Torture: CIA Interrogation, from the Cold War to the War on Terror.* New York: Metropolitan Books, 2006.

Meir, Golda. *A Land of Our Own: An Oral Autobiography.* Edited by Marie Syrkin. New York: Putnam, 1973.

Minear, Richard H. *Victors' Justice: The Tokyo War Crimes Trial.* Michigan Classics in Japanese Studies. Ann Arbor: Center for Japanese Studies, University of Michigan, 2001.

Moghalu, Kingsley. *Rwanda's Genocide: The Politics of Global Justice.* New York: Palgrave Macmillan, 2005.

Moore, Robin. *Task Force Dagger: The Hunt for Bin Laden.* New York: Random House, 2003.

Musharraf, Pervez. *In the Line of Fire: A Memoir.* New York: Free Press, 2006.

Neier, Aryeh. *The International Human Rights Movement: A History.* Princeton, NJ: Princeton University Press, 2012.

Nettelfield, Lara J., and Sarah E. Wagner. *Srebrenica in the Aftermath of Genocide.* Cambridge: Cambridge University Press, 2014.

Neuffer, Elizabeth. *The Key to My Neighbor's House: Seeking Justice in Bosnia and Rwanda.* New York: Picador, 2001.

Newton, Ronald C. *The "Nazi Menace" in Argentina, 1931–1947.* Stanford, CA: Stanford University Press, 1992.

Nowak, Manfred. *U.N. Covenant on Civil and Political Rights: CCPR Commentary.* Arlington, VA: N.P. Engel, 1993.

Off, Carol. *The Lion, the Fox and the Eagle: A Story of Generals and Justice in Rwanda and Yugoslavia.* Toronto: Random House Canada, 2000.

Ogata, Sadako. *The Turbulent Decade: Confronting the Refugee Crises of the 1990s.* New York: W. W. Norton, 2005.

Organization for Security and Co-operation in Europe. *Delivering Justice in Bosnia and Herzegovina: An Overview of War Crimes Processing from 2005 to 2010.* Sarajevo: Organization for Security and Co-operation in Europe (OSCE) Mission to Bosnia and Herzegovina, May 2011.

Overy, Richard. *Interrogations: The Nazi Elite in Allied Hands, 1945.* New York: Viking, 2001.

Owen, Mark, and Kevin Maurer. *No Easy Day: The Firsthand Account of the Mission That Killed Osama Bin Laden.* New York: Penguin, 2012.

Palmer, Michele, and Bruce M. Stave. *Witnesses to Nuremberg: An Oral History of American Participants at the War Crimes Trials.* Twayne's Oral History Series. New York: Twayne, 1998.

Paulussen, Christophe. *Male Captus Bene Detentus? Surrendering Suspects to the International Criminal Court.* School of Human Rights Research. Antwerp: Intersentia, 2010.

Pavlaković, Vjeran. "Croatia, the International Criminal Tribunal for the Former Yugoslavia, and General Gotovina as a Political Symbol." *Europe-Asia Studies* 62, no. 10 (2010): 1707–40.

Pearlman, Moshe. *The Capture and Trial of Adolf Eichmann.* New York: Simon & Schuster, 1963.

Pelton, Robert Young. *Licensed to Kill: Hired Guns in the War on Terror.* Reprint ed. New York: Broadway Books, 2007.

Peskin, Victor. "Caution and Confrontation in the International Criminal Court's Pursuit of Accountability in Uganda and Sudan." *Human Rights Quarterly* 31, no. 3 (August 2009): 655–91.

———. *International Justice in Rwanda and the Balkans: Virtual Trials and the Struggle for State Cooperation.* New York: Cambridge University Press, 2008.

———. "Rwandan Ghosts." *Legal Affairs*, September/October 2002.

———. "The International Criminal Court, the Security Council, and the Politics of Impunity in Darfur." *Genocide Studies and Prevention* 4, no. 3 (December 2009): 304–28.

Peskin, Victor, and Mieczysław P. Boduszyński. "Balancing International Justice in the Balkans: Surrogate Enforcers, Uncertain Transitions and the Road to Europe." *International Journal of Transitional Justice* 5, no. 1 (March 2011): 52–74.

Pham, Phuong, and Patrick Vinck. *Transitioning to Peace: A Population-Based Survey on Attitudes about Social Reconstruction and Justice in Northern Uganda.* Initiative for Vulnerable Populations. Berkeley: Human Rights Center, University of California, Berkeley, School of Law, December 2010.

Pham, Phuong, Patrick Vinck, Eric Stover, Andrew Moss, Marieke Wierda, and Richard Bailey. *When the War Ends: A Population-Based Survey on Attitudes about Peace, Justice, and Social Reconstruction in Northern Uganda.* Berkeley-Tulane Initiative on Vulnerable Populations. Berkeley: Human Rights Center, University of California, Berkeley; New Orleans, LA: Payson Center for International Development, Tulane University; New York: International Center for Transitional Justice, December 2007.

Phayer, Michael. *Pius XII, the Holocaust, and the Cold War.* Bloomington: Indiana University Press, 2007.

———. *The Catholic Church and the Holocaust, 1930–1965.* Bloomington: Indiana University Press, 2000.

Pilger, John, ed. *Tell Me No Lies: Investigative Journalism and Its Triumphs.* London: Vintage, 2005.

Posner, Gerald L., and John Ware. *Mengele: The Complete Story.* New York: Dell, 1986.

Powell, John W. "A Hidden Chapter in History." *Bulletin of the Atomic Scientists*, October 1981, 44–52.

Power, Samantha. *Chasing the Flame: One Man's Fight to Save the World.* New York: Penguin Press, 2008.

Randall, Kenneth C. "Universal Jurisdiction under International Law." *Texas Law Review* 66, no. 4 (March 1988): 785–841.

Raub, Lindsey. "Positioning Hybrid Tribunals in International Criminal Justice." *New York University Journal of International Law and Politics* 41, no. 4 (Summer 2009): 1013–53.

Rejali, Darius. *Torture and Democracy.* Princeton, NJ: Princeton University Press, 2007.

Reydams, Luc. "Let's Be Friends: The United States, Post-Genocide Rwanda, and Victor's Justice in Arusha." Discussion paper, Institute of Development Policy and Management, University of Antwerp, 2013.

Reydams, Luc, and Jan Wouters. "The Politics of Establishing International Criminal Tribunals." In *International Prosecutors*, edited by Luc Reydams, Jan Wouters, and Cedric Ryngaert, 6–80. Oxford: Oxford University Press, 2012.

Reydams, Luc, Jan Wouters, and Cedric Ryngaert, eds. *International Prosecutors*. Oxford: Oxford University Press, 2012.

Risen, James. "Psychologists Approve Ban on Role in National Security Interrogations." *New York Times*, August 7, 2015.

Robinson, Mary. "Foreward." In *The Princeton Principles on Universal Jurisdiction*, by Princeton Project on Universal Jurisdiction, edited by Steven Macedo, 15–18. Princeton, NJ: Princeton University, 2001.

Rohde, David. *Endgame: The Betrayal and Fall of Srebrenica, Europe's Worst Massacre since World War II*. New York: Farrar, Straus & Giroux, 1997.

Romano, Cesare P.R., André Nollkaemper, and Jann K. Kleffner, eds. *Internationalized Criminal Courts: Sierra Leone, East Timor, Kosovo, and Cambodia*. International Courts and Tribunal Series. Oxford: Oxford University Press, 2004.

Runkle, Benjamin. *Wanted Dead or Alive: Manhunts from Geronimo to Bin Laden*. New York: Palgrave Macmillan, 2011.

Russell, Steve. *We Got Him! A Memoir of the Hunt and Capture of Saddam Hussein*. New York: Pocket Books, 2012.

Ryan, Allan A., Jr. *Klaus Barbie and the United States Government: A Report to the Attorney General of the United States*. Washington, DC: U.S. Department of Justice, Criminal Division, August 1983.

———. *Quiet Neighbors: Prosecuting Nazi War Criminals in America*. San Diego, CA: Harcourt Brace Jovanovich, 1984.

Ryngaert, Cedric, and Jan Wouters. "Arrest and Detention." In *International Prosecutors*, edited by Luc Reydams, Jan Wouters, and Cedric Ryngaert, 647–99. Oxford: Oxford University Press, 2012.

Sadat, Leila Nadya, ed. *Forging a Convention for Crimes against Humanity*. Cambridge: Cambridge University Press, 2011.

Sayer, Ian, and Douglas Botting. *America's Secret Army: The Untold Story of the Counter Intelligence Corps*. New York: Franklin Watts, 1989.

Scheffer, David. *All the Missing Souls: A Personal History of the War Crimes Tribunals*. Princeton, NJ: Princeton University Press, 2012.

Schiff, Benjamin N. *Building the International Criminal Court*. Cambridge: Cambridge University Press, 2008.

Schroen, Gary C. *First In: An Insider's Account of How Seven CIA Officers Spearheaded the War on Terror in Afghanistan*. New York: Presidio Press, 2005.

Segev, Tom. *Simon Wiesenthal: The Life and Legends*. New York: Doubleday, 2010.

———. *The Seventh Million: The Israelis and the Holocaust*. Translated by Haim Watzman. New York: Henry Holt, 1993.

Shattuck, John. *Freedom on Fire : Human Rights Wars and America's Response.* Cambridge, MA: Harvard University Press, 2003.

Shawcross, William. *The Quality of Mercy: Cambodia, Holocaust and Modern Conscience.* New York: Simon & Schuster, 1984.

Silber, Laura, and Allan Little. *Yugoslavia: Death of a Nation.* New York: Penguin Books, 1997.

Silvers, Jonathan, dir. *Elusive Justice: The Search for Nazi War Criminals.* DVD, Documentary. Saybrook Productions, 2011.

Simpson, Christopher. *Blowback: America's Recruitment of Nazis and Its Effects on the Cold War.* New York: Weidenfeld & Nicolson, 1988.

Singer, P. W. *Wired for War: The Robotics Revolution and Conflict in the 21st Century.* New York: Penguin Press, 2009.

Slye, Ronald C., and Beth Van Schaack. *International Criminal Law: The Essentials.* New York: Aspen, 2008.

Smith, Bradley F. *The American Road to Nuremberg: The Documentary Record, 1944–1945.* Stanford, CA: Hoover Institution Press, Stanford University, 1982.

Steinacher, Gerald. *Nazis on the Run: How Hitler's Henchmen Fled Justice.* Oxford: Oxford University Press, 2011.

Stover, Eric. "International Criminal Justice." In *World at Risk: A Global Issues Sourcebook,* 2nd ed. Washington, DC: CQ Press, 2009.

Stover, Eric, and Gilles Peress. *The Graves: Srebrenica and Vukovar.* Zurich: Scalo, 1998.

Stover, Eric, and Harvey M. Weinstein, eds. *My Neighbor, My Enemy: Justice and Community in the Aftermath of Mass Atrocity.* Cambridge: Cambridge University Press, 2004.

Straus, Scott. *The Order of Genocide: Race, Power, and War in Rwanda.* Ithaca, NY: Cornell University Press, 2006.

Sudetic, Chuck. "The Reluctant Gendarme." *Atlantic Monthly,* April 2000.

Taylor, Telford. *The Anatomy of the Nuremberg Trials: A Personal Memoir.* New York: Alfred A. Knopf, 1992.

Totani, Yuma. *The Tokyo War Crimes Trial: The Pursuit of Justice in the Wake of World War II.* Cambridge, MA: Harvard University Press, 2008.

Trevor-Roper, Hugh. *The Last Days of Hitler.* 6th ed. London: Papermac & Macmillan Press, 1995.

Trueheart, Charles. "A New Kind of Justice." *Atlantic Monthly,* April 2000.

Umutesi, Marie Beatrice. *Surviving the Slaughter: The Ordeal of a Rwandan Refugee in Zaire.* Madison: University of Wisconsin Press, 2004.

Van Tuyl, Penelope. *Effective, Efficient, and Fair? An Inquiry into the Investigative Practices of the Office of the Prosecutor at the Special Court for Sierra Leone.* Berkeley: War Crimes Studies Center, University of California, Berkeley, September 2008.

Walters, Guy. *Hunting Evil: The Nazi War Criminals Who Escaped and the Quest to Bring Them to Justice.* New York: Broadway Books, 2010.

Weschler, Lawrence. *Vermeer in Bosnia: Cultural Comedies and Political Tragedies.* New York: Pantheon Books, 2004.

West, Rebecca. *A Train of Powder.* New York: Viking Press, 1955.

Whiting, Charles. *The Hunt for Martin Bormann.* New York: Ballantine Books, 1973.

Wiesenthal, Simon. *Justice, Not Vengeance.* Translated by Ewald Osers. New York: Grove Weidenfeld, 1989.

———. *The Murderers Among Us: The Simon Wiesenthal Memoirs.* Edited by Joseph Wechsberg. New York: McGraw-Hill, 1967.

Wieviorka, Annette. *The Era of the Witness.* Translated by Jared Stark. Ithaca, NY: Cornell University Press, 2006.

Wilson, Chris. "Searching for Saddam: The Social Network That Caught a Dictator." *Slate,* February 22, 2010.

Wilson, Richard Ashby. *Writing History in International Criminal Trials.* Cambridge: Cambridge University Press, 2011.

Wittmann, Rebecca. *Beyond Justice: The Auschwitz Trial.* Cambridge, MA: Harvard University Press, 2005.

Wood, Nancy. "The Papon Trial in an 'Era of Testimony.'" In *The Papon Affair: Memory and Justice on Trial,* edited by Richard J. Golsan, translated by Lucy B. Golson and Richard J. Golsan, 96–114. New York: Routledge, 2000.

Wright, Lawrence. *The Looming Tower: Al-Qaeda and the Road to 9/11.* New York: Vintage, 2007.

Yee, James. *For God and Country: Faith and Patriotism Under Fire.* New York: PublicAffairs, 2005.

Zimbardo, Philip. *The Lucifer Effect: Understanding How Good People Turn Evil.* New York: Random House, 2007.

Zuroff, Efraim. *Operation Last Chance: One Man's Quest to Bring Nazi Criminals to Justice.* New York: Palgrave Macmillan, 2009.

Index

204; transfer to domestic courts, 220; in
Zaire, 198
Hutu interim government, 190, 191, 192,
193, 194–95, 205–6, 211
Hutu Revolution of 1959, 189
hybrid tribunals, international, 8, 186–88,
231–76, 380, 419n22; challenges of,
235–38; comparisons to, 9, 282, 283;
defined, 8, 235; and human rights
NGOs, 275–76; and legal authority, 10;
Special Tribunal for Lebanon, 418n17;
success of, 3. *See also* Cambodia hybrid
court; East Timor hybrid court; Kosovo
hybrid court; Lebanon hybrid court;
Senegal hybrid court; Sierra Leone
hybrid court

ICC (International Criminal Court). *See*
International Criminal Court (ICC)
ICG (International Crisis Group), 427n201
ICJ (UN International Court of Justice),
176, 177
ICRC (International Committee of the Red
Cross), 5, 36, 59, 64, 363
ICTR, budget statistics, 423n98
ICTY, budget statistics, 422n98
Idema, Jonathan "Jack or Keith", 367
identity reinvention: Eichmann, Adolf, 61,
62; German Nazis, 14, 61; identity
papers, 64; Karadzic, Radovan, 14; and
Vatican ratlines, 63
illegal abductions, Cold War era, 11
Im Chaem, 248
Immigration and Naturalization Service
(INS), 121–22, 403n5
Immigration Subcommittee of the Judiciary
Committee, 121
immunity: and African Union, 326; bilateral
immunity agreements, 285, 356, 378,
386; Holtzman on, 122; ICC staff, 318;
and ICC trials, 326; and informants,
212, 220; sovereign-immunity, 6, 203,
235, 355; and universal jurisdiction,
359–61; for war criminals, 55–56
improper capture defense, 10
impunity, 8, 11, 12, 15, 225–30, 378
in absentia trials, 418n17; Barbie, Klaus,
103, 111; Bormann, Martin, 43;
convictions of CIA operatives, 12;
Lischka, Kurt, 106; prohibition of, 9
India, 9, 26, 46, 205, 206
indictments: on 2001 conflict in Macedonia,
413n110; custody of indictees, 3;
Haradinaj, Ramush, 185; Hutu genocide

suspects, 218; and international
community, 3; Kosovo Liberation Army,
162; Milosevic, Slobodan, 163–64;
Mladic, Ratko, 148; Nuremberg Trial,
43; ratings on, 409n137; in Rwanda,
198; Rwanda tribunal, 202, 204;
Serbian officials, 162; Serbian war
crimes suspects, 170; top-down
approach, 203; transfer of suspects, 220;
UN members and, 143; war crimes, 145;
Yugoslavia tribunal, 149
Indonesia, 9, 46
INS (Immigration and Naturalization
Services), 121–22
intelligence agencies, 30–31, 135–36. *See
also specific agencies*
intelligence assets, German, Cold War
recruitment of, 4
intelligence informants, 124–27; Bosnian
Serb, 160; in Burkina Faso, 259; and
Cold War era politics, 137; Eastern
European, 127; German, 31, 39, 67–68,
75, 80, 126–27; Hutu genocide suspects,
211–13; in Japan, 55; on Kabuga, 219;
and Morrisette, 208, 211–13, 215, 261;
war criminals, 69; in West Africa, 260
intelligence reports, Ustasha war criminals, 66
Interahamwe (anti-Tutsi militia), 190, 192,
203, 208, 211–12, 217, 218
Inter-Allied Commission on the Punishment
of War Crimes, 25
International Committee of the Red Cross
(ICRC), 5, 36, 59, 64, 253, 363
International Covenant on Civil and
Political Rights, 12, 215
International Criminal Court (ICC),
279–332, 380, 434n127; and Africa, 9;
appeals, 288, 318–19; and al-Bashir,
Omar, 305–10, 324, 325, 381, 386;
bloggers, 450n18; and Bush, George W.,
285–86; and Bush administration,
George W., 283, 285–86, 305, 331; and
Central African Republic, 329–30; and
China, 9, 331–32; comparisons to ad
hoc tribunals, 9, 282, 283, 287–88, 297,
306; comparison to hybrid tribunals,
282, 283; and Congo, Democratic
Republic of the, 9, 329, 330; and Côte
d'Ivoire, 319–23, 329; criticism of, 281,
290, 292–94, 301, 307, 313, 321; and
Darfur, 304–11; and diplomats, 14;
due-process protections, 35; establishment of, 9; and European states, 14;
foundations of, 287–91; and France,

Israeli Justice Ministry, 97
Israeli Reparations Mission, 80
Israeli secret service (Mossad), 80
Israel secret service (Mossad), 97
Italy, 66, 71
Ivan the Terrible, 131. *See also* Demjanjuk, John
IWG (Nazi War Criminal and Japanese Imperial Government Records Interagency Working Group), 124–27
IWG historians, 124–27, 132–33, 136
Izieu orphanage, 405n31

Jackson, Jessie, 250–51
Jackson, Robert, 43–44, 48, 49
Jallow, Hassan, 219–20, 227, 228
al-Jamadi, Manadel, 352, 442n95
Jänish, Rudolf, 60–61
Janjic, Janko, 158
Japan: Allied Occupation of, 47, 49–51, 53–57; and German specialists, 37; nationalism in, 137; post-WWII, 57, 380; surrender, 46; and wartime atrocities, 46. *See also* Tokyo war crimes trials
Japanese government: accountability, criminal, 136; and OSI watch list, 129
Japanese war criminals: arrests, 49; and Cold War, 7; indictment of, 46; and OSI watch list, 129; pursuit of, 3, 49–51; suicides, 51–52; trials of, 5; Unit 731, 129
Jasenovac concentration camp, 66, 135, 147
Jeffreys, Alec, 96–97
Jerusalem, 72, 85, 98, 133
Jerusalem District Court, 85–86
Jessen, Bruce, 364–65, 366
Jewish defense force (The Haganah), 61
Jewish Historical Documentation Center, 73, 74
Jewish World Congress, 26
Jintao, Hu, 280
JIOA (Joint Intelligence Objectives Agency), 37–38
Johnston, George H., 49
joint criminal enterprise doctrine, 131–32, 185
Joint Intelligence Objectives Agency (JIOA), 37–38
Joint Special Operations Command, 372
Jones, Alan, 261
Junger, Sebastian, 159, 253
Junkers, Werner, 90

Kabbah, Ahmed Tejan, 249, 250–51, 253–55, 258, 262, 263

Kabila, Joseph, 218
Kabuga, Félicien, 14, 201, 214, 218–19
Kabuga case, 218
Kabul, 366
Kagame, Paul, 194, 199–200, 227–28, 230, 326
Kailahun District, 253
Kaing Guek Eav. *See* Duch (Cambodian prison commander)
Kajelijeli, Juvenal, 215–16
Kallon, Morris, 262, 265–66
Kaltenbrunner, Ernst, 33–34, 60, 393n59
Kambanda, Jean, 201, 202, 213–14
Kansteiner, Walter, 267
Kaplan, Alice Y., 120, 123–24
Karadzic, Radovan, 14, 145–46, 148–49, 150–51, 152, 157–61, 166, 173–75, 176, 177–78, 183; Anderson on, 412n61; arrest of, 178; and Serbian government, 178
Karadzic trial, verdict in, 183
Karamira, Froduald, 206–7, 211
Karamira trial, 206, 207
Karpinski, Jane, 350, 351, 354, 358, 442n81
Katanga, Germain, 330
Katyn massacre, 42
Kayani, Ashfaq Parvez, 375
Kayishema, Clement, 203, 204
Keane, Fergel, 192
Kearns, Michael, 364–65
Keenan, Joseph B., 49
Kennan, George, 48
Kennedy, Edward M. "Ted", 122
Kentarō Awaya, 57
Kenya, 323–27; arrests in, 212; Hutu genocide suspects, 209–12; Hutu suspects pursuit in, 207; and ICC investigations, 9; Interahamwe (anti-Tutsi militia), 190, 192, 203, 208, 211–12, 217, 218; Kabuga in, 201, 218; Kenyan police, 210, 213; noncooperation, 209; refugees in, 201
Kenyatta, Uhuru, 290, 323–27
Kenyatta case, 323–27
Kerry, John, 286
Kersten, Mark, 450n18
al-Khatab, Abid Hamid Mahmoud, 345
Khmer Rouge regime: and China, 240–41; crimes of, 234; death statistics from, 232; defense attorneys, 119; Dunlop and, 231; Khmer Rouge forces, 15, 119, 239; *The Killing Fields* (film), 232; mass graves, 231; Nhem Ein, 238–39; Pol Pot, 239–41, 242, 243, 246; and